EDUCATING
STRATEGIES
STUDENTS
AND
WITH MILD
METHODS
DISABILITIES

SECOND EDITION

EDITED BY

EDWARD L. MEYEN
University of Kansas

GLENN A. VERGASON
Georgia State University

RICHARD J. WHELAN
University of Kansas Medical Center

LOVE PUBLISHING COMPANY©
Denver • London • Sydney

Chapter 6, from "Behavior Management in Inclusive Classrooms" by S. L. Carpenter and E. McKee-Higgins, July, 1996, *Remedial and Special Education*, Vol. 17, No. 4, pp. 195–203. Copyright 1996 by PRO-ED, Inc. Reprinted by permission.

Chapter 8, adapted from "Strategies for Adapting Science Textbooks for Youth with Learning Disabilities" by T. Lovitt and S. Horton, March, 1994, *Remedial and Special Education*, Vol. 15, No. 2, pp. 105–116. Copyright 1994 by PRO-ED, Inc. Reprinted by permission.

Chapter 9, from "Teaching Students with Learning Problems in Math to Acquire, Understand, and Apply Basic Math Facts" by C. Mercer and S. Miller, May/June 1992, *Remedial and Special Education*, Vol. 13, No. 3, pp. 19–35. Copyright 1992 by PRO-ED, Inc. Reprinted with permission.

Chapter 12, from "Curriculum and Instructional Issues in Teaching Secondary Students with Learning Disabilities" by H. Rieth and L. Polsgrove, Spring, 1994, *Learning Disabilities Research and Practice*, Vol. 9, No. 2, pp. 118–126. Copyright 1994 by Lawrence Erlbaum Associates, Inc. Reprinted by permission.

Chapter 18, from "Teaching Concepts: Procedures for the Design and Delivery of Instruction" by M. Prater, September/October 1993, *Remedial and Special Education*, Vol. 14, No. 5, pp. 51–62. Copyright 1993 by PRO-ED, Inc. Reprinted by permission.

Chapter 19, from "Educational Interventions for Students with Attention Deficit Disorder" by T. A. Fiore, E. A. Becker, and R. C. Nero, October/November 1993, *Exceptional Children*, Vol. 60, No. 2, pp. 163–173. Copyright 1993 by The Council for Exceptional Children. Reprinted by permission.

Most of the other chapters in this book are from selected issues of *Focus on Exceptional Children*. Copyright by Love Publishing Company. Reprinted with permission.

Published by Love Publishing Company
Denver, Colorado 80222

Library of Congress Catalog Card Number 97-74579

Contents

Part Two—Curriculum Strategies Introduction 131

EDWARD L. MEYEN
UNIVERSITY OF KANSAS

7   Preferred and Promising Practices for Social Skills Instruction 137

GEORGE SUGAI AND TIMOTHY J. LEWIS

8   Strategies for Adapting Science Textbooks for Youth with Learning Disabilities 163

THOMAS C. LOVITT AND STEVEN V. HORTON

9   Teaching Students with Learning Problems in Math to Acquire, Understand, and Apply Basic Math Facts 177

CECIL D. MERCER AND SUSAN P. MILLER

Part Three—Instructional Strategies for Students with Mild Disabilities

301

GLENN A. VERGASON, GEORGIA STATE UNIVERSITY
M. L. ANDEREGG, KENNESAW STATE COLLEGE

Preface

You are about to read a book composed of chapters organized around the themes of management, curriculum, and instructional strategies. If you already are involved in the education of children and youth with disabilities, many of the authors will be familiar to you. You may know their work and where they are from. You may even have met some of them personally and know that what they have to say makes a difference to teachers.

If you are new to the field or if your background is in general education, you are about to be introduced to the work of individuals who have devoted their careers to studying the instructional challenges presented by students with disabilities, and who have the ability to translate their research into messages that are easily understood and directly applicable to the role of teachers in the classroom today. Although each selection has its own contribution to make, the collection and the organization of the selections is what makes this book a unique resource for teachers, teacher educators, and others whose primary interest is to improve instruction for children and youth with disabilities.

At a time when information in all fields is exploding and sophisticated electronic systems are becoming available for disseminating information almost instantaneously, the need remains for resources that systematically pull together information on validated interventions for teaching students with disabilities. This book was designed to help fill this need by presenting a series of sound and effective instructional and curricular solutions to the challenges posed by students with mild disabilities in the classroom.

The editors were motivated to create this resource because of the expanding opportunities presented by reauthorization of IDEA and the continual need of classroom teachers for interventions that work and that help accommodate the needs of students with disabilities. As more students with mild disabilities are integrated into general education classrooms, the level of diversity among learners increases and teachers have a greater need for effective interventions.

The context for this book is the reform movement in education. Most reference the beginning of the reform movement with the release of the *Nation at Risk* report by the Commission on Excellence in Education in 1983. After 15 years of effort and endless reports, one would assume that conditions in today's classrooms would be far more favorable for the teaching-learning process than what characterized classrooms of the 1960s and 1970s. To some extent they are, but many of the reform initiatives undertaken to date have altered the instructional environment in ways that have added to the demands on the teacher without offering interventions designed for these new circumstances. One example of the reform movement that many view as a progressive step, but one that has placed increased demands on the teacher, is the inception of inclusive instructional environments and a shifting of instructional responsibility for students with mild disabilities to the general classroom teacher.

Inclusion is one of the few reform initiatives that specifically addresses students with disabilities. Even though other reforms such as national assessment, world-class curriculum standards, choice, and site-based management have implications for students with disabilities, they were not conceived to benefit this group of students. In examining the context of inclusion, it becomes clear that one cannot simply make the classroom teacher responsible for developing the interventions and strategies that are effective in meeting the needs of students with mild disabilities in inclusive instructional environments. Teachers always have dealt with diverse needs among their students. The presence of student with disabilities in their classrooms, however, has broadened the range of diversity and redefined the extremes of diversity from an instructional perspective. What has emerged, therefore, is the need for strategies that have been validated as being effective and that are applicable to this new environment. Although teachers historically had applied, and will continue to apply, best practices and develop their own practices, a larger community of professionals now must share in the responsibility for creating the needed solutions.

Researchers and others who engage in curriculum development are among that expanded group who must become part of the solution. What is known about instructional and curriculum strategies must be made easily accessible to teachers and teacher educators. At the same time, there is a strong need to stimulate researchers to investigate strategies for meeting the needs of students with mild disabilities in inclusive environments and to accept responsibility for translating the results of their research into interventions designed specifically for teachers to implement and teacher educators to use in preparing teachers for the future.

The emphasis on management, instruction, and curriculum in selecting strategies and authors for this book reflects a commitment to the classroom teacher. Today's teachers need access to practical and validated strategies specific to their expanded roles in working with parents, collaborating with colleagues, conducting their own action research, and making more effective use of technology in their classrooms.

Part One *Caring for Joe*

RICHARD J. WHELAN
THE UNIVERSITY OF KANSAS MEDICAL CENTER

Let's set the scene. Joe is a 10-year-old fifth-grade student in an elementary school. Overall, he has the cognitive ability to be an above-average student in academic subject matter. His IQ is 119, with no great difference between verbal and performance scores. Yet, the fifth-grade teacher, and all of the teachers from prior years, describe Joe as a "puzzle." His daily work and periodic achievement measures are well below expectations based upon cognitive ability. During classroom instruction Joe often is unresponsive, distracted, and, with ever increasing frequency, abandons self-control and civility in favor of an angry, confrontational style of relating to peers and teachers. Joe's behavior is truly perplexing to the teacher and has not abated with the imposition of general behavior management procedures from the school district's policy handbook.

Consider this episode. Joe's teacher is prepared to present a lesson in science, specifically on how electricity functions in our environment. The teacher has prepared all of the process steps for presenting this to a class of 20 students. These steps include the following components of effective instruction (Rosenshine & Stevens, 1986):

1. Reviewed past lesson on electric devices in the home.
2. Described the new content to be learned—characteristics of magnets, demonstrating how unlike poles attract each other, and how like poles repel each other.
3. Established student pairs to conduct small experiments with magnets—one doing and one observing and recording.
4. Provided feedback and answered questions asked by the student pairs.
5. Students continued with experiments and written descriptions of the results.
6. Teacher checked for student understanding of polarity, lines of force, and making a magnet from a magnet.

Joe wasn't a very good partner in his pair. He didn't pay attention, whispered to classmates instead of listening, became angry when he couldn't do the experiments, and finally "blew-up," with associated screaming, breaking pencils, throwing workbooks, and directing hurtful words at peers and the teacher. Joe had a tantrum for all to see and experience.

What Now, Effective Teacher?

Doyle (1986) made the point that teachers are responsible for learning and for order, which are reciprocal events in that both are necessary for instruction to take place. Learning occurs when the above six teaching functions are carried out. Order occurs when the teacher uses management skills to (a) establish peer groups, (b) post rules and consequences, (c) respond to student deviation from the rules, and (d) make sure the teaching functions are sequential and applied consistently. Finally, learning focuses upon individual students, whereas order is concerned with group process.

Joe's teacher understands the distinction between learning and order and has demonstrated good management skills to the extent that the general education class usually is engaged with the content to be learned. In brief, the teacher uses the instructional system to maintain order and only rarely resorts to rules and consequences to enforce it. Generally, Joe's teacher maintains a high percentage of on-task behaviors, and a low percentage of discipline problems.

Joe is different, though. He doesn't respond to the general framework of teaching and order that most students do. The "desist" (Kounin, 1970) techniques that prevent disorder do not work with Joe. He has all of the characteristics of a student with emotional or behavior disorders (EBD).

Joe's teacher now must go beyond the generally effective group-oriented management techniques to use those tailored to individual applications. One approach is to offer "praise" when Joe is on-task and behaving appropriately. Upon first inspection, this is a good idea. Students with EBD, however, often take the obvious and do the reverse. A general education student does the obvious in response to praise; he or she continues with the task or increases efforts. The student with EBD often reverses the obvious and stops responding after the teacher delivers praise (Levin & Simmons, 1962). Now Joe's teacher will need to complete some research to find individualized behavior management models that might just enable Joe to rejoin the classroom group as a contributor instead of a detractor.

The Research Journey

A first step in the research journey is to review models of behavior management that provide application guidelines for individuals as well as groups. Joe's teacher will find out quickly that the existing classroom organization is designed to prevent problems and to provide support to keep students on the appropriate side of acceptable behavior. It is not organized to correct misbehavior as exemplified by Joe (Charles, 1992). Therefore, Joe's teacher can narrow the search to procedures that will (a) decrease or stop Joe's outbursts, and (b) enable Joe to engage constructively with the curriculum content and the peer group.

One model that Joe's teacher will encounter in the research literature is the contingent use of consequences for inappropriate and appropriate behaviors. The model, however, addresses much more than the unscientific use of rewards and punishers to shape behavior. Instead, Joe's teacher will find a model that stresses the relationship among—the analysis of—events that occur *before the behavior* and those that occur *after the behavior*, and how those events can be arranged for Joe to acquire success in learning.

This model is not without its critics. For example, Kohn (1993, p. 47) equates rewards with bribes. He uses the term "bribes" recklessly and incorrectly. Bribes are characterized by:

> Any money, goods...promised, given and accepted...to induce action...(Black, 1979)

A bribe is a promise to give a person something to act in ways he or she shouldn't—a practice that Kohn and professional educators unambiguously reject. But is it a bribe when payment is given for an act that most people believe should be performed without payment? Kohn probably would say *yes*. The real question in regard to Joe, however, must be: Does he engage the task in a manner consistent with his abilities, and does he, along with his peers, find that task intrinsically motivating (rewarding)? The answer is *no!* as verified by his acting-out responses to the instructional context. If Joe's teacher currently is using Kohn's alternatives to contingent consequences—content that is meaningful, teacher-student problem-solving, increased self-efficacy through informed choices—and they are not working for Joe, the next research step is to go beyond the "pop" uses of rewards and punishment to the scientific analysis of Joe's behavior and the condition present when it occurs.

If Joe's teacher does arrange environmental events to decrease excessive negative behaviors and increase personal and academic behavior, will Joe continue to exhibit these new skills when he once again is expected to function with the general teaching and order context of the classroom? The answer is a "clear maybe"; it all depends. If Joe falls back into old patterns of reacting, one interpretation is that he is lacking intrinsic motivation because contingent consequences are detrimental to self-efficacy (Kohn, 1993). Is this interpretation valid? Absolutely not. First of all, consequences do not ruin intrinsic motivation (Cameron & Pierce, 1996; Eisenberger & Cameron, 1996). Second, well-learned behaviors acquired by planned consequences can be maintained by naturally occurring events (e.g., advanced reading competence increases what some may label as internal locus of control and others might refer to as habitual).

In the long run, if Joe succeeds in acquiring and maintaining skills for success in school, attributing that result to (a) intrinsic motivation, (b) internal locus of control, or (c) unobservable naturally occurring contingent consequences is probably of little relevance to Joe. It is, however, of relevance to his teacher, who undertook and completed the research journey successfully.

No Miracle

Establishing classroom learning and order is not an easy task. It requires highly refined knowledge and skills. And, for the students who do not respond appropriately to general classroom organization, or cannot cope with it, teachers must acquire new sets of knowledge and skills that will help them earn the school success they deserve. Joe's teacher did it, and so can other teachers of the so many Joes in our schools.

The six selections that follow provide substantial guidance for Joe's teacher to select a managerial strategy that can be tailored to his needs. Again, the teacher may have to experiment with various strategies, including involving Joe in developing a plan of action. Joe and his teacher soon will know if the plan is working. If it is not, it's time to try another way. In this context, Joe's responses or lack of them constitute the evaluation of the strategy. Joe knows best and in that sense is truly the teacher of his teacher.

References

Black, H. (1979). *Black's law dictionary* (5th ed.). St. Paul, MN: West Publishing.

Cameron, J., & Pierce, W. (1996). The debate about rewards and intrinsic motivation: Protests and accusations do not alter the results. *Review of Educational Research, 66*(1), 39–51.

Charles, C. (1992). *Building classroom discipline* (4th ed.). White Plains, NY: Longman.

Doyle, W. (1986). Classroom organization and management. In M. C. Wittrock (Ed.), *Handbook of research on teaching* (3d ed., pp. 392–432). New York: Macmillan.

Eisenberger, R., & Cameron, J. (1996). Detrimental effects of rewards: Reality or myth? *American Psychologist, 5*(11), 1153–1166.

Kohn, A. (1993). *Punished by rewards*. New York: Houghton Mifflin.

Kounin, J. (1970). *Discipline and group management in classrooms*. Huntington, NY: Robert E. Krieger Publishing.

Levin, G., & Simmons, J. (1962). Response to food and praise by emotionally disturbed boys. *Psychological Report, 11*, 539–546.

Rosenshine, B., & Stevens, R. (1986). Teaching functions. In M. C. Wittrock (Ed.), *Handbook of research on teaching* (3d ed., pp. 376–391). New York: Macmillan.

Discipline in Special Education and General Education Settings

**DEBORAH DEUTSCH SMITH
AND DIANE PEDROTTY RIVERA**

THE DISCIPLINE (think "ordered learning") plan described in this selection is one that Joe's teacher should consider thoughtfully. It provides an enlightening description of the procedures to use when classroom order begins to crumble for the group or the individual. It addresses the causes of problems and ways to prevent them. If prevention fails, however, the authors provide a specific plan for proactive intervention. Again, Joe's teacher should review and, possibly adopt the plan described here.

Discipline is of utmost concern to educators and is viewed by the American public as a major problem in education (Gallup, 1984, 1994). State legislators and Congress also view it as a major problem in our nation's schools—one that must be solved. Many reasons are cited for the lack of discipline in school settings: for example, low teacher salaries, insufficient funding for education, lack of parental support, and a disregard for authority by students. Many of these problems are beyond the control of educators but must not be used as an excuse for why discipline problems cannot be ameliorated. Rather, educators must focus on identifying and addressing the individual needs of students, improving the educational environment, using effective prevention and intervention techniques, and building collaborative partnerships.

Although the majority of students do not present discipline problems, even a small number of students who engage in negative behavior can disrupt the learning environment and divert teacher time from instruction to manage the situation. Therefore, educators must establish a system of order that clearly defines the boundaries for acceptable behavior and provides consequences for appropriate and inappropriate behavior.

Discipline can be defined as "...order among pupils so learning can take place without competition from unproductive factors. It is a system of rules for conduct and a mechanism for ensuring that conduct codes are followed" (Smith & Rivera, 1993, p. 2). A system of classroom order can be achieved when principles of effective discipline are implemented:

1. Establish a positive climate.
2. Build a foundation for a positive learning environment.
3. Use prevention techniques.
4. Establish collaborative relationships with parents and other professionals for dealing with discipline concerns and promoting a positive learning climate.
5. Match intervention to behavior problem.
6. Establish an evaluation system to monitor student progress frequently.

When these principles are incorporated into educators' instructional repertoires, an environment for success and learning can be fostered and more time can be devoted to teaching. Providing a learning environment based on the principles of effective discipline can help students understand the relationship between specific behaviors and their consequences and can result in all students learning important social skills.

Today's educators must consider many factors when planning their discipline programs (for example, students' cultural and linguistic diversity or disabilities). Educators from various fields (special education, general education, counseling, remedial reading) must work collaboratively to accommodate the needs of all students. As students with disabilities spend more of their school day in the general education setting, special education and general education professionals must develop discipline plans collaboratively. General education teachers need to be comfortable with the needs of students with disabilities as they implement their discipline programs. The purpose of this chapter is to present what we believe are the components of an effective discipline program. We begin by providing possible reasons for discipline problems, followed by a discussion of prevention and intervention techniques. We conclude by explaining some techniques for evaluating discipline programs.

Why Discipline Problems Occur

Just as students come to America's public schools with a great variety of learning styles and needs, some have a variety of reasons for not conforming to school rules and expectations. A few of those are briefly discussed in the following sections.

Types of Disruptions

Almost all students exhibit some kind of discipline problem or disruptive behavior during their 13-year school career. It is the *kind, degree, place,* and *amount of disruption* that determine whether the behavior requires a comprehensive discipline plan. Often there is a fine line between what is acceptable deportment and what is not, and many students have difficulty understanding where the line falls and what behavior crosses it (Krumboltz & Krumboltz, 1972). In many cases, school personnel need to help students understand the subtle discriminations required to meet the behavioral demands of the various educational settings they experience. Students need to learn when it is appropriate to talk in class and when it is not. They must learn which teachers tolerate a noisy class and which do not. Educators must help students learn to discriminate between the behavioral demands of each school situation and match that situation with the proper behavior pattern. Effectively matching the situation with the appropriate behavior pattern is an important skill to learn. In other words, some conduct problems occur simply because students do not know how to read the environmental cues—some subtle and some not so subtle—that indicate the acceptability of behavior.

Circumstances

Sometimes conduct problems occur because teachers' expectations are unrealistic. For example, expecting a class of first-graders to sit quietly for a symphony orchestra's hour-long rehearsal is probably unreasonable, as it is unreasonable to expect bright students to sit and wait 20 minutes for the rest of the class to complete a seatwork assignment. Teachers who judge the attention span of their students will help avoid conduct difficulties.

The arrangement of the environment should also be considered. Sometimes behavior problems occur because traffic patterns are congested or seating arrangements are poorly arranged. Simply observing how students interact socially can help teachers decide what might be appropriate seating arrangements.

Transitional times also can invite disruption. When students are free to move about the classroom from one activity to the next, change from one lesson to another, or freely line up to go from the classroom to another area without supervision or clear rules or expectations, the result is often confusion and disruption.

Instructional Procedures

Effective instructional procedures include practices that minimize behavioral problems. For example, when students are left to complete work independently when they are not equipped to do so, the environment is open for disruption. Sometimes students are disruptive because they don't understand what is being taught and fail to ask questions for clarification. For other students the lesson may move too slowly, allowing students time to create diversions to occupy their attention until the teacher is ready to move on to the next activity.

Boredom or Frustration

Many behavioral problems occur because students are either bored with an activity that is too easy or frustrated because it is too difficult. One important study (Center, Deitz, & Kaufman, 1982) evaluated the relationship between task difficulty and inappropriate behavior. The relationship is dramatic and clear. When there is a mismatch between student ability and academic assignments, disruption occurs at a high level. The need for flexible educational programming is a pervasive reality in today's schools because of federal requirements to include students with disabilities, to bus pupils to achieve social integration, and not to track or group students by ability. Because of these mandates, teachers must now accommodate students with an increasingly wider range of abilities and plan flexible activities that will hold the interest of diverse class members.

Motivation

Admittedly, many students come to school with a well-developed ability to disrupt the learning atmosphere. These students know how to read the environmental cues and determine what the behavioral expectations are in various school settings. They are neither bored nor frustrated. For whatever reasons, they are not motivated to become active participants in the learning situation and instead seek to disrupt the learning climate. Their behavioral repertoires are counterproductive to their own and their classmates' learning. Because even one student can destroy the learning environment for an entire class, behavior problems must be confronted. Although many preventive measures are sufficient to encourage most students to behave appropriately, many students are candidates for more direct intervention procedures.

Students with Behavioral Disabilities

Some students are the source of considerable disruption. Many of these students have disabilities and are included in general classes. They seem unable to meet the behavioral expectations of typical classroom situations for extended periods of time. Their inability to conform, their frequent frustration over learning activities, and the recognition by their peers that they are different often lead to disruptive situations. Although many of these students need a considerable amount of structure to meet setting demands, they are integrated during parts of the school day when the structure is at a minimum. This may contribute to their difficulties in meeting behavioral expectations. They also are easy targets for teasing and rebuff by general education students, which often leads to further disruptive occurrences. When these students are the center of disruption, there are generally two basic reasons for the disturbance: their inability to act appropriately and their nondisabled counterparts' temptation to bait, chide, and encourage inappropriate behavior from these students. An analysis to determine the causes of inappropriate school behaviors can help educators select specific preventive and intervention measures aimed at reducing disruption.

Prevention Techniques

Successful discipline plans are based on a foundation of prevention. These techniques require teachers to be familiar with the strengths and weaknesses of their students, curriculum, instruction, and classroom management. Prevention techniques establish the foundation on which teachers can implement additional interventions and promote a positive classroom environment. Several prevention techniques are highlighted for consideration, along with some guiding principles that foster effective discipline programs.

Rules

Students must be aware of the teacher's expectations of acceptable and unacceptable conduct. These expectations typically are addressed through the use of classroom rules—an important prevention technique because they provide parameters of acceptable behavior. Without rules students are left on their own to devise guidelines for establishing predictability and a sense of security in their environment (Windell, 1991). Most students follow the rules; however, teachers should schedule classroom time for the discussion, implementation, and enforcement of the rules if they are to be an effective part in the discipline plan.

Specific suggestions for establishing and implementing rules are provided by Smith and Rivera (1993):

1. *Establish a list of rules.* Keep the list short and positive (e.g., instead of "No talking," try "Raise your hand to speak"). Be sure the rules can be enforced, are age-appropriate, and are general enough to encompass several behaviors.

2. *Involve students in developing the classroom rules.* Students can assist in establishing classroom rules at the beginning of the school year and as the need arises. Students can discuss their classroom environment and how specific rules can create a positive climate for learning.

3. *Promote student understanding of the rules.* Ensure that students understand teachers' expectations by stating the rules, providing specific examples of following and breaking the rules, and practicing the application of the rules. Intermittently praise students who follow the rules, and implement consequences for those who break the rules.

4. *Provide students with reminders about the classroom rules.* Several occasions may arise that warrant reminders about proper classroom conduct. For example, when rules are first initiated, students may need cues and warnings. Pairing reminders with specific praise is a good strategy to teach the rules. At times of high probability of rule violations, reminders may prevent problems from occurring.

Manage the Environment

The classroom environment can play a major role in the management of student behavior and the prevention of discipline problems. Teachers who are well prepared and cognizant of student interactions within the environment can create a physical environment and implement management techniques that promote discipline. For instance, high traffic areas are good opportunities for disruptive behavior to occur. Students can talk to each other, initiate physical contact, and be disruptive just in the course of sharpening a pencil or walking to their desks. To prevent such problems, teachers can (a) observe traffic patterns and determine high frequency areas that could be problematic, (b) keep work areas separated to minimize excessive student movement, (c) provide plenty of space, and (d) ensure that areas have easy access (Evertson, Emmer, Clements, Sanford, & Worsham, 1984).

Teachers can also better manage student learning by organizing the materials to be used by students or teachers during instruction. Classroom organization also promotes more engaged instructional time, minimizes "down time," and increases opportunities for students to initiate appropriate behavior.

Plan for Transitions

Transitions between lessons and activities or physical environments can be successful or disastrous. The key to effective transitions, and thus appropriate conduct, is planning. Several steps can ensure smooth transitions. For instance, teachers can provide a readiness signal so students know it is time to finish their activity. "In 10 minutes we will go to lunch" is an example of a signal that prepares students for the upcoming transition. A second step is for teachers to tell students how the transition will be made (e.g., line up by rows or students with last names beginning with M through Z) and what behavior is expected (e.g., no talking, have all materials ready). Finally, teachers should provide reinforcement for students who conduct themselves appropriately during transitions.

Guiding Principles

Some basic principles help establish effective discipline practices. Although many of these principles have been noted in the discipline and behavior management literature for years, they warrant mention because of their effectiveness. The principles include (a) "with-it-ness" or "eyes in the back of your head" technique, (b) "ripple effect" (Kounin, 1970), (c) avoidance of power struggles, (d) avoidance of grudges, (e) focus on student's behavior, not on their character, (f) preparation to teach, (g) anticipation of problems, and (h) implementation of stress management techniques.

Intervention Techniques

Discipline problems often occur or continue to occur even though teachers have implemented preventive measures as part of the overall discipline plan and system of order in the classroom. Teachers should address disruptions of classroom rules directly and shape and encourage an instructional environment conducive to learning. There are many ways of achieving discipline and reducing or eliminating behavior problems. For example, mild and positive forms of intervention can be used when preventive measures have proven unsuccessful. The use of severe and negative measures should be kept to a minimum to avoid a serious long-term impact on the climate of the school, overuse of punitive techniques, and the perception that the one who administers the negative procedure is a punitive person.

The most important technique for promoting a climate for learning is to match the disciplinary infraction with the intervention. To do this, educators must be fully aware of many different intervention techniques and intervene systematically and sensibly. The Intervention Ladder (see Figure 1.1) graphically depicts a hierarchy of disciplinary interventions that can be used as a guide for selecting an appropriate disciplinary action. The interventions are arranged in a hierarchy from mild to intrusive interventions. Tactics that are found lower on the ladder should be selected first

Figure 1.1 *Intervention Ladder*

Source: From *Effective Discipline* (p. 17) by D. D. Smith and D. M. Rivera, 1993, Austin, TX: Pro-Ed.

because they tend to remediate a large number of behavioral problems. Those interventions on the higher rungs are more intrusive and should be reserved for use only when other tactics have not been successful. Table 1.1 presents a definition and an example of each intervention on the ladder.

Table 1.1 *Glossary for the Intervention Ladder*

Tactic	Definition	Example
SPECIFIC PRAISE	Providing students with positive statements and feedback about their appropriate conduct.	"Juan, thank you for waiting until everyone has finished their work to sharpen your pencils."
IGNORING	Systematically and consistently not paying attention to each occurrence of the target behavior.	When Susan came to the teacher's desk and interrupted Ms. Miller and Pete, who were working together on a special assignment, Ms. Miller and Pete paid no attention to her.
RULES	The entire class (teacher and pupils) determines a code of conduct for all to follow.	After several weeks of school, the class reviewed and finalized the guidelines about the behavior expected from each member. In addition to establishing a classroom code of conduct, they decided on some consequences for infractions of the rules.
CONTINGENT INSTRUCTIONS	After an occurrence of the target behavior, the teacher quietly and on a one-to-one basis tells the individual specifically not to engage in that activity.	While Steven was chewing gum in class, the teacher went to his desk and said to him quietly, "Don't chew gum at school, Steven."
CONTINGENT OBSERVATION	Removal of a disruptive student from a group activity, but still allowing the individual to observe the proceedings.	During a group science activity, Bill was disruptive. His teacher had him return to his desk for 5 minutes while the others continued the science experiment.
CRITERION-SPECIFIC REWARDS	The student earns a special privilege only for reaching the desired behavior.	Because Tyler was not absent for a week of school, he was allowed 10 minutes of extra gym time on Friday afternoon.
FINES	The student loses privileges for engaging in the target behavior.	Emily became ineligible for this week's monitor duty because she was disruptive in the hall before school.

(continued)

■ **Table 1.1** *(continued)*

Tactic	Definition	Example
GROUP CONTINGENCIES		
Dependent	A person earns privileges or rewards by behaving appropriately.	Susan earned the entire class 5 minutes of extra lunch time because she didn't argue with her teachers all morning.
Independent	Individuals earn reinforcement when they achieve a goal established for the group.	Each student who returned to campus on time after lunch break for 2 school weeks is rewarded with bonus points toward their semester grade.
Interdependent	The class or group earns a special reward when the entire class meets the established goal.	When the entire class was not disruptive during history period Monday through Thursday, the weekly history test was canceled.
PEER MANAGEMENT		
Tutoring	One student proficient in an academic assignment serves in the role of teacher for a classmate who needs additional assistance.	Sally had difficulty learning her arithmetic facts and, therefore, was very disruptive during the time scheduled for arithmetic. Her teacher paired her with a classmate for extra drill and practice, which resulted in less disruption and Sally's mastery of arithmetic facts.
Behavioral manager	One whose classroom behavior is usually appropriate earns the privilege of becoming the dispenser of praise and rewards for a peer.	After training in behavioral techniques, Brian became the behavioral manager for Kevin. Brian modeled correct behavior and reinforced Kevin when he acted appropriately.
Environmental restructuring	The class is instructed and reinforced for encouraging a classmate's appropriate behavior.	Franklin had a history of disturbing class during study and seatwork assignments. In the past, the class laughed at Franklin and encouraged his disruption. After discussion and training sessions, the class learned to praise his quiet working behavior and ignore his disruptions.
SELF-MANAGEMENT		
Self-regulation	Individuals monitor their own behavior, seek to avoid those situations that precipitate inappropriate behavior, and stop that behavior if it is initiated.	When Bill realized that he and Lonnie were about to begin to fight, Bill left the playground and returned to his classroom.

(continued)

■ **Table 1.1** *(continued)*

Tactic	Definition	Example
Self-evaluation	Correcting one's own performance, recording the frequency, and graphing the resulting data.	Judy marked each time she talked out during school on a score sheet kept on her desk. At the end of each day, she totaled the tallies and graphed the score.
Self-reinforcement	Rewarding oneself for correct behavior.	Because Leroy did not get into trouble that day in the lunchroom, he stopped at a convenience store after school and treated himself to a soda.
PARENT ACTION	Involves parents in the design and implementation of an intervention plan.	Young-il's parents worked with his teacher to develop a plan to promote homework completion at home with reinforcement by the teacher.
OVERCORRECTION		
Positive practice	Extreme practice of the desired forms of the target behavior.	Megan pushed and shoved her way into class after recess. For the next 5 school days, she had to hold the classroom door open for her classmates. This made her the last one returning to class after recess and lunch breaks.
Restitution	When the environment is destroyed or altered, the student must restore it to an improved state.	In a mood of defiance, Gail tipped over her desk. As her consequence, she had to straighten the entire classroom.
Exclusion	Upon substantial disruption, the student is excused from class.	Sarah was too noisy during music, so the music teacher had her return to her homeroom.
Seclusion	For severe, out-of-control behavior, the pupil is placed in an isolated room.	Whenever John had a violent temper tantrum, he was sent to a time-out room for a minimum of 3 minutes.
TIME-OUT		
Exclusion	Upon substantial disruption, the student is asked to leave the class.	Reginald was loud and uncooperative during science class. The teacher's attempts to curb the behavior failed, resulting in Reginald being asked to report to the principal's office.

(continued)

■■ **Table 1.1** *(continued)*

Tactic	Definition	Example
Seclusion	As a result of severe, disruptive, out-of-control behavior, the student is placed in an isolated room for a short period of time until the behavior is brought under control.	Elizabeth became extremely angry as a result of an altercation with another student. She became verbally abusive, threatened other students, and refused to cooperate with the teacher by sitting down and returning to her task. Elizabeth was removed to the isolation room to allow her time to calm down and regain her composure.
PUNISHMENT	The application of an aversive event after an occurrence of an undesired behavior.	For refusing to do her seatwork assignment, Nancy had to stay after school and wait for her parents to pick her up, after her parents consulted with the teacher about Nancy's inappropriate behavior.
EXCLUSION		
In-school supervision	Removal of a student from one or more classes while requiring him or her to spend the time in a designated school area.	After considerable unruly and disruptive conduct in Algebra and English, Mary Jane was assigned to spend that time in the counselor's office for 3 school days.
Suspension	The removal of an individual from school for a specified number of days, not usually longer than 10 school days.	After a variety of interventions were scheduled unsuccessfully and a hearing was held, Nathan was suspended for 1 week because he defiantly disobeyed his teachers, destroyed school property, and threatened other students.
Expulsion	Removal of a student from school either permanently or for an indefinite time, usually exceeding 10 school days.	School personnel had tried all means available to them to control Mark's conduct. Despite their attempts, Mark fought with other students, threatened his teachers, and destroyed the learning environment for his classmates. After a formal hearing, Mark was expelled from school.

Source: From *Effective Discipline* (pp. 96–97, 154–156) by D. D. Smith and D. M. Rivera, 1993, Austin, TX: Pro-Ed.

Prevention is the foundation of the ladder and consists of the techniques discussed in previous sections. Sometimes, however, preventive measures are not applied soon enough to avoid the development of discipline problems. If direct intervention becomes necessary, educators should select techniques that reflect a sensitive match between infractions and the intervention procedures. We selected several intervention techniques from the Intervention Ladder in Figure 1.1 that have been used effectively to manage an individual's or group's behavior in both general and special education settings to discuss here as illustrative examples.

Specific Praise

Specific praise means giving students positive feedback about their appropriate behavior. It is specific in the sense that students are told which behaviors they engaged in that were appropriate and they are praised for those actions as well. The following examples illustrate both the correct and incorrect applications of specific praise.

The secondary teacher tells a student privately, "Samantha, I appreciate your coming to class on time and bringing all of your books." This statement tells the student specifically what she has done that meets the teacher's expectations.

Brian was able to read quietly for one-half hour without disturbing his neighbors. The teacher commented to Brian, "I appreciate how quietly you have been reading without talking to your neighbors this afternoon."

Mrs. Dodger, the second-grade teacher, thanked Alexandra, Mikayla, and Samuel for coming to the reading table for instruction the first time she called them.

"Brett, you certainly did well today" is not specific. A comment such as "Brett, thanks for remembering to raise your hand when you wanted to speak" is specific to the expected performance.

Specific praise is easy to use and when used correctly has a powerful effect on behavior. It can be provided in writing or verbally, publicly or privately, depending on the student who is being praised. At first, specific praise should be used each time the targeted behavior occurs; later, as the student learns the desired behavior, it should be intermittently delivered.

Specific praise can serve both an instructional and reinforcing role. For example, the specific feedback students receive about their positive performance tells them what behavior is expected and desired. This is important for those students who do not fully understand what is expected of them because they have not completely mastered the unspoken rules of conduct. Also, the student is given attention and positive comments about the desired or expected behavior, which can be very reinforcing to some youngsters. This tactic also often produces a "ripple effect" (i.e., other students engage in the behavior that was praised to earn their own praise from the teacher). Following are some ideas for implementing the specific praise intervention technique.

1. Identify the target behavior.
2. Provide a positive comment about the expected behavior.
3. Make the statement specific to the behavior.
4. Provide specific praise orally or in writing, publicly or privately depending upon the situation and the student.
5. Apply specific praise consistently and then intermittently.
6. Evaluate the effectiveness of the intervention frequently.
7. Develop a plan of how to increase the use of specific praise in the classroom.
8. Consider how the "ripple effect" and the use of specific praise could change students' behaviors.

Ignoring

Ignoring requires educators to systematically withdraw attention for every occurrence of the problem behavior. It can be a powerful intervention when used correctly in appropriate situations. For example, it is effective only when the person whose attention is being sought is the one who withholds attention. In the following example, ignoring Jim's talking behavior worked only when the attention of the students around him in study hall was withdrawn and he was aware of this situation.

Jim talked to several students around him during study hall. The study hall teacher chose to ignore Jim's disruption, but the behavior only worsened. When the teacher told the students privately that they were not to talk to Jim and when he realized that he was being ignored, Jim's disruptive behavior ceased.

Below are guidelines for the use of ignoring. Teachers must use discretion when ignoring behaviors (Sabatino, 1983). Some behaviors (e.g., tattling, whining) indeed can be ignored safely without risk to instruction. Other behaviors (e.g., throwing objects, hitting), however, can interfere with instruction or pose a threat to the student, teacher, or other students. In these cases, ignoring is obviously not the appropriate intervention to use.

1. Identify the behavior of concern.
2. Identify whose attention the student is seeking; that person should implement the intervention.
3. Ignore the student when the target behavior occurs.
4. Provide attention and praise to the student when the target behavior does not occur.
5. Use the "ripple effect" to obtain appropriate behavior.
6. Identify ways that nonverbal communication can be used as part of the ignoring technique.
7. Identify behavior problems where specific praise paired with ignoring would be effective interventions.
8. Consider ways to teach students to ignore the target student.

Criterion-Specific Rewards

Teachers can encourage discipline by implementing various reinforcement procedures. The use of criterion-specific rewards implies that the student earns a privilege only for reaching the desired level of the target behavior, such as increasing academic performance or decreasing inappropriate behaviors. Rewarding students for engaging in appropriate behavior is positive and most often successful. If reinforcement is used to reduce disruption, it should be used to improve academic performance as well. When implementing a criterion-specific reward system, several considerations must be addressed: selecting reinforcers, establishing criterion for earning reinforcers, and identifying schedules of reinforcement.

Rewards selected for students do not have to be expensive or tangible, and the system for earning rewards does not need to be complicated. (See Table 1.2 for examples.) Simple systems are often more effective than complex ones. The following suggestions are offered for identifying reinforcers and rewards:

1. Determine the activities students prefer through observation and questioning.
2. Have a variety of age-appropriate reinforcers available to meet individual preferences and to provide options.
3. Try new rewards as student preferences change.
4. Select reinforcers that are inexpensive, are easy to locate and implement in the classroom, and can be enjoyed in a short amount of class time.
5. Schedule time daily or weekly for students to enjoy the earned reinforcers.

The criteria for earning a reward will vary. Criteria can often be determined from behavioral objectives, teacher's guides, or common sense. For example, most academic skills should be taught to mastery, which means from 85% to 95% accu-

■■■ **Table 1.2** *Examples of Rewards*

Elementary-Level Students	Secondary-Level Students
Happy face stars and stickers	Grades
Student of the week	Certificate of recognition
Super stars	Honor roll club recognition at the end of each grading period
Good work displayed on bulletin board	Bulletin board decoration
Puzzles and games	Age-appropriate board games
Choice of playground equipment	Library pass
Assignment reduction	Choice of seat
Principal's helper	No homework

Source: Adapted from *Effective Discipline* (p. 77) by D. D. Smith and D. M. Rivera, 1993, Austin, TX: Pro-Ed.

racy. However, certain academic skills, such as counting money and telling time, should be taught to a 100% criterion level. Criteria for decreasing disruptive behavior also varies. Some behaviors (e.g., hitting, stealing) must be reduced to 0% occurrence, whereas others (e.g., out of seat, talking out) may be acceptable at just a few occurrences during a certain period of time. Criteria for decreasing or extinguishing inappropriate behavior can be determined from behavioral objectives, social skills programs, and experience.

The schedule of reinforcement used depends on the individual needs of the students. For example, some students need continuous reinforcement contingent on achieving the specified criterion for performance when they are first acquiring a new skill. Some students who have recently learned a skill still require reinforcement on an intermittent, unpredictable basis to maintain the criterion level.

Interdependent Group Contingency

A group contingency involves a reward being given to students based on the behavior of other students. An interdependent group contingency is when the class or group earns a reward when the entire class meets the established goal. That is, everyone must perform the behavior in order for all students to reap the benefit of the reward. In this intervention, the entire group either does or does not benefit from the actions of the group. In other words, all who participate in the appropriate or inappropriate activity participate in its consequences. Classic research (e.g., Barrish, Saunders, & Wolf, 1969; Broden, Hall, Dunlap, & Clark, 1970; Sulzbacher & Houser, 1968) has demonstrated the efficacy of the interdependent group contingency to manage student behavior and establish an environment of discipline. Additionally, this technique has been recommended for use in cooperative learning teams to minimize disruptive group behavior (Maurer, 1988).

Interdependent group contingencies have several advantages. First, they can be used to manage student behavior in large- and small-group situations. Secondly, they work effectively with all age groups, including high school students, to foster improved academic or social performance. Third, interdependent group contingencies can be fun and result in effective discipline and management without the heavy atmosphere that a rule-laden environment can foster. Below are several ideas for implementing this intervention technique.

1. Identify a target behavior maintained by the group.
2. Determine implementation details (e.g., game-like format, points).
3. Identify the criterion level and a reward.
4. Establish the reward schedule.
5. Tell students that to earn the reward, everyone is accountable for the target behavior.
6. Collect data to determine the success of the interdependent group contingency.
7. Think of ways an interdependent group contingency can be implemented schoolwide by faculty working together to eliminate problems.

Peer Management: Peer Tutoring

Whether in the general or in the special education setting, students can be a very valuable resource in attaining academic and social skills. Peer tutoring implies that students proficient in certain academic skills assist other students who need additional help. This technique can be useful in meeting individual needs of students with disabilities, promoting academic achievement, and thus diminishing disruptive behavior. Peer tutors are beneficial in several situations: (a) working together to finish tasks; (b) assisting other students when the teacher is involved with small-group instruction; (c) serving as group leaders at learning centers, in committees, and in the library; and (d) helping other students who require assistance (Evertson et al., 1984). Once the decision has been made to institute a peer tutoring program in the classroom, teachers must address several considerations. Smith and Rivera (1993) offer the following guidelines for establishing a peer tutoring program.

Guidelines for Tutoring Situations

Regardless of the tutoring assignment a student is given (academic tutor or behavioral manager), some important factors relating directly to the success of tutoring situations must be included:

1. *Select the tutors carefully.* Select students who want to engage in tutoring relationships and have a good command of the content to be taught. Also be sure there is a good match between tutors and tutees.
2. *Train the tutors.* Tutors must receive instruction in effective techniques to impart subject matter, to manage behavior, and to reinforce the tutee. Teacher modeling and tutor role-playing can be used in practice situations to help tutors acquire effective techniques for working with tutees.
3. *Provide incentives and rewards for tutors.* Students selected as tutors may be motivated and inspired at the onset of the tutoring experience and then lose interest. Tutors must be provided with reinforcement for doing their job successfully.

Evaluation

We have described a number of proven intervention procedures for modifying disruptive and disobedient behavior, but these strategies are not always effective with all children all of the time. We advocate the use of tactics lower on the Intervention Ladder first and the application of more stringent procedures only when less intrusive techniques are not sufficient to change the target behavior to meet the requirements of desired school and classroom deportment. Educators need to use evaluation procedures that provide immediate feedback about the influence of the tactics applied. Therefore, we suggest that evaluation be concurrent with the implementation of intervention techniques. The evaluation methods discussed here are simple but powerful enough for the purposes of judging the effectiveness of intervention procedures and communicating those effects to others. For those unfamiliar with plotting student data, numerous sources of information are available, but see especially Cooper, Heron, and Heward (1987) and Gardner et al. (1994).

What Should Be Measured?

The behaviors of primary concern should be the targets of the measurement. Measurement should center directly on the behavior the educator seeks to change. That behavior must be defined carefully and in observable terms. It must be something that can be consistently observed over a period of time. Moods, feelings, and self-concepts are very difficult to measure this way, but the ways in which they are manifested are not difficult to measure. A child might be called "moody," but when that child verbally assaults her classmates and teachers, swears at classmates, or announces that she will not do her work or follow classroom rules, measurement is an easy task.

Identification of the target behavior(s) can be easily accomplished by informal observations and anecdotal recordkeeping. Notes about what specific behaviors comprise disobedient acts can be very helpful in determining exactly what behaviors need remediation. During this observation period, many teachers often find that the behaviors of concern are neither as pervasive, general, or unmanageable as they had thought. This identification period must be complete. Its main purpose is to identify what is to be measured. If the teacher changes his or her mind in the middle of the evaluation phase, the data gathered become useless. One key to successful evaluation is consistency in what behaviors are measured and the strategy scheduled. Thus, to determine what to measure:

1. Select a behavior of great concern (e.g., causing destruction, interfering with instruction, hurting self or another student).
2. Define precisely the behavior to be measured (i.e., must be observable, countable, and have a beginning and end).
3. Observe consistently over a period of time (i.e., observe the same time each day for the same amount of time).

How Should Behavior Be Measured?

Behavior should be measured in the simplest way possible and with as much immediacy as possible. Evaluations of intervention programs should not become terribly complex. Evaluation of a behavioral intervention is not inherently better because it took hours to complete and involved an unwieldy measurement system requiring outside data takers. Often a simpler system results in easier application and communication.

Once the behavior or set of behaviors targeted for remediation is identified precisely, the teacher must decide what measurement system to use. The measurement system to be selected depends on the type of behavior change desired (e.g., Is the teacher concerned with the *frequency* or with the *duration* of the behavior?). The amount or frequency of the following behaviors is usually what constitutes the problem: littering on school grounds, defacing or destroying property, talking back to the teacher, not completing homework or seatwork assignments, or not returning library books. However, for some behaviors teachers are more concerned about the duration of the target behavior: for example, the amount of time wasted during class or spent changing from class to class or activity to another activity, preparing to leave school at the end of the day, or coming from the school bus to the classroom.

In some cases, both the frequency and duration of the behavior can be of concern. In these situations the educator should decide which aspect is more important (or take both frequency and duration data concurrently). Although often related, the frequency and duration of behaviors are not necessarily dependent on each other. For example, a student can be out of his or her seat once, but for the entire class period. Thus, when determining how to measure behavior: (a) use the simplest technique and (b) select a system that is sensitive to the target behavior.

When Should Behavior Be Measured?

Behavior should be measured in the same way and at the same time each day the teacher and student work together. The notion of consistent and daily (or very frequent) applications of tactics and measurement systems is critical to successful intervention. The purpose of collecting precise information about student performance is to determine whether the infraction is serious and whether the scheduled intervention causes the desired improvement. To judge the effectiveness of the intervention, the teacher must be able to compare one day's performance with another and one week's performance with the next. For this to occur, the measures of the target behavior must be equivalent. They must be taken frequently (preferably daily) on the same behavior or set of behaviors with the same measurement system under similar conditions. Frequent measurements provide a more accurate and complete picture of the student's behavior patterns. Teachers need to know as soon as possible whether the initiated programs are producing the intended results, particularly for serious infractions. Pre- and posttesting with several months between each evaluation is a luxury educators and school environments cannot afford. Also, subsequent educational planning is best when information is readily available. When deciding when behavior should be measured:

1. Use the measurement the same way and same time each day.
2. Select a consistent time daily to measure the behavior.
3. Compare the data from one day and week to the next.
4. Measure frequently, preferably daily.

Who Should Conduct the Measurement?

The school day is filled with many noninstructional tasks, and teachers' time is consumed with activities that limit their abilities to concentrate on instruction. The elimination or reduction of various behavioral distractions results in increased instructional time; however, it is not necessary for only teachers to spend time collecting information about student deportment.

There is no mystique about measuring student performance or collecting data on students' school behavior. Once the target behavior has been identified, the proper measurement system selected, and the time period for measurement determined, the collection and display of the evaluation data are relatively simple tasks. With some initial guidance and periodic monitoring, practically anyone can be assigned the task of collecting the data on which evaluation decisions will be made. Both experience and research indicate that people other than teachers—parent volunteers, para-educators, the targeted students, other students—can collect accurate information. If students are used, however, they might initially need assistance so they will be neither too stringent nor too lenient.

Measurement Systems

Many different measurement systems are available for evaluating the effectiveness of intervention procedures on the improvement of student performance. Some of these (e.g., correct and error rate scores, percentage correct scores) are more applicable to instructional situations; others are more complicated than necessary for most instructional or discipline situations. Simple data collection systems usually meet the need. In particular, three measurement systems are most useful to assess student deportment: frequency, duration, and the percentage of those two indicators of performance.

Frequency indicates how many times the student engaged in the target behavior. It is a tally or count of the number of times the behavior occurred over a constant period of time or of how many students engaged in the target behavior.

Duration data answer the question "How much time did the student engage in a certain activity?" The person collecting the data should be given a stopwatch that can accumulate time. Each time the targeted behavior begins, the stopwatch is started, and each time the episode concludes, the stopwatch is stopped. At the end of the period, the total amount of time spent engaged in the target behavior appears on the face of the stopwatch, and that becomes the day's data to record. When this method of collecting duration data is used, the teacher knows only the total time the student engaged in the undesirable behavior for the observation period, not how long each episode lasted. Because, however, the major concern usually is the total amount of instructional time being misused, information about the time involved for each occurrence of the target behavior during the period is not as important.

In middle and high schools, academic periods last for fairly consistent lengths of time. On the rare days when the schedule is altered, those data could be discounted and not entered into the permanent record. Tardiness is usually observed under constant conditions, and simple duration data are sufficient for the purposes of daily and weekly comparisons. In elementary schools, teachers usually schedule their school day according to a constant set of time periods. Some keep records of school deportment for the entire school day. In these cases simple frequency and duration data suffice.

Percentage of occurrence is a type of measurement system that adjusts for observation times that are not consistent. As just mentioned, if frequency or duration data are collected, the time period for data collection must be constant because the purpose of data collection and the application of a measurement system is for a comparison of one day's data with another. In many school situations, observation times cannot be consistent. Many factors contribute to this problem, including abbreviated school days and inconsistent class periods. When consistent observation times are not possible on a daily basis, simple frequency and duration data are not useful without an additional calculation turning the raw data into percentage scores.

Evaluation Phases

Four basic phases comprise most behavioral evaluation plans: assessment, intervention, maintenance, and follow-up. The *assessment phase* has many obvious purposes: identification of the seriousness of the infraction, the intensity of its occurrence, and the conditions under which it occurs. Consistent daily assessment before interventions are scheduled has many benefits. Often the teacher finds that the correct behavior for change has not been identified and other behaviors need to be identified and measured precisely. Sometimes the seriousness of the problem leads to selection of a procedure higher on the Intervention Ladder than originally planned. Of course, the primary benefit of the assessment phase is for later comparisons. Only when teachers know the original levels of the behavior under consideration can an evaluation of long- and short-term effects be made.

The *intervention phase* follows the assessment or baseline period. The intervention selected should be in effect each observation day during this phase. After several days of explaining the intervention strategy to the students, daily instructions are not necessary. The intervention phase should last as long as necessary. There are two fundamental reasons for terminating an intervention: either a criterion has been met or the intervention is unsuccessful. Data should guide teachers making such determinations. Sometimes an intervention is effective initially but loses its power with time. When the evaluation data indicate that this has occurred, another intervention strategy should be planned that adds to or replaces the first. Unfortunately, not all interventions work as hoped or expected. If evaluation data indicate that the behavior worsened or that the intervention did not produce the desired results, another plan must be put into effect. Therefore, many remediation programs include more than one intervention phase.

When interventions are terminated, the previous undesirable behavior patterns may return. Thus, it is necessary to implement a *maintenance phase* by continuing to measure the target behavior after the intervention phase is concluded. For several weeks the teacher in charge of the project should continue measurement of the target behavior according to the schedule followed during the assessment and intervention conditions. If the desired deportment is maintained, periodic checks should ensue in a *follow-up phase*.

When designing an intervention plan for a targeted behavior, remember to:

1. Conduct an assessment phase (baseline) to obtain information about initial performance.

2. Select a measurement system that is sensitive to the targeted behavior.
3. Measure daily at the same time.
4. Graph and utilize decision rules.
5. Implement the intervention systematically and on a daily basis.
6. Establish a criterion for mastery.
7. Compare assessment with intervention phase data to determine if progress is being made.
8. Conduct periodic checks to assure maintenance.
9. If students don't maintain their performance, intervene immediately and consistently so data can guide decision-making.
10. Match infraction and intervention using data collected.

Displaying Data

For ease of analysis and communication with other educators, the school community, parents, and students, the display of the evaluation data need not be complicated. Graphs do not have to be constructed or maintained only by the adult supervising the intervention project. Students can contribute to this task while applying the basic mathematics skill of graphing. A disruptive student could earn the privilege of keeping a class graph for a period of time, or a responsible student can be assigned the task. Students whose behavior has been targeted for remediation could chart the evaluation data gathered on themselves. Although not terribly time-consuming, constructing and keeping graphs current can be one more unnecessary task to ask teachers and other school personnel to assume. Therefore, whenever possible, consider asking students to construct and enter the data on the graphs.

Conclusion

With recent calls for more inclusive schools (NASBE, 1992; Sailor, 1991), general education teachers are seeing a higher rate of integration of students with disabilities in their classrooms. One result is a greater diversity of ability, motivation, skills, and achievement. A frequent by-product of such diversity is higher levels of disruption, which, unfortunately, can negatively impact the learning environment. All teachers, and particularly those working in inclusive classrooms, must work diligently to ensure that students receive as much instructional time as possible. Without direct attention to this factor, positive instructional time can drop to extremely low levels (Pemberton, 1994) and negatively influence students' academic achievements.

High levels of disruption can alter the positive learning environment, remove the teacher from instruction, and result in classroom chaos. In this chapter, we suggest that discipline intervention can and should be helpful. Teachers must create learning environments that prevent and deter disruption. They must be armed with a wide array of interventions ranging from mild to severe and subtle to intrusive. When administered in a systematic and hierarchical fashion, intervention can result in an exciting situation where students are free to explore and learn to their levels of ability. We hope that this brief exploration of the context of discipline, the creation of positive learning environments, and the Intervention Ladder will assist you in developing a rich classroom where discipline is not a concern.

References

Barrish, H. H., Saunders, M., & Wolf, M. M. (1969). Good behavior game: Effects of individual contingencies for group consequence on disruptive behavior in a classroom. *Journal of Applied Behavior Analysis, 2,* 119–124.

Broden, M., Hall, R. V., Dunlap, A., & Clark, R. (1970). Effects of teacher attention and a token reinforcement system in a junior high school special education class. *Exceptional Children, 36,* 341–349.

Center, D. B., Deitz, S. M., & Kaufman, M. E. (1982). Student ability, task difficulty, and inappropriate classroom behavior: A study of children with behavior disorders. *Behavior Modification, 6,* 355–374.

Cooper, J. O., Heron, T. E., & Heward, W. L. (1987). *Applied behavior analysis.* Columbus, OH: Merrill.

Evertson, C. M., Emmer, E. T., Clements, B. S., Sanford, J. P., & Worsham, M. E. (1984). *Classroom management for elementary teachers.* Englewood Cliffs, NJ: Prentice Hall.

Gallup, A. M. (1984). The Gallup poll of teachers' attitudes toward the public schools. *Phi Delta Kappan, 65,* 97–107.

Gallup, A. M. (1994). *Results of the Annual Gallup Poll.* Lincoln, NE: Gallup Organization.

Gardner, R., et al. (1994). *Behavior analysis in education: Focus on measurably superior instruction.* Pacific Grove, CA: Brooks/Cole.

Kounin, J. S. (1970). *Discipline and group management in classrooms.* NY: Holt, Rhinehart, & Winston.

Krumboltz, J. D., & Krumboltz, H. B. (1972). *Changing children's behavior.* Englewood Cliffs, NJ: Prentice Hall.

Maurer, R. (1988). *Special education discipline handbook.* West Nyack, NY: Center for Applied Research in Education.

National Association of School Boards of Education (NASBE). (1992). *Winners all.* Alexandria, VA: NASBE.

Pemberton, J. (1994). *An analysis of teacher time during the school day: A study comparing five service delivery models available to students identified as having disabilities.* University of New Mexico: Unpublished doctoral dissertation.

Sabatino, A. (1983). Prevention: Teachers' attitude and adaptive behavior—Suggested techniques. In D. A. Sabatino, A. C. Sabatino, & L. Mann (Eds.), *Discipline and behavioral management* (pp. 29–84). Austin, TX: Pro-Ed.

Sailor, W. (1991). Special education in the restructured school. *Remedial and Special Education, 12,* 8–22.

Smith, D. D., & Rivera, D. M. (1993). *Effective discipline.* Austin, TX: Pro-Ed.

Sulzbacher, S. I., & Houser, J. E. (1968). A tactic to eliminate disruptive behaviors in the classroom: Group contingent consequences. *American Journal of Mental Deficiency, 73,* 88–90.

Windell, J. (1991). *Discipline: A source of 50 fail-safe techniques for parents.* New York: Macmillan.

2 The Missing Link: Students Discuss School Discipline

SUE THORSON

AS POINTED OUT in the introduction to this section, involving students in establishing and maintaining an orderly learning environment is a productive procedure in classroom organization. Students generally can and will work with peers and teachers to plan how content can be learned through collaboration and cooperative effort. Joe may just be able to provide the keys to his own self-control curriculum.

All too often students are studied, tested, and acted upon without acknowledgment of their own experiences and ideas. Procedural decisions are based upon the conceptual frameworks of adults who may have had very different school experiences from those of the students they are analyzing. This causes misperceptions and misunderstandings, misplacement, and sometimes even mistreatment. Therefore, asking the students themselves about a common experience may be valuable.

To this end, I began a discussion with students about their experiences in a Saturday detention. The conversation expanded to include the school's discipline and then to the school as a part of the community. The experiences the students related ranged from amusing to disturbing. Their provocative insights will be useful to educational planners.

Besides the information it produced, this form of research seemed to have intrinsic value. The students reported that they enjoyed the opportunity for individual discussions on serious topics. Even the most playful individuals took the time and made an effort to seriously consider the topics we discussed. They read their transcripts, even when reading was difficult for them. They reported having complementary discussions of our conversations with family and friends.

The Project

Student placement often was precipitated by behavior problems in general classes, so discipline was a major concern in my high school resource room. Long before they reached high school, my students had learned how to beat the system, drive teachers crazy, and tune out of any experience that remotely resembled academic learning. Of course, good pedagogy increased attention, and behavioral techniques decreased behavior problems, but neither immediately resulted in acceptable behavior outside our room. Detentions and suspensions were assigned frequently, but they seemed to have little effect on these students.

When I served my triennial duty as detention supervisor, or I discussed school life with my colleagues in general education, I found that they had the same experiences with some of their students. More specifically, good lessons were useless when a student wouldn't pay attention; relationships were difficult to build in large, brief class sessions; and behaviorism was tricky to integrate into the secondary school environment. The result was that students were sent to the office and given either a detention or a suspension.

Although replete with theories about and suggestions for effective discipline, research did not provide any new information. Effective discipline has been an educational issue for Mediterranean-European cultures since ancient Egyptian times (Butts, 1947). Jewish traditions also provided a foundation for our educational practices. Hebrew teachers were encouraged to punish wrongdoing (Barclay, 1959); the Hebrew word *musar*, which means education, discipline, and chastisement, appears in the book of *Proverbs* (circa 900 B.C.E.) 30 times (Brubaker, 1947). Discipline, including punishment, has been an integral part of American education since colonial times and still is espoused by many parents, administrators, and teachers. Keeping students in school after dismissing the others is a punishment long accepted in our schools.

Many researchers maintain that punishment is ineffective, community members question its morality, and judges increasingly rule against it. Some researchers blame society, and more specifically the parents, for children's misbehavior. Others say that adolescence is a stage characterized by rebellious, antisocial behavior. Alternative theories suggest that the school, the teaching, or the curricula should be changed to eliminate discipline problems.

Even though all of this information was interesting, it didn't answer my question about how to maintain discipline in my resource room and in general programs. I don't like to punish, but it does seem to have the desired effect at times (Millman, Schaefer, & Cohen, 1980; Weber, 1984), although in other instances misbehavior actually increases (Gretzinger, 1988; Kreisberg, 1990). I, too, wonder at the state of society and the way some parents do or do not rear their children, but I can do very little about it. And, though adolescents do seem to go through stages, high school teachers do not have the luxury of waiting for them to reach adulthood.

The only hope seemed to be a change of pedagogy, but how? Expand the curriculum or go back to basics? Get stricter or become more student-centered?

Technology or relationships? The choices are infinite, the answers are contradictory, and I have a student climbing up the air shaft now.

After getting him down, I asked Harry (not his real name) why he did that and he explained that, like Mount Everest, it was there. Knowing that it would contribute to my growing discomfort was an added bonus, although Harry did not have malicious intent. So off he went to the office while I retrieved my temper. Although I yelled at him often and sent him to the office at least once a week, Harry later confided that my caring and high expectations had stopped him from making a suicide attempt on more than one occasion. This and similar student-teacher interactions led me to believe that the students and I had very different understandings of the world and the discipline process. Kreutter's (1983) research suggested that students and teachers do indeed perceive discipline differently.

After a move to university teaching, I had the opportunity to further my inquiries with students and the time to organize and reflect upon their responses. The results indicated that my question was all wrong. Although they don't like it, most secondary students I talked to saw a need for discipline. They saw its administration, however, as symptomatic of the problems of the school community as a whole.

The Process

Qualitative researchers study people's understandings of their worlds (Bogden & Biklin, 1992). Ethnography is a specific method used to investigate the complex meaning systems of behavioral organization, self-concept, and societal structure (Spradley, 1979). Husserl (in Barritt, Beekman, Bleeker, & Mulderij, 1985) described phenomenology as an attempt to understand the constitution of the conscious mind, which is the basis of all knowledge. To understand life, we must turn to experience, forgetting our preconceived ideas and looking at occurrences with fresh eyes (Barritt et al., 1985).

The attempt to look at an experience through another's eyes enables the researcher to begin to achieve an awareness of different ways of thinking and acting, to identify new possibilities. Barritt et al. (1985) suggested that these might best be discovered by attending to *variations* in behavior rather than the norm. Thus, the initial attempt to understand the student's point of view was made using an ethnographic method of research based on the philosophy of phenomenology. Detention results from many types of students' deviation from the behavioral norm, so students in detention were good candidates to interview.

To understand a student's constructions of meaning, the inquirer must be aware of many factors, including the individual's life outside of school, nonacademic strengths, and the perception of obstacles (Gay & Williams, 1993). Therefore, although each student was asked to respond to core issues and participate in the same series of conversations, deviations from the topic of detention also were pursued, to discover other issues that might affect the student's perceptions of discipline. To respond to student direction, a conversational rather than an interview technique was constructed. Although the conversations were only loosely directed by common social reactions, they were similar in general content, indicating that the students had similar concerns.

I was able to meet with students assigned to Saturday School detention in a large Southern California high school. The reasons they were assigned to detention were similar to those identified nationally: tardiness, truancy, and disrespect (Dinkins, 1981; Duncan, 1991). Fourteen students, seven from general education and seven from special education, volunteered to talk with me. The students included ninth through twelfth graders and one graduate of the special education program. Both young men and young women participated. Although all had lived in the United States for all or most of their lives, they were of African, African American, Asian, Latino, Mexican, and European American heritages.

After hearing an explanation of the study, the students chose a pseudonym and we began the individual conversations. The earliest discussions revolved around my concern with discipline. I asked all the students individually why they received the detention, why their friends received detentions, and how they would deal with these misbehaviors if they were the principal. After reading the transcription of our first meeting, the students scheduled a second discussion during lunch or after school. At that time I asked about the roles of teachers, administrators, friends, and family in their education and in their decisions about behavior. I tried to elicit a continuum of misdemeanors and consequences, but each student moved to explore issues of communication and community instead.

The third visit aimed to clarify the previous transcription and to develop a description of the school and the participants. Finally, we had lunchtime pizza parties for all of the participants, at which time they were given a copy of the summary of their conversations and discussed how they felt about the process. They also were invited to contact me if they wanted to change their part of the summary, and they all received a letter of recommendation describing their role in the research.

The conversations were strikingly similar across placement, age, gender, and ethnic lines. The students' comments about rule orientation, strictness, and student responsibility reflected the same continuum from conservative to liberal that we see in society at large, but their desire to please their parents and their concerns about communication and relationships within the school community were unanimous.

The Research Is Right

As the discussions progressed, the research I had reviewed was verified. Although the students contradicted each other and themselves, they clearly supported all of the theories. Appropriate discipline, it seems, depends upon the situation and the individual.

The students agreed that, in general, rules are necessary and that rules should be followed. They were assigned detention because they did not understand the rules, or the teacher was unfair, or the specific rule was not appropriate.

Chaquan, a general education freshman, complained, "They've got rules for everything you do." She explained that she got in trouble because she didn't always know the rules on a new campus, "because on the first one [misdemeanor], you're dazed...the first one you're supposed to tell them, or talk to them, [but] they're ready to give you a referral or detention, right away."

Johnny, a ninth-grade special education student with bilingual skills, was disciplined often because he misunderstood directions or did not understand rules. Once his PE teacher gave him detention for not following instructions. "Well," claimed Johnny, "I did follow [the directions]. He told us, 'Go around.' Well, around where? And like, that's it. That's how I got in trouble." Sometimes, the teachers misunderstood him. For example:

> ...she said I cussed her out, but I didn't cuss her out. I was cussing this kid out. And she thinks I cussed her out, but I didn't. I didn't say her name. I just said this kid's name. So I got in trouble, I got suspended for two days.

Nivek, a tenth-grade special education student, compounded his problems when he lost his temper because the proctors misunderstood him:

> I got it [detention] because I was just walking around the school and everything like that...cuz I went to the restroom. And the proctors didn't believe me, that I had a pass...and they sent me to ABC [the school discipline room].... So I got mad about it...and they told me, "You better calm down." I said, "No. It's not fair just bringing me over here, just cuz I went to the restroom." ...so they gave me Saturday detention because I wasn't supposed to be mad. This is a weird school, man.

Tom, a general education sophomore, has received only one detention this year. It was because he returned to school late after an appointment. After he was assigned the detention, his mother attempted to provide an excuse for him, but after several unsuccessful contacts with the school, she asked him to go ahead and serve the detention.

Rebecca, a general education junior, and her friends were assigned detention because they frequently were late to class. She explained that they were meeting at a far corner of the campus during the mid-morning break and couldn't hear the late bell. After the detention they changed their meeting place.

Several students had been assigned detention for leaving campus during the lunch hour, a privilege reserved for seniors. All of the students believed this rule was unfair. Some stayed on campus after getting caught; others maintained that the food was not good and the rule was unjust, so they were resolved to go out to lunch. Antashia's mother requested an off-campus pass so her daughter could eat lunch elsewhere, but it was denied because she was not a senior. Antashia said:

> Forget it. I'm gonna eat either way it goes. That's me. I like to eat. I could eat some food, and I'm not gonna stop eating for nobody. You can punish me, they can have me in Saturday School every Saturday, but if I'm hungry, I'm gonna leave and go get some food.

Students who spoke of leaving campus habitually for lunch were careful to add that it was important to return to campus in plenty of time to get to class promptly, because they didn't want to miss learning opportunities.

Other students worried about the conflict of school rules with their personal priorities. Rebecca eventually failed her first-period class because she could not get her little brother to child care and then get to school on time. Both special and general education students disagreed with the school rules against fighting. They agreed that fighting on campus was not desirable but explained that in some situations they had to defend their honor or physical well-being. Casper, a special education sophomore, told of being maneuvered into fighting in the office:

> I got in a fight with this kid in the office, in front of the security guard. I didn't plan it that way. I was in my class and the kid, when he told on me, cuz he was messing with me and he said that, he told on me that I was always messing with *him*. And so I went in the office and he was in the principal's office and I was sitting down, and he all, like mumbling some stuff and he asked the lady, "Can I go get a drink? Can I go get a drink by the drinking fountain?" The lady said, "Yeah." He walked by me, he started to, he like said something. I ignored him, then he came back in and he got in my face and so I stood up and he started talking and then he pushed me...so I pushed him and he tried swinging and he hit me in the side of the head. And then I hit him in his face and the security guard jumped over and I almost hit the security guard.
>
> ...the kid pushed me, then he swung at me. Then I hit him...Cuz then everybody in the school would be like, "You didn't swing back,"...even my mom said, "After the first swing, don't stand there. "

Tracy, a general education sophomore, was one of the students who agreed with Casper: "Sometimes you got to fight...Sometimes you can't help it. Somebody go up to you; they swing at you, what you gonna do then? Stand there and say, 'I won't fight,' and get beat up?"

A few students believed detention was a deterrent to their own future misbehavior, although they did not think it was effective for others. They generally said they would avoid detention in the future because it was a waste of time.

Stephanie, an 18-year-old special education sophomore, said, "It stopped me...I learned from it that I shouldn't go back in that place again." She added, "...it was too boring for me. I couldn't stand it. When I get bored, I just want to walk out."

Alissa and Angela, both in general education, agreed that they did not want to repeat the experience because they had better things to do with their time. Larson and Karpas (1967) seem to be correct when they refer to detention as a procedure designed to "annoy the annoyer."

Don, a special education junior, saw detention as an opportunity to reflect:

> Just to get away from the students, and you know, keep you by yourself in a quiet place...it helped me a lot. Cuz I'd be like, "Man, I gotta do better so I won't go back in here no more. I miss all my friends."...[It's] kinda like a little jail. Not a bad one. It's just a place to keep you until you think you have learned your lesson, not to get in trouble, not to be bad, talk back to the teachers or anything.

Johnny, too, said a detention experience is punishing to him and makes him want to behave better. Unfortunately, both young men have trouble following through with their good intentions and are assigned detentions frequently.

Most of the students did not see detention as a real deterrent. Chaquan said, "I'm going to be here for the next three weeks. So if it would have had an effect, then nobody would be here the second time." Angela, the general education sophomore mentioned earlier, does not see punishment as a change agent. She explained:

> All of the punishments that we've had, none of the kids respond to, I mean, not one of them do. And if they really wanted to stop, they'd stop on their own. This wouldn't make them stop.

Antashia, the general education junior, agreed:

> OK, I left to go get something to eat, OK, punish me...I mean, Saturday School, to me, and probably to basically everybody else, was just like, "Oh, I'm not gonna go to class. I can just go and get that little detention over with in Saturday School."...It's no big deal... It wouldn't stop me from doing the things that I do....

Like many researchers (e.g., Block, 1987; Brown & Payne, 1988; Feldhusen, 1978), the students identified parents as important contributors to school discipline problems, but only in the case of *other* families, not their own. They were pessimistic about the futures of friends without parental support.

Carla, a special education sophomore, talked about her friend Mike, who dropped out:

> It's cuz like, I don't know, it seems like it's the way the parents are with you when you're little. They got raised with gangs, their parents were in gangs and drugs and all that. And they were never respectable to people...And at school, you know, they don't care. They'll talk back to whoever they want, whenever they want.
>   ...Some people just drop out, and they never do nothing for their life. They think it's so easy, just dropping out. And they say, well, you know, "I'll have money later; watch, I'll get a job." And they can't and you know, they sell drugs and things like that and stuff.

Antashia disagreed:

> I've been knowing some of them since the fourth grade and up...It's like, they have those parents that don't care....
>   You can't blame nobody but yourself. I can't simply say it's my mom's fault that I'm here [in Saturday School]. She didn't have anything to do with it. She's not the one I got in the car with...She raised me, and she's not done raising me. But when I'm at school and she's at work, I know what I have to do, and I just chose to do the wrong thing that day. I can't blame her for it.

Instead of blaming her mother, Antashia emphasized the positive effect her mother has had on her school experience. Her mother helped her with homework, taught her to respect her teachers, and continues to encourage her when school becomes too frustrating.

Schoolwork was both cited and implied as a reason for misbehavior. Kratzert and Kratzert (1991) claimed that changes in methodology would reduce frustration and thus improve discipline. Some students complained about boring classes and uncaring teachers. Others had no compunctions about missing classes to go to a party, visit friends, or just "hang out."

The students agreed that it is the teacher's job to maintain control. Good teachers, who teach interesting materials clearly, rarely have discipline problems. Don said, "If they're so good with kids, they shouldn't have no problems with their detention and giving them ABC."

Rebecca told of an algebra teacher who does not do so well:

....my teacher was doing this problem, and she just started talking about it, how to do it, and all of a sudden she started going somewhere else, explaining something else....I got lost. So I started falling asleep, and I fell asleep. She was talking too much. Then by the time I woke up, I guess it was five minutes later, or ten, she was still talking about the same problem...nobody did the homework last night. Everybody came today with the same question, "How do you do it?" Cuz nobody understood it, and then she tried to explain it again today.

Her history teacher keeps Rebecca interested by discussing campus events and current issues along with the standard history curriculum.

Chaquan, does her work for biology, but not Spanish, because:

My biology teacher, she's good. She teaches us, she explains it, when she goes to the notes, she'll tell us how to do those, she shows movies and all that; I mean movies [about] insects and reptiles and all that.... But my other teachers, I don't understand what they're saying. Like my Spanish teacher, I didn't even know what she was talking about. She would give us, like, nine assignments to do in one week. And then didn't explain how to do most of them. And she wanted to know why [we got] low grades in the class.

When students decided to improve their behavior, the reason was to get credits for graduation, grades, or employment. Don summarized, "So I thought about it to myself, and I'm gonna behave myself. If I could ace those classes, get out of school, go where I've gotta go, do what I've gotta do. No problem."

Students who are unhappy with the quality of their education may exhibit maladaptive behaviors as a form of resistance (Kampol, 1994; Shor, 1992; Willis, 1981). Special education students were especially resentful of the poor quality of education they were receiving, and they talked about misbehaving in response.

Carla, who is disciplined frequently in school, explained:

Like, since I started going to high school, I was like, "...I'm gonna drop out.... What's the big thing about dropping out? I don't have to go to school; I don't have to do homework; I don't have to do nothing." And when I went to ninth grade, there was just nothing.... I had to wake up early and go to school and not do nothing. I didn't have to even carry books, or pencils, or paper, nothing. I never did carry nothing. And I don't know if it's just only the Special Ed, or other people, cuz I used to see, like some of my friends they would carry books, they would carry, you know, like, a folder and two books. And me, it was like, I never carried nothing. Like, you know, I don't know, I felt like I'm not going to learn nothing when I get out of high school.

Casper also is in trouble constantly with the school and municipal authorities. He described a teacher who:

> ...wouldn't give no one homework, cuz like no one ever did it. And I was like, "Can I have homework?" He's all, "No, I don't want to give out homework." I was like, "Well, can I take the math book home, for I can do some math." "No, I can't give out the math books. You won't bring it back." And so I never really had work.... And if I don't get homework and everything, how am I supposed to learn and stuff?

Casper went on to explain that, although he enjoys playing Monopoly and watching popular movies, he wonders how these activities contribute to his learning. He also gleefully described the many ways he and his friends devised to get even with teachers who were rude to them or who talked to their friends instead of teaching the class:

> Sometimes, when the teacher would be on the phone, we knew she'd be on there for a while, so we'd start talking, "What are we doing tomorrow; what are we doing now," and talk around and making jokes and stuff.... Then, like we'd get loud and stuff. And she'd like, "I'm on the phone!" And some kid would come out with a smart remark and stuff. And she'd like, "Who said that?!" And she'd turn her back so she didn't know who it was, and we're, "We don't know." And one time, some kid threw a bottle of glitter and it hit her...and it hit the board. She was all, "Well, who was that?"
>
> It's like, if we're just sitting there, we can't, if we're sitting there and everything, and she's on the phone, we're not learning anyway, so we start....

Tracy, a sophomore in the general education program, has a teacher who singles her out for discipline. She explained:

> You can't just talk to yourself, unless I'm going crazy.... So I don't see how he can just single out one person and just give them detention, and not give the other person detention that they was talking to, or that was talking to them.

The problem is compounded because:

> I figure if I'm going to get in trouble, I'm gonna annoy him as much as I can. I'm already going to get in trouble, he deserve it, if he gonna keep singling me out, so I get on his nerves! ...If you know you're already getting in trouble, why shut up?

Not surprisingly, students often cited friends as a reason for getting in trouble. Truancy, especially, was a group activity. Students skipped or left school to be with their friends, attend "ditching parties," or spend private time with girlfriends or boyfriends. Students, however, also cited friends and peers as a motivation for behaving well. Alissa saw herself as a potential role model:

> I hope by my attitude that I can influence people around me; if they're my age or my friends who might be acting rowdy or whatever. I hope that they can look at me

and settle down a little bit. You know, just try and be a good example for every people; not necessarily to walk around and say, "Oh well, look at me. I'm doing this and that!" but, just hold myself, the way I carry myself and be a good person.

Don is another student who saw a responsibility to be a role model for his peers:

My job as a student is to do my work, be the best I can be, make other people look at me and want to try to be like me, you know, do the things I do. Like if they see, like say you used to be a bad person, and then all of a sudden, you change yourself around, and like, you're doing good. So then, like the people that's still being bad, they'll look at you like, "Aw, you used to be bad like me. So now, I think I want to get like that, and be smart." Have a little sense, you know.

...I'm trying to follow it through...leave a good footprint there, another person can follow.

The Missing Links: Fun, Parents, Community

Although pieces of the students' beliefs can be found in the research about discipline, some factors were interpreted quite differently. For example, the students claimed that sometimes they misbehaved purely for the fun of it, without ulterior motive or concern. Although many student problems theoretically are caused by parents, these students looked to their parents for support as they pursued their educations. Most surprising to me were the sophisticated theories of educational communities evolving from their discussions of discipline.

Many expressed the belief that rules are made to be broken; rules exist as a challenge to creative minds. They enjoyed breaking rules and confessed that they would fight control, even when they knew it was in their best interest. These students saw school as boring, getting around the rules as a sport, and detention the penalty for getting caught. They were firm in their claim that they intended no malice toward teachers when they broke rules or disrupted class.

Casper wanted to give his teachers a hard time sometimes because otherwise "there'd be no fun in going to school." He continued, "[We would], just out of fun, turn out the lights, and throw a desk over, no one...knows who did it!"

Carla, who enjoyed her biology class because she learned things, also liked a class in which the students misbehaved regularly. She explained, "...and they would start throwing papers and keep on doing things, you know? And I liked that class, because we never did nothing, and I got used to it.... He was my best teacher!"

Robert, a graduate of the special education program, and Johnny agreed that the pleasure of truancy is in the chase rather than the day off. Johnny said, "Running away from proctors, you know, that's fun." Robert complained:

Some of the proctors let you leave...But, I mean, when they let you leave, that's no fun.... [I would rather] send somebody to go talk to a proctor, tell the proctor, "Hey, there's somebody over here, doing this." Proctor turns around, walks that way, and you walk right behind the proctor, out the gate...to get by the proctor, or like that, it was just like a big game, pretty much.

[Once you're off campus] it gets boring. During the day, nothing.... You can't go out, school police sees you, you're in trouble. Now if they see and you run from them, now that's fun. You have them chasing you and they're pissed off like hell.

Casper explained that eliminating weapons on campus was difficult, partially because, although students might understand the wisdom of the policy, many could not resist the challenge of smuggling in any contraband:

> They might have metal detectors at the front gate and stuff, but a kid could always have a friend go in with no weapon or nothing, then go to the back gate, when no one's around, and then hand them a gun, couple of guns or something, then the other kid is gonna go through the metal detector, how can they get busted or stuff?... It's just more challenge for the kid to get in. And they'll be like, "Well, let's see if we can get something in today," and it's the challenge, cuz when someone says, "You can't bring this, or you're gonna get busted." Like Walkmans you can't bring; people are like, "Well, we're gonna bring them in our bag anyway, it's like...Well, let's see if we can get past all this," or hop over the fence or something, or throw them over the fence and then go pick them up or something. It's easy, like it can be done at any school.

The students I talked to were adamant about their responsibility to control themselves. They denied that any outside agent actually could change their behavior but cited parents and other family members as primary influences in their lives. They saw family members as sources of inspiration and encouragement; above all, they wanted to please and impress their parents. The main reason for trying to behave, and even for staying in school, was concern for parents. All of the students spoke respectfully of their parents and initiated a discussion about how important it was to make them happy or at least protect them from disappointment. Because the parents were notified of the detention assignment, some students resolved not to repeat the experience.

Angela's mother was angry because her daughter left campus, but explained her anger and the reason for the on-campus rule. Angela said she won't leave campus again until she has a pass, partially because she prefers to follow the rules, partially to avoid Saturday School, "but mostly because of my mom, because I'm supposed to listen to her."

All of the students were concerned about parental reactions to their school performance. Rebecca tries to stay out of trouble because, "every time I do something like that, they lose more confidence." She and her younger brother are the only two members of the family who have not dropped out of school.

Like Rebecca, Nivek is determined to graduate, "Not for me. But for them, so they'll be proud of me."

Chaquan is not afraid of punishment, because her mother discusses behavior problems and advises Chaquan how to avoid them, but she doesn't like it when the office calls and bothers her mother about misbehavior. When Johnny's mother got upset about the number of times he was suspended, he stopped doing things that would result in suspension.

Angela concludes:

Well, I think that we should all respect each other, because, I mean, that's the way my mom teaches me. My parents are from Africa, and they teach respect. My mom has taught me to respect everybody, all my elders.... And it's just that I think we all need respect, to respect our elders mostly. And then our peers also. I think that's the best way to get across with people. If you respect them and they respect you back....

The students agreed on the importance of parent involvement. They emphasized repeatedly the importance of contacting parents frequently and courteously. Because they thought parents ideally should make decisions about punishment, they were frank in admitting that they would (and do) attempt to interfere with school contacts by erasing answering machines and intercepting mail. The school is responsible, however, to continue to call, write, or even visit until contact is made. Chaquan added:

But some parents don't really care. There's a lot of kids up here, they come to school when they want to, and they leave and whatever, and their parents don't care...I don't think there is nothing to do...If they don't care, then there's nothing you [as an administrator] can do.

Even then, Chaquan concluded, it may be that the parents just don't understand the importance of the problem, so administrators should continue to work with the family while pursuing other ways of dealing with the student.

Students who received support from their teachers noticed it and appreciated it. These students expressed concern about disrespectful behavior toward adults and wished some teachers would discourage it more firmly. Others saw the lack of communication as an important reason for ongoing behavioral problems.

Although students did not credit teachers as a primary influence in their lives, the special education students clarified that teacher support was important to their growth. Don explained:

They say, "You got the talent, you can do what you want to do. But you know, you gotta ace this class too, along with what you want to do. If you don't ace this class, you ain't gonna get nowhere you want to be.... Mr. Forrest will push you, and make you understand, you know, like these are things you gotta do, then they'll work. They'll keep on pushing you and pushing you until you want to go the right way.

Like Mr. Forrest. Now there's a good teacher. You know, he'll look out for every student. Try to make sure you're doing the right thing. Keep you in line and all that kind of good stuff. Make sure you don't drop out.

Ana, a special education junior, added:

Ms. Guerrero...She's a good teacher. She helps you any way she can.... She tries to push you, but not towards where you're gonna think, "She's annoying me" or "bothering me." She's not like that. She's like, if you want the help, you'll take it. If not, then just turn away the other way, don't take it; but she's like holding it for you....

Well, you have to change personally first, you know, then to change everything later.... You'll start getting on the right track; you'll want to do more things, and then they'll want to help you more. More and more.

Stephanie talked about inappropriate student behavior in the classroom:

They argue with the teacher, they say bad words in front of them.... For some reason this kid popped up and said, "Mr. Smith, I need your blanking help." And he sent him out of class. Mr. Smith is a real nice guy and I don't think anybody should treat him like that. You gotta respect elders. That's what I usually do.

She added that when she disagrees with a teacher, she does so politely and usually is able to resolve the problem amicably. Chaquan also told about a teacher whose students make her cry but "she don't ever do nothing about it...she lets them run over her. They say something to her, she just let it pass. She in bed crying about them."

Tom explained that the teachers in his school are "not that bad," but:

They have to act like some way that they're really taking care of their business.... Most teachers, kids don't respect them cuz they're not scared of the teacher. Some teachers are respectful (sic). You can just see it, when you go to that class. All of the...I mean, even if they're bad, they won't disrespect that teacher, if they know how.... It depends on the teacher.

Rebecca agreed that the teacher has to try to keep the students under control so they can "learn the best they can." Alissa, an honors program senior, added:

I think it's their responsibility, if they're [the students] disrupting the class, to let them know, "You're disrupting my class, I don't appreciate it. Sometimes you [the teacher] just have to tell a student, "You need to sit down and be quiet; if you have a problem with it, we'll discuss it after class. Or if you really don't like it, you can leave and go to the office."

...[There's a] separation from being in a training camp or like a strict academy or something. I think it's important to get to voice your opinion, and just share with other people, help you get to know them. Not really to be, not necessarily to be social, but, it's just important to...I think it might teach a little bit of consideration, to say, "Wait a minute, this is what they're thinking. So, maybe I can do something to change, to make them feel more comfortable."

Lack of communication occurs when the teacher refuses to listen to the student. Chaquan tried to clarify a situation with a substitute but "she just said, 'Just gimme your number!' and I was like, 'What number you have so I could tell you if that's the right one or not?' And she wrote me up a referral." Casper's friends tried to explain what happened, getting the whole group into trouble:

...then that one other kid, he even said, "He didn't flip off the lights." And then those two kids that didn't get in trouble, cuz they sat down,...and then both of them said, "He didn't flip off the lights." But she didn't want to believe me. Cuz they all sticking up for me, she says. So everybody else got Saturday School and they're all trying to say, "Yeah, he wasn't even in the classroom at the time."... And she blamed me and I couldn't argue with her. And my whole class, even the two girls who weren't even my friends, they said I didn't do it. But she didn't want to agree.

Tracy reminded adults, "Don't always jump to believe the teacher, listen to the student, too, cuz they're people too."

The students' responses to my questions were interesting and, I think, informative. Even more significant were their spontaneous references to community. The students had a clear vision of the school's role in society, the micro society of the school itself, and the function of a discipline program in that society.

Since Plato's *Republic*, social philosophers have examined the role of schools in training future citizens. Antashia explained, "You're supposed to come here and get an education. If you're tardy and you're ditching, you're not getting it...."

Thompson and Dodder (1986) implied that, besides education, the school's function is to contain students so they stay out of trouble. Carla agreed:

> When they suspend you, you get in more trouble, cuz you're out in the street...And that's what happened to me once.... I got into trouble one day cuz there was a party and they arrested everybody in that party; cuz there was a d.p., a ditching party, and that day I got in trouble more than I get in trouble at school, because I got arrested and everything.

Angela wondered how, then, students can be kept in school except to socialize:

> I know everybody, even if you're smart, even if you know that you need to be in school, you still don't like school. The only part you like about school is socializing with your friends and stuff. That's about it. All the work you have to do and everything. Unless the class is fun or something like that; maybe a few wouldn't mind going to class. Because I notice that people do that. The classes that they like, they go to, but the ones they don't like, they ditch. [It should be] a little more interesting. Cuz some teachers just give you book work. They just give you the work, they say, "Here, this is what you've gotta do; do it." And...that's boring.

The school itself is seen as a society. Although they agreed that the purpose of the institution is education, the students' comments usually revolved around opportunities to socialize, the dearth of extracurricular activities, and the unsafe environment. Alissa described the school in terms of an extended metaphor:

> This school...it's like a little city. Some areas have the gangsters, the upper-class people, the brainy people, the people in between.... It's just like its own little separate world. You came in, you're in one place, you go home, you're in another place.
>   You go in the office, they're in the government.
>   It's a city that definitely needs help. It needs a lot of rearranging, everything: attitudes, colleagues. I know we have a lot of new policies this year, but it always needs more work.
>   [The community needs to] be more interactive with the government, just like how it is in the real world. I think that a lot of the time, the government has too much power, and the community doesn't have enough sayso. Or you know, when we're talking, it's just like we're talking to hear ourselves talk, there's not nobody listening. But, I mean, it could be a good city.

Antashia agreed that the lack of community feeling is a cause of disagreement and discipline problems:

Like, you know, start making the school better for us. We sit here, we come to school all day. I know, in some parts, in some part of the day, we're gonna leave school and go have fun on our own. And go get some excitement on our own. And we come to school, it's no fun, it's boring.

We'll have lunch dances. But at lunch dances, they play like three, four English songs; lunch is thirty minutes long, but when we have that, it's extended lunch. So it's probably like an hour. And the rest is Spanish songs. Which makes people mad, which starts a fight, cuz they be like, "Ew. Why they playing that?" Then the Mexicans, you know, "That's our kind of music."

Although Robert understood the school's financial limitations, he suspected that monies spent enforcing rules and punishing offenders might be better spent in enabling taggers to use their artistic talents to beautify the school, or equipping athletes so they can contribute to school spirit instead of finding sport in harassing and evading proctors.

Discipline is a form of guidance whereby students learn the rules and procedures of society. Continuing her metaphor, Alissa explained why things could be better:

Because I know there's a lot of people here with potential that they don't even know they have. But it takes the teachers and the people in the office to bring it out of them. Because if you don't know it's there, but somebody can recognize that in you, they know what activities and assignments to give you to bring it out of you, you know, to make you a better person. That should be the focus, to keep the city going, to make it a place where somebody else might hear about it and say, "You know, that's a good place to be."

In another conversation, she addressed discipline specifically:

The teacher draws the line. Because, you know, [as a teacher] I can understand where the students need to interact with each other, and feel like they're having more responsibility, but there's a certain point, you know, you're [as a student] a child. You don't know everything. You may feel like you do. You may feel like you're misunderstood or whatever, but for right now, there's someone older than you who has been through more than you have, and they're in control....

So what are the students learning from the school discipline procedure? Alissa observed:

The guy that runs it [Saturday School], he was telling us that it's supposed to be a punishment and stuff, and he was like asking us, "Well, what are you in here for?" and some people said, "Cuz we got in trouble," and another person said, "Cuz we got caught." So it wasn't that he did something wrong, it was just that he got caught. So, I think that a lot of people's attitude is like, "Well, you know, I can do, if I can get away with it, then it's no big deal." And it's not that they feel bad about doing it, they feel bad about getting caught. If they had the chance to do it again, and they knew they wouldn't get caught, then they probably would.

After discussing the procedure as another learning experience to prepare her for adulthood Alissa concluded:

> We can only take what's there for us; if we find a way around it and change it and make it work for us, not necessarily hurting anybody, but, making it work for us, that's part of becoming an adult.

Rebecca agreed that warnings and punishments are a necessary component of learning about life skills. She saw warnings as a form of advice that informs students about the consequences of their actions. Punishment also is necessary, although not always effective:

> Because you can't get away with everything, just like that, just so easy. Cuz if he gets away with it, without nobody telling him anything, or punishing him, he'll just keep doing it. He'll go, "Well, this is OK. So nobody's going to tell me anything, so I can just do it over again." ...For some people.... It doesn't work on all people.

The students realized that schools can't do everything. A few students will never change, for many reasons. Don explained, "There's gonna be somebody in the group that's gonna start something. So you can't...there's bad people everywhere you look and go...."

They suspected that the focus needs to change. Nivek said students, himself included, should concentrate on "learning, and finish[ing] school."

Antashia concluded, "No, it's not really about punishment.... Punishment's not always the answer. It could be about other things."

Alissa finished her metaphor with the comment:

> You know, we come here and meet somebody, because everything is a cycle. I don't think anything is a coincidence. Cuz I move a lot, I just ended up here. Well, something good will come out of it cuz you're there for a reason. Like a big city that will help.

All of the students said that if they were in charge, they would talk to students who break rules, then consider adjusting schedules, changing teachers, or making other adaptations in the school or student program. They agreed that some form of punishment eventually might be necessary but were adamant in their belief that detention and suspension should be used as last resorts rather than an automatic consequence of certain behaviors.

When asked how they would handle discipline if they were administrators, the first reaction of every participant was that the administrator should talk to the student. Stephanie said, "I would tell them that teachers don't like the way they're behaving, and that when the teachers tell you what to do, you follow that."

Don added, "Actually, you gotta listen to both of the sides. If you just take the teacher's side all the time, the student may be right and the teacher would be wrong at times....Teachers have to understand kids too."

Alissa emphasized:

> I think each case, I mean, it might be time-consuming, but I think each case should be looked at...I think I'd go into details on everything. I'd look at that person's record, to see if their attendance is up, and how their citizenship is, does this person really care, or are they just doing it to be rebellious? What?... I just couldn't

punish everybody.... I would just have to look at each and every circumstance before I applied that rule. That I wouldn't just say, "everybody," that I would listen first.

Angela thought administrators should be active in solving the problem. For example, she would work with fighters:

> I guess they need to talk to whoever they're having problems with, they're supposed to see what's going on, because if you sent somebody to detention, that didn't solve anything, because whenever they meet again, they'll just bring it back up, they'll start it all over again. So I don't think detention is helping fighting, if people get in fights, they need to get the two people who are in the fight and sit down and talk to them to see what's going on.

Parent involvement also is an essential factor in school-student interactions. Alissa explained:

> I think it's important for parent involvement, whether you have to call the house, or you know, invite them to the school.... I think if something...was going on, you have to start talking to the parents, or whoever is in charge of them, before they leave.... I just really think it should be as much as you can do to help the student.... I think it should be more parent involvement. Administration and parents and students; everybody should be interacting.

Many students said that even the threat of parent involvement is an effective deterrent. When discussing ditching, Carla said:

> I would just call their parents. And then you would get in trouble for that. Cuz like my friends are like, "Uh uhh, they're gonna call my parents, I'm not gonna go." And they do, and they won't ditch any more cuz their parents....

The students agreed that a punitive procedure might be necessary on rare occasions, after extensive counseling, schedule changes, and other school adaptations. They also agreed that a form of removal from school would be effective because of social isolation, loss of credit, and missed learning opportunities. They indicated that they believe strongly that, to be effective, the consequences have to be given consistently and fairly harshly. They also said they would include a constructive activity, such as campus clean-up or academic work, to help them learn positive behaviors and improve their sense of value to the community.

For learning to take place, some standard of behavior must be maintained. Nivek said, "I don't feel comfortable about it when kids mess around and everything like that. I try to put my mind on one thing or another.... Without being a bother to anyone, I want to study." He did not suggest that we punish students who are not quiet; rather, there should be a separate place for each group to learn.

Chaquan agreed, maintaining, "I wouldn't kick no kids out of school, cuz everybody needs their education."

Don recommended a strict alternative school, but "for like two weeks; they come back out of that school learning something," ready to behave in their classes.

Carla had the same idea, but wanted a strictly enforced in-school suspension with no socializing and appropriate academic assignments. She pointed out that rules must be enforced consistently.

Antashia also believed, "If you're gonna punish somebody...you never stick to it. That's why people take advantage of punishment, or the punishment's not harsh enough."

Stephanie and Chaquan wanted students to be involved in campus clean-up and maintenance activities.

Alissa added:

Something positive can come out of it too. They're negative in their class, and inconveniencing the teachers and the other people around them. Take that and do something good with it. Put them to work.... Show, help the school look nicer, do something productive.... I think the work would get out and they'd be like, "Man, you know, two steps away from the trash can and you just want to throw it down on the ground. Go to the trash can and put it in the trash!"

Conclusions: More Questions

How might these students' ideas affect discipline in their school? Primarily, I think, they cried out for liberation from rote enforcement and standard procedures. They believed that good educational practices and honest communication would avert many situations and solve some problems without the need for punishment. They admitted freely that their youth and inexperience led them to make foolish mistakes, and they looked to teachers and administrators for advice and counseling.

The students agreed that they wanted to have fun—sometimes inappropriately. Although they hoped for some latitude in expressing their exuberance, they realized that if respectful counseling did not cause a change in behavior, a negative consequence might be in order. Parent contact (which they believed should be constant throughout the education experience) was judged to be the most effective way to initiate behavior change. In a few cases, a time-out, similar to Glasser's (1990) model, or a *brief* alternative placement might be necessary.

The interactive research process seems to have immediate positive results. The students complained consistently about lack of communication with adults. Our conversations were structured carefully so their thoughts were valued. How did the opportunity to interact on an adult level affect these students? They demonstrated development of reflective skills as they considered their own situation in conjunction with their expressed philosophies. Reading transcripts of our conversations gave poor readers practice and encouraged the more academic students to examine their own styles of self-expression. All of the students expressed pride in their ideas and enjoyment of the interactive process.

Finding the time to discuss issues with students is difficult, but it is valuable not only for the student but also for the teacher. Jackman (1995) noted that an extended conversation with a student gave her many valuable insights. I asked secondary teachers from other districts to read the transcription to validate my understandings. They commented upon the value to them as reminders of the difference in teachers' and students' perceptions and vowed to make time to initiate conversations with their students whenever possible.

These were 14 students from a population of several thousand, in one school among thousands, at one point in time. Although their concerns may echo throughout the secondary school system, their specific priorities and suggestions probably are unique. To truly understand student reactions to discipline, one must ask the students involved, not generalize from one's own experience or the experiences of others.

References

Barclay, W. (1959). *Train up a child*. Philadelphia: Westminster Press.

Barritt, L., Beekman T., Bleeker, H., & Mulderij, K. (1985). *Researching educational practice*. University of North Dakota: Center for Teaching and Learning.

Block, J. (1987, April). *Longitudinal antecedents of ego-control and ego-resiliency in late adolescence*. Paper presented at Biennial Meeting of Society for Research in Child Development, Baltimore.

Bogden, R. C., & Biklen, S. K. (1992). *Qualitative research for education: An introduction to theory and methods*. Boston: Allyn & Bacon.

Brown, W. E., & Payne, T. (1988). Policies/practices in public school discipline. *Academic Therapy, 23*(3), 297–301.

Brubaker, J. S. (1947). *A history of the problems of education*. New York: McGraw-Hill.

Butts, R. F. (1947). *A cultural history of education*. New York: McGraw-Hill.

Dinkins, H. K. (1981). *Disciplinary problems and corrective measures in South Carolina secondary schools* (doctoral dissertation, University of South Carolina). Dissertation Abstracts International, 42, AAC8129452.

Duncan, M. P. A. (1991). *Perceptions of South Carolina public secondary school administrators toward major student discipline problems* (doctoral dissertation, University of South Carolina). Dissertation Abstracts International, 52, AAC9200797.

Feldhusen, J. F. (1978). Behavior problems in secondary schools. *Journal of Research & Development in Education, 11*(4), 17–28.

Gay, J. E., & Williams, R. B. (1993). Case study training for seeing school through adolescent's eyes. *Adolescence, 28*(109), 13–19.

Glasser, W. (1990). *The quality school: Managing students without coercion*. New York: Harper Perennial.

Gretzinger, B. Q. (1988). *System-wide implementation of an assertive discipline-based behavior management plan: A program evaluation* (doctoral dissertation, University of Southern Mississippi). Dissertation Abstracts International, 49, AAC8902491.

Jackman, J. (1995). In knowing our students ourselves. *Journal of Learning Disabilities, 28*(9), 569–574.

Kampol, B. (1994). *Critical pedagogy: An introduction*. Westport, CT: Bergin & Garvey.

Kratzert, W. R., & Kratzert, M. Y. (1991). Characteristics of continuation high school students. *Adolescence, 26*(101), 13–17.

Kreisberg, S. (1990). *Transforming power: Domination, empowerment, and education*. Albany: State University of New York Press.

Kreutter, K. J. (1983). *Student and teacher attitudes toward disciplinary practices in a junior high setting* (doctoral dissertation, Temple University). Dissertation Abstracts International.

Larson, K. A., & Karpas, M. R. (1967). *Effective secondary school discipline*. Englewood Cliffs, NJ: Prentice Hall.

Millman, H. L., Schaefer, C. E., & Cohen, J. J. (1980). *Therapies for school behavior problems*. San Francisco: Jossey-Bass.

Shor, I. (1992). *Empowering education: Critical teaching for social change*. Chicago: University of Chicago Press.

Spradley, J. P. (1979). *The ethnographic interview*. Ft. Worth: Harcourt Brace Jovanovich.

Thompson, W. E., & Dodder, R. A. (1986). Containment theory and juvenile delinquency: A reevaluation through factor analysis. *Adolescence, 21*(82), 365–376.

Weber, T. R. (1984). *Perceptions of superintendents, principals, assistant principals, deans, counselors, and teachers concerning discipline in selected Illinois high schools* (doctoral dissertation, Northern Illinois University). Dissertation Abstracts International, 45, AAC8503860.

Willis, P. (1981). *Learning to labor: How working class kids get working class jobs* (2d ed.). New York: Columbia University Press.

3

Courage for the Discouraged: A Psychoeducational Approach to Troubled and Troubling Children

LARRY K. BRENDTRO
AND STEVEN VAN BOCKERN

THESE AUTHORS HAVE ADDED yet another dimension to the distinguished literature of psychoeducational ways to help students like Joe. The model described in this selection provides a gestalt to many psychoeducational practices. The gestalt is *The Circle of Courage*, which includes the outcomes of an empowered person. That is, the outcomes become the goals for Joe and other students who have similar needs. Acquiring the parts of the Circle is an indication of menal health by anybody's definition.

> *The way one defines a problem will determine in substantial measure the strategies that can be used to solve it.*
> —*Nicholas Hobbs*

In the three decades since the Council for Children with Behavior Disorders was formed, research about this population has exploded. Professionals working with these challenging children have encountered a cacophony of competing theories and methodology. Too often, proponents for purist viewpoints have been intolerant of other perspectives, berating alternative approaches as unscientific, dehumanizing, or obsolete. Most practitioners, however, have been skeptical of narrow approaches that offer a panacea. When facing a furious student, a single theory offers a slim shield indeed. Now, as our field matures, we finally are moving away from simplistic "one-size-fits-all" mindsets. The term *psychoeducational* has been used to describe approaches that blend multiple strategies of intervention.

Psychoeducational approaches planfully combine a variety of methods to meet the diverse needs of troubled children. These eclectic models can create a synergy wherein the whole is greater than the parts, but only if the diverse theoretical components are synthesized carefully (Macmillan & Kavale, 1986). We will review existing psychoeducational approaches and present a new model grounded in practice wisdom and modern developmental theory. At the onset, we must make a distinction between psychoeducation and unstructured eclecticism.

Pitfalls of Green Thumb Eclecticism

In an early study of services for emotionally handicapped children, Morse, Cutler, and Fink (1964) found that in many settings no organized philosophy of treatment could be detected. Instead, staffs followed intuitive approaches that observers classified as naturalistic, primitive, or chaotic. Most seemed to use a "green thumb" eclecticism, trying out various procedures without apparent consistency or depth. Their style was neither organized nor proactive but, rather, consisted of spur-of-the-moment responses to individual academic or behavioral problems.

Without a guiding theory to influence selection of interventions, "try anything" eclecticism is like choosing a potluck meal while blindfolded. Among the pitfalls of green thumb eclecticism are:

1. *The flaws of folk psychology.* "Doing what comes naturally" with troubled and troublesome youth often entails attacking or avoiding them. These fight/flight responses are highly counterproductive. Harsh punishment easily escalates into hostility, and kindness often is exploited. If a whipping or a dose of love were all that were required, these kids would have been cured long ago.

2. *Contradictions in methodology.* If techniques drawn from different models are mixed together in potluck fashion, confusion sets in about what to do when theories suggest prescriptions that run counter to one another (Quay & Werry, 1988). For example, is planfully ignoring angry behavior better, or should one see this anger as a cry for help and communicate with the child?

3. *Incompatibility with teamwork.* When various team members invent idiosyncratic models of treatment, conflict and chaos reign. Russian youth work pioneer Makarenko (1956) observed that five weak educators inspired by the same principles is a better configuration than 10 good educators all working according to their own opinion.

4. *Inconsistency with children.* In programs in which adults are confused or inconsistent, anxious students become more agitated and antisocial students

more manipulative. The most volatile possible combination is a dysfunctional staff team confronting a cunning and cohesive negative peer group.

Fortunately, we are not confined to naive "green thumb" eclecticism, as a number of thoughtful approaches merge multiple methods. Before presenting our own model, we briefly highlight four major approaches to the reeducation of troubled children.

Perspectives on Psychoeducation

In his book, *Caring for Troubled Children*, Whittaker (1980) identified four principal approaches that have shaped practice in North American programs of reeducation. These all represent different ways of defining emotional and behavioral problems, and they lead to different intervention strategies. Listed in historical sequence, the four models are:

1. *Psychodynamic:* Children are viewed as "disturbed" because of underlying emotional problems and unmet needs.
2. *Behavioral:* Children are viewed as "disordered" because of maladaptive patterns of learned behavior.
3. *Sociological:* Children are viewed as "maladjusted" because of association with peers who embrace negative values and behavior.
4. *Ecological:* Various ecosystems in the child's environment are seen as creating conflict and "dis-ease" in children.

Although each model has continued to develop with a separate tradition and literature, these approaches all have become more eclectic over time. Actually, as each model has become more comprehensive, it has been labeled as "psychoeducational" by at least some of its proponents:

1. *Psychodynamic psychoeducation places major emphasis on resolving inner conflicts of troubled children.* This blending of mental health concepts with education is tied to the early work of a number of outstanding European specialists who emigrated to North America around the time of World War II. Exemplary of this tradition is Fritz Redl (1902–1988), who was trained by August Aichorn and Anna Freud in Austria. Redl and Wineman (1957) worked with what they called highly aggressive youth in Detroit and co-authored the classic book, *The Aggressive Child*. Collaborating with William Morse at the University of Michigan Fresh Air Camp for troubled youth, they trained an entire generation of professionals in this model of psychoeducation.

    Redl saw emotional disturbance as an exaggeration of feelings common to all individuals. What distinguishes the troubled child was the inability to manage those feelings. Redl also was concerned with behavior, but primarily as a way of understanding the "inner life" of children. His comprehensive approach includes some 20 techniques for "managing surface behavior," and a system for de-escalating crisis situations. He also designed the "life space interview," a counseling strategy used by front-line staff (e.g., teachers, youth workers) to transform naturally occurring problems into opportunities for correcting distorted thoughts, feelings, and behaviors. Leading psychoeducational theorists include William Morse (1985) and Nicholas Long, who directs the Institute for Psychoeducational Training in Hagerstown, Maryland.

2. *Behavioral psychoeducation uses learning principles to modify the disordered behavior of children.* A prominent spokesperson for this version of psychoeducation is Arnold Goldstein of Syracuse University. His data-based belief is that disordered behavior has complex causes and thus is treated best with comprehensive interventions. He contends that powerful and lasting change requires methods that are both *multilevel* (directed both at the youth and at the system) and *multimodal* (combining cognitive, affective, and behavioral interventions).

Goldstein (1988) has combined a variety of behavioral skill training methods into *The Prepare Curriculum* for teaching prosocial competence. Another widely used example of this merger of methods is *Aggression Replacement Training*, designed to address the deficits in social skills, anger control, and moral reasoning that characterize aggressive youth (Goldstein & Glick, 1987).

The eclectic behavioral approach known as the Boys Town Teaching Family Model (Coughlin & Shanahan, 1991) also qualifies for our definition of psychoeducational. This approach systematically integrates methods including social skills training, relationship building, nonaversive crisis intervention, and structured verbal interventions called "teaching interactions." The Boys Town model is used widely in both residential and public school settings. This model has been subjected to extensive research, and The Boys Town National Training Center in Boys Town, Nebraska, offers professional certification programs (Tierney, Dowd, & O'Kane, 1993).

3. *Sociological psychoeducation utilizes peer groups as a primary agent of change in values and behavior of troubled youth.* These programs grew from research showing that delinquent behavior develops through association with peers who support antisocial beliefs and behavior. The impact of peers is strong, particularly among youth with weak parental attachments and controls. Unlike traditional group therapy, which treats individuals within a group, the aim of guided group interaction (GGI) is to win over the entire group to prosocial values and behavior, thereby encouraging change in individuals (Empey & Rabow, 1961).

Harry Vorrath extended the original GGI model into a comprehensive system for reeducation known as PPC, or *positive peer culture* (Vorrath & Brendtro, 1985). Peer group models are used most widely in residential treatment (Brendtro & Wasmund, 1989) and alternative schools and classes for troubled youth (Carducci & Carducci, 1984; Garner, 1982). PPC also has been proposed as an alternative approach to school discipline (Duke & Meckel, 1984). Positive peer culture groups identify problems and develop strategies to solve them. The goal is to create a prosocial ethos by making caring fashionable, demanding greatness instead of obedience, and challenging youth to assume responsibility for their lives. Brendtro and Ness (1983) described a "psychoeducational" approach using peer group strategies with other methods, which has been developed at the Starr Commonwealth Schools for troubled youth in Michigan and Ohio. The National Association of Peer Group Agencies provides research and training on this treatment model (Kern & Quigley, 1994).

4. *Ecological psychoeducation has been the most actively eclectic approach, borrowing freely from the more traditional models.* The leading author of this approach was Nicholas Hobbs (1918–1983) who created the Re-ED model at Vanderbilt University. (Re-ED is an acronym for Reeducation for Emotionally Disturbed Children.) The most recent model to develop, Re-ED borrows generously from each of the foregoing models and is described as both *ecological* and *psychoeducational* (Lewis & Lewis, 1989). Hobbs was influenced strongly by European and French-Canadian psychoeducation, and he blended education, child care, and treatment into the role of "teacher-counselor."

   A past president of the American Psychological Association, Hobbs was a powerful advocate for focusing on strength, health, and joy, rather than deviance and pathology. In *The Troubled and Troubling Child*, Hobbs (1982) argued that most emotional disturbance is not a symptom of individual pathology but, rather, a sign of malfunctioning human ecosystems. Re-ED professionals strive to develop competence in restorative relationships, working in close liaison with families and communities (Lewis & Lewis, 1989). The American Re-ED Association, a nationwide network of residential and school-based Re-ED programs, has grown from this ecological tradition. The Re-ED philosophy now is being applied to the challenging problems of urban schools in settings such as the Positive Education Program in Cleveland, Ohio (Cantrell, 1992).

Cross-fertilization has increased among all of these theories, albeit much of it random, as practitioners intuitively tinker with once pure models. Today, we find behaviorists advocating relationship building, psychodynamic programs using reinforcement concepts, and nearly universal recognition of the importance of group and ecological dynamics. In the face of this intermingling of theories, traditional concepts such as "behavioral" and "psychodynamic" no longer convey a clear meaning at the level of practice.

The Search for a Unifying Theme

A rich array of specialized methods now is available for treating troubled children and youth. What has been missing is a conceptual framework to bind together these separate components into a coherent system. As Yochanan Wozner (1985) of Israel observed, a "powerful reclaiming environment" for troubled youth requires a "unifying theme." This is a shared set of beliefs about program goals that gives consistency and cohesiveness to elements of the program. A unifying theme is essential to mold a common consensus among staff and youth about program mission.

We now propose a unifying theme for psychoeducation that grows from "empowerment" philosophy and psychology. This "new" paradigm challenges the deviance and deficit model that is common in many approaches to troubled children. Our model seeks to address the question, "What do all successful approaches have in common?"

In visiting an air show, one might see machines as diverse as biplanes and bombers, but each is able to fly only because it has been designed to the same fundamental principles of flight. Likewise, in spite of variations, all successful models of psychoeducation with troubled children must address the same fundamental needs of children. We have sought to identify these common principles that transcend successful work with children regardless of setting or theoretical model.

In our book, *Reclaiming Youth at Risk* (Brendtro, Brokenleg, & Van Bockern, 1990), we proposed a unifying theme for the education and treatment of troubled children. Dr. Brokenleg, a Lakota Sioux psychologist, introduced us to sophisticated Native American child-rearing systems that created courageous, respectful children without the use of harsh punishments. We integrated this native wisdom with the practice wisdom of great European pioneers in work with troubled youth. A note about each of these traditions will serve as an introduction to our model.

Psychologists Rogoff and Morelli (1989) contended that, to fully understand child development, one must break free of cultural biases and explore other cultural models. Centuries before European and American reformers would challenge Western patriarchal models of obedience, Native American tribes of North America had developed elaborate democratic institutions, governance systems, and models of education. These "primitive" peoples actually were far more advanced than the conquering Europeans in their understanding of child and youth development. When Europeans settled this new land, however, they imposed their obedience training system on Indian children, who were placed forcibly in militaristic boarding schools.

Martin Brokenleg's father was captured by the boarding school staff, who traveled the reservation each fall to harvest the next crop of first-graders. Now, several generations of Indian youth have been parented artificially in this environment, where they were beaten if they spoke their native language. Our research sought to reclaim traditional native empowerment philosophies for use in developing contemporary approaches to youth at risk.

We also were intrigued to find great similarity between native concepts of education and ideas expressed by Western educational reformers who challenged traditional European concepts of obedience training. These youth work pioneers worked at a time when democracy was replacing dictatorship in many nations. Attacking traditional authoritarian pedagogy, they included:

- *Maria Montessori,* Italy's first female physician, who created schools for disadvantaged youth and wrote passionately about the need to build inner discipline.
- *Janusz Korczak,* Polish social pedagogue, who proclaimed the child's right to respect and created a national children's newspaper so the voices of children might be heard.
- *John Dewey*, American pioneer of progressive education, who saw schools as miniature democratic communities of students and teachers working to pose and solve problems.
- *Anton Makarenko,* who after the Russian Revolution brought street delinquents into self-governing colonies where youth took turns as leaders of youth councils.

Now the wisdom of these early pioneers is being validated by modern psychological researchers.

The Circle of Courage

Early European anthropologists described Native American children as radiantly happy, courageous, and highly respectful, noting that their elders never subjected them to harsh punishment. The professional literature, however, shows little understanding of how tribal cultures could rear children with prosocial values and positive self-esteem. Long before the term "self-esteem" was coined, European youth work pioneers used a similar concept, which they called "discouragement." The obvious solution to discouragement is to help children develop courage. As we discovered, building courageous children was a central focus of Native American tribal cultures. Our modern "civilization," in contrast, produces millions of children of discouragement. How might we go about rearing courageous and respectful children?

In his definitive work, *The Antecedents of Self-Esteem,* Stanley Coopersmith (1967) concluded that childhood self-esteem is based on significance, competence, power, and virtue. Traditional Native child-care philosophy addresses each of these dimensions:

1. *Significance* is nurtured in an environment in which every child is treated as a "relative" and is surrounded by love and affection. This fosters a sense of *belonging*.
2. *Competence* is enhanced by nurturing each child's success and by celebrating the success of others. This provides all children abundant opportunities for *mastery*.

3. *Power* is fostered by practicing guidance without coercion. Even the youngest children learn to make wise decisions and thus demonstrate responsible *independence*.
4. The highest *virtue* is to be unselfish and courageously give of oneself to others. Children reared in altruistic environments learn to live in a spirit of *generosity*.

Lakota artist George Bluebird portrayed these concepts in a drawing of a medicine wheel called the "circle of courage," featured in Figure 3.1.

Patriarchal values and the developmental needs of children are strikingly disharmonious.

At first glance, the foregoing principles hardly seem debatable. They fit with humanistic values, psychology, and our own experience. After all, who would advocate the opposite of these concepts—alienation, failure, helplessness, and egotistic selfishness? Further, convincing youth themselves that these are important values is not difficult. Young people want to belong, succeed, have power over their lives, and be needed in the world. *Once these values are given primacy in our programs, their revolutionary quality becomes apparent.*

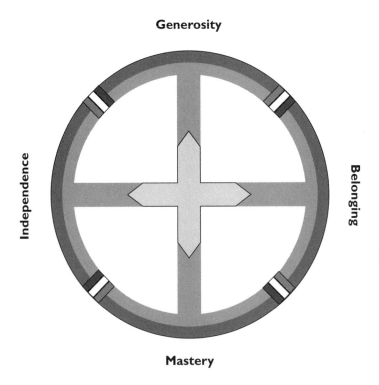

Figure 3.1 *Circle of Courage*

Whereas most of our traditional systems have been anchored in adult dominance, the Circle of Courage is a youth empowerment model. Table 3.1 shows how Native empowerment values mirror the foundations of self-esteem identified by Coopersmith (1967) and challenge the values of the dominant culture.

1. Instead of belonging, the hyperindividualism of Western society breeds an "ecology of alienation" (Bronfenbrenner, 1986).
2. In the place of mastery, traditional schools play a competitive zero-sum game in which enthroning "winners" ensures abundant losers.
3. When one's need for power is expressed by dominating others, all who are subjugated are disempowered.
4. A culture that equates worth with wealth provides its young a sanction for selfishness.

Successful programs for at-risk youth embody a unifying theme of values grounded in the holistic needs of children. Wozner (1985) defined the key difference among educational environments as whether they are "reclaiming" or "nonreclaiming." Reclaiming schools are organized to meet the needs both of the young person and of society. Nonreclaiming schools operate to perpetuate the system. The distinction is whether one is teaching students or tending school.

Blueprint for a Nonreclaiming School

These abstractions can be operationalized by examining some attitudes and practices of nonreclaiming schools. Next, with some hyperbole, we offer a compilation of comments we have heard in various schools.

Anti-Belonging

Greet newcomers with "report to the office" warning signs. Orient new students and their probably irresponsible parents by making them sign the discipline policy manual. Emphasize that the automatic response to "serious" behavior is exclusion in its many forms including in-school suspension (ISS), out-of-school suspension (OSS),

Table 3.1 *Empowerment Versus Patriarchal Values*

Foundations of Self-Esteem	Native American Empowerment Values	Western Patriarchal Values
Significance	Belonging	Individualism
Competence	Mastery	Winning
Power	Independence	Dominance
Virtue	Generosity	Affluence

or after-school and Saturday (ASS) detention. If students quit, call them "dropouts" (pejorative). Be very businesslike lest you get entangled in "unprofessional" relationships. If kids don't respond, ship them to segregated "alternative" and special education programs to "get them out of our classrooms."

Teachers should not have to wet-nurse students, so get rid of that values clarification crap we are supposed to handle in homerooms. Put troublemaking special ed students, who can't be expelled, on homebound. [Authors' note: 40% of all students on homebound instruction are those with emotional and behavioral problems.] Make schools as large as possible to build better bands and ball teams. Ring bells every 50 minutes to mix 2,000 kids in narrow hallways. If they become hard to manage, hire more security guards so teachers are free to "teach."

Anti-Mastery

Organize instruction tightly around separate specialized subjects. Switch to a different group of students each period. You won't know them well, but at least one kid can't ruin your whole day. If students say they are having fun in a class, or if a teacher takes field trips, spread word in the lounge that no learning is going on. Make them work by themselves so they don't copy one another, follow a tight schedule, and have the shortest possible breaks between periods. Fill the policy manual with get-tough rules such as, "Students who skip school will be suspended" and "in-school suspension days will be counted as unexcused absences" and "students with 12 unexcused absences will fail the semester."

Emphasize competition with tough grading systems, tracking, and reduced expectations for difficult students. In all "real" classes make all students listen to professor-like lectures that are brain-antagonistic even in the university. Of course we don't mean those "popular" shop, art, and PE classes, because they are activity courses, not real education. If they don't hate it, they won't learn anything. What's all the fuss about outcome-based education? Let's stick to what has worked in the past. Use only the textbook and the "approved" curriculum. Maybe we need some more trophies for the top "winners" in sports and studies.

Anti-Independence

Impose systemwide discipline policies so we know who really runs this place. Give students a token student-government game to play so they won't challenge our control of really important issues. Make examples of troublemakers by announcing detention lists on the intercom. One thing we don't want is violence, so come down hard on bullies and let them know who's boss so they learn not to pick on others. Assume that if students engage in a spirited discussion about some current event, they are dodging real learning. Pace the room to keep on top of the class. Keep students anchored in their desks. Impose rules by fiat, put names on the board, and have surprise locker searches to keep them off-guard.

Use computers to schedule students because they probably just want to choose classes with their friends. Keep students in submissive roles so they learn to "respect" authority. (Years later the only teachers they will remember are the ones who don't take any crap.) Limit student choice of curriculum, because they aren't mature enough to make those decisions. I think it's time for another of those assertive discipline seminars. I felt so good after the last one, being reassured that this was my class and I was in charge.

Anti-Generosity

We have to do something to derail this foolish proposal that all students participate in volunteer service learning activities. This only steals time from real learning. Sure, maybe students need to feel needed, but if they want to be bleeding-heart social workers, let them do this on their own time. We have to do something about this cooperative learning movement. It's just a way of letting smart kids do the work for slow ones. Stop cross-age tutoring, because the older youth may take advantage of the younger ones.

And the notion of peer counselors really turns me off. Can you imagine what they would tell each other? Let them bring their problems to a trained guidance counselor. We shouldn't get into controversial social issues in school or teach values, except for the flag and patriotism. We have enough to do in the cognitive domain, so leave affective issues to parents. Also, put a stop to this multiculturalism in curriculum. Immigrant children should become American just as we had to. Today's kids will not produce unless you give them some reward or payoff, but, hey, that's the American system.

Although these comments may not be typical of most schools, a war undoubtedly is going on between tradition and reform in contemporary education. We believe, however, that conflict is the predictable reaction to the real changes sweeping education, and today's reform will be the mode of the future. The empowerment movement in schools must be seen as part of a broader cultural paradigm shift that is unsettling the established power relationships in Western culture.

Many traditionally powerless groups (e.g., women, people of color, ethnic minorities, and now children) are achieving fuller participation in an increasingly democratic world. A prominent example is the recent U. N. document on the rights of children, which has gained the status of international law. This shift to empowerment is a grassroots democracy movement that will impact all social institutions, including the school.

Mending Broken Circles

Only as we abandon our preoccupation with the control of deviance can we nurture the unmet developmental needs that drive most problem behavior. A growing research base shows that successful psychoeducational programs must nurture belonging, mastery, independence, and generosity in troubled children. Of course, other underlying physical and safety needs exist, but from the perspective of psychosocial development, these are four anchor points.

Belonging, mastery, independence, and generosity define social and mental health. As such, these are universal needs for all children and critical unmet needs for damaged children. Many students come to school already having experienced this "circle of courage" in their lives. Many others, however, come to us discouraged, with long histories of unmet needs.

- Instead of belonging, they are guarded, untrusting, hostile, withdrawn; or they seek attention through compensatory attachments.
- In place of mastery, they have encountered perpetual failure leading to frustration, fear of failure, and a sense of futility.
- Not having learned independence, they feel like helpless pawns, are easily misled, or seek pseudopower by bullying or defiance.
- Without a spirit of generosity, they are inconsiderate of others, self-indulgent, and devoid of real purpose for living.

Recently one of our graduate students surveyed high school students and asked them to "grade their schools" according to the criteria of belonging, mastery, independence, and generosity (Odney & Brendtro, 1992). Some of their comments will be used to introduce the following sections. After hearing their voices, we will identify a range of intervention techniques for mending broken circles of courage.

Fostering Belonging

Some of the teachers think they are too cool to talk to us.
If you're walking down the hall, the teachers will put their heads down
and look at the floor and keep walking.

—Helen

Pioneer Native American educator and anthropologist Ella Deloria described the central value of belonging in traditional Indian culture in these simple words: "Be related, somehow, to everyone you know." Treating others as kin forged powerful social bonds of community that drew all into the circle of relatives. From the earliest days of life, all children experienced a network of nurturance, wherein every older member in the tribe felt responsible for their well-being.

Theologian Martin Marty of the University of Chicago observed that throughout history the tribe, rather than the nuclear family, ultimately ensured survival of a culture. When parents faltered in their responsibility, the tribe always was there to nourish the new generation. The problem today is that we have lost our tribes. The school is the only institution beyond the family that provides ongoing relationships with all of our young. Schools could become the new tribes to support and nurture children at risk.

Early educational pioneers saw positive human attachments as the *sine qua non* of effective teaching. Johann Pestalozzi declared that love, not teaching, is the essence of education. In his classic book, *Wayward Youth*, Austrian August Aichorn

(1935) argued that relationship was the heart of the reeducation process. His ethic was that affection rather than punishment must be dispensed to difficult youth because this is their primary unmet need. As educational literature became more "professional," however, relationship building was ignored temporarily. Now the importance of human attachment is the focus of a revival of interest.

Research shows that the quality of human relationships in schools and youth service programs may be more influential than the specific techniques or interventions employed (Brophy, 1986). Teachers with widely divergent instructional styles can be successful if they develop positive classroom climates. Building successful relationships, however, takes time and effort.

The late eminent psychiatrist Karl Menninger often noted that many of today's youth do not experience a sense of belonging at home. When they come to school and behave in unacceptable ways, they get another unbelonging message: "People who act like that don't belong here." Some youth quit trying to build human bonds and begin to protect themselves with a guarded, suspicious, withdrawn manner. Others do not give up seeking attention, recognition, and significance. Instead they pursue "artificial belongings" in gangs, cults, or sexual promiscuity.

Hostile or withdrawn youth often are signaling to adults that they have learned by experience to expect rejection, and untrained people almost invariably give them what they are used to receiving. Many ways of reaching out to these unloved and sometimes unlovable children are possible if adults can overcome the fight or flight reactions that come so naturally. Following are strategies for meeting the needs for attachment and belonging, which have developed in various theoretical traditions.

1. *Psychodynamic programs* long have posited that strong, trusting relationships between troubled youth and adults are prerequisites to effective reeducation. Youth work pioneer August Aichorn concluded that love is the primary unmet need of many troubled children. Morse emphasized the importance of "differential acceptance," in which we accept the child but not the behavior. To accurately decode "testing" behaviors also is important. Many troubled children initially provoke well-meaning adults to see if they will become hostile.

2. *Behavioral research* by Phillips and colleagues (1973) reported a failure to replicate their *achievement place model* when positive staff-student relationships were missing. Now called the *teaching family model*, relationship building components are central to this approach. The staff is trained to begin all corrective teaching interactions with a positive or empathy statement.

3. *Sociological models* use peer relationships as the foundation for treatment. This method is powerful particularly with youth who initially are inclined to trust peers more than adults. Peer concern rather than peer pressure is the basis for program success. Adults must model caring relationships and monitor confrontations carefully so students don't become targets of counteraggression (Brendtro & Ness, 1982).

4. *Ecological models* developed by Hobbs (1982) presume that the disturbed youth begins with a belief that most adults cannot be trusted. Only the people who can break down this barrier of trust can become predictable sources of support, affection, and learning. In Re-ED programs, "trust...is the glue that holds teaching and learning together, the beginning point of reeducation."

The emphasis on fostering attachments is also prominent in the middle school movement. Typically, schedules are designed so frequent and sustained contact between students and teachers is possible. Maeroff (1990) described one program in which a small team of four to five adults, including teachers, administrators, and counselors, serves 45 students. Each adult meets twice daily with a smaller advisory group of 8–10 students. In another middle school teachers greet their students as the buses arrive. Bells are eliminated, team-teaching is used, four award assemblies are held throughout the year, and F's have been changed to U's (Raebuck, 1990).

The celebration of belonging to a caring community is a central theme of effective schools. O'Gorman, a Catholic high school in Sioux Falls, South Dakota, invites new freshman students to a "unity weekend" retreat over the Labor Day holiday. Some of the 90 trained senior volunteers welcome the new students, helping them carry sleeping bags and luggage into the school and providing leadership for the weekend activities. Students from outlying communities who have no preexisting peer relationships at this school receive a special invitation to a picnic and waterslide party hosted by a school counselor and the natural peer helper organization. Here, too, a strong advising system anchors each student in a close relationship with a small cadre of peers and a teacher-counselor.

Teachers in American schools traditionally have been attached to grade levels or subjects, not to cohorts of students. In contrast, Norwegian elementary school teachers often progress through the grades, remaining with one group of students for several years. In like manner, Holweide, a comprehensive secondary school in Cologne, West Germany, assigns teachers to teams of six or eight, which follow the same 120 students over the course of 6 years. In this structure the beginning and year-end rituals are eliminated, freeing more time for instruction. These teachers come to know their students in ways that tests never can approach (Shanker, 1990).

Positive attachments between adults and youth are the foundation of effective education. These individual bonds, however, must be part of a synergistic network of relationships that permeate the school culture. These include positive peer relationships among students, cooperative teamwork relationships among school staff, and genuine partnerships with parents. Administrators also must see their roles as co-workers in support of their staff, not as superiors trying to dominate. In the final analysis, only adults who are themselves empowered will be free to build empowering relationships with youth.

Fostering Mastery

I was walking down the hall and said "hi" to Mr. Nilson. He looked at me
and said, "Oh, you're still here. You haven't dropped out yet, huh?"
I know people have this in their head and think of me as being less than them.
I would like to put Mr. Nilson in the situation I've had in my life,
and I'll bet any amount of money he'd fold his cards.

—*Lincoln*

In traditional Native American culture, children were taught to celebrate the achievement of others, and a person who received honor accepted this without arrogance. Someone more skilled than oneself was seen as a model for learning, not as an adversary. The striving was for personal mastery, not to become superior to one's opponent. Recognizing that all must be nourished in competency, success became a possession of the many, not of the privileged few.

Maria Montessori, Italy's first female physician, decried the obedience tradition of schooling in which children sit silently in rows like "beautiful butterflies pinned to their desks." She tried to revolutionize learning with the belief that curiosity and the desire to learn come naturally to children.

The desire to master and achieve is seen in all cultures from childhood onward, a phenomenon that Harvard psychologist Robert White called "competence motivation." People explore, acquire language, construct things, and attempt to cope with their environments. It is a mark of humanness that children and adults alike desire to do things well and, in so doing, gain the joy of achievement.

Tragically, though, something often happens to the child's quest for learning in school, the very place where mastery is supposed to be nourished and expanded. Schooling in the traditional setting often fragments learning into subject areas, substitutes control for the natural desire to learn, co-opts naturally active children for hours in assembly line classes, ignores both individual and cultural differences, and is structured on competitive learning (Overly, 1979).

Children who lack skills in social or academic realms often appear resistant to learning. They withdraw from challenge and risk, avoiding most what they understand least. As Mary MacCracken (1981) said in her book, *City Kid*, "When you have failed often and painfully enough, you will do almost anything to avoid having to try again" (p. 152).

Each of the treatment models has sophisticated strategies for breaking patterns of failure and futility. All address the crucial task of teaching social skills. Sometimes this is highly structured, as in direct instruction using formal curricula of social skills. In some models the demonstrated problem itself becomes the curriculum for teaching new ways of coping, as in life space interviews or peer counseling groups. Instead of communicating "I don't want to see any problems," educators and therapists are learning to use naturally occurring incidents as the basis for instruction. A sampling of promising methods for helping children achieve mastery and social competence follows.

1. *Psychodynamic* methods encourage creativity and self-expression in the curriculum to create a sense of mastery. Art, drama, music and poetry, literature—all can help youth connect with their feelings and surmount their problems. If problems cannot be eliminated immediately, they should be recast as learning opportunities. In the life space interview (LSI), real-world problems are grist for learning more adaptive ways of thinking, feeling, and acting. Instead of withdrawing from youth in times of crisis, the staff sees this as a unique window of opportunity for teaching coping skills.

2. *Behavioral* programs, of course, are grounded in learning theory. Among the most useful contributions are systematic social skills instruction to develop social competence and teach adaptive skills. These skills can be as diverse as asking for help and making friends. Students entering a *teaching family* program are taught up front how to accept criticism, using role-playing and other realistic methods. Even before their first encounter with an adult, they are being given new coping strategies. Cognitive behavioral techniques are employed to replace irrational thinking or destructive self-talk with more accurate and adaptive thinking.

3. *Sociological* models train youth to assume problem-solving roles. The treatment group provides feedback about hurtful or inconsiderate behavior of members and encourages positive alternatives. For example, easily angered youth are taught to understand and disengage from the put-down process, thereby inoculating themselves from the negative behavior of others. Of course, positive groups also foster positive attitudes toward school and teachers.

   We recall a substitute teacher who most reluctantly accepted her first assignment to a class of delinquent youth in a peer treatment program. She was dumbfounded when the first discipline problem of the day was solved instantly by peers with a chorus of "leave the teacher alone so she can teach!"

4. *Ecological* Re-ED programs assume that competence and intelligence can be taught. Academic success itself is seen as a powerful therapy. By helping youth be good at something, especially schoolwork, one impacts a person's self-worth and motivation. Students also need opportunities for problem solving in interpersonal relationships in which they display "conspicuous ineptitude." This model also uses extensive adventure and outdoor education activities to reach students who don't respond to typical school structures.

Traditional educational approaches were developed centuries before any scientific understanding of the human brain. With increased knowledge of how the human brain functions, we now are able to restructure schooling so it is "brain friendly." Leslie Hart (1983), who has synthesized brain research related to education, suggests that the brain is designed to detect patterns and works best in nonthreatening, active, and social settings.

Writing in 1909 in *The Spirit of Youth and the City Streets,* Jane Addams observed that many of the difficulties of youth are related to the reality that they are highly spirited and adventurous. A distinctive feature of much youthful delinquency is the celebration of prowess. These youth are not motivated by the humdrum routine of most schools. Their search for fun and adventure often leads to excitement and kicks through risk-seeking behavior.

Wilderness education programs build on this spirit of adventure. When struggling against the elements of nature, even the most resistant youth has no need to defy the law of natural consequences (Bacon & Kimball, 1989). The Eckerd Wilderness Educational System operates a network of programs for youth at risk across the eastern United States. While totally abandoning the traditional classroom structure, its staff is able to make formidable academic and social gains with previously nonachieving youth.

Fostering Independence

This is probably the biggest part of school that I don't like.
All through school, kids are herded around like sheep and are left with
almost nothing to decide upon.

—Travis

Traditional Native culture placed a high value on individual freedom. In contrast to "obedience" models of discipline, Native education was designed to build "respect" by teaching inner discipline. Children were encouraged to make decisions, solve problems, and show personal responsibility. Adults modeled, taught values, and provided feedback and guidance, but children were given abundant opportunities to make choices without coercion.

Horace Mann once declared schooling in a democracy to be "an apprenticeship in responsibility." Early in the century Janusz Korczak of Poland founded a system of student self-governance in his orphanage for Warsaw street children. "Fifty years from now, every school in a democracy will have student self governance," he declared. But America continues to be uniquely out of step with many other nations that have implemented the principles of "democracy in education" for which American John Dewey is famous. We remain tethered to the obedience model, causing anthropologist Ruth Benedict to exclaim that our culture systematically deprives young people of the opportunity for responsibility and then complains about their irresponsibility.

A 6,000-year-old Egyptian stone bears the inscription: "Our earth is degenerate. Children no longer obey their parents." Similar calls are heard today, and those who think we have been too permissive could be expected to object to the notion of giving power to youth. The choice, however, is not between demanding obedience or total permissiveness. As Mary Wood says, adults need to continue to be in control—but of the learning environment rather than of the children. Put another way, we must make demands; however, we need to demand responsibility instead of obedience. Even when we intervene in behavior, the tone can be, "Why must adults handle this problem when you are mature enough to handle it yourselves?"

Youth deprived of power will get it somehow, often in a delinquent underground as they bully the weakest in their midst and sabotage our adult-dominated programs. Fortunately, all treatment models are recognizing the need to listen to the voices of youth, as seen in these strategies for teaching independence and self-control.

1. *Psychodynamic* approaches assume that many aggressive children lack sufficient self-management of emotions and behavior. The goal is to develop "controls from within." Redl and Wineman (1957) offered detailed behavior management strategies for providing external controls temporarily while at the same time using "clinical exploitation of life events" to teach the youth self-responsibility. Wood and Long (1991) outlined counseling methods to help children "master the existential crisis" of gaining responsible independence from adults.

2. *Behavioral* approaches to aggression also teach youth self-management skills for dealing with anger. These include recognizing "triggers" and "cues" for anger arousal, using self-administered "reminders" and "reducers" to lessen anger, and self-evaluation and reinforcement (Goldstein & Glick, 1987). Boys Town uses procedures whereby youth help decide the rules by which they will live in teaching family homes. Cognitive behavior theorist Meichenbaum (1993) now emphasizes that individuals construct their own personal realities, and the therapist's task is to help them take charge of reconstructing more positive personal outlooks to manage life stress.

3. *Sociological* models of group treatment reject the "patient" role and empower students to become agents of their own healing. Individuals are held accountable for behavior, and excuses are turned back to the individual in a verbal technique called the "reversal of responsibility." For example, if a student rationalizes a fight, saying, "Well, he said things about my mother that were lies!" the group may respond, "Well, that's his problem, so why did you make his garbage yours?" By helping others with similar problems, youth develop a sense of control over their own destiny.

4. *Ecological* programs also use self-governing groups to implement behavioral programming (Lewis & Lewis, 1989). Any member can call together a problem-solving group. These groups often are led by youth. The group helps the member learn new strategies for avoiding the problem, thereby encouraging responsible behavior in all members. Rhodes (1992), a co-founder of the Re-ED model, has developed a life-impact curriculum that empowers children's thinking so they can "reconstruct their own reality."

The German youth work pioneer Otto Zirker once observed that when surrounded by walls, young people make wall climbing a sport. Faced with authoritarian structures, youth willingly enter into the counter-control game. Adults who struggle to manage behavior by power assertion believe they are engineering an orderly environment. The reality is more often a submerged negative subculture marked by chaos and disorganization (Wasmund, 1988).

In their study of effective alternative schools, *Expelled to a Friendlier Place*, Gold and Mann (1984) challenged the common practice of employing highly developed formal codes of conduct to manage behavior. Although these rule books make some adults feel secure, they are likely to be ignored or outmaneuvered if they are not owned by front-line staff and youth. Effective alternative schools are able to adapt flexibly to the needs of youth rather than make every decision "by the book." The emphasis shifts from pursuing rule violators to teaching values that foster inner control. Such is the case at the Thomas Harrington School in Harrisonburg, Virginia, where one rule applies equally to all students and staff: Respect people, respect property (Raebuck, 1990).

Independence for many youth is thwarted by inflexible and uncompromising structures. At the Jefferson County High School in Louisville, Kentucky, success with at-risk youth comes from flexible schedules (school is open from 8 a.m. to 9:30 p.m., 12 months a year), promise of success, treating students with respect, and awarding a regular high school diploma. The director of this alternative school, Buell Snyder, said, "I hire only teachers who agree to treat students with respect at all times, and I discard those who, despite their good intentions, infantilize or ridicule students" (Gross, 1990).

Fostering Generosity

I would have liked to tutor something or been a peer counselor.
I could have helped someone and benefited from it myself if I had
been given the chance to participate.

—Sondra

A central goal in Native American child-rearing is to teach the importance of being generous and unselfish. Children were instructed that human relationships are more important than physical possessions. Describing practices a century ago, Indian writer Charles Eastman tells of his grandmother teaching him to give away what he cherished the most—his puppy—so he would become strong and courageous.

Pioneering German educator Kurt Hahn once observed that all young people desperately need some sense of purpose for their lives. Youth in modern society, however, do not have roles in which they can serve, and thus they suffer from the "misery of unimportance." Hahn advocated volunteer activities that tap the need of every youth to have some "grande passion." During the Hitler years he went to England, where he developed the basis of the Outward Bound movements.

Rousseau, Pestalozzi, Korczak, and many others also wrote of the importance of teaching youth the values of compassion and service to others. A century ago, William James noted that war always has fulfilled young men's need to be valuable to their community. He proposed a "moral equivalent to war" by involving youth in volunteer civic service. Although we seem to have lost sight of these basic truths for a time, there is now a healthy revival of the concept that we must offer opportunities to develop altruism, empathy, and generosity in modern youth (Kohn, 1990).

The following discussion highlights the increasing emphasis being placed on developing prosocial values and behavior as an antidote to hedonistic, antisocial lifestyles that characterize many modern youth.

1. Redl's *psychodynamic* model departs from traditional Freudian views that children experience too much guilt. Today, many youth seem not to have acquired the most basic sense of human concern. They suffer from too little guilt, and they can hurt or exploit others with impunity. Treatment for these children might involve "guilt-squeeze" life space interviews to foster empathy with victims, or "massaging numb values" to foster internalization of caring values.

2. *Behavioral* research suggests that teaching techniques to manage anger is not enough. Youth will choose prosocial alternatives only if they can move beyond egocentric moral reasoning. Thus, cognitive moral education is part of Goldstein's aggression replacement training. Everson (1994), from the Boys Town program, advocates teaching social skills as a way of fostering moral development. The goal is to create moral dilemmas in once self-centered youth. Now empowered with prosocial skills, youth have new options to act in caring ways.

3. *Sociological* group treatment models seek to "make caring fashionable" and to make youth uncomfortable with selfish, hurting behavior and thinking patterns. Positive peer culture programs teach youth to show concern by helping group members and then give them abundant opportunities to generalize helping behavior through service learning. For example, delinquent youth at Starr Commonwealth regularly "adopt" residents of nursing homes as grandparents, and they serve as basketball coaches to younger community children.

4. *Ecological* programs address the children and families who are alienated from community bonds. Re-ED involves students in community service in a variety of ways including helping the elderly, operating a "roadblock" to solicit funds for a hospital, and distributing food and toys to needy families.

Every level of education has seen a revival of interest in volunteer service learning as an antidote to the narcissism and irresponsibility of modern lifestyles. All over the country in alternative and some traditional settings, examples of service learning can be found. At Chadwick School in Los Angeles, privileged students run a soup kitchen, help the mentally ill put on plays, work with disturbed children, and campaign for environmental protection. At Harlem's Rice High School in New York, students work with the sick and needy. In Connecticut students serve as the professional rescue squad for a semirural area. In all of these programs, young people's abilities to participate and help are valued (Lewis, 1990).

For 6 to 8 weeks in Shoreham-Wading River, students spend a double period, twice a week, in some community service activity. Students, for example, may work with elderly people or those with handicaps (Maeroff, 1990). Students in Petaluma, California, worked hard to clean up the endangered Adobe Creek. They hauled out

20 truckloads of junk, including washing machines, sofas, two beds, and 36 old tires. They planted willow trees. Now the group is trying to raise $200,000 for a fish hatchery. At least 25 ex-students are studying natural resources and wildlife at Humboldt State University in northern California. Three others are majoring in environmental law at other schools (Sims, 1990).

Service learning opens unusual programming possibilities with troubled children and youth who heretofore have seen themselves as "damaged goods." As they reach out to help others, they create their own proof of worthiness (Brendtro & Nicholau, 1985). Diane Hedin (1989) summarized various research studies supporting the positive results of volunteer service. These include increased responsibility, self-esteem, moral development, and commitment to democratic values.

Putting It All Together: The Michigan Study

Our thesis has been that reclaiming programs must address the critical variables of belonging, mastery, independence, and generosity. We close this chapter by highlighting a recent study of more than 300 delinquent youth in Michigan correctional facilities (Gold & Osgood, 1992). The programs encompassed two state and two private treatment centers using positive peer culture (PPC) treatment methodology.

The Michigan researchers gathered exhaustive data from records, referral agencies, staff, students, and caregivers. They observed each youth from arrival until 6 months' follow-up after release. The population consisted of boys, generally 15 or 16 years old, who had been arrested from one to 20 times. The typical student was remarkably unsuccessful in school, with average academic achievement 4.2 grade levels below expectation. A third had not even attended in the period before placement. These youth are representative of those served currently by North American juvenile corrections programs.

The youth lived in 45 separate self-contained treatment/classroom groups, each with its own interdisciplinary staff team. This enabled researchers to study the impact of these different treatment environments. Thus, though all programs used peer group treatment, they differed on variables such as the amount of autonomy given to youth and the closeness of staff and youth relationships. Variations in the group culture were related to success in the program and in the community after release.

Gold and Osgood reviewed prior research showing that homogeneous settings for aggressive youth typically spawn strongly negative youth countercultures. Instead of cooperating with treatment goals, students resist adult control, develop a code of silence against informing on one another, go underground to circumvent institutional rules, and use physical coercion to maintain a peer subculture committed to delinquent values and behavior. An ongoing debate in the research literature is considering why these negative subcultures form. Two competing explanations have been proposed:

1. Negative youth traits: Delinquent youth "import" into the reeducation setting their dysfunctional character traits. This is a collective example of the "bad apple" notion.
2. Negative institutional milieu: Depriving environments create aggressive countercultures. Harsh, coercive settings strip youth of autonomy and decision making, thus fostering rebellion.

Contrary to what might have been expected, Gold and Osgood found that delinquents in the Michigan settings regularly viewed their environments as safe and supportive. Although full consideration of their exhaustive study is beyond the scope of our current discussion, we highlight their findings related to the principles of belonging, mastery, independence, and generosity.

- *Belonging:* The more troubled and beset youth are, the more they need close personal attachments to reconstruct their lives. Adults who do not form these bonds distance themselves from delinquent youth and thereby diminish their ability to influence them.
- *Mastery:* Delinquent behavior often is provoked by scholastic failure. Teachers in successful school programs give students "uncommonly warm emotional support" and prevent them from failing. Youth who become interested in school and make achievement gains have better subsequent community adjustment.
- *Independence:* Involving delinquent youth in decision-making, even in highly secure settings, fosters the turn around to prosocial behavior. Adult domination and authoritarian control feeds negative peer subcultures, which sabotage treatment goals.
- *Generosity:* High value is placed on caring in peer-helping programs, and a key measure of progress is showing concern for other group members. Students who adopt prosocial norms have more positive experiences during treatment and gain access to more prosocial reference groups after leaving the program.

The Michigan research also shows that the "treatment versus custody" debate is bogus, as concern and control are both essential. Successful programs find ways to address developmental needs of youth as well as societal needs to stop destructive behavior. This requires adults who are authoritative but not authoritarian. These data contradict the currently popular boot-camp notion that the harsher the institutional experience, the greater is the deterrent effect. In reality, troubled youth need safe, positive environments where they can form corrective social bonds with caring adults and peers.

References

Addams, J. (1909). *The spirit of youth and the city streets*. New York: Macmillan.
Aichorn, A. (1935). *Wayward youth*. New York: Viking Press.

Bacon, S. B., & Kimball, R. (1989). The wilderness challenge model. In R. Lyman, S. Prentice-Dunn, & S. Gabel (Eds.), *Residential and inpatient treatment of children and adolescents*. New York: Plenum Press.

Brendtro, L., Brokenleg, M., & Van Bockern, S. (1990). *Reclaiming youth at risk: Our hope for the future*. Bloomington, IN: National Educational Services.

Brendtro, L., & Ness, A. (1982). Perspectives on peer group treatment: The use and abuse of guided group interaction/positive peer culture. *Children & Youth Services Review, 4*(4), 307–324.

Brendtro, L., & Ness, A. (1983). *Re-educating troubled youth: Environments for teaching and treatment*. New York: Aldine du Gruyter.

Brendtro, L., & Nicholau, A. (1985). *Service learning with behaviorally disordered students*. [Monograph on severe behavior disorders of children and youth]. Council for Children with Behavior Disorders, Arizona State University, Tempe.

Brendtro, L., & Wasmund, W. (1989). The peer culture model. In R. Lyman, S. Prentice-Dunn, & S. Gabel (Eds.), *Residential and inpatient treatment of children and adolescents*. New York: Plenum Press.

Bronfenbrenner, U. (1986). Alienation and the four worlds of childhood. *Phi Delta Kappan, 67*, 430–436.

Brophy, J. (1986). Teacher influences on student achievement. *American Psychologist, 41*, 1069–1077.

Cantrell, M. (1992). Guns, gangs and kids. *Journal of Emotional & Behavioral Problems, 1*(1), Special issue.

Carducci, D., & Carducci, J. (1984). *The caring classroom*. Palo Alto, CA: Bull Publishing.

Coopersmith, S. (1967). *The antecedents of self-esteem*. San Francisco: W. H. Freeman.

Coughlin, D., & Shanahan, D. (1991). *Boys Town family home program training manual* (3rd ed.). Boys Town, NE: Father Flanagan's Boys' Home.

Duke, D., & Meckel, A. (1984). *Teacher's guide to classroom management*. New York: Random House.

Empey, L., & Rabow, J. (1961). The Provo experiment in delinquency rehabilitation. *American Sociological Review, 26*, 683.

Everson, T. (1994). The spiritual development of youth at risk. *Journal of Emotional & Behavioral Problems, 3*(10).

Garner, H. (1982). Positive peer culture programs in schools. In D. Safer (Ed.), *School programs for disruptive adolescents*. Baltimore: University Park Press.

Gold, M., & Mann, D. (1984). *Expelled to a friendlier place: A study of effective alternative education*. Ann Arbor: University of Michigan Press.

Gold, M., & Osgood, D. W. (1992). *Personality and peer influence in juvenile corrections*. Westport, CT: Greenwood Press.

Goldstein, A. (1988). *The prepare curriculum: Teaching pro-social competence*. Champaign, IL: Research Press.

Goldstein, A., & Glick, B. (1987). *Aggression replacement training: A comprehensive intervention for aggressive youth*. Champaign, IL: Research Press.

Gross, B. (1990). Here dropouts drop in—and stay! *Phi Delta Kappan, 71*(8), 625–627.

Hart, L. A. (1983). *Human brain and human learning*. New York: Longman.

Hedin, D. (1989). The power of community service. *Proceedings of Academy of Political Science, 31*(2), 201–213.

Hobbs, N. (1982). *The troubled and troubling child*. San Francisco: Jossey-Bass Publishers.

Kern, D., & Quigley, R. (1994). *Developing youth potential* [video]. National Association of Peer Group Agencies, Woodland Hills, 4321 Allendale Ave., Duluth, MN 55803.

Kohn, A. (1990). *The brighter side of human nature: Altruism and empathy in everyday life*. New York: Basic Books.

Lewis, A. (1990). On valuing young people. *Phi Delta Kappan, 71*(6), 420–421.

Lewis, W., & Lewis, B. (1989). The psychoeducational model: Cumberland House after 25 years. In R. Lyman, S. Prentice-Dunn, & S. Gabel (Eds.), *Residential and inpatient treatment of children and adolescents*. New York: Plenum Press.

MacCracken, M. (1981). *City kid*. New York: Signet Books.

Macmillan, D. L., & Kavale, K. A. (1986). Educational intervention. In H. Quay & J. S. Werry (Eds.), *Psychopathological disorders of childhood*. New York: John Wiley & Sons.

Maeroff, G. (1990). Getting to know a good middle school: Shoreham-Wading River. *Phi Delta Kappan, 71*(7), 505–511.

Makarenko, A. S. (1956). *Werke [Works]* (Vol. 5). Berlin: Volk & Wissen Volkseigener Verlag.

Meichenbaum, D. (1993). Changing conceptions of cognitive behavior modification: Retrospect and prospect. *Journal of Consulting & Clinical Psychology, 62*(2), 202–204.

Morse, W. C. (1985). *The education and treatment of emotionally impaired children and youth.* Syracuse, NY: Syracuse University Press.

Morse, W. C., Cutler, R., & Fink, A. (1964). *Public school classes for emotionally handicapped children.* Washington, DC: Council for Exceptional Children.

Odney, J., & Brendtro, L. (1992). Students grade their schools. *Journal of Emotional & Behavioral Problems, 1*(2), 2–9.

Overly, N. (Ed.). (1979). *Lifetime learning.* Alexandria, VA: Association of Supervision & Curriculum Development.

Phillips, E., et al. (1973). Achievement place: Behavior shaping works for delinquents. *Psychology Today 7*(1), 74–80.

Quay, H., & Werry, J. S. (Eds.). (1988). *Psychopathological disorders of childhood.* New York: John Wiley & Sons.

Raebuck, B. (1990). Transformation of a middle school. *Educational Leadership, 47*(7), 18–21.

Redl, F., & Wineman, D. (1957). *The aggressive child.* New York: Free Press. (Combined version of two earlier books, *Children who hate and Controls from within.*)

Rhodes, W. C. (1992). Empowering young minds. *Journal of Emotional & Behavioral Problems, 1*(2). (special issue on Life-Impact Curriculum)

Rogoff, B., & Morelli, G. (1989). Perspectives on children's development from cultural psychology. *American Psychologist, 44*(2), 343–348.

Shanker, A. (1990). The end of the traditional model of schooling and a proposal for using incentives to restructure our public schools. *Phi Delta Kappan, 71*(5), 345.

Sims, C. (1990). Teens mop up. *Outdoor, 5*(2), 23–24.

Tierney, J., Dowd, T., & O'Kane, S. (1993). Empowering aggressive youth to change. *Journal of Emotional & Behavioral Problems, 2*(1), 41–45.

Vorrath, H., & Brendtro, L. (1985). *Positive peer culture* (2nd ed.). New York: Aldine du Gruyter. (First edition published 1967)

Wasmund, W. (1988). The social climates of peer group and other residential programs. *Child & Youth Care Quarterly, 17*, 146–155.

Whittaker, J. (1980). *Caring for troubled children.* San Francisco: Jossey-Bass Publishers.

Wood, M., & Long, N. (1991). *Life space intervention: Talking with children and youth in crisis.* Austin, TX: Pro-Ed.

Wozner, Y. (1985). Institution as community. *Child & Youth Services, 7*, 71–90.

Management of Aggressive and Violent Behavior in Schools

ROBERT B. RUTHERFORD, JR., AND C. MICHAEL NELSON

UNFORTUNATELY, THE JOES OF THE CLASSROOM can show episodes of violent behavior. This selection offers educators an understanding of these stressful acts of aggression. And it goes beyond understanding to specific guidelines for responding to violence in the classroom. The authors also address the importance of prevention strategies through anger control and aggression replacement training programs.

Aggressive and violent behaviors are increasing among children and youth in America's schools. Although many children and adolescents occasionally exhibit aggressive and sometimes antisocial behaviors in the course of development, an alarming increase is taking place in the significant number of youth who confront their parents, teachers, and schools with persistent threatening and destructive behaviors. Students who exhibit chronic patterns of hostile, aggressive, and defiant behaviors frequently are characterized as having *oppositional disorders* or *conduct disorders* (Horne & Sayger, 1990; Kazdin, 1987), and their behaviors are increasingly identified as antisocial (Walker, Colvin, & Ramsey, 1995).

The *Diagnostic and Statistical Manual of Mental Disorders (DSM-III-R)* (American Psychiatric Association, 1987) defines oppositional defiant disorder as

> a pattern of negativistic, hostile, and defiant behavior.... Children with this disorder commonly are argumentative with adults, frequently lose their temper, swear, and are often angry, resentful, and easily annoyed by others. They frequently actively defy adult requests or rules and deliberately annoy other people. They tend to blame others for their own mistakes or difficulties. (p. 56)

Conduct disorder, a more serious and disruptive aggressive behavior pattern, is defined in the *DSM-III-R* as

> a persistent pattern of conduct in which the basic rights of others and major age-appropriate societal norms or rules are violated.... Physical aggression is common. Children and adolescents with this disorder usually initiate aggression, may be physically cruel to other people or animals, and frequently destroy other people's property. (p. 53)

Antisocial behavior has been defined as "recurrent violations of socially pre-scribed patterns of behavior" (Simcha-Fagan, Langner, Gersten, & Eisenberg, 1975, p. 7), and antisocial patterns of behavior have been described as the polar opposite of prosocial patterns, which are composed of cooperative, positive, and mutually reciprocal social behaviors (Walker et al., 1995). According to Walker et al., "Antisocial behavior suggests hostility to others, aggression, a willingness to com-mit rule infractions, defiance of adult authority, and violation of the social norms and mores of society" (p. 2).

Whether students are formally diagnosed as having oppositional defiant disorders or conduct disorders is of less relevance to many educators and school staff than is the increase they are seeing in the number of students, with and without formal diagnoses, who are exhibiting aggressive and violent antisocial behaviors in the schools. A sub-stantial body of research indicates that antisocial behavior problems are significant and durable conditions in many children and adolescents (Nelson & Rutherford, 1990). For example, from their series of longitudinal assessments of antisocial behavior of boys in school settings, Walker and his colleagues (Shinn, Ramsey, Walker, Stieber, & O'Neill, 1987; Walker, Shinn, O'Neill, & Ramsey, 1987; Walker, Stieber, & O'Neill, 1990; Walker, Stieber, Ramsey, & O'Neill, 1991) found that students who exhibited antiso-cial behavior experienced significantly greater school failure than other students. Specifically, these students exhibited significantly less academically engaged time in academic settings, initiated and were involved in significantly more negative interac-tions with peers, had more school discipline contacts, were perceived by teachers as less socially skilled, and experienced lower school attendance than their peers.

Walker et al. (1987; 1995) suggested that students who continue to exhibit anti-social behaviors over time will be at increased risk not only for continued school fail-ure but also for membership in deviant peer groups, school dropout, and eventual delinquency and adult criminal careers. They concluded that "the long-term develop-mental implications for children who display this behavior pattern are extremely seri-ous" (Walker et al., 1987, p. 15). Walker and his colleagues (Bullis & Walker, in press; Walker et al., 1995) provided evidence that if antisocial behavior patterns are not iden-tified and treated before children reach the age of 8, these patterns are considered to be chronic and are much more difficult to ameliorate than when they are identified and treated before that time. In fact, antisocial behaviors that are present in childhood have been found to be remarkably durable over time. In her classic follow-up study of chil-dren exhibiting deviant behavior, Robins (1966) found that childhood antisocial status was the most powerful predictor of adjustment problems in adults.

The focus of this chapter is on the spectrum of behaviors judged by others as aggressive or violent. Students who exhibit these patterns may or may not be assigned formal diagnostic labels such as conduct disorder, oppositional defiant disorder, or emotional and behavioral disorder. Antisocial behavior patterns, assessment methodologies, and intervention strategies are described.

Aggression and Violence

Aggressive and violent tendencies are the defining characteristics of most students who have been identified as antisocial. Overt forms of antisocial behavior are characterized by aggressive acts directed against persons and include verbal or physical assault, oppositional-defiant behavior, use of coercive tactics, and humiliation of others (Walker, 1993). From a social learning perspective, aggression is defined as gestural, verbal, and physical behaviors that result in physical, material, or psychological pain or injury to another person. Younger aggressive students demonstrate higher rates of such behaviors as humiliating, biting, being destructive, whining, yelling, teasing, being noncompliant, and being negative than their nonaggressive peers (Patterson, Ray, Shaw, & Cobb, 1969). A defining characteristic of older aggressive students is the persistence of these behaviors over time. Although most children demonstrate a significant decrease in aggressive behavior as they mature, aggressive children maintain a consistently high rate of aggressiveness as they grow older.

The student's social environment greatly influences the level and intensity of his or her aggressive and violent behaviors in the school and classroom. Social learning may be the most important determinant of both aggressive and prosocial behavior. According to Bandura (1973) aggression is learned through the observation of aggression and its consequences and through experiencing the direct consequences of aggressive and nonaggressive behaviors. Kauffman (1993) made the following generalizations about the effects of social learning on aggression and violence:

- Children learn many aggressive responses by observing models or examples.
- Children are more likely to imitate aggressive models when the models are of high social status and when they observe the models receiving reinforcement or not receiving punishment for aggression.
- Children learn aggression when their aggressive acts do not lead to aversive consequences or succeed in obtaining reinforcement by harming others.
- Aggression is more likely to occur when children are aversively stimulated by physical assault or verbal threats, taunts, or insults; by thwarting goal-directed behavior; or by decreased positive reinforcement.
- Three types of reinforcement may maintain aggressive behavior: external reinforcement (tangible rewards or increased social status for aggression, removal of aversive conditions, victim pain or suffering); vicarious reinforcement (gratification from observing others rewarded for aggression); and self-reinforcement (self-reward following successful aggression).

- Aggression may be perpetuated by cognitive processes and rationales that justify hostile behavior.
- The punishment of children by adults may result in aggression when it causes pain, when there are no positive alternatives to the punished behavior, when punishment is delayed or inconsistent, or when punishment provides a model of aggressive behavior. (p. 321)

Kerr and Nelson (1989) suggested three functional explanations for aggression in the classroom. First, the aggressive behavior may be under inappropriate stimulus control. Whereas certain forms of hurtful behavior may be deemed appropriate under specific conditions (e.g., self-defense, with mutual consent, for the protection of others), the students who are antisocial may exhibit these behaviors in situations that do not warrant aggression. In addition, such students may lack the ability to discriminate the environmental cues or prompts that set the occasion for prosocial rather than antisocial behaviors. Second, aggressive behaviors often are reinforced by tangible reward or personal gain, by the reaction of others, or by the avoidance of aversive, undesired, or unpleasant situations or consequences. Third, aggressive behavior may be imitated. If the student who is antisocial is a member of a group that places value on aggression and toughness, he or she may imitate the aggressive behavior exhibited by peers or other high-status models.

Thus, from a social learning perspective, student aggression may occur as a result of a complex interaction of any of the following three factors: inappropriate or ineffective stimulus control, direct or indirect reinforcement of aggression, and modeling of aggression. To develop and implement effective intervention strategies to ameliorate antisocial behaviors, and to identify and teach prosocial skills in lieu of aggressive and violent acts, it is important to conduct functional assessments of aggressive behavior across classroom and school contexts. Assessment is accomplished through a functional analysis of the antecedents and consequences of both antisocial and prosocial behaviors.

Assessment of Aggressive Behavior

The most successful strategies for managing aggressive behavior are based on early identification and intervention. Children who are likely to develop chronic patterns of aggressive behavior are identifiable at an early age. Because the roots of chronic aggression are in early socialization experiences, behavior patterns leading to this condition often are evident before children enter school (Kazdin, 1987). In fact, two stable patterns of behavioral disorders emerge during the preschool years: internalizing or withdrawing and externalizing or acting out (Achenbach & McConaughy, 1987; Walker & Bullis, 1991). Externalizing behavior patterns are more prevalent and may involve or lead to aggression, noncompliance, and delinquency.

Systematic Schoolwide Screening

Systematic screening procedures have been developed that reliably identify students who are at risk for the development of aggressive behavior patterns (McConaughy & Achenbach, 1989). One of these procedures, developed by Walker and Severson (1990), is called Systematic Screening for Behavior Disorders (SSBD). This multiple gating procedure begins with the classroom teacher nominating up to 10 students who are at risk for externalizing behavior disorders and then rank-ordering them according to their degree of acting-out behavior. The same procedure is used for screening pupils at risk for internalizing behavior disorders. However, because the focus of this chapter is on externalizing behavior, screening for internalizing disorders will not be described. The second gate involves the teacher completing two brief rating scales for the three highest-ranked pupils. Those students who exceed local norms are advanced to the next gate, in which trained observers make two sets of controlled, 15-minute observations of the students in structured academic activities and unstructured play activities. Students who exceed age- and sex-appropriate norms may be assessed through standardized diagnostic procedures and may receive early intervention services. The SSBD procedure offers the advantage of exposing all students to systematic screening (Walker et al., 1988).

In terms of intervention, the great advantage of systematic screening programs is that they identify aggressive and violent behavior problems early on, at a time when these problems are most responsive to intervention efforts. As mentioned earlier, abundant research supports Bullis and Walker's (in press) contention that antisocial behavior, if not addressed by the time children reach the age of eight, is extremely durable and resistant to treatment.

Assessment Methodology

Significant advances in behavioral assessment procedures have been made in recent years. The technology includes the careful study of both behavior and the contexts in which it occurs. The strategy of behavioral-ecological assessment, for example, involves the evaluation of observable student behaviors over the range of environmental settings in which they occur (Kerr & Nelson, 1989). The goals are to (a) identify the specific interpersonal and environmental variables within each setting that influence behavior; (b) analyze the behavioral expectations for various settings; and (c) compare those expectations with the student's behavior across the settings (Polsgrove, 1987). This strategy has yielded a rich supply of information about the environmental factors that influence aggressive behavior as well as the functions that such behavior serves for the student.

Wehby (1994) identified four hypotheses about the factors that lead to aggressive behavior that have emerged from the available research. Aggressive behavior may be the result of (a) a social skills deficit; (b) positive or negative reinforcement; (c) environmental deficits; or (d) deficits in the cognitive processing of social stimuli. Although these hypotheses overlap and are not inclusive of all the possible causes of aggressive behavior, each has been supported by research. For example, some children engage in aggressive behavior because they lack the appropriate social skills to gain entry into peer activities and to negotiate conflicts. Aggressive behavior also may be supported by attention from others or by access to desired materials or activities (positive reinforcement) as well as by escape from or avoidance of undesired activities, such as difficult tasks (negative reinforcement). The environmental-deficit hypothesis is supported by research demonstrating that aggressive children are more likely to display higher rates of aggression in settings characterized by low densities of positive reinforcement for desired behaviors or by low levels of structure.

Finally, research by Dodge and his colleagues (Dodge & Coie, 1987; Dodge, Petit, McClaskey, & Brown, 1986; Dodge & Tomlin, 1987) has revealed that some aggressive children attend to irrelevant cues, fail to encode relevant information, misinterpret the intentions of others, make hostile attributions of intent, and are unable to develop competent solutions to problems.

These findings suggest that both the context and function of aggressive behavior must be considered when developing interventions. Too often, the only interventions used with aggressive behavior involve punishment tactics, which do not address the function the behavior may serve for the student. A thorough behavioral analysis of aggression should address its antecedents and consequences as well as the behavior itself.

Antecedents of Aggression

Typically, assessments of aggression have focused on the immediate antecedent events. Although such antecedents often are important factors in provoking aggression, Conroy and Fox (1994) have noted that more complex events or combinations of events, known as setting events, may be what sets the occasion for the display of aggression. These events may occur within the same setting as, and immediately precede, the aggressive behavior (e.g., a noisy, crowded room) or they may be temporally more remote (e.g., events occurring in the home before school). By noting the nature of the aggressive behavior, its time of occurrence, the other persons present, and the activities taking place, the interventionist can identify potential relationships between setting events and behavior. Conroy and Fox also recommended that interviews be conducted with persons who know the student and are familiar with his or her behavior and suggested the use of behavioral checklists and rating scales as alternatives to direct observation for identifying setting events. Again, knowledge of these antecedent variables may be important in designing effective interventions.

Topography of Aggressive Behavior

The topography, or form, of aggressive behavior may range from verbal taunts or insults to physical attacks on other persons or property (Kerr & Nelson, 1989). It is important to assess and document the topographies of aggression displayed by the student as well as the sequence of behaviors leading to an aggressive act. For example, a child may exhibit a pattern of displaying agitation and then noncompliance before engaging in verbal or physical aggression. If such a pattern can be identified, it is possible to intervene early in the sequence before it has reached the point at which the environment will be severely disrupted or persons are in physical danger. Early intervention in a chain of behaviors leading to aggression is more likely to be effective than waiting until the behavior has escalated to the point at which the student has lost all control.

Consequences of Aggression

The communicative function of behavior has been studied by a number of researchers. Carr, Durand, and their colleagues initiated a line of applied behavior analytic research examining the communicative function of the behavior of persons with severe and profound disabilities (Carr & Durand, 1985; Carr, Newsome, & Binkoff, 1980; Durand & Carr, 1987). This research is based on the limited verbal abilities of such individuals, which creates a need to understand the communicative purposes served by aberrant behavior. Donnellan, Mirenda, Mesaros, and Fassbender (1984) identified three categories of behaviors that serve communicative functions: (a) behaviors that express requests for attention, interactions, or items; (b) behaviors that express protests, refusals, or the desire to terminate an activity; and (c) behaviors that express declarations or comments or have personal meaning. Dunlap and his colleagues (Dunlap et al., 1993; Foster-Johnson & Dunlap, 1993) focused on two major categories: behaviors that produce a desired event and behaviors that serve to escape or avoid an undesired event. By systematically observing the rate of undesired behaviors under different task and reinforcement conditions, researchers can test hypotheses regarding the functions these behaviors serve. Through the teaching of desired behaviors that serve the same communicative function, it has been possible to reduce the rates of undesired behaviors.

Dunlap and his colleagues have extended this research strategy to the communicative function of the behaviors of students with emotional and behavioral, but not cognitive, disabilities (Dunlap, Kern-Dunlap, Clarke, & Robbins, 1991; Dunlap et al., 1993). This research holds great promise for the design of more effective interventions for students exhibiting aggressive and violent behavior, because it offers a proactive alternative to waiting until the aggressive behavior occurs and then punishing it.

When Shores and his colleagues (Gunter, Denny, Jack, Shores, & Nelson, 1993; Shores, Gunter, & Jack, 1993; Shores et al., 1993) examined the interactions between students with emotional and behavioral disabilities and their teachers, they found low rates of teacher reinforcement of desired student behavior, high rates of aversive interactions, and higher probabilities of teacher avoidance and escape behavior in the presence of pupils with aggressive behavior patterns. Their body of research compellingly demonstrates that aggressive and other undesired student behaviors may be strengthened because they produce desired outcomes or reduce the likelihood of undesired outcomes.

Tools for the Functional Analysis of Aggressive Behavior

Behavior analysts traditionally have advocated an assessment model that examines the immediate antecedents and consequences of behavior (Kerr & Nelson, 1989). The value of such an analysis is indisputable, but the model requires full attention to the student during the observation period—something that is difficult for teachers to accomplish. Alternative strategies that are often more practical for busy practitioners include behavioral interviews (Gross, 1984), ratings that estimate the strength of behaviors across time and activities (Touchette, MacDonald, & Langer, 1985), and after-the-fact behavior incident logs (Kerr & Nelson, 1989). Data collected from all of these strategies are useful for intervention planning.

Relationship of Assessment to Intervention

As indicated earlier, a comprehensive behavioral-ecological assessment can be used to identify the variables that are functionally related to the targeted behavior and the standards and expectations of the settings in which the behavior occurs. With this information, augmented by data indicating specific conditions affecting the rate of behavior, interventionists can design strategies tailored to the unique characteristics of the student, the behavior, and the settings in which it occurs. In particular, by analyzing the setting events and stimuli preceding an episode of student aggression, interventionists can become more sensitive to these variables and apply more appropriate treatments. If these strategies include teaching the student to recognize his or her indicators of agitation, to understand the communicative purpose of the behavior, and to employ more adaptive means of achieving the function served by the maladaptive behavior, the needs of the pupil and others in the setting will be better served.

Monitoring the Effectiveness of Interventions

Practitioners often object to collecting data on targeted student behaviors because such activities add to the burden of their already busy schedules. However, as White (1986, p. 522) indicated, "To be responsive to the pupil's needs, the teacher must be a student of the pupil's behavior, carefully analyzing how that behavior changes from day to day and adjusting the instructional plan as necessary to facilitate continued learning." Although White was referring to students in general, the statement also pertains to students with serious behavior problems, such as aggression and violence. Whether the intervention involves reducing the frequency or intensity of aggressive acts, increasing alternatives to aggressive behavior, or both, it is important to monitor the student's (and the teacher's) progress toward the desired behavioral goals and objectives. Failure to do so involves the risk of prolonging an ineffective intervention or of continuing an intervention strategy that no longer is necessary. Formative evaluation of intervention strategies against objective data decision rules is required practice.

Intervention Strategies

Teacher-Mediated Interventions

Two primary types of intervention enable teachers to manage aggressive behaviors: rearranging behavior enhancement and behavior reduction contingencies for aggression and teaching appropriate, prosocial skills that are incompatible with antisocial acts. These two approaches are based on a social learning theory model that presumes that aggressive behaviors are learned and that prosocial skills that are incompatible with aggressive behaviors can be taught (Bandura, 1971).

Behavioral interventions derived from applied behavior analysis (Baer, Wolf, & Risley, 1968, 1987) and social learning theory emphasize the use of overt, objectively observable behaviors as dependent measures. Such behavioral interventions may be represented on two continua: one depicting behavior enhancement procedures and one depicting behavior reduction procedures (Nelson & Rutherford, 1988).

Behavior Enhancement Contingencies

Six levels, or types, of behavior enhancement procedures have been documented in the applied behavior analysis literature. When combined with behavior reduction procedures, these strategies have proven to be effective tools for ameliorating aggressive and violent behavior in the classroom and school. The six levels are tangible reinforcement, activity reinforcement, token reinforcement, behavioral or contingency contracting, modeling, and social reinforcement.

Tangible Reinforcement. Tangible reinforcers are material items that have reinforcing value for particular students. Although they frequently are used as backup reinforcers in token economies (as described later), they also may be delivered immediately following desired student behavior. In their study of tangible reinforcement, Dewhurst and Cautela (1980) found that 5- to 12-year-old students with behavior problems rated stickers as their most preferred reinforcers. Rhode, Jenson, and Reavis (1993) suggested that tangibles tend to be more effective with younger students who may not initially respond consistently to teachers' social reinforcement.

Activity Reinforcement. The opportunity to engage in desired or high-probability behaviors (Premack, 1959) has been shown to be an effective reinforcement procedure with students exhibiting mild to moderate behavioral problems in school. For example, Jackson, Salzberg, Pacholl, and Dorsey (1981) effectively reduced the aggressive school-bus-riding behaviors of a 10-year-old boy by making afternoon privileges at home (watching TV and playing outside) contingent upon successively (progressively) lower rates of occurrence of targeted behaviors on the bus that included yelling, name-calling, moving from seat, grabbing and throwing objects, spitting, hitting, pinching, and pushing.

Token Reinforcement. Token economies have been used effectively with a wide range of student populations and age-groups and in numerous educational and treatment settings (Kazdin, 1982). For example, Deitz, Slack, Schwarzmueller, Wilander, Weatherly, and Hilliard (1978) demonstrated the positive effects of a token system in which a 7-year-old student received stars exchangeable for time on the playground for every 2-minute period in which she exhibited one or zero aggressive behaviors, including shoving, pushing, hitting, throwing objects, and destroying objects. Tokens can be exchanged for a variety of tangible and activity reinforcers, and they often can be delivered more quickly and easily than tangible reinforcers.

Behavioral or Contingency Contracting. Behavioral contracting involves the negotiation and implementation of a formal written agreement between a student and a teacher, parent, peer, or other person. A typical contract specifies the behavior(s) to be increased or decreased, the student goals with respect to the behaviors, and the consequences associated with goal attainment or nonattainment (Rutherford, 1975). Contracting has been effective in modifying a variety of desired and undesired behaviors in students of all ages. Rutherford and Polsgrove (1981), who reviewed 35 studies in which contracts were made with children and youth who exhibited behaviorally disordered, antisocial, or delinquent behavior, concluded that "contracting has contributed to behavioral change in a number of instances" (p. 64).

Modeling. With this behavior enhancement procedure, students observe adult or peer models performing and being reinforced for demonstrating prosocial behaviors and strategies. When students then imitate these modeled behaviors, they are reinforced as well. Modeling has the potential for reinforcement at two stages—at the point of observing the model being reinforced (vicarious reinforcement) and at the point when the student performs the same behaviors.

Modeling has been used mainly for teaching complex prosocial behaviors and typically is implemented in conjunction with other behavior enhancement and reduction procedures, such as behavior rehearsal and role-playing interventions. Modeling is an important component of Goldstein's (1987) program for teaching prosocial skills to adolescents who exhibit antisocial behavior. Through the use of live acting by trainers or of audiovisual modeling displays, models demonstrate the skill steps necessary to expertly perform such aggression-relevant prosocial skills as responding to failure, responding to anger, dealing with being left out, dealing with an accusation, and dealing with group pressure.

Social Reinforcement. Social reinforcement consists of the teacher giving positive verbal and physical feedback, attention, and approval for desired student behavior. When used in combination with other behavior enhancement and reduction procedures, this type of intervention often is effective for developing the prosocial behaviors of students who behave antisocially (Rutherford, Chipman, DiGangi, & Anderson, 1992). Walker et al. (1995) pointed out that behavior-specific adult praise is an extremely powerful form of focused attention that communicates approval and positive regard. They noted that although students who behave antisocially initially may not be responsive to adult praise because of a history of negative adult interactions, social reinforcement paired with other behavior enhancement procedures eventually will increase the positive valence of praise.

Behavioral Reduction Contingencies

Because the antisocial aggressive behavior patterns of children and youth often are so well developed, aversive, and resistant to behavior enhancement procedures used in isolation, interventions are most effective when they combine behavior enhancement and reduction techniques (Nelson & Rutherford, 1988; Walker et al., 1995). A substantial body of research has identified several behavior reduction procedures, including differential reinforcement, response cost, and time-out.

Differential Reinforcement. Four strategies have been developed for reducing undesired behaviors through differential reinforcement. Differential reinforcement of incompatible behavior (DRI) and differential reinforcement of alternate behavior (DRA) involve, as their names imply, reinforcing behaviors that are incompatible with or merely alternatives to problem behaviors. Differential reinforcement of low rates of behavior (DRL) involves providing reinforcement when problem behavior occurs less than a specified amount in a period of time. Differential reinforcement of the omission of behavior (DRO) requires that the problem behavior be suppressed for an entire interval of time (Deitz & Repp, 1983).

DRI and DRA have been effective with a variety of student populations and problem situations when the behaviors that are incompatible with or alternative to aggression, for example, prosocial skills and strategies for social interaction, have been systematically reinforced. DRL has been used primarily to reduce minor classroom misbehaviors or to eliminate in a stepwise process the limited number of aggressive responses that may be initially tolerated. Using DRL procedures, Deitz et al. (1978) reduced to nearly zero the number of antisocial and other inappropriate behaviors exhibited by a 7-year-old boy in a special class. Epstein, Repp, and Cullinan (1978) and Trice and Parker (1983) successfully used DRL to reduce the obscene and aggressive verbal responses of six behaviorally disordered 6- to 9-year-olds and two disruptive 16-year-olds, respectively. DRO has been used successfully to reduce the occurrence of a number of severe behavior problems, although it usually is employed in combination with other behavior enhancement and reduction procedures (Stainback, Stainback, & Dedrick, 1979). Rose (1979), Rapoff, Altman, and Christopherson (1980), and Dorsey, Iwata, Ong, and McSween (1980) successfully used DRO alone or in combination with other behavior reduction techniques to significantly reduce self-aggressive and self-injurious behaviors of students with severe disabilities.

Response Cost. Research involving the removal of reinforcers following the occurrence of undesired target behaviors has indicated that this strategy is a powerful, cost-effective procedure for preventing and suppressing the occurrence of a variety of aggressive and violent behaviors (Walker, 1983). The two most common applications of response cost involve removal of the opportunity to participate in specified activities and token removal, for example, the imposition of fines within token economy systems following inappropriate behavior (Rutherford, 1983). Walker et al. (1995) suggested that response cost contingencies usually are necessary, in combination with other interventions, to produce socially valid reductions in aggressive and violent antisocial behaviors. The research literature supports the combined application of limit setting, reinforcement contingencies, and aversive consequences, such as time-out and response cost. Examples of response cost contingencies with students with behavior problems include a group contingency of 1-minute reductions in a special 10-minute recess for each instance of a "naughty finger" (raised fist with middle finger extended), a verbal reference to it, or "tattling" about another child's use of the naughty finger (Sulzbacher & Houser, 1968); a response cost lottery in which adolescent students begin the day with a fixed number of reward tickets, lose tickets contingent upon misbehavior, and exchange remaining tickets for rewards (Proctor & Morgan, 1991); and token loss contingent upon the aggressive behaviors of predelinquent boys (Phillips, 1968).

Time-Out. Response contingent time-out, or time-out from positive reinforcement, is a behavior reduction procedure whereby access to the sources of reinforcement is removed for a period of time following the occurrence of maladaptive or antisocial behaviors (Rutherford & Nelson, 1983). This complex intervention may be implemented at several different levels, ranging from planned ignoring to seclusion (Nelson & Rutherford, 1983). Research has shown time-out to be effective with children with moderate to severe behavior problems, but many factors appear to influence its success, including the level of time-out used, how it is applied, the schedule under which it is administered, procedures for removing the student from time-out, and the concurrent use of other behavior enhancement and reduction interventions (Gast & Nelson, 1977; Rutherford & Nelson, 1983).

Substantial empirical evidence supports the use of planned ignoring time-out plus social reinforcement for reducing the aggressive behaviors of young children (Pinkston, Reese, LeBlanc, & Baer, 1973; Sibley, Abbott, & Cooper, 1969; Wasik, Senn, Welch, & Cooper, 1969). Also proven successful for young children exhibiting aggressive behavior have been planned ignoring and restraint plus social reinforcement (Noll & Simpson, 1979); contingent observation time-out plus social reinforcement (Porterfield, Herbert-Jackson, & Risley, 1976); reduction of response maintenance stimuli time-out plus group free time (Devine & Tomlinson, 1976); exclusion time-out plus social reinforcement (Firestone, 1976; Mace & Heller, 1990); and seclusion time-out plus social reinforcement (Sachs, 1973; Sloane, Johnstone, & Bijou, 1967; Webster, 1976).

Extinction, Verbal Aversives, Physical Aversives, and Overcorrection

Four behavior reduction contingencies that generally have not proven to be effective in reducing antisocial behavior patterns are extinction, verbal aversives, physical aversives, and overcorrection.

Extinction. Although withholding reinforcers (e.g., attention) that are thought to be maintaining undesired behavior following the occurrence of that behavior has proven to be a successful strategy with a variety of behaviors and students (Polsgrove & Reith, 1983), Stainback et al. (1979) concluded that extinction is one of the least effective procedures for controlling severe maladaptive behavior. Further, they stated that it is an inappropriate strategy for reducing behaviors reinforced by consequences other than those controlled by the teacher (e.g., severe aggressive and disruptive behaviors).

Verbal Aversives. Verbal reprimands have proven effective for reducing mild and moderate behavior problems (Nelson, 1981; Rutherford, 1983), but, unless used with other strategies, they are not likely to be effective in reducing more serious forms of maladaptive behaviors. However, when verbal reprimands are associated with other punishing consequences, such as response cost or time-out, they may acquire aversive properties and subsequently be effective when used alone (Gelfand & Hartman, 1984).

Physical Aversives. Substances with aversive tastes and odors, electric shock, and slaps, pinches, and spankings constitute the range of physical aversive procedures that have been investigated as ways to reduce problem behaviors. In general, these forms of punishment have been found to be efficient and effective means of weakening severe maladaptive behaviors, such as self-injurious and extreme assaultive behaviors of individuals with severe disabilities in institutional settings (Rutherford, 1983; Stainback et al., 1979). However, because parents and community groups frequently object to the use of such extreme interventions, alternative procedures are required in public school settings.

In addition, physical aversives may not be effective for reducing students' serious aggressive and violent antisocial behavior when that behavior is rooted in physical abuse and violence. For such students, aggression may be a response learned through modeling of the physically punitive behaviors of adults. To use physical aggression to control aggression is paradoxical and, as noted by Rose (1983), not empirically validated. Physical aversives, in the form of corporal punishment, have failed to produce sustained suppression of inappropriate behaviors (Rose, 1981), increase the likelihood that the student will behave aggressively in other settings (Maurer, 1974), and make no contribution to the development of new, appropriate behaviors (Goldstein, Apter, & Harootunian, 1984).

Overcorrection. This complex procedure involves components of restraint and guided practice, social punishment, extinction, and time-out. Both restitutional and positive practice overcorrection have been effective in reducing a wide variety of self-stimulatory and self-injurious behaviors (Stainback et al., 1979), as well as the behavior problems of students with mild disabilities (Nelson, 1981). In addition, restitutional overcorrection has been effective in reducing aggressive behavior (Gelfand & Hartman, 1984). However, claims that overcorrection is superior to other techniques for reducing aggressive behavior have not been substantiated. Further, the unacceptability of overcorrection to many practitioners, and student resistance to overcorrection procedures are obstacles to its effectiveness (Axelrod, Brantner, & Meddock, 1978).

Teaching Alternative Behaviors

This component of teacher-mediated intervention involves teaching alternative prosocial skills and anger-control strategies to replace aggressive and violent behaviors in the classroom and school. The contingency management procedures reviewed earlier will help manage the outbursts of an aggressive student but may fall short of offering the student new and better ways to solve problems with others. Behavior enhancement and reduction procedures can be used, however, to both manage aggression and violence and teach replacement responses. Through the functional assessment procedures described earlier, practitioners can formulate hypotheses regarding what purposes the undesired behavior serves the student and can then identify and teach the student an alternative, prosocial response. Naturally, it is important to provide systematic positive reinforcement of prosocial skills, especially when they are first acquired. Two primary intervention approaches have been designed for teaching alternative behaviors to student aggression: social skills training and anger management training.

Social Skills Training. The basic goal of social skills training is to help the student who behaves antisocially acquire the social skills needed to avoid interpersonal rejection and gain acceptance by significant peers and adults. Aggressive students often are at a serious disadvantage with regard to both peer and teacher social interactions because of their deficits in the areas of social perception and social skills. Walker et al. (1995) pointed out that peer and teacher rejection is nearly an inevitable consequence of displaying antisocial behavior in school.

Walker et al. (1995) defined social skills for students as a set of competencies that allow students to initiate and maintain positive social relationships with others, contribute to positive peer acceptance and satisfactory school adjustment, and cope effectively and adaptively with the larger social environment. Social competence is a judgment-based evaluation of the student by peers, teachers, parents, and other adults showing recognition that the student exhibits persistent and generalized social skills and strategies across multiple settings and with multiple individuals.

A number of social skills training programs have been developed to promote the social competence of aggressive and socially deficient children and youth. Four of these programs are Goldstein's Structured Learning curriculum (Goldstein, 1987; Goldstein, Sprafkin, Gershaw, & Klein, 1980; McGinnis & Goldstein, 1984); The Boys Town Teaching Social Skills to Youth curriculum (Dowd & Tierney, 1992); The Walker Social Skills curriculum (Walker, Todis, Holmes, & Horton, 1988); and the Teaching Social Skills: A Practical Instructional Approach curriculum (Rutherford et al., 1992).

All social skills curricula offer a similar format. The Teaching Social Skills: A Practical Instructional Approach curriculum, which focuses on teaching prosocial skills to elementary-aged students who are aggressive, immature, or withdrawn, can serve as an illustration. Each of its interventions follows a standard format that incorporates effective components of behavioral intervention. In each case, the student is taught to eventually self-manage prosocial behaviors and effective and positive social interactions. Although the interventions are teacher-directed at first, they are structured to ensure that control is placed eventually with the student. The student is provided with the tools to evaluate the environment, consider the alternatives, choose prosocial behaviors or strategies, monitor the effects of those behaviors, and adjust his or her behavior accordingly.

The five components of the Teaching Social Skills program include:

1. Teach the student to identify alternative prosocial behaviors and strategies.
2. Provide the student with models demonstrating prosocial behaviors and strategies.
3. Provide the student with opportunities to practice prosocial behaviors and strategies in nonthreatening role-play and real-life situations.
4. Socially reinforce the student in a direct manner for demonstrating prosocial behaviors and strategies.

5. Teach the student how to self-control the continued use of prosocial skills and strategies through self-monitoring, self-evaluation, and self-reinforcement (Rutherford et al., 1992).

Anger Management Training. Although the teacher-mediated contingency management approaches identified earlier may help manage and control aggressive and violent behavior effectively in the school, students who behave antisocially often continue to be persistently angry in out-of-school interactions with both peers and adults. Feindler and Ecton (1986) emphasized the following impediments to successfully implementing contingency management interventions with these students: (a) competing peer reinforcement contingencies; (b) lack of powerful competing reinforcers; (c) low-frequency or covert aggressive behaviors that go undetected or unconsequented; (d) inconsistent behavior change agents; and (e) lack of maintenance and generalization of treatment effects.

An important addition to teacher-mediated contingency management interventions that target antisocial behavior is the direct treatment of high anger arousal, which may accompany impulsive and explosive behavior. As Feindler and Ecton (1986) pointed out, although aggressive behavior is not always accompanied by anger arousal, most theorists agree that a state of anger often is an antecedent to aggressive behavior. Therefore, despite the difficulties in operationalizing or measuring a hypothetical construct such as anger, a primary focus of the treatment of aggression should be on anger control.

Anger control programs that have been developed for aggressive and violent children and adolescents include stress inoculation training (Maag, Parks, & Rutherford, 1988; Meichenbaum, 1985); the "Think-Aloud" cognitive-behavioral approach (Camp, Blum, Hebert, & van Doornick, 1977); Adolescent Anger Control (Feindler & Ecton, 1986); Anger Management for Youth (Eggert, 1994); and Aggression Replacement Training (Goldstein & Glick, 1987).

Aggression replacement training combines the contingency management procedures and prosocial skills development of Goldstein's Structured Learning curriculum (Goldstein, 1987) with cognitive-behavioral anger control training strategies and interventions (Finch, Moss, & Nelson, 1993). Anger control training teaches antisocial behavior inhibition—that is, the reduction, management, or control of anger and aggression. Students are taught to respond to provocations that previously resulted in anger with a chain of responses consisting of the following:

1. Triggers—identifying internal and external events that stimulate anger.
2. Cues—identifying physiological factors that signal anger arousal.
3. Reminders—generating anger-reducing self-statements.
4. Reducers—using techniques such as backward counting, deep breathing, peaceful imagery, and reflection on long-term consequences.
5. Using prosocial skill alternatives to anger and aggression.
6. Conducting self-evaluations of the use and results of the anger control sequence (Goldstein & Glick, 1987).

Schoolwide Interventions

Aggression and violence are becoming increasingly prevalent in individual students and groups of students in U.S. schools (Goldstein, Harootunian, & Conoley, 1994). Although these antisocial behaviors often are serious, persistent, and well entrenched in students' patterns of social interaction with peers, teachers, and other adults, strong empirical evidence indicates that the teacher-mediated interventions reviewed in this chapter can have a significant impact on ameliorating these behaviors in the context of a schoolwide intervention plan. Research by Walker et al. (1995), Simpson, Miles, Walker, Ormsbee, and Downing (1991), and Sprick, Sprick, and Garrison (1993) presents a strong case for proactive rather than reactive schoolwide programming that targets aggressive and violent behavior.

Walker et al. (1995) described procedures for developing a proactive schoolwide discipline program whereby school staff collaborate to design and implement an instructional plan for teaching expected prosocial behaviors to and correcting the inappropriate behaviors of students who behave antisocially. They described a system for implementing a continuum of preestablished rules and consequences for managing minor rule infractions, serious school violations, and illegal behavior. In addition, they described procedures for providing individual assistance to students who do not respond to teacher-mediated or general schoolwide interventions. The keys to the success of schoolwide procedures that effectively deal with aggression and violence are that they are proactive rather than reactive in their approach to discipline and that they involve the entire school staff in the design and implementation of the discipline plan.

Sprick et al. (1993) and Simpson et al. (1991) emphasized the collaborative aspect of developing plans for schoolwide intervention for antisocial behavior. Sprick et al. suggested that a schoolwide plan is most effective when school personnel organize to develop collaborative interventions for students. Simpson et al. recommended the development of transdisciplinary programming for dealing with aggressive and violent behavior in the schools. Unlike the traditional "pull-out" model in which professionals work with students on isolated skills and provide segregated instruction, transdisciplinary educational and treatment programs are structured so that multiple interventions can occur simultaneously. Professionals operating within such transdisciplinary programs work together to determine students' needs and to evaluate progress within and between programs.

Conclusions

Abundant technology exists for assessing and successfully intervening with aggressive and violent behavior in the schools. In most cases, the behavior patterns that lead to chronic aggression are evident before children enter school. Systematic screening procedures that effectively identify students at risk for aggressive and violent behavior are available and should be used on a schoolwide basis as part of a system of early intervention.

Studies of aggression have led to the development of strategies for identifying the functional relationships between patterns of aggressive behavior and the environmental antecedents and consequences of that behavior. Identification of these functional relationships is essential to the design of interventions that not only are effective but also are least intrusive and proactive. A student's aggressive behavior may serve either of two purposes: to gain something the student wants or to escape something that the student does not want (Foster-Johnson & Dunlap, 1993). By understanding the function of the behavior for the student, practitioners can design proactive interventions, such as modifying a curriculum that is too difficult or teaching prosocial skills to replace undesired behavior the student uses to fulfill his or her wants.

Proactive interventions, in which new skills are taught systematically, offer an advantage over reactive strategies (e.g., punishment) because the instructional interventions are not dependent upon the occurrence of the undesired behavior. Because the undesired behavior is likely to occur at low rates, proactive strategies that teach appropriate and replacement behaviors or adaptive coping skills have the further advantage of allowing instructional trials to be delivered much more frequently. Finally, proactive strategies that focus on early identification and prevention are less intrusive and more effective than interventions applied after the behavior has occurred.

It is important to carefully monitor aggressive behavior (or earlier behavior patterns that are the targets of intervention) during the systematic application of intervention strategies. Only through formative evaluation procedures can practitioners adjust and adapt interventions to improve their effectiveness.

Finally, it is important to recognize that most students with aggressive and violent patterns of behavior are aggressive out of school as well as in school. Therefore, educators should establish links to family members and community professionals to extend the analysis of the student's behavior and to allow for the design of interventions that can be applied consistently across multiple settings. Comprehensive, ecologically based intervention is critical to the successful treatment of established patterns of aggressive and violent behavior.

References

Achenbach, T. M., & McConaughy, S. M. (1987). *Empirically based assessment of child and adolescent psychopathology*. Newbury Park, CA: Sage.

American Psychiatric Association. (1987). *Diagnostic and statistical manual of mental disorders* (3d ed.-rev.). Washington DC: Author.

Axelrod, S., Brantner, J. P., & Meddock, T. D. (1978). Overcorrection: A review and critical analysis. *Journal of Special Education, 12*, 367–391.

Baer, D. M., Wolf, M. M., & Risley, T. R. (1968). Some current dimensions of applied behavior analysis. *Journal of Applied Behavior Analysis, 1*, 91–97.

Baer, D. M., Wolf, M. M., & Risley, T. R. (1987). Some still current dimensions of applied behavior analysis. *Journal of Applied Behavior Analysis, 20*, 313–328.

Bandura, A. (1971). *Social learning theory*. Morristown, NJ: General Learning.

Bandura, A. (1973). *Aggression: A social learning analysis*. Englewood Cliffs, NJ: Prentice Hall.

Bullis, M., & Walker, H. M. (in press). Characteristics and causal factors of troubled youth. In C. M. Nelson, R. B. Rutherford, & B. I. Wolford (Eds.), *Developing comprehensive and collaborative systems that work for troubled youth: A national agenda.* Richmond, KY: National Coalition for Juvenile Justice Services.

Camp, B. W., Blum, G., Hebert, F., & van Doornick, W. (1977). "Think-Aloud": A program for developing self-control in aggressive young boys. *Journal of Abnormal Child Psychology, 5*, 152–169.

Carr, E. G., & Durand, M. (1985). Reducing behavior problems through functional communication training. *Journal of Applied Behavior Analysis, 18*, 111–126.

Carr, E. G., Newsome, C. D., & Binkoff, J. A. (1980). Escape as a factor in the aggressive behavior of two retarded children. *Journal of Applied Behavior Analysis, 13*, 101–117.

Conroy, M. A., & Fox, J. J. (1994). Setting events and challenging behaviors in the classroom: Incorporating contextual factors into effective intervention plans for children with aggressive behaviors. *Preventing School Failure, 38*(3) 29–34.

Deitz, D. E., & Repp, A. C. (1983). Reducing behavior through reinforcement. *Exceptional Education Quarterly, 3*(4), 34–46.

Deitz, S. M., Slack, D. J., Schwarzmueller, E. B., Wilander, A. P., Weatherly, T. J., & Hilliard, G. (1978). Reducing inappropriate behavior in special classrooms by reinforcing average interresponse times: Interval DRL. *Behavior Therapy, 9*, 37–46.

Devine, V. T., & Tomlinson, J. R. (1976). The "workclock": An alternative to token economies in the management of classroom behaviors. *Psychology in the Schools, 13*, 163–170.

Dewhurst, D. L., & Cautela, J. R. (1980). A proposed reinforcement schedule for special needs children. *Journal of Behavior Therapy and Experimental Psychiatry, 2*, 109–113.

Dodge, K. A., & Coie, J. D. (1987). Social information processing factors in reactive and proactive aggression in children's peer groups. *Journal of Personality and Social Psychology, 53*, 1146–1158.

Dodge, K. A., Petit, G. S., McClaskey, C. L., & Brown, M. (1986). *Social competence in children.* Monographs for the Society for Research in Child Development, 51 (2, Serial No. 213).

Dodge, K. A., & Tomlin, A. (1987). Cue utilization as a mechanism of attributional bias in aggressive children. *Social Cognition, 5*, 280–300.

Donnellan, A. M., Mirenda, P. L., Mesaros, R. A., & Fassbender, L. L. (1984). Analyzing the communicative functions of aberrant behavior. *Journal of the Association of the Severely Handicapped, 9*, 201–212.

Dorsey, M. F., Iwata, B. A., Ong, P., & McSween, T. E. (1980). Treatment of self-injurious behavior using a water mist: Initial response suppression and generalization. *Journal of Applied Behavior Analysis, 13*, 343–353.

Dowd, T., & Tierney, J. (1992). *Teaching social skills to youth: A curriculum for child-care providers.* Boys Town, NE: Boys Town Press.

Dunlap, G., Kern, L., dePerczel, M., Clarke, S., Wilson, D., Childs, K. E., White, R., & Falk, G. D. (1993). Functional analysis of classroom variables for students with emotional and behavioral disorders. *Behavioral Disorders, 18*, 275–291.

Dunlap, G., Kern-Dunlap, L., Clarke, S., & Robbins, F. R. (1991). Functional assessment, curricular revision, and severe behavior problems. *Journal of Applied Behavior Analysis, 24*, 387–397.

Durand, V. M., & Carr, E. G. (1987). Social influences of self-stimulatory behavior: Analysis and treatment application. *Journal of Applied Behavior Analysis, 20*, 119–132.

Eggert, D. L. (1994). *Anger management for youth: Stemming aggression and violence.* Bloomington, IN: National Educational Service.

Epstein, M. H., Repp, A. C., & Cullinan, D. (1978). Decreasing "obscene" language of behaviorally disordered children through the use of a DRL schedule. *Psychology in the Schools, 15*, 419–423.

Feindler, E. L., & Ecton, R. B. (1986). *Adolescent anger control: Cognitive-behavioral techniques.* New York: Pergamon.

Finch, A. J., Moss, J. H., & Nelson, W. M. (1993). Childhood aggression: Cognitive-behavioral therapy strategies and interventions. In A. J. Finch, W. M. Nelson, & E. S. Ott (Eds.), *Cognitive-behavioral procedures with children and adolescents: A practical guide* (pp. 148–205). Boston: Allyn & Bacon.

Firestone, P. (1976). The effects and side effects of time-out on an aggressive nursery school child. *Journal of Behavior Therapy and Experimental Psychiatry, 6,* 79–81.

Foster-Johnson, L., & Dunlap, G. (1993). Using functional assessment to develop effective, individualized interventions for challenging behaviors. *Teaching Exceptional Children, 25*(3), 44–50.

Gast, D. L., & Nelson, C. M. (1977). Time-out in the classroom: Implications for special education. *Exceptional Children, 43,* 461–464.

Gelfand, D. M., & Hartman, D. P. (1984). *Child behavior analysis and therapy* (2nd ed.). New York: Pergamon.

Goldstein, A. P. (1987). Teaching prosocial skills to antisocial adolescents. In C. M. Nelson, R. B. Rutherford, & B. I. Wolford (Eds.), *Special education in the criminal justice system* (pp. 215–250). Columbus, OH: Merrill.

Goldstein, A. P., Apter, S. J., & Harootunian, B. (1984). *School violence.* Englewood Cliffs, NJ: Prentice Hall.

Goldstein, A. P., & Glick, B. (1987). *Aggression replacement training.* Champaign, IL: Research Press.

Goldstein, A. P., Harootunian, B., & Conoley, J. C. (1994). *Student aggression: Prevention, management, and replacement training.* New York: Guilford.

Goldstein, A. P., Sprafkin, R. P., Gershaw, N. J., & Klein, P. (1980). *Skillstreaming the adolescent: A structural learning approach to teaching prosocial skills.* Champaign, IL: Research Press.

Gross, A. M. (1984). Behavioral interviewing. In T. H. Ollendick & M. Hersen (Eds.), *Child behavioral assessment: Principles and procedures* (pp. 61–79). New York: Pergamon.

Gunter, P. L., Denny, R. K., Jack, S. L., Shores, R. E., & Nelson, C. M. (1993). Aversive stimuli in academic interactions between students with serious emotional disturbance and their teachers. *Behavioral Disorders, 18,* 265–274.

Horne, A. M., & Sayger, T. V. (1990). *Treating conduct and oppositional defiant disorders in children.* New York: Pergamon.

Jackson, A. T., Salzberg, C. L., Pacholl, B., & Dorsey, D. S. (1981). The comprehensive rehabilitation of a behavior problem child in his home and community. *Education and Treatment of Children, 4,* 195–215.

Kauffman, J. M. (1993). *Characteristics of emotional and behavioral disorders of children and youth.* New York: Macmillan.

Kazdin, A. E. (1982). The token economy: A decade later. *Journal of Applied Behavior Analysis, 15,* 431–445.

Kazdin, A. E. (1987). *Conduct disorders in childhood and adolescence.* Newbury Park, CA: Sage.

Kerr, M. M., & Nelson, C. M. (1989). *Strategies for managing behavior problems in the classroom* (2nd ed.). Columbus, OH: Merrill.

Maag, J. W., Parks, B. T., & Rutherford, R. B. (1988). Generalization and behavior covariation of aggression in children receiving stress inoculation therapy. *Child and Family Behavior Therapy, 10*(2/3), 29–47.

Mace, F. C., & Heller, M. (1990). A comparison of exclusion time-out and contingent observation for reducing severe disruptive behavior in a 7-year-old boy. *Child and Family Behavior Therapy, 12*(1), 57–68.

Maurer, A. (1974). Corporal punishment. *American Psychologist, 29,* 614–626.

McConaughy, S. M., & Achenbach, T. M. (1989). Empirically based assessment of serious emotional disturbance. *Journal of School Psychology, 27,* 91–117.

McGinnis, E., & Goldstein, A. P. (1984). *Skillstreaming the elementary student.* Champaign, IL: Research Press.

Meichenbaum, D. (1985). *Stress inoculation training.* New York: Pergamon.

Nelson, C. M. (1981). Classroom management. In J. M. Kauffman & D. P. Hallihan (Eds.), *Handbook of special education* (pp. 663–687). Englewood Cliffs, NJ: Prentice Hall.

Nelson, C. M., & Rutherford, R. B. (1983). Time-out revisited: Guidelines for its use in special education. *Exceptional Education Quarterly, 3*(4), 56–67.

Nelson, C. M., & Rutherford, R. B. (1988). Behavioral interventions with behaviorally disordered children. In M. C. Wang, M. C. Reynolds, & H. J. Walberg (Eds.). *Handbook of special education: Research and practice: Mildly handicapping conditions* (Vol. 2, pp. 125–143). New York: Pergamon.

Nelson, C. M., & Rutherford, R. B. (1990). Troubled youth in the public schools: Emotionally disturbed or socially maladjusted? In P. E. Leone (Ed.), *Understanding troubled and troubling youth* (pp. 38–60). Newbury Park, CA: Sage.

Noll, M. B., & Simpson, R. L. (1979). The effects of physical time-out on the aggressive behaviors of a severely emotionally disturbed child in a public school setting. *AAESPH Review, 4*, 399–406.

Patterson, G. R., Ray, R. S., Shaw, D. A., & Cobb, J. A. (1969). *Manual for coding of family interactions*. New York: Microfiche Publications.

Phillips, E. L. (1968). Achievement Place: Token reinforcement procedures in a home-style rehabilitation setting for "pre-delinquent" boys. *Journal of Applied Behavior Analysis, 1*, 313–323.

Pinkston, E. M., Reese, N. M., LeBlanc, J. M., & Baer, D. M. (1973). Independent control of a preschool child's aggression and peer interaction by contingent teacher attention. *Journal of Applied Behavior Analysis, 6*, 115–124.

Polsgrove, L. J., & Reith, H. (1983). Procedures for reducing children's inappropriate behavior in special education settings. *Exceptional Education Quarterly, 3*(4), 20–33.

Polsgrove, L. J. (1987). Assessment of children's social and behavioral problems. In W. H. Berdine & S. A. Meyer (Eds.), *Assessment in special education* (pp. 141–180). Boston: Little, Brown.

Porterfield, J. K., Herbert-Jackson, E., & Risley, T. R. (1976). Contingent observation: An effective and acceptable procedure for reducing disruptive behavior of young children in a group setting. *Journal of Applied Behavior Analysis, 9*, 55–64.

Premack, D. (1959). Toward empirical behavior laws: I. Positive reinforcement. *Psychological Review, 66*, 219–233.

Proctor, M. A., & Morgan, D. (1991). Effectiveness of a response cost raffle procedure on the disruptive behavior of adolescents with behavior problems. *School Psychology Review, 20*, 97–109.

Rapoff, M. A., Altman, K., & Christopherson, E. R. (1980). Suppression of self-injurious behavior: Determining the least restrictive alternative. *Journal of Mental Deficiency Research, 24*, 37–46.

Rhode, G., Jenson, W. R., & Reavis, H. K. (1993). *The tough kid book: Practical classroom management strategies*. Longmont, CO: Sopris West.

Robins, L. N. (1966). *Deviant children grown up*. Baltimore: Williams & Wilkins.

Rose, T. L. (1979). Reducing self-injurious behavior by differentially reinforcing other behaviors. *AAESPH Review, 4*, 170–186.

Rose, T. L. (1981). The corporal punishment cycle: A behavioral analysis of the maintenance of corporal punishment in the schools. *Education and Treatment of Children, 4*, 157–169.

Rose, T. L. (1983). A survey of corporal punishment of mildly handicapped students. *Exceptional Education Quarterly, 3*(4), 9–19.

Rutherford, R. B. (1975). Establishing behavioral contracts with delinquent adolescents. *Federal Probation, 34*(10), 28–32.

Rutherford, R. B. (1983). Theory and research on the use of aversive procedures in the education of moderately behaviorally disordered and emotionally disturbed children and youth. In F. H. Wood & K. C. Lakin (Eds.), *Punishment and aversive stimulation in special education* (pp. 41–64). Reston, VA: Council for Exceptional Children.

Rutherford, R. B., Chipman, J., DiGangi, S. A., & Anderson, K. (1992). *Teaching social skills: A practical instructional approach*. Ann Arbor, MI: Exceptional Innovations.

Rutherford, R. B., & Nelson, C. M. (1983). Analysis of the response contingent time-out literature with behaviorally disordered students in classroom settings. In R. B. Rutherford (Ed.), *Severe behavior disorders of children and youth* (Vol. 5, pp. 79–105). Reston, VA: Council for Children with Behavioral Disorders.

Rutherford, R. B., & Polsgrove, L. J. (1981). Behavioral contracting with behaviorally disordered and delinquent children and youth: An analysis of the clinical and experimental literature. In R. B. Rutherford, A. G. Prieto, & J. E. McGlothlin (Eds.), *Severe behavior disorders of children and youth* (Vol. 4, pp. 49–69). Reston, VA: Council for Children with Behavioral Disorders.

Sachs, D. A. (1973). The efficacy of time-out procedures in a variety of behavior problems. *Journal of Behavior Therapy and Experimental Psychiatry, 4*, 237–242.

Shinn, M. R., Ramsey, E., Walker, H. M., Stieber, S., & O'Neill, R. E. (1987). Antisocial behavior in school settings: Initial differences in an at-risk and normal population. *Journal of Special Education, 21*, 69–84.

Shores, R. E., Gunter, P. L., Jack, S. L. (1993). Classroom management strategies: Are they setting events for coercion? *Behavioral Disorders, 18*(2), 92–102.

Shores, R. E., Jack, S. L., Gunter, P. L., Ellis, D. N., DeBrier, T. J., & Wehby, J. H. (1993). Classroom interactions of children with behavior disorders. *Journal of Emotional and Behavioral Disorders, 1*, 27–39.

Sibley, S. A., Abbott, M. S., & Cooper, B. P. (1969). Modification of the classroom behavior of a disadvantaged kindergarten boy by social reinforcement and isolation. *Journal of Experimental Child Psychology, 1*, 203–219.

Simcha-Fagan, O., Langner, T., Gersten, J., & Eisenberg, J. (1975). *Violent and antisocial behavior: A longitudinal study of urban youth* (OCD-CB-480). Unpublished manuscript. Washington, DC: U.S. Office of Child Development.

Simpson, R. L., Miles, B. S., Walker, B. L., Ormsbee, C. K., & Downing, J. A. (1991). *Programming for aggressive and violent students*. Reston, VA: Council for Exceptional Children.

Sloane, H. N., Johnstone, M. K., & Bijou, S. W. (1967). Successive modification of aggressive behavior and aggressive fantasy play by management of contingencies. *Journal of Child Psychology and Psychiatry, 8*, 216–226.

Sprick, R., Sprick, M., & Garrison, M. (1993). *Interventions: Collaborative planning for students at risk*. Longmont, CO: Sopris West.

Stainback, W., Stainback, S., & Dedrick, C. (1979). Controlling severe maladaptive behaviors. *Behavioral Disorders, 4*, 99–115.

Sulzbacher, S. I., & Houser, J. E. (1968). A tactic to eliminate disruptive behaviors in the classroom: Group contingent consequences. *American Journal of Mental Deficiency, 73*, 88–90.

Touchette, P. E., MacDonald, R. F., & Langer, S. N. (1985). A scatter plot for identifying stimulus control of problem behavior. *Journal of Applied Behavior Analysis, 18*, 343–351.

Trice, A. D., & Parker, F. C. (1983). Decreasing adolescent swearing in an instructional setting. *Education and Treatment of Children, 6*, 29–35.

Walker, H. M. (1983). Applications of response cost in school settings: Outcomes, issues, and recommendations. *Exceptional Education Quarterly, 3*(4), 47–55.

Walker, H. M. (1993). Antisocial behavior in school. *Journal of Emotional and Behavior Problems, 2*(1), 20–24.

Walker, H. M., & Bullis, M. (1991). Behavior disorders and the social context of regular class integration: A conceptual dilemma. In J. W. Lloyd, N. N. Singh, & A. C. Repp (Eds.), *The regular education initiative: Alternative perspectives on concepts, issues, and models* (pp. 75–94). Sycamore, IL: Sycamore Press.

Walker, H. M., Colvin, G., & Ramsey, E. (1995). *Antisocial behavior in school: Strategies for practitioners*. Pacific Grove, CA: Brooks/Cole.

Walker, H. M., & Severson, H. (1990). *Systematic screening for behavior disorders*. Longmont, CO: Sopris West.

Walker, H. M., Severson, H., Stiller, B., Williams, G., Haring, N. G., Shinn, M. R., & Todis, B. (1988). Systematic screening of pupils in the elementary age range at-risk for behavior disorders: Development and trial testing of a multiple gating model. *Remedial and Special Education, 9*(3), 8–14.

Walker, H. M., Shinn, M. R., O'Neill, R. E., & Ramsey, E. (1987). A longitudinal assessment of the development of antisocial behavior in boys: Rationale, methodology, and first year results. *Remedial and Special Education, 8*(4), 7–16.

Walker, H. M., Stieber, S., & O'Neill, R. E. (1990). Middle school behavioral profiles of antisocial and at-risk control boys: Descriptive and predictive outcomes. *Exceptionality, 1*, 61–77.

Walker, H. M., Stieber, S., Ramsey, E., & O'Neill, R. E. (1991). Longitudinal prediction of the school achievement, adjustment, and delinquency of antisocial versus at-risk boys. *Remedial and Special Education, 12*(4), 43–51.

Walker, H. M., Todis, B., Holmes, D., & Horton, G. (1988). *The Walker Social Skills curriculum: The ACCESS program*. Austin, TX: Pro-Ed.

Wasik, B. H., Senn, K., Welch, R. H., & Cooper, B. R. (1969). Behavior modification with culturally deprived school children: Two case studies. *Journal of Applied Behavior Analysis, 2*, 181–194.

Webster, R. E. (1976). A time-out procedure in a public school setting. *Psychology in the Schools, 13*, 72–76.

Wehby, J. H. (1994). Issues in the assessment of aggressive behavior. *Preventing School Failure, 38*(3), 24–28.

White, O. R. (1986). Precision teaching—precision learning. *Exceptional Children, 52*, 522–534.

5 Classroom Interventions for Students with Attention Deficit Disorders

KAREN J. ROONEY

IN ADDITION TO ANGRY OUTBURSTS in the classroom, Joe has difficulty attending to important features of instruction. Does he have an attention deficit disorder (ADD)? This chapter provides a diagnostic system a teacher can use to answer the ADD question. It goes beyond diagnosis. The intervention section is rich in methodology, instruction, and content. Joe's teacher will be doubly empowered with this selection in the professional development notebook.

To work effectively with students with attention disorders in the classroom, a diagnostic/prescriptive approach is necessary for the teacher to understand the student and develop appropriate interventions. The disorder increases the complexity of the teaching process because the attentional problems result in gaps in learning, different processing styles, and behaviors that interfere with learning and academic performance. For example, Jimmy was sitting in class listening to a lesson on farm animals. His reaction to the lesson was to ask his teacher if she had ever been to the Empire State Building, which certainly gave the impression that Jimmy had not been paying attention. The teacher responded, "Jimmy, why would you ask that question now?" Jimmy explained, "You were talking about farm animals, and my uncle used to have a farm that I visited every summer. Last year, he sold his farm and moved to New York City, so I went there instead of the farm, and he took me to the Empire State Building." Jimmy taught his teacher that students with attention disorders do not always process information the way their parents or teacher think they should and that behavior is not always what it seems to be.

During a well-intentioned spelling lesson, Sarah taught her teacher the second lesson, which demonstrates the necessity for ongoing monitoring and diagnostic teaching. Sarah's teacher taught her to use small words within words to help her with spelling. Sarah spelled the word brown as "brone." She was asked to identify a small word within brown to help her spell the word correctly. She identified the word "ow" in brown, and teacher was quite satisfied until Sarah wrote "brone" on the retest. The teacher asked Sarah if she remembered the small word she had identified, and Sarah said, "Yes—the word 'ow.'" The teacher pointed to Sarah's word and queried, "Do you see 'o-w' in brown?" Sarah gave the teacher an exasperated look and said, "Well, you didn't tell me that 'c (see)-o-w' was in the word, so that's why I got it wrong."

Sarah taught her teacher that working with students with attention disorders is not always easy and that interventions have to take into account the individual's unique characteristics as well as the situation. No program or intervention will magically cure an attention disorder. An in-depth understanding of the student's attention disorder is needed to develop classroom interventions that support attention, fill in gaps in learning, and provide feedback to the teacher for continuing and changing interventions. The use of descriptors to describe the attention disorder will help teachers understand the disorder better.

Descriptors of Attention Disorders

The definition of attention frequently has been described in generic terms as though attention were a singular construct, but the literature has not supported this approach (Goldstein & Goldstein, 1990; Kietzman, Spring, & Zubin, 1980; Posner & Snyder, 1975; Rosenthal & Allen, 1978). In contrast, Postle (1988) described attention as "the process through which we construct the world we experience." Thus, a multifactorial definition of attention is necessary for understanding the construct (Halperin et al., 1990). In spite of this data, when a child is diagnosed as having an attention deficit, little attention is given to the description of the attention problems involved. Typically, the diagnosis of attention deficit disorder is treated as a definitive, singular construct as though the label will explain the individual's disorder. Subtype descriptors can prevent the oversimplification of a complicated construct and make the diagnosis of an attention disorder a more salient description that can be translated into appropriate educational and behavioral interventions.

Attention can be divided into two categories that describe specific types of attentional weaknesses: (a) encoding, or problems with incoming stimuli and the storage of this stimuli for processing; and (b) the selection of stimuli to process further.

Encoding

Attention span refers to the length of time an activity is pursued. Switching from task to task without completing the task is one example of a weakness in attention span. A child is not able to continue attending long enough to complete the task or process successfully.

Focusing attention refers to the ability to tune out distracting or irrelevant stimuli so attention is directed toward the appropriate stimuli. This type of attention deficit is exacerbated as the complexity of the task increases (Kietzman et al., 1980; Zentall, 1983).

Divided attention refers to the ability to split attention between two or more inputs or aspects of a task. Impairment in the ability to "split" or allocate attention results in deterioration in speed and accuracy of attentional processing (Kietzman et al., 1980). If a teacher is giving an example of gravity by describing a ride at an amusement park, the attention should focus on the message, and distracting, irrelevant conversations or environmental noises have to be ignored. Focused attention requires the elimination of distracting or irrelevant stimuli. For example, if a teacher is demonstrating a math problem and teaching the steps verbally, the student has to divide or allocate attention between the problem being worked and the message being delivered.

Sustained attention is the ability to maintain the focus of attention over time and is related to arousal or activation of the nervous system. Kahnehan (1973) stated that arousal is the amount of effort required for attentional processing. If arousal is low, motivation, alertness, and processing capacity are diminished and sustained attention is impaired. Many students with ADD become fatigued because of the greater demands on energy when they process information or pay attention.

Intensity of attention has been shown to have an influence on focus as well as memory storage (Pettijohn, 1987). The greater the intensity of the attention from factors such as interest, motivation, or novelty, the greater is the ability to focus and sustain attention. Weaknesses in intensity are similar to widespread underarousal, which interferes with attentional processing capacity. Research on students with ADD indicates that the students perform better under novel, highly stimulating conditions and less well under routine, boring conditions (Zentall, 1983).

Sequential attention is the ability to focus attention on the stimuli in the order necessary to successfully complete the task or accurately comprehend the information. For example, if instructions are being given, attention must be directed to the stimuli in correct order for accurate comprehension and execution to take place. Accuracy of sequential attention affects comprehension of behavioral situations as well as academic processing because of the importance of sequential order in comprehension, application, and generalization.

Selection

Selective attention is the ability to choose the appropriate stimuli for processing. After attention is focused and sustained, certain pieces of information or stimuli are chosen for further processing. For example, in a textbook some terms are put in bold print to help students select these words, rather than other words in the text, for processing. Students with ADD have more difficulty than non-ADD students with the selection process (Hallahan & Reeve, 1980). The concept of selective attention is important in terms of educational intervention because of its implications for studying and test-taking.

Involuntary attention is an automatic response to a stimuli. For example, if someone calls a person's name, the attentional response is immediate.

Voluntary attention is conceptually driven and refers to "the allocation of attention to stimuli that are relevant to current plans, expectations and intentions" (Kietzman et al., (1980). This type of attentional processing is intentional, deliberate, and conscious. The process of choosing relevant stimuli requires excessive energy and demands extensive practice but can become more automatic over time. Driving a car is an example of a task involving voluntary attention that becomes an automatic process. As the car leaves the motor vehicle department, the new driver is thinking of every detail related to the driving process, but with experience the driver can look at scenery, recognize familiar friends, and listen to the news while driving, without interference in the driving process.

Filtering is the process of weeding out irrelevant stimuli from relevant stimuli. Theories such as the "bottleneck" suggest that information is narrowed to the most critical stimuli. This filtering process also has been viewed in terms of "set." *Schema set* (Broadbent, 1971) is a filtering process that targets appropriate stimuli because of the physical properties of the stimuli.

A second filtering process called *response set* selects stimuli for further processing based on the similarity between the stimuli and the conceptual expectation. For example, if a child is told to attend to the teacher with the blue dress, the schema set controls the selection. If the child is told to attend to the teacher who is talking about space, the response set controls the selection. Because students with ADD have difficulty with schemas, the filtering process is complicated by the organizational weaknesses as well as the attentional focus.

The use of these descriptors of attention has been well documented in the literature. Encoding descriptors such as short-term/working memory deficits have been reviewed by Baddeley (1986), Torgeson, Kistner, and Morgan (1987), and McIntyre, Murray, and Blackwell (1981). Selective attention deficits have been analyzed from an educational perspective in some of the most interesting studies (Hallahan & Reeve, 1980; Hallahan, Tarver, Kauffman, & Graybeal, 1978; Richards, Samuels, Turnure, & Ysseldyke, 1990). An understanding of these descriptors of attentional disorders enables educators to understand the nature of the disorder as manifested in the individual so intervention planning will be a "better fit" and more successful.

Intervention Planning

In regard to intervention planning, knowledge of two techniques for behavioral analysis and two important approaches to intervention can be useful. Behavioral observation and behavioral analysis are important techniques to enable a teacher to analyze a student's individual needs, as well as environmental dynamics that have to be addressed during intervention planning. In addition, behavior management and organizational training should be addressed in the intervention program.

Behavioral Observation

Behavioral observation systems are valuable tools to collect information about a student's behavior. The techniques are simple and depict behavior over time so the practitioner can view the behaviors more objectively than with less structured approaches. Many checklists are available that can be used for assessment (Goldstein & Goldstein, 1990), but observation is necessary to determine how the disorder presents itself in the individual student. The observational techniques discussed next represent some simple methods to obtain behavioral information

Strength/Weakness Chart

A simple chart made from teacher perceptions of the individual's strengths and weaknesses can facilitate educational/behavioral planning. Teacher comments often have less impact because the comments are narrative in nature and are not organized succinctly. The comments may be from current teachers or may be compiled from comments and/or grades in the student's cumulative record. Charts can clearly convey the perceptions of a teacher or multiple teachers concerning a student's strengths and weaknesses as well as the teachers' concerns. Solutions using the strengths can be generated for each weakness. An example of such a chart for a tenth-grader is given in Figure 5.1.

Strengths	Weaknesses	Accommodations/Recommendations
Discussion in class	Sustained attention	Oral test alternatives
Leader in cooperative learning	Fatigue	Eliminate rote copying tasks
		Frequent breaks
Oral responses	Written language	Practice essay questions
Multiple-choice tests	Essay tests	Use pictorials/diagrams for concepts
Memorization	Integration	Use graphic organizers that force attention to detail and identification of the concept
		Key word note-taking
		Prepare study materials in cooperative learning groups
		Use review systems consistently
		Use multiple-choice tests with essays that have been organized in advance

Figure 5.1 *Sample Strengths/Weaknesses Chart*

Tracking Cards

Tracking the frequency of the behaviors sometimes can be difficult for teachers who are actively involved in the teaching process. Easy access to a card with designated spaces representing specific behaviors may enable the teacher to record a quick check-mark as a frequency tally. Manipulatives such as moving the pieces of an abacus, moving colored macaroni from one container to another, or shifting rubberbands from one wrist to another are examples of creative substitutes for written tallies. The frequency number then is recorded on the daily card, and the data from daily cards can be graphed or tabulated to provide a more objective view of the severity of the problem and is useful for parent or student conferences. A second type of card simply makes a record of daily comments by the teacher. Examples of these cards are given in Figure 5.2.

Time Sampling of Attention

Attention has been defined as on-task behavior that can be measured through the use of a time-sampling method to identify the occurrence and nonoccurrence of on-task behavior representing attention (Hallahan, Kneedler, & Lloyd, 1982; Hallahan, Lloyd, Kosiewicz, Kauffman, & Graves, 1979; Rooney, Hallahan, & Lloyd, 1984). Observing on-task behavior is particularly useful when looking at student levels of attention in the classroom. The task that will be observed is defined in behavioral terms so the definition of on-task behavior is clear. If the student is supposed to be reading a book, on-task behavior may be defined as eyes being on the book. If the student should be listening to the teacher, the student's eyes should be on the teacher. If a student should be writing, the pencil should be moving on the paper. The behavioral definitions make the judgments more objective, uniform, and accurate.

In addition to the target student, a sample of students is selected randomly. Usually the observational sample consists of five students, consisting of four randomly selected students plus the target student. Each student is given a number, and a recording sheet with the numbers of each child and Yes/No columns for each is created. The observer looks at each child at consistent intervals (i.e., every two seconds) and places a checkmark in the "yes" column if the student is on-task, or places a checkmark in the "no" column if the student is not doing the behavior identified by on-task criteria. The recording sheet may look like the one in Figure 5.3.

Behavioral observation systems are valuable tools to collect information about a student's behavior. These techniques are just a sample of simple observational techniques that depict behavior over time so the behaviors can be viewed more objectively, accurately, and systematically over time than with less structured approaches.

Behavioral Analysis

When observing students with attention disorders, visual organizers can facilitate the process of behavioral analysis. The organizers help focus attention on the dynamics of the behavior by forcing consideration of the situation prior to the occurrence of the behavior and after the occurrence of the behavior, which can change the intervention planning dramatically. For example, if the behavior of concern is that Bill yelled out in class, the intervention will be geared toward Bill, but if the analy-

Narrative Cards	Quantitative Cards

November 10
Sue had trouble starting her classwork
   immediately.
Sue had difficulty finishing her seatwork and
   had to take classwork home to finish.
Sue was involved in a disagreement on the
   playground. She and Marta fought over
   their turn on the swing. They were
   separated and put in time-out until
   they could control their behavior.
Did not have papers signed by parents.

Did Sue finish her work this week?

	Yes	No
Monday		x
Tuesday	x	
Wednesday	x	
Thursday		x
Friday		x

November 11

Sue did not finish seatwork again today
   and had to take work home. She did
   not have her book for reading so
   could not complete reading assignment.
Had to borrow a pencil.
Did well on the playground today.

Was Sue working?   November 10

9:00	yes	9:50 yes
9:10	no	10:00 yes
9:20	yes	10:10 yes
9:30	no	10:20 no
9:40	no	10:30 no

November 12

Had Pair Instruction activity, and work
   was completed.
Did well on playground.
Recommendation: More pair instruction
   for both social and academic reasons.

Was Sue working?   November 11

9:00	yes	9:50 yes
9:10	yes	10:00 no
9:20	yes	10:10 no
9:30	yes	10:20 no
9:40	yes	10:30 no

Figure 5.2 *Narrative and Quantitative Cards*

sis reveals that Steve punched Bill on the back first, the targets of the intervention should be both Steve and Bill.

Without sufficient analysis, even the target of the intervention can't be identified accurately. If the analysis discloses that Bill yelled out and after class Bob and Sarah told him how funny he was when he yelled and dared him to do it again, the intervention should take into account the peer pressure that is causing the behavior to continue. Figure 5.4 gives examples of some visual organizers—the Three, Four, and Five Square approaches.

Was Bob paying attention (eyes on book while reading)?									
Bob		Sammy		Jonah		Jonathan		Francis	
Yes	No	Yes	No	Yes	No	Yes	No	Yes	No
x		x		x		x		x	
x		x		x		x		x	
x		x			x	x		x	
x		x		x		x		x	
x		x		x		x		x	
	x	x		x		x		x	
	x	x		x		x		x	
x			x	x		x		x	
	x	x		x		x		x	
	x	x		x		x		x	
x		x		x		x		x	
x		x			x		x	x	
Percentages on-task:									
67%		92%		83%		92%		100%	

Figure 5.3 *Time Sample Recording Sheet*

The situation prior to occurrence of the behavior must be identified to put the behavior in the appropriate context. In the situation depicted in Figure 5.4, Bill received a negative consequence and probably was angry because Jim started the episode but got away with it. Bill's anger likely will affect future interactions with the teacher. Jim likely will continue the behavior because he did not receive any consequence at all and probably enjoyed getting away with the kicking.

In the Three Square approach, the behavior is analyzed in its context to arrive at causative factors that are making the behavior occur or dynamics that are making the behavior continue. The fourth square generates solutions, and the fifth square tracks effective interventions for the individual student.

Behavior Management

Behavior management depends on the predictability of behavior, on the premise that people learn behavior, and on the assumption that programs can be devised to change behavior.

Two common behavior management formats used to change behavior must be examined in light of the characteristics used to describe attention disorders. The first format is geared to the individual: Mrs. Jones, the teacher, would like Jane to volunteer more often in class. She sets up a system that will give Jane a star on a chart

Three Square Approach

Before	Target	After
Jim kicks Bill in the hall.	Bill slaps Jim on the back when he enters class.	Bill gets a detention.

Four Square Approach

Before	Target	After	Solutions
Jim kicks Bill in the hall.	Bill slaps Jim on the back when he enters class.	Bill gets a detention.	Give Jim a detention. Apologize to Bill for being unfair. Have conference with both boys. Next time find out what actually happened.

Five Square Approach

Before	Target	After	Solutions	What Works
Jim kicks Bill in the hall.	Bill slaps Jim on the back when he enters class.	Bill gets a detention.	Give Jim a detention. Apologize to Bill for being unfair. Have conference with boys. Next time find out what actually happened.	Apology.

Figure 5.4 *Examples of Visual Organizers*

taped to her desk each time she volunteers for an answer. When Jane has all 10 squares filled in on the chart, she will earn a special eraser for her pencil.

The second format, called a *token economy* system, is geared to the group and often is used in classrooms and residential settings. A list of behaviors and reinforcers for the group is compiled so the individual operates within the system set up for the group. Typical classroom activities and reinforcers are listed in Figure 5.5.

The students receive points as the behaviors occur so the tallies result in the number of points the child has to spend. The student is free to spend the points any way he or she wishes.

Though these plans seem simple and straightforward, human behavior and its management are complex. When impulsivity, need for immediate gratification, and rapid satiation rates are involved, behavior management techniques may not work as well as expected. Cost-response techniques in which the students have the reward and only lose the reward through inappropriate behavior have been found to be effective for some students (Swanson, Kitkin, Pfiffner, & McBurnett, 1992).

Another alternative is to use techniques that involve the student in the process. The student is given models of solutions to the identified problem and asked to come up with a workable solution. The student may use one of the models or generate a new solution. Role-playing solutions or alternative behaviors can also be helpful. Students brainstorm all the possible behavior choices for an identified situation, role-play each option and its consequences, and choose the best solution.

Even when new behaviors are learned, generalization of the behaviors has been difficult to achieve without additional intervention such as the technique Swanson and his colleagues have successfully developed (Swanson et al., 1992). The trainer was used as an effective generalization cue by having the trainer actually be present in the new setting to act as a stimulus to generalize the new behavior.

Organizational Strategy Training

Teachers need to tell students with attention disorders how to learn as well as what to learn without using complicated, step-by-step strategies that do not accommodate

Activities	Points	Reinforcers	Points
On time for class	10	Prize bag	200
Has materials	20	Computer time (15 min.)	100
Completes work	30	Activity table (15 min.)	100
Raises hand for question	10	Conversation time (15 min.)	100
Test grade A	50	Daily messenger	200
Test grade B	40	Listen to music	200
Test grade C	30	Library time (15 min.)	100
Takes turn	20		

Figure 5.5 *Typical Activities and Reinforcers*

the characteristics of students with attention disorders and are not flexible enough to generalize easily to a variety of situations. Appropriate interventions should:

1. Be systematic to minimize judgment and organizational demands.
2. Be simple and dependable.
3. Be manipulative (active involvement).
4. Build the necessary base of information (not activate prior knowledge).
5. Identify missing skills.
6. Force conceptual understanding or recognition of instructional needs.
7. Be concrete and visual.
8. Provide advance organization so multiple passes through material is not required.
9. Help break down processes into manageable units.
10. Guide the learning process.
11. Force attention to critical detail.
12. Result in review systems consisting of the critical pieces of information.
13. Accommodate nonlinear or associational styles of thinking.
14. Guide memory storage and practice specific retrieval in a study system.

If interventions do not meet these criteria, the effectiveness of the approach will be diminished by the interaction of the characteristics of attention disorders and the characteristics of the situation or the academic task. The following strategies (Rooney, 1990) support attention, guide information processing, and facilitate memory storage/retrieval. They were designed to accommodate the cognitive and behavioral characteristics associated with attention deficit disorders.

Content Reading

For students with ADD, certain concerns related to content reading have to be addressed. These students have difficulty with the accuracy of prior knowledge and compilation of the critical detail that successful students attend to automatically. To do this, strategies that guide the selection of the appropriate detail must be taught, as opposed to approaches that define the process after selection of the important detail has taken place. To accomplish this, the student:

1. Reads the subtitle and the section under the subtitle. As the student is reading, he or she writes the *names* of people and places, and important *numbers* and *terms* on separate index cards. Only the word or number by itself should be on a card. For example, if the words *Ireland, 2500 B.C.,* and *Urquhart Castle* were in a passage, each would appear on a separate card.
2. Returns to the subtitle and turns it into the best test question possible. The words of the subtitle must be in the question. He or she writes the question on one side of an index card and answers the question on the back of the same card.
3. Repeats steps 1 and 2 on all the sections to be covered, producing two types of cards, one with *main idea questions* and *answers* and the other with *specific details*.

4. Studies the cards by looking at them one by one. For the detail cards the student asks the question, "How is this related to the material?" or "What does this have to do with the material?" For the main idea cards the student tries to answer the question from memory.

If the student is not sure of an answer for any of the cards, the card is placed in one pile. If the student is sure of the answer, the card is placed in a second pile. The cards will be sorted into two piles, one called "not sure" and the other called "sure." The student sets the "sure" pile aside and continues working with the pile called "not sure." For the unknown detail cards, he or she goes back into the material or asks someone for the answer and writes the answer on the back of the card. The student reviews the detail cards as well as the main idea cards (which already have the answer on the back) until all cards are in the "sure" pile.

For a comprehensive review for semester examinations, all the cards are reviewed, as the system automatically has accumulated all the details and main ideas presented during the semester. The cumulative nature and the card-sort as a manipulative process support review and study, which is even more problematic for students with ADD if a long delay occurs between the instruction and the evaluation. A sample from a ninth-grade handout is presented in the accompanying box. A student's cards for that sample are shown in Figure 5.6.

THE LOCH NESS MONSTER

Over the years, people in all countries have been fascinated by reportings of monsters that seem to date from prehistoric times or the age of the dinosaurs. Sightings of the Abominable Snowman, Big Foot, and the Loch Ness Monster have intrigued journalists, explorers, and scientists for many years. Recently, new scientific equipment has focused renewed interest in the legend of the Loch Ness Monster.

A Description of Loch Ness

In Scotland lies a very famous lake called Loch Ness. The lake is about 24 miles long, about a mile wide, and approximately 650 feet deep. Overlooking the lake are several local castles such as the famous Urquhart Castle and the Aldourie Castle. The presence of the castles adds a mystique to the area, which increases interest in the area. The main attraction of Loch Ness, however, is the reported presence of a huge, serpent-like monster named "Nessie."

Nessie

The Loch Ness Monster may be the most famous sea serpent in the world. It is described as being 40 to 60 feet long with a head about the size of a horse's head. Its thin neck is about six feet long and is attached to a fat body with an eight-foot-long tail. The description is similar to a dinosaur known as the plesiosaurus. Scientists think that Nessie is a plesiosaurus that has survived since prehistoric times.

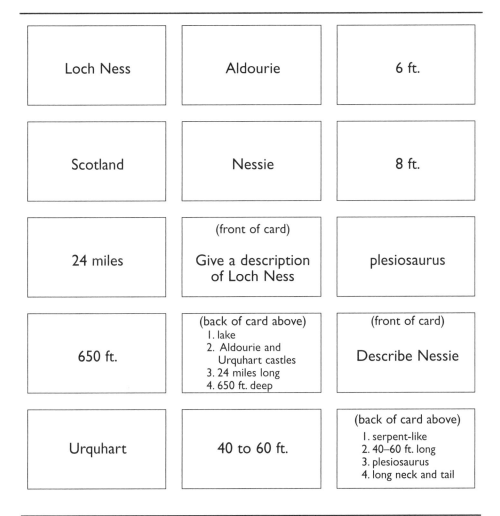

Loch Ness	Aldourie	6 ft.
Scotland	Nessie	8 ft.
24 miles	(front of card) Give a description of Loch Ness	plesiosaurus
650 ft.	(back of card above) 1. lake 2. Aldourie and Urquhart castles 3. 24 miles long 4. 650 ft. deep	(front of card) Describe Nessie
Urquhart	40 to 60 ft.	(back of card above) 1. serpent-like 2. 40–60 ft. long 3. plesiosaurus 4. long neck and tail

Figure 5.6 *Reading Cards for Loch Ness Monster Example*

Visual Organizers for Reading

In order to minimize the organizational demands of techniques described as mapping, mindmapping, or "spidering," a strategy called "Wheels for Reading" was developed. The strategy uses the wheel, which is simply an oval, as the basis of organization for tracking main ideas and details in a visual format. The approach is simple. While reading the material, the student puts the main ideas in the wheel and attaches the details spoke-like around the wheel. The details that have to be attached are names of people and places, important numbers and terms. Any other important material can be attached as well. The wheels always are placed one under the other, producing a linear pattern so no organizational decisions are required.

The wheels are developed as the student reads, producing a visual organizer for efficient review as soon as the reading is completed. If students have good visualization skills, the visual format of the wheel and spokes makes recalling the information from memory easier. An example, for the Loch Ness reading passage, is given in Figure 5.7.

Wheels for Literature

The wheel (oval) organizer for general reading can provide a concise summary of the details and main ideas if the student knows in advance the type of information to track during the story. The wheel set-up depends on the type of literature being read.

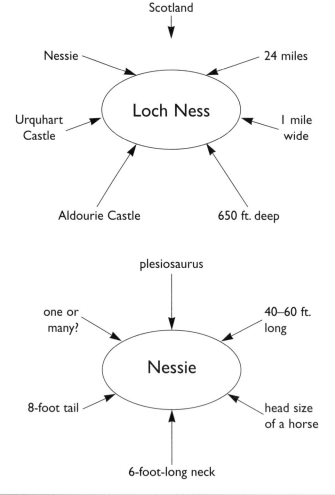

Figure 5.7 *Reading Wheels for Loch Ness Monster Example*

The basic organization of the literature provides the format for the wheels and wheels can be added according to specific class assignments. For example, a poem may have four wheels representing stanza 1, stanza 2, stanza 3, and theme. A short story may use three wheels to track characters, setting, and plot. Novels may use a wheel for each chapter. Details and main ideas are attached to the wheel so the result is a short, visual summary of the important information.

Advance visual organizers for literature may be as simple as putting the assigned topic/question that must be tracked (such as examples of good versus evil) in a wheel and, while reading the literature, attaching ideas, details, or page numbers that relate to the question. When the reading is done, all the information related to the assigned topic is readily available for use in discussion or essay answers. An example for a short story is given in Figure 5.8.

Writing Strategy

Students with ADD find the writing process difficult because they have to attend to so many different components when writing (causing problems in divided attention, selective attention, sequential attention, attention to detail, and organization). Traditional outlining makes heavy demands on attentional processing and can be overwhelming for students with ADD. To facilitate the writing process and bypass excessive demands on memory and sequential processing, advance visual organizers can be used to break the writing process into manageable units.

Furthermore, many prewriting strategies deplete the student's energy during the prewriting stage. The process can be laborious and may not result in a better product but, instead, in the student's avoiding similar tasks. To rectify this, advance visual organizers can be used effectively to simplify the process. The basic strategy for a composition or a paper is presented below. The student is to:

1. Place the title at the top of a sheet of paper.
2. Draw five oval shapes (wheels) on the first sheet. Write *start* in the first oval and *end* or *therefore* in the last oval. Place a word, a phrase, or a sentence in the first wheel to identify the idea or ideas that will be used to start the paper (introduction). Write one main idea to be developed inside each of the three middle wheels. In the last wheel, mark *end* or *therefore,* write a word, a phrase, or a sentence to identify the conclusion.
3. Reproduce each oval on a separate sheet of paper. Around each oval attach all possible details, ideas, or thoughts related to the idea around the wheel in a spoke-like fashion.
4. When all the ideas are around the appropriate wheels, number the ideas in the order they will be written about in the paper.

The strategy results in a set of six pages. The first page has the five-wheel overview, and each of the other pages has an individual wheel on it, as illustrated in Figure 5.9. The wheels can be used to develop an outline or to write a rough draft.

The wheels provide structure to brainstorm ideas in any order, organize information without excessive demands on memory, and sequence ideas as separate steps

Title:_____ Author:_____

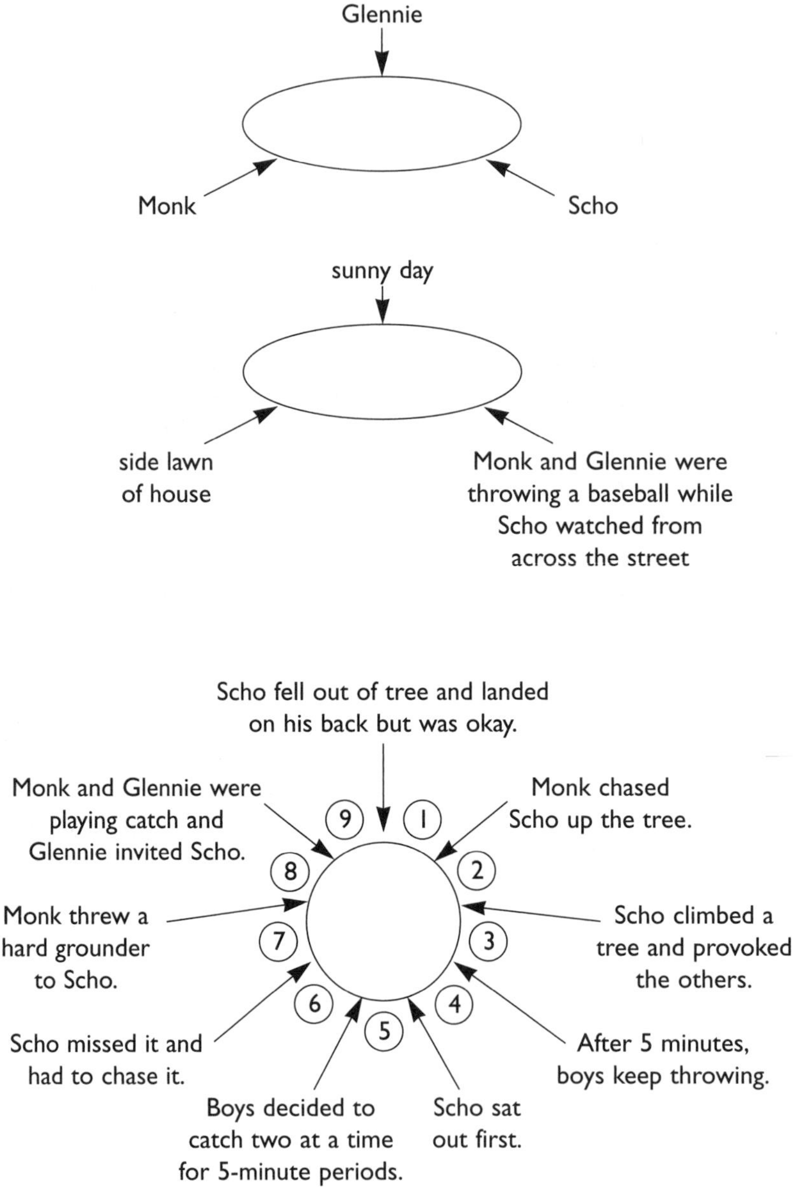

Glennie

Monk

Scho

sunny day

side lawn
of house

Monk and Glennie were
throwing a baseball while
Scho watched from
across the street

Scho fell out of tree and landed
on his back but was okay.

Monk and Glennie were
playing catch and
Glennie invited Scho.

9

1

Monk chased
Scho up the tree.

8

2

Monk threw a
hard grounder
to Scho.

7

3

Scho climbed a
tree and provoked
the others.

6

4

5

Scho missed it and
had to chase it.

After 5 minutes,
boys keep throwing.

Boys decided to
catch two at a time
for 5-minute periods.

Scho sat
out first.

Figure 5.8 *Sample Literature Wheels*

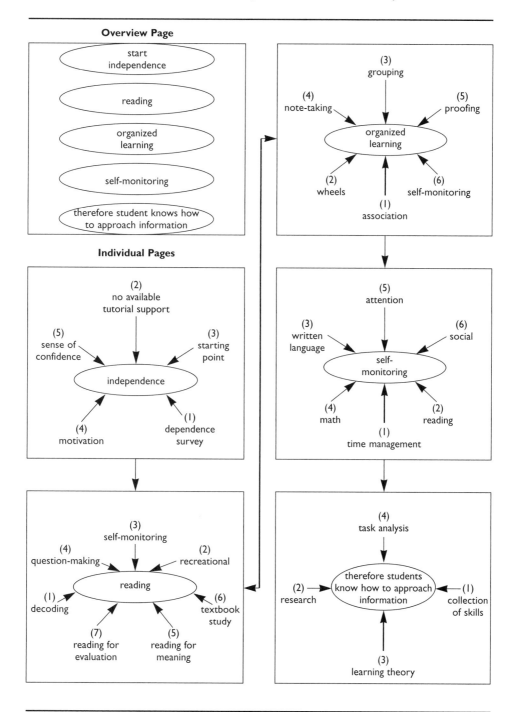

Figure 5.9 *Visual Depiction of Writing Strategy*

before the student actually produces the written language. The student can work on the material one wheel at a time without losing the organization. The number of wheels varies to meet the demands of the assignment:

Essay test	One wheel with the question in the center and ideas to be developed attached around the wheel.
Paragraph	Three wheels with the topic sentence in the first, the main idea in the second, and the clincher sentence in the third. The ideas are attached around the second wheel and numbered in sequential order.
Composition	Five wheels—for introduction, three main ideas, and conclusion.
Research Paper	Five basic wheels, but, for a long paper, additional sets of wheels in groups of three can be added.

Mathematics

Attentional deficits impact math performance in three basic ways:

1. Students have difficulty handling the sequential processing demands.
2. Students have trouble with specific application of the concept.
3. Students have a hard time attending to the details (such as sign of operation) involved.

To accommodate these weaknesses, application study cards made from the math textbook may help. The student uses the information at the beginning of the section or chapter to identify the concept being explained then writes the topic and page number in the book at the top of an index card. Then the student takes notes on the instructions in the book in his or her own words. The student makes up an original example and works out the example.

A teacher or tutor checks the student's example for accuracy. If the example has an error, the error is highlighted and corrected so the study cards draw the student's attention to "careless errors" that have a high possibility of recurrence in the future.

This procedure supports conceptual understanding, specific application, and attention to detail. The cards can be used for frequent repetition to review information prior to new learning, as well as to promote automaticity. An example of a math card is given in Figure 5.10.

Vocabulary

Vocabulary weaknesses often stem from a lack of conceptual understanding or from the absence of visual images behind the words. To provide a visual base for a verbal concept, students write the vocabulary word to be learned on one side of an index card. On the back of the card, they write the definition and immediately draw a simple picture of the first association they made after reading the word and its definition. Figure 5.11 uses the example of the word *belligerent*, meaning argumentative, and pulls up the image of two children fighting. The strategy produces a visual association that comes from the student's general knowledge base, so unknown information is linked to known information.

Front of Card	Back of Card
p. 52. First-degree equations having two variables A first-degree equation having two variables is one that can be written in this standard form. Ax + By = C ABC = constants x & y = variables	2x + 3y = 12

Figure 5.10 *Sample Math Card*

Spelling

The spelling strategy does not replace spelling instruction but does provide a structured way of processing words using a multisensory approach. The strategy should be used to learn spelling words, content area terms, or the spelling of vocabulary words. As with the vocabulary strategy, the spelling strategy uses index cards to maintain a cumulative review system. On the front of the card, the student:

1. Writes the correct spelling of the word.
2. Spells the word out loud.
3. Spells and writes the word in its parts.
4. Marks visual clues such as small words within the word.

Front of Card	Back of Card
belligerent	

Figure 5.11 *Sample Vocabulary Card*

Turns the card over and:

5. Writes the word from memory.
6. Marks the visual clues again.
7. Writes the word with eyes closed.

The strategy, illustrated in Figure 5.12, supports sequential processing as well as attention to detail, and it provides multisensory processing and utilizes global associative strengths. Words misspelled in writing should be emphasized over low-frequency words from the lists.

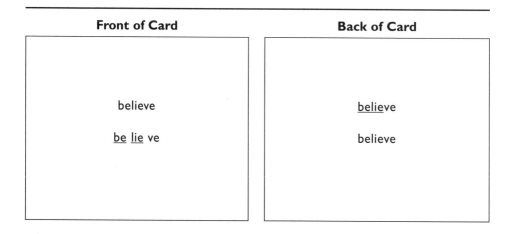

Figure 5.12 *Sample Vocabulary Card*

Conclusion

Working with students who have attention disorders can be challenging, but it also can be extremely rewarding when interventions enable students to improve their behavior and academic performance. To be successful, teachers need to examine the characteristics of the disorder present in the individual student and be knowledge-able about the impact of these characteristics on behavior, performance, and instruction.

Techniques for observation and behavioral analysis allow the teacher to gain the insight necessary to understand the student and the dynamics of the situation. The tools of behavior management and organizational training enable the teacher to design interventions to accommodate individual needs. Observation and behavioral analysis must clarify the issues that need to be addressed in the intervention planning, and behavior management programs and academic strategies must take the identified characteristics and dynamics into account. This approach should produce "goodness of fit," which results in greater success for students with attentional disorders.

References

Baddeley, A. D. (1986). *Working memory*. New York: Oxford Press.

Broadbent, D. E. (1971). *Decision and stress*. New York: Academic Press.

Goldstein, S., & Goldstein, M. (1990). *Managing attention disorders in children*. New York: John Wiley & Sons.

Hallahan, D. P., Kneedler, R. D., & Lloyd, J. W. (1982). Cognitive behavior modification techniques for learning disabled children: Self-instruction and self-monitoring. In J. D. McKinne, & L. Feagans, *Current topics in learning disabilities* (Vol. 1, pp. 207–244). New York: Ablex Publishing.

Hallahan, D. P., Lloyd, J. W., Kosiewicz, M. M., Kauffman, J. M., & Graves, A. W. (1979). Self-monitoring of attention as a treatment for a learning disabled boy's off-task behavior. *Learning Disability Quarterly, 2*, 24–32.

Hallahan, D. P., & Reeve, R. E. (1980). Selective attention and distractibility. In B. K Keogh (Ed.), *Advances in special education* (Vol. 1, pp. 141–181). Greenwich, CT: JAI Press.

Hallahan, D. P., Tarver, S. G., Kauffman, J. M., & Graybeal, N. L. (1978). Selective attention abilities of learning disabled children under reinforcement and response cost. *Journal of Learning Disabilities, 11*, 42–51.

Halperin, J. M., Newcorn, J. H., Sharma, V., Healey, J. M., Wolf, L. E., Pascualvaca, D. M., & Schwartz, S. (1990). Inattentive and noninattentive ADHD children: Do they constitute a unitary group? *Journal of Abnormal Child Psychology, 18*, 437–450.

Kahnehan, D. (1973). *Attention and effort*. Englewood Cliffs, NJ: Prentice Hall.

Kietzman, M. L., Spring, B., & Zubin, J. (1980). Perception, cognition and information processing. In H. I. Kaplan & B. J., Saddock (Eds.), *Comprehensive textbook of psychiatry, 4*, 157–178.

McIntyre, C. W., Murray, M. E., & Blackwell, S. L. (1981). Visual search in learning disabled and hyperactive boys. *Journal of Learning Disabilities, 14*(3), 156–158.

Pettijohn, T. F. (1987). *Psychology: A concise introduction*. Guilford, CT: Dushkin Publishing Group.

Posner, N. I., & Snyder, C. R. (1975). Attention and cognitive control In R. Solso (Ed.), *Information processing and cognition: The Loyola symposium*. Hillsdale, NJ: Earlbaum Press.

Postle, D. (1988). *The mid gymnasium*. London: Macmillan.

Richards, G. P., Samuels, S., Turnure, J. E., & Ysseldyke, J. E. (1990). Sustained and selective attention in children with learning disabilities. *Journal of Learning Disabilities, 23*(2), 129–135.

Rooney, K. J. (1990). *Independent strategies for efficient study*. Richmond, VA: Educational Enterprises.

Rooney, K. J., Hallahan, D. P., & Lloyd, J. W. (1984). Self-recording of attention by learning disabled students in the regular classroom. *Journal of Learning Disabilities, 17*, 360–364.

Rosenthal, R., & Allen, T. (1978). An examination of the attention arousal and learning dysfunctions of hyperactive children. *Psychological Bulletin, 85*, 689–716.

Swanson, J. M., Kitkin, R., Pfiffner, L., & McBurnett, K. (1992). School-based interventions for ADD students. *CHADDER, 6*(1), 8–9, 22.

Torgeson, J. K., Kistner, J. A., & Morgan, S. (1987). Component processes in working memory. In J. Borkowski & J. D. Day (Eds.), *Memory and cognition in special children: Perspectives on retardation, learning disabilities and giftedness*. Norwood, NJ: Ablex.

Zentall, S. S. (1983). Learning environments: A review of physical and temporal factors. *Exceptional Education Quarterly, 4*, 90–115.

6. Behavior Management in Inclusive Classrooms

STEPHANIE L. CARPENTER
AND ELIZABETH McKEE-HIGGINS

IS JOE IN A GENERAL OR A SPECIAL EDUCATION
instructional setting? Our Joe could be in either one. The situational
context has to be considered when managerial strategies are
developed, used, and evaluated. For this selection, assume that Joe
is in a general education classroom. Actually, that is what the law
(IDEA) requires unless a more restrictive placement can be
validated. The general education teacher can use the guidelines
presented here to develop prosocial behaviors of the group and
respond to Joe's many needs at the same time.

A primary measure of effectiveness for instructional programs is student academic achievement. However, teachers identify behavioral dimensions as a high priority for the success of students with disabilities and students at risk for school failure in general education classrooms—often as a higher priority than academic skills (Blanton, Blanton, & Cross, 1994; Ellett, 1993; Hanrahan, Goodman, & Rapagna, 1990; Mayer, Mitchell, Clementi, Clement-Robertson, Myatt, & Bullara, 1993). Indeed, students' behaviors during instruction may impact the classroom climate and the extent to which all students are actively engaged in instruction, an indicator of achievement outcomes (Christenson, Ysseldyke, & Thurlow, 1989). A classroom climate characterized by learning and cooperative interactions with groups of students who are motivated, responsive to traditional authority figures and systems (e.g., teachers and schools), and compliant with established rules and routines may be jeopardized by the presence of students who have not learned or adopted behaviors that are compatible with performing within a classroom community of learners. At times the misbehavior of one student or a small group of students seems to spread to other students even when classwide or schoolwide behavioral expectations are established and communicated to students (Smith & Rivera, 1995). When teachers take excessive time to respond to inappropriate student behaviors, valuable instructional momentum and time may be lost. As the diversity of students' characteristics within classrooms increases, the need increases for classroom behavior management systems that are responsive to group and individual student characteristics (Lewis, Chard, & Scott, 1994).

The purpose of this chapter is twofold. First, proactive behavior management programs are described as an effective means to respond to diverse behavioral characteristics among all students, both those with and without disabilities. Second, one teacher's experiences are described; she incorporated components of a proactive behavior management plan to address both her students' and her own behaviors in order to minimize the negative impact of students' misbehavior on instruction and achievement. An underlying premise is that it is by changing their own behaviors that teachers may have the greatest impact on their students' classroom behaviors.

Proactive Behavior Management Programs

Traditional approaches to managing problem behavior have not been responsive to the behavioral and learning characteristics of students with chronic behavior problems (Colvin, Kameenui, & Sugai, 1993). Despite evidence that effective discipline programs recognize and reward appropriate behavior to promote a positive school climate (Colvin et al., 1993; Mayer et al., 1993), many school or classroom management procedures are reactive, punitive, or control oriented (Colvin et al., 1993; Reitz, 1994). The assumption is that punishment will change behavior in desirable directions. Colvin et al. stated:

> To manage behavior school discipline plans typically rely on reprimands, penalties, loss of privileges, detention, suspension, corporal punishment, and expulsion. By experiencing these reactive consequences it is assumed that students will learn the "right way" of behaving and be motivated sufficiently to comply to the expectations of the school. (p. 364)

Conversely, *effective behavior management programs* that are responsive to individual and group behaviors for classroom or school interactions and participation are proactive in nature. Proactive behavior management programs

- Use instructional techniques to develop desired behaviors;
- Promote a positive climate to motivate students;
- Are dynamic and responsive to students' changing behavioral skills; and
- Use collegial interactions to support teachers' use of effective procedures.

Instructional Approach

In an instructional (Colvin et al., 1993) or educative (Reitz, 1994) approach to addressing behavior management, educators view students' participation and interaction behaviors in a way that is similar to their view of students' academic behaviors. The focus is on providing students with structured opportunities to learn and practice desirable behaviors rather than using negative consequences to eliminate undesirable behaviors. The main components of an instructional approach to behavior management include "teaching objectives, explanation of procedures, practice activities, prompts, reinforcement, feedback, and monitoring" (Colvin et al., 1993, p. 366). Colvin and his colleagues developed a model for addressing chronic behavior problems that parallels instruction to remediate chronic academic problems. In this model, teachers (a) identify the functional relationships between behavior and the environment, (b) identify expected or acceptable behaviors, (c) modify the environment so that students can practice expected behaviors in the absence of stimuli that are likely to elicit the inappropriate behavior, (d) reinforce correct responding by using differential reinforcement, and (e) move toward less restrictive or more naturally occurring programming to foster generalization and maintenance of acceptable behaviors.

By using an instructional approach to behavior management, teachers ensure that students understand not only what behaviors are desirable within a classroom learning environment but also how to perform the behaviors within the context of instructional activities and interactions within the classroom. An instructional approach provides the foundation for creating a positive learning climate that will motivate students to learn and perform.

Positive Climate

A positive learning climate is one in which the classroom environment is a desirable place to work and to interact with others. For some students, school is not a pleasant place to be because they engage in behaviors that are viewed as undesirable in the classroom environment. When these undesirable behavior patterns are coupled with academic difficulties, a cycle of school failure often emerges that leads many students to stay away from school or ultimately to drop out. Redesigning behavior management programs to create environments that are more desirable places in which to learn should promote greater student motivation to participate in school programs (Dunlap et al., 1993; Mayer et al., 1993). Teachers enhance the learning climate when they recognize the desirable aspects of students' behaviors and structure the classroom environment to facilitate productive work habits and positive interpersonal interactions.

Mayer et al. (1993) incorporated academic and behavioral techniques and consultant support to create a climate that was a pleasant and rewarding place for students. Academic components of the program included peer tutoring during the academic year, an intensive summer school program, and a career development program for students. Behavioral techniques targeted both teacher behaviors and student behaviors for intervention. "The emphasis was on recognizing, teaching, and following classroom rules" (p. 140). Students' on-task behaviors were targeted. Tangible reinforcers and verbal praise were given for "rule-following" behavior. Teachers sought to increase their approval responses to students' behaviors and decrease disapproval responses. Approval responses included verbal praise, approving gestures, physical contact, recognition of interaction initiated by a student, and delivery of tangible reinforcers to an individual, subgroup, or the entire class. Disapproval consisted of disapproving gestures or verbal statements (e.g., criticism, reproach, or request for behavior change) and punitive contingencies (e.g., time-out, response cost, or overcorrection procedures). Outcomes of the program included increased use of approval by teachers, increased amount of on-task behaviors for students, and a 35.5% decrease in student suspensions.

Reitz (1994) proposed a model for designing comprehensive classroom-based programs for students with emotional and behavioral problems that also included academic and behavioral techniques. Of 10 components presented as essential, five directly or indirectly addressed the creation of a positive class climate:

1. Consistent classroom schedule and structure in which rules, expectations, consequences, and routines are clearly communicated to students and consistently followed by the teacher. Students may be involved in developing classroom procedures. The teacher should maintain positive focus by emphasizing desired behaviors and their consequences.
2. High rates of student academic involvement and achievement in which the curriculum (content) and instructional delivery (teacher behavior) focus on high rates of student engagement during instruction and practice.
3. High rates of social reinforcement from teachers to promote the learning of new behaviors. Teachers' use of approval statements is an effective teaching tool.
4. System to ensure high rates of tangible reinforcement in which points or "tokens" are given immediately following the occurrence of a desired student behavior and exchanged later by the student to obtain predetermined privileges, activities, or items.
5. A repertoire of teacher responses to mild disruptive behavior that keeps minor problems from escalating into major ones. Combinations of praise for appropriate behavior and ignoring of inappropriate behavior (e.g., differential reinforcement) are effective in maintaining a focus on the positive.

Teachers promote a positive class climate by structuring the learning environment, emphasizing the desirable aspects of students' behaviors, and engaging in positive interpersonal interactions with all students. Both an instructional orientation and a positive classroom climate are necessary in order for behavioral interventions to be dynamic and responsive to students' changing behavioral skills.

Dynamic and Responsive Interventions

Effective behavior management programs are dynamic processes whereby teachers adjust interventions in response to students' changing behaviors. The premise is that behavior management systems, while maintaining a positive orientation, should impose only as much teacher or outside influence as is necessary to achieve desirable student behaviors and a positive learning climate. Knowing "how much is enough" is a function of experience and knowing students' behavioral characteristics. However, when teachers are faced with classrooms composed of diverse student populations, beginning with more structure paired with ample reinforcement and moving toward less permits teachers the opportunity to set the stage for desirable student behaviors early on.

Smith and Rivera (1995) have proposed that when problem behaviors persist despite preventive and proactive procedures for teaching appropriate behavior and maintaining a positive class climate, teachers should respond to misbehavior by using a continuum of behavior management techniques that corresponds to the severity (e.g., kind and degree) and importance (e.g., location and amount of disruption) of the problem. Less intrusive procedures, such as prevention, praise, and ignoring, are used for relatively mild behavior disturbances; more intrusive procedures, such as contingencies, parent action, and exclusion, are used for more problematic behaviors. Less intrusive techniques include consequences for behavior that are both naturally occurring within general education classrooms and positive in nature. As techniques become less positive and less available (in terms of access or immediacy) across a variety of general settings, they become more intrusive. The use of observation and measurement techniques concurrent with behavior management procedures is useful for evaluating the effectiveness of interventions and communicating results to others (Alberto & Troutman, 1990; Smith & Rivera, 1995). Procedures such as recording the occurrence of target behaviors and graphing the data assist teachers in making intervention adjustments that are responsive to students' current performance.

Viewing interventions along a continuum may be useful when a classwide plan is effective for most students but is not sensitive to an individual student's needs for structure and reinforcement (e.g., type and frequency). If less intrusive procedures prove ineffective for increasing specific desirable behaviors, then more intrusive procedures may be considered. When more intrusive behavior management procedures are deemed appropriate, teachers should have a plan for changing to less intrusive techniques once students have attained the desired performance levels. For instance, specific verbal praise may not be a powerful reinforcer for some students. A tangible reinforcer may be warranted until the expected behaviors become part of the students' repertoire of skills. Once performance levels are well established, students would be gradually "weaned" to less tangible rewards, such as verbal praise.

So far the discussion of behavior management programs has focused on the teacher's role in developing desirable or expected student behaviors. However, if the goal is for behavior management systems to be instructional, then it follows that procedures should foster students' behavioral skills that will enable them to function not only successfully but also independently in school and community settings. Students' self-management of their behaviors to correspond to expectations within particular settings is consistent with an instructional focus for behavior management techniques. Self-management—the application of behavior change processes to modify or maintain one's own behavior (Hughes, Korinek, & Gorman, 1991)—ultimately empowers students to be independent performers across settings and people. Within a self-management paradigm, teachers transfer ownership of behavior interventions to students (Cole & Bambara, 1992). Similar to teacher-directed behavior management techniques, procedures for implementing self-management systems may be viewed as instructional, proactive, or educative in nature (Clark & McKenzie, 1989; Kern, Dunlap, Childs, & Clarke, 1994; Prater, Hogan, & Miller, 1992).

Teachers' ability to plan and implement interventions that address students' changing behavioral skills is key to effective behavior management programs that focus on developing appropriate behaviors and maintaining a positive learning climate. For many educators, the opportunity to interact with their colleagues provides a resource that further enhances the effectiveness of behavior management programs for students with challenging behaviors.

Collegial Interactions

Collegial interactions serve two primary purposes during the development and implementation of proactive behavior management systems: (a) support for changes in teacher behaviors and (b) programming consistency. Strong collaborative relationships among school staff facilitates commitment to developing, implementing, and maintaining schoolwide plans for proactive behavior management programs (Colvin et al., 1993; Mayer et al., 1993; Reitz, 1994). Cheney and Harvey (1994) found that teachers desired consultations and feedback so that they could ensure that they were making correct decisions. Indeed, understanding behavioral interventions is a prerequisite for effective implementation (Reimers, Wacker, & Koeppl, 1987). Other teachers, administrators, support personnel, or university faculty may provide ongoing feedback, dialogue, and assistance for teachers as they attempt to adapt their behavior management practices (Dettmer, Thurston, & Dyck, 1993; Idol, Nevin, & Paolucci-Whitcomb, 1994). Reimers et al. reported that teachers who implement behavioral programs proficiently and experience benefits in terms of improved student behaviors rate behavioral interventions as more acceptable and are more likely to use them consistently. Taken together, the research suggests that collegial relationships can influence the success teachers experience with behavior management systems, the consistency of implementation, and ultimately the effectiveness of the program.

Collegial interactions and communication about behavior management also create consistency for students in terms of behavioral expectations and supports. When all staff commit to proactive and instructional behavior management approaches, a united front is presented to students that creates a consistent, predictable school environment (Colvin et al., 1993).

Classroom Behavior Management: A Ripple Effect

The behavior management challenges experienced by one first-grade teacher as she included students with disabilities and diverse learning needs are presented here. Her story is not unlike that of other teachers who find that chronic minor behavior problems somehow seem to gradually increase from minor to major proportions that threaten the positive atmosphere of the classroom as well as the effectiveness of instruction. In the present case, however, the application of proactive behavior management principles occurred in conjunction with an ongoing dialogue with an outside observer (i.e., university supervisor); this collaboration led to a classroom in which students and teacher were focused on instruction (both academic and behavioral).

Twenty-five students were in the class. Six students with disabilities, such as speech/language delays, learning disabilities, hearing impairment, and/or emotional impairments, were full-time members of the class. In the second semester, one student with severe emotional disturbance began as a part-time class member. All students were in the first grade. Support instruction included both plug-in and pull-out arrangements. For example, specialists such as the speech and language therapist came into the general education classroom to work with students within the academic and behavioral context of the first-grade curriculum (i.e., the plug-in approach). The speech and language therapist also worked one-on-one or in small groups with students in a separate classroom for some of their educational objectives (i.e., pull-out). A set of rules termed the "Magic Five" served as the basis for class behavior: feet flat, hands in lap, eyes on teacher, mouth closed, and ears listening. The teacher was also implementing several new teaching procedures to address diverse learner characteristics. A university supervisor visited the classroom periodically to consult or collaborate about teaching practices and their effects on student performance.

The Problem: On the Surface

At the beginning of the year several students displayed tendencies toward acting out, but with the help of the Magic Five and many students who were responsive to teacher directions, the classroom routine ran smoothly. Then, in October, Alex arrived. Alex wandered around the room during seatwork, squirmed on the carpet, touched other students, and blurted out comments and questions when others were speaking. He had a way of distracting his classmates and seemed to incite off-task behavior. To complicate matters, Alex's basic skills lagged behind expected levels. He seemed immature and unready for first grade.

By February, the behavior of students who had been only mildly disruptive earlier in the year seemed to escalate. By March, despite the teacher's encouraging students to use the Magic Five and directing students to stop disruptions or "get on-task," off-task behavior had spread to even more students. At any one time, seven or eight children seemed to be off-task. Inappropriate behaviors that had been evident primarily during "carpet-time" instruction were prevalent during cooperative groups and independent seatwork as well. Problem behaviors seemed to overshadow desirable behaviors and also to disrupt instruction.

Meanwhile, Alex was experiencing increasing academic and behavioral difficulties. He seemed to need a less demanding environment for part of the day. Afternoon activities in kindergarten were arranged while he continued mornings in the first grade. Alex seemed much happier. The rest of the class was still misbehaving. The teacher felt tired and discouraged.

The Problem: Looking Deeper

As the teacher and the university supervisor discussed the learning climate of the class, it was apparent that unacceptable student behaviors were undermining instructional efforts. Off-task behaviors seemed so pervasive that it was difficult to know where to begin. We used a four-step approach to gather information and narrow the scope of the problem:

1. Determine when behaviors seem to present the greatest barrier to instruction and learning.
2. Determine which behaviors are most problematic and identify alternative behaviors that are desired.
3. Identify teacher, classmate, or environmental variables that precede and/or follow the undesired and desired behaviors.
4. Collect data on student and teacher behaviors.

Synthesizing information about the problem proved helpful in identifying patterns associated with the inappropriate behaviors. Patterns of student behaviors and teacher responses emerged that were useful in designing a comprehensive intervention.

Off-task behaviors were most disruptive during large-group instruction (five times/day) when students were seated on the carpet in the front of the class. Off-task behaviors consisted of talking without permission, moving out of the assigned place, and touching other students. The entire class averaged over 200 off-task behaviors across these activities, and Alex contributed between 80 and 100 of these disruptions (see Figure 6.1) (McKee, 1994). Data were also collected for the types of verbal statements made by the teacher to students during large-group instruction. Comments that were negative or corrective in nature (disapproval statements) were far greater in number than were comments about students' appropriate behaviors (approval statements), averaging a 6:1 ratio of negative to positive comments.

Solving the Problem

A comprehensive behavior management plan was developed that targeted teacher and student behaviors. The aim was to design an intervention that was simple, that reinforced appropriate behaviors, that taught students to recognize their behavior, that involved them in setting goals for their behavior, and that was responsive to individuals' different performance levels for behavioral skills. The role of the teacher was to set up the management structure, maintain a positive instructional focus on student behaviors, provide rewards, and involve students. The role of the students was to self-evaluate their behavior and participate in goal setting for behavior parameters.

Teacher Behavior Change

The teacher targeted specific times during the day to teach, practice, and reinforce desirable student behaviors. Five activity times in which students were grouped on

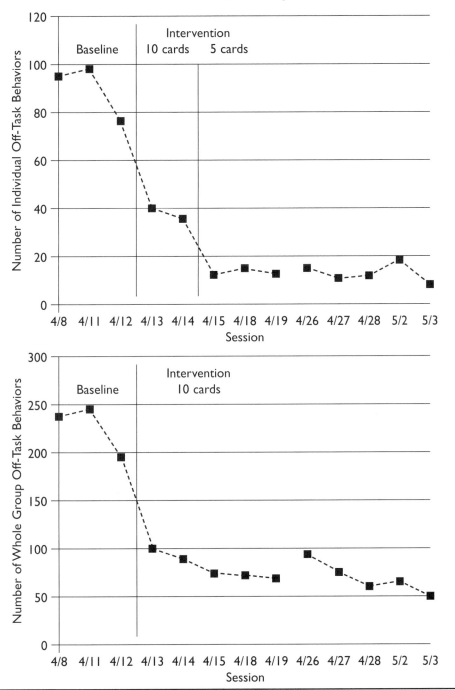

![Figure icon] **Figure 6.1** *First-Grade Students' Group and Individual Off-Task Behaviors During Five Daily Whole-Group Instruction Activities*

Note: The teacher was absent between sessions 4/19 and 4/26.

the carpet for instruction provided the backdrop for implementing the behavior management plan. The teacher sought to (a) increase her use of approval statements to respond to appropriate behavior and (b) ignore or redirect inappropriate behavior. A minimum ratio of three approval statements to one disapproval statement was desired. The teacher generated a list of possible responses to appropriate and inappropriate student behaviors so that she would be prepared with a variety of specific comments that were not only positive but also informational (see Table 6.1).

Table 6.1 *Positive Teacher Comments for Use in Response to Student Classroom Behaviors*

Student Behaviors		
Appropriate/ Desired	**Inappropriate/ Undesired**	**Teacher Responses**
Sitting with bottoms flat on carpet	Kneeling up	"I'm glad so many people remember how to sit in Magic Five."
Raising hand to speak	Calling out a response	"It really helps me know if you have something to say when you raise your hand."
Sitting inside the tape	Sitting outside the tape/ leaning on the wall	"It's important to sit inside the tape because it helps you remember what you're supposed to be looking at and thinking about."
Looking in the direction of whoever is speaking	Talking to another person or playing with something	"It's so polite to look at someone when it's their turn to speak."
Walking quickly and quietly to desk	Running to desk or stepping on and over a chair. Yelling to friends while going to desks.	"I like how _____ went to her desk so quickly and got started. _____ did a great job walking quietly to his desk."
Working on the right assignment	Drawing instead of working on assignment	"People are working so hard on this assignment."
Using quiet voices	Yelling or talking too loudly	"It's so important to use quiet voices at our desks so we don't disturb our friends who are working."
Finding something appropriate to do when work is done	Wandering around the room when work is done or drawing or playing an inappropriate game	"_____ is a great thing to do when all your work is done. Good idea."

Student Behavior Change

A three-part behavior management system was implemented in which group, individual, and special individual plans operated concurrently during the five carpet-time activities. Three activities occurred in the morning and two in the afternoon. The group contingency provided an opportunity for students to work together for a common goal and to support each other in using appropriate behaviors. Individual contingencies were used to give recognition to students who displayed desirable behaviors, to give specific individual feedback to all students, and to encourage students to self-evaluate.

Reinforcers were identified from a menu of reinforcers that were available for use in the classroom. Students participated in the choice of reinforcers that would be used for group and individual contingencies. An activity reinforcer in the form of class games played on the chalkboard was chosen for the group contingency. Advantages of the activity reinforcer were that it could be easily administered at two times during the day, the students enjoyed whole-class games, and playing games promoted group interaction behaviors that were related to the desired classroom participation behaviors. An edible reinforcer in the form of small pieces of candy was chosen for the individual contingencies. The primary advantage of the edible reinforcer was that because most students in the class considered candy to be a treat, it represented a reinforcer that might quickly result in a positive behavior change while giving the teacher an opportunity to use positive verbal statements to shape and maintain desired student behaviors. Thus, the edible reinforcer was chosen as a temporary measure with a plan for gradually decreasing and eventually eliminating its use once student behaviors began to improve.

Prior to each activity time, students were asked to determine an acceptable level of off-task behavior for the group. The goal and actual number of off-task behaviors were displayed on a chart (see Figure 6.2). Each time the group goal was met, a check was placed on the chart and a portion of a favorite cartoon character was uncovered. If the students in the group reached their goal for two out of three morning activities and/or both afternoon activities, then they played a game such as hangman or 7-Up before lunch and/or before afternoon dismissal. The teacher encouraged students to set goals that were reasonable in relation to previous levels of off-task behavior, gradually decreasing the number. At least some off-task behaviors were considered acceptable throughout.

At the conclusion of each activity, students placed a card in a name pocket displayed on the bulletin board if they thought they had used on-task behaviors during the activity. In the beginning, the teacher and students briefly discussed the on-task behaviors and reached consensus about the students' performance. When individual students had earned 10 cards, they were rewarded with a few pieces of candy. Alex and several other students were having difficulty earning 10 cards at the rate of other children, and although their behavior had improved, it was still at unacceptable levels. When this situation occurred, the teacher lowered the number of cards required to receive candy to 5 for these students, producing more acceptable results (see Figure 6.1).

How are we doing?

Today is <u>Tuesday</u>.

Activities	Goal		Clicks
1. <u>Opening</u>	<u>10</u>	✔	<u>6</u>
2. <u>Story</u>	<u>15</u>	✔	<u>10</u>
3. <u>Math</u>	<u>12</u>		<u>14</u>

Did we make it?   Yes or No

⟨ Lunch ⟩

4. <u>D.E.A.R.</u>   __   __

5. <u>Poem</u>   __   __

Did we make it?   Yes or No

⟨ Home ⟩

Figure 6.2 *Poster and Cartoon Figure Used to Record Students' Goals for Decreasing Off-Task Behavior During Whole-Group Instruction Activities*

Reflections: Then and Now

Student response to teacher approval and rewards for on-task behavior was almost immediate. Group off-task behaviors decreased to 10 to 15 occurrences per activity. This level was considered acceptable on the basis of the characteristics of young children, the goals set by the group, and the nature of the activities. Alex's off-task behaviors decreased to approximately 2 per activity, a significant decrease from the baseline levels of 15 to 20 per activity. As the teacher refocused her responses to emphasize approval statements, the classroom climate became more relaxed and pleasant. Eventually the daily use of the activity reward and candy was phased out. Goal setting for group behaviors and cards for individuals continued; the students seemed to feel rewarded by meeting their goals. Alex seemed motivated. The rest of the class seemed much happier. The teacher felt energized and effective.

Alex had another interesting response to the new behavior management system: He no longer wanted to go to kindergarten in the afternoon because he wanted to stay with his first-grade class all day. He began completing assignments, his reading and math skills improved, and he and his teacher developed a congenial relationship. When the school's placement team met at the end of the school year to make a decision about whether or not he should be retained, the decision was made based on results of the interventions described here: Alex was promoted to second grade because he had demonstrated academic and behavioral skills that were typical for other first graders who were proceeding to the second grade.

The following year the teacher continued a positive instructional focus that was responsive to individual student needs. Rules were written positively and posted in the classroom. In addition to the schoolwide Magic Five, rules included the following: (a) When you want to speak, raise your hand; (b) when someone else is speaking, look and listen; and (c) when someone does something you like, give them a compliment. During the first quarter of school, individual and group behaviors were recognized with cards and points exchanged for activities (edible rewards were not needed). Lastly, the teacher continued to self-monitor her use of approval statements.

At the beginning of the year I rewarded kids like crazy for good behaviors. Having a structured behavior management plan works like a charm. Every time I see a student who could be another Alex I look for what they're doing right. Telling kids what they're doing right instead of telling them what they're doing wrong really works well—for me and them.

—First-grade teacher

Conclusions

For many educators the prospect of educating children with disabilities (and possibly a greater variability of behavioral challenges) in general education classrooms is daunting when (a) the numbers of students in classes are increasing, (b) behavior management procedures are taxed by the range of unacceptable behaviors exhibited by students without disabilities, and (c) supports for using new teaching practices are minimal. From such a perspective, undesirable student behavior is viewed as the problem within classrooms and schools. An alternative perspective is to view student behavior as integrally related to the context of the classrooms and schools. In other words, a more fundamental consideration may be the way educators respond to students' behaviors, both desirable and undesirable. The "instructional" methods used, class climate created, individuality supported, and collegiality practiced by educators can significantly influence the behavioral and achievement outcomes for the individual child.

Several lessons emerged as young students with disabilities were included in a first-grade classroom. First, when behavior management procedures only marginally (and perhaps negatively) address the behaviors of students without disabilities, including students with disabilities may amplify existing problems. Proactive behavior management programs that are systematically and thoughtfully implemented provide structure and reinforcement that is beneficial for the class as well as the individual child. Second, even though educators may already know about behavior management methods that work, sometimes individual teachers are too close to challenging classroom situations to see clearly what is happening. The collaboration and encouragement of a trusted colleague, or just seeing things through a different lens, can lead to improved outcomes for students and teachers. A final related issue may be the importance of intensive and appropriate intervention at a young age for students, with and without disabilities, who may be at the beginning of a cycle of school failure. Traditionally, the response has been to place such students in separate classes or programs without consideration for how the current environment might be modified and whether modifications are implemented effectively. However, as teachers are encouraged and supported to use known, effective practices in order to be more responsive to all students' learning characteristics, the focus for managing students' behaviors may shift (a) from where interventions occur to what interventions are effective and (b) from viewing students as the problem to viewing educators as the solution.

References

Alberto, P. A., & Troutman, A. C. (1990). *Applied behavior analysis for teachers* (3rd ed.). Columbus, OH: Merrill.

Blanton, L. P., Blanton, W. E., & Cross, L. E. (1994). An exploratory study of how general and special education teachers think and make instructional decisions about students with special needs. *Teacher Education and Special Education, 17*, 62–74.

Cheney, D., & Harvey, V. S. (1994). From segregation to inclusion: One district's program changes for students with emotional/behavioral disorders. *Education and Treatment of Children, 17*, 332–346.

Christenson, S. L., Ysseldyke, J. E., & Thurlow, M. L. (1989). Critical instructional factors for students with mild handicaps: An integrative review. *Remedial and Special Education, 10*(5), 21–31.

Clark, L. A., & McKenzie, H. S. (1989). Effects of self-evaluation training of seriously emotionally disturbed children on the generalization of their rule following and work behaviors across settings and teachers. *Behavioral Disorders, 14*, 89–98.

Cole, C. L., & Bambara, L. M. (1992). Issues surrounding the use of self-management interventions in the schools. *School Psychology Review, 21*, 193–201.

Colvin, G., Kameenui, E. J., & Sugai, G. (1993). Reconceptualizing behavior management and school-wide discipline in general education. *Education and Treatment of Children, 16*, 361–381.

Dettmer, P., Thurston, L. P., & Dyck, N. (1993). *Consultation, collaboration, and teamwork for students with special needs*. Boston: Allyn & Bacon.

Dunlap, G., Kern, L., dePerczel, M., Clarke, S., Wilson, D., Childs, K. E., White, R., & Falk, G. D. (1993). Functional analysis of classroom variables for students with emotional and behavioral disorders. *Behavioral Disorders, 18*, 275–291.

Ellett, L. (1993). Instructional practices in mainstreamed secondary classrooms. *Journal of Learning Disabilities, 26*, 57–64.

Hanrahan, J., Goodman, W., & Rapagna, S. (1990). Preparing mentally retarded students for mainstreaming: Priorities of regular class and special school teachers. *American Journal on Mental Retardation, 94*, 470–474.

Hughes, C. A., Korinek, L., & Gorman, J. (1991). Self-management for students with mental retardation in public school settings: A research review. *Education and Training in Mental Retardation, 26*, 271–291.

Idol, L., Nevin, A., & Paolucci-Whitcomb, P. (1994). *Collaborative consultation* (2nd ed.). Austin, TX: Pro-Ed.

Kern, L., Dunlap, G., Childs, K. E., & Clarke, S. (1994). Use of a classwide self-management program to improve the behavior of students with emotional and behavioral disorders. *Education and Treatment of Children, 17*, 445–458.

Lewis, T. J., Chard, D., & Scott, T. M. (1994). Full inclusion and the education of children and youth with emotional and behavioral disorders. *Behavioral Disorders, 19*, 277–293.

Mayer, G. R., Mitchell, L. K., Clementi, T., Clement-Robertson, E., Myatt, R., & Bullara, D. T. (1993). A dropout prevention program for at-risk high school students: Emphasizing consulting to promote positive classroom climates. *Education and Treatment of Children, 16*, 135–146.

McKee, E. E. (1994). *Using edible reinforcement to decrease the number of inappropriate verbalizations of a first grade student.* Unpublished manuscript, Johns Hopkins University, Rockville, MD.

Prater, M. A., Hogan, S., & Miller, S. R. (1992). Using self-monitoring to improve on-task behavior and academic skills of an adolescent with mild handicaps across special and regular education settings. *Education and Treatment of Children, 15*, 43–55.

Reimers, T. M., Wacker, D. P., & Koeppl, G. (1987). Acceptability of behavioral interventions: A review of the literature. *School Psychology Review, 16*, 212–227.

Reitz, A. L. (1994). Implementing comprehensive classroom-based programs for students with emotional and behavioral problems. *Education and Treatment of Children, 17*, 312–331.

Smith, D. D., & Rivera, D. P. (1995). Discipline in special education and general education settings. *Focus on Exceptional Children, 27*(5), 1–14.

Part Two — *Curriculum Strategies Introduction*

EDWARD L. MEYEN
UNIVERSITY OF KANSAS

Educational Concerns

As teachers, teacher educators, administrators, parents, or citizens we find our-selves increasingly in situations that cause us to be concerned about what is occurring in the public schools. Often the issues that catch our attention—whether through the media or less formal venues—are problems that require solutions. Examples range from concerns about students being assigned to read books that parents or others don't accept for one reason or another, international comparisons of how American students perform in selected academic fields, the need for a better balance of diversity in the classroom, and students graduating from school unprepared for the world of work, to increases in teen drug use and school violence. In addition, those of us who are concerned with the education of children and youth with disabilities have more specific concerns. This does not mean we are less sensitive to the issues facing education in a global context. Rather, we are focused on ensuring that the curriculum being taught to children with disabilities and the techniques applied in the classroom are appropriate to their needs and effective in enhancing their performance.

To some extent, special educators have become indistinguishable from the general public in terms of the way in which their concerns have evolved. From being concerned initially with equity and instructional practices, both substantive and pedagogical, we now hear concerns that challenge the value of special education, question past practices, and argue that the primary factor in educating students with disabilities is the setting in which they are educated.

Real as these concerns are, they are somewhat minor. Those in the public who have called into question the quality of public education often focus on the principles upon which public education was founded, expressing, at best, modest confidence in the nation's ability to prepare teachers effectively for the classroom. If allowed to persist, this line of thinking can shift the attention of the public and professional educators alike away from the concerns that are truly central to what and how children are taught.

Each problem, whether addressing education as an enterprise or the education of children and youth with disabilities, is serious and warrants attention. The challenge is not to reach consensus on identifying legitimate concerns. Rather, the challenge is to energize the appropriate groups—stakeholders, policymakers, individual professionals, and researchers—to respond to the problems. As always, the problem is easy to identify, but not the solution.

In special education we long have espoused the need for researched-based interventions designed to assist teachers and teacher educators in teaching students with disabilities. Yet, when interventions become available, they often do not find their way into the classroom. This realization raises the question of what kind of problems we really are facing. In an age of information science, once the target audience is identified, dissemination should be fairly simple and straightforward. Further, the problem is particularly perplexing because dissemination of interventions can take place either through the professional preparation of teachers or the curricula they implement in the classroom. Neither strategy seems to have worked or been employed effectively, through. The reason for this discrepancy may be that insufficient attention has been given to translating the results of research into instructional material in a manner that is meaningful and easily accessible by teachers.

The nature of the problem dictates the solution. The expertise to address the problem may rest with individuals or groups who possess certain knowledge and experience. The latter may consist of individuals whose roles are related to improving education but who are remote from the classroom. Although ownership of educational problems is not a high priority for most people or groups, educational problems are elusive to educators until these problems are owned or assigned.

The tendency is to label most educational concerns as curriculum problems or issues—both on the part of the general public and, to some extent, individuals familiar with the challenges of education. This attitude promotes the view that responsibility for finding solutions rests with those who design or acquire curricula. But the problem may not be the curriculum. And the required solution may not even relate to curriculum! Instead, it may be more instructional or resource-based. In special education, the focus historically has been on curriculum—ensuring that students receive an appropriate education. But simply because there is a tendency to judge them to be so does not mean that all problems associated with teaching children with disabilities are curricular in nature.

With the movement toward inclusive instructional environments, the challenges all teachers face are changing. Certainly, teacher always have had to attend to the diverse needs of students. Today, however, with students with disabilities in general education classrooms, the extremes of diversity have increased as these children bring instructional needs to the classroom that extend the array of strategies teachers need to be responsive. As teachers respond to this expanded instructional diversity, the attributes of students, which previously presented modest instructional challenges, now take on a different meaning. The context of the classroom has changed, and the attributes of each student are adding to the teacher's challenges.

Faced with these challenges, many teachers assign responsibility for solutions to someone else. This occurs mainly because most people have not thought through what curriculum means and have only a general view of what the curriculum covers. The public and the profession are quick to assign responsibility to the classroom teacher when, in reality, this responsibility should be shared by teachers, curriculum developers, researchers, and even those who make decisions on the availability of fiscal resources.

In analyzing who is responsible for providing the curriculum solutions teachers need as they encounter the increasingly diverse attributes of students in their classrooms, it becomes clear that this responsibility also is shared but the partnerships are loosely formed. Obviously, the teacher must have the knowledge and skill to make curriculum decisions, adapt materials, and match instructional resources and approaches to the needs of individual students. The teacher's responsibilities for curriculum/instructional solutions, however, pale when compared to the responsibilities of those who design curriculum, produce instructional resources, market instructional materials, and conduct research on instruction for students with disabilities. The latter group disseminates its work, which then becomes part of the knowledge base teachers select from when they build a repertoire of strategies for coping with the instructional challenges they face in the classroom. Contributing to this knowledge base is a significant responsibility and should not be taken lightly. Translating that knowledge base into validated interventions is an even greater responsibility.

The selections in this section represent an effort by several authors to present research on curriculum in a manner that is meaningful to teachers who are faced daily with a need for curriculum strategies in their classrooms. The selections are representative of a wide range of research-based interventions in the special education literature.

Curriculum Solutions

Preferably, the curricula implemented in classrooms where children with disabilities are placed incorporate the results of research such as the findings reported in this section. Although that typically is the goal of curriculum developers, much of the research escapes those who develop curriculum. As a result, teachers are left to their own resourcefulness when having to identify and translate research to the classroom. When we talk about curriculum development, we need to talk about *all* students, but more important, we need to talk about the generic process of designing curriculum. One approach to resolving curriculum problems and stimulating the creation of more solutions is to ensure that curriculum development focuses on the full range of student attributes represented in the classroom.

Too often, discussions of curriculum center on the development of curriculum for specific student populations based on the presumption that how one goes about designing curriculum varies depending on the group for whom the curriculum is being designed. Certainly, the curriculum may have to vary to meet the needs of students with disabilities, but the *process* of curriculum development need not differ.

In special education, we historically have been guilty of this kind of parochial thinking. Instead, for the most part, the process of designing curriculum is generic. That does not mean everyone involved in developing curriculum must follow the same steps or use the same process. Even so, certain steps generalize across the process. This core is what we need to focus on as we advocate for better designed curriculum. Curriculum development is analogous to designing and drawing blueprints for a house. You want the house design to meet the needs of those who are going to live in it. Although the ultimate design may be unique, the process for designing most homes is largely the same.

In regard to students with disabilities, American schools traditionally have centered on differences. The assumption has been that differences observed in he performance of children with disabilities has exceeded in importance the attributes they share with all other learners. As a result, educators have approached curriculum for students with disabilities as a unique process, and, at the same time, those who design curriculum for general education often have overlooked opportunities to accommodate the needs of students with disabilities in the curricula they design.

It is important to think of the students who historically have been served through special education as contributors to diversity in the classroom and not as a group of students who are separate and require a different approach to curriculum development. Students with disabilities must be viewed as one of several groups who contribute to diversity in the classroom, and curricula must be designed to accommodate the broadest range of diversity in instructional settings.

Contributors to Curricular/Instructional Diversity

As part of the education bureaucracy, special education represents one of the earliest attempts to accommodate diversity in the classroom. When special education was first implemented, the focus was on students who were outside the norm—students whose presence in the classroom presented instructional problems beyond those that most teachers considered to be part of their responsibility.

What is different today in most schools is that, with the growth in minority populations, we have many more groups of children bringing to the classroom backgrounds, personal cultures, and language differences, which have added significantly to the diversity in schools. The major contributors to the extreme range of instructional diversity, however, remain students with disabilities.

This is not to suggest that ethnic or cultural differences are not significant but, rather, that students with disabilities add a new dimension to diversity. In the context of learning and teaching, meeting the demands presented by this added dimension of diversity is not longer a philosophical issue. It represents an unparalleled challenge in American education as was true in the traditional delivery systems of special education.

A Perspective

Much of what has been written and has occupied the attention of educators and policymakers has emphasized social issues in the guise of seeking better education for students with disabilities. Historically, an element of faith has undergirded special education. That same optimism must characterize our commitment to educating *all* children—the optimistic belief that all students can learn to their potential. If we begin from the belief that our responsibility is to ensure that all children achieve their potential, we have a better chance of succeeding. That is different from saying that all students must achieve world-class standards. In addition, it created different conditions for curriculum developers.

An optimistic view holds that all students have the opportunity to achieve and that we should strive to create more powerful interventions to help them reach their full potential in all aspects of their development. Sometimes we become confused in planning instructional programs for students with disabilities because we tend to look at special education from an organizational perspective rather than an instructional perspective. Yet, the only reason special education has evolved over the years is that these students are difficult to teach and present unique instructional demands.

When we analyze the diversity that a child with a disability brings to the classroom, we have to start by raising questions: Do we need curricular or instructional solutions? What specifically are the needs of the students? Certainly, many students with disabilities primarily need curricular modifications. A larger group of students with disabilities need changes in methodologies that allow them to benefit from the general curriculum. Finally, some need a totally different curriculum. These students are small in number, but they represent the greatest challenge.

Summary

Traditionally, the goal of special education has been to match curriculum and instruction to student needs. For a host of reasons, however, we have moved away from the curricular and instructional concerns that guided the early years of special education. That shift is one of the reasons for this book. We need to pay more attention to providing teachers and teacher educators with resources on curriculum and instructional interventions that have been researched and found to be effective with special-needs students.

7 Preferred and Promising Practices for Social Skills Instruction

GEORGE SUGAI AND TIMOTHY J. LEWIS

SOCIAL SKILLS are an instructional concern for most teachers. Here is an overview of social skills assessments, also detailing a number of instructional strategies for teaching social skills. Particular attention is given to the needs of classroom teachers.

Teaching children and youth to be socially competent is a central theme within schools. As Odom, McConnell, and McEvoy (1992) stated, "Humans enter a social world at birth and make their way through the world by successfully negotiating decades of social exchange" (p. 7). An estimated 10% of school-age children, however, have social skill difficulties significant enough to lead to peer rejection (Asher, 1990). For children with disabilities, the problem is even worse. Early education teachers have indicated that up to 75% of children with disabilities need remediation in social skills (Odom et al., 1992). Teaching social skills directly is one strategy to provide children with the social behaviors they need to successfully interact socially with peers with and without disabilities (Hops, Finch, & McConnell, 1985).

Most published social skills curricula fail to meet the specific needs of students with disabilities and lack information about assessment, teaching, and generalization strategies (Maag, 1989). The need for effective social skills curricula is highlighted by teacher surveys that overwhelmingly indicate that special and general educators alike believe social skills training should be an integral part of the curriculum (Bain & Farris, 1991; Fuller, Lewis, & Sugai, 1995; Meadows, Neel, Parker, & Timo, 1991).

The focus of this chapter is on the strategies and structures necessary for fostering social competence in all children, and, in particular, children who are at risk of academic or social failure. These include strategies for assessing and understanding social skills problems, strategies for teaching social skills, and preferred practices for achieving generalized responding. Guidelines for developing, examining, and selecting a social skills curriculum are provided.

Clarification of Terms

Social Competence

If a dozen individuals were asked how they would define social competence, 12 different definitions would likely emerge. The professional literature provides a variety of overlapping definitions (e.g., Elliott & Gresham, 1991; Gresham, 1986; Hollinger, 1987; Maag, 1989; Walker, McConnell, Holmes, et al., 1983). At one end of the continuum, definitions of social competence focus on large attributes (e.g., empathy, cooperativeness, sensitivity), which tend to be "owned" by or associated specifically with the child or youth. At the other end of the continuum are definitions that focus on specific, overt behaviors or actions (e.g., saying "thank you," walking away when angry, waiting one's turn, raising one's hand for help). In between are definitions integrating the two extremes (e.g., anger management, coping, life skills, problem solving, building friendships).

For the purposes of this chapter, we use Gresham's definition of social competence, as it contains representative elements from the range of definitions, operates efficiently within his definition of social skills, and highlights the importance of social validation.

> Social competence [is] an evaluative term based on judgments (given certain criteria) that a person has performed a task adequately. These judgments may be based on opinions of significant others (e.g., parents, teachers), comparisons to explicit criteria (e.g., number of social tasks correctly performed in relation to some criterion), or comparisons to some normative sample. (Gresham, 1986, p. 146)

Social Skills

Like the wide range of definitions for social competence, the range of definitions for social skills is broad. Some definitions focus on the expression of positive and negative feelings; other definitions focus on the discrete behaviors the person exhibits. For purposes of this chapter, social skills are "those behaviors which, within a given situation, predict important social outcomes" (Gresham, 1986, p. 5). This definition is appealing for a variety of reasons.

1. The definition emphasizes the actions or behaviors children display in their interactions with others. When focusing on behaviors, we gain greater precision in assessing and evaluating the presence or absence of a social skill and, therefore, social competence.
2. The definition includes an emphasis on the specific context or situation in which the social skill is required or used. Children and youth must become fluent at discerning the critical features of the context in which a specific social skill is required so they can discriminate what skill or skill variation is required for a successful social interaction or outcome.
3. The definition directs attention to the relationship between a given social skill and the social outcomes associated with using that social skill.

Two basic social outcomes must be considered: (a) positive peer relations/interactions, and (b) favorable adult judgments about the social skill (Gresham, 1986). The former outcome acknowledges the importance of the influence of the child's or youth's peer group in shaping and changing his or her social behavior and interactions. The latter recognizes that adults (e.g., teachers, parents, administrators, psychologists, other community people) are the ultimate judges of whether a child or youth is using appropriate social skills, especially with respect to educational decisions (e.g., instructional placements, behavior management).

Social Skills Instruction

Like definitions for social competence and social skills, definitions of social skills instruction are diverse and vary according to how the person conceptualizes social skills and social competence. Given that the main mission of the schools is seen as preparing students to become academically competent so they can become contributing members of our society, and that social skills instruction does have its conceptual variations, a more educational definition for social skills instruction is suggested. In this chapter, we use a definition for social skills instruction by Fuller, Lewis, and Sugai (1995): "Direct and planned instruction designed to teach specific social behavior that, when displayed by the student, results in positive judgments of social competence from peers and adults."

Social skills instruction should be "direct" in that students engage in overt behavior (e.g., verbalizations, behavioral rehearsal, written products) and teachers lead the student through the process in much the same way that academic facts, skills, and concepts are taught and acquired. Social skills instruction should be "planned" in that instructional sequences are prepared carefully to lead the student systematically and efficiently toward specific, planned instructional goals and objectives.

This definition aligns with the Gresham definition of social skills and considers how relevant individuals in the student's social environment judge the student's performance (Hollinger, 1987; Meadows et al., 1991). In addition, this definition assumes that social skills and social competence are acquired in ways similar to how academic skills, concepts, and competence are acquired.

Assumptions

Before discussing preferred assessment and instructional and generalization strategies, we discuss six assumptions and summary statements regarding social skills instruction (Sugai, 1990).

1. *Social skills are learned behaviors and can be taught.* Although some children are predisposed to learn some behaviors more readily than others because of living conditions, biophysical features, prior learning histories, and so forth, we suggest that social skills are learned responses acquired in the same manner as other skills (e.g., academic, vocational, daily living). In addition, regardless of whether social skills are considered a single response, a sequence of responses, or a collection of related responses, they are learned. Sometimes this learning is unplanned

(e.g., watching the actions of others, trial and error), and sometimes it is planned (e.g., taught directly and explicitly), but in all cases children and youth can be and have been taught.

2. *Behavior management problems are social skills problems.* When children or youth exhibit inappropriate social behavior and fail to display appropriate social skills, we are quick to label this as a behavior management problem and to prescribe consequence-based strategies designed to eliminate the problem behavior (e.g., isolation, reprimands, restrictions, privilege loss) (Colvin, Kameenui, & Sugai, 1993). This reactive approach fails to emphasize the importance of giving the student a suitable replacement or alternative response (i.e., social skill) that renders the inappropriate behavior less useful and effective in achieving the same outcome.

A more proactive approach focuses on strengthening or teaching an effective and efficient replacement response—that is, social skills instruction (Colvin, Sugai, & Patching, 1993; Sugai, 1992). From this perspective, behavior problems are conceptualized as learning errors, and social skills instruction is considered an essential feature of a behavior management or an intervention plan. In the case of students with disabilities who also have identified emotional and behavioral disabilities, goals and objectives for behavior should be included on individualized education plans (IEPs).

3. *Social skills are necessary prerequisites for academic skills.* Social competence and academic competence are closely related and dependent. Asking permission, raising one's hand before speaking, working with peers, waiting one's turn, and seeking assistance from others are just a few of the social skills children must display to be academically successful in school settings. Many students have the opportunity to observe, practice, and receive feedback on their displays of these behaviors; however, many other students are disadvantaged in their academic teaching/learning environment because they have not learned, are not supported for displays of, or are not fluent in these academically supporting skills. Students who have not learned the prerequisite skills necessary to benefit from teacher-directed instruction, independent study, or cooperative learning activities are likely to experience academic and social failure.

4. *The initial steps in setting up a social skills curriculum are time- and energy-consuming.* Most teachers receive four or more years of formal preservice training, and participate in many inservice training activities throughout their teaching career. Most of this training is based on content associated with academic instruction and curriculum. Some of this time is spent on standard classroom and behavior management techniques (e.g., enforcing rules, preventing and reducing interfering behaviors, maintaining classroom order) that usually emphasize consequences. The time given to teaching social skills often is limited to describing packaged social skills programs and involving non-classroom-based resources (e.g., counselors, school psychologists, social workers, nurses).

To become competent in teaching social skills, teachers must learn about assessing and teaching social skills, practice what they have learned, and receive regular feedback on their attempts. In the best of all worlds, this training would be at the preservice and inservice levels, similar to experiences teachers receive when they learn to teach reading, science, or any other academically related skill.

Learning to implement a social skills program requires more than just reading the teacher's manual and starting with Lesson One on Monday and progressing to Lesson Two on Tuesday. For social skills to be effective and efficient, substantial time must be spent assessing individuals or groups of children; designing or modifying published curricula; planning for the integration of the social skills curriculum into other content areas and activities; assessing student progress toward specific learner outcomes; and evaluating the effectiveness of one's instructional design, materials, and implementation. A social skills program will likely fail if consideration is not given to the skills, time, and energy required to learn and implement the program.

5. *The ideal curriculum does not exist.* Although many curricula are instructionally sound and reasonably complete, they cannot accommodate the full range of social skills problems and social skills settings that students and teachers are likely to experience. Teachers will be required to modify or expand most of the available published curricula to meet the situation-specific needs of their students. The time invested in adapting a curricula, however, will be well spent because students will be more likely to use personally meaningful social skills, teachers will be less likely to see problem behavior at school, and peers and adults will be more likely to have rewarding interactions with students. In addition, students with disabilities who display more adaptive social skills will be viewed more positively by their nondisabled peers than students who continue to display inappropriate social behaviors (Coie, Dodge, & Kupersmidt, 1990).

6. *The approach and components of social skills instruction are fundamentally the same as academic instruction.* As we have stressed, we believe that the basic instructional skills required to teach social skills are functionally the same as those used to teach academic skills. In general, when teaching academic and social skills, teachers must be efficient in how they (a) design their instruction (e.g., specify learner outcomes, assess student performance relative to expected outcomes, select and design effective instructional sequences and materials); (b) present their instruction (e.g., oral and written presentations, models, demonstrations); (c) arrange opportunities for students to practice (e.g., oral and written assignments, behavioral rehearsals); (d) assess and evaluate student learning/performance (e.g., outcome indicators, valid assessment protocols); and (e) provide informative feedback (e.g., positive reinforcement, proactive error corrections). Although the content of instruction varies, the instructional practices and techniques are the same.

Preferred Strategies for Assessing and Understanding Social Skill Problems

Successful social skills instruction is directly related to the extent to which we can conduct accurate and functional assessments (Carter & Sugai, 1989; Haring, 1992; Lewis, 1994; Lewis & Sugai, 1993, 1996a, 1996b; Sugai & Fuller, 1991). Accurate and functional assessments permit us to identify who requires social skills instruction, understand problem social behaviors, identify functional replacement social skills, plan useful social skills instructional plans, and monitor and evaluate the effectiveness of these plans. If social skill information is not collected and considered in the development and implementation of social skills instruction, learning outcomes are likely to be irrelevant, ineffective, and inefficient (Horner, O'Neill, & Flannery, 1993).

In this section we present a review of the purposes, types, and preferred methods of social skills assessment. Attention is directed to preferred, behaviorally oriented assessment practices that result in more effective and efficient instructional practices. Strategies that emphasize classification, diagnosis, and labeling outcomes are not included in this discussion.

Purpose

Social skills assessments are conducted for a number of important purposes:

1. *Social skills assessments are used to screen the general social competence of individual students or groups of students.* This information is used to determine generally where a social skills instructional program should begin. For example, a school has developed four rules or behavioral expectations that will be used to shape a positive schoolwide climate: (a) respect each other, (b) manage yourself, (c) work cooperatively, and (d) be safe. Each classroom teacher assesses the extent to which his or her students display behaviors that indicate they have mastered these skills. The teachers determine that most of their students have not learned the schoolwide rules and that a schoolwide social skills program should be implemented at the beginning of the school year for all students.

In a second example, a teacher screens her students to identify which students display significant social skill deficits and could benefit from an intensive social skills training program. Using criteria that identify students who display internalizing (e.g., withdrawn) and externalizing (e.g., acting out) problem behavior, the teacher selects about a fourth of the students as possible candidates for the social skills instruction.

2. *Assessment strategies are used to collect information about the nature of a student's social skill problem.* In general, we examine what seems to be maintaining the problem social behavior (e.g., peer/adult attention, activity escape), what kind of social skills problem the student displays (e.g., acquisition, fluency, maintenance, generalization), and what instructional strategies are likely to be most effective with a specific student or group of students. For example, a teacher learns that his student avoids social contact with peers because they tease her. When he evaluates his assessment information, he determines that the student has a limited number of appropriate social skills for responding to teasing. He develops a plan to teach the student a way to protest, a skill that results in the termination of peer teasing.

3. *Social skills assessments are conducted to assist in selecting and modifying curriculum and design and delivery of instruction.* Assessment information about

the social skills strengths and weaknesses of individual students or large groups of students is used to select the most compatible, effective, and efficient social skills program (published and teacher-made). A number of important decisions can be considered. For example, are the skills that have to be taught included in a curriculum? Are teaching examples and non-examples relevant to the age/grade level and settings of the target students? Are necessary teaching strategies included, supported, and described?

For instance, a teacher determines that four of her students do not have an acceptable strategy for managing their anger. She uses this assessment information to select a published social skills program with anger and conflict management strategies. She also uses assessment information to modify the examples and non-examples found in the curriculum and to make the lessons more relevant to the students' learning histories.

4. *Assessment information is used to monitor and evaluate the progress students make in their social skills instruction.* This information can be used to decide whether to continue, discontinue, or change a social skills intervention. In general, evaluation information should be based on actual behavior or performance changes (i.e., what the student does) or on judgments made by others (i.e., social validation). For example, based on 5 days of assessment information a teacher notices that a student's use of a certain social skill is inaccurate, inconsistent, and deteriorating steadily. As a result, he introduces a change in the social skills instructional program, and sees an improvement in the student's performance.

Assessment Methodologies

In this section we address the purpose, outcomes, and technical adequacy of each type of assessment, shown in Table 7.1, to illustrate the range of assessment types and their similarities and differences across the four purposes described in the previous section (screening, problem analysis, curriculum selection and instructional development, and progress monitoring). With respect to outcomes, two categories are differentiated. The first, behaviors and skills, refers to an emphasis on what the student does. The second category, nonbehaviors, refers to judgments, perceptions, and interpretations made by relevant others (e.g., educators, parents, peers, student). Finally we discuss broadly the technical adequacy (i.e., how much confidence we have in the assessment methods and outcomes) of each assessment type.

Teacher Rankings

One of the most common types of assessment for identifying students with social skills problems and for obtaining a general perception about how students generally relate to one another is through teacher rankings. With this sociometric strategy, teachers typically rank-order their students from most to least against a specified criterion. Information about the specific behavioral strengths and weaknesses (i.e., performances) of students is not obtained through teacher rankings. For example, to identify popular and unpopular students, a classroom teacher might list students from most liked to least liked by peers. This list would be used to determine whether

Table 7.1 *Overview of Social Skill Assessment Types*

SOCIAL SKILL ASSESSMENT TYPE	MEASURE OF BEHAVIOR	OUTCOMES[1]		TECHNICAL ADEQUACY[2]	PURPOSE[3]			Progress Monitoring	
		Behavior/ Skills	Nonbehaviors		Screening	Problem Analysis	Curriculum Selection and Instructional Development	Performance	Social
Teacher Rankings	Indirect	Low	High	Moderate	High	Low	Low	Low	High
Others' Ratings	Indirect	Moderate	Moderate	Moderate	High	Moderate	Moderate	Moderate	Moderate
Peer Nominations	Indirect	Low	High	Moderate	Moderate	Low	Low	Low	High
Self-Ratings	Indirect	Moderate	Moderate	Low	Low	Low	Low	Low	Moderate
Behavioral Interviews	Indirect	Moderate	Moderate	Moderate	Moderate	Low	Low	Low	Low
Behavioral Role Plays/Analogues	Indirect	Moderate	Low	Low	Moderate	Moderate	Moderate	Moderate	Moderate
Direct Observation									
Frequency/Tally	Direct	High	Low	High	Moderate	Moderate	Low	High	Low
Functional Assessment	Direct	High	Low	High	Low	High	High	High	Low

[1] High/moderate/low = extent to which behavioral and nonbehavioral outcomes are assessed

[2] High/moderate/low = extent to which technical adequacy is known about assessment type

[3] High/moderate/low = extent to which a specific assessment purpose is addressed

an all-class social skills program is needed, which smaller group of students might benefit from a social skills lesson that builds peer friendships, or to assess the effects of a social skills program.

Although easy to administer, outcome information is limited to general orderings or groupings of students and general interpretations of pre- and post-intervention effects. Gresham's (1992) review of the assessment literature indicates that "teacher rankings correspond fairly well to naturalistically observed behaviors" (p. 158), students with nonproblematic behavior often are overlooked, and evidence about the level of agreement between teachers and peers and parents is lacking.

Peer Nominations

Another sociometric method for assessing social competence involves having students nominate or rate their peers against selected criteria. These criteria tend to be nonbehavioral in form (e.g., best or worst friend, best or worst worker, least or most helpful) and focus on student's perceptions of peer acceptance/rejection or popularity/unpopularity. Like teacher rankings, peer nominations are most useful for screening and social validation (e.g., has the student become more/less popular? more/less rejected?).

Peer nomination procedures are easy to implement; however, their technical adequacies are unclear. Gresham (1992) indicates that weak correlational relationships seem to exist between positive and negative nominations and that it is unclear whether peer acceptance or peer popularity is being assessed.

Ratings by Others

Ratings by others are useful because more emphasis is placed on behavioral outcomes than broad perceptions of a child or youth's status. With this emphasis, ratings by parents, teachers, peers, and others result in information about target social behaviors, both problematic and appropriate, and social validations for nonbehavioral correlates (e.g., peer acceptance and popularity). Rating approaches usually consist of a list or collection of behavioral factors or descriptors (e.g., converses with others, makes positive self-statements, works independently, negotiates effectively with others, expresses anger appropriately) against which teachers, parents, peers, and others rate the extent to which a student displays or has those attributes (e.g., *The Walker-McConnell Scale of Social Competence and School Adjustment,* Walker & McConnell, 1988). Because ratings of behavioral correlates by peers and adults correlate with other nonbehavioral sociometric tools, Gresham (1992) suggests that the assessment of social acceptance and rejection is possible.

Self-Ratings

Self-rating methods involve asking students to rate their own status (nonbehavioral) among peers (e.g., popularity, rejection, acceptance) or competence (behavioral) on specific social skills. Although appealing from a social validation perspective (i.e., how students perceive their own social competence), little evidence supports its use. Gresham (1992) indicates that, "In short, children's self-report measures have not shown to be useful in predicting peer acceptance, peer popularity, teacher rations of social skills, role-play performance, or social behavior in naturalistic settings" (p. 163).

Behavioral Interviews

Behavioral interviews are verbal (written or oral) reconstructions of behavioral events developed by students or their peers, teachers, and parents. Because these accounts are separated in time and place from actual behavioral events, the resulting information is an indirect measure of the student's social competence. Behavioral interview data, which can be behavioral or nonbehavioral in nature, are useful to define social behaviors, identify the context in which appropriate and problem social behaviors are occurring, and develop more direct observation systems and social skills interventions. Gresham's (1992) review of the research reveals relatively strong support for the use of behavioral interviews, but their utility as a method of assessing children's social competence is relatively unknown, especially how interview findings correlate with measures from teacher and peer ratings and behavioral observations.

Behavioral Role Plays/Analogues

Behavioral role plays consist of having the student practice or perform the desired social skill in an analogue (test) context to determine what the student can and cannot do under controlled conditions. Behavioral role plays are a popular method when natural opportunities to observe the student's performance are difficult to access (time, personnel, place) and infrequent. Role play assessments, however, are extremely limited in that students may know the skill and demonstrate it appropriately but continue to demonstrate inappropriate behavior in the natural setting because of competing contingencies, leading the teacher to a false conclusion that the student does not require intervention on a specific skill or set of skills (Walker, Irvin, Noell, & Singer, 1992).

Direct Observation

Although more time and resources are required than with other assessment methods, one of the most useful means of assessing social competence is direct observation (Sugai, Maheady, & Skouge, 1989; Walker & Fabre, 1987). Direct observation consists of going to the "natural" setting (e.g., playground, hallway, cafeteria, bus) in which a social skills problem is occurring, noting the features of that setting, watching the student interact with others in the environment, and recording the events and the contexts in which they occur. Information might include with whom the student interacts, the nature of the interactions (e.g., socially appropriate versus inappropriate, cooperative versus antisocial), how long the interaction lasts, where the interaction occurs, what behaviors the student displays during the interaction, and so forth.

Traditional direct methods of assessment measure one or more dimension of the social skill or behavior problem of interest (i.e., frequency, duration, latency, locus, force, topography). In recent years, however, attention has centered on functional assessment procedures that examine setting, antecedent, and consequent factors that are associated predictably with specific behavioral events. These assessments target factors that trigger, predict, or maintain behavioral events. Functional assessment results are analyzed to produce hypotheses that describe possible relationships between environmental events and problem behavior and the likelihood that a behavior will occur. If these hypotheses describe the problem situation reliably, useful interventions (i.e., social skills programs) can be developed. Because of its practical utility and technical adequacy, the functional assessment technology has been identified as a preferred practice when assessing social behaviors.

Because most social skills programs are initiated in response to a pattern of inappropriate student behavior, functional assessment represents a useful method of assessing and understanding problem behavior (Lewis & Sugai, 1993, 1996a, 1996b). Functional assessments focus our attention on the settings in which inappropriate behavior is most likely to be displayed (e.g., playground, bus, hallway). In addition, they can identify skills each child will need to be successful in targeted problem settings (Hops et al., 1985). For example, if a child has a high rate of inappropriate peer interactions at recess (e.g., derogatory name calling, pushing children, interrupting games), assessments would focus on what the child has to do instead of the inappropriate behaviors (e.g., initiate appropriate peer interactions, comply with playground rules). Functional assessments produce an estimate of the frequency or duration of both appropriate and inappropriate behaviors. If information about comparable peer behaviors is collected, assessments can be made about the relative severity and intrusiveness of the behavioral events.

Finally, the results from functional assessments increase our understanding about what predictable outcomes (maintaining consequences) are associated with problem behaviors (e.g., escape, attention, avoidance) and what social skills (i.e., functional equivalents, fair-pair) we need to select to compete with contingencies that maintain the problem behavior.

Information from functional assessments is useful in determining the type of social problem or skill error (Lewis, Heflin, & DiGangi, 1991; Wolery, Bailey, & Sugai, 1988). Students who have not learned to produce or display socially correct responses (i.e., skill deficit) should be differentiated from students who have acquired appropriate social behaviors but do not display the behavior in the target setting (i.e., performance problem). This differentiation is important in determining the amount and type of instruction. A skill deficit requires direct instruction to focus on skill accuracy and fluency, whereas a performance problem requires increasing positive contingencies and practicing the skill in the target setting.

Functional assessment information also is useful in identifying teaching examples and in determining how socially competent children respond and interact under similar conditions. The examples selected should represent the range of settings and conditions under which the social skill is and is not required. These examples can assist students in determining when and where a specific social skill should be used. In addition, the examples can provide opportunities for students to learn when specific variations of a given social skill class (e.g., managing anger, initiating interactions) are and are not required for successful social interactions. Effective examples should sample and represent the full range of setting conditions, response variations, and actual versus contrived social situations. Systematically selecting and carefully sequencing effective examples combine to reduce the possibility of the student's acquiring misrules about when and under what conditions a given social skill should be used or displayed.

Preferred Methods of Social Competence Assessment

To summarize, social skills assessment information is critical for (a) a complete understanding of the nature of the social skill problem, (b) the selection of an appropriate social skill to be taught, (c) the design of an appropriate social skills lesson, (d) the selection or modification of a social skills curriculum, and (e) an adequate evaluation of the effectiveness of a social skills lesson. At a minimum, methods of social skills assessment should focus on observing the student's behaviors and his or her interactions with others. These observations should occur directly in the targeted settings and center on displays of appropriate and inappropriate social skills, the conditions under which the appropriate and inappropriate social skills are displayed, and the responses of socially competent students under similar social situations. To determine if the problem is a skill deficit or a performance problem, observations also should take place in settings where the student is not having social skills problems.

Because social competence is determined by relevant others in the social environment (i.e., peer acceptance and adult judgments), indirect assessment methods (e.g., interviews, rating scale) also should be used. Because the criterion for social competence varies by individual, over time, and across conditions, social perceptions from adults and peers should be collected by direct observation of actual social interactions in targeted settings. Although a student increases his or her use of conflict management skills in "nine out of 10 opportunities" (i.e., behavioral objective is achieved), success may not be realized if adults or peers identify one of 10 occurrences of the problem behavior as being unacceptable.

Preferred Instructional Strategies for Teaching Social Skills

After assessment information has been collected and a need for teaching social skills has been determined, social skills instruction can begin. Social skills instruction is defined as *direct and planned instruction designed to teach specific social behavior that, when displayed by the student, results in positive judgments of social competence from peers and adults.* Like instruction involving academic, vocational, community, life, or any other type of skill, social skills instruction has five basic phases:

1. Selecting the curriculum
2. Designing the instruction
3. Preparing for presentation of instruction

4. Presenting the instruction
5. Monitoring student performance, evaluating instructional effectiveness, and modifying instruction.

Each of these phases is described briefly, followed by recommendations for preferred practice. This discussion is based on the following assumptions:

1. Teaching social skills is fundamentally the same as teaching academic skills.
2. A set of effective teaching skills has been identified.
3. Social skills instruction has to be integrated into the overall school and classroom curriculum and cannot be taught in isolation.
4. Social skills instructors must have opportunities to practice teaching social skills.
5. Assessment information is necessary to develop effective instruction in social skills and to evaluate whether social competence has been achieved.

Selecting the Curriculum

When the need to teach social skills is indicated, most teachers initially look toward published social skills curricula. A variety of published social skills training programs are available to address different age groups, social skills, teaching approaches, and settings. Published programs provide teachers with a basic structure from which to assess and teach social skills. These can be useful when teaching large numbers of students relatively generic social skills such as greeting others and managing stress. This sort of program also can serve as a starting point upon which to build more intensive individualized social skills plans for small groups of students or individual students who have serious social skill deficits or competing behavior problems.

Given the variety and range of available programs, selecting an appropriate social skills program is a challenging endeavor. In general, four basic questions should be considered (Cohen, Alberto, & Troutman, 1979):

1. Who is the target population of students?
2. What is the purpose of the curriculum?
3. What are the structural and administrative features of the curriculum?
4. What methods are used to teach social skills?

Carter and Sugai (1988, 1989) extended these questions to include an examination of specific curricular elements:

1. What instructional components are included in the curriculum? (a) modeling, (b) strategic placement, (c) direct instruction, (d) correspondence training, (e) rehearsal/practice, (f) prompting/coaching, (g) positive reinforcement/shaping, or (h) positive practice?
2. Are the following programming considerations covered? (a) Are assessment procedures/instruments included? (b) Is the curriculum adaptable to indi-

vidual needs? (c) Can the curriculum be used with small groups? (d) Can personnel implement the curriculum without specialized training beyond that described in the curriculum? (e) Is the cost reasonable and manageable? (f) Are strategies included that will promote maintenance and generalization of skills? (1989, p. 38)

If a published curriculum is not selected and a teacher-made curriculum is considered, the same questions should be applied. Whatever the curriculum choice, teachers must adjust the curriculum to the student's learning needs determined previously through systematic assessment.

Designing the Instruction

As stressed throughout this chapter, instruction should be designed to meet the learning needs presented by the student within the context of a specifically delineated problem or target setting. In this section we present an overview of a basic approach—model-lead-test—to designing and teaching social skills and give a brief description of the key components of a complete social skills lesson.

Although variations are found across approaches to teaching social skills, instructional models of teaching and designing social skill lessons generally follow the basic model-lead-test format (Engelmann & Carnine, 1982; Lewis, Heflin, & DiGangi, 1991; Sugai, 1990). In general, students are presented with a demonstration of the skill to be learned (model). Next, opportunities are arranged for students to practice or rehearse the skill with assistance (e.g., verbal prompts) from the teacher (lead). Finally, students are checked to verify what they have learned and can do without assistance (test). This format of teaching social skills is generally the same as the format used to teach academic skills in a direct instruction approach.

Essential to designing social skills instruction effectively and applying the model-lead-test format is the selection and use of teaching examples. Students learn to use and not use a range of social behaviors that represent a social skill across settings from the teaching examples used during demonstration and practice activities (Engelmann & Carnine, 1982; Scott & Sugai, 1995). In general, the following rules (Engelmann & Carnine, 1982; Kameenui & Simmons, 1990) should be applied in selecting and using teaching examples to maximize opportunities for students to learn how to make discriminations in social skills:

1. Use both positive and negative examples of a social skill and the contexts in which the skill should or should not be applied.
2. Use a full range of positive and negative examples to represent social skill variations and the contexts in which the skill variations should and should not be used.
3. Sequence positive and negative examples that are minimally different to maximize discriminations about when and where a social skill should be used.

The model-lead-test format is applied within lessons that have eight major components. A brief example of a lesson designed to teach "greeting others" is illustrated in the following box, in which each of the eight major components is described briefly in relation to the example.

1. *Name of skill.* Each social skill should be given a clear name or label to assist in communication during and about instruction (e.g., anger management, greeting others, initiating a conversation, accepting criticism).

2. *Critical rule.* Students must be taught a rule that represents discrimination about when a social skill should be or not be used. This rule includes a description

---

Sample of a Model-Lead-Test Instructional Lesson for Teaching "Greeting Others"

1. *Name the skill:* How to greet other students.

2. *Define the skill (critical rule):* When you see a person you know for the first time that day, greet him (her).

   Ask each student to state the rules for greeting.

3. *Introduce the skill components:* The first thing we do when we want to greet someone is to look at the person. Second, we wait for the appropriate time to speak. Third, we state our greeting.

4. *Define the skill component for the day:* Today we're going to talk about the rule for greeting, "When you see a person you know for the first time that day, greet him (her)."

   Ask each student: "What is the rule?"

5. *Demonstrate the critical rule:* Set up role plays with the educational assistant in which someone wishes to greet someone.

   Prompt students to observe, and following the role play, ask the students if you demonstrated the skill appropriately.

   Give several appropriate and inappropriate examples.

   Be sure to include all students by assigning observation tasks.

6. *Practice/role play examples:*

   Be sure to include all students by assigning observation tasks.

7, *Test:* Set up new untrained role plays for each student. Ask students to state the critical rule: "What do you do when you see someone for the first time that day?" or "What is the rule about greeting people?"; "What's the first thing to do when you want to greet someone?"

8. *Assign a homework task:* Tonight I want you to greet someone. Tomorrow I will ask you whom you greeted and what you said.

of the set of conditions that occasion or signal a student to use or not use a specific social behavior. For example, the critical rule for managing anger might be "When angry, stop what you're doing and manage your anger." This rule is used to disengage the student from a problematic interaction and initiate a different response (e.g., take a deep breath, leave the situation, problem solve, manage conflict). A critical rule is used as a way for the student to learn (discriminate) when a social skill should and should not be used. The discrimination is acquired through a series of systematically sequenced positive and negative examples and the practice of a specific behavior that occasions the social skill. The acquisition and effective use of a critical rule is especially important for students who can demonstrate the social skill (e.g., four-step problem solving sequence, five-step conflict management process) in isolation but cannot or do not demonstrate the skill when it is required.

3. *Description of skill and skill components.* Every social skill lesson should include an operational (measurable, observable) description of the social skill. Depending on the student's learning history, more complex social skills may have to be broken down (task-analyzed) into smaller teaching units. For example, greeting a person might include the following steps: (a) look at the person, (b) wait for the appropriate time to speak, and (c) state your greeting. This sequence would be preceded by the critical rule for when to use the skill and would include a set of useful skill variations (Lewis, 1991b, 1992; Sugai, 1990). In our "greeting others" example, the critical rule for using the skill could be, "When you see a person for the first time that day, greet him (her)."

Skill variations are topographically different ways of engaging in the same social behavior or skill, but all serve the same function or have the same effect. For example, variations in how students greet peers and how they greet adults should be taught. Friends can be greeted with a "high-five," a friendly nickname, a facial expression, or hand gesture; whereas adults should be greeted more formally (e.g., "Good morning, Ms. Fernandez").

4. *Model/demonstration.* Social skill lessons should be designed to include a model/demonstration instructional activity. Modeling strategies are important but not sufficient instructional strategies for teaching social skills (Barton, 1986; Carter & Sugai, 1988, 1989; Kratochwill & French, 1984; Michelson & Mannarino, 1986). Models and demonstrations of the social skill are useful ways for students to see what the social skill and its variations look like and to learn about the conditions under which the social skill should and should not be used (i.e., critical rule). Using examples from the students' natural environment will ensure that they are culturally and age-appropriate demonstrations.

Demonstrations should be presented by individuals who are competent at the skill, are respected by the observing students, and are members of the students' normal social community (e.g., educational assistant, adult, or peer). With respect to time constraints, allow at least two examples and two non-examples of the skill or skill component to be presented. For example, during demonstrations, appropriate (e.g., "what's up?" "yo") and inappropriate (e.g., "hey jerk," "get lost") greetings that have been observed on the playground or other common school settings also should be collected and used.

To increase the salience of the relevant features of a demonstration, teachers should describe or point out the critical features of the demonstrations as they are being presented. Descriptions can be provided by the person doing the demonstration (e.g., "Now I'm looking at the person I'd like to talk to") or by an observer (e.g., "See how she's taking a deep breath as she notices her anger rising"). In addition, before the demonstration begins, observing students should be given specific tasks to do during and after the demonstration. For example, a student might be asked to identify the conditions under which the teacher was using the anger management social skill. These kinds of assignments highlight the critical features of the social skill and the conditions under which it is required; they keep students engaged; and they teach them to focus on the important aspects of the social demonstration.

5. *Role play/behavioral rehearsal.* Modeling procedures are enhanced when followed by role-play or behavioral rehearsal activities in which students have the opportunity to receive guided practice (lead). Guidelines for setup, development, and selection and use of examples are the same as those used for modeling and demonstration activities. The difference is that target students are given the opportunity to practice the social skill and to receive specific feedback (reinforcement and corrective feedback) about their use of the skill.

The goal of behavioral rehearsals is to arrange opportunities for students to demonstrate the social skill in the most errorless manner possible. Initial role play attempts should be monitored closely, and students should be given early and frequent feedback about their performance. To the greatest extent possible, role plays should be orchestrated so the target student engages in the social skill successfully. If mistakes or chronic errors are expected, precorrections or reminders are useful. A precorrection is a prompt provided before and early in a problem context to minimize the occurrence of an error (Colvin, Sugai, & Patching, 1993). For example, a student could be told to take a deep breath and to show the teacher what he or she will do just before the role play begins. Precorrections are designed to minimize having the student practice errors and to increase the probability of receiving positive reinforcement for appropriate display of the social skill. During role plays the target student should model or practice only positive examples of social skills. Students who have been identified as needing social skills training do not need to practice inappropriate or incorrect social behaviors; they already have demonstrated their mastery of the wrong skill!

As in modeling and demonstration activities, participants or observers can describe or point out what they are doing during the role play. Before the role play begins, nonparticipating students should be given specific tasks or activities that will engage them during the role play. For example, a nonparticipating student could be asked to prepare to report on what the target student did to greet others. Another nonparticipating student could be asked to describe the conditions under which the target student used the greeting response. Target students participating in role plays can be asked to verbalize their actions as they are practicing the social skill. The teacher can use this information to assess what is being learned and to what the student is attending.

Following the role play, teachers should focus their discussion directly on essential features of the social skill that were displayed and the conditions under which they should be displayed. To prevent students from learning misrules, irrelevant features of the role play should not be addressed. For example, after a cafeteria-greeting role play, discussions should target whether the student demonstrated the skill component of the day (e.g., "Look at the person"), not whether he or she carried a cafeteria tray or lined up appropriately. Students who display the social skill correctly during the role play and students who display approximations to the correct social skill should receive positive reinforcement. When social behavior errors are observed, proactive (informative) corrections should be provided. During discussions, common terms, phrases, and key words should be used (e.g., "That's right. Mary looked at the person when she said 'hello'").

6. *Review.* To prevent students from learning isolated social behaviors and to increase exposure to the social skill, social skill lessons should allow frequent opportunities to review what has been learned. These reviews should occur within lessons, especially after demonstration and role-play activities in which social behavior components of a larger social skill are being taught in isolation. For example, "checking to see if the other person is talking" is being taught in isolation of the larger social skill of "maintaining conversations." Previous lessons should be reviewed at the beginning of each new lesson to maintain continuity. Conducting review sessions outside the context of formal social skill lessons (e.g., at other times of the day, in other locations, during other activities) is useful to facilitate generalized responding (responding across settings, people, or times). Reviews should include opportunities for students to interact actively with the teacher by answering questions, demonstrating skills, or describing contexts in which a skill might be used or has been used.

7. *Test.* At the end of a social skill lesson, students should be asked to demonstrate what they have learned. This information is important for determining the extent to which a student has benefited from a lesson and the extent to which progress is being made toward mastery of the social skill (i.e., instructional objective). Tests (probes, quizzes) should consist of activities or items that have not been used in demonstrations and role-play activities. Although assessing a student's performance using test items that are identical to instructional conditions is useful for examining maintenance effects, a better indicator of generalized student responding outside the instructional context is information about the extent to which students can generalize or adapt their responses.

Depending upon the student's learning history, the complexity of the skill being taught, and the like, test items can involve oral questioning, role-play analogues, written responses, or other typical assessment strategies. Testing, however, should provide students with opportunities or simulations to engage in the actual behavior. This behavioral examination allows the teacher to see the accuracy and quality of what the student is likely to say or do. Tests should be given without precorrections or assistance because the aim of the tests is to examine the extent to which the student responds accurately and independently. After each response, corrective feedback should be given for errors. Positive reinforcement should be given for partially or totally correct responses. Testing also should occur randomly at other times of the day, in other locations, and under natural conditions to obtain a judgment of how the student might respond outside the instructional context.

8. *Homework assignment.* Achieving a high accuracy level in social skill performance during social skill lessons is desirable because it is an indicator of the extent to which the student is benefiting from instruction and the extent to which instruction is effective. Even so, display of the social behavior in other settings, with other people, and over time is more desirable. Assigning homework is one strategy for bridging the gap between the social skill lesson, which consists of many contrived examples and activities, and the real world, which is where these social skills must ultimately be displayed.

Similar to academic instruction, homework assignments should be designed so students can practice aspects of the social skill lesson independently, successfully, and outside of the formal instructional context of the social skill lesson. Homework activities should require the student to identify examples of situations in which a social skill might be used, identify the relevant features of those situations, look for correct and incorrect displays of the social skill, determine the consequences of appropriate and inappropriate use of a social skill, and practice the social skill in situations that are likely to be supportive and to provide positive reinforcement for attempts to use the social skill. Other strategies for facilitating generalized responding and response maintenance are covered next.

Preparing for the Presentation of Instruction

After social skills instruction has been designed, several logistical considerations should be considered before actually administering a social skills lesson:

1. Collect or prepare materials (e.g., curriculum, teacher-made materials, other school supplies).
2. Establish a schedule and location for teaching the social skills lesson (e.g., daily, weekly; morning, afternoon; within other lessons; duration).
3. Determine group membership (minimum of two, same age versus multi-age, with or without disabilities, socially competent and incompetent).
4. Determine adult participants (e.g., teaching assistants, administrators, teachers, parents).
5. Develop and teach rules for participating in the group (e.g., attendance, on time, asking questions or requesting for assistance, getting teacher attention, consequences for rule-following and violating).
6. Teach prerequisite skills for participating in a social skills lesson (e.g., participating and observing modeling or role play activities, turning in homework assignments).

Rules for participating in the group and prerequisite skills for participating in social skills activities should be taught at the beginning of a social skills sequence and should be reviewed and reinforced regularly. In general, the same routines, rules, and structures used during other regularly scheduled academic or school lessons or activities should be followed during social skills instruction.

Preparing for the presentation of instruction also involves specifying and reviewing the behavioral objectives established for individuals or the group as a whole. A means of assessing progress toward the mastery of objectives should be developed. Using actual student performance to evaluate the effectiveness and efficiency of a social skills instructional lesson is essential. As indicated previously, student performance should be assessed during social skill lessons to determine the extent to which students are benefiting from the instruction. More important, however, is a routine for assessing student performance in natural classroom or school contexts (e.g., playground, hallways, lunchrooms) to assess the extent to which students are applying what they have learned to real social problem contexts.

Presenting the Instruction

The actual presentation of a social skills lesson should be similar to the presentation of other classroom and school-related instruction. Consistent attention should be given to the rules, expectations, and routines identified and taught in the course of preparing the social skills lesson. Effective teaching strategies and practices should be implemented and monitored on an ongoing basis.

Monitoring Student Performance and Implementation of Social Skills Instruction and Modifying Instruction

Student performance should be monitored on an ongoing basis with regular cumulative review. Attention should be given to the student's actual social behavior, the effect of the student's behaviors on the environment and on the behavior of others in the environment, and the perceptions or judgments of relevant peers and adults. Because social skills are, by definition, social in nature and because social validation statements by relevant others often determine whether the student is considered socially competent, collecting information from individuals in the student's social community is important.

The most appropriate curriculum and the most perfectly designed instructional plan are only as good as the accuracy and quality of their implementation. Teachers should arrange regular opportunities to evaluate their social skills teaching practices, especially at the beginning of a social skills instructional program. A teaching colleague, supervisor, administrator, teaching assistant, parent, or other respected adult might observe the presentation of instruction and give the teacher feedback about instructional strengths and weaknesses. Alternatively, teachers can videotape themselves teaching and self-evaluate their performance later. Ultimately, one of the best indicators of the success of implementation is student performance. Students indicate their response to strong and weak assignments by the extent to which they remain actively on task, engage in disruptive or cooperative behavior, and progress toward learning and performance outcomes.

An analysis of the types of performance errors students make can indicate what adjustments have to be made in social skills instruction. In general, at least eight different instructional decisions can be made (Haring, Liberty, & White, 1980; White & Haring, 1980):

1. Make no change because adequate progress is indicated.
2. Change the date when instruction is expected to be completed because more or less time is needed.
3. Slice back to a previous skill in the task analysis that was not mastered.
4. Step back to teach a missing prerequisite skill.
5. Try a different instructional strategy because the current strategy is ineffective.
6. Adjust instruction to accommodate a different phase of learning (i.e., acquisition, fluency, maintenance, generalization, adaptation).
7. Change to a new skill.
8. Implement a compliance training program to respond to interfering or competing behavior.

Preferred Practices for Achieving Generalized Responding

One of the most important and desirable outcomes of a social skills training program is generalized responding—seeing the student apply a social skill learned in one setting to another setting, with other individuals, or at a different time. Although training should continue until the student can state or demonstrate the critical rule and show the skill during social skills training, the success of a social skills training program should be judged ultimately by the extent to which students can generalize their practiced or newly learned skills to the original problem setting or context. As discussed in the introduction, social skills trained in one setting typically do not generalize beyond that setting or context (Berler, Gross, & Drabman, 1982; Hops, Walker, & Greenwood, 1988; Krauter, McLaughlin, & Williams, 1986; Lewis, 1994; Lewis, Sugai , Mercer, & Heilman, 1995; Walker, McConnell, Holmes, et al., 1983) *unless* training is extended to that setting or context (Kim & Sugai, 1995; Lewis, 1994; Scott & Lewis, 1994; Scott & Sugai, 1995).

Although the empirical identification of effective generalization strategies is relatively sparse, some promising techniques can be employed to promote generalized responding throughout the social skills program. In this section, techniques that can be employed to increase the likelihood of generalized responding are described briefly.

Selection of Relevant Examples

Generalized responding can be facilitated by using training examples taken from the student's natural environment (Carter & Sugai, 1989; Haring, 1992; McConnell,

1987; Steere, Pancsofar, Powell, & Butterworth, 1989). These examples are found by conducting direct observations of target students and socially competent peers in various social situations, asking relevant others (e.g., peers, parents, teachers) about situations in which students have demonstrated social skill deficits, and interviewing target students about situations in which they have experienced problems or difficulties. By incorporating these examples into the design of social skills instruction, teachers can highlight the critical features of the contexts in which specific social skills and their variations should be used. Applying examples that have common features to relevant social situations enhances the likelihood of generalized responding.

Involving Relevant Others in Training

Including relevant staff and peers in social skills training also can help promote generalized responding (Brady et al., 1984; Scott, Himadi, & Keane, 1983). When individuals whom students are likely to encounter in their daily routines are involved in social skills instructional activities (e.g., demonstrations, role plays), students have opportunities to become familiar with the physical and behavioral features of these social agents and to learn what to expect when they encounter these individuals outside the training context. An additional benefit of including others in social skill activities is that these individuals also are exposed to what students are being taught and can anticipate and prepare for how they might respond when they encounter the student outside the training context. These individuals can be taught to assist target students when specific social skills are needed, provide positive reinforcement when appropriate social skills are displayed, and provide positive corrections when social skill errors are made.

Training in the Natural Environment

Because the research evidence about effective generalization strategies is limited, specific interventions should be developed for direct implementation in the target generalization setting (where the student is having social behavior difficulties) (Carter & Sugai, 1989; Chandler, Lubeck, & Fowler, 1992; Lewis, 1994; Scott, Himadi, & Keane, 1983). The simplest direct intervention is to prompt the student to use a targeted skill and reinforce the student in the generalized setting when an appropriate social skill is displayed (i.e., precorrection) (Chandler et al., 1992; Colvin, Kameenui, & Sugai, 1993; Lewis, 1994). When appropriate, behavioral contracts should be used to organize the social skill expectations for the student, peers, and adults involved in the social activities of the target student. Contracts specify what social skills are expected, where and when the social skills should be displayed, and the consequences for appropriate and inappropriate social skill displays.

Other interventions that can be applied in the target problem setting and that have been shown to be effective include self-management strategies (Hops, Walker, & Greenwood, 1988; Lewis, 1991a; Sugai & Tindal, 1993; Wolery, Bailey, & Sugai,

1988). Self-management strategies include self-recording, self-selection and self-administration of consequences (positive reinforcers and punishers), and self-instruction. Each of these strategies is designed to give the student a response that can be used in nontraining contexts in which the usual forms of assistance are not available but that prompt or signal the desired social skill to be displayed. Like any social behavior, self-management skills have to be taught (a) directly, (b) to a high degree of mastery to increase the likelihood that the student will use the skill, and (c) in conjunction with the social skill to be managed.

Conclusion

Although social skills, social skills instruction, and social competence are conceptualized differently, having and using social skills clearly are important prerequisites for success in a variety of social settings. Many students learn easily how to be successful socially across a variety of settings because their learning histories enable them to benefit from relatively informal models of learning (e.g., observation, trial-and-error learning, vicarious reinforcement). Teachers can teach social skills, but learning how to teach a social skills program requires time, effort, practice, and careful attention to detail. This article has emphasized (a) the importance of teaching social skills directly and systematically and including social skills in the classroom and school curriculum, (b) preferred strategies for assessing and understanding social skill problems, (c) preferred strategies for teaching social skills, and (d) preferred practices for achieving generalized responding.

We acknowledge the following individuals for their assistance in the preparation of this document: Rollen Fowler, Hwangyong Kim, Myounghee Kim, David Knox, Lance Schnacker, Terry Scott, and Tary Tobin. Preparation of this manuscript was supported in part by the National Center for the Improvement of Tools in Education through a grant (H180M10006) from the U.S. Department of Education, Office of Special Education Programs, Washington DC. Opinions expressed in this manuscript do not necessarily represent the position of the National Center for the Improvement of Tools in Education or the U.S. Department of Education.

References

Asher, S. R. (1990). Recent advances in the study of peer rejection. In S. Asher & J. Coie (Eds.), *Peer rejection in childhood* (pp. 3–14). New York: Cambridge University Press.

Bain, A., & Farris, H. (1991). Teacher attitudes toward social skills training. *Teacher Education & Special Education, 14*, 49–56.

Barton, E. J. (1986). Modification of children's prosocial behavior. In P. S. Strain, M. J. Guralnick, & H. M. Walker (Eds.), *Children's social behavior: Development, assessment, and modification* (pp. 331–371). Orlando, FL: Academic Press.

Berler, E. S., Gross, A. M., & Drabman, R. S. (1982). Social skills training with children: Proceed with caution. *Journal of Applied Behavior Analysis, 15*, 41–53.

Brady, M. P., Shores, R. E., Gunter, P., McEvoy, M. A., Fox, J. J., & White, C. (1984). Generalization of an adolescent's social interaction behavior via multiple peers in a classroom setting. *Journal of the Association for Persons with Severe Handicaps, 9*, 278–286.

Carter, J. & Sugai, G. (1988). Teaching social skills. *Teaching Exceptional Children, 20*(3), 68–71.

Carter, J. & Sugai, G. (1989). Social skills curriculum analysis. *Teaching Exceptional Children, 22*(1), 36–39.

Chandler, L. K., Lubeck, R. C., & Fowler, S. A. (1992). Generalization and maintenance of preschool children's social skills: A critical review and analysis. *Journal of Applied Behavior Analysis, 25*, 415–428.

Cohen, S. B., Alberto, P. A., & Troutman, A. (1979). Selecting and developing educational materials: An inquiry model. *Teaching Exceptional Children, 12*(1), 7–11.

Coie, J. D., Dodge, K. A., & Kupersmidt, J. B. (1990). Peer group behavior and social status. In S. A. Asher & J. D. Coie (Eds.), *Peer rejection in childhood* (pp. 17–59). New York: Cambridge University Press.

Colvin, G., Kameenui, E. J., & Sugai, G. (1993). School-wide and classroom management: Reconceptualizing the integration and management of students with behavior problems in general education. *Education & Treatment of Children, 16*, 361–381.

Colvin, G., Sugai, G., & Patching, W. (1993). Pre-correction: An instructional strategy for managing predictable behavior problems. *Intervention, 28*, 143–150.

Elliott, S. N., & Gresham, F. M. (1991). *Social skills intervention guide: Practical strategies for social skills training.* Circle Pines, MN: American Guidance Service.

Engelmann, S., & Carnine, D. (1982). *Theory of instruction: Principles and applications.* New York: Irvington Publishers.

Fuller, M., Lewis, T. J., & Sugai, G. (1995). *Social skills instruction in schools: A survey of teachers in Oregon public schools* (Behavior Disorders Research Report No. 4). Eugene: University of Oregon, Behavior Disorders Program.

Gresham, F. M. (1986). Conceptual and definitional issues in the assessment of children's social skills: Implications for classification and training. *Journal of Clinical Child Psychology, 15*(1), 3–15.

Gresham, F. M. (1992). Social skills and learning disabilities: Causal, concomitant, or correlational? *School Psychology Review, 21*, 348–360.

Haring, N. G. (1992). The context of social competence: Relations, relationships, and generalization. In S. L. Odom, S. R. McConnell, & M. A. McEvoy (Eds.), *Social competence of young children with disabilities: Issues and strategies for intervention* (pp. 307–320). Baltimore: Paul H. Brookes.

Haring, N. G., Liberty, K. A., & White, O. R. (1980). Rules for data-based strategy decisions in instructional programs. In W. Sailor, B., Wilcox, & L. Brown (Eds.), *Methods of instruction for severely handicapped students* (pp. 159–192). Baltimore: Paul H. Brookes.

Hollinger, D. (1987). Social skills for behaviorally disordered children as preparation for mainstreaming: Theory, practice, and new directions. *Remedial & Specific Education, 8*, 17–27.

Hops, H., Finch, M., & McConnell, S. (1985). Social skill deficits. In P. H. Bornstein & A. E. Kazdin (Eds.), *Handbook of clinical behavior therapy with children* (pp. 543–598). Homewood, IL: Dorsey Press.

Hops, H., Walker, H. M., & Greenwood, C. R. (1988). *PEERS: Procedures for establishing effective relationship skills—A program for children with socially withdrawn behaviors.* Del Ray, FL: Educational Achievement Systems.

Horner, R. H., O'Neill, R. E., & Flannery, K. B. (1993). Building effective behavior support plans from functional assessment information. In M. E. Snell (Ed.), *Systematic instruction of persons with severe handicaps, 4th ed.* (pp. 184–214). Columbus, OH: Merrill.

Kameenui, E. J., & Simmons, D. C. (1990). *Designing instructional strategies: The prevention of academic learning problems.* Columbus, OH: Merrill.

Kratochwill, T. R., & French, D. C. (1984). Social skills training for withdrawn children. *School Psychology Review, 13*, 331–337.

Krauter, R., McLaughlin, T., & Williams, R. (1986). The effects of social skills training on mildly handicapped youngsters in the natural setting using the ACCEPTS program. *B. C. Journal of Special Education, 10*(3), 279–288.

Lewis, T. J. (May, 1991a). *Social withdrawal assessment/intervention strategies: An investigation in maintaining treatment effects.* Posterboard presentation, 17th Annual Association for Behavior Analysis: International Convention, Atlanta, GA.

Lewis, T. J. (September, 1991b). *Designing effective social skills.* Paper presented at Illinois Council for Children with Behavioral Disorders Conference, Chicago.

Lewis, T. (1992). Essential features of a social skills instructional program. In J. Marr, G. Tindal, & G. Sugai (Eds.), *The Oregon Conference monograph* (pp. 32–40). Eugene: University of Oregon, College of Education.

Lewis, T. J. (1994). A comparative analysis of the effects of social skills training and teacher directed contingencies on the generalized social behavior of pre-school children with disabilities. *Journal of Behavioral Education, 4,* 267–281.

Lewis, T. J., Heflin, J, & DiGangi, S. A. (1991). *Teaching students with behavioral disorders: Basic questions and answers.* Reston, VA: Council for Exceptional Children.

Lewis, T. J., & Sugai, G. (1993). Teaching communicative alternatives to socially withdrawn behavior: An investigation in maintaining treatment effects. *Journal of Behavioral Education, 3,* 61–75.

Lewis, T. J., & Sugai, G. (1996a). Functional assessment of problem behavior: A pilot investigation of the comparative and interactive effects of teacher and peer social attention on students in general education settings. *School Psychology Quarterly, 11,* 1–19.

Lewis, T. J., & Sugai, G. (1996b). Descriptive and experimental analysis of teacher and peer attention and the use of assessment based intervention to improve the pro-social behavior of a student in a general education setting. *Journal of Behavioral Education, 6,* 7–24.

Lewis, T., Sugai, G., Mercer, M., & Heilman, J. (1995). *An examination of reviews of social skill research: Summary of preferred practices.* Eugene, OR: National Center for Improving the Tools of Educators.

Maag, J. (1989). Assessment in social skills training: Methodological and conceptual issues for research and practice. *Remedial & Special Education, 10*(4), 6–17.

McConnell, S. R. (1987). Entrapment effects and the generalization and maintenance of social skills training for elementary school students with behavioral disorders. *Behavioral Disorders, 12,* 252–263.

Meadows, N., Neel, R. S., Parker, G., & Timo, K. (1991). A validation of social skills for students with behavioral disorders. *Behavioral Disorders, 16,* 200–210.

Michelson, L., & Mannarino, A. (1986). Social skills training with children: Research and clinical application. In P. S. Strain, M. J. Guralnick, & H. M. Walker (Eds.), *Children's social behavior: Development, assessment, and modification* (pp. 373–406). Orlando, FL: Academic Press.

Odom, S. L., McConnell, S. R., & McEvoy, M. A. (1992). Peer-related social competence and its significance for young children with disabilities. In S. L. Odom, S. R. McConnell, & M. A. McEvoy (Eds.), *Social competence of young children with disabilities: Issues and strategies for intervention* (pp. 3–36). Baltimore: Paul H. Brookes.

Scott, R. R., Himadi, W., & Keane, T. M. (1983). A review of generalization in social skills training: Suggestions for future research. In M. Hersen, R. M. Eisler, & P. M. Miller (Eds.), *Progress in behavior modification* (Vol. 15, pp. 113–172). New York: Academic Press.

Scott, T. M., & Lewis, T. J. (1994). Promoting generalized social skills among mildly disabled elementary school students. In J. Marr, G. Sugai, & G. Tindal (Eds.), *The Oregon Conference '94 monograph* (pp. 121–128). Eugene: University of Oregon, College of Education.

Scott, T. M., & Sugai, G. (1995). *Facilitating generalized social inter action in children: The effects of general case instruction and reinforcement.* Unpublished manuscript, University of Oregon, Eugene, Behavioral Research and Teaching.

Steere, D. E., Pancsofar, E. L., Powell, T. H., & Butterworth, J. (1989). Enhancing instruction through general case programming. *Teaching Exceptional Children, 22*(1), 22–24.

Sugai, G. (1990). *Social skill analysis.* Unpublished manuscript. Division of Learning and Instructional Leadership, University of Oregon, Eugene.

Sugai, G. (1992). The design of instruction and the proactive management of social behavior. *Learning Disabilities Forum, 17,* 20–23.

Sugai, G., & Fuller, M. (1991). A decision model for social skills curriculum analysis. *Remedial & Special Education, 12*(4), 33–42.

Sugai, G., Maheady, L., & Skouge, J. (1989). Best assessment practices for students with behavior disorders: Accommodation to cultural diversity and other individual differences. *Behavior Disorders, 14*, 263–278.

Sugai, G., & Tindal, G. (1993). *Effective school consultation: An inter active approach.* Monterey, CA: Brooks/Cole.

Walker, H. M., & Fabre, T. R. (1987). Assessment of behavior disorders in the school setting: Issues, problems, and strategies revisited. In N. Haring (Ed.), *Assessing and managing behavior disorders* (pp. 198–234). Seattle: University of Washington Press.

Walker, H. M., Irvin, L. K., Noell, J., & Singer, G. H. S. (1992). A construct score approach to the assessment of social competence: Rationale, technological considerations, and anticipated outcomes. *Behavior Modification, 16*, 448–474.

Walker, H. M., & McConnell, S. R. (1988). *The Walker-McConnell scale of social competence and school adjustment: A social skills rating scale for teachers.* Austin, TX: ProEd.

Walker, H. M., McConnell, S., Holmes, D., Todis, B., Walker, J., & Golden, N. (1983). *The Walker social skills curriculum: The ACCEPTS program.* Austin, TX: ProEd.

Walker, H. M., McConnell, S., Walker, J., Clarke, J., Todis, B., Cohen, G., & Rankin, R. (1983). Initial analysis of the Accepts Curriculum: Efficacy of instructional and behavior management procedures for improving the social adjustment of handicapped children. *Analysis & Intervention in Developmental Disabilities, 3,* 105–127.

White, O. R., & Haring, N. G. (1980). *Exceptional teaching* (2d ed.). Columbus, OH: Merrill.

Wolery, M., Bailey, D. B., & Sugai, G. M. (1988). *Effective teaching: Principles and procedures of applied behavior analysis with exceptional students.* Boston: Allyn & Bacon.

8 Strategies for Adapting Science Textbooks for Youth with Learning Disabilities

THOMAS C. LOVITT AND STEVEN V. HORTON

THE ADAPTATION OF TEXTBOOKS has become an important strategy for enhancing the success of students with disabilities in general education classes, particularly in subjects such as science. Lovitt and Horton draw upon research conducted at the University of Washington in offering suggestions to classroom teachers regarding the process of adapting textbooks in science to meet the needs of students with disabilities. Special attention is given to study guides, graphic organizers, and vocabulary drills as approaches to adaptation.

This chapter reviews selected approaches for adapting textbook passages for low-achieving and remedial students and pupils with learning disabilities. Our emphasis in this article is on research we have carried out at the University of Washington in the past dozen or so years. Moreover, the studies reviewed here were conducted in secondary programs, and with the exception of one study, have to do with scientific topics. We provide information on how to carry out these adaptations in general and special education classes.

In our research, we restricted our interest to textbooks rather than other sources of information such as lectures, workbooks, and films because textbooks represent the primary means of presenting new information to students, beginning in the intermediate grades and continuing through secondary programs. The methods for adapting textbooks that are discussed in this chapter, however, are applicable to those other sources of information.

There are two primary reasons for adapting textbooks for pupils with learning disabilities and other low-achieving students. The first, and perhaps the most important, is that the majority of those students are unable to read assigned textbooks with the proficiency required to gain information from them and to assimilate that information with previously learned material. Lovitt, Horton, and Bergerud (1987), in a study involving pupils with mild disabilities and general education students enrolled in science and social studies classes in middle school and high school, reported a significant correlation between the rate at which students read textbooks orally and scores on written tests based on textbook information. Of 72 students sampled, the 27 who read orally at a rate of 135 words per minute or higher, averaged 60% correct or higher on written tests. Conversely, the 24 students who read at a rate of fewer than 135 words per minute averaged less than 60% correct on the tests. Not many students with learning disabilities are able to read orally at a rate of 135 words per minute.

A second and related reason for adapting textbooks for adolescents with mild disabilities is that many of those books are poorly organized. As Kantor, Anderson, and Armbruster (1983) put it, many textbooks are "inconsiderate." Those authors maintained that when textbooks were evaluated on the basis of structure, coherence, unity, and audience appropriateness, great numbers of them fell short. Kantor et al. estimated that textbooks were appropriate for only the top 50% of the students.

Review of Selected Research

The section that follows is a review of selected studies on three ways in which to adapt textbooks: study guides, graphic organizers, and vocabulary drill.

Study Guides

One modification technique that has been successfully applied with pupils with mild disabilities and general education students is the writing of study guides. Study guides are questions or statements that appear on worksheets to help students learn content information during or after they have read a passage (Cheek & Cheek, 1983; Lovitt & Horton, 1987). They are abstracts of important pieces of information from larger contexts.

In several studies researchers have demonstrated that study guides are effective in assisting students through secondary textbooks, many of which contain numerous facts and details. In one such study, Lovitt, Rudsit, Jenkins, Pious, and Benedetti (1985) reported significant academic improvement of mainstreamed students with learning disabilities and general seventh-grade science students by providing teacher-directed study guides that presented sequenced main ideas from a chapter. Bergerud, Lovitt, and Horton (1988), in another investigation, reported favorable effects resulting from student-directed study guides, in comparison with a self-study condition, for high school students with learning disabilities who were taught science in a resource room.

In the research by Lovitt and colleagues, study guide materials were presented as part of comprehensive reading activities that consisted of reading textbook passages, completing comprehension questions, and taking written tests. When presented in that manner, study guide materials resemble adjunct questions that appear in text immediately following a passage. A written response to such questions in text has been shown to improve significantly the reading comprehension of general education students, particularly when questions relate directly to criterion test items (e.g., Hamaker, 1986).

Horton and Lovitt (1989a) arranged a two-experiment study to respond to three research questions regarding the applicability of study guides to heterogeneous groups in mainstream secondary classes: (a) Are study guides more effective than a self-study condition for students of three types—students with learning disabilities, general education pupils, and students characterized as remedial? (b) Do study guides produce similar effects in middle school and high school, and in science and social studies? (c) Are the effects of study guides consistent when administered by either teachers or students? In arranging these studies, we took several variables into account to ensure the ecological validity of the research, including keeping intact such circumstances as the teachers, settings, textbooks, grouping arrangements, and the sequences of instruction that were normally used.

To carry out that research, we requested students in the experimental conditions to read 1,500-word passages from texts and then gave them study guides over the material. In the first experiment, teachers directed the activity as their students studied from the guides. Specifically, teachers placed a transparency of the study guide questions without answers on an overhead projector and lectured from it. The study guides were made up of short-answer questions based on main ideas from selected text passages. As the teachers directed the discussion by calling on students to read and answer questions, they wrote the answers on their study guide and instructed the pupils to do likewise. Following that teacher-directed activity, students studied their completed guides for a few minutes and then responded to a multiple choice test over the material from their text and their study guides.

At another phase of the experiment, these students were involved in an alternate condition. At that time, they also read passages from texts, but instead of being given study guides, they were provided self-study time in which to reread the material and take notes prior to taking the tests.

In the second experiment of their study, Horton and Lovitt (1989a) investigated the effects of student-directed study guides with the same individuals in the same classes. For this experiment, students were given study guides like those in the first experiment, but now they were requested to look up the answers themselves. To assist them, page numbers were printed alongside each study guide item to indicate where the missing information was located. As the students scanned through their books looking for answers and writing them on the guides, teachers circulated throughout the classrooms and assisted those who were having trouble with the assignment. Following this exercise, teachers placed a transparency of a completed study guide on the overhead and reviewed the items. If pupils had written incorrect information or were unable to answer a question, they were given time to complete their guides correctly.

As was the case in the first experiment, these pupils were involved in an alternate treatment, taking notes from their reading and studying those notes. Furthermore, the dependent measures in this second experiment were the same as those in the first experiment, pupils' scores on multiple choice tests.

The results of those study guide experiments led to affirmative conclusions for all three research questions: Study guides were significantly more effective than self-study for secondary students of three types; study guides were superior to self-study in middle school and high school and in science and social studies; and study guide material resulted in consistent effects for heterogeneous groups of students, whether they were primarily teacher directed or student directed.

In previous study guide research, teachers presented only one level of a textbook modification. This common approach does not address the fact that in many instances the textbook information is too easy for some students, about right for others, and too difficult for yet others. A more refined technique is to match pupils to differential levels of textbook instruction so that each learner interacts with subject matter at his or her highest level of ability. With that in mind, Horton, Lovitt, and Christensen (1991) sought to extend previous study guide research by addressing the following research questions, among others: (a) Are study guides more effective for secondary students when they are presented through a single level of instruction, or through multilevel instruction in which students are differentially matched to one of three instructional groups? (b) Are the effects consistent in science and social studies and in middle school and high school? (c) Are the effects consistent for low-, average-, and high-performance students?

There were 82 pupils in the study: 17 with learning disabilities, 18 remedial, and 47 without disabilities. They were enrolled in science and social studies classes in middle school and high school. In one treatment, students were assigned multilevel study guides containing different levels of referential clues, with the guides implemented through three instructional groups: teacher directed, dyadic, and independent. The basis for placing the pupils in one of the three instructional groups was their score on reading inventories that were developed from reading passages in their respective textbooks.

The multilevel study guides contained three levels that differed only in referential cues: the lowest level (teacher directed) contained both the paragraph number and the page number in the text where the answer could be found to the question; the middle level (dyadic) contained only the page number after the question; and the highest level (independent) contained only the question. The single-level study guides did not contain referential cues.

Following are procedures for implementing the multilevel study guide: (a) direct students to read a 1,200-word passage of text; (b) form three groups of students, and then complete and study a multilevel study guide using the textbook; and (c) administer a multiple choice test. Prior to the multilevel treatment, the teachers instructed the students working in dyads to complete the study guide by cooperatively answering the questions one at a time. The independent students completed and studied the guide materials on their own.

In the single-level study guide condition the students were not grouped for instruction. Instead, the teacher followed these procedures: (a) directed students to read a 1,200-word passage; (b) requested them to complete and study a single-level study guide without assistance, using their textbooks; and (c) administered a multiple choice test.

We drew the following conclusions from this study, among others. First, the diagnostic-prescriptive strategy was an effective method of matching secondary students to appropriate levels of study guides. Second, the multilevel study guides generally produced the greatest benefits among low-performing students. Third, each secondary teacher successfully managed three skill groups simultaneously.

To assist school personnel to develop study guides, we offer the following steps. They are from suggestions of Tierney, Readence, and Dishner (1985) and from our research (e.g., Lovitt & Horton, 1987):

1. Analyze the material to be read for both subject matter and level of difficulty.
2. Select the content to be emphasized during the lesson.
3. Decide on the processes that students must use in acquiring that content (e.g., comprehending the material with respect to literal, interpretive, or applied responses).
4. Consider students' abilities to read, write, listen, and organize in relation to the content and processes to be emphasized. Vary the structure of study guides with respect to question type, format, and method of implementation to increase chances that the effects of the treatment will generalize.
5. Make the study guides as aesthetically pleasing as possible (e.g., avoid overcrowding the print).

Graphic Organizers

The term *graphic organizer* (GO) refers to both verbal and visual representation of key vocabulary or content information. Graphic organizers visuospatial arrangements of information containing words or statements that are connected graphically in a meaningful way. Horton, Lovitt, and Bergerud (1990) arranged a set of three experiments to study the effects of GOs on middle school and high school students in science and social studies classes. These researchers obtained data from general and remedial students and pupils with learning disabilities. In the first experiment, the teacher directed most aspects of the treatment, whereas in the second and third experiments the students were given more responsibility for developing and studying from the GOs.

Two conditions constituted the first experiment. In one, students were given GOs after they had read a passage in their assigned textbook. All of the boxes and interconnecting lines were available for those GOs, but much of the information pertaining to subordinate categories was left out. During instruction, the teacher placed an identical copy of the GO on the overhead projector and conducted a lecture from it over material that had been read. While lecturing, the teacher called on pupils and they filled in the missing information as a class. When the GOs were completed, students were given a few minutes to study the material on their own and then were given a test. The format of the test was the incomplete version of the GO.

In the second condition of the experiment, the students were not given a GO. Instead, they were allowed time to study the passage after they had read it. During that time they were encouraged to make an outline, write and answer questions, define terms, or use any other strategy as long as they produced a written product. Students were given as much time for self-study as they had during the GO condition. Following these sessions, the same type of test was administered that had followed GO sessions; students were given a blank GO and asked to fill it in.

During the second and third experiments in this series, students were granted more responsibility for developing the GOs. In Experiment 2, students were provided a cover sheet on which the page and paragraph numbers for the answers in the textbook were printed, rather than being told which pieces of information belonged in the various spaces. In Experiment 3, the students were simply given a sheet on which clues regarding the facts and concepts required to complete the diagram were printed at the bottom of the page. While the students filled in the missing information, their teacher circulated about the room and assisted those who were having trouble. Following periods of self-directed activity, the teacher placed a completed GO on the overhead and asked students to check theirs and make the necessary adjustments. Students were then given a few minutes to study the GOs before taking the tests. The alternate treatment in Experiments 2 and 3 was the same as that described for Experiment 1.

Our findings from the three GO experiments indicated that this form of textbook modification was effective for students with learning disabilities and for remedial and general education students. Students' average correct scores on tests across the three experiments were significantly higher when GO treatments were in effect than in self-study conditions. Furthermore, the performances were comparable within each student classification whether GOs were completed through teacher- or student-directed procedures.

Horton and Lovitt (1989b) have suggested a four-step process to assist teachers in constructing GOs from textbooks:

1. Select and divide the chapters to be modified into reading passages of about 1,500 words. Choose material that has been difficult for students to understand, or that clearly lacks organization.
2. Construct an outline of the main ideas in the reading passage.
3. Select a GO format that matches the structure of the information; that is, top down/bottom up, compare and contrast, sequence, or diagram.
4. Prepare a teacher's version of the GO that includes all the information in the diagram, and a student's version for which information from certain categories (e.g., superordinate-subordinate) is missing. Several commercial software programs are available for developing graphics, such as MacPaint (Atkinson, 1985), MacDraw (Cutter, 1985), MORE (Living Videotext, 1987), and Superpaint (Snider, Zocher, & Jackson, 1986).

Although we have presented examples of teachers implementing GOs almost exclusively after students have read a unit of text, teachers may choose to present GOs before students read an instructional unit or during the presentation of the material. Moreover, GOs can be completed as a teacher-directed activity, as a student-directed activity with text references (i.e., page or paragraph numbers), or as a student-directed activity with a list of clues attached (e.g., answers that complete the diagram are provided on a cover sheet).

Vocabulary Drill in a Precision Teaching Model

Whereas the first two approaches for adapting textbooks focused on the main ideas, concepts, and relationships of those features, vocabulary drill in a precision teaching model is designed to enhance the development of vocabulary. The verbal technique described here for adapting textbook material consists of a series of 1-minute timed drills in which students write terms that match definitions or vice versa. Given a sheet of definitions from a unit on biology that are placed on a worksheet and a list of terms at the top of the worksheet, for example, students match vocabulary to their definitions by writing the terms on lines that precede their appropriate meanings. Rate data from these exercises are commonly plotted on Standard Behavior Charts, affording evaluation as per the conventions of precision teaching (White & Haring, 1980).

Our rationale for supporting the use of this method to adapt textbook information is based on the fact that key vocabulary serves as a foundation on which facts, concepts, and relationships are built. Even the most cursory inspection of secondary science textbooks reveals that they are brimming with idiosyncratic vocabulary. Students who have command of a subject's vocabulary will undoubtedly stand a greater chance of mastering that subject than will pupils who lack familiarity with the key terms.

Lovitt, Horton, and Bergerud (1987) examined the extent to which vocabulary knowledge related to other measures of academic performance among students with learning disabilities and general education students enrolled in science and social studies classes in middle school and high school. The investigators ran correlations between vocabulary scores (based on terms selected from their respective textbooks) and the following: (a) measures of test performance on specific content following instruction, (b) oral reading rates, (c) oral comprehension scores, and (d) teachers' rankings of student progress throughout the school year. Results indicated a significant correspondence between all variables for high-, average-, and low-achieving students.

The effects of vocabulary drills using the precision teaching approach on comprehension of textbook information was investigated in a study by Lovitt, Rudsit, Jenkins, Pious, and Benedetti (1986) involving seventh-grade students enrolled in physical science classes. The participants in this research were four classes of general education students, as well as students with learning disabilities mainstreamed into those classes.

For purposes of analysis, the students in each class were rank ordered according to their accumulated test scores in their respective classes. From those listings, experimental groups of 6 students were formed for each class: 2 from the "high" third, 2 from the "middle" third, and 2 from the "low" third. The other students in the four classes were considered as the contrast group.

Throughout a 2-week period one of the researchers took the experimental groups from the general classes into an adjoining room and administered the vocabulary drills. During that time, he conducted a series of exercises with the vocabulary sheets that included the scheduling of several 1-minute timings and providing correction and feedback. Over the course of that experimental phase the students did timings on two sheets, each of which contained eight vocabulary words. Meanwhile, as this instruction was being delivered, the classroom teacher provided instruction based on a lecture and discussion format to the other students in the general classroom. The students in both settings were instructed on the same general topic and for the same amount of time.

In order to determine the relative effects of the treatments, students in the experimental groups and the contrast pupils were given a multiple choice test on science information from the section of the textbook from which the vocabulary items were drawn, prior to and following the 2-week period. Analysis of those data revealed the gain scores for experimental pupils were significantly higher than those of the contrast students. This finding was true in all four classes and for all ability levels: high, middle, and low.

Only ordinary 8 -inch   11-inch sheets of paper are required to develop precision teaching vocabulary sheets. Following are steps for constructing and using those sheets:

1. Identify the important vocabulary in a passage.
2. Select about eight terms.
3. Write clear and brief definitions for those terms.
4. Print the eight vocabulary words on the top left corner, one word under the next, on Side 1 of the sheet (see Figure 8.1).
5. Design a matrix of five rows and five columns to make up 25 squares.
6. Write the definitions of the vocabulary words in each of the 25 squares, leaving a blank for the vocabulary word. If a word was "meter," then the definition with the blank might appear as "A _____ is a SI unit of length."
7. Print those definitions randomly on the page, three or four times per vocabulary word.
8. Print the words again on Side 2 (reverse side) of the vocabulary sheet on the top of the page, and write the definitions along the words. Below these construct a 25-square matrix made up of five columns and five rows (see Figure 8.2).
9. Print the vocabulary words in these boxes.
10. Give each student a manila folder with an acetate sheet attached to one flap.
11. Ask students to place the vocabulary sheet beneath the acetate with Side 1 showing (definitions without vocabulary words).
12. Give them special marking pens for writing the vocabulary words.

UNIT 1, SHEET #1   Chapter 1: Measuring and Experimenting

buoyancy (buo)
displacement (dis)   Student_____
SI (SI)
standard (stan)   Date_____
hypothesis (hyp)
observing (ob)   Teacher_____
inference (in)
scientific method (s.m.)   Period_____

_____ is an international system of units (Metric System).	_____ is taking notice and gathering data; using senses to find out things.	A fixed quantity used in measuring is a _____.	_____ is a way to determine the volume of an odd-shaped piece of matter.	_____ is an international system of units (Metric System).
A _____ is a proposed answer to a questions or tentative solution to a problem.	The upward push on an object placed in a liquid is called _____.	A conclusion based on observation is called an _____.	A _____ is a proposed answer to a questions or tentative solution to a problem.	The _____ is a way to solve problems: observing, measuring, explaining, and testing.
_____ is a way to determine the volume of an odd-shaped piece of matter.	A fixed quantity used in measuring is a _____.	The _____ is a way to solve problems: observing, measuring, explaining, and testing.	A conclusion based on observation is called an _____.	_____ is a way to determine the volume of an odd-shaped piece of matter.
A conclusion based on observation is called an _____.	The _____ is a way to solve problems: observing, measuring, explaining, and testing.	_____ is an international system of units (Metric System).	_____ is taking notice and gathering data; using senses to find out things.	A _____ is a proposed answer to a questions or tentative solution to a problem.
A fixed quantity used in measuring is a _____.	The upward push on an object placed in a liquid is called _____.	A fixed quantity used in measuring is a _____.	_____ is taking notice and gathering data; using senses to find out things.	The upward push on an object placed in a liquid is called _____.

Figure 8.1 *Side 1 of a Precision Teaching Sheet Containing Textbook Terms at the Top Left and Their Definitions Below, Printed Randomly Three or Four Times Across Five Columns*

buoyancy   — upward push on an object placed in a liquid
displacement   — way to determine the volume of an odd-shaped piece of matter
SI   — international system of units (Metric System)
standard   — fixed quantity used in measuring
hypothesis   — measuring proposed answer to a question or tentative solution to a
                  problem senses
observing   — taking notice and gathering data; using to find out things
inference   — conclusion based on observation
scientific method   — orderly way to solve problems: observing, measuring, explaining, and testing

SI	observing (ob)	standard (stan)	displacement (dis)	SI
hypothesis (hyp)	buoyancy (buo)	inference (in)	hypothesis (hyp)	scientific method (s.m.)
displacement (dis)	standard (stan)	scientific method (s.m.)	inference (in)	displacement (dis)
inference (in)	scientific method (s.m.)	SI	observing (ob)	hypothesis (hyp)
standard (stan)	buoyancy (buo)	standard (stan)	observing (ob)	buoyancy (buo)

Figure 8.2 *Side 2 of a Precision Teaching Sheet Containing Textbook Terms and Their Definitions at the Top, and the Terms That Match the Definitions Presented on Side 1.*

13. Inform students to proceed from left to right on the top row, then move to the next row, and so forth. Tell them not to skip around as they fill in the words.

14. Inform students that if they can't remember a word to look at the top of Side 1 and read the vocabulary words.

15. Remind the students that if that doesn't help, they should turn the sheet over and look at the top of Side 2 where the words and definitions are printed. They are not to resort to either of these aids unless they have to.

16. Conduct a series of 1-minute timings with these sheets. Ask students to fill in as many answers as they can in that time.

17. Following the timings, request students to turn their sheets over and place them underneath the acetate sheet so that Side 2 is showing. When this is done, the answers on Side 2 match the squares in which the students wrote their answers; thus they are able to check their own work.

18. Tell students to circle the answers that were incorrect and to write in the correct answers as they check their papers.

19. Inform them, finally, to count the number of correct and incorrect answers and to record that number on the chart attached to their manila folder.

Recommendations and Considerations

In the past, one of the primary responsibilities of special education teachers who served students with mild disabilities in the public schools was to recommend the placement of those students to the extent possible in general education classes. While the need for such advocacy still exists, there is, or should be, a concomitant concern for issues of curriculum and instruction. A common problem today is how to help students with learning disabilities and other low-achieving students comprehend material from their textbooks. To the extent that educators can achieve such a task, there is a greater likelihood that those youth will stay in school and feel reasonably good about it. According to Rumberger (1987), the two prime reasons for dropping out of school are poor performance and disliking school, both of which are related to grades.

The biggest problem in adapting materials or modifying other instructional features is that many teachers, particularly those at the secondary level where there is the greatest need for modifications, are not inclined to do so. Unlike their counterparts at the elementary level, secondary teachers are not generally as sensitive to individual differences. Hence, they are not as inclined to make adjustments in their materials and styles of teaching for their pupils. Certainly, there is reason for secondary teachers to feel this way: They ordinarily have class loads of from 100 to 150 students and three or four different subjects for which to prepare.

The most common response we receive in workshops designed to train secondary teachers in the various methods of adapting textbook materials is: "I can see that it would really help my students, particularly the slow ones, if I modified certain of their materials, but when will I find the time to do it?" Admittedly, this is a troublesome issue.

On the bright side, we have found that when teachers are first assisted to develop study guides and carry out other modifications, they find it is not as difficult or as time-consuming a process as they thought it might be. Moreover, when teachers are reminded of the fundamental reason for modifying the textbooks, many of them will make the effort to do so. That rationale is that if textbooks and other means of presenting materials are modified and made more accommodating to youth, the chances of their participating in classes and enjoying the instructional sessions are improved. And, their attendance may improve, as might their grades, thus encouraging them to stay in school longer and increasing chances of their graduating.

Looking at this situation realistically and with an eye to the future, it is imperative that general education teachers become willing to modify textbooks, and other aspects of instruction, for not only will students classified as having learning disabilities be placed in their classes, but also pupils classified as having mental retardation, as well as others. In order to make science, social studies, language, and mathematics classes interesting and meaningful for many of those latter students, teachers will need to make adjustments beyond simply modifying their textbooks. Returning to the matter of adjusting textbooks, following are six effective approaches for efficiently modifying materials:

1. Modify only textbook chapters or passages within chapters that have proven difficult for students or that clearly lack organization.
2. Collaborate with other teachers who use the same text by dividing the modification load and sharing materials.
3. Use curriculum-based assessments prior to instruction to determine which students can interact with the text at an independent level and which students will need materials modifications.
4. Computerize the materials adaptation process by using commercial software, thereby developing a continuous store of materials.
5. Encourage general and special education teachers to co-teach certain subjects and to modify the materials cooperatively.
6. Urge teachers, through textbook adoption committees, to demand that textbook publishers offer study guides, graphic organizers, vocabulary exercises, computer programs, or other adaptations of material in addition to basic textbooks and supplementary materials.

Perhaps the line of least resistance for improving the performance of students with mild academic disabilities in general education classrooms is to use modification techniques that are suitable and powerful enough to help all students. Each of the techniques we reviewed—study guides, graphic organizers, and vocabulary drills—either in paper-and-pencil or computerized form, have been shown to improve the academic performance of low-achieving and general education students.

A question related to the willingness and ability of teachers to modify textbooks and other materials has to do with students. That question might be posed as follows: "How will students get along in classes where their teachers do not modify the textbooks, when they have been in situations where teachers did make the proper adjustments?" Our first response to that question is that every effort should be made to see that all teachers are able and willing (with assistance and encouragement from others) to modify textbooks and make other instructional adjustments. Beyond that, we suggest that students receive instruction on a few select methods of comprehending expository materials that have recently been substantiated by research: summarizing, locating main ideas, and constructing questions. Yet another strategy to consider for youth who enter situations where teachers are unwilling or unable to make adjustments would be to teach them to ask for assistance, when it is acceptable to do so, and from whom. Indeed, the ability to seek assistance and the confidence to do so is a strategy that would serve youth well, far beyond their years in middle and high school classes.

If we could make only one recommendation concerning the several techniques we have discussed, we would suggest using *study guides* because of their versatility and ease of construction. To develop a study guide, the teacher selects the most critical information and places it on a worksheet in either a question or statement format and directs the student to learn it, either independently as a cooperative effort, as in a study by Meadows (1988), or as a teacher-directed activity. The key to using study guides effectively is for teachers to construct test items that relate directly to the guide material.

Generally, modifying materials through visual techniques requires more labor than verbal methods, but they have the added benefit of student appeal. We have found that student interest in these types of materials is quite high, possibly because they represent a welcome change from a steady diet of verbally oriented lessons. With practice, teachers develop a critical eye for which types of materials lend themselves to modification by a visual method. Textbooks in biology, physical and environmental science, and health are laced with sections that can be neatly organized by *graphic organizers* of one type or another.

Vocabulary drills are fast-paced activities that teach the language of a subject, and are often enjoyable for students when they are presented in a precision teaching format. A simple variation of the vocabulary drill we described would be to use flash cards with terms written on one side and their definitions on the other. Using them, students can practice by themselves or in pairs. A clever technique described by Eshleman (1985) is the SAFMEDS approach (Say All Fast a Minute Each Day Shuffled). For this, the student identifies as many of the cards as possible in 1 minute, then counts the number correct and incorrect and charts those numbers. On the next day the student shuffles the cards so that they do not appear in the same order and takes another timing with them. Typically, the student stays with the same set of words until a desired rate was reached and then switches to a new set of words.

Underlying the various methods for modifying textbooks that we have discussed, and the arguments we have made for the necessity of such material adjustments for low-achieving students, is the reality that rarely can all of the pertinent information in textbooks be successfully taught to heterogeneous groups in an unmodified state. To accept this premise is to elevate the organization of information to an equal status with its content and to increase the probability that more individuals with disabilities will gain more from their instruction.

References

Atkinson, B. (1985). *MacPaint* [Computer program]. Cupertino, CA: Apple Computer.

Bergerud, D., Lovitt, T. C., & Horton, S. V. (1988). The effectiveness of textbook adaptations in life science for high school students with learning disabilities. *Journal of Learning Disabilities, 21*, 70–76.

Cheek, E. H., & Cheek, M. C. (1983). *Reading instruction through content teaching*. Columbus, OH: Merrill.

Cutter, M. (1985). *MacDraw* [Computer program]. Cupertino, CA: Apple Computer.

Eshleman, J. W. (1985). Improvement pictures with low accelerations: An early foray into the use of SAFMEDS. *Journal of Precision Teaching, 6*(3), 54–55.

Hamaker, C. (1986). The effects of adjunct questions on prose learning. *Review of Educational Research, 56*, 212–242.

Horton, S. V., & Lovitt, T. C. (1989a). Using study guides with three classifications of secondary students. *The Journal of Special Education, 22,* 447–462.

Horton, S. V., & Lovitt, T. C. (1989b). Construction and implementation of graphic organizers for academically handicapped and general secondary students. *Academic Therapy, 24*, 625–641.

Horton, S. V., Lovitt, T. C., & Bergerud, D. (1990). The effectiveness of graphic organizers for three classifications of secondary students in content area classes. *Journal of Learning Disabilities, 23*, 12–22, 29.

Horton, S. V., Lovitt, T. C., & Christensen, C. (1991). Matching three classifications of secondary students to differential levels of study guides. *Journal of Learning Disabilities, 24*, 518–529.

Kantor, R. N., Anderson, T. H., & Armbruster, B. B. (1983). How inconsiderate are children's textbooks? *Journal of Curriculum Studies, 15*, 6–72.

Living Videotext. (1987). *MORE* [Computer program]. Mountain, CA: Author.

Lovitt, T. C., & Horton, S. V. (1987). How to develop study guides. *Journal of Reading, Writing and Learning Disabilities, 3*, 333–343.

Lovitt, T. C., Horton, S. V., & Bergerud, D. (1987). Matching students with textbooks: An alternate to readability formulas and standardized tests. B. C. *Journal of Special Education, 2*, 49–65.

Lovitt, T., Rudsit, J., Jenkins, J., Pious, C., & Benedetti, L. (1985). Two methods of adapting science materials for learning disabled and general seventh graders. *Learning Disability Quarterly, 8*, 275–285.

Lovitt, T. C., Rudsit, J., Jenkins, J., Pious, C., & Benedetti, D. (1986). Adapting science materials for general and learning disabled seventh graders. *Remedial and Special Education, 7*(1), 31–39.

Meadows, N. (1988). *The effects of individual teacher-directed and cooperative learning instructional methods on the comprehension of expository text.* Unpublished doctoral dissertation, University of Washington, Seattle.

Rumberger, R. (1987). High school dropouts: A review of issues and evidence. *Review of Educational Research, 57*, 101–121.

Snider, B., Zocher, E., & Jackson, C. (1986). *Superpaint* [Computer program]. San Diego, CA: Silicon Beach Software.

Tierney, R. J., Readence, J. E., & Dishner, E. K. (1985). *Reading strategies and practices: A compendium* (2nd ed.). Boston: Allyn & Bacon.

White, O. R., & Haring, N. G. (1980). *Exceptional teaching.* Columbus, OH: Merrill.

9 Teaching Students with Learning Problems in Math to Acquire, Understand, and Apply Basic Math Facts

CECIL D. MERCER AND SUSAN P. MILLER

MATH REPRESENTS a challenging area of academic instruction for students with disabilities, as it is for many nondisabled students. In offering suggestions to teachers, Mercer and Miller relate research findings to 10 components of math instruction. In doing so, they demonstrate strategies for enhancing the performance of students with disabilities in math and provide significant service in translating research into instructional practices. The results of field testing the Strategic Math Series also is discussed.

Many students with learning problems have math deficiencies that result in practical and emotional problems. Daily living requires the application of math skills, for example, planning and monitoring time, computing percentages for on-sale purchases, making estimations, interpreting recipe measurements, measuring for carpet purchases, computing scores in games, handling banking transactions, and maintaining a checkbook. In school settings, math problems often result in school failures and lead to high levels of anxiety. Bartel (1990) stated that students with math deficiencies are as disabled as individuals with reading problems.

Research suggests that the math deficiencies of students with learning problems emerge in the early years and continue throughout secondary school. Cawley and Miller (1989) reported that the mathematical knowledge of students with learning disabilities tends to progress approximately 1 year for every 2 years of school attendance. Warner, Alley, Schumaker, Deshler, and Clark (1980) found that the math progress of students with learning disabilities reaches a plateau after seventh grade. The students in their study made only 1 year's total growth during Grades 7 through 12. Both studies report that the mean math scores of students with learning disabilities in the 12th grade is high-5th-grade.

In a survey of students with learning disabilities in Grade 6 and above, McLeod and Armstrong (1982) found that two of every three students are receiving special math instruction. From his survey of resource teachers, Carpenter (1985) found that both elementary and secondary learning disabilities teachers use one third of their instructional time to teach math. The importance of providing effective instruction for students with math difficulties is apparent; however, the challenge of improving instruction for these students intensifies when one examines the reforms being considered in math education. For example, the National Council of Supervisors of Mathematics (1988) and the National Council of Teachers of Mathematics (1989) are calling for reforms in math education that endorse higher standards of math achievement. Reforms that produce higher standards are certain to frustrate teachers and students who are struggling with current standards and the traditional curriculum.

Although many students with math deficiencies exhibit characteristics that predispose them to math disabilities (e.g., problems in memory, language, reading, reasoning, and metacognition), their learning difficulties are often compounded by ineffective instruction. Many authorities (Carnine, 1991; Cawley, Fitzmaurice-Hayes, & Shaw, 1988; Cawley, Miller, & School, 1987; Kelly, Gersten, & Carnine, 1990; Scheid, 1990) believe that poor or traditional instruction is a primary cause of the math problems of many students with learning problems. Numerous studies support the position that students with math disabilities can be taught to improve their mathematical performance (Kirby & Becker, 1988; Mastropieri, Scruggs, & Shiah, 1991; Peterson, Mercer, & O'Shea, 1988; Rivera & Smith, 1988; Scheid, 1990).

Given the poor math progress of students with learning problems and the call for a reform in math education to increase standards, a need clearly exists to design an effective math curriculum for these students. Without better math instruction, these youngsters will continue to face much frustration and failure. This chapter reports on the results of field-testing a math instructional design that incorporates research-supported procedures for teaching basic math facts to students with learning problems.

Components of Effective Math Instruction

The amount of research on teaching math has dramatically increased in the last decade, and it is now clear that both curriculum design and teacher behavior directly influence the mathematics achievement of students with learning problems (Good & Grouws, 1979; Kameenui & Simmons, 1990; Kelly et al., 1990; Mastropieri et al., 1991; Scheid, 1990). Although much remains to be learned about teaching math, it is important for educators to examine existing research and literature to determine *what* should be taught in a math curriculum and the best practices for *how* to teach it. Only through the systematic examination and application of what is known about math instruction can educators ensure that the achievement of students with learning problems is commensurate with their potential. The components of effective math instruction are presented next.

Select Appropriate Math Content

Math educators are recommending reforms in the content of the math curriculum. Although computation remains a vital component, experts agree that obtaining answers via written work is not sufficient. The ability to think critically and understand concepts, operations, and real-life applications are important goals of a math curriculum. In 1988, the National Council of Supervisors of Mathematics released its official statement, *Twelve Components of Essential Mathematics*. The statement includes four components that directly relate to teaching facts to students with learning problems:

1. *Problem solving.* Learning to solve problems by applying previously acquired information to new and different situations is one of the primary reasons for studying math. Problem solving involves solving verbal (text) problems as well as nonverbal problems.
2. *Communicating mathematical ideas.* Students must learn the language and notation of math. They should present math ideas via manipulative objects, drawings, writing, and speaking.
3. *Applying mathematics to everyday situations.* Students should be encouraged to translate daily experiences into mathematical representations (i.e., graphs, tables, diagrams, or math expressions) and interpret the results.
4. *Focusing on appropriate computational skills.* Students must gain proficiency in using operations (i.e., addition, subtraction, multiplication, division) with whole numbers and decimals. Knowledge of basic facts is essential, and mental arithmetic is important.

Daily living requires the application of math skills, for example, planning and monitoring time, computing percentages for on-sale purchases, making estimations, interpreting recipe measurements, measuring for carpet purchases, computing scores in games, handling banking transactions, and maintaining a checkbook.

Establish Goals and Expectancies

The teacher's effort to achieve an instructional match between student and task characteristics results in goal-setting. Thus, appropriate instructional goals are based on careful assessment of a student's learning needs. Basically, goals provide the basis for instruction. Student attention and achievement improve when teachers present clear goals and precise directions (Berliner, 1982). Moreover, goals communicate teacher expectancies, which, in turn, strongly influence student achievement. In their synthesis of research on good teaching, Porter and Brophy (1988) reported that good teachers are clear about their instructional goals and communicate both their expectancies and why the specific expectancies exist. In presenting goals, effective teachers explain what the student needs to do to achieve the goal and what he or she will learn in the process (Christenson, Ysseldyke, & Thurlow, 1989).

There is growing support for the premise that teachers tend to make goals too easy for students with learning problems (Anderson & Pellicer, 1990; Clifford, 1990; Fuchs, Fuchs, & Deno, 1985). Clifford (1990) reported that students need a challenge rather than easy success, and that tasks involving moderate risk-taking provide the best level of difficulty in setting goals. She recommended that instructional environments feature error tolerance and reward for error correction. A substantial research base (Locke & Latham, 1990; Locke, Shaw, Saari, & Latham, 1981) documents the premise that difficult but attainable goals lead to higher effort and achievement than do easier goals.

Provide Systematic and Explicit Instruction

Christenson et al. (1989) discussed four elements that relate to the quality of systematic instruction. First, a demonstration-prompt-practice sequence enhances student outcomes (Carroll, 1985; Rosenshine & Stevens, 1986). This sequence occurs within an interaction format that involves the active participation and involvement of students and active teaching and monitoring by teachers. Second, explicit instruction is important for facilitating positive academic growth. Explicitness involves highly organized, step-by-step presentations that identify the target skill, cover why the skill is important, and discuss when the skill is useful and how to apply it. Third, effective instruction enables students to understand the directions and demands of the task. It is not sufficient for teachers to assume that students understand. It is important for teachers to conduct periodic checks (especially during independent practice) to ensure that students understand directions and task demands (Good, 1983). Fourth, the systematic use of learning principles is characteristic of effective instruction. Positive student outcomes occur when attention is maintained, positive reinforcement is used, spaced and varied practice occurs, and motivation is high.

Numerous investigators (Blankenship & Lilly, 1981; Deshler, Schumaker, & Lenz, 1984; Rosenshine & Stevens, 1986) support the use of systematic instructional procedures. Rosenshine and Stevens reported that an efficient teaching process involves three steps: demonstration, guided practice with prompts and feedback, and independent practice with feedback. These steps, coupled with an advance organizer, are inherent in the validated teaching sequence developed at the University of Kansas Institute for Research in Learning Disabilities. Moreover, these procedures (i.e., demonstration and practice) are consistent with the emphasis on teaching mastery of the skill at a generalization level. Some research suggests that demonstration, modeling, and feedback enhance the acquisition and generalization of academic skills (Deshler et al., 1984).

Numerous researchers have used these steps, and variations of them, to produce excellent mathematics achievement with students who have learning problems. For example, Blankenship (1978), Sugai and Smith (1986), and Rivera and Smith (1987) used a demonstration and permanent model technique to teach computation skills to students with learning disabilities. The technique involved a step-by-step teacher demonstration with the teacher leaving the completed problem with the student for use as a permanent model. The demonstration and permanent model technique proved to be very effective with students with learning disabilities. Also, Rosenshine (1983) reported that an 80% accuracy rate during the learning of new material is an important factor in improving the performance of low-achieving students.

Teach Students to Understand Math Concepts

During the acquisition of a computational or problem-solving skill, it is essential that the student be instructed in such a way that understanding is assured. Many authorities (Reisman, 1982; Suydam & Higgins, 1977; Underhill, Uprichard, & Heddens, 1980) believe that the use of the concrete-representational-abstract (CRA) sequence is an excellent way to teach students with learning problems to understand math concepts, operations, and applications. Several research studies (Hudson, Peterson, Mercer, & McLeod, 1988; Mercer & Miller, 1991; Peterson et al., 1988) reveal that the CRA sequence is an effective way to teach math to students with learning problems. Results indicate that large numbers of formal experiences at the concrete and representational levels are not necessary for students with learning problems to understand the basic facts. In this research, within six 30-minute lessons (three concrete and three representational), students at risk for school failure and students with learning and emotional problems demonstrated an understanding of the targeted math concept and generalized their learning to abstract-level (numbers only) problems. Moreover, the students retained the targeted skills during follow-up testing.

The learning of concepts and rules is also germane to facilitating a student's understanding of math. If a student memorizes that $8 + 6$ is 14 but sees $6 + 8$ as a new problem to memorize, he or she needs to understand a basic concept (in this case, the commutative property of addition) to learn addition effectively. Likewise, if a student understands the inverse relationship of addition and subtraction (i.e., $a + b = c$; $c - b = a$), the learning of subtraction is facilitated. Moreover, the concept of place value is difficult for many students and deserves much teacher attention. Finally, rules such as "Any number times zero is zero" help with learning multiplication facts. Concrete and representational experiences are excellent for demonstrating concepts and rules to students.

Monitor Progress

Monitoring progress involves the teacher frequently checking on the behavior and academic work of students and making instructional adaptations based on observations, to ensure that an appropriate instructional match is being maintained. Good and Brophy (1986) noted that active, frequent monitoring is the key to student learning. Active monitoring includes checking to see if students understand the task requirements and the procedures needed to complete the task correctly. To check understanding, the teacher asks the student to demonstrate how to complete the task. When the student performs the task, the teacher is able to pinpoint errors and help the student make corrections. Because these procedures enable the teacher to catch errors prior to extensive practice, high success rates are maintained (Christenson et al., 1989). Moreover, Rieth and Evertson (1988) reported that active teacher monitoring (i.e., moving rapidly around the classroom, checking work, and engaging in substantive interactions with students) increases the on-task academic responding of students with learning problems. In a review of programs for at-risk students, Slavin and Madden (1989) reported that the most effective programs involve frequent assessment of student progress and use of the results to modify programs according to individual needs. In a review of academic monitoring procedures, Fuchs (1986) reported that when students' academic programs were systematically monitored and developed formatively over time, the students achieved an average of .7 standard deviation units higher (equivalent to 26 percentage points) than those students whose programs were not monitored systematically. The research is replete with the positive effects of monitoring the math progress of students with learning problems and giving feedback (Fuchs, 1986; Lloyd & Keller, 1989; Miller & Milam, 1987; Robinson, DePascale, & Roberts, 1989).

Provide Feedback

A significant finding of the Beginning Teacher Evaluation Study (Fisher et al., 1980) is that academic feedback is positively associated with student learning. Rieth and Evertson (1988) noted that all major reviews of effective teaching report that feedback is among the most essential teacher behaviors for promoting positive learning outcome. In a synthesis of research on good teaching, Porter and Brophy (1988) reported that good teachers monitor students' understanding via regular, appropriate feedback. Wang (1987) reported that feedback is important to promoting the following student outcomes: (a) mastery of content and skills for further learning, (b) ability to study and learn independently, (c) ability to plan and monitor learning activities, (d) motivation for continued learning, and (e) confidence in one's ability as a learner.

Gersten, Carnine, and Woodward (1987) reported that teachers who provide immediate corrective feedback on errors produce higher student achievement. Robinson et al. (1989) found that feedback helped students with learning disabilities complete more mathematics problems and improve accuracy from 73% to 94%. Moreover, Collins, Carnine, and Gersten (1987) noted that basic and elaborate feedback significantly improved student performance on reasoning skill tasks. In a comparison of basic and elaborative feedback, they found that elaborative feedback produced the greatest skill acquisition. Kline, Schumaker, and Deshler (1991) reported that elaborative feedback routines greatly improved the efficiency of academic instruction to students with learning disabilities. Although the literature is replete with studies that document the importance of feedback, studies analyzing the behavior of general and special education teachers report low frequencies of feedback to special education students (Rieth & Evertson, 1988).

Teach to Mastery

In this discussion, *mastery learning* refers to teaching a skill to a level of automaticity, which is usually obtained when an individual continuously responds to math problems without hesitating to think about computing the answer. (Most people operate at a level of automaticity when responding to questions such as "What is your address?" or "What is 6 + 2?") Rate of responding is regarded as an effective measure of automaticity (Hasselbring, Goin, & Bransford, 1987; Kirby & Becker, 1988; Lovitt, 1989). Reaching mastery on a skill provides numerous benefits, including improved retention and ability to compute and/or solve higher level problems. Other benefits include finishing timed tests, completing homework faster, receiving higher grades, and developing positive feelings about math.

Before mastery instruction or techniques are used, it is essential that the student possess the preskills and understand the concept related to the targeted skill. Once an understanding of a skill is achieved, mastery-level instruction becomes appropriate. Independent practice is the primary instructional format used to acquire mastery. Given that practice can become boring, the teacher must put forth an effort to make practice interesting or fun. Instructional games, peer teaching, computer-assisted instruction, self-correcting materials, and reinforcement are helpful in planning practice-to-mastery activities.

In establishing mastery rate levels for individuals, it is important to consider the learner's characteristics (e.g., age, academic skill, motor ability). For most students, a rate of 40 to 60 correct digits per minute with two or fewer errors is appropriate. Once a mastery level is achieved, the teacher and student are able to move to the next level skill with appropriate preskills and more confidence.

Teach Problem Solving

Since the National Council of Teachers of Mathematics (1980) made a statement noting that problem solving should be a top priority in math instruction, it has received more attention. Although problem solving has received a decade of attention from educators, its exact nature remains ambiguous (Engelmann, Carnine, & Steely, 1991). From an inspection of 10 books and problem-solving articles about students with learning problems, 37 different descriptors of problem solving were identified (Mercer, 1992). In addition, no definitions were offered, although some authors did infer that problem solving is analogous to doing word problems. The National Council of Teachers of Mathematics (1989) described problem solving as it relates to word problems and computation problems. It seems reasonable that a problem-solving activity is needed for any task that is difficult for the student. Thus, computation and word problems could both require problem-solving procedures. For skills in which automaticity has been achieved, problem solving is probably not a necessary procedure.

Most authorities (Cawley et al., 1987; Fleischner, Nuzum, & Marzola, 1987; Kameenui & Simmons, 1990) interpret problem solving within the context of word problems. From an analysis of the literature, it is apparent that problem solving includes some unifying components; for example, the student must (a) have a mathematical knowledge base, (b) apply acquired knowledge to new and unfamiliar situations, and (c) actively engage in thinking processes. These thinking processes involve recognizing a problem, planning a procedural strategy, examining the math relationships in the problem, determining the mathematical knowledge needed to solve the problem, representing the problem graphically, generating the equation, estimating the answer, sequencing the computation steps, computing the answer, checking the answer for reasonableness, self-monitoring the entire process, and exploring alternative ways to solve the problem.

Fortunately, in spite of the complexity of the concept, the problem-solving emphasis is generating research that provides insights into how to reach students with learning problems to solve word problems (Case & Harris, 1988; Montague & Bos, 1986; Nuzum, 1983). Paralleling the emphasis on problem solving has been a focus on strategy instruction. In this instruction, a strategy is taught that helps the student engage in the appropriate steps needed to recognize and successfully solve a word problem.

Teach Generalization

Generalization refers to the performance of the targeted behavior in different, non-training conditions (i.e., across subjects, settings, people, behaviors, and/or time) that do not involve the same events that were present in the training conditions (Stokes & Baer, 1977). Students with learning problems typically have difficulty generalizing skills. A lack of instruction aimed at teaching these students to generalize math skills has contributed to their generalization problems. Ellis, Lenz, and Sabornie (1987a, 1987b) reported that generalization must be taught throughout the instructional process. Selected instructional practices to help students generalize math skills include:

1. Develop motivation to learn. It is believed that students who desire to learn a skill or strategy are most likely to generalize it. Motivation helps students feel responsible for their own learning and helps establish the independence needed to apply the new skill in settings without teacher support.
2. Throughout the instructional process, hold periodic discussions with students about the rationale for learning the math skill and in which situations (e.g., homework, recreational activities, shopping, etc.) it is useful.
3. Throughout the instructional process, provide students with a variety of examples and experiences. For example, vary the manipulative objects (such as cubes, checkers, and buttons) in concrete activities, and use a variety of pictures, drawings, and tallies in representational activities.
4. Teach skills to a mastery level so students can concentrate on using, rather than remembering, the skill.

5. Teach students to solve problems pertinent to their daily lives. This connects the skill to functional uses and promotes motivation and the need to generalize.

Promote a Positive Attitude Toward Math

Many students with learning problems have a history of mathematics failures. Consequently, they develop negative attitudes toward math learning and feel insecure about their capabilities to succeed in math. Attitudes, beliefs, and motivation play an important role in the learning of math. The National Council of Teachers of Mathematics (1989) and the National Council of Supervisors of Mathematics (1988) stressed the need to focus on the affective side of mathematics instruction. It is apparent that math instruction must be designed to ensure success and promote positive attitudes. Selected guidelines for promoting positive attitudes toward math learning include the following:

1. Involve students in setting challenging but attainable instructional goals. Goal-setting exerts a powerful influence on student involvement and effort (Locke & Latham, 1990).
2. Provide students with success via building on prior skills and using task analysis to simplify the instructional sequence of a math skill or concept.
3. Use progress charts to provide students with feedback on how well they are doing.
4. Discuss the relevance of a math skill to real-life problems. Use word problems that are part of a student's daily life.
5. Communicate positive expectancies of students' abilities to learn. Students need to sense that the teacher believes they will achieve in math.
6. Help students understand the idea that their own effort affects outcomes regarding achievement. Constantly point out that what they do influences both their success and their failure. This helps students realize that their behavior directly influences what happens to them and, consequently, that they are in control of their own learning.
7. Model an enthusiastic and positive attitude toward math and maintain a lively pace during math instruction.
8. Reinforce students for effort on math work.

Basic Math Facts and Students with Learning Problems

Math has a logical structure. Students construct simple relationships first and then progress to more complex tasks. As the student progresses in this ordering of math tasks, the learning of skills and content transfers from each step to the next. Reisman and Kauffman (1980) discussed the progression of math learning and its relationship to cognitive factors. The abilities to form and remember associations, understand basic relationships, and make simple generalizations appear to be basic cognitive factors that are needed before formal math instruction begins (Bartel, 1990). More complex cognitive factors are needed as the student progresses from lower level math skills to higher order ones. Moreover, the mastery of such lower level skills is essential to learning higher order ones; thus, the concept of *learning readiness* is important in math instruction. In their *Twelve Components of Essential Mathematics*, the National Council of Supervisors of Mathematics (1988) highlighted the need for students to be knowledgeable about basic facts and proficient in basic operations (addition, subtraction, multiplication, division). Many authorities (Kirby & Becker, 1988; Reisman, 1982; Underhill et al., 1980) claim that failure to understand basic concepts in beginning math instruction contributes heavily to later learning problems. Unfortunately, many students with learning problems fail to achieve an understanding of basic math facts or develop fluency in using facts.

Cox (1975) conducted a study of error patterns across skill and ability levels among students with and without disabilities. She found that the average percentages of systematic errors in multiplication and division were much higher for exceptional education students compared to nondisabled students. The majority of errors for all students occurred because of a failure to understand the concepts of multiplication and division. Moreover, Cox found that without intervention, many of these youngsters persisted in making the same systematic errors for a long period of time.

In a study of multiplication and division errors committed by students with learning disabilities, Miller and Milam (1987) found that the majority of the errors were due to a lack of prerequisite skills. Errors in multiplication were primarily due to a lack of knowledge of multiplication facts and inadequate addition skills. Errors in division included many subtraction and multiplication errors. The most frequent error in division was failure to include the remainder in the quotient. Miller and Milam concluded,

> Many of the errors discovered in this study indicated a lack of student readiness for the type of tasks required. Students were evidently not being allowed to learn and practice the skills necessary for higher order operations. The implications are obvious: students must be allowed to learn in a stepwise fashion or they will not learn at all. (p. 121)

Fleischner, Garnett, and Shepherd (1982) noted that the inability to acquire and maintain math facts at fluency levels sufficient for acquiring higher level math skills is common among students with learning problems. De Corte and Verschaffel (1981) and Russell and Ginsburg (1984) reported that unfamiliarity with basic number facts plays a major role in the math difficulties of students with math learning problems. Other researchers (Garnett & Fleischner, 1983; Thornton & Toohey, 1985) report that many students with learning disabilities lack proficiency in basic number facts. They note that these youngsters are unable to retrieve answers to math facts efficiently.

As noted previously, it is anticipated that reforms in math education will increase the overall complexity of the mathematics curriculum. It is essential that general and special educators work together to ensure that students with learning problems do not become victims of instructional reforms that are insensitive to their unique learning and emotional needs. Cawley and Miller (1989) reported that students with learning disabilities are capable of making progress in math throughout the school years, and comprehensive programming is needed to ensure their math progress. Given the problems that students with learning problems exhibit with lower level math skills (many students do not know the 390 basic math facts after 5 or more years of school) and the importance of these skills in overall math achievement, it is apparent that comprehensive programming to teach basic math facts is needed.

Strategic Math Series: Programming for Teaching Basic Math Facts

Educators who have examined the mathematical deficits of students have suggested a number of initial teaching and remediation methods. Many of these methods feature the concrete-representational-abstract teaching sequence that has been found to facilitate math learning. Implicit in this method of instruction is an emphasis on teaching students to understand the concepts of mathematics prior to memorizing facts, algorithms, and operations. Although the CRA sequence is widely advocated for mathematical learning, it is rarely used in a systematic manner during math instruction. The Strategic Math Series (SMS) (Mercer & Miller, 1991) provides a systematic means of CRA instruction.

According to the CRA sequence, instruction begins at the *concrete level*, where the student uses three-dimensional objects to solve computation problems. For example, in solving the problem 5 2, the student is instructed to look at the first number, 5, and count that many groups, using circles or paper plates to represent the groups. Next, the student is instructed to look at the second number, 2, and place that many objects in each group (i.e., circle or plate). After being instructed to count or add the number of objects in all the circles, 10, the student says and writes the answer to the problem. After successfully solving several multiplication problems at the concrete level, the student proceeds to the representational level.

At the representational level, drawings are used to solve computation problems. For example, in solving the problem 7 3, the student is instructed to look at the first number, 7, and draw that many groups using circles, Next, the student is instructed to look at the second number, 3, and draw three tallies in each circle. The student then counts the tallies in the circles, 21, to arrive at the answer. Finally, the student says and writes the answer to the problem. After successfully solving several multiplication problems at this level, the student begins to work at the next level, the *abstract level*.

At the abstract level, the student looks at the computation problem and tries to solve it without using objects or drawings. The student reads the problem, remembers the answer or thinks of a way to compute the answer, and writes the answer. No objects or drawings are used in the computation unless the student is unable to answer a problem. Because success in math requires the ability to solve problems at the abstract level, it is essential that students achieve mastery at this level.

The Instructional Sequence

As presented in Table 9.1, the instructional sequence of SMS is divided into seven phases with 21 basic lessons. Student completion of all 21 lessons is important for two reasons. First, the lessons are sequenced and build upon each other in terms of complexity. Second, although most students acquire the respective computation skill (e.g., multiplication facts) when they reach the posttest, they need additional practice to maintain their knowledge and skills, to increase their fluency, and to ensure further development of their problem-solving skills.

Phase 1: Pretest

During this instructional phase a pretest is administered to the student to determine whether instruction is needed. Before the pretest, a rationale for assessing the respective basic facts is discussed with the student. If his or her score on the pretest falls below the mastery criterion (i.e., 80%), the student is informed that he or she needs to work on the targeted basic facts. The need for instruction is discussed, and a commitment to learn is obtained from the student via a signed contract.

Phase 2: Teach Concrete Application

The concrete phase of instruction includes Lessons 1 through 3. For each lesson, a sample script and learning sheets guide the teacher through the instructional sequence. During these lessons, students manipulate concrete objects to solve basic facts on their learning sheets. (A separate curriculum manual is used for each skill area—for example, addition, subtraction, multiplication, or division.) Students also begin to solve word problems in which the numbers are vertically aligned, but blank spaces are provided after the numbers for students to write the name of the manipulative object (see Table 9.2). These concrete lessons act as a springboard for learning facts at the representational and abstract levels.

Table 9.1 *Instructional Phases of the Strategic Math Series*

Phase	Purpose	Lessons
1	Pretest	Pretest Lesson
2	Teach concrete application	Lessons 1–3
3	Teach representational application	Lessons 4–6
4	Introduce the DRAW strategy	Lesson 7
5	Teach abstract application	Lessons 8–10
6	Posttest	Posttest Lesson
7	Provide practice to fluency	Lessons 11–21

■■■ **Table 9.2** *Multiplication Problem-solving Sequence in Strategic Math Series*

Lesson and Description	Example	Lesson and Description	Example
Lessons 1–3 (two word problems)		**Lessons 9–10 (three word problems)**	
A computation problem is presented with the word *groups* written to the right of the first number and blanks beside the second number and the answer space.	6 groups of 3 _____ _____	A computation problem is presented with a noun or phrase (adjective-noun) written to the right of the first and second numbers and the answer space.	6 brown bags × 3 red apples red apples
The student writes the name of the manipulative objects used in the lesson in the blanks, solves the problem, and reads the statement, "Six groups of 3 checkers is 18 checkers."	6 groups of 3 checkers 18 checkers	The student solves the problem and reads the statement, "Six brown bags of 3 red apples is 18 red apples."	6 brown bags × 3 red apples 18 red apples
Lessons 4–6 (two word problems)		**Lesson 11 (three word problems)**	
A computation problem is presented with the word groups written to the right of the first number and blanks beside the second number and the answer space.	6 groups of 3 _____ 18 _____	A computation problem is presented with words on both sides of the numbers and the answer space. The numbers remain lined up in a vertical format.	Sue has 6 bags of 3 apples. She has __ apples.
The student writes the name of the drawings used in the respective lesson in the blanks, solves the problem, and reads the statement, "Six groups of 3 circles is 18 circles."	6 groups of 3 circles 18 circles	The student solves the problem and reads the statement.	Sue has 6 bags of 3 apples. She has __ apples.
Lesson 7 (no word problems)		**Lesson 12 (three word problems)**	
Lesson 8 (two word problems)		A regular sentence word problem is presented in which the numbers are not aligned.	Sue has 6 bags. There are 3 apples in each bag. How many apples does Sue have?
A computation problem is presented with the word groups written to the right of the first number and common words written to the right of the second number and the answer space.	6 groups × 3 apples apples	The student solves the problem and writes the equation.	6 x 3 = 18
The student solves the problem and reads the statement, "Six groups of 3 apples is 18 apples."	6 groups × 3 apples 18 apples	**Lesson 13 (three word problems)**	
		A sentence word problem including extraneous information is presented.	Sue has 6 bags. There are 3 apples in each bag. Bill has 2 pet turtles. How many apples does Sue have?

(continued)

◾ **Table 9.2** *(continued)*

Lesson and Description	Example	Lesson and Description	Example
(Lesson 13 continued)		Lessons 15–21 (three problems)	
The student crosses out the extraneous information, solves the problem, and writes the equation.	Sue has 6 bags. There are 3 apples in each bag. *Bill has 2 pet turtles.* How many apples does Sue have?	Three types of word problems are presented, each including: 1 problem without extraneous information 1 problem with extraneous information 1 problem to be created by the student	
Lesson 14 (three problems) The student is instructed to write or dictate his or her own multiplication word problems.	_____ _____ _____ _____	The student writes or dictates the "creation" problem, solves the problem, and writes the equation.	
The student writes or dictates a multiplication word problem, solves the problem, and writes the equation.	There are 3 puppies. Each puppy has 2 spots. How many spots are there altogether? $3 \times 2 = 6$		

Phase 3: Teach Representational Application

The representational phase of instruction includes Lessons 4 through 6. Again, a sample script and learning sheets guide the teacher through each lesson. In this phase, students use drawings and tallies to solve basic facts on their learning sheets. Moreover, they continue to solve word problems in which the numbers are vertically aligned, but now they fill in the blanks after the numbers with the name of the drawing (see Table 9.2). Representational lessons help students understand the respective facts as they move toward the abstract level.

Phase 4: Introduce the "DRAW" Strategy

Many students with learning difficulties are passive when faced with a problem-solving situation (i.e., they tend to guess or quit working). However, these same students can become active, independent learners when they master a problem-solving strategy to facilitate computation. Thus, Lesson 7 introduces a math strategy called DRAW to help students solve facts at the abstract level. Each letter of DRAW cues students to perform certain procedures:

1. *D*iscover the sign.
2. *R*ead the problem.
3. *A*nswer, or DRAW a conceptual representation of the problem using lines and tallies, and check.
4. *W*rite the answer.

Phase 5: Teach Abstract Application

This phase of instruction is presented in Lessons 8 through 10. For each lesson, a script guides the teacher through the instructional sequence. Again, a learning sheet is provided to facilitate continued student practice of the targeted facts. During this time, students use the DRAW Strategy to solve abstract-level problems when they are unable to recall an answer. Students also begin to solve word problems in which the numbers are still vertically aligned but now include the names of common objects or phrases after the numbers instead of blank spaces (see Table 9.2).

Phase 6: Posttest

During this phase of instruction, a posttest is administered to each student to determine whether he or she has learned the basic facts and is ready to proceed to the phase of instruction designed to increase fluency (speed of computation) and further develop problem-solving skills. If the student's score on the posttest is below 90% he or she repeats one or more of Lessons 8 through 10. When the student achieves a score of 90% or higher, the teacher informs the student that he or she is doing well and is ready for lessons in which students learn to increase their computation speed and solve more challenging word problems. The teacher also explains the need to solve facts at a rate that ensures success in various situations (e.g., classroom tests, classroom seatwork, homework, shopping, minimum competency tests, basal tests, and standardized tests).

Phase 7: Provide Practice to Fluency

The practice to fluency phase takes place in Lessons 11 through 21. Each lesson features a script to guide the teacher through the instructional sequence, plus a learning sheet to facilitate student practice of facts and word problems. Students work on three primary skills: (a) solving word problems, which become increasingly complicated as the lessons progress; (b) increasing the rate at which they can compute facts; and (c) discriminating previously learned facts from the newly acquired facts and accurately computing those problems.

To help students solve more complicated word problems, specific practice is provided in Lessons 11 through 21. Problems are presented in sentence form (as opposed to the numbers being vertically aligned with phrases written to the right of the numbers). As the lessons progress, students learn to filter out extraneous information and to create their own word problems (see Table 9.2).

To help students increase their rate of computation, a 1-minute timed probe, called *Addition, Subtraction, Multiplication,* or *Division Minute,* is given during selected lessons of this phase. A student is considered to be fluent or to have reached mastery on the Minute probes when he or she is able to write the answers to problems at the rate of 30 digits per minute with no more than two errors.

Finally, to help students discriminate between types of facts, during selected lessons of this phase all students receive a one-page Facts Review, containing two or more types of facts. Such practice not only checks the student's ability to discriminate facts when presented on the same page, but also provides important practice of previously learned facts.

The Instructional Procedures

To help teach basic facts, all lessons include a sequence of procedures that has proven to be effective with students who have learning difficulties. The primary instructional procedures are as follows: Give an Advance Organizer, Describe and Model, Conduct Guided Practice, Conduct Independent Practice, Conduct Problem-Solving Practice, Administer Minute Probe, Administer Facts Review, Conduct Pig Game Practice, and Provide Feedback.

Give an Advance Organizer

The first component in each lesson, the Advance Organizer, prepares the student for specific lesson activities. As presented in this curriculum, the Advance Organizer serves three purposes: (a) It connects the existing lesson to the previous lesson, (b) it identifies the target lesson skill, and (c) it provides a rationale for learning the skill.

Describe and Model

The Describe and Model section follows the Advance Organizer section in Lessons 1 through 10 only. Because students usually understand the target facts by Lesson 10, demonstrations are no longer necessary after Lesson 10. As a result, this section is omitted in Lessons 11 through 21.

The Describe and Model component provides the teacher with an opportunity to describe and model the computation process, following two basic procedures. In Procedure 1, the teacher asks and answers questions aloud while demonstrating how to compute the answer for one or more problems on the learning sheet. In computing the problem, the teacher verbalizes his or her thoughts so students can better understand the thought processes involved. When the teacher arrives at an answer, he or she tells students the answer and instructs them to write it on their learning sheets. To enhance generalization across stimulus configurations, both horizontally and vertically configured problems are used as bases for the teacher's demonstrations.

In Procedure 2, the teacher continues to demonstrate how to solve one or more problems. While doing so, she or he asks questions and solicits student responses, using prompts and cues to facilitate correct responses. Thus, in Procedure 2, the teacher and the students work a problem together. When an answer is computed, the students say the answer and write it on their learning sheets. Again, to enhance generalization across stimulus configurations, both horizontally and vertically configured problems are used.

Conduct Guided Practice

Guided Practice follows the Describe and Model procedures in Lessons 1 through 10 only. Students solve facts independently by Lesson 11; thus, Guided Practice is not included in Lessons 11 through 21. Guided Practice provides the teacher with the opportunity to instruct and support students as they move toward solving problems on their learning sheets independently. To enhance generalization across stimulus configurations, problems are written in both horizontal and vertical formats. During this time, the teacher follows two basic procedures designed to facilitate student independence in computing subtraction problems.

In Procedure 1, the teacher's role is to prompt and facilitate students' thought processes. Thus, the teacher no longer demonstrates the process unless further demonstration appears necessary. To facilitate correct responses, the teacher asks questions and solicits student responses, using prompts and cues. Through the use of this procedure, students are guided through each problem in a way that ensures success.

In Procedure 2, the teacher instructs students to solve the next few problems on the learning sheet, and offers assistance to individual learners only if needed. Thus, the teacher's role now is to step back, monitor student work, and provide assistance with thought processes only if needed.

Conduct Independent Practice

Independent Practice of facts is an integral component of the 21 basic lessons. It enables the teacher to determine if students can independently solve problems. The scripts for this component consist of simple directions, including a statement that reminds students to use previously learned skills and techniques to solve problems. During this time, the teacher does not provide any assistance.

Conduct Problem-Solving Practice

Like Independent Practice of computation facts, Problem-Solving Practice is an integral component of all lessons. To teach students the thought process involved in problem solving, the teacher uses a graduated sequence of word problems. For example, in Lesson 1, students begin solving problems involving three words, and by Lesson 21 they are writing their own word problems. Along the way, students learn to extract any information that is irrelevant to a problem. Thus, when they complete a facts program, they are able to solve word problems with and without extraneous information and to write their own word problems.

Administer Minute Probe

To help students increase their rate of computation, a 1-minute timed probe is given to them during Lessons 11, 13, 15, 16, 18, 20, and 21. (Depending on the needs of the students, the probe may be given during additional lessons in this phase.) The purpose of this probe is to provide the student with independent practice in quickly computing the respective facts. A student is considered to be fluent or to have reached mastery on a probe when he or she is able to write the answers to problems at the rate of 30 digits per minute with no more than two errors. For students with fine motor problems, this rate may be modified. Because each student is unique, some students will achieve mastery on the probe before completing all 21 lessons, while others will need to extend practice beyond the 21st lesson.

Once students have achieved mastery on their probe, instruction is altered in two ways. First, students who have reached mastery are allowed to skip the Independent Practice of computation facts in all following lessons, but not the Problem-Solving Practice. Second, after mastery is reached, the students' computation rates are checked using a probe at least every three lessons to ensure maintenance.

Administer Facts Review

To help students discriminate different facts from each other, a one-page Facts Review, containing both newly acquired and previously learned facts, is given to all students in Lessons 14, 17, and 19. (Again, depending on individual students' needs, the Facts Review may be given during additional lessons in this phase.) Such practice not only acts as an independent check of the student's ability to discriminate facts when presented on the same page, but also provides important practice of previously learned addition facts.

Conduct Pig Game Practice

Beginning in Lesson 11 and continuing through Lesson 21, additional practice of the respective facts is encouraged on the learning sheets under the heading, "Pig Game Practice." These problems are to be completed while playing one of several "Pig Games." These games feature the use of dice that include five numbers and one pig drawing on each die. The chance factor of the game (e.g., losing a turn, gaining an extra roll of the dice) is involved when the pig drawing appears. Although considered to be optional activities, Pig Games serve as an entertaining way to further practice the target facts.

Provide Feedback

Because proper feedback is critical to learning, a feedback component is found in all 21 lessons. This component allows the teacher to recognize and praise correct student responses, thereby preventing future errors. Feedback is facilitated through use of the Facts Progress Chart, whereby the teacher and the student plot the student's scores for the last 10 problems on a learning sheet, plus the total number of completed problems on the Minute Probe and the Facts Review.

Research has shown that if teachers follow certain steps when giving corrective feedback, students will reach mastery in half the instructional time otherwise required when the steps are not used (Kline et al., 1991). Thus, the steps are important when giving feedback about a student's learning sheet, Minute Probe, or Facts Review. To further facilitate student learning during instruction, the teacher should decrease her or his involvement in each phase of the feedback process and increase the students' involvement in assessing their progress through questioning techniques. The steps are as follows:

1. *Score the product for correct and incorrect responses; determine the total percentage of correct responses.* Ideally, scoring is completed as soon as the student has turned in the product. The teacher ensures that students understand the scoring system—how he or she marks errors, indicates the total number of correct and incorrect responses, and obtains the final percentage score.

2. *Individually meet with each student; help the students plot their scores on Progress Charts.* At the beginning of each meeting, the teacher makes at least one specific, positive statement about the student's work. For example, "John, you've really got a good handle on subtracting zero from any number." Next, the teacher helps the student plot his or her score on the Progress Chart. The teacher compares the student's score to the mastery goal line, noting any progress.

3. *Specify incorrect responses and corresponding error patterns, if they exist.* The teacher explains where errors have occurred and tries to avoid using the word you. For example, the teacher says, "These problems are incorrect." If an error pattern exists, the teacher might say something like, "John, I've noticed that these problems involving the number 9 are incorrect."

4. *Show the student how to perform the task.* For at least one problem missed, the teacher shows the student how to compute the problem correctly using the most recently instructed phase of the CRA sequence. For example, the teacher demonstrates how to compute the problem with concrete objects if she or he has been teaching the concrete lessons, with pictures or tallies if she or he has been teaching the representational lessons, or with the DRAW Strategy if she or he has been teaching the abstract lessons.

5. *Ask the student to practice the application.* The teacher asks the student to show how he or she will proceed in the future, using a different problem. "Okay, John, now you try it using this problem. Think aloud so I can hear your thoughts as you do the problem." The teacher checks to see that the student correctly applies the current phase of the CRA sequence.

6. *Close the feedback session.* The teacher makes a positive statement about the student's performance in the feedback process and notes expectations for the future, for example, "John, you've done a super job and I know that the next time you see a 0, you'll do great."

Relationship of SMS and Components of Effective Math Instruction

An inspection of Table 9.3 reveals how the 10 components of effective math instruction were incorporated into the SMS instructional design. For each component, SMS includes from one to six instructional procedures or activities. Placement of effective teaching routines within a curriculum helps teachers translate research into classroom practices. In addition to facilitating best practices in math instruction, this procedure enabled teachers to provide feedback concerning how to improve the application of the components in their classrooms.

Strategic Math Series: Field Test Results
Concrete-Representational-Abstract Sequence

Although the CRA instructional sequence has been recommended in the math literature for decades, limited empirical data exist to support it. Thus, the initial stage of

Table 9.3 *Research Areas of Effective Math Instruction and Related SMS Curriculum Components*

Research Areas	Related Curriculum Components
Select appropriate math content	A graduated word problem sequence is used. Use of the mnemonic DRAW activates computation strategies. Computation problems are solved via objects, pictures, drawings, and numbers. Word problems are created. Basic facts are the target skill.
Establish goals and expectancies	Pretest ensures essential preskills. Pretest establishes need for target skill. Student signs a commitment to learn. Mastery or goal criteria are set. Progress on each goal is monitored.
Provide systematic and explicit instruction	Each lesson features the following steps: give an advance organizer, describe and model, conduct guided practice, conduct independent practice, and provide feedback.
Teach students to understand math concepts	The instructional sequence features the CRA sequence and the teaching of relationships and rules.
Monitor progress	Progress of each lesson is monitored on a chart. Percentage and rate scores are monitored against a mastery criterion.
Provide feedback	A teacher-directed, six-step elaborated feedback routine is used in each lesson.
Teach to mastery	After an understanding of the targeted concept is achieved, practice-to-mastery lessons are used to achieve a fluency criterion.
Teach problem solving	Problem-solving activities are used in each lesson. Students learn to solve problems with and without extraneous information and to create their own word problems.

(continued)

■ **Table 9.3** *(continued)*

Research Areas	Related Curriculum Components
Teach generalization	Students are provided multiple examples of the targeted math concept at the concrete, representational, and abstract levels. Problems are presented in vertical and horizontal formats. Students learn to a mastery criterion. Teachers and peers provide instruction. Rationales for the skill are discussed in each lesson.
Promote a positive attitude toward math	Success on each lesson is facilitated via explicit and carefully sequenced instruction. Goal-setting and goal attainment are included in each lesson. Elaborated feedback is provided in each lesson. Targeted math concepts are applied to students' daily lives. Practice-to-mastery activities feature high interest formats (e.g., Pig Games, peer teaching). Charts of progress provide visual displays of progress and encourage students to comprehend the relationship between their behavior and learning outcomes.

field-testing the Strategic Math Series involved testing the effectiveness of the CRA sequence.

A curriculum consisting of three concrete lessons, three representational lessons, and three abstract lessons was designed. Each lesson included a script that featured the following instructional sequence: Give an advance organizer, describe and model, conduct guided practice, conduct independent practice, and provide feedback. The lessons were used to teach place value (ones and tens) and basic facts (addition, subtraction, multiplication, and division) to students with learning problems. Each student was given a pretest, a posttest, and a retention test. The retention test was administered 5 to 10 school days after instruction was terminated. The results of the place value instruction are reported in several sources (Hudson et al., 1988; Peterson et al., 1988), and a summary of the place value data is presented in Table 9.4. The findings indicate that the mean gain on the place value scores was 68% and the mean retention score was 8% higher than the mean posttest score. The sample included 21 students with learning disabilities, 3 students with emotional handicaps, and 6 students identified as at risk for academic failure. Altogether, six teachers participated in field-testing place value. Given that students across all teachers and settings made substantial gains in 4 hours of instruction (nine lessons, 30 minutes each), it was concluded that the CRA sequence holds promise for teaching place value.

Table 9.4 *Field-Test Results of CRA Sequence of Place Value and Basic Facts*

	Pretest	**Posttest**	**Retention**
Place value	20% $n = 30$	88% $n = 30$	96% $n = 30$
Basic facts	16% $n = 40$	86% $n = 40$	82% $n = 36$

Next, the CRA sequence was tested for teaching basic facts (addition, subtraction, multiplication, and division). Again, nine scripted lessons were tested, and pretest, posttest, and retention measures were used. The results reported in Table 9.4 indicate a mean percentage increase of 70% from pretest to posttest. Also, the mean retention score reveals that the posttest achievement level was maintained. Altogether, eight teachers participated in the field testing. The student sample included 18 students identified as at risk for academic failure, 15 as learning disabled, 4 as emotionally disabled, and 3 as severely emotionally disturbed. Because the students made substantial gains across all teachers and settings with a 4 hours of instruction, it was concluded that the CRA sequence is effective for teaching the acquisition of basic facts. These results led to the inclusion of the CRA sequence in the Strategic Math Series curriculum for teaching basic facts.

Basic Facts Curriculum

The Strategic Math Series curriculum for basic facts has been field-tested primarily in special education settings. A total of 22 teachers from seven Florida school districts used SMS. Of the 109 elementary students who participated, 102 were identified as learning disabled, 5 as emotionally handicapped, and 2 as at risk for school failure. Field testing took place in small group (less than 7 students) and large group (7 to 18 students) instructional arrangements. Of the 22 teachers who participated, 21 (96%) indicated they would use the SMS curriculum again. Of the 75 students who were asked to complete follow-up questionnaires, 60% rated SMS as better than other math instruction and 31% rated it as equal to other math instruction. Thus, 91% rated the curriculum as equal to or better than other math instruction. Given the teacher and student satisfaction, it was concluded that SMS has positive consumer satisfaction.

Computation Acquisition and Generalization Data

Inspection of the results in Table 9.5 indicates that students were able to acquire the respective facts within Lessons 1 through 10 (i.e., 5 hours of instruction). For example, the total mean scores demonstrate that the average gain across skills was 59%. Moreover, the findings reveal that the students in the subtraction and multiplication groups were able to apply the DRAW Strategy to solve computation problems that they were not taught. For example, during the DRAW lesson, the students were taught to solve 3   4 by drawing lines to represent groups, and tallies to represent the number in each group:

$$3 \quad 4 = \frac{/\ /\ /\ /}{/\ /\ /\ /} = 12$$

After the completion of all 21 lessons, students were asked to solve multiplication operations such as 12   3. Of the 65 students in multiplication and subtraction who were tested for the response generalization task, 62 performed the task successfully. Moreover, generalization testing was conducted by examiners whom the students did not know, in library, cafeteria, or classroom settings.

Word Problem Data

An examination of Table 9.5 indicates that students in subtraction and multiplication were able to learn word problems successfully. The pretest was conducted prior to Lesson 1, and the posttest was administered within 1 to 5 days after Lesson 21 was completed. The posttest included two problems with extraneous information and two problems without extraneous information, and it required the students to create two word problems and solve them. The posttest was conducted in library, cafeteria, or classroom settings by examiners whom the students did not know.

Table 9.5 *Percentage Scores for Computation and Word Problem Data*

	Computation			Word Problem	
Fact	**Pretest**	**Posttest**	**Generalization**	**Pretest**	**Posttest**
Addition 0–9	40 $n = 4$	98 $n = 4$			
Subtraction 0–9	17 $n = 14$	95 $n = 14$	92 $n = 13$	28 $n = 9$	84 $n = 9$
Multiplication	43 $n = 52$	91 $n = 52$	96 $n = 52$	36 $n = 40$	92 $n = 40$
Division	9 $n = 19$	81 $n = 19$			
Total	32 $n = 89$	91 $n = 89$	95 $n = 65$	34 $n = 49$	91 $n = 49$

Note: The number of students in addition is low because fewer students in the field-test sites needed instruction in that skill. Data are not reported in selected areas due to absences, school-wide testing, field trips, and the ending of the school year.

Computation Mastery Data

The initial rate data were collected after Lesson 8 (the first abstract lesson), and the posttest rate data were collected after Lesson 21. The follow-up data were gathered in library, cafeteria, or classroom settings 3 to 5 days after Lesson 21 by examiners whom the students did not know. Inspection of Table 9.6 indicates that the students were able to increase their rates for all skills. Across all skills the mean rate improvement was 132% after Lessons 9 through 12. Given that 15% to 25% weekly improvement is considered an excellent criterion for improving rate of correct responses (White & Haring, 1980), these data are very positive. The mean weekly percentage increase was 51 across skills, with a range of 31% to 69%. In multiplication, the students significantly reduced their error rates and increased their digits-correct rates. In other skill areas, the beginning error rates were minimal. These data suggest that the students need additional practice to reach the target rate of 30 digits correct per minute with two or fewer errors.

Data Summary

Overall, the field test data indicate that students with learning problems were able to (a) acquire computational skills across facts, (b) solve word problems with and without extraneous information, (c) create word problems involving facts, (d) apply

Table 9.6 *Rate-Per-Minute Scores for Mastery Data*

Fact	Pretest	Posttest	Rate Correct Increase Follow-up	% Increase Per Week	Total % Per Week	Increase
Addition 0–9	10/.5 n = 8	18/.1 n = 8	18/0 n = 8	3.1	31	80
Subtraction 0–9	11/.9 n = 28	24/.4 n = 28	18/.6 n = 5	4.8	45	118
Multiplication	5/8 n = 46	14/2 n = 46	14/2 n = 37	3.5	69	180
Division	8/.6 n = 13	15/.4 n = 123		2.7	34	88
Totals	7.6/4 n = 95	17.6/1.2 n = 95	15/1.6 n = 45	3.8	51	132

Note: Number/number represents correct responses/incorrect responses.

a mnemonic strategy to difficult problems, (e) increase rate of computation, and (f) generalize math skills across examiners, settings, and tasks.

These results were obtained with each student receiving approximately 11 hours of instruction within a group setting. This finding is significant in that many students with learning problems continue to have difficulty with these skills after years of traditional instruction. Moreover, consumer satisfaction data from teachers and students were positive. Finally, teachers in the field-test sites provided many recommendations for making SMS more "user friendly." Their changes have been incorporated into revised teacher manuals.

Discussion

The SMS for basic facts represents an effort to incorporate research-based instructional factors into a curriculum for students with learning problems. The results of field testing indicate that SMS holds promise for teaching students with learning problems to acquire and understand basic facts and to apply them in problem-solving activities. Although these field test results are encouraging, several issues and questions need to be addressed

1. The establishment of a rate criterion for mastery remains difficult. There is much variability in the findings on the fluency rate of specific math skills; however, the rate of 30 correct digits per minute with two or fewer errors is at the lower end of suggested fluency rates (Mercer & Mercer, 1989). In two studies (Gayler, 1988; Jones, 1990), the number of trials needed by nine first and second graders with learning problems to reach 30 digits correct per minute with two or fewer errors on subtraction facts 0 to 9 ranged from 632 to 1,168, with a mean of 840. More research is needed to guide the establishment of mastery rate criteria for specific math skills across individual learners of different ages and motor skills.

2. The most efficient applications of concrete, representational, and abstract level procedures continue to be examined. In teaching subtraction with regrouping, Evans and Carnine (1990) found that concrete representations and symbolic (abstract) activities were both effective, but symbolic instruction was more efficient. Moreover, they suggested that the symbolic-concrete sequence is more efficient than the concrete-symbolic sequence. The entire CRA sequence has been recommended in the literature for decades, but its effectiveness has not been systematically examined. As with the Evans and Carnine study, most researchers have compared components of the SRA sequence (concrete and abstract versus abstract; representational and abstract versus concrete and abstract, etc.) but have not systematically examined the three-component sequence. More research is needed to determine if the entire CRA sequence is more effective than any two-part combinations of the sequence, and if a different order of the three parts is more effective. Moreover, the CRA sequence and its various two-part and three-part combinations need to be examined in relation to math skills that vary in difficulty, maintenance of skills, generalization of skills, and problem solving. The field-test data for SMS sug-

gest that the CRA sequence holds promise for teaching place value and basic facts to students with learning problems. Perhaps the progressive experiences coupled with the multiple examples across the various modalities enable students with learning difficulties to learn.

3. Although the individual components of SMS have research support, the relative effectiveness of the separate components on student outcomes is unknown. Script-guided explicit teaching, elaborated feedback, monitoring of progress, the DRAW strategy, the word-problem sequence, the Pig Games, the concrete lessons, the representational lessons, and the practice-to-mastery lessons are some components that warrant study. Investigations in these areas could lead to more efficiency.

4. SMS needs to be compared to other curricula to determine its relative effectiveness.

5. After students reach the practice-to-mastery lessons, alternative instructional delivery systems need to be explored to facilitate independent practice. From their research review, Mastropieri et al. (1991) reported that cooperative learning, computer-assisted instruction, peer tutoring, and interactive videodiscs have produced positive student outcomes in math.

6. When students reach mastery in fact computation, the inclusion of word problems that involve solving for different unknowns appears warranted. Also, word problems that require multisteps (e.g., addition and subtraction) are needed.

Many students with learning problems enter the upper grades without a functional knowledge of lower level math skills, such as place value and basic facts. Moreover, higher standards in math are likely to make the situation more threatening to these students. The research regarding how to teach math to these students is extensive. Educators are challenged with the task of putting best practices in the schools. One logical plan for promoting these practices is to develop and field test a curriculum that incorporates effective teaching routines. Sprick (1986) noted that less than 3% of commercial materials are field-tested before being published. For the benefit of all students and teachers, math materials that incorporate effective teaching practices need to be established in the nation's schools. If this happens, perhaps future efforts will not be directed toward reforming an ineffective math curriculum but toward refining quality instructional practices.

References

Anderson, L. W., & Pellicer, L. O. (1990). Synthesis of research on compensatory and remedial education. *Educational Leadership, 48*(1), 10–16.

Bartel, N. R. (1990). Problems in mathematics achievement. In D. D. Hammill, & N. R. Bartel, *Teaching students with learning and behavior problems* (5th ed., pp. 289–343). Austin, TX: PRO-ED.

Berliner, D. C. (1982, March). *The executive functions of teaching.* Paper presented at the annual meeting of the American Educational Research Association, New York.

Blankenship, C. S. (1978). Remediating systematic inversion errors in subtraction through the use of demonstration and feedback. *Learning Disability Quarterly, 1*, 12–22.

Blankenship, C., & Lilly, M. S. (1981). *Mainstreaming students with learning and behavior problems: Techniques for the classroom teacher.* New York: Holt, Rinehart & Winston.

Carnine, D. (1991). Curricular interventions for teaching higher order thinking to all students: Introduction to the special series. *Journal of Learning Disabilities, 24*, 261–269.

Carpenter, R. L. (1985). Mathematics instruction in resource rooms: Instruction time and teacher competence. *Learning Disability Quarterly, 8*, 95–100.

Carroll, J. B. (1985). The model of school learning: Progress of an idea. In L. W. Anderson (Ed.), *Perspectives on school learning: Selected writings of John B. Carroll* (pp. 82–108). Hillsdale, NJ: Erlbaum.

Case, L. P., & Harris, K. R. (1988, April). *Self-instructional strategy training: Improving mathematical problem solving skills of learning disabled students*. Paper presented at the annual meeting of the American Educational Research Association, New Orleans.

Cawley, J., Fitzmaurice-Hayes, A., & Shaw, R. (1988). *Mathematics for the mildly handicapped—A guide to curriculum and instruction*. Boston: Allyn & Bacon.

Cawley, J. F., & Miller, J. H. (1989). Cross-sectional comparisons of the mathematical performance of children with learning disabilities: Are we on the right track toward comprehensive programming? *Journal of Learning Disabilities, 23*, 250–254, 259.

Cawley, J. F., Miller, J. H., & School, B. A. (1987). A brief inquiry of arithmetic word-problem solving among learning disabled secondary students. *Learning Disabilities Focus, 2*, 87–93.

Christenson, S. L., Ysseldyke, J. E., & Thurlow, M. L. (1989). Critical instructional factors for students with mild handicaps: An integrative review. *Remedial and Special Education, 10*(5), 21–31.

Clifford, M. M. (1990). Students need challenge, not easy success. *Educational Leadership, 48*(1), 22–26.

Collins, M., Carnine, D., & Gersten, R. (1987). Elaborated corrective feedback and the acquisition of reading skills: A study of computer-assisted instruction. *Exceptional Children, 54*, 254–262.

Cox, L. S. (1975). Diagnosing and remediating systematic errors in addition and subtraction computations. *The Arithmetic Teacher, 22*, 151–157.

De Corte, E., & Verschaffel, L. (1981). Children's solution processes in elementary arithmetic problems: Analysis and improvement. *Journal of Educational Psychology, 73*, 765–779.

Deshler, D. D., Schumaker, J. B., & Lenz, B. K. (1984). Academic and cognitive interventions for LD adolescents: Part I. *Journal of Learning Disabilities, 17*, 108–117.

Ellis, E. S., Lenz, B. K., & Sabornie, E. J. (1987a). Generalization and adaptation of learning strategies to natural environments. Part I: Critical agents. *Remedial and Special Education, 8*(1), 6–20.

Ellis, E. S., Lenz, B. K., & Sabornie, E. J. (1987b). Generalization and adaptation of learning strategies to natural environments. Part II: Research into practice. *Remedial and Special Education, 8*(2), 6–23.

Engelmann, S., Carnine, D., & Steely, D. G. (1991). Making connections in mathematics. *Journal of Learning Disabilities, 24*, 292–303.

Evans, D., & Carnine, D. (1990). Manipulatives—The effective way. *Direct Instruction News, 10*(1), 48–55.

Fisher, C. W., Berliner, D. C., Filby, N. N., Marliave, R., Cahen, L. S., & Dishaw, M. M. (1980). Teaching behaviors, academic learning time, and student achievement: An overview. In C. Denham, & A. Lieberman (Eds.), *Time to learn*. Washington, DC: National Institute of Education.

Fleischner, J. E., Garnett, K., & Shepherd, M. J. (1982). Proficiency in arithmetic basic facts computation of learning disabled and nondisabled children. *Focus on Learning Problems in Mathematics, 4*(2), 47–56.

Fleischner, J. E., Nuzum, M. B., & Marzola, E. S. (1987). Devising an instructional program to teach arithmetic problem-solving skills to students with learning disabilities. *Journal of Learning Disabilities, 20*, 214–217.

Fuchs, L. S. (1986). Monitoring progress among mildly handicapped pupils: Review of current practices and research. *Remedial and Special Education, 7*(5), 5–12.

Fuchs, L. S., Fuchs, D., & Deno, S. L. (1985). The importance of goal ambitiousness and goal mastery to student achievement. *Exceptional Children, 52*, 63–71.

Garnett, K., & Fleischner, J. E. (1983). Automatization and basic fact performance of normal and learning disabled children. *Learning Disability Quarterly, 6*, 223–230.

Gayler, S. K. (1988). *The effect of the concrete to abstract mathematic instructional sequence with first graders.* Unpublished master's thesis, University of Florida, Gainesville.

Gersten, R., Carnine, D., & Woodward, J. (1987). Direct instruction research: The third decade. *Remedial and Special Education, 8*(6) 48–56.

Good, T. L. (1983). Classroom research: A decade of progress. *Educational Psychologist, 18*(3), 127–144.

Good, T. L., & Brophy, J. E. (1986). School effects. In M. C. Wittrock (Ed.), *Handbook for research on teaching* (3rd ed., pp. 570–602). New York: Macmillan.

Good, T. L., & Grouws, D. A. (1979). The Missouri Mathematics Effectiveness Project: An experimental study in fourth-grade classrooms. *Journal of Educational Psychology, 71*(3), 355–362.

Hasselbring, T. S., Goin, L. I., & Bransford, J. O. (1987). Developing automaticity. *Teaching Exceptional Children, 19*(3), 30–33.

Hudson, P. J., Peterson, S. K., Mercer, C. D., & McLeod, P. (1988). Place value instruction. *Teaching Exceptional Children, 20*(3), 72–73.

Jones, D. S. (1990). *Trials to mastery of basic subtraction.* Unpublished master's thesis, University of Florida, Gainesville.

Kameenui, E. J., & Simmons, D. C. (1990). *Designing instructional strategies: The prevention of academic learning problems.* Columbus, OH: Merrill.

Kelly, B., Gersten, R., & Carnine, D. (1990). Student error patterns as a function of curriculum design: Teaching fractions to remedial high school students and high school students with learning disabilities. *Journal of Learning Disabilities, 1*, 23–29.

Kirby, J. R., & Becker, L. D. (1988). Cognitive components of learning problems in arithmetic. *Remedial and Special Education, 9*(5), 7–15, 27.

Kline, F. M., Schumaker, J. B., & Deshler, D. D. (1991). Development and validation of feedback routines for instructing students with learning disabilities. *Learning Disability Quarterly, 14*, 191–207.

Lloyd, J. W., & Keller, C. E. (1989). Effective mathematics instruction: Development, instruction, and programs. *Focus on Exceptional Children, 21*(7), 1–10.

Locke, E. A., & Latham, G. P. (1990). *A theory of goal setting and task performance.* Englewood Cliffs, NJ: Prentice-Hall.

Locke, E. A., Shaw, K. N., Saari, L. M., & Latham, G. P. (1981). Goal setting and task performance: 1969–1980. *Psychological Bulletin, 90*, 125–152.

Lovitt, T. C. (1989). *Introduction to learning disabilities.* Boston: Allyn & Bacon.

Mastropieri, M. A., Scruggs, T. E., & Shiah, S. (1991). Mathematics instruction for learning disabled students: A review of research. *Learning Disabilities Research & Practice, 6*, 89–98.

McLeod, T., & Armstrong, S. (1982). Learning disabilities in mathematics—Skill deficits and remedial approaches. *Learning Disability Quarterly, 5*, 305–311.

Mercer, C. D. (1992). *Students with learning disabilities* (4th ed.). New York: Macmillan.

Mercer, C. D., & Mercer, A. R. (1989). *Teaching students with learning problems* (3rd ed.). Columbus, OH: Merrill.

Mercer, C. D., & Miller, S. P. (1991). *Strategic math series: Multiplication facts 0–81.* Lawrence, KS: Edge Enterprises.

Miller, J. H., & Milam, C. P. (1987). Multiplication and division errors committed by learning disabled students. *Learning Disabilities Research, 2*(2), 119–122.

Montague, M., & Bos, C. S. (1986). The effect of cognitive strategy training on verbal math problem solving performance of learning disabled adolescents. *Journal of Learning Disabilities, 19*, 26–33.

National Council of Supervisors of Mathematics. (1988). *Twelve components of essential mathematics.* Minneapolis, MN: Author.

National Council of Teachers of Mathematics. (1980). *An agenda for action: Recommendations for school mathematics of the 1980's.* Reston, VA: Author.

National Council of Teachers of Mathematics. (1989). *Curriculum and evaluation standards for school mathematics.* Reston, VA: Author.

Nuzum, M. (1983). *The effects of a curriculum based on the information processing paradigm on the arithmetic problem solving performance of four learning disabled students.* Unpublished doctoral dissertation, Teachers College, Columbia University, New York.

Peterson, S. K., Mercer, C. D., & O'Shea, L. (1988). Teaching learning disabled children place value using the concrete to abstract sequence. *Learning Disabilities Research, 4*(1), 52–56.

Porter, A. C., & Brophy, J. (1988). Synthesis of research on good teaching: Insights from the work of the Institute for Research on Teaching. *Educational Leadership, 45*(8), 74–85.

Reisman, F. K. (1982). *A guide to the diagnostic teaching of arithmetic* (3rd ed.). Columbus, OH: Merrill.

Reisman, F., & Kauffman, S. (1980). *Teaching mathematics to children with special needs.* Columbus, OH: Merrill.

Rieth, H., & Evertson, C. (1988). Variables related to the effective instruction of difficult-to-teach children. *Focus on Exceptional Children, 20*(5), 1–8.

Rivera, D. M., & Smith, D. D. (1987). Influence of modeling on acquisition and generalization of computational skills: A summary of research findings for three sites. *Learning Disability Quarterly, 10,* 69–80.

Rivera, D., & Smith, D. D. (1988). Using a demonstration strategy to teach midschool students with learning disabilities how to compute long division. *Journal of Learning Disabilities, 21,* 77–81.

Robinson, S. L., DePascale, D., & Roberts, F. C. (1989). Computer-delivered feedback in group-based instruction: Effects for learning disabled students in mathematics. *Learning Disabilities Focus, 5*(1), 28–35.

Rosenshine, B. (1983). Teaching functions in instructional programs. *The Elementary School Journal, 83,* 335–351.

Rosenshine, B., & Stevens, R. (1986). Teaching functions. In M. C. Wittrock (Ed.), *Handbook of research on teaching* (3rd ed., pp. 376-391). New York: Macmillan.

Russell, R., & Ginsburg, H. (1984). Cognitive analysis of children's mathematical difficulties. *Cognition and Instruction, 1,* 217–244.

Scheid, K. (1990). *Cognitive-based methods for teaching mathematics to students with learning problems.* Columbus, OH: LINC Resources.

Slavin, R. E., & Madden, N. A. (1989). What works for students at risk: A research synthesis. *Educational Leadership, 46*(5), 4–13.

Sprick, R. S. (1986). *Solutions to elementary discipline problems* (Cassette tapes). Eugene, OR: Teaching Strategies.

Stokes, T. F., & Baer, D. M. (1977). An implicit technology of generalization. *Journal of Applied Behavioral Analysis, 10*(2), 349–367.

Sugai, G., & Smith, P. (1986). The equal additions method of subtraction taught with a modeling technique. *Remedial and Special Education, 7*(1), 40–48.

Suydam, M. N., & Higgins, J. L. (1977). *Activity-based learning in elementary school mathematics: Recommendations from research.* Reston, VA: National Council of Teachers of Mathematics.

Thornton, C. A., & Toohey, M. A. (1985). Basic math facts: Guidelines for teaching and learning. *Learning Disabilities Focus, 1,* 44–57.

Underhill, R. G., Uprichard, A. E., & Heddens, J. W. (1980). *Diagnosing mathematical difficulties.* Columbus, OH: Merrill.

Wang, M. C. (1987). Toward achieving educational excellence for all students: Program design and instructional outcomes. *Remedial and Special Education, 8*(3), 25–34.

Warner, M., Alley, G., Schumaker, J., Deshler, D., & Clark, F. (1980). *An epidemiological study of learning disabled adolescents in secondary schools: Achievement and ability, socioeconomic status and school experiences* (Report No. 13). Lawrence: University of Kansas Institute for Research in Learning Disabilities.

White, O. R., & Haring, N. G. (1980). *Exceptional teaching: A Multimedia training package* (2nd ed.). Columbus, OH: Merrill.

10 Strategies for Teaching Social Studies

KATHLEEN McCOY

McCOY ADDRESSES the challenge that teachers face in providing access to instruction in social studies to students with mild disabilities. She reminds readers of the themes that form the framework for teaching social studies. Models of social studies instruction and instructional formats are presented. The author does an excellent job of integrating theory with practice by offering suggestions to ensure student access to instruction in social studies. Readers will find implications for instruction in general.

Picture this. Elizabeth, a seventh grader complete with technicolor nails and braces on her teeth, twirls her hair and tries to look attentive. Her teacher, Mr. Bogel, is waxing poetic about the marvels of the West Indies. In theory, Elizabeth is taking careful notes, recording Mr. Bogel's lecture. In practice, Elizabeth is compiling a list of cosmetic products that are prerequisites for the spring dance. Somewhere on the edge of her consciousness Elizabeth hears, "...Chapter 13 on next Tuesday's quiz." Elizabeth is fully aware that receiving poor grades in Social Studies results in mall restrictions. Somewhat reluctantly, Elizabeth leaves the world of make-up and trods page by page through the chapter to discover the wonders of Central America as defined by the Chapter Review on page 120. To find the answers to the chapter questions, Elizabeth reads line by painful line. Too bad that she doesn't know how to use section headings to locate information, an activity that takes most kids 30 minutes takes a whopping 4 hours for Elizabeth. No wonder she hates social studies.

In the next room, Jorge has just finished placing the final sugar cube on top of the Great Pyramid. Last week he mummified a cornish game hen, and next week he is going to finish writing a play about ancient Egypt. His part is that of a pharaoh called Ramses who meets aliens from outer space. Jorge is not quite sure who Ramses is or even if Egypt exists, but he is thrilled that his mother made him a costume decorated with gold and jewels. Jorge also is happy because his teacher, Ms. Goodwind, likes arts and crafts projects and doesn't like textbooks or tests. No written records of Jorge's progress in social studies will ever be unearthed.

Student Diversity

How common are these two scenarios in today's social studies classes? In an area of study where diversity is respected, how disparate can instructional methods be to honor the Expectations of Excellence, curriculum standards set by the National Council for the Social Studies (NCSS, 1994)? How disparate can instructional methods be to meet the diverse needs of today's students? As a result of inclusion, more than 70% of students with learning disabilities (LD), mild mental handicaps (MH), and behavior disorders (BD) are being educated in the general education setting (Ysseldyke & Algozzine, 1990). In addition, many students with mild disabilities who also are limited in using English as their primary language of instruction are included in general education settings (Gersten, Brengelman, & Jimenez, 1994). Given the diversity represented by children with mild disabilities, the 10 themes that form the framework of the social studies standards (NCSS 1994) almost seem to have been designed specifically for them (pp. x–xii):

1. Culture
2. Time, Continuity, and Change
3. People, Places, and Environments
4. Individual Development and Identity
5. Individuals, Groups, and Institutions
6. Power, Authority, and Governance
7. Production, Distribution, and Consumption
8. Science, Technology, and Society
9. Global Connections
10. Civic Ideals and Practices

The Need for Social Studies

Students with mild learning problems, such as Elizabeth and Jorge, need to understand how culture accepts or rejects their special needs and who they are relative to others in the room and the world. A knowledge of historical roots related to disabilities in society can help students with mild learning problems connect to others in the class and develop a sense of relatedness. Students need to learn about people, places, and human-environment interactions and discover how their personal identity is shaped by their culture, by groups, and by institutional influences such as schools, churches, families, and government systems. They need to understand how their individual rights can be protected within the context of majority rule and how goods and services can be distributed. They need to learn about their role as citizens and how they can make a positive difference in their class and in their community. In sum, students with special learning problems, like all children, need to learn social studies.

Social Studies Defined

The area of social studies, as can be seen from the 10 themes from *Expectations for Excellence*, is a complex area of study focusing on the integration of social science, behavioral science, and humanities that forms the basis of civic competence in the United States. The Board of Directors of the NCSS (1994), the primary membership organization for social studies educators, has adopted the following definition:

> Social studies is the integrated study of the social sciences and humanities to promote civic competence. Within the school program, social studies provides coordinated, systematic study drawing upon such disciplines as anthropology, archaeology, economics, geography, history, law, philosophy, political science, psychology, religion, and sociology as well as appropriate content from the humanities, mathematics, and natural sciences. The primary purpose of social studies is to help young people develop the ability to make informed and reasoned decisions for the public good as citizens of a culturally diverse, democratic society in an interdependent world (NCSS, p. 3).

Social Studies Instruction for Children with Mild Disabilities

The Challenge

The challenge is how to provide access to social studies content in a general education setting to children with mild disabilities. For at least 20 years the traditional textbook-based instructional approach has been found to be ineffective (Goodlad, 1984; Turner, 1976). The traditional method of lecture-read-group discussion is likely to miss the needs of many students with learning problems (Horton, Lovitt, & Slocum, 1988), especially those at the middle and secondary level, where textbooks are heavily used. Overwhelming numbers of students with learning problems are reading two or more years below grade level—never mind that they lack strategies for comprehension skills such as drawing inferences or locating main ideas to apply to real-world situations (Ellis, 1994). If the model of instruction, traditional or otherwise, does not match the needs of children with mild disabilities, what model for social studies instruction can be used?

Accommodations in General Education Settings

Use of Instructional Interventions

Before attempting to implement instructional strategies specific to social studies, we might want to find out what light research findings can shed upon accommodating student needs in general. Results of research conducted to determine the extent to which accommodations for individual differences have occurred have been somewhat dismal.

For example, in a detailed analysis of the first year of a mainstreaming project, Baker and Zigmond (1990) examined the educational practices in general education classes in grades K–5. They were documenting changes necessary to facilitate full-time inclusion for students with learning disabilities. The overall impression was of undifferentiated group instruction—so much for meeting individual needs. Teachers essentially followed district mandates and lesson plan guides. Instruction was directed to the whole class. The teachers acknowledged diversity, but provided lessons based on uniformity.

Unfortunately, Baker and Zigmond's observations are supported by the results of many surveys designed to poll teachers about their experiences and attitudes concerning the inclusion of children with special needs in their classes. Questionnaires typically address attitudes toward modifying or identifying strategies that could be used in the general education setting with children with mild disabilities. Results across studies find that, though teachers indicate the value of providing interventions, they generally don't find such provision feasible (Bender & Ukeje, 1989; Schumm & Vaughn, 1991; Whinnery, Fuchs, & Fuchs, 1991).

Acceptable Accommodations in General Education Settings

According to Schumm and Vaughn (1991), the kinds of adaptations that teachers perceive as most desirable are providing reinforcement and encouragement, establishing a personal relationship with a student with special needs, and involving the student in whole-class activities—the same behaviors that would be expected to be found toward children without special needs. Teachers are least likely to accept strategies that require systematic evaluation of goals or adjustment of materials and instructional practices for learners with special needs. The likelihood of adapting long-range plans, adjusting physical arrangements of the room, or modifying scoring and grading criteria is minimal.

Without some type of intervention, implementation of individualization or accommodation in the general education setting is unlikely. The question now becomes not only what strategies to implement but also how to implement these strategies. Research results suggest strongly that instructional strategies can be utilized to teach content areas such as social studies to children with mild learning problems (Bulgren, Schumaker, & Deshler, 1994; Carnine, Crawford, Harniss, & Hollenbeck, 1995) but must be implemented with a minimum of disruption to normal classroom routine. Students with mild learning problems, like all children, need instruction to become better citizens by developing a sound knowledge base in social studies. To receive instruction in social studies in an inclusion setting, students with mild disabilities need personalized modification of materials that is not disruptive or difficult to implement.

Increasing Acceptance of Providing Accommodation

Acceptance and utilization of strategies for instructional accommodation may be increased by making the students aware of possible strategies, providing experience with the strategy, and increasing opportunities for the students to practice the strategy (Schumm & Vaughn, 1991). Special education teachers are the ones responsible for providing awareness and in class experiences with accommodation strategies. As a member of an instructional team, the special educator has the responsibility for modeling strategies, leading other team members through these strategies, and testing how well these strategies work within the context of social studies in the general education setting. To make suggestions or recommendations to the general educator without field-testing in the general education classroom is like asking the CEO of General Motors to mass-produce a solar car without a prototype—a nice concept but, without evidence of financial success, not likely to be marketed. The inclusionary yellow-brick road leads back to Kansas or, in this case, the special education teacher.

Social Studies Knowledge Base: Preparation of Teachers

Roles

The role of the special education teacher is to be the instructional strategist, not the content specialist. The content specialist, usually the general education teacher, theoretically is grounded with a sound knowledge base in social studies. More than likely at grades kindergarten through fifth or sixth grade, however, the special educator and the elementary education teacher have about the same amount of background knowledge—a methods course in teaching elementary-age students social studies and whatever general studies courses their university or college requires for graduation. Teachers with a degree in elementary education are prepared in programs heavily weighted in educational methods, usually at the expense of depth of understanding of the course content to be taught (National Commission on Excellence in Education, 1983); the social studies background of most special education majors is not much different from elementary education majors.

Self-contained General Education Classrooms

When general educators and special educators have comparable backgrounds, either or both can assume the planning, delivering, and evaluating of instruction. With a common knowledge base modifications to content are one step closer to reality. Planning is simplified because the step of teaching each other the social studies content can be bypassed. Given most teachers' lack of expertise in social studies at the elementary level, the district curriculum guide, topic coverage in texts, or unit topics designed by expert teachers probably should be used as guides for planning activities. A review of such guides can be completed outside of joint planning time. Because the special education teacher has the same level of expertise as the classroom instructor, joint preparation time for accommodations can be focused on the when and the how but not the what. To the extent that each teacher or group of teachers is flexible and communicates student and classroom needs, accommodations are possible.

Departmentalized Instruction

When social studies is departmentalized, the content specialist is more likely to have a fairly extensive background in social studies, whereas the special educator's knowledge base in social studies is minimal (Bulgren & Lenz, 1996). The content specialist must assume responsibility for developing social studies competence in students. The social studies specialist will have to identify critical content for the support teacher, who then will have to find ways to teach students remedial or compensatory strategies using key content in the social studies area.

Identification of Content

Textbook-Driven Instruction

When social studies is departmentalized or taught as a separate subject, a text-driven approach supported by teacher-made activities is still the most common format (Bracey, 1993). In addition, many elementary and secondary social studies teachers believe overwhelmingly that the social studies emphasis for students with mild disabilities should be the same as for all students in the class (Passe & Beattie, 1994) This is not an unreasonable thought considering that when students with special needs grow up, they will be expected to participate as citizens with the same responsibilities as other adults.

Critical knowledge is identified more easily for nonspecialists in settings that use a social studies text as a basis for instruction. The content is in the book and usually has been developed by experts in social studies. If Mr. Atwood wants to teach a unit on critical thinking, for example, all he has to do is turn to Chapter 6, "Whose View of the World? Maps and Their Uses," in the text. Chapter 6 has been thoughtfully labeled "Critical Thinking Activities." Though it is difficult to determine if the chapter content is driving Mr. Atwood or Mr. Atwood is driving the chapter content, the essential ideas are clearly presented, as can be seen a portion of the chapter outline "Critical Thinking Activities," presented in Figure 10.1.

Because Mr. Atwood is following the chapter outline, Mrs. Carpenter, the special education teacher, is able to design modified materials for the students in Mr. Atwood's social studies class. Instead of spending a lot of planning time trying to identify content, she can spend her time modifying content to meet student needs. Because the whole idea of inclusion is to educate children with special needs in the general education setting, Mrs. Carpenter can develop small-group or whole-class activities that reinforce the content presented in Chapter 6 without becoming a social studies specialist. This is a good idea because Mrs. Carpenter is not a social studies expert, nor is she likely to become one.

Mrs. Carpenter can complement Mr. Atwood's lesson on reading map symbols by providing material that moves the children gradually from pictorial and semipictorial symbols on maps. These first maps may be made by the children and, in addition to drawing, cutting and pasting, Mrs. Carpenter can provide cues, prompts, or models for the children who need them. Matthew, for example, may benefit from having models of pictorial representations attached to his drawing paper. The models representing real-life encounters, such as those presented in Figure 10.2, can be a first step in helping Matthew understand symbols before he moves to more abstract legends.

Mrs. Carpenter next shapes instruction to lead to the more abstract symbols used on conventional wall maps, globes, and maps that are included in the textbook. She either can take materials developed by Mr. Atwood and adapt them or she can

(continued)

Figure 10.1 *Partial Outline from Chapter on Critical Thinking Activities*

provide adapted material for Mr. Atwood to be used with children like Matthew and Sammy. Mr. Atwood and Mrs. Carpenter both know which children need modification, but Mrs. Carpenter's role is to go beyond the norm, because she is the teacher of children with special education needs, and include modified materials embedding basic skill instruction. No one said inclusion was easy, but having a text as a guide can be extremely efficient.

■ **Figure 10.1** *(continued)*

Source: From M. G. Allen & R. L. Stevens, Chapter outline for "Critical Thinking Activities," *Middle grades social studies*. 1994, ix-xii, Boston: Allyn & Bacon.

Value of Textbooks

Even though the traditional method of lecture-read-groups discussion may not be effective (Horton, Lovitt, & Slocum, 1988), textbooks need not be abandoned. In fact, for teachers trained in elementary education, logic dictates use of a social studies text in some way. The text may be used as a primary resource, as a supplemental text, or as a reference manual. How the text is used depends on the delivery system in the classroom and the extent to which the teacher is responsible for the curriculum in the text. For some teachers, especially those whose primary education has been in special education or elementary education, and for some students who need structure, the text provides an excellent organizational and content resource.

Social Studies Content Across Curricula

When social studies is presented as part of a basic core, cross-over or integration with other core content, such as literature or science, is to be expected. Key content

■ **Figure 10.2** *Pictorial Symbol System Representing Real-Life Encounters*

can be more difficult to determine in the social studies areas when it is infused with other content. In an integrated approach, social studies is viewed as a composite subject. The various elements of social studies are history, geography, economics, political science, anthropology, sociology, and psychology. Morals and ethics are included from philosophy, and elements from the humanities and fine arts such as literature, art, and art history also are part of this composite. Because social studies is a blend of many disciplines, the focus of social studies becomes human behavior—how people interact with the environment and with the innumerable ways in which people live in society (Welton & Mallan, 1996).

In this model of social studies, content cuts across disciplines. The area of humanities, for example, is often integrated with social studies as a means of understanding cultural aspects of people or periods of time (Smith, Monson, & Dobson, 1992). In the study of westward expansion in the United States, for example, the book *Long Ago in Oregon* (Lewis, 1987) can be used to reveal the daily lives of people in a town in Oregon during the early 19th century. The poetic vignettes in the book can be integrated with more literal concepts presented through history texts or guides. The content emphasis in an interdisciplinary approach varies with the interests, needs, and knowledge base of the instructor or instructors. The integrated approach to social studies instruction is delivered most often in elementary schools and in junior-high settings that use a thematic core approach.

Whole-Language and Integrated Curriculum

Integrated instruction often is paired with a whole-language orientation. Choosing and elaborating on a theme in social studies through literature, reading, and writing represents the heart of whole language (James & Zarrillo, 1989). To a greater or lesser extent, whole-language integration with social studies translates to minimal or no use whatsoever of textbooks. These instructors believe students will develop and sustain interest in social studies by engaging in democratic processes such as collaboration, discussions, cooperative learning, problem resolution and so on. Overuse of the text prevents active engagement in these democratic processes. Whether use of a textbook leads or does not lead to active participation is not the issue; the point is that many classes using an integrated approach do not use textbooks as a major source of content.

Teacher planning in an integrated model first must identify which social studies concepts should be introduced to students. Planning time, as all teachers know, is a precious commodity, most often absorbed in conferences, grading, and administrative tasks (Bulgren & Lenz, 1996). Insufficient planning time makes the integrated/whole-language model difficult to implement for students with special needs.

Next, the type of learning experiences have to be outlined in social studies as well as other content area. Skills accompanying the lesson also must be identified. The learning climate must encourage both inquiry and choice. Suggested informal guidelines for planning an integrated social studies and whole language unit (Routman, 1994) are as follows.

1. Develop a semantic web as the class or group brainstorms the topic.
2. Have students select a subtopic by listing their first, second, and third choices of subtopics.
3. Divide the students into small groups of up to four students per subtopic.
4. Have the groups develop questions to research for their subtopic of study.
5. Have each group meet with another group to confer over the questions each group generated for their respective subtopics.

6. Have each group establish a format for using resources to discover the answers to the questions they generated about their subtopic.
7. Have all of the students take notes on their subtopics.
8. Ask students to use their notes to write rough drafts.
9. Have each group present the information its members gathered to the entire class. (A variety of formats may be used: quiz shows, radio shows, festivals, plays, travelogues, etc.)
10. Have classmates make oral presentations. Students must give at least two positive statements before a student can make positive suggestions for improvement.
11. Evaluate group interactions and content learned. This is done by the teacher and through student self-evaluations. In addition, an essay test given by the teacher may be included at this point.

As can be seen from a brief analysis of these guidelines, the special education teacher has quite a challenge. Not only must the content be identified, but strategies for teaching children with mild disabilities also must include instruction in social skills (recommendations 1–5, 10, and 11), writing strategies (recommendations 5, 6, 8), notetaking strategies (recommendations 4, 7, 8), and public speaking strategies (9, 10, 11). For students who have mild learning problems, almost all these areas require instructional guidance, and almost all of these strategies will be needed within 2 to 3 weeks.

The good news is that once the special education teacher has developed instructional techniques for delivering these strategies, the approaches can be used repeatedly for whatever topics follow. The bad news is that development of these strategies in a whole-language setting is teacher-intensive and not that many teachers are available (McCoy, 1996). Often, instruction is left to peers who may or may not have the skills themselves. Learning under these guidelines is indeed a social activity.

Models of Social Studies Instruction

Respecting the Model

The challenge facing the special education teacher is twofold.

1. The student's needs must be respected and accommodated.
2. The social studies teacher's needs must be respected and accommodated.

No matter how the special education teacher feels about traditional instruction or arts and crafts as an instructional approach to social studies, if the method is being used in the classroom, accommodations must account for the approach as well as the student's instructional needs.

Ignoring diversity or, at the other extreme, being paralyzed by differences found in students and instructional approaches is dysfunctional. Ms. McLooney, the special education teacher, a recently converted true believer of whole-language philosophy, is horrified to team with Mr. "King of the Textbooks" Parker. She thinks no real learning can come from a classroom that uses basal social studies texts and requires that children learn facts through the dreaded "m word" (memorization, for those of you too young to remember!). Mr. Parker is so repelled by McLooney that he shuts her out, literally and figuratively, from the class. Too bad for Al, Stan, and Rob, whose IEP goal of receiving equal access to social studies content in the general education setting is highly improbable. The challenge is to find a flexible path between the McLooneys and the Parkers—instruction that accounts for student need more than for instructor bias.

Basic Social Studies Models

Three models used frequently in social studies instruction are (a) textbook-based plans (b) theme or topic-oriented plans, and (c) child-centered plans. At the heart of each of these models is the application of democratic beliefs and values (Saxe, 1994). Each of the three basic models may have one or many types of focus (e.g., awareness of self in a social setting or sharing earth space with others). Examples illustrating applications of democratic beliefs and values within the three basic models are found in Table 10.1.

Textbook-based plans are developed by teachers who use the textbook or other curriculum guides to determine the nature and content of the program. Theme or topic-oriented plans are similar to textbook plans, but they rely less on the text. More of the teacher's and students' influence is found in topic-oriented planning. Students, for example, are more involved in focus activities and questions. Of the three models, child-centered plans are the least structured. Children help decide the study units with the teacher. Jointly, they plan how they will work, activities to do, and how to share ideas with class members.

Characteristics of Models

Each model has strengths and limitations. Consequently, many social studies instructors combine or use elements of all three approaches, depending upon instructional content and class make-up. Text-based or text-driven instruction is more common at upper elementary and secondary levels; theme instruction often is integrated with content from other subject areas, such as literature, and typically is found in middle schools and junior-high schools that use a team approach. Child-centered plans are associated most often with lower elementary grades and with teachers who hold a whole-language philosophy. In a text-driven approach, students will need to learn from lectures and textbooks. In a more child-centered approach, students will need to learn from each other as well as printed material. Depending on the teacher's philosophy and background, blends of both approaches in social studies instruction can be found at any level in any model and accommodations can be made within and across models.

Commonalities in Models

Most approaches to social studies instruction attempt to teach students how to think critically when evaluating information, to problem solve, and to hypothesize, and

■■■■ **Table 10.1** *Illustrative Examples of Applications of Democratic Beliefs and Values*

Grade	Central Focus	Democratic Rights, Freedoms, Responsibilities, or Beliefs Addressed	Illustrations of Opportunities
K	Awareness of self in a social setting	1. Right to security 2. Right to equal opportunity 3. Respect for others' rights 4. Honesty	1. Explore how rules make a room safe for everyone. 2. Every child is scheduled to be a leader for a day. 3. Focus on common courtesies; e.g., when someone speaks, one should listen. 4. The teacher reinforces honesty as exhibited by children.
1	The individual in primary social groups	1. Impartiality 2. Freedom of worship 3. Consideration for others	1. When an altercation is reported, the teacher tries to find out exactly what happened before taking action. 2. Stress that each family decides whether or not or how to worship. 3. Everyone has a right to a turn.
2	Meeting basic needs in nearby social groups	1. Respect for property 2. Respect for laws 3. Value personal integrity	1. Discuss vandalism in neighborhoods. 2. Laws protect the safety of people. 3. Explore the importance of keeping promises.
3	Sharing earth space with others	1. Pursuing individual and group goals 2. Government works for the common good	1. Goods are exchanged with other places to meet the needs of the people. 2. Government is concerned about the unemployed and works to reduce unemployment.
4	Human life in varied environments	1. Respect for the rights of others. 2. Respect for different ways of living	1. Respect the right of individuals from other cultures to have different values. 2. Appreciate that life-styles of people in other places are different from ours.
5	People of the Americas	1. Freedom to worship 2. Right of privacy 3. Freedom of assembly	1. People came to the Americas because of religious persecution. 2. A home cannot be searched without a warrant except under most unusual circumstances.

Source: From National Council for the Social Studies Task Force on Early Childhood Elementary Education, *Social Studies Curriculum Planning Resources* (Washington, DC: Author, 1990), p. 33.

infer information about how people act and react to their world. Projects that reflect students' reasoning abilities often require utilization of reading, writing, and organizational skills.

Reading Material. In text-driven approaches, students are expected to read texts, answer study questions, often taken from the book, and complete reports on some aspect of study (e.g., "Our Home and Families" or "Native American Beliefs about the Earth"). In lieu of textbooks or to complement textbooks, the more child-centered or topic-oriented approach relies heavily on tradebooks chosen by teachers to represent the theme of study (e.g., *Josefina Story Quilt* by Coerr, 1986; *Loving the Earth: A Sacred Landscape Book for Children* by Lehrman, 1990).

The ultimate goal of reading in social studies areas is how to comprehend and apply social studies content to life issues. The guiding principles for engaging in reading activities apply equally to textbooks, tradebooks, magazines, newspapers, or any other form of printed material. Teachers guide reading by first activating prior knowledge and setting the purpose for reading. Strategies for reading the material are set by reviewing the title and subheadings, looking at pictures, asking questions about the content before reading or inspecting questions that may accompany the text.

As students read content, teachers monitor comprehension by asking questions and clarifying concepts. Contextual analysis is used to understand new terms and integrated new information. After reading has been completed, teachers provide opportunities for students to think about what was read and summarize major concepts and details. Teachers guide students to sources that could provide additional information about aspects of the material that are particularly interesting or confusing.

The role of the special education teacher is to ensure that students with mild learning problems are exposed sufficiently to principles of reading to meet their needs. The basis for reading instruction shifts to the required reading material in the class, whether tradebook or textbook. The extent to which the special education teacher must augment instruction is in direct relationship to the extent to which the social studies teacher applies principles of good reading instruction to the material used to teach social studies concepts.

Projects. Projects, whether formal reports or student-created dramas or dioramas, require organizational skills to complete. Checksheets are simple, yet powerful guides that can assist students with mild learning problems in organizing projects. Checksheets are simply written task analyses with a means to indicate that the task has been completed. The checksheets for the same task, just as a task analysis for the same task, can be modified according to student skill.

Suppose the class is assigned a project to create a collage representing diversity in their class. For some children a step-by-step procedure can serve as an organizational guideline. Shelley, for example, has great ideas but doesn't know how to focus to get started. Her checksheet might place greater emphasis on the steps needed to get started; for example:

Step 1: Brainstorm about what you like best about five of the boys and five of the girls in the class.

Step 2: Combine your brainstormed ideas into five or fewer categories.
Step 3: Find or create a picture or symbol to represent the categorical headings.

Michael, who has problems with task completion, may need more steps indicating what is expected in the final product (e.g., a step directing him to complete at least five pictures or symbols, a step directing him to label each picture with a student's name, a step telling him to glue each labeled picture onto the base sheet, and a final step reminding him to place the finished collage in the teacher's "work completed" basket). For Brianna, who has problems with pace, a checksheet could be modified to indicate task time required for clusters of steps (e.g., 5 minutes for steps 1–3, 10 minutes for steps 4 and 5, and so forth).

Writing. Often social studies classes, integrated or not, require a heavy emphasis on writing, including spelling, punctuation, and reference skills such as location and documentation. Techniques that have been found successful in teaching these basic skills out of context also can be applied to teaching them in the context of social studies content. When writing a story, for example, key vocabulary terms specific to the content can be listed in a prominent place in the classroom. For students who do not read well, pictures or cues next to terms can help them identify words without excessive teacher contact. The list serves as a reference point and frees children to express their ideas without being limited because of poor spelling skills. Attribute planning forms (Ellis, 1993) such as the one presented in Figure 10.3 or story maps like those in Figure 10.4 have been used successfully for a long time. Techniques such as these lend themselves easily to social studies content.

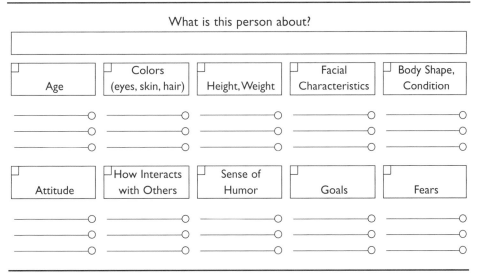

Figure 10.3 *Attribute Planning Form*

Source: From *Writing Strategies for Thought-Full Classrooms* by E. S. Ellis (Tuscaloosa, AL: SMART Strategy Associates, 1993).

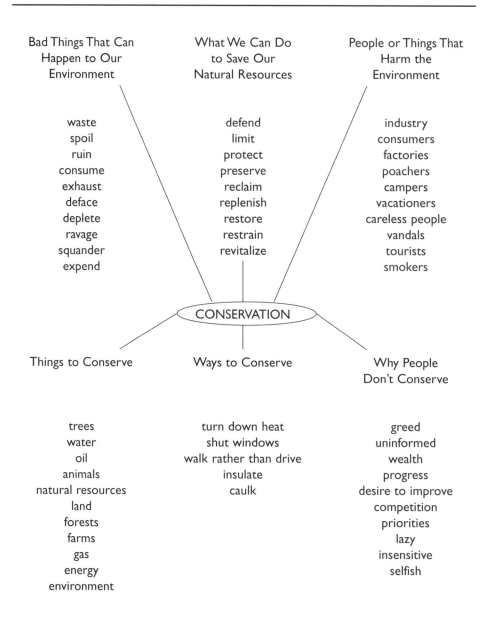

Figure 10.4 *Semantic Map: Conservation*

Source: From D. D. Johnson, S. Toms-Bronowski, & S. D. Pittleman, "Vocabulary Development," in R. E. Kretschmer (Ed.). *Reading and the Hearing Impaired Individual* (Monograph), *Volta Review, 1982, 84,* 11–24.

Instructional Formats

Cooperative Activities

More often than not, text-based theme-oriented and child-centered instruction in social studies borrow heavily from instructional formats for group activity. Activities often range from cooperative groups, in which children work together to complete tasks, to large-group or whole-class formats, in which a lot of independent work is completed.

Structuring Cooperative Group Activities

Cooperative group work can be structured in many different ways, such as cooperative learning, the jigsaw method, and Student Teams Achievement Division (STAD). The assumption behind cooperative approaches is that teamwork is innately more motivating and instructional than blanket group work. The power of social interactions and cooperation found in cooperative formats are posited to be mini-reflections of society at large, that is, citizens working together in task-oriented groups.

Cooperative Learning. In cooperative learning, children work in small groups to accomplish a common goal. The teacher acts as a facilitator and the students serve as resources to each other. Roles are assigned, and together the group produces a project or completes a task. Often everyone in the group receives the same grade. The basic principle of group composition in cooperative learning is to provide the greatest mix possible given the student population. This mix includes academic, interpersonal skills, gender, ethnicity, disability, language, race, and social class. Small groups reflect the composition of the whole class. Ability grouping is not acceptable because homogeneous grouping minimizes the mix. All the most popular students cannot be in one group; neither can all the less academically able students constitute a group.

Heterogeneous grouping lends itself well to inclusionary instruction. Deciding how to form groups is not without precedent. In general, some social and academic talents that are helpful in assigning children to groups are skills in reading, writing, planning, decision making (comparing alternatives), notetaking, brainstorming, and using reference material such as the internet. The following six guidelines for forming groups have been suggested by Parker and Jarolimek (1997):

1. *Work, not play.* The purpose of cooperative grouping is work, not play. When placed in the same group, friends tend to play, so they usually should not be placed together.
2. *Random assignment.* To result in mixed groups, they can be formed alphabetically or by numbers in birthdays until the teacher learns the characteristics of the students. Adjustments can be made as need arises.
3. *Purposeful mixing.* As the teacher becomes familiar with students' work habits and interpersonal skills, groups can be mixed purposefully. Mixing

students who are strong and weak on each of these characteristics is one way to balance groups. Students, with poor interpersonal skills or poor academic histories, however, should not be placed together.

4. *Special helper*. A variation on purposeful mixing is to select one or more students for each group to act as a special helper. Suppose the teacher has decided that groups of four children are to write historical fiction about Harriet Tubman or James Madison. Each student is to do a different chapter, but the group would be more efficient if someone who likes to sketch is in each group, or someone who is a strong planner (i.e., a member who can help the group decide on four different chapters topics).

5. *Index cards*. The teacher writes each student's name on an index card, piece of construction paper or tagboard, or popsicle stick or tongue depressor. Based on the type of group work, a special helper is chosen according to the strengths most necessary for that task for each group. Next, the other children are sorted in the greatest mix possible to each of the special helpers. A random technique obtained by shuffling the deck of namecards or picking popsicle sticks also can be used to form groups around the special helper.

6. *Duration*. Group membership lasts until the cooperative task is completed or until the group has learned how to work cooperatively. Although the group remains the same, the task changes (e.g., from making a paper machè globe to writing a biography of Martin Luther King. A new task is a chance for the teacher to choose a different set of helpers.

The Jigsaw Method. The jigsaw method is a variation of cooperative learning. In this approach, each group produces some aspect of a project. When all the groups have finished their project, the jigsaw puzzle is complete. In Mr. Brenes's class, for example, the students have been divided into six heterogeneous groups of six students each. He gives each group or team the same assignment: to produce a short report that shows examples of, and clearly distinguishes among goods and services in six different areas in Spain: health, food, transportation, recreation, housing, and education. Each team member is responsible for one area. Pedro, for example, must research health, Antonia has food, and so forth. To complete the puzzle takes all six collages; each member contributes one part of the puzzle. Before the puzzle is completed, the teams split up into topic areas. Now Pedro, who is from Team A, meets with all the other children on the other five teams who have been assigned the topic of health. This temporary "health team" meets and plans how to find information that represents the topic of health services in Spain. Members of the temporary "health team" can work together or alone and, once the task is completed, return to the original teams to assemble the whole report representing the six topic areas.

STAD. In the STAD approach to cooperative group work, the students first listen to the teacher present information, then begin cooperative work. Before the teacher lectures or presents, the students are placed in groups. Then the teacher presents the rationale and content of the lesson. Suppose, in a lesson on map legends, Ms. Soroka takes 15 minutes or so to display three different maps, explaining the design and function of the legend on each. Next, she gives the group one handout with questions and another with responses. Only one copy of either the questions or the responses is given to each group so that group members must share materials. Each group is given 20 minutes to accomplish their assignment: to understand why the answers are correct. Finally, the students are given a short quiz over the questions and answers. The group with the highest average score (or that shows the greatest improvement over the last quiz average) is rewarded with special certificates and honorable mention in the class newsletter.

Cooperative Group Model. Cooperative group activities mirror society. The positive effects of group activities on the achievement and self-image of children with mild learning problems is clear. Students assist each other, working together to complete class activities of high caliber. Strengths are emphasized, and differences are minimized. When cooperative learning groups increase the participation of low-status children, their achievement level is raised. Four factors that influence positive academic achievement for children with mild learning problems in cooperative learning groups have been identified in Cohen and Lotan (1990) and Cohen, Lotan, and Cantanzarite (1990):

1. Opportunity for multiple roles in the group
2. Learning tasks involving multiple abilities
3. Teacher intervention for low-status children
4. Simultaneous groups and concept emersion.

A Model Cooperative Group Lesson

Using an example designed for teaching fourth graders responsibility (Fernlund & Crowell, 1990) demonstrates how the achievement levels and self-esteem of Jenny, Sammy, Bridget, and Carmella are influenced as they work cooperatively on this unit. The basis for the unit is the story of the little match girl, a poor child who was sent to sell matches in the cold. In the original story, this sad little girl went to sleep in the snow and died.

Experiences. The teacher, Ms. Martinez, encourages multiple roles by asking the children to participate in three different experiences with the concept of responsibility as related to the story. One experience is a role-playing task in which the four children write a story ending, or if told the ending, make up a new one. Another experience is the creation of decision trees in which the children depict the choices the girl faces and the consequences of each choice. The four girls then dramatize the story's new ending. A third experience requires the children to produce a short narrative in which they must reflect on the match girl's life, followed by small-group discussion guided by the following questions:

> In the story of the little match girl, we find her sad, cold, and lonely. Who do you think should have taken responsibility for her? Was it the girl herself, her parents, her relatives, people passing by? Decide for yourself, and write your thoughts before you discuss them with your group.

Jenny, Sammy, Bridget, and Carmella then discuss their opinions.

Highlighting Abilities. Ms. Martinez designed experiences that immersed Jenny, Sammy, Bridget, and Carmella in the concept of responsibility, as well as highlighted their different abilities: acting for Jenny, writing for Sammy, discussing and speaking for Bridget, and drawing for Carmella. The tasks are open-ended, and the students are encouraged to rely on their group, rather than their teacher, for direction.

Limited teacher interaction provides recognition and praise for Bridget's discussion talents and Carmella's drawing skills and thus builds their self-esteem. Their teacher provides status intervention for Carmella, who has problems writing, when assigning the decision drawing tree. The decisions are listed, and a happy face or sad face, indicating the worth of the choice, is drawn beside the decision. Bridget, who struggles with reading, is quite skilled at role playing and creating new endings for stories. Ms. Martinez has designed a unit with lessons valuable for building students' participation skills and creating a positive social studies environment (Farris & Cooper, 1994).

Potential Problems

The bright side of group cooperative lessons is seen in the model lesson on responsibility. Now for a word from the dark side: At times cooperative group work breaks down because some of the children, often those with mild learning or social disabilities, do not do any of the work. Some of the children accomplish little or nothing and by default force others in the group to carry them through the activity. As part of the cooperative group, these children earn high grades, but individually they may have learned nothing related to the social studies content. The danger in cooperative group instruction is that some children's problems are hidden sufficiently by group participation so that the teacher's attention is not directed to their needs.

Whole-Class Activities: Large Group

Text-based or Theme-oriented Plans

Even before instruction begins, the text-based social studies teacher decides the basic approach to take with the subject. In broad terms, two approaches are used: depth or breadth.

1. In the narrow and deep approach, a lot of time is spent on one particular subject, such as 10 weeks on ancient Egypt, which ensures depth of thought.
2. The alternative is to spend less time on a broader range of subjects (e.g., 2 weeks on ancient Egypt, 2 weeks on ancient India, 2 weeks on ancient China, 2 weeks on ancient Europe, and 2 weeks on ancient Rome). This ensures breadth.

The social studies teachers' reason for choosing one or the other of the approaches depends on the purpose of instruction.

The in-depth approach uses social studies content as a way to develop thinking skills. The topic is not as important as the need to expand students' ability to develop concepts and problem-solving skills. As a result instruction aims at providing an in-depth look at a culture or place by including art, literature, and beliefs and practices, as well as more traditional social studies content, by limiting exposure to a few topics.

While also valuing higher level outcomes, the second approach reflects a more traditional view that teachers are to provide the background—that is, a broad knowledge base—for the next teachers of the same or related subject. In this approach, social studies teachers want to provide or instill the fundamental concepts necessary to familiarize students with topics they will revisit in greater depth as they mature. The broad-based approach to social studies represents a spiraling curriculum model. Many different topics are introduced in a given school year. In subsequent years the same topics are presented again in more depth. Thus, in-depth learning builds upon a prior knowledge base. Achieving familiarity with a wide range of topics puts the historical period or geographic place in the context of what came before and what follows. Essential vocabulary to understand the period or place is contextualized and forms the basis for conceptualization.

Understanding the essential vocabulary and key ideas are important in the textbook-based or theme-based approach for all students. For instance, if the topic is the Middle Ages, students have to understand what a castle is or what nobility means, or the basic social structure of the Middle Ages. For students with mild learning problems, basic vocabulary becomes pivotal for concept development. Some children with mild learning problems will need support in identifying, reading, and understanding the fundamental vocabulary and related concepts. Vocabulary and concept development can be done several ways and should include a variety of practice opportunities.

Vocabulary. Social studies is vocabulary-intensive. One of the major causes of poor comprehension and faulty reading is the nature and type of vocabulary found in social studies content. Limits must be placed on simplifying the specialized terms or the meaning necessary for more complex understanding will be nonfunctional or misleading. Parker and Jarolimek (1997) have identified seven areas of vocabulary that must be considered in social studies instruction: technical terms, figurative terms, words with multiple meanings, terms peculiar to a locality, words easily confused with other words, acronyms, and quantitative terms. Examples of these specialized words are presented in Figure 10.5. Words representing these categories need special attention in social studies.

In many textbook-based units, students are given a list of terms. The students research or are instructed in definitions for those terms. Written drill or practice often is given to reinforce retention. Students work with terms presented in a variety of formats (e.g., writing definitions or using the word in context). Vocabulary also can be used to describe situations or representations of content in the unit (e.g., students might be given a picture and asked to label or describe objects depicted, such as a castle, a knight, or a joust). A variety of practice activities on essentially the same material assists in comprehension and retention. These vocabulary study techniques are simple in nature and, with a minimum of guidance, can be completed successfully by children with mild learning problems.

Technical terms—Words, terms, and expressions peculiar to social studies and usually not encountered when reading selections from other fields of knowledge. *Examples:* veto, meridian, frontier, latitude, longitude, legislature, polls, franchise, temperate, plateau, hemisphere, mountainous, balance of power, capitalism, democracy, nationalism, civilization, century, ancient, decade, pueblo, fjord, iceberg.

Figurative terms—Expressions that are metaphorical; having a different connotation from the literal meaning usually associated with the word. *Examples:* political platform, cold war, closed shop, Iron Curtain, pork barrel, open door, hat in the ring, domino theory, Sunbelt.

Words with multiple meanings—Words that have identical spelling but whose meaning is derived from context. *Examples:* cabinet, belt, bill, chamber, mouth, bank, revolution, fork, court, assembly, range.

Terms peculiar to a locality—Expressions peculiar to a specific part of the country that are not commonly used elsewhere. *Examples:* truck, meeting, borough, gandy, draw, coulee, right, prairie, section, run, butte, arroyo, geoduck, goobers, grits, potlatch, bayou, haul cane road.

Words easily confused with other words—Words that are closely similar in general configuration. *Examples:* continent for country, alien for allies, principal for principle, longitude for latitude, executive for execution, conversation for conservation.

Acronyms—Words that are abbreviated expressions. *Examples:* NATO, NASA, OPEC, SALT, NOW, UNICEF, AIDS, MADD.

Quantitative terms—Words and terms signifying amounts of time, space, or objects. *Examples:* shortly after, century, fortnight, several years later, score, 150 tons.

■ Figure 10.5 *Specialized Terms in Social Studies*

Source: From W. C. Parker & J. J. Jarolimek, "Reading to Learn Social Studies," *Social studies in Elementary Education* (10th ed., Chapter 11, pp. 322–350), (Columbus, OH: Merrill, 1997).

At the end of instruction, some kind of evaluation for vocabulary comprehension is given. The object of the evaluation is twofold: (a) to determine what students have learned and (b) to provide students with positive views of themselves as learners. Students with mild learning problems can be successful with drill-and-practice activities with minimum guidance from teachers. Multiple exposure to vocabulary seems to be an effective way for many students with disabilities to learn. When students with mild learning problems learn these essential vocabularies, as reflected by a good score on a social studies quiz, they can experience a sense of accomplishment.

Special education teachers' tasks are to ensure that students understand and complete the drill-and-practice activities the social studies teacher provides.

Modifications such as rewording directions, changing print size, or teaching students organizational skills for meeting deadlines become part of the accommodation responsibility of special education teachers. Task monitoring, that accounts for teaching students how to attend and complete tasks that exceed normal classroom demands also becomes part of the responsibility of special education teachers.

Concept Formation. Students with mild learning problems, as with all students, must have acquired and retained knowledge of the basic vocabulary before they can understand higher level concepts within a unit. For example, students are likely to have great difficulty comprehending the social hierarchy of the Middle Ages without understanding the vocabulary used to describe the time period. Many students with mild learning problems have trouble deducing meaning from the context. By building on vocabulary that they know, they can incorporate new associations.

A Model for Large-Group Instruction

Organization, organization, organization. One of the often-cited weaknesses of students with mild learning problems is lack of organizational skills. Given the extensive amount of content delivered in a text-based model of social studies, students who are not organized are often at a loss for identifying key vocabulary and concepts, assignments, and due dates for projects, readings, and quizzes. In a text-driven social studies model, many students with organizational problems would benefit from a fairly standardized and predictable unit format.

Predictability. In a standardized format, activities basically are presented in a predictable order, (e.g., students know for better or worse what to expect instructionally). In Mr. Maher's sixth grade class, for example, each lesson is designed for a 2-week period. Each lesson has a vocabulary list of 20 words, and four essay questions. For a history or geography unit, Mr. Maher typically gives students a blank map, which is used throughout the unit. The students are required to identify and locate nine to 12 places related directly to the unit of study. Mr. Maher's pattern of instruction is to work with the vocabulary words for a certain number of days until all the students understand all the key words, to work on map identifications, and near the end of the unit to discuss and outline the answers for the essay questions.

The student's responsibility is to write out the definitions and the essay questions in sentence form and to learn the places on the map. Within the 2-week unit, students engage in at least one, but usually two or three, high-interest, low-accountability activities (e.g., coloring a map to show a historical period or building a model in which the effort and the attempt are as important as the results). For Mr. Maher, the high-interest activities do not represent a large percentage of the grade. The focus of accountability is on the vocabulary, map identification, and essays.

At the end of each 2-week unit, Mr. Maher gives a quiz that essentially covers the vocabulary, places on the map, and concepts in the essays. Information from the essays is presented in a multiple-choice format. If the students have completed four essays, they can expect at least four of the quiz questions to be based on the essays.

Positive Self-Image. Any student who has done the essay and mapping assignments and learned the vocabulary in a 2-week period can do well. The focus of the test on the vocabulary and map balances the skills of the remedial student with the interests and needs of the higher level students in the same class. Students with poor academic records know they can be successful in the class by focusing time and energy on the basics. They can do as well as the students who typically are high achievers. Students who complete basic vocabulary activities, map identification, and essays rapidly can spend more time on high-interest activities.

Task Completion. Most assignments are not collected or graded until the end of the unit. This 2-week period allows for differences in rate of task completion. Students can take from 1 to 10 days to define terms, identify locations, and complete essays. Students with problems in reading, writing, or study skills are not likely to write assigned definitions in 1 day. Students with mild disabilities often need time accommodations to complete the required assignments. One suggested accommodation is to assign less content to students with mild disabilities (Henley, Ramsey, & Algozzine, 1996), an accommodation that is not acceptable to most social studies teachers (Passe & Beattie, 1994). Another suggested accommodation is to lessen the amount of practice time with key concepts, an accommodation that is contrary to instructional research findings. Accommodations like Mr. Maher's may be the middle ground—and an instructionally sounder path for students with mild learning problems under a text-based social studies model.

Organizational Needs. In keeping with students' organizational needs, Mr. Maher requires that all written work be kept in a single folder. The purpose of the folder is to keep the students organized by requiring them to arrange all written work in a standardized format. For example, on the first day for each unit, they are given a notetaking sheet with vocabulary printed on one side and essay items on the other, which they immediately place on the first page of the folder. Words are presented in vertical lists, with spaces for writing definitions or notes for definitions. As students read texts or listen to lecture, they can take notes on this sheet.

Page 2 of the folder is reserved for the blank map to be used in the unit to label required places. As the unit progresses, the students are expected to produce the required places or formations. Following the map page are rewritten definitions that the students produce in complete sentences. Rewriting reinforces what was learned during the notetaking, and the complete sentence format is necessary so the students later can understand what they have written. Following the rewritten definitions is a page for rewritten essays; complete sentences and standard paragraph form are required for the rewritten essay notes. Following the written vocabulary and essays are whatever written activities were done with the unit.

Activities. The purpose of the activities is to allow greater in-depth participation in the topic for students who have acquired the basic unit content. By the simple nature of the required tasks (e.g., in writing definitions, students who need more time to finish required content can do so on their own time as homework or in study hall). The activities provide these students with a change of pace from application of basic skills and even can account for differences in learning styles or talents.

In the study of the Middle Ages, for example, an activity could be one centering on how occupations formed the basis of assigning last names. Students could match the occupation to the name (e.g., "Carter" is a person who hauls things in wagons, or "Smithe" is the last name of a person who works with iron). Other examples of high-interest activities include drawings depicting the relationship between the serfs and their lords and poems describing life as a knight. Activities such as these can be used to expand the knowledge base of the unit through personally meaningful projects.

Review. Next in the folder usually would be a cloze review using all or most of the vocabulary words in a narrative context. For example:

> "During the Middle Ages, the _____ were the agricultural workers (serfs). These workers were bound to a _____ manor, the land owned by a member of the _____ (nobility)....

The students fill in the blanks, and class discussion ensues, if necessary, to clarify or expand responses. The completed responses are:

> During the Middle Ages, the serfs were the agricultural workers. These workers were bound to a manor, the land owned by a member of the nobility...."

Accountability. The quiz for the unit is the last entry in the folder. Using the concept of completed folders, students are accountable for all assignments, and each assignment is weighted approximately the same. As a result, students who have problems taking tests find less emphasis on testing and more focus on written work.

Mr. Maher has provided an organizational framework that accounts for individual differences and leads to conceptual block-building in social studies. The 2-week timeframe provides structure and predictability. Flexibility within the structure also allows students with mild learning problems more time for instruction, practice, and assistance with the content of the unit. Students with mild learning problems can be successful in acquiring a knowledge base for future classes and develop positive self-esteem through awarded grades.

Potential Problems

The bright side of text-based group lessons was seen in the model unit on the Middle Ages. Now for a word from the dark side: At times group work breaks down because some of the children, often those with mild learning or social disabilities, do not do any of the work. Some of the children accomplish little or nothing and by default earn failing grades. As a result, these children may have learned nothing related to the social studies content. The danger in large-group instruction is that some children's problems are so serious that teacher intervention is directed more to task completion and motivation than to instruction in social studies content. Potential problems under a large group or whole-class text-based model of social studies seem familiar to potential problems found in a child-centered model. Is it possible that many models, or at least aspects of models, are necessary to meet students' divergent needs? By embedding aspects of models that match students' entry skills, many potential problems can be reduced or eliminated.

Knowledge Acquisition

Prerequisite Skills

The more a model employs a text-driven approach, the greater is the risk that "It's boring!" will become the social studies motto (at least until success can or cannot be demonstrated). The greater the emphasis on the child-centered approach, the greater is the possibility of developing arts and crafts skills at the expense of a sound knowledge base in social studies. Yet, a striking similarity exists between potential problems across all basic models of social studies instruction. The problematic aspects of group activities, cooperative or not, stem from the same source as situations in which children do not stay on task, do not complete assignments, refuse to hand in homework, fail quizzes, and decline to participate in group discussion. In these cases, low grades flash like a beacon, highlighting failure and promoting low self-esteem. Who's to blame for poor achievement across these very different social studies instructional models and philosophies? Elementary, my dear Watson. The invisible villain is the missing prerequisite skill.

Entry Skill

To be successful in learning social studies concepts under any model, task demands must match the student's skill level. This is not new information. Students need not stay at a low level, but to require them to learn new concepts through activities that exceed their skill levels is to doom them and their teachers to the tragedy of Sisyphus—always condemned to reach that impossible mountaintop. Just as Sisyphus is a myth, so is success in social studies for children with mild learning problems without the appropriate instructional support.

Abundance of Instructional Resources

There is no lack of sources for instructional strategies either for identifying prerequisite skills or for locating strategies of instruction for acquisition, retention, or generalization to new content. Textbooks for teaching children with mild learning problems are easily accessible. Techniques for teaching social studies under a variety of models also are available. The classic best seller *Social Studies in Elementary Education* (10th ed.) by Parker and Jarolimek (1997) is bursting with ideas, as is *Middle Grades Social Studies* by Allen and Stevens (1994).

Representative texts emphasizing a more child-centered approach or the "new social studies" are *Children and Their World: Strategies for Teaching Social Studies* (5th ed.) by Welton and Mallan (1996) and *Elementary Social Studies: A Whole Language Approach* by Farris and Cooper (1994). The National Council for the Social Studies (NCSS) (Evans & Saxe, 1996) has produced a 406-page bulletin, *Handbook on Teaching Social Issues*, which describes an "issues-centered" curriculum.

Inclusion Paradigm Shift Revisited

A diverse student population has become the norm in any social studies class. When trying to accommodate the wide range of ethnic, physical, intellectual, and social differences of students, a variety of administrative approaches has been used. Ironically, these approaches have done little to foster diversity in the classroom. Typical approaches have included grouping, special classes, and pull-out programs (Welton & Mallan, 1996). These exclusionary techniques are being replaced by instruction or attempts at instruction in the general education setting.

Limited Services

School districts often provide full- or part-time aides to assist children with severe to moderate disabilities. Juan, for example, who has muscular dystrophy, has an aide, and Patrick, who has a hearing disability, has an interpreter. For Tim, who can't organize his thoughts, or for Daniel, who is prone to outbursts, support personnel is more limited.

Ideally, Tim and Daniel, and all other students with mild disabilities, have access to a special education teacher or a classroom teacher highly skilled in teaching techniques that accommodate their students' needs. The picture of the ideal team approach—the special education teacher and general education teacher collaborating hand-in-hand, side-by-side, day-by-day, sharing compatible philosophies—is more surreal than real. Anyone who buys this educational picture is ready to purchase the Brooklyn Bridge at cost.

Collaboration

Accommodating the needs of children with mild disabilities under the "romancing the team" approach simply is not feasible for all teachers or all students. One of the widely accepted practices of the 1990s has been collaboration between general and special educators. Although the collaboration model has been applied successfully in some situations (Idol, Nevin, & Paolucci-Whitcomb, 1994), the stamina of teachers in terms of time and opportunity has been strained severely. Not enough special education teachers are being educated to fill the growing demands of children with mild disabilities (McCoy, 1996).

Inclusion

Inclusion, the movement designed to bring special education services to the general classroom, changed the instruction paradigm of moving children with special needs into special settings for special instruction by special teachers. This shift also means that most children with mild learning problems will be instructed directly by the general education teacher in all areas, including social studies. The inclusion paradigm left the collaboration role of teachers "to be determined."

Special Education Presence

The problem with inclusion is one of special education presence. Special education teachers are assigned to students who are enrolled in a variety of classrooms. No matter how skilled special education teachers are, they physically cannot be in more than one room at a time. The solution lies in how special educators can modify the environment while reducing the time they are present physically in the classroom. With respect for the classroom social studies model, the presence and the influence of special techniques accommodating students' needs is possible at most times given proper planning and a paradigm shift in roles. Special educators will reduce their direct instructional contact with students, but services and instructional impact must equal or exceed past service models of delivery. Under the inclusion model, students with mild learning problems will need more access with carefully constructed or orchestrated instructional modifications and less time with direct instruction from teachers with special training.

Modified materials, models of expected products, and guidelines for completing tasks are only three of many techniques that can provide the special presence needed without providing the continuous presence of the special education teacher. Special education teachers may find themselves less and less involved in providing instruction directly to students and more and more involved in providing instructional materials that can be used independently.

The New Inclusion Model

To be in five classrooms at one time, the special education teacher of the future will have to become a specialist within the instructional design field. Fortunately, technological advances have made creation of materials and modification of material less time-intensive. The special educator will have to design materials and environmental settings that provide access to social studies content by taking into account the instructional skills of the students and classroom demands. So far, no large-scale model of this "new inclusion" paradigm exists.

The new inclusion model has put educators at a crossroad where preparation and opportunity meet. To paraphrase John Maynard Keynes, "I do not know which makes a teacher more conservative—to know nothing but the present or nothing but the past." For certain, teachers engaging in the new inclusion paradigm will have to be far from conservative as they dare to invent models of inclusion that account for diversity in students and diversity of service delivery. As Thoreau said, "If you have built castles in the air, your work need not be lost; that is where they should be. Now put the foundations under them."

References

Allen, M. G., & Stevens, R. L. (1994). *Middle grades social studies: Teaching and learning for active and responsible citizenship*. Boston: Allyn & Bacon.

Baker, J. M. & Zigmond, N. (1990). Are regular education classes equipped to accommodate students with learning disabilities. *Exceptional Children, 56*(6), 515–526.

Bender, W. N., & Ukeje, I. C. (1989). The other side of placement decisions: Assessment of the main-stream learning environment. *Remedial & Special Education, 9*(5), 28–33.

Bracey, G. W. (1993). Elementary curriculum materials: Still a long way to go. *Phi Delta Kappan, 74*(8), 654, 656.

Bulgren, J., & Lenz, K. (1996). Strategic instruction in the content areas. In D. D. Deshler, E. S. Ellis, & B. K. Lenz, *Teaching adolescents with learning disabilities* (2d ed.). Denver: Love.

Bulgren, J. A., Schumaker, J. B., & Deshler, D. D. (1994). The effects of recall enhancement routine on the test performance of secondary students with and without learning disabilities. *Learning Disabilities Research & Practice, 9*(1), 1–11.

Carnine, D., Crawford, D., Harniss, M., & Hollenbeck, K. (1995). *Understanding U.S. history: Vol 1. Through the Civil War.* Eugene, OR: Considerate Publishing.

Coerr, E. (1986). *The Josefina Story Quilt.* Illus. B. Begen. Harper & Row.

Cohen, E., & Lotan, R. (1990). Teacher as supervisor of complex technology. *Theory into Practice, 29*(1), 78–84.

Cohen, E., Lotan, R., & Catanzarite, L. (1990). Treating status problems in the cooperative classroom. In S. Sharan (Ed.), *Cooperative learning: Theory and research* (pp. 203–229). New York: Praeger.

Ellis, E. S. (1993). *Writing strategies for thought-full classrooms.* Tuscaloosa, AL: SMART Strategy Associates.

Ellis, E. S. (1994). An instructional model for integrating content-area instruction with cognitive strategy instruction. *Reading & Writing Quarterly: Overcoming Learning Difficulties, 1,* 63–90.

Evans, R. W., & Saxe, D. W. (1996). *Handbook on Teaching Social Issues* (NCSS Bulletin 93). Washington, DC: NCSS.

Farris, P. J., & Cooper, S. M. (1994). *Elementary social studies: A whole language approach.* Madison, WI: Brown & Benchmark.

Fernlund, P., & Crowell, S. (1990, November 18). *Complex instruction in elementary social studies.* Paper presented at meeting of National Council for the Social Studies, Anaheim, CA.

Gersten, R., Brengelman, S., & Jimenez, R. (1994). Effective instruction for culturally and linguistically diverse students: A reconceptualization. *Focus on Exceptional Children, 21*(1), 1–16.

Goodlad, J. (1984). A place called school. New York: McGraw-Hill.

Henley, M., Ramsey, R., & Algozzine, R. F. (1996). *Characteristics of and strategies for teaching students with mild disabilities* (2d. ed.). Boston: Allyn & Bacon.

Horton, S. W., Lovitt, T. C., & Slocum, T. (1988). Teaching geography to high school students with academic deficits. *Learning Disability Quarterly, 11,* 371–379.

Idol, L., Nevin, A., Paolucci-Whitcomb, P. (1994). *Collaborative consultation* (2d ed.). Austin: Pro-Ed.

James, M., & Zarrillo, J. (1989). Teaching history with children's literature: A concept based, interdisciplinary approach. *Social Studies, 80,* 153–158.

Johnson, D. D., Toms-Bronowski, S., & Pittleman, S. D. (1982). Vocabulary development. In R. E. Kretschmer (Ed.), *Reading and the hearing impaired individual* (monograph). *Volta Review, 84,* 11–24.

McCoy, K. M. (1996). *Teaching special learners in the general education classroom* (2d ed.), Denver: Love.

Lehrman, F. (1990). Loving the earth: A sacred landscape book for children. *Celestial Arts. 1,* 48 pages.

Lewis, C., (1987). *Long ago in Oregon* (J. Fontaine, Illus.). New York: Harper & Row.

National Commission on Excellence in Education. (1983). *A nation at-risk: The imperative for educational reform.* Washington, DC: Author.

National Council for the Social Studies Task Force. (1994). *Expectations of excellence: Curriculum standards for social studies.* Washington, DC: Author.

National Council for the Social Studies Task Force on Early Childhood Elementary Education. (1990). *Social studies curriculum planning resources.* Washington, DC: NCSS.

Parker, W. C., and Jarolimek, J. (1997). *Social studies in elementary education.* Columbus, OH: Merrill.

Passe, J., & Beattie, J. (1994). Social studies instruction for students with mild disabilities: A progress report. *Remedial & Special Education, 4*(15), 227–233.

Routman, R. (1991). *Invitations: Changing as teachers and learning K–12.* Portsmouth, NH: Heinemann.

Routman, R. Invitations: Changing as teachers and learners K–12 in P. J. Farris & S. M. Cooper, *Elementary Social Studies: A whole language approach*, City: Publisher, 1994, p. 38.

Saxe, D. W. (1994). *Social studies for the elementary teacher.* Needham Heights, MA: Allyn & Bacon.

Schumm, J. S., & Vaughn, S. (1991). Making adaptations for mainstreamed students: General classroom teachers' perspectives. *Remedial & Special Education, 12*(4), 18–27.

Smith, J. A., Monson, J. A., & Dobson, D. (1992). A case study on integrating history and reading instruction through literature. *Social Education, 56*(7), 370–375.

Turner, T. N. (1976). Making the social studies textbook a more effective tool for less able readers. *Social Education. 40*, 38–41.

Welton, D. A., & Mallan, J. T. (1996). *Children and their world* (5th ed.). Geneva, IL: Houghton Mifflin.

Whinnery, K. W., Fuchs, L. S., & Fuchs, D. (1991). General, special, and remedial teachers' acceptance of behavioral and instructional strategies for mainstreamed students with mild handicaps. *Remedial & Special Education, 12*(4), 6–17.

Ysseldyke, J., & Algozzine, B. (1990). *Introduction to special education*. Boston: Houghton Mifflin.

Curriculum Considerations in an Inclusive Environment

CYNTHIA L. WARGER
AND MARLEEN C. PUGACH

WITH THE TREND toward more inclusive placements for students with disabilities, the nature of collaboration changes. The authors discuss the nature of this change and the need for what they describe as "curriculum-centered collaboration." They provide examples appropriate at the classroom level in curriculum planning. Embedded in the chapter is a reader-friendly table of curriculum trends by subject field.

Ms. Grant has taught special education for more than a decade. This year her school moved to an inclusive model. Students who previously had been assigned to Ms. Grant's resource room are going to be included fully in a fifth-grade classroom taught by Ms. Howard. Ms. Grant has collaborated in the past with Ms. Howard, primarily in applying behavior management techniques to solving students' problems. Given this new arrangement, however, she knows that more is needed to support the students' progress.

At Stone Middle School, eighth-grade teachers want to implement an interdisciplinary curriculum unit for students across classrooms. Teachers feel strongly that special education students should be included in the project work. They have called upon Mr. Pack, the special education teacher, to assist with the planning and instruction. In the past Mr. Pack worked with special education students on basic literacy skills but now realizes that to pull his weight on the interdisciplinary team, he will have to do more.

Special education teacher Ms. Barker and history teacher Mr. Marley have been co-teaching for the last year. Occasionally Ms. Barker provides actual instruction to the class, but her role consists primarily of tutoring individual students. The district just announced that the social studies curriculum will undergo renewal next year. Although Ms. Barker is pleased with the progress students have been making as a result of her interventions, she is beginning to think that much more could be done if certain changes were made to curriculum before presenting it. She wishes there would be a way to contribute to curriculum planning.

As these vignettes suggest, the movement toward increased inclusive placements for students with disabilities is changing the role of the special education teacher. As special educators are expected to deliver more and more of their educational support within the general classroom context, new opportunities to reconfigure traditional specialized services abound. Collaboration between general and special educators has long been an important means of fostering this change. Unlike the collaboration typically found in noninclusive programs, in which the major focus is on the special educator solving individual student problems, however, collaborative partnerships now face the challenge of expanding to include curriculum planning and implementation. As educators share responsibility for all students, what students know and are expected to do—which are fundamental questions of curriculum—have become the concern of all educators.

In this article, we explore how teacher collaboration can be expanded specifically to include curriculum considerations and to offer a process by which teachers can work together to address these concerns. Whether the special educator is serving as a co-teacher, a teacher consultant, or a member of a prereferral team, issues related to curriculum should be moving to the forefront of discussions in inclusive contexts.

Curriculum as the New Target of Collaboration

In the context of inclusive schools, students with a wide range of learning and behavioral characteristics are not themselves considered so much a part of the problem. Instead, the challenge is to create learning environments that promote success for all students. As a result of the focus shifting from problems within students to how classroom work is designed, the relationship between students, particularly those with mild disabilities, and the curriculum requires a reconceptualization as well (Pugach & Warger, 1993; Warger & Pugach, 1996).

Curriculum, after all, is at the heart of schooling. As many special educators often have observed, students who increasingly are being included in general education classes are the same students who were excluded in the first place because of their unsuccessful performance in the standard curriculum. So if special education teachers are to make serious contributions to the success our students achieve in inclusive settings, they must be prepared to address the curriculum itself.

The standard curriculum continues to pose problems for students with disabilities, and thus affects the ease and success with which integration can take place (McLaughlin & Warren, 1992; NASBE, 1992). Too often, students are denied access to the curriculum simply because they do not have the prerequisite skills that will allow them to participate in the lesson. In other cases the problem lies with the structure and content of the curriculum itself. Difficulties arise when the content is at a cognitive level that is too high, requires analytic skills that the student does not have, or assumes a certain knowledge base that is not present. If the curriculum is deemed the problem, the challenge that ought to take priority is to rethink what the student is being asked to do and whether it is appropriate given students' unique learning and behavioral characteristics.

For many special and general educators this description of curricular problems may seem obvious. What creates the current challenge for educators working in inclusive settings is to frame classroom dilemmas from a proactive perspective in which the target of the intervention is the curriculum and its relationship to the student rather than the student alone. The goal becomes one of planning learning environments that, from the onset, result in the highest learning achievement for the most students possible. At the same time, emphasis is placed on identifying how the curriculum might be making unreasonable demands on learners, rather than assuming that "this growing number of students" is what is presenting unreasonable instructional challenges to teachers.

This seemingly subtle distinction has some significant implications for how special and general education approach "business as usual." In traditional, noninclusive programs, when a student is not achieving the curriculum goals, the tendency is to look at the deficit behavior or learning characteristic as the sole source of the problem. To improve inclusive programs so they support student success, we can shift the source of the problem to the curriculum itself and how it is delivered in the classroom. The goal is to reassess what the student is being asked to learn and how the knowledge and skills are being presented. In doing this, special and general education teachers ask themselves what they can do together to improve the student's relationship with the curriculum. The role of special education support personnel takes on new meaning when interventions are framed from the perspective of (a) how reasonable the curriculum is in the first place, and (b) how to adapt and modify the curriculum based on a sound understanding of curriculum goals.

Over the last few years we have worked with special and general educators alike to refocus their thinking about inclusion onto curriculum (Pugach & Warger, 1993; Pugach & Warger, in press; Warger & Pugach, 1993) and to use it as an entry point when collaborating about how to redesign classrooms to accommodate a wider range of learners. We have found that, by targeting curriculum rather than student deficits as the jumping-off point for discussions between general and special educators, we have a much better chance of eliminating barriers to student success— whose origins more often than not can be traced to rigid conceptions of curriculum in the first place.

Collaborative Partnerships: A Logical Starting Point

Children's unique learning needs finally are being recognized as the norm rather than the exception in our nation's schools. For several years, one way that school districts have been addressing the ever widening diversity of student needs in general education classrooms is through collaborative partnerships between general and special educators. Co-teaching, collaborative consultation, peer collaboration, pre-referral teams, teacher assistance teams—to name a few—are among the most widely practiced methods for promoting successful inclusion of students with mild learning and behavioral disabilities (Laycock, Gable, & Korinek, 1991; McLaughlin & Warren, 1992; National Association of School Boards of Education, 1992).

The intent of these collaborative partnerships undoubtedly has been to put energy and resources into preventing school failure by implementing modifications or accommodations of standard, normative practice in general education classrooms specifically to meet the needs of students who are experiencing academic or behavioral difficulties. Most collaborative interactions, however, still revolve around the old special education paradigm in which the focus of problem solving is on the individual characteristics or performance deficits that pose instructional dilemmas for teachers.

As we move toward more inclusive classrooms and schools, professional collaboration between special and general education teachers is more important than ever. Because the basic structure and content of general education classrooms will without question determine the success of inclusion, however, we can no longer simply move students with disabilities out of resource rooms and into the mainstream, tinkering with accommodations to and modifications of the existing curriculum along the way. Instead, inclusive education demands that we rethink our basic conceptions of teaching and learning, which essentially means rethinking the curriculum itself—not only for students with disabilities, but for all students. Collaboration provides an ideal vehicle through which deliberations might take place. This represents a fundamental change in how the roles of special and general educators are viewed in the school setting, whose task becomes one of pooling knowledge about curriculum and current curriculum trends, along with knowledge about how diverse characteristics of learners are expected to interact with the content. The purpose of collaborative discussions and action is to shape the basic structure of what goes on in the classroom to the advantage of all students before the content is presented rather than after the student has failed. As such, collaboration moves us squarely into the realm of curriculum reform.

Maintaining this level of involvement in curriculum reform requires a conscious focusing on the part of both special and general educators on how they interpret the place of curriculum—both past and present—in their shared work. Most likely, general educators will arrive at the curriculum question from a reform context that calls for more rigorous content and increased academic standards for all students by emphasizing in-depth coverage of content, students' abilities to think critically and creatively to solve problems, and integration into the curriculum of concepts that are connected across subject areas (see, for example, Lewis, 1990; Newman, 1988; O'Neil, 1990). Special educators, who tend to have less knowledge about the scope and sequence of the various academic areas, will bring their own agenda, most often reflected in concerns that these curriculum reforms will result in more student failure (see, for example, Carnine & Kameenui, 1990; Glatthorn 1985;

Sapon-Shevin, 1987; Shepard, 1987). Special educators' conceptions of curriculum traditionally treat it either as remedial practice or as whatever has been stated in the individualized education program (for a more thorough discussion, see Pugach and Warger, 1996). If a curriculum that respects diversity in learning is to be achieved, both views must be pursued actively, debated, and integrated.

Making such a shift is hard work for all teachers. Collaboration between special and general education, however, already affords built-in professional support that can be drawn upon for making the structural and conceptual changes that curriculum planning and renewal requires (Pugach & Wesson, 1995). Making the commitment to becoming knowledgeable about and participating in curriculum in the broad sense enables the development of educational programs in which students can learn challenging, interesting, and motivating content. Defining educational outcomes for students with disabilities from a point of greater curriculum understanding, rather than from the narrow framework that has been traditional in special education, provides educators with unlimited opportunities to set higher expectations and design innovative strategies for reaching them.

In the following examples we describe how collaborative practices between general and special educators can be redesigned as curriculum-centered collaboration both for preventive curriculum planning and for trouble-shooting curriculum problems in the classroom as they arise. Classroom-based curriculum trouble-shooting occurs when special and general education teachers focus specifically on curriculum as the point of problem solving at the classroom level in anticipation of or in response to student difficulty. In contrast, preventive planning comes about through joint participation of special and general education teachers on school or district-wide curriculum planning or renewal teams.

In both examples, what is central is how knowledge and skills can be made more accessible to a wider range of students. By refocusing the traditional source of the problem away from the student and onto the curriculum, the conversation between special and general educators is concerned with broad instructional changes that will be necessary given the new curriculum goals and objectives they choose to enact.

Curriculum-Centered Collaboration at the Classroom Level

In developing a curriculum-centered approach to solving specific classroom problems, we drew on a generic process that already is typical of many collaborative partnerships and is composed of four phases: (a) establishing rapport and setting up the boundaries for collaboration; (b) identifying the problem; (c) developing an intervention plan; and (d) evaluating the collaboration (Aldinger, Warger, & Eavy, 1991). In each step of this generic process, we have shifted the attention of the conversation away from the student's presenting problem to the curriculum itself. Figure 11.1 illustrates this curriculum-centered problem-solving process.

Stage One: Orientation
  Establish rapport
  Set limits for collaboration

Stage Two: Problem Identification
  Identify new curriculum goals, instructional strategies, and assessment techniques.
  Identify new relationships between student, curriculum, teacher, and peers.
  Discuss potential mismatch with student characteristics.
  Present relevant data.
  State potential difficulty area.

Stage Three: Intervention
  Brainstorm suggestions: curriculum, instruction, assessment.
  Select strategies.
  Identify support practices for students and/or teachers.
  Develop and implement plan.

Stage Four: Closure
  Review student progress.
  Evaluate.

Figure 11.1 *Curriculum-Centered Problem-Solving Process*

In this section we present a description of each phase, along with a vignette depicting how two collaborating teachers might interact. We offer two examples. In the first, the special and general education teachers are planning classroom activities from a curriculum perspective to avoid problems. In the second, teachers collaborate from a curriculum perspective about a classroom situation gone awry.

Classroom Trouble-Shooting

Phase One

In the first phase of our curriculum-centered approach, teachers establish rapport and set the expectations for collaboration. If the special and general education teachers are co-teaching or when the special educator is providing services in the classroom regularly, beginning this phase at the start of the school year is best. By beginning early, the special educator has an opportunity to gain familiarity with the curricular goals and outcomes for the students in that classroom. In addition, the special educator begins to understand the general educator's teaching style and instructional preferences. Tasks might include surveying materials and giving attention to assessing the learning and behavioral characteristics of the total student group. Similarly, general education teachers make it a point to learn about the special educator's skills and experience and begin thinking in terms of how those assets might be utilized best.

At this time, coming to a preliminary agreement on roles and responsibilities is helpful. Hard questions have to be addressed regarding beliefs and expectations. For example, the perception may linger that the special education teacher will serve primarily as a glorified aide in the classroom. This perception can undermine future efforts to focus jointly on curriculum because the special education teacher pulls away "the kids with problems," placing primary attention back within an individual-deficit orientation.

Early on, the understanding should be that both special and general education teachers bring expertise to the conversation. Although the content knowledge of special educators is often not as extensive as that of the general educator, the special educator still brings a wealth of knowledge to the partnership, not to mention key expertise in making modifications and adaptations. Now is not the time to "defer" to the general educator, as commonly was the case during mainstreaming collaborations. In those collaborations, keeping the child in the general education placement—no matter how much of a problem the standard curriculum was overall—was the overt goal. In contrast, the goal of curriculum-centered problem solving is to pool expertise to improve learning outcomes for all students. The knowledge that special educators bring, particularly with respect to modification and adaptation, becomes much more meaningful if it is implemented through a lens of deep curriculum knowledge.

Jan has been teaching third grade for several years. This will be the first year that Barbara, a special education teacher, has been assigned a teaming placement, so she is not quite sure what to expect.

At the first planning meeting the two went over their expectations. Barbara expressed her apprehensions about being in the general education classroom but emphasized that in no way was her enthusiasm diminished as a result. Jan took the opportunity to spell out her high expectations for student success, particularly as related to the eight special education students on the class roster. Barbara listened and assured Jan that she, too, was committed to providing a strong educational program for all kids. Having found a similar goal upon which to focus, the two teachers began discussing how each could contribute to achieving their joint purpose of student learning.

Clearly, building rapport does not happen overnight. It involves a long-term commitment between the professionals. Even so, there is much to be said for first impressions. The efforts that transpire during this phase can either advance or harm the impending collaborative work. In the conversation between Barbara and Jan, neither made the assumption that Jan was interested only in curriculum or that Barbara was interested only in bringing her "bag of special education tricks" into the classroom.

Phase Two

In the next phase, problem identification, the goal is to identify potential areas of difficulty in the curriculum for the student(s). The discussion is to include topics such as new curriculum goals, instructional strategies the teachers wish to use to support those goals, and preferred assessment techniques. Take some time to explore the rationale for each point of discussion. At this step, questions for discussion might include the following.

- Are the goals representative of new curriculum standards? For instance, in mathematics, the curriculum might depart from an emphasis on computational skills to problem-solving skills. In language arts, students might be expected to fine tune their oral discourse skills in addition to their written skills. In science, students might be expected to move beyond completing experiments to generating their own hypotheses for investigation. In social studies, students might be asked to apply their learnings beyond paper-and-pencil tests to solving real problems in the community.

- What prerequisite knowledge and skills do the goals require? Many of the new curriculum trends emphasize the ability to analyze, synthesize, and create (for a thorough discussion, see Pugach and Warger, in press). Application of knowledge is another major focus, especially as it relates to problem solving across disciplines. Many of the new standards also expect students to be able to gather, integrate, evaluate, and present information in a variety of formats. The use of technology often is assumed in higher grades, particularly for tasks such as word-processing and using databases.

- What social skills are needed for the student to participate in the lesson? For instance, cooperative learning assumes a number of critical social skills such as listening, waiting one's turn, taking responsibility, initiating conversation, asking questions, and making group decisions.

- What level of independence is required for students to complete the learning tasks? For example, many inquiry-based lessons rely on students to sustain interest over time, to have the necessary cognitive capacities to recall information pertaining to the topic over several days, and to think critically about the information being gathered.

This kind of discussion provides a framework within which the special and general education teachers can reach a clear understanding of student expectations. From this point, teachers are ready to predict potential student difficulties with the curriculum.

Instead of making the assumption that a given student will have difficulty—and having teachers revert to a deficit problem-solving process—the focus of the collaborative dialogue remains on the curriculum goal and instructional strategies the teachers have selected to carry it out. The question becomes: Do the students have the necessary skills and knowledge to succeed in the lesson? To answer this question, teachers scan the group, targeting students who, they speculate, will have particular difficulty because of a mismatch between the goal/instructional approach and the students' skills. At this point additional data might have to be gathered to support their hypotheses. Or the teachers might wish to review students' portfolios or previous work samples to confirm their hunches.

Teachers also need to identify any new relationships that new curriculum goals create among student, teacher, and peers. For example, if the students are expected to solve problems collaboratively, a new relationship—one of interdependency—must be formed between classmates. Or, if students are expected to complete an indepth analysis of a topic, their relationship to the material must be more personal to ensure that they sustain interest over time. In addition, in both cases the traditional relationship between teacher and learner is altered as students are expected to take on more responsibility for their learning.

Jan and Barbara decided that, because the district had moved to a whole-language approach to teaching literacy, this might be a good place to start their work. They planned for a literature-circle activity in which the students would be invited to share their opinions and thoughts about a story. It ends with a clear delineation of potential areas of student difficulty.

The literature-circle activity requires students to sit, wait their turn, and answer when the teacher calls upon them. During the proposed literature-circle activity, students are encouraged to use their critical thinking skills to analyze story elements such as character, plot, and setting. The goal of the activity is for students to use oral discourse skills to share their thinking about the story.

Barbara knew that several of the students had difficulty reading at third-grade level. She also knew that the story Jan wanted to use dealt with concepts that would be new to about a fourth of the class. Finally, Barbara was concerned that if students came to the literature circle without being able to answer the questions, they might react by acting out. Jan agreed with the analysis.

After much discussion, Jan decided that, to her, the most important goal of the lesson was for students to share their learning in a group. She was less concerned with how the students obtained the information, although she did want to encourage a positive attitude toward reading. As a result of the collaborative problem identification, the problem was defined as:

- The lesson requires students to read a story written at a third-grade reading level and to analyze the characters, plot, and setting. Some of the students, however, cannot read independently at that level.
- The lesson requires students to comprehend a story in which many of the concepts are new. Further, some of the students, as a result of their life experiences, will have no context for understanding these concepts.

- The lesson requires students to share their thoughts about the story orally with the class in a group-discussion format. Students who have not read the material might become bored and, thus, demonstrate inappropriate behavior.

Phase Three

With these problem statements in hand, the teachers now are ready to develop ideas to expand, modify, or enhance the curriculum for all students. The teachers also should identify and offer multiple possibilities for enriching the curriculum. If they have to introduce more intensive strategies for certain students, this work should be done only in the context of the specific curriculum goal. Thus, a student might need additional support on a goal this week but not need any help on next week's goal.

In contrast, in traditional problem-centered collaboration, once a student's problem is identified, he or she is almost always expected to need special assistance. The resulting plan should incorporate all of the ideas and suggestions for making the curriculum more accessible to the students. It should draw on the strengths and talents of both collaborating educators.

Jan and Barbara have been brainstorming ideas for how to enhance the lesson to ensure that all students are successful. Here is what they decided:

On Monday, Barbara will introduce the new concepts in the book to the students prior to reading. She will conduct a hands-on activity in which students become familiar with the concepts by relating them to something in their own lives. After this initial activity, she will introduce the story and give them several thought questions to help focus their reading. Students then will be divided into cooperative learning groups to read the story. Members of each group will be allowed to select how they read the material. One student reads while the others listen; each takes turns reading. Once finished, the individual groups will discuss the thought questions the teacher posed earlier. Students will be given time to write their thoughts about the story in their reading logs. Children also will be encouraged to write their opinions about the story in the log, along with any questions they still have. During free time, students can ask either teacher for input on the task.

On Tuesday, students will be invited to participate in the literature circle. The first question Jan will ask the students is whether they liked or disliked the story. Because this question is open-ended, all students will have an immediate chance to participate. She will use a technique called a "whip," in which she goes from child-to-child with the question. During this exchange Barbara will record the students' answers on a flip chart. Next Jan will ask the students to relate what they learned about the new concepts in the story. Finally she will ask the students to think analytically about the characters. Before she calls on a student to answer, however, she will have the students do "think-pair-share," a strategy in which they first think about the answer, then share it with a partner, and finally share it with the entire group.

Phase Four

In the final phase teachers need a plan for assessing how well students are able to achieve the curriculum outcomes, how students reacted to the new instructional strategies, and whether the assessment captured students' learning well. Questions to be posed at this phase include the following.

- What did the students learn, and how well?
- What did we learn about our students' learning and behavioral characteristics that will help us plan better lessons next time?

In the example, Barbara and Jan built in a number of tactics to be used as performance-based assessment. First, during the warm-up activity Jan took detailed anecdotal notes in the form of a running record. She made notes about which children raised their hands when asked if they had ever heard of a particular concept. She compared these notes to notes taken during the literature-circle discussion. Students in the cooperative groups also were asked to record their group's answers to the challenge questions. Their answers, along with their learning logs, gave the teachers a more detailed account of how students were progressing. Finally, during the literature circle, Barbara kept a record of participating students and their answers.

During the next planning session, Barbara and Jan compared their notes. They found that they had been correct in assuming that a large number of students had no prior experience with the concepts. They also found that all but three students were able to answer questions during the literature circle. In looking back over the data, they found that the three students all had been in the same cooperative learning group. This opened up a new line of discussion as it related to future instructional modifications.

Classroom Trouble-Shooting After-the-Fact

At times even the best planned curriculum lesson "fails" in terms of expectations. Planning curriculum to meet students' needs, even planning it collaboratively, does not necessarily guarantee success, although it does tend to increase the probability of success. When a lesson or curriculum unit does not seem to work, the focus still can remain on the curriculum, not the individual students. To identify what should be improved, teachers again can look to the interaction between the curriculum plans and the instructional approach.

At such times, especially if students have gotten out of control, focusing on the child as the source of the problem becomes easy. Our focus on curriculum should not be misconstrued to imply that a student has no responsibility for problems that occur in the learning setting. Rather, our perspective is that the curriculum and its appropriateness or inappropriateness should be considered as one of the first sources of problems. It also is a source over which teachers probably have the largest measure of control.

In addressing a "failed" lesson, we suggest that the collaborating teachers again use the problem-solving process described. This time, though, they are trying to analyze a problem that has occurred already, with the intent of preventing its recurrence.

Students in Bill Rodman's fourth-grade class have just come in from the playground. Mr. Rodman has asked them to pick up math materials laid out on the table in front of the room. He stands at the table, monitoring the students as they come up and get their materials. As Dennis and Carl come up, they trip each other. Mr. Rodman immediately directs both boys to "sit down." Carl starts to complain that "Dennis started it." Mr. Rodman interrupts him and says that if Carl doesn't want to lose his afternoon recess that he needs to sit down. As he sits down, Carl glares at Dennis. Dennis makes a face at him. Carl jumps up and exclaims to Mr. Rodman, "Dennis is making faces."

Mr. Rodman takes a deep breath and tells both boys that their names will go up on the board if he hears another word. Dennis whines, "But I didn't do anything. You're always taking Carl's side against me." Carl makes a face back at Dennis.

Finally, the last student has gotten the materials to be used in a measuring activity. Mr. Rodman orients the students to the assignment, which is to sort the materials by length. Just as he finishes, Dennis takes a measuring stick off Carl's desk, puts it in his nose, and then back onto Carl's desk. Carl mimics loudly: "All right, I told you boys, one more peep and your names go on the board." Carl screams, "I didn't do anything. Dennis picked his nose with my stick, and I ain't gonna use it now."

The class erupts into laughter. Mr. Rodman raps on the table with his ruler to quiet the class. He orders the students to take their rulers and begin measuring the sticks. LaShonda raises her hand and asks, "Which one should we measure first?" Carl calls out, "I'm not measuring the stick Dennis had in his nose." Mr. Rodman glares at Carl and snaps at LaShonda, "the longest one first." LaShonda replies, "but how do we know which one is longest until we measure them?" Mr. Rodman tells the students to put the sticks aside and take out their math books. They will complete a page of multiplication and division problems instead.

Now suppose that you, as a collaborating teacher, had observed this scene and were meeting with Mr. Rodman to go over the lesson. How would you describe the problem? Most likely, Mr. Rodman will see the problem as being Dennis and Carl—"they're constantly fighting and disrupting the class." You might see the problem as Mr. Rodman's inability to manage the classroom and his ineffective instructional techniques. How should this be discussed?

From a curriculum-centered approach, the content of collaboration would focus on what Mr. Rodman wanted his students to know and be able to do. This is not to ignore the issues of classroom management, but the discussion would start with the curriculum. Here's how the problem statements might look:

- The goal is to have students measure real objects. Some students, however, don't have the self-control to handle manipulatives.
- The lesson requires students to exercise independence and respect for each other as they retrieve materials for the task. Some students, however, may not have learned appropriate routines for getting materials.
- The lesson requires students to measure real objects. For most students, this is a new concept they are unfamiliar with.

Given these problem statements, Mr. Rodman and the teacher he collaborates with are in a position to brainstorm solutions. For instance, the students might benefit from seeing him demonstrate the measuring task prior to trying it out themselves. Moreover, he might introduce the measurement task by drawing attention to the purpose of measurement in daily life. Students first might be instructed to measure their desk—a stationary object—before being given other objects. To structure the measuring task, Mr. Rodman might assign students to small groups in which they measure a large object together. Finally, he likely needs to teach directly the routine to be followed when getting up to get materials.

Exploring the problem through a curriculum lens allows teachers the opportunity to see how instruction can be enhanced and improved. Further, it helps teachers focus on the goals and outcomes of the instruction as the major consideration. If other specific individual interventions are required, they should be initiated only in relationship to an effective curriculum in the first place. Most important, a curriculum focus makes "trying another way" the norm in a collegial setting. All of us make mistakes. None of us are perfect teachers. By taking the judgmental quality out of our collaborations and focusing on the goal of improving student learning, we can move the process of improvement forward more quickly and professionally.

Curriculum-Centered Collaboration for Broad-Based Curriculum Planning

At the classroom level, curriculum-centered collaboration can go a long way in improving teaching and learning for all students. In schools where this sort of collaboration is occurring already, teachers are finding that extending these collegial exchanges to curriculum planning or renewal teams is a logical next step. Acting in advance to prevent problems from a broader perspective redirects the focus to creating positive learning environments that lead to success for all students. Thus, another way to expand the role of special educators is by including them on curriculum renewal teams.

Traditionally, special educators do not participate on curriculum redesign or renewal teams, whether school- or district-wide. Classroom teachers sometimes have not even been offered opportunities to serve on these work groups. Yet these teams typically are where the real proactive, collaborative curriculum work occurs—work that can prevent some of the most common curriculum problems. As new curriculum trends make their way into the district's scope and sequence, prior discussions regarding how that curriculum trend will affect learning are critical to the eventual success of all students.

Understanding curriculum trends is not always easy, especially when the trends themselves may not be consistent. Further, the unprecedented curriculum reform activity that is being undertaken in the various content areas deserves much attention before it can be understood fully. The summary of trends in Table 11.1 illustrates the sometimes conflicting and controversial nature of some current trends. A clear picture of the meaning and intent of these trends for everyone on the team is essential for responsible curriculum renewal to occur. In the current curriculum reform climate, this means being familiar with the new frameworks in each of the subject areas, as well as the purpose and structure of interdisciplinary approaches to delivering curricula.

When including special and general education classroom teachers on curriculum renewal or redesign teams, the goal is to identify, from a global perspective, whether the knowledge and skills deemed critical for the district's students are really accessible to them. During classroom-based collaborative trouble-shooting, teachers refocus their views about the role curriculum plays in helping or hindering student success. The same concept applies here. Curriculum renewal teams must determine whether students across the district will be able to succeed with the new curriculum goals. The emphasis is still on success, and not on setting up conditions where we know in advance that large numbers of students most likely will fail. If team members suspect that students will not be able to master the goals, the team has to determine how best to address this situation. Curriculum decisions have to be made from the perspective of all the district's students.

A process that we have found to work in directing the discussions follows:

- Clearly identify and define new curriculum trends. The team identifies the specific trends and how they differ from current curriculum practice.
- Determine the impact of these new trends on the curriculum. The trends should be discussed in relationship to the total scope and sequence of the district curriculum.
- Review scope and sequence and determine how and where the new trends best fit.
- Identify specific goals representative of curriculum trends, and infuse them into the scope and sequence.

Here the discussion also should cover prerequisite skills in the sequence that supports attainment of goals at various levels.

- Identify and discuss potential areas of mismatch. What effect will these new goals have on student learning? What will students need to master the goals? From here, the discussion should focus on how the district can build in supports to ensure that all students are successful.

■■■ **Table 11.1** *Summary of Current Curriculum Trends*

Subject	Trends
Mathematics	Mathematical literacy Conceptual understanding Technology Problem solving Improving attitudes and expectations about mathematics Mental computation and estimation Relationships among concepts Mathematics across disciplines Communicating mathematically
Science	Clarifying misconceptions Scientific literacy Science in society Science and job skills Communicating about science Incorporating scientific material Process science experiences Technology Confronting religion and other ways of knowing
Social Studies	History and geography as core Integrated themes Values education Citizenship Critical thinking Global interdependence Understanding individual differences Integration with other disciplines Career education/world of work
Language Literacy	Whole language/whole literacy* Writing as a process Writing across the curriculum Using language arts to enhance self-esteem Critical thinking Focus on social, political, and moral issues Censorship Oral discourse/speaking Return to basics (phonics, skill-based instruction)*

*Often interpreted/implemented as conflicting trends

Basically, any curriculum renewal process can be adapted to foster collaboration between special and general educators. The important consideration is to make an explicit effort to consider up front how the curriculum fits the learning and behavioral characteristics of the students and what the district can do to support learning.

Schools can do several things to support teachers who are collaborating around curriculum. Prevention and the long-term goal of improving educational outcomes for all students do not come cheaply. First and foremost, teachers must be afforded time to plan curriculum. To expect teachers to find time "on-the-fly" between classes or before school is not enough. Scheduled blocks of time have to be made available regularly for teachers who are collaborating. Equally important, teachers should be provided professional development around curriculum issues. School districts should devote as much attention to the curriculum as they typically do to new instructional techniques. Further, from our experience in introducing new curriculum frameworks, teachers need adequate time to reflect on what the changes mean to teaching and learning.

Finally, incentives should be built into the system directly. Whether it be released time from mundane tasks such as hall or recess duty to honoraria for participation in extra staff development activities, teachers deserve to be compensated and acknowledged for the additional time and effort they take to revamp classroom practices through curriculum reform.

Making a Real Difference Through Collaboration

Although many special and general education teachers engage in collaboration already, the convergence of reform in special education and reform in curriculum provides a unique opportunity to push that collaboration farther than ever before toward meeting students' needs. By pooling their expertise, special and general education teachers can refocus their collective energies on the underlying barriers to student success and begin to design responsive educational programs based on a clear understanding of the goals of the curriculum, and a willingness to rethink the curriculum itself.

Special education has a long tradition of worrying about the quality of the general education program. This issue is all the more critical as the philosophy of inclusion becomes more prevalent. Special educators often have struggled with how best to contribute to improving the educational landscape. Refocusing the process and dynamics of collaboration onto the curriculum itself unveils the potential for literally expanding the range of learning opportunities for students with disabilities—and for all students as well.

As we move toward a curriculum focus for our collegial deliberations, we must think about the meaning of what we ask students to do in school. Once the goals are on the table, special education teachers can take on the role—now redefined—of figuring out what supports will be necessary to assist children in achieving them.

We always have asked the question, "What is this student unable to do?" Now the time has come to ask a different set of questions: "Is what we are asking this student to do reasonable?" "Will it lead to important learning?" Finally, "If we agree that the learning goal is important, how do we design the curriculum and classroom tasks to ensure that students are successful?" These are the kinds of questions a curriculum-centered structure for collaboration enables teachers to ask—and to answer together.

References

Aldinger, L. E., Warger, C. L., & Eavy, P. W. (1991). *Strategies for teacher collaboration.* Ann Arbor, MI: Exceptional Innovations.

Carnine, D., & Kameenui, E. J. (1990). The general education initiative and children with special needs: A false dilemma in the face of true problems. *Journal of Learning Disabilities, 23*(3), 141–144, 148.

Glatthorn, A. A. (1985). *Curriculum reform and at-risk youth. Philadelphia: Research for Better Schools.*

Laycock, V. K., Gable, R. A., & Korinek, L. (1991). Alternative structures for collaboration in the delivery of special services. *Preventing School Failure, 35*(4), 15–18.

Lewis, A. C. (1990). Getting unstuck: Curriculum as a tool of reform. *Phi Delta Kappan, 71*(7), 534–538.

McLaughlin, M. J., & Warren, S. H. (1992). *Issues and options in restructuring schools and special education.* College Park, MD: Center for Policy Options in Special Education.

National Association of School Boards of Education. (1992). *Winners all: A call for inclusive schools.* Alexandria, VA: Author.

Newman, F. M. (1988). Can depth replace coverage in the high school curriculum? *Phi Delta Kappan, 69*(5), 345–348.

O'Neil, J. (1990). Drive for national standards picking up steam. *Educational Leadership, 48*(5), 4–8.

Pugach, M. C., & Warger, C. L. (1993). Curriculum considerations. In J. I. Goodlad & T. C. Lovitt, (Eds.), *Integrating general and special education* (pp. 135–148). New York: Charles E. Merrill.

Pugach, M. C., & Warger, C. L. (1996). *Curriculum trends, special education, and reform: Refocusing the conversation.* New York: Teachers College Press.

Pugach, M. C., & Wesson, C. L. (1995). Teachers' and students' views of team teaching of general education and learning disabled students in two fifth grade classes. *Elementary School Journal, 95,* 279–295.

Sapon-Shevin, M. (1987). The national education reports and special education: Implications for students. *Exceptional Children, 53*(4), 300–306.

Shepard, L. (1987). The new push for excellence: Widening the schism between regular and special education. *Exceptional Children, 53,* 327–329.

Warger, C. L., & Pugach, M. C. (1993). A curriculum focus for collaboration. *Learning Disabilities Focus, 18*(4), 26–30.

Warger, C. L., & Pugach, M. C. (1996). Forming partnerships around curriculum: A new focus for inclusion. *Educational Leadership, 53*(5), 62–65.

12 Curriculum and Instructional Issues in Teaching Secondary Students with Learning Disabilities

HERBERT J. RIETH AND LEWIS POLSGROVE

THE EDUCATION OF STUDENTS with learning disabilities at the secondary level has become the focus of research only recently. Consequently, any serious discussion of instructional issues related to teaching secondary students with learning disabilities must address ongoing research and identify needed areas of research. The authors effectively place issues and research implications in perspective—in the areas of program models, curriculum content, and classroom environments.

In this chapter we present a perspective on current curriculum and instructional issues related to teaching students with learning disabilities (LD) in secondary schools. First, we discuss issues concerning the impact of traditional secondary school programs on students with LD. Second, we identify some promising lines of ongoing research focusing on three areas: model programs, curriculum content, and classroom environmental variables pertaining to the education of students with mild disabilities in secondary school programs. Third, we suggest promising research, development, and model demonstration activities that might compose a research agenda for enhancing knowledge of effective educational practices for this population.

Impact of Secondary Special Education

Only recently have adolescents and young adults begun to receive a fair share of special education services (Halpern & Benz, 1987; Patton & Polloway, 1992; Schloss, Smith, & Schloss, 1990). Despite this recent trend toward increasing services for disabled students in secondary school programs, students continue to experience extensive academic and social difficulties (Maheady, Sacca, & Harper, 1988). The difficulties are well-documented and include:

1. Severe deficits in basic academic skills such as reading, spelling, and math.
2. Generalized failure and below-average performance in content area courses such as science, social studies, and health.
3. Deficient work-related skills, such as listening well in class, note-taking, study, and test-taking skills.
4. Passive academic involvement and a pervasive lack of motivation.
5. Inadequate interpersonal skills.

Such difficulties contribute to disabled students' general lack of academic progress during high school (Schumaker, Deshler, & Ellis, 1986). Adolescents with mild disabilities also are at greater risk than "normal" or slow-achieving peers to fail classes: Almost one in three received at least one failing grade in their most recent school year (Wagner, 1990). Zigmond, Levin, and Laurie (1985) reported that 20% of secondary school students with LD in their study failed more mainstream courses than they passed. Although approximately 75% of Donahoe and Zigmond's (1990) sample of learning disabled ninth graders passed mainstream health courses, only 60% passed science, and less than 50% earned passing grades in social studies.

Wagner (1990) published results of a 5-year longitudinal study involving 531 adolescents with LD ages 3 to 21. A national sample of school districts stratified with regard to region, wealth, and size provided subjects for the study. Parent telephone interviews, teacher surveys, and school records analyses composed the data. Wagner found, first, that most secondary students with LD spend half to full time in general education classes. In most cases, these students experience failure prior to reaching high school: Seventy-three percent in this sample were at least 1 year older than their nondisabled peers. Moreover, students with LD were significantly more likely to fail in general than in special classes. The likelihood of their failure increased significantly in relation to both the number of general classes they were assigned and the length of time they remained in these classes.

The most probable factors contributing to course failures by students with LD in Wagner's (1990) study were, in order of significance: absences totaling more than 8 days and disciplinary problems. School policies and limitations in special services may also increase the probability of their failure; for example, the majority of these students were graded on the same standards as their nondisabled classmates and they generally were not provided with tutoring services or other assistance outside of their special education classes. Moreover, a majority of general education teachers reported receiving little support in instructing these students.

Other studies corroborate these findings. Zigmond, Kerr, Brown, and Harris (1984), for example, reported that failing grades among adolescents with disabilities could be traced primarily to frequent class absences and tardiness. Teachers reported that these students often come to classes unprepared (i.e., without a writing implement, notepaper, or textbook at least 30% of the time). The teachers characterized the students with LD as poorly organized and inept at taking notes, identifying main ideas in lectures and texts, and following directions. In addition, the students had difficulty completing and turning in assignments (Zigmond, Kerr, & Schaeffer, 1988).

These results indicate that it is not enough to merely place students with LD in general class settings without providing appropriate training, materials, and support to them and to their teachers. To do so surely invites their failure. As Wagner (1990) observed, "Encouraging greater instruction of students with disabilities in regular education classes, without serious attention to the instruction that goes on in these classes, would seem simply to encourage greater rates of academic failure" (p. 28).

The consequences of failing courses are serious, particularly those courses needed for graduation. Students who fail to accumulate sufficient numbers of required credits to pass ninth grade frequently drop out of high school before graduation (Thornton & Zigmond, 1986). Although passing ninth grade does not guarantee successful completion of high school, failing at this grade level increases the likelihood of dropping out. By leaving school early, they may miss educational experiences most important for their transition to adulthood (Wagner, 1989).

Why do students with LD quit school in high numbers? Although a completely clear relation between school failure and high dropout rates for students with LD cannot be established, current information strongly suggests that this is a major influential variable. Failure of one or more courses and having disciplinary problems were the two most common reasons students gave in Wagner's (1990) study for deciding to quit school.

A consistent finding across a number of studies indicates that learning disabled students quit school with greater frequency than their nondisabled counterparts. For example, Hasazi, Gordon, and Roe (1985) reported that 34% of their sample of Vermont special education students left school prior to graduation. Lichtenstein (1988) reported a 40% dropout rate for learning disabled students in New Hampshire. Even higher dropout rates of 42% (Cobb & Crump, 1984), 47% (Levin, Zigmond, & Birch, 1985), 42% (Edgar, 1987), and 53% (Zigmond & Thornton, 1985) have been reported in some urban school districts.

Students with disabilities are, in general, significantly less likely than nondisabled students to graduate from high school, get any postsecondary education, find employment, or become engaged in any productive activity after high school (Wagner, 1989). These outcomes assume greater importance because successful postschool transition appears strongly related to success in school.

Although remaining in school does not assure that students with disabilities will meet with later success, those that do "tough it out" may have a better chance of making the transition from student to employee. Edgar (1987) reported in his study of 827 adolescents with learning and behavioral handicaps that the employment rate for dropouts was about half that (30%) of those who graduated (61%). It is not clear whether these results indicate that graduation led to better jobs, created a higher skill level, or was viewed more favorable by potential employers, or whether students who remained in school were more capable. Nevertheless, the employment picture even for those who graduated was not encouraging: Only 23% of them had jobs paying more than minimum wage.

It is clear from a number of studies that programs for students with LD characteristically focus on teaching academics with a goal of mainstreaming these students. Edgar (1987) and Zigmond (1990), for example, both observed that the bleak results yielded by this approach warrant a reappraisal of the secondary special curriculum. Edgar argued that if the ultimate goal of special education is to prepare students with mild disabilities to be productive and independent citizens, there must be a radical modification of the curriculum away from academics toward developing vocational, functional, and independent living skills. Short of a complete restructuring of the current special education curriculum, it seems clear that research on model demonstration programs is required to develop and evaluate effective alternative educational curricula to meet the long-term needs of this population.

Fortunately, there exist prototypic models that program developers and investigators can use as an initial framework for generating a more viable curriculum for students with LD. We review three of these: the first described by Schumaker et al. (1986); the second, which is closely related to the first, described by Ellis (1993); and one discussed by Zigmond (1990).

Alternative Secondary Program Models

Strategies Intervention Model

Based on work emerging from Office of Special Education Programs—funded research institutes on LD, Deshler and his colleagues (e.g., Schumaker et al., 1986) developed an elaborate Strategies Intervention Model (SIM) for teaching secondary students with LD. The major goal of this model is to provide students with a set of cognitive and metacognitive strategies that will improve their coping and problem-solving skills in academic, social, and vocational settings.

Core Curriculum

The core curriculum of the SIM consists of instruction on five types of strategies: task-specific learning, executive, social, motivation, and transition (see Figure 12.1). Task-specific learning strategies are related to content areas such as reading, listening and note-taking, writing, memory, and test-taking. Executive strategies focus on developing independent problem solving. Social skills strategies facilitate social communication, resistance to peer pressure, and conflict resolution. A set of motivational strategies teaches students to set realistic goals and to monitor and

Curriculum Component	Instructional Component	Organizational Component
• Task-Specific Learning Strategies • Executive Strategies • Social Skill Strategies • Motivation Strategies • Transition Strategies	• Acquisition Procedures • Generalization Procedures • Maintenance Procedures • Groups Instructional Procedures • Material and Instruction Modification Procedures	• Communication Procedures • Management Procedures • Evaluation Procedures • Teacher Training and Adoption Procedures

Figure 12.1 *The Strategies Intervention Model, Showing the Three Major Components and Their Subcomponents*

Source: "Intervention Issues Related to the Education of LD Adolescents," by J. B. Schumaker, D. D. Deshler, & E. S. Ellis in *Psychological and Educational Perspectives on Learning Disabilities*, edited by J. K. Torgesen and B. Y. L. Wong (Orlando, FL: Academic Press, 1986), pp. 329–365.

evaluate their progress. Finally, transition strategies provide instruction on how to meet challenges that students will face moving from school to daily living and vocational situations.

Instructional Component

In addition to the strategy training curriculum component, the SIM consists of two additional pieces: the Instructional component and the Organizational component. The Instructional component consists of a set of procedures specifying how strategies will be taught—procedures for facilitating acquisition, generalization, and maintenance of strategies; group instructional methods; and necessary materials and instruction modifications. Guidelines and procedures for implementing appropriate instructional practices in this component have been reported in several studies (Schumaker et al., 1986).

Organizational Component

The Organizational component concerns a set of procedures for introducing the curriculum to the school setting, managing its implementation, evaluating it effects, and training school personnel to implement it. Procedures contained in this component of the curriculum include a set of communication steps for developing cooperative planning among school personnel. The management procedures subcomponent provide guidelines for operating within specific settings. A set of evaluation procedures provides feedback to teachers implementing the interventions and staff regarding the effectiveness of the program. Finally, a set of training and adoption procedures serves to promote fidelity of implementation of the SIM.

In addition to the central components, Schumaker et al. (1986) outlined a broad perspective of procedures they recommend as appropriate practices in secondary school programs for students with LD. They favor the use of direct over indirect instruction with carefully sequenced and individualized objectives. Second, they advocate that teachers attend to macroinstructional variables such as allocating and managing time efficiently, maximizing opportunities for students to learn through careful planning, appropriate pacing, and establishing high performance expectancies. Third, they advocate the use of empirically validated methods. Finally, they recommend using techniques for enhancing students' motivation through self-regulation techniques.

Integrated Strategy Model

Ellis (1993) proposed a variant of the SIM, which he labeled the Integrated Strategy Model, that combines content instruction with general strategy instruction as key activities in teaching adolescents with LD. Ellis's model, which Scruggs and Mastropieri (1993) suggested differs only slightly from Deshler's model, endeavors to integrate teacher-directed instruction to facilitate students' use of effective and efficient information-processing skills to master content-area subject knowledge. The goal is to enable students to become good information processors, which is viewed as an essential skill in school and subsequently in employment settings. The core of the model consists of four hierarchically ordered instructional processes that teachers employ to teach content strategically. They include orienting process, framing process, applying process, and extending process.

The orienting process involves the teacher employing the target-information processing strategy to teach specific academic content. However, the teacher never specifically labels the strategy process being modeled. The intent is to facilitate student mastery of the target academic content area and enable the student to develop an experiential base for using the target-information processing strategy to learn content knowledge.

In the framing process, the teacher directly models and provides an ongoing narrative description of the use of the target-information processing strategy to foster academic-content learning. The goal of this phase is for the student to understand how and when to employ the information-processing strategy to obtain specific content information.

The applying process is designed to enable students to independently use the target-learning strategy to acquire content knowledge. Ideally, the student will apply the learning strategy in multiple contexts and can discriminate when to apply the strategy, and why, within and across subject matter content areas.

Finally, during the extending process phase the student is taught to extend or transfer her or his knowledge into additional content and problem-solving areas. Students are encouraged to create and use new strategies based on the previously learned strategy.

Although Ellis's model is designed to be widely applicable for teaching adolescents with LD in special and general education settings and is built on reasonably sound learning principles, it has not been empirically evaluated. Its promise for instructing adolescents with LD warrants extensive empirical verification.

Zigmond's Model Program

Zigmond (1990) proposed a prototype comprehensive alternative model program for secondary students with LD. This model, which also contains some similarities to the SIM, focuses on four components: intensive instruction in reading and mathematics, training in survival skills, concentration on passing courses required for graduation, and planning for life after high school.

Intensive Instruction

Academic deficits in reading, writing, and math contribute substantially to students failing mainstream courses such as English, social studies, and science (Donahoe & Zigmond, 1990). Traditional secondary programs for students with LD must therefore provide intensive and efficient instruction in basic skills; this training will also be essential to students for success in employment and independent living settings.

Survival Skills

A second component of Zigmond's (1990) model involves explicit instruction in survival skills including behavior control, social skills, teacher-pleasing behaviors, and study skills. This content is deemed important because of the well-documented social skill deficits among high school students with mild disabilities and the disabilities' detrimental impact on academic, social, and vocational outcomes (Walker, 1988).

Zigmond (1990) suggested that behavior control activities must be designed to help students who are often in trouble and who are frequently suspended or punished. The students require explicit instruction to understand the relation between their behavior and these outcomes. They must be instructed in alternative ways (a) of responding to particular situations and (b) to forecast the consequences of behaving one way or another.

A second subcomponent of survival skills identified in Zigmond's (1990) model involves social skills training. Walker (1988) suggested that providing direct instruction in social skills to adolescents with disabilities is essential for them to gain maximum benefit from academic instruction. Having appropriate interpersonal skills contributes to greater acceptance by teachers, peers, and significant others; as these skills span multiple settings and enable students to establish social support networks, the students may substantially improve their prospects of being successful in mainstreaming, vocational, and transition efforts. Walker regarded social skills training as an instructional as opposed to a behavioral intervention, although he advocated the use of traditional stimulus control and reinforcement procedures to facilitate the display, generalization, and maintenance of mastered social skills in target environments.

In addition to broad social skills, Zigmond (1990) recommended teaching secondary students with LD in teacher-pleasing behaviors. These include skills—making eye contact, looking interested in a lesson, volunteering an answer, and looking busy—that lead teachers to consider the students more positively. Other investigators have observed that these students often need to be taught, explicitly, how to act like good students (P. J. Schloss & Sedlak, 1986; Schumaker et al., 1986).

As a vehicle for teaching teacher-pleasing behavior, Zigmond (1990) suggested having students record their performance of target behavior daily on self-monitoring forms that are checked by their teachers at regular intervals. The number of skills that students self-monitor increases gradually until students are recording their performance on as many as seven or eight skills.

Both Schumaker et al. (1986) and Zigmond (1990) considered study skills essential for students with LD. Study skills instruction should focus on metacognitive skills, class attendance, assignment completion, attentiveness, and compliance behavior. Metacognitive instruction focuses on teaching students general techniques for remembering and summarizing content area material, how to proofread a paper, and how to take notes from lectures (Schumaker et al. 1986).

Vocational Skills

Zigmond (1990) observed that an increasing number of educators are recognizing the need to prepare adolescents for successful transition to life after high school through formal vocational counseling and instruction. Vocational counseling targets two distinct groups of students with mild disabilities.

The first, a relatively small segment of students, includes those who are planning to attend college and who need help in selecting appropriate schools, arranging for adapted versions of college entrance examinations, and completing admissions applications. The second group consists of non-college-bound students who need help in planning training that might be needed during high school that will lead to rewarding postschool occupations and employment.

Many students with disabilities are counseled into vocational education track as part of transition planning, but this solution does not guarantee successful transition. In this regard, Phelps (1985) stated that in

> most states, the access to and the quality of vocational programs has already been significantly reduced and eroded...without rigorous and occupationally-specific vocational education programs at the secondary level, it is highly unlikely that either the education or employment needs of disadvantaged or handicapped youth will be adequately met during the decade ahead. (p. 5)

Studies by Thornton (1987) and Zigmond and Thornton (1985) reinforce Phelps's view as they found no evidence that mainstream vocational education programs actually provided disabled students with better preparation for employment than did the more traditional academic curriculum. The failure of vocational education programs to better prepare students for postschool employment suggests the need to develop and analyze alternative approaches to vocational education.

Curriculum Content Research

In this section, we discuss issues related to curriculum content relevant to teaching secondary students with LD. Here we focus on ongoing studies related to teaching basic academic skills that will enable these youngsters to have successful general class and transition experiences.

Goal and Standard Setting

Despite the pivotal role of goals in education, there are very few reported systematic investigations that have examined the process, procedures, and criteria used to set goals for student performance at the classroom, school, district, and state levels in special education.

At the classroom level, we know very little about the procedures and decision-making processes that teachers employ to establish daily, weekly, monthly, or yearly academic goals for students. In fact, Fuchs (1986) found that despite the apparent importance of goals, the goal-specification literature provides little useful information about guidelines for setting academic and social behavior performance goals for individual students.

The absence of guidelines has serious implications for practice. For example, individualized educational programs (IEPs) are employed ubiquitously in special education, but empirically guided procedures for identifying appropriate goals are not available. Fuchs, Fuchs, and Hamlett (1989) reported that IEPs are frequently set before the efficacy of the students academic program has been established; this practice makes it difficult to develop attainable but ambitious goals for students. In fact, they observed that selected goal standards usually underestimate student performance, and special education teachers specifically must be prompted to raise goals to more realistic levels. Thus, existing professional practices that lead to the establishment of underestimated performance goals for disabled students may be contributing inadvertently to the students' lack of academic progress.

Fuchs, Bahr, and Rieth (1989) found that high school students who set their own performance goals improved their math computation performance more than students with assigned goals. These findings suggest that student participation in the goal-selection process (a) improves performance outcomes, (b) enhances goal commitment, and (c) may enhance the sense of potential accomplishment.

Thinking Skills

One of the primary and perhaps more promising research foci in this area concerns developing students' thinking skills. Carnine (1991) and Ellis (1993) advocated for major curricula modifications to enhance the acquisition of higher order thinking processes by all students. They argued that many interventions including efficient teaching techniques, cooperative learning, and metacognitive strategy training are undermined when curricular materials are organized to focus on rote learning. Although they consider the acquisition of basic requisite knowledge as important, they observed that it is equally important to expose students with disabilities to instructional materials that require higher order thinking. Carnine suggested that students should have an opportunity to master, apply, and memorize important relations among concepts as well as "sameness" knowledge.

Sternberg (1990) argued that styles of thinking and learning are as important as levels of ability, and he observed that teachers often ignore these variables as they structure learning tasks. Resnick and Klopfer (1989) also indicated that educators must develop students' thinking abilities. They suggested the need for developing a new instructional theory concerned with methods of presenting and sequencing information, organizing practice and feedback, motivating students, and assessing learning. They argued that a fundamental principle of cognition is that learning requires background knowledge that cannot be imparted directly to students. Rather, students must play an active role in acquiring knowledge by questioning the instructor and relating new information to their existing knowledge base. This process develops generative knowledge that students can use to interpret new situations, solve problems, think and reason, and learn.

A major characteristic of students with LD, however, is that they are typically passive and unmotivated learners who do not fare well in unstructured learning situations. For these reasons, Harris and Pressley (1991) cautioned against taking an extreme constructivist approach in teaching these students. Although discovery learning may be motivating to these students, without guidance in this process they may very well engage in "errorful knowledge construction" based on misunderstanding or incorrect information (p. 393). They argued that direct instruction in cognitive and metacognitive strategies is necessary to avoid this pitfall. Indeed, this approach appears to hold considerable promise (Deshler & Schumaker, 1986; Pressley et al., 1990).

One interesting line of research on thinking skills has been followed by Bransford and his colleagues. To develop meaningful knowledge accessible by disabled learners, Bransford, Sherwood, Hasselbring, Kinzer, and Williams (1990) advocated using real-world problem situations as instructional "anchors." In this approach, a contextual anchor such as a popular videodisc movie was repurposed as an instructional platform. This approach is used to generate interest and motivate students to identify, define, and attempt to solve problems using academic skills. In addition, it requires them to attend to their perceptions and comprehension of these problems in the process. This approach holds promise for the simultaneous instruction of problem-solving and cognitive strategies in a variety of applied situations (Cognition and Technology Group at Vanderbilt, 1990).

Although videodisc technology represents an advanced new approach, using visual imagery to teach concepts to students with LD may be the powerful underlying principle. For example, Scruggs and Mastropieri (1992) demonstrated that the use of simple overhead projector transparencies of pictures incorporating mnemonic cues was effective in helping secondary students with LD recall science facts.

On another level, Prawat (1989) urged adopting strategies that look beyond instructional approaches to the organization of the curriculum content. Specific foci include: developing correspondence between various ways of representing concepts and procedures, making explicit how important elements of the knowledge base interrelate, and acknowledging and being sensitive to students' simplistic knowledge or misconceptions.

Another issue related to teaching thinking skills concerns how best to impart to students certain metacognitive skills. Schumaker et al. (1986) suggested a three-step sequence. First, specific learning strategies are taught to enable students to deal with specific tasks they encounter. Second, planned opportunities for generalization are arranged so that students can apply the strategies learned in one situation or task to others. Third, students are taught to invent their own strategies in response to a particular situation. Along these lines, Harris and Pressley (1991) outlined a seven-stage procedure for teaching students self-instructional strategies involving: (a) developing essential preskills, (b) evaluating the student's current performance, (c) describing the strategy, (d) modeling the strategy with self-instructions, (e) memorizing the strategy steps, (f) practicing the strategy with feedback, and (g) performing the strategy independently. Such a set of procedures, of course, assumes that teachers can identify which tasks in their curriculum would be best to introduce these procedures. Unfortunately, little information is available to guide teachers in this effort.

Academic Content Areas

Reading and Language Arts

Taylor (1989) argued that emerging research and principles of efficient instruction support the practice of combining reading, writing, and language development instruction. He observed that there is an infinite variety of patterns that students might use in becoming literate, and he recommended studies on these patterns to establish a framework for broader interventions that could then be evaluated in a variety of secondary school settings.

After reviewing research on teaching basic reading, Turner (1989) concluded that phonics instruction falls into the vast category of weak instructional treatments that perennially plague the field of education. This suggests that time spent devoted to improving phonics instruction might be better spent searching for more powerful methods for beginning reading instruction and other techniques that could accelerate literacy in secondary settings.

Spelling

A major aspect of writing involves correct spelling. Although many educators do not consider this an important skill, poor spelling skills may impede a reader's interpretation of written text. Sporadic attention has been given to developing effective methods for teaching spelling skills, but some recent evidence suggests that spelling ability may be vastly facilitated through the integration of spelling and other meaning-based language arts instruction (Dixon, 1991). Such integration may enhance overall language arts understanding as well.

Math

School mathematics learning goals appear to have shifted over the last 5 years from learning basic skills using direct instruction to facilitating higher order thinking and problem solving (Porter, 1989). Although this approach might be productive for nondisabled students, studies have not established the value of this approach with disabled students. However, Porter's method has intuitive logic, in that unless students are taught to apply their conceptual skills in mathematics to higher level skills, their development in this important area will be severely limited.

Although it seems obvious, the more time students spend engaged in actual instruction, the more they achieve. Yet, studies have revealed that teachers using the same mathematics textbook may substantially vary the amount of time they allocate to mathematics and thus the amount of content they cover (Barr, 1988; Freeman & Porter, 1989; Porter, 1989). Regulating such variables is important as they have been shown to affect achievement outcomes. Although a relatively small number of studies have been conducted in this area, findings suggest the importance of additional research.

Lloyd and Keller (1989) identified two key points from research on cognitive processes in arithmetic. First, as children become more proficient in addition, they develop strategies based on previous strategies that are more efficient than earlier ones. These strategies emulate patterns of development in other individuals. Second, conceptual and procedural knowledge appear linked and thus change together. They concluded by suggesting that research is needed on the effects of teaching concepts in combination with procedural strategies.

An emerging approach to providing mathematics instruction for secondary students with LD involves the use of videodisc technology. Kelly, Carnine, Gersten, and Grossen (1986) reported significant achievement improvements in learning fraction concepts among a group of secondary students with LD using a commercial videodisc program. This approach promises to change the way teachers provide instruction in special education classrooms. In a related study, Woodward and Gersten (1992) reported that the use of a commercial videodisc instructional approach in mathematics improved student performance and significantly increased the instructional interactions between teachers; moreover, teachers found this approach to be highly acceptable.

Social Studies

The National Assessment of Education Progress of student knowledge of democratic principles and history reported that a sample of 17-year-old students enrolled in general education could answer correctly only 54.5% of the test items (Kinder & Bursuck, 1991). In one of the few analyses of the social studies performance of students with disabilities, Patton, Polloway, and Cronin (1987) found that 36% of secondary special education teachers did not teach social studies. Foley (1990) reported that only 55 of 120 middle and junior high school students were placed in mainstreamed social studies or history classes. Thus, studies suggest that students with mild disabilities may not receive adequate instruction in history or social studies.

One promising social studies instructional strategy developed by Kinder (1989) consists of a complete instructional program that includes preskills instruction, problem-solution-effect note-taking, timelines, vocabulary, and a reciprocal questioning components. Preliminary data reported by Kinder and Bursuck (1991) suggested that this approach may be successful in teaching American History content to students with mild disabilities. Whether students can independently apply this strategy in other settings, however, is unclear and should be examined further.

Brophy (1990) observed that although the literature on social studies education has produced many useful ideas, it has yet to produce an extensive empirical knowledge base. He found little research linking specific curriculum, instruction, or evaluation practices to measured student outcomes. Further, few studies have attempted to systematically compare theoretically optimal programs with plausible alternatives. These issues as well as research on the role of teaching students with LD thinking skills in social studies constitute important prospects for research in this area.

Science

Science education has also received little emphasis in special education research although recent research in cognition makes a compelling case for teaching higher order thinking with the essential science facts and concepts (Mastropieri & Scruggs, 1992; Woodward & Noell, 1991). The advantages of providing science instruction to students with disabilities include: (a) expanded experiential repertoire, (b) skills learned are often related to adult functioning, (c) instruction frequently includes concrete manipulations, and (d) science offers a context for teaching problem-solving skills (Mastropieri & Scruggs, 1992).

Woodward and Noell (1991) advocated a thorough revamping of the science curriculum to focus on the principles of sameness coupled with relevant, coherent explanations that help students understand, think systematically, and apply their knowledge to a range of problems. Their model involves judicious selection of concepts that would then be taught explicitly. In this model, concepts are carefully sequenced, and students are continually tested for mastery of the material. They observed that these objectives parallel those found in general secondary education and this approach combined with videodisc-based instruction offers students with disabilities more opportunities to learn the content. Further, they argued that students with disabilities would also benefit from this kind of instruction because they are required to apply higher order thinking skills to solve domain specific problems. Finally, Mastropieri and Scruggs (1992) showed that science instruction featuring intensive teaching, highly structured presentations, frequent organizational pictures, and mnemonics pairing unfamiliar labels with meaningful words may facilitate acquisition of concepts by students with disabilities.

Classroom Environment

Procedures and Presentations

Brophy and Good (1986); Rieth and Evertson (1988); and Christenson, Ysseldyke, and Thurlow (1989) provided comprehensive reviews of classroom environmental variables that were found to be correlated with student achievement outcomes. Rieth and Evertson reported that a number of pre- and postinstructional variables provide the essential staging area from which effective instruction is launched. These include the arrangement of classroom space and student seating, development of rules and procedures for behavior and academic work, academic content, communicating learning goals, pacing, and the careful allocation of instructional time.

Christenson et al. (1989) reported that well-organized and efficiently run classrooms result when students are informed of specific behavioral expectations and classroom routines and when teachers monitor student behavior and follow through on expectations. These procedures set the stage for critical teaching variables such as effective demonstration, modeling procedures, and lesson pacing, which in turn increase student attention and academic engaged time. Rieth and Evertson (1988) reported that effective teachers create attractive, efficient learning environments. They make a number of organizational decisions, prior to the start of the school year, about (a) room arrangement including seating and desk placement; (b) needed rules and procedures; and (c) routines for accomplishing academic tasks and activities. Christenson et al. indicated that the creation of a positive climate in the classroom and the school is an important correlate of student learning. Student achievement is also related to the teachers' ability to match students' skill repertoires and task difficulty. Effective teachers provide clear learning goals and effectively communicate to students the rationales for academic tasks (Anderson, Evertson, & Brophy, 1979).

Evertson (1982) reported that sequencing the delivery of lesson content into several presentation-demonstration-practice-feedback cycles to be more effective with lower ability students rather than developing plans requiring students to attend to a presentation or to work for 25 to 30 minutes on the same seatwork activity. Further, Barr (1988) reported that pacing instruction and student work can account for as much as 80% of the difference in achievement among high and low performers.

Opportunities to Learn

Rieth and Evertson (1988) observed that time and learning research consistently has demonstrated significant relations between time spent on learning and student achievement. Rieth and Frick (1983) reported that the amount of instructional time is influenced by effective classroom management skills that not only increased the amount of time available to spend on instruction but also ensured that the time is continuous and relatively free of distractions, interruptions, and disruptions. Other research has demonstrated that students who engage in active academic responses make greater gains in achievement than students whose responses are passive (Greenwood, Delquadri, & Hall, 1984).

Christenson et al. (1989) indicated that teachers have a direct influence on students' opportunity to respond by interacting more with students, using error correction procedures, and calling on all students during instruction. They suggested that alternative teaching strategies such as choral responding, peer tutoring, and cooperative learning structures might increase the number of opportunities students have to respond. Available information therefore suggests that the educational environment should be structured to incorporate frequent evaluation that must be congruent with what is taught.

In one of the few research studies investigating the secondary classroom environment, Rieth, Bahr, Polsgrove, Okolo, and Eckert (1987) analyzed teacher and student behavior in high school resource room programs. In general, the teachers used instructional approaches associated with general high school classrooms. They included substantial dependence on paper-and-pencil materials, considerable confusion in the directions and content of instructional tasks, and low rates of academic feedback, all of which added up to less than ideal instructional environments for the students in this sample. These data suggest the need for extensive research and development projects that extensively analyze the regular and special education instructional environments.

Summary and Recommendations

The picture unveiled in this review is both bleak and promising: bleak in the sense that the impact of schooling on secondary students with LD is neutral, at best, and promising in the sense that research in this area over the past decade has generated interventions that produce positive outcomes among this population. Unfortunately, the dearth of basic and applied studies with this population suggests the need for an ambitious agenda of research studies and demonstration projects that focus on enhancing the acquisition, maintenance, and transfer of academic skills by these students.

We suggest a three-tiered agenda to organize needed research for the field. At Level 1, basic research studies are needed that would help clarify the nature of thinking skills and learning potential of the LD population. Swanson (1987) deftly outlined a prospective approach that spans the gamut from basic studies that compare ability groups to field trials that evaluate potentially effective interventions. He argued that development of a metatheory explaining cognitive styles of students with LD is prerequisite to developing viable field interventions.

Although one might disagree with Swanson's position, we can envision how research under controlled conditions might provide analogue information that would lead to improved instructional methods. A second level of research is required, however, that would focus on promising *in situ* interventions for teaching and motivating secondary students with LD.

At Level 2 in our proposed agenda, studies are needed that address the perennial question of whether to focus on remediating academic problems of students with LD or concentrate on teaching them minimal academic survival skills and/or vocational training. The dearth of intervention studies rationalizes assigning high priority to this question. Also at the second level, recent work in cognitive psychology focusing on the higher order thinking and problem-solving strategies appears particularly lucrative. Further effort might be invested in discerning the instructional, teaching, and curricular strategies that enable adolescents with mild disabilities to acquire, maintain, and transfer academic and social skills in an effort designed ultimately to help reduce the rate of failure, increase skill repertoires, and improve chances of graduation and employment for students with LD. In particular, work related to teaching content, information-processing strategies and usage, and mnemonic instruction appears promising.

Finally, a third tier of research studies that focus on broader variables pertaining to the instructional needs of the population of secondary students with LD appears to be required. This level would include evaluation context variables (Rieth et al., 1987), effective program components (Ellis, 1993; Schumaker et al., 1986; Zigmond, 1990), and school policies on student and teacher behavior.

At Level 3, studies are also needed to further characterize the dynamics of classroom ecologies and context variables that facilitate the student's acquisition of academic, social, and vocational skills. Studies evaluating the role of technology to enhance skill acquisition, maintenance, and transfer are also needed. Level 3 research might also focus on identifying appropriate curriculum, curriculum content, curricular sequence, and the delivery mechanisms and support services necessary for creating ideal learning environments. Finally, studies that explore the relation of outcome variables to program content, field experience, and student behavior are recommended at this level.

Because so much work needs to be done at all levels, it is difficult to identify and establish priorities regarding specific studies that might be undertaken within each. However, our review has highlighted some of the more promising lines of research currently being conducted at Levels 2 and 3 of our proposed agenda. We think that the next decade holds considerable hope for advancing practices in this critical area.

References

Anderson, L. M., Evertson, C. M., & Brophy, J. E. (1979). An experimental study of effective teaching in first grade reading groups. *Elementary School Journal, 79*, 193–223.

Barr, R. (1988). Conditions influencing content in nine fourth grade mathematics classrooms. *Elementary School Journal, 88*, 387–411.

Bransford, J. D., Sherwood, R. S., Hasselbring, T. S., Kinzer, C. K., & Williams, S. M. (1990). Anchored instruction: Why we need it and how technology can help. In D. Nix & R. Spiro (Eds.), *Cognitive, education, and multimedia exploration in high technology* (pp. 115-142). Hillsdale, NJ: Lawrence Erlbaum Associates, Inc.

Brophy, J. (1990). Teaching social studies for understanding and higher-order applications. *The Elementary School Journal, 90*, 351–417.

Brophy, J. E., & Good, T. (1986). Teacher behavior and student achievement. In M. C. Wittrock (Ed.), *Handbook of research on teaching*. New York: Macmillan.

Carnine, D. (1991). Curricular interventions for teaching higher order thinking to all students: Introduction to special series. *Journal of Learning Disabilities, 24,* 261–269.

Christenson, S. L., Ysseldyke, J. E., & Thurlow, M. L. (1989). Critical instructional factors for students with mild handicaps: An integrative review. *Remedial and Special Education, 10*(5), 21–31.

Cobb, R. M., & Crump, W. D. (1984). *Post-school status of young adults identified as learning disabled while enrolled in public schools: A comparison of those enrolled and not enrolled in learning disabilities programs*. Washington, DC: U.S. Department of Education.

Cognition and Technology Group at Vanderbilt. (1990). Anchored instruction and its relationship to situated cognition. *Educational Researcher, 19*(6), 2–10.

Deshler, D. D., & Schumaker, J. B. (1986). Learning strategies: An instructional alternative for low-achieving adolescents. *Exceptional Children, 52,* 583–590.

Dixon, R. C. (1991). The application of sameness analysis to spelling and integrated language arts. *Journal of Learning Disabilities, 24,* 285–291.

Donahoe, K., & Zigmond, N. (1990). Academic grades of ninth-grade urban learning-disabled students and low-achieving peers. *Exceptionality, 1,* 17–27.

Edgar, E. (1987). Secondary programs in special education: Are many of them justifiable? *Exceptional Children, 53,* 555–561.

Ellis, E. S. (1993). Integrative strategy instruction: A potential model for teaching content area subjects to adolescents with learning disabilities. *Journal of Learning Disabilities, 26,* 358–383.

Evertson, C. (1982). Differences in instructional activities in higher- and lower-achieving junior English and Math classes. *Elementary School Journal, 80,* 329–350.

Foley, R. (1990). *Correlates of academic achievement of adolescents with behavioral disorders.* Unpublished doctoral dissertation, Northern Illinois University, Dekalb.

Freeman, D. J., & Porter, A. C. (1989). Do textbooks dictate the content of mathematics instruction in elementary schools? *American Educational Research Journal, 26,* 403–421.

Fuchs, L. S. (1986). Monitoring the performance of mildly handicapped students: Review of current practice and research. *Remedial and Special Education, 7,* 5–12.

Fuchs, L. S., Bahr, C., & Rieth, H. J. (1989). Effects of goal structures and performance of adolescents with learning disabilities. *Journal of Learning Disabilities, 29*(9), 554–560.

Fuchs, L. S., Fuchs, D., & Hamlett, C. L. (1989). Effects of alternative goal structures within curriculum-based measurement. *Exceptional Children, 55,* 429–438.

Greenwood, C. R., Delquadri, J., & Hall, R. V. (1984). Opportunity to respond and student academic performance. In W. Heward et al. (Eds.), *Focus on behavior analysis in education* (pp. 58–88). Columbus, OH: Merrill.

Halpern, A. S., & Benz, M. R. (1987). A statewide examination of secondary special education for students with mild disabilities: Implications for the high school curriculum. *Exceptional Children, 52,* 122-129.

Harris, K. R., & Pressley, M. (1991). The nature of cognitive strategy instruction: Interactive strategy construction. *Exceptional Children, 57,* 392–404.

Hasazi, S. B., Gordon, L. R., & Roe, C. A. (1985). Factors associated with the employment status of handicapped youth exiting high school from 1979-1983. *Exceptional Children, 51,* 455–469.

Kelly, B., Carnine, D., Gersten, R., & Grossen, B. (1986). The effectiveness of videodisc instruction on teaching fractions to learning handicapped and remedial high school students. *Journal of Special Education Technology, 8,* 5–17.

Kinder, D. (1989). *Teacher's guide.* Unpublished manuscript, Educational Research and Services Center, DeKalb, IL.

Kinder, D., & Bursuck, W. (1991). The search for a unified social studies curriculum: Does history really repeat itself? *Journal of Learning Disabilities, 24,* 270–275.

Levin, E., Zigmond, N., & Birch, J. (1985). A follow-up study of 52 learning disabled students. *Journal of Learning Disabilities, 18,* 2–7.

Lichtenstein, S. (1988). Dropouts: A secondary special education perspective. *Counterpoint, 8*(3), 13.

Lloyd, J. W., & Keller, C. E. (1989). Effective mathematics instruction: Development, instruction, and program. *Focus on Exceptional Children, 21*(7), 1–10.

Maheady, L., Sacca, M. K., & Harper, G. F. (1988). Classwide peer tutoring with mildly handicapped high school students. *Exceptional Children, 55*(1), 52–59.

Mastropieri, M. A., & Scruggs, T. E. (1992). Science for students with disabilities. *Review of Educational Research, 62*, 377–411.

Patton, J. R., & Polloway, E. A. (1992). Learning disabilities: The challenges of adulthood. *Journal of Learning Disabilities, 25*, 410–415.

Patton, J. R., Polloway, E. A., & Cronin, M. E. (1987). Social studies instruction for handicapped students: A review of current practices. *The Social Studies, 78*, 131–135.

Phelps, L. A. (1985). An agenda for action: Excellence in education. *Journal for Vocational Special Needs Education, 7*, 3–6.

Porter, A. C. (1989). A curriculum out of balance: The case for elementary school mathematics. *Educational Researcher, 18*, 9–15.

Prawat, R. S. (1989). Promoting access to knowledge, strategy, and disposition in students: A research synthesis. *Review of Educational Research, 59*, 1–42.

Pressley, M., Burkell, J., Cariglia-Bull, T., Tysynchik, L., McGoldrick, J. A., Schneider, B., Snyder, B. L., Symons, S., & Woloshyn, V. E. (1990). *Cognitive strategy instruction that improves children's academic performance*. Cambridge, MA: Brookline.

Resnick, L. B., & Klopfer, L. E. (1989). Toward the thinking curriculum: An overview. In L. B. Resnick & L. E. Klopfer (Eds.), *Toward the thinking curriculum: Current cognitive research*. Pittsburgh, PA: Association for Supervision and Curriculum Development.

Rieth, H. J., Bahr, C., Polsgrove, L., Okolo, C., & Eckert, R. (1987). The effects of microcomputers on the secondary special education classroom ecology. *Journal of Special Education Technology, 8*, 36–45.

Rieth, H., & Evertson, C. (1988). Variables related to the effective instruction of difficult to teach children. *Focus on Exceptional Children, 20*(5), 1–8.

Rieth, H. J., & Frick, T. (1983). *An analysis of the impact of instructional time with different service delivery systems on the achievement of mildly handicapped students*. (Final Grant Research Report). Bloomington: Indiana University, Center for Innovation in Teaching the Handicapped.

Schloss, P. J., & Sedlak, R. A. (1986). *Instructional methods for students with learning and behavioral problems*. Boston: Allyn & Bacon.

Schloss, P. J., Smith, M. A., & Schloss, C. N. (1990). *Instructional methods for adolescents with learning and behavior problems*. Boston: Allyn & Bacon.

Schumaker, J. B., Deshler, D. D., & Ellis, E. S. (1986). Intervention issues related to the education of LD adolescents. In J. K. Torgesen & B. Y. L. Wong (Eds.), *Psychological and educational perspectives on learning disabilities* (pp. 329–365). Orlando, FL: Academic Press.

Scruggs, T. E., & Mastropieri, M. A. (1992). Classroom applications of mnemonic instruction, acquisition, maintenance, and generalization. *Exceptional Children, 58*, 219–231.

Scruggs, T. E., & Mastropieri, M. (1993). Special education for the twenty-first century: Integrating learning strategies and thinking skills. *Journal of Learning Disabilities, 26*, 392–398.

Sternberg, R. J. (1990). Thinking styles: Keys to understanding student performance. *Phi Delta Kappan, 71*, 366–371.

Swanson, H. L. (1987). *Memory and learning disabilities: Advances in learning and behavioral disabilities*. Greenwich, CT: JAI.

Taylor, D. (1989). Toward a unified theory of literacy learning and instructional practices. *Phi Delta Kappan, 71*(3), 184–193.

Thornton, H. (1987). *A follow-up study of learning disabled young adults who participated in mainstream vocational educational programs*. Unpublished doctoral dissertation, University of Pittsburgh.

Thornton, H. S., & Zigmond, N. (1986). Follow-up of post-secondary age LD graduates and dropouts. *LD Research, 1*, 50–55.

Turner, R. L. (1989). The great debate: Can both Carbo and Chall be right? *Phi Delta Kappan, 71*, 276–283.

Wagner, M. (1989, March). *The transition experiences of youth with disabilities: A report from the national longitudinal transition study.* Paper presented at the meetings of the Division of Research, Council for Exceptional Children, San Francisco.

Wagner, M. (1990, April). *The school programs and school performance of secondary students classified as learning disabled: Findings from the national longitudinal transition study of special education students.* Paper presented at the meetings of Division G, American Educational Research Association, Boston.

Walker, H. (1988). Special educational curriculum and instruction: Social skills. In T. Husen & N. Postlethwaite (Eds.), *International encyclopedia of education.* Oxford, England: Pergamon.

Woodward, J., & Gersten, R. (1992). Innovative technology for secondary students with learning disabilities. *Exceptional Children, 58*, 407–421.

Woodward, J., & Noell, J. (1991). Science instruction at the secondary level: Implications for students with learning disabilities. *Journal of Learning Disabilities, 24*(5), 277–284.

Zigmond, N. (1990). Rethinking secondary school programs for students with learning disabilities. *Focus on Exceptional Children, 23*, 1–14.

Zigmond, N., Kerr, M. M., Brown, G. M., & Harris, A. L. (1984). *School survival skills in secondary school age special education students.* Paper presented at the meeting of the American Educational Research Association, New Orleans.

Zigmond, N., Kerr, M. M., & Schaeffer, A. L. (1988). Behavior patterns of learning disabled adolescents in high school academic classes. *Remedial and Special Education, 9*, 6–11.

Zigmond, N., Levin, E., & Laurie, T. E. (1985). Managing the mainstream: An analysis for teacher attitudes and student performance in mainstream high school programs. *Journal of Learning Disabilities, 18*, 535–541.

Zigmond, N., & Thornton, H. (1985). Follow-up of post-secondary age learning disabled graduates and dropouts. *Learning Disabilities Research, 1*, 50–55.

13. A Focus on Curriculum Design: When Children Fail

DEBORAH C. SIMMONS
AND EDWARD J. KAMEENUI

SIMMONS AND KAMEENUI address the topic of academic failure and describe ways in which curriculum can add to learning problems. Specific attention is given to curriculum factors over which teachers have control as well as factors related to learners' that are beyond teachers' control. They argue for greater national and local attention to design and offer perspectives on principles of curriculum design. This selection is especially appropriate for teacher educators and those responsible for assisting teachers in curriculum planning.

In a preview to the "Reading Report Card," U.S. Department of Education Secretary Richard Riley profiled recent national scores indicating that only one-third of high school seniors read proficiently (*Register Guard*, 1995, p. A7). In addition, approximately 75% of fourth and eighth graders scored below the proficient range—which represents a significant decline in reading performance from previous years. A conspicuous finding revealed that, while scores for the top quarter of students remained stable from previous years, the most significant decline involved children at the bottom of the achievement scale.

General and special educators can easily assign faces and names to the children profiled in the national statistics. Some we know as students with specific learning disabilities and language disorders; others are considered at-risk for reading failure, and still others may have no identified disability, yet have consistently struggled throughout their academic careers to keep up with their age-level peers. Though varieties of nomenclature are used to identify these children and many characteristics used to describe their behaviors, their common denominator is failure (Kameenui, 1993). More specifically, they are failing to achieve from traditional curriculum and instruction.

This chapter is devoted broadly to the topic of academic failure, and specifically to the role of curriculum design in either intercepting or exacerbating learning difficulties. A focus on curriculum design does not discount the fact that learners in the bottom of the achievement rankings may differ along biological, neurological, experiential, sociological, and psychological dimensions from those who rank consistently near the top. Rather, this emphasis acknowledges the real differences these learners bring to instruction and to the body of knowledge and science of instruction professional educators possess to address these needs.

The emphasis on curriculum design shifts the focus from factors over which teachers have little control (e.g., neurology) to those that are amenable and capable of preventing and remediating failure. Our goals in this article are to (a) provide a demographic and instructional context for the need to attend to curriculum design at both a national and a local level, (b)define and specify the dimensions of curriculum design, (c) apply curriculum design principles to select academic contents, and (d) discuss implications of poorly designed instruction for students with diverse learning needs.

From our perspective, this is not a problem about *where* special education is delivered, *who* is certified as a professional educator to deliver the instruction, or *how* publishers market their curriculum materials. Rather, our primary interest is on the features of instructional tools, how they are implemented, and their effect on children with diverse learning needs.

Why Children Fail: The Demographic/Instructional Context of General Education

The heart of scientific inquiry rests in the search for and discovery of causes. It is human nature to ask why, and when children fail, the areas to indict and investigate are seemingly infinite. In 1992, Phi Delta Kappa published a study of students at risk titled, *Growing up Is Risky Business and Schools Are Not to Blame.* The authors reported researchers' reluctance to pin down causes, because specifying causation implies personal responsibility and "researchers are hesitant to take such steps" (Frymier et al., 1992, p. v). The report concluded that children's problems, including academic failure, are not attributable to schools but instead to the broader context of the culture in which they live. Precisely, society, in which schools are a part, is responsible, and to understand children's failure, we must address the larger context of society. If society is to blame, the following statistics confirm that general and special education have an ominous task ahead.

Changing Demography and Increasing Complexity

Today, many more students bring linguistic, experiential, cognitive, and sociological differences to school that require more of teachers and the instructional curriculum. The following data from the *Sixteenth Annual Report to Congress* substantiate this increasing trend. In 1992–93, more than five million children birth through age 21 received services under Part B of the Individuals with Disabilities Act (IDEA) and Chapter I of the Elementary and Secondary Education Act—an increase of 3.7% from the previous year. The change in total number of children served from the previous year parallels recent trends of 2 to 3 percent increases per year since 1988–89. Approximately half of these students were classified as having learning disabilities and received much of their instruction in general education (U.S. Department of Education, 1994).

More children with disabilities and diverse learning needs are being educated in general education than ever before (Fuchs & Fuchs, 1994; McLeskey & Pacchiano, 1994). Estimates of the range of instructional levels within general education already are high, with more than five grade levels represented per classroom in some schools (Jenkins, Jewell, Leceister, Jenkins, & Troutner as cited in Fuchs & Fuchs, 1994). In general, teachers and classrooms in general education are not prepared to address the learning and curricular needs that children bring to classrooms (Baker & Zigmond, 1990). Observational and self-report data indicate that the type and quantity of instructional adaptations in general education are insufficient to effect "optimal growth" for many low-performing students in general education (Zigmond et al., 1995).

The portrait of the typical American classroom is changing dramatically. Some of the changes indicate that a growing number of students, including those with disabilities, may not acquire basic, fundamental academic skills and strategies. Perhaps never before have the demographics of an individual classroom presented such complex and diverse demands on teachers and the curricula. Those responsible for addressing the unique and varying needs of learners may find the complexity unwieldy in the face of growing class sizes and reduced instructional support.

These conclusions highlight that classrooms are becoming more complex and traditional curriculum and instruction are unlikely to address students' diverse needs. Recognizing that children's academic failure is a complex challenge undoubtedly complicated by social problems, poverty, deteriorating family structures, and so forth, we are compelled to examine the role of schools and the role of curriculum design in understanding why children do not profit from unspecialized or general instruction. In this chapter, we describe how instructional tools, when designed properly, can mediate the learning demands and difficulties of students with disabilities and other students with diverse learning needs.

Curriculum Design: A National Concern

The educational imperative is clear, though the focal point is obscured by the myriad of factors that influence learning. Mosenthal (1982) proposed that models of learning (and failure) can never be specified fully. More likely, a search for causation and intervention will focus on "partial specifications" of factors most proximal and amenable to change.

More than three decades ago, Carroll (1963) suggested that student learning was based on (a) characteristics of the learner, (b) the time devoted to learning an objective, and (c) the quality of instruction. In addressing learning problems, to assert that educators tend to focus primarily on the learner is fair even though variables within the learner are the most resistant to change because they are unobserved, private, and entirely outside teachers' influence. The second factor, time devoted to learning, is limited by the number of hours in a school day, as well as the range of objectives and activities in the curriculum. Although efficiencies can be achieved to make instructional time more effective, instructional time is often a fixed variable.

More important, diverse learners and children with disabilities

> constantly face the *tyranny of time* in trying to catch up with their peers, who continue to advance in their literacy development. Simply keeping pace with their peers amounts to losing more and more ground for students who are behind. (Kameenui, 1993, p. 379, emphasis added)

Playing "catch up" in school requires using time and every learning opportunity judiciously, strategically, and preciously. Moreover, playing catch-up exacts an enormous cost on students, teachers, administrators, and parents, and the gains are not likely to occur unless the pedagogical machinery is precisely tuned, performance-based, instructionally oriented, and almost free of instructional and curricular error. Finally, the opportunities for these students to advance or catch up diminish greatly over time, and the cognitive and emotional fatigue in trying to catch up is also high. Given the extraordinary challenges inherent in playing catch-up, the best strategy is not to get behind in the first place; to intervene early, frequently, and purposefully to get ahead and stay ahead.

The final factor, quality of instruction, has the greatest potential to affect the needs of students with diverse learning needs. Quality of instruction is influenced by the quality of *instructional tools* available to teachers and the quality of *instructional techniques* used to deliver the instruction.

Interestingly, the quality of instruction component of Carroll's (1963) model is central to the concept of "special education" and is implicated, albeit indirectly, in the federal statutory definition of special education. Specifically, special education is defined in the Individuals with Disabilities Education Act (IDEA) (20 USC 1401 *et seq.*) as specially designed instruction, at no cost to parents, to meet the unique needs of a child with a disability (Bateman, in press). Citing this statutory definition is much easier than interpreting what it means, which, according to Bateman's (in press) most recent legal analysis, is akin to untying the Gordian knot with one hand restricted.

Although the legal interpretation of what "specially designed instruction...to meet the unique needs of a child with a disability" means is beyond the scope of this article, suffice it to say that the instructional program must be "reasonably calculated" to allow the child to benefit. The standard for gauging whether a child benefits is determined on a case-by-case basis and influenced substantially by many factors (e.g., documented lack of progress under alternative instructional conditions, controlling legal precedent, current state laws, suitable balance between goals of academic progress and least restrictive environment).

The legal and statutory complexities in determining what passes for quality instruction notwithstanding, some special educators have called for reforming special education by relying on instructional and educational tools and curricular programs with the "strongest support in theory and reliable empirical research" (Kauffman, 1994, p. 616). In other words, quality instruction should be determined not by what is popular, but by what is tested, evaluated, and proven to be effective for all students, especially diverse learners (Carnine, 1993; Worrall & Carnine, 1994). As Kauffman (1994) implored in his recent call for reforming special education, "Special education carries special responsibility for care in teaching or it has no meaning, regardless of where or by whom it is offered" (p. 616–617).

Responding to Failure: The Role of Educational Tools

For several decades researchers have investigated the relation of curriculum design and instruction to learner outcomes. Findings from studies in content areas ranging from history to vocabulary learning to mathematics indicate a class of variables that consistently and positively affect academic performance for children with diverse learning needs. The primary source that defines instruction in classrooms is the published curriculum and, specifically, textbooks.

The role of textbooks as the main vehicles of information is well documented (Armbruster & Ostertag, 1993; Baker & Zigmond, 1990; Hoffman et al., 1994). In reading, more than 90 percent of classroom instruction is based on commercial educational materials and, specifically, the basal reader (Komoski, cited in Kameenui, 1993). Mayer, Sims, and Tajika (1995) have noted that textbooks actually may serve the role as a "national curriculum" (p. 456) because of their widescale adoption and influence.

Observational and student achievement data indicate that the type and quantity of instruction based on basal programs and traditional adaptations are insufficient to effect optimal or even satisfactory growth for many students with learning disabilities (Baker & Zigmond, 1990). In a study of kindergarten through fifth-grade reading instruction, Baker and Zigmond found that instruction was taught "by the book," largely undifferentiated, and conducted in large groups. Inclusion of students with increasingly diverse learning needs, reliance on a predominant instructional tool, and modest to limited instructional adaptations in general education seemingly call for a ratcheting up of the overall quality of conventional instruction. For example, one strategy for improving instruction is to enhance the quality of the "tools" most commonly used as the base of reading instruction.

Improving the Quality of Instructional Tools: A National Agenda

The diverse and changing demography of today's classrooms places increasing responsibility on developers and publishers to produce educational tools that effect positive change in all learners. Recognizing the widespread use of published curricula and their impact on students with diverse learning characteristics, the Office of Special Education Programs (OSEP) of the U.S. Department of Education announced a series of research priorities to investigate the quality of instructional tools. The first of these cooperative agreements was awarded to the University of Oregon in 1991, with a specific emphasis on improving the quality of instruction tools for students with diverse learning needs. The National Center to Improve the Tools of Educators (NCITE) was established at the University of Oregon, College of Education, in September, 1991, and is directed by Douglas Carnine and Edward Kameenui. Kauffman (1994) has recognized the work of NCITE in his call for special education reform.

NCITE's position is that quality tools that effect positive change in all learners can be identified and advanced by relying on scientifically derived knowledge based on methodologically sound research. Holding to these criteria, NCITE is conducting comprehensive analyses of research on the characteristics of students with diverse learning needs, field testing educational tools in authentic contexts, and soliciting feedback from users of educational tools (e.g., teachers, developers, and publishers) to construct a scientific knowledge base. Three interdependent goals frame NCITE's strategy to improve the quality of educational tools:

1. To establish an empirical knowledge base that articulates the relation between attributes of quality technology, media, and materials and increased attainment of various valued outcomes for students with diverse learning needs
2. To advance the knowledge of publishers, developers, and the education marketplace about the attributes of quality educational tools
3. To increase awareness and support for the use of high-quality educational tools.

NCITE's mission is to increase awareness and promote the use of high-quality educational tools by providing publishers and developers information about the attributes of quality education tools. These attributes have been derived from research on curriculum design variables and the field testing and analyses of educational tools. NCITE has conducted extensive research syntheses in the academic areas of mathematics, beginning reading (e.g., phonological awareness, emergent literacy, word recognition), text structure, language arts (e.g., integrating reading and writing), social studies, and science.

Based on these research syntheses, NCITE has identified six generic principles that traverse a range of academic content areas and are sufficiently encompassing, sensitive, and flexible to capture the distinct and critical features of varying academic domains and cognitive constructs (e.g., phonological awareness, metacognition). The six principles include *big ideas, conspicuous strategies, mediated scaffolding, strategic integration, judicious review*, and *primed background knowledge*. These curriculum design principles provide a framework for examining and fortifying instruction in ways that improve the overall quality of instruction and mediate some of the difficulties that students with disabilities encounter.

Defining Curriculum Design

Curriculum design refers to the way information in a particular domain (e.g., social studies, science, reading, mathematics) is selected, prioritized, sequenced, organized, and scheduled for instruction within a highly orchestrated series of lessons and materials that make up a course of study. Curriculum design provides a broader context for instructional design, which, according to Smith and Ragan (1993), refers to the "systematic process of translating principles of learning and instruction into plans for instructional materials and activities" (p. 2). As Smith and Ragan pointed out:

> An instructional designer is somewhat like an engineer—both plan their works based on principles that have been successful in the past—the engineer on the laws of physics, and the designer on basic principles of instruction and learning. (p. 2)

Whereas the engineer, to extend Smith and Ragan's analogy, is concerned with developing the architectural, electrical, and mechanical plans for building physical structures, the instructional designer is concerned with developing the architectural pedagogy for the communication of symbolic information that has a high probability of preventing learner errors and misconceptions and misrules (Tennyson & Christensen, 1986). Primarily because instructional design is concerned with the communication of symbolic information mediated by a learner, however, it is difficult to appreciate fully what curriculum design looks like, how it fits a particular instructional situation, whether it works for all learners or just some, or how it is related directly to student performance.

Perhaps an important feature of curriculum design is that it is concerned with the intricacies of analyzing, selecting, prioritizing, sequencing, and scheduling the communication of information *before* it is packaged for delivery or implemented. It is the behind-the-scenes activity that appears as the sequence of objectives, schedule of tasks, components of instructional strategies, amount and kind of review, number of examples, extent of teacher direction, and support explicated in teachers' guides and lesson plans. Curriculum design is the blueprint for instruction that carries significant potential for students with diverse learning needs.

Some blueprints are skeletal, providing little instructional specification, and others have fundamental flaws that fail to provide an adequate foundation on which to build further skills and future learning success. For example, consider the following modified directions illustrative of a current commercial reading program:

> *Have children look at the illustration and name the pets in the picture. Elicit the word **pig** and write it on the board. Tell children they will learn about the sound they hear at the beginning of **pig** and the letter that stands for that sound. Ask children to read the first line of the poem. Have them find the word **pig** and match it with the word on the board. Then, as you read the words, ask children to tell which word in the pair begins with the same beginning sound as **pig**.*

This excerpt may seem a benign exercise in beginning reading. Nevertheless, for children at-risk for reading failure, with language delays, or with identified reading disabilities, this activity and those of comparable instructional design can exact pervasive and negative consequential effects on long-term academic development. Because this is an excerpt from a larger reading lesson, we cannot evaluate the lesson fully and perhaps fairly. Select features, however, may complicate learning unintentionally and in a sense promote failure.

We will discuss specifics of curriculum design in subsequent sections. Suffice it to say, though, that the activity makes far too many assumptions about learner preskills, promotes inefficient and ineffective strategies, and relegates teaching to assessment. Moreover, if individuals have not been prepared to evaluate curriculum from a design perspective, the more subtle design problems of the activity may go unnoticed although the effects on learners are likely to be evident in their inability to perform the associated tasks.

If this example is representative of contemporary curricula, and given the importance of curriculum design in preempting learning problems, how does one go about evaluating curriculum systematically and sufficiently? What criteria do you use to evaluate curriculum to determine whether the instructional tool is likely to structure information in ways that are memorable, manageable, and meaningful for students with diverse learning needs? To answer these questions, we recommend the six principles NCITE uses as minimum criteria for evaluating curricula. Carnine (1994) noted that these criteria are not fully specified. Rather, they are offered in the spirit of initiating a dialogue about how educators can make instructional decisions for students who have diverse learning needs. They do not represent a definitive guide to developing, selecting, or modifying curricula but, instead, a starting point for evaluating and selecting instructional tools.

Principles of Effective Curriculum Design

Big Ideas

Big ideas are concepts and principles that facilitate the most efficient and broadest acquisition of knowledge across a range of examples in a domain (Carnine, 1994). Big ideas enable students to learn the most and learn it as efficiently as possible by serving as anchoring concepts by which "small" ideas often can be understood. For students with diverse learning needs, these conceptual anchors are becoming more important in this age of information proliferation.

The growing amount of information to be learned is a source of heavy pressure on educators. In their book, *Curriculum for a New Millennium,* Longstreet and Shane (1993) estimated that by the late 1990s, the quantity of available information will double every 24 months. In effect, this means that learners in today's schools will be exposed to more information in a year than their grandparents were in a lifetime. For students who have difficulty acquiring and maintaining information, a focus on big ideas seems pivotal to manage the amount of information in textbooks.

The tendency of American education to expose students to concepts and information is not new and, unfortunately, not restricted to a particular subject area. In

1989 Porter discussed the consequences of curricula that teach for exposure, and the impending compromises on depth of understanding. An article in *Education Week* (1994) also profiled the tendency of United States textbooks to emphasize breadth over depth.

> We cover lots and lots of things, more than anybody else in the world, but we don't do anything in great depth.... Science textbooks in the United States typically are two to four times longer than those in other countries... and yet it's just those constant snippets of information. While some countries expect 13-year-olds to cover 10 to 15 scientific topics in depth, U.S. textbooks rush them through 30 or 40 topics. (p. 10)

How publishers select, prioritize, and connect information is a design issue, and one that warrants serious consideration of big ideas. The major assumptions of big ideas are that (a) not all curriculum objectives and related instructional activities contribute equally to academic development, and (b) more important information should be taught more thoroughly than less important information (Carnine, 1994). Although some information is fundamental to a domain, other ideas are simply *not* essential, particularly for students with diverse learning needs who face the tyranny of time and must catch up with their peers. For these learners, in particular, big ideas have to be prominent features of instructional tools in the respective content areas. Big ideas should be the instructional anchors of programs for students with diverse learning needs. This does not suggest other information should not be taught, simply that it should not have equal weight or equal time.

Conspicuous Strategies

Strategies are a general set of steps that students follow to solve problems. Many students induce the steps in a strategy on their own. Inducing learning strategies, however, may require a considerable amount of time before the student identifies the optimum strategy. For students with diverse learning needs, this approach is highly problematic because instructional time is a precious commodity and these learners may not induce an effective or efficient strategy. Learning is most efficient when strategies are made explicit. In addition, strategies are most effective when they are of medium breadth and can be generalized.

When applied to a process such as reading comprehension and a specific skill such as determining the main idea, a conspicuous strategy is the set of steps that leads to effective and efficient comprehension and identification of the main idea. Unfortunately, many students with diverse learning needs do not intuit or figure out that the main idea tells about the whole paragraph or story until much time has passed and many opportunities for learning have been exhausted. Moreover, published curricula may not provide the strategic steps necessary for teachers to communicate the process adequately.

Teachers, then, must make explicit the steps proficient readers use to determine whether the main idea is stated explicitly or implicitly, discriminate most important from less important information, summarize ideas, and come to a reasonable conclusion. If educational tools do not provide these steps explicitly either in teacher directions or in printed examples, the burden rests on the teacher to devise and communicate these strategies.

Mediated Scaffolding

Mediated scaffolding refers to the personal guidance, assistance, and support that a teacher, peer, materials, or task provides a learner. It should be seen as temporary support to assist during initial learning. On new or difficult tasks, scaffolding may be substantial and then removed systematically as learners acquire knowledge and skills. Scaffolding can be accomplished through multiple formats including the careful selection of examples that progress from less difficult to more difficult, the purposeful separation of highly similar and potentially confusing facts and concepts (e.g., /p/ and /b/ in early letter-sound correspondence learning), the strategic sequencing of tasks that require learners to recognize then produce a response, or the additional information that selected examples provide, such as highlighting the digits used in a division problem.

American texts are qualitatively different from the instructional tools of other nations in the types of scaffolded examples. Specifically, Mayer, Sims, and Tajika (1995) compared American and Japanese textbooks in teaching mathematical problem solving. They commented, "Japanese textbooks contained many more worked-out examples...than did the U.S. books." One of the primary conclusions was the Japanese textbooks tend to support learners in the learning process by providing multiple examples of successful problem solving strategies, whereas "in the U.S., textbooks are more likely to provide lots of exercises for students to solve on their own without much guidance" (p. 457). This type of guidance seems critical for students with diverse learning needs.

Finally, scaffolding is not a static, predetermined instructional condition. Rather, the degree of scaffolding covaries with the learner's abilities, the goals of instruction, and the complexities of the task. Educators must determine the level and degree of scaffolding necessary. Nonetheless, the extent to which published curricular materials build in support structures will facilitate teachers' ability to provide the scaffolding that learners need.

Strategic Integration

Strategic integration involves the careful combination of new information with what the learner already knows to produce a more general, higher-order skill. Integrating new information with existing knowledge increases the likelihood that information will be understood at a deeper level. The integration must be strategic so new information does not become confused with what the learner knows already. Likewise, it must be parsimonious, emphasizing critical connections.

For new information to be understood and applied, it should be integrated with what a learner knows and understands already. For example, narrative composition seems to invite a logical sequence for integrating story grammar elements strategically across reading comprehension and written composition based on identification, application, and generation activities. In beginning reading, once learners can hear sounds in words and recognize letter-sound correspondences, those skills can be integrated to recognize words. These powerful and often logical connections comprise strategic integration.

Judicious Review

Successful learning also depends on a review process to reinforce the essential building blocks of information within a content domain. According to Dempster (1991), the pedagogical jingle of "practice makes perfect" is not a reliable standard to ensure successful learning. Simple repetition of information will not ensure efficient learning.

Dixon, Carnine, and Kameenui (1992) identified four critical dimensions of judicious review:

1. Sufficient to enable a student to perform the task without hesitation
2. Distributed over time
3. Cumulative with information integrated into more complex tasks
4. Varied to illustrate the wide application of a student's understanding of the information.

So how does a teacher select information for review, schedule review to ensure retention, and design activities to extend a learner's understanding of the skills, concepts, or strategies?

According to Dempster (1991), "spaced repetitions," in which a learner is asked to recall a learning experience, are more effective than "massed repetitions," if the "spacing between occurrences is relatively short" (p. 73). As early as 1917, Edwards (cited in Dempster, 1991) observed that elementary school children who studied academic information once for 4 minutes and again for 21 minutes several days later retained about 30 percent more information than students receiving one continuous 61 minute session. Repeated presentations of shorter time increments distributed over time, therefore, should be considered when scheduling instruction.

Primed Background Knowledge

Successful acquisition of new information depends largely on (a) the knowledge the learner brings to a task, (b) the accuracy of that information, and (c) the extent to which the learner accesses and uses that information. For students who have diverse learning needs, priming background knowledge is critical to success, as it addresses the memory and strategy deficits they bring to tasks. In effect, priming is a brief reminder or prompt that alerts the learner to task dimensions or to retrieve known information.

For example, if learners are facile in hearing and manipulating sounds in words and can identify letter-sound correspondences reliably, they are prepared to learn how to apply that information to identify words. Students with diverse learning needs, however, may not access information in memory as efficiently and effectively or may not rely consistently on effective strategies to identify unknown words. In these cases, the task of priming background knowledge is paramount to subsequent reading success.

A minimum of three guidelines should be considered when priming background knowledge:

1. Identify essential preskills or background knowledge most proximal to the new task
2. Once proximal tasks are identified, determine whether the background knowledge needs to be primed or taught
3. Provide the priming necessary to elicit the correct information or ready the learner by focusing attention on a difficult task or component of a task.

Summary of Curriculum Design Principles

These six instructional principles serve as the primary guidelines for designing tools to promote learning for students with diverse learning needs (see Table 13.1). All too often, tools for most students do not consider the unique characteristics and needs of an increasing number of students who demand higher quality instruction (e.g., Kameenui & Simmons, 1990).

As expectations for students increase, accountability for achievement also increases. As classrooms become more complex environments and the needs of learners more diverse, teachers must rely on effective instructional tools, based on quality curriculum design principles, to increase the likelihood that students will attain and maintain information successfully. In the next section, we illustrate the application of curriculum design principles to selected content areas.

Application of Curriculum Design Principles to History, Mathematics, Beginning Reading, and Writing

The six principles serve as the minimum pedagogical framework for design of a curriculum for all learners, especially students with diverse learning and curricular needs. Developing a pedagogical framework around these six principles is an enormously complex task that involves expert knowledge of a domain (e.g., earth science, geometry) and expertise in instructional design for diverse learners. We do not expect classroom practitioners or curriculum development specialists to have all this knowledge. Nor do we expect teachers to design curriculum materials from scratch or redesign and modify existing curricula in substantial ways. The following applications of the six principles in the areas of history, mathematics, reading, and writing exemplify curriculum design that is both possible and necessary for the full range of learners.

■ **Table 13.1** *Summary of Critical Dimensions of Curriculum
Design Principles*

Principle	Criteria/Features
Big Idea: Concepts, principles, or heuristics that facilitate the most efficient and broad acquisition of knowledge	1. Focus on essential learning outcomes 2. Capture rich relationships 3. Enable learners to apply what they learn in varied situations 4. Involve ideas, concepts, principles, and rules central and fundamental to higher-order learning 5. Form the basis for generalization and expansion
Conspicuous Strategies: Useful steps for accomplishing a goal or task	1. Planned 2. Purposeful 3. Explicit 4. Of medium-level application 5. Most important in initial teaching
Mediated Scaffolding: Instructional guidance provided by teachers, peers, materials, or tasks	1. Varied according to learner need and experiences 2. Based on task (not more than learner needs) 3. Provided in the form of tasks, content, and materials 4. Weaned or removed according to learner proficiency
Strategic Integration: Integrating knowledge as a means of promoting higher-level cognition	1. Combines cognitive components 2. Results in a new and more complex knowledge structure 3. Aligns naturally with information (i.e., not "forced") 4. Involves meaningful relationships 5. Links essential big ideas across lessons within a curriculum
Primed Background Knowledge: Preexisting information that affects new learning	1. Aligns with learner knowledge and expertise 2. Considers strategic and proximal preskills 3. Readies learner for successful performance
Judicious Review: Structured opportunities to recall or apply information previously taught	1. Sufficient 2. Varied 3. Distributed 4. Cumulative 5. Judicious

As Smith and Ragan (1993) noted, selecting *what* to teach (e.g., the big ideas in a specific domain) and specifying the intricate requirements of *when* (e.g., strategic integration, judicious review) and *how* (e.g., conspicuous strategies, mediated scaffolding, primed background knowledge) to teach is akin to pedagogical engineering. This engineering is predicated on the presumption that a fundamentally sound curriculum design increases the probability that the information will be communicated to all learners successfully. Although the big ideas across the various domains are necessarily different, the principles for how and when to teach those ideas share a procedural sameness; that is, understanding mediated scaffolding and judicious review in the context of teaching phonological awareness in beginning reading, should facilitate the understanding of mediated scaffolding and judicious review in the context of teaching concepts in other content areas including history, mathematics, writing, etc. In the following examples, we illustrate the covariation of curriculum design principles and content.

History

Big ideas can be critical in content areas such as social studies, history, and science. Expository or content area texts typically are complicated if not unmanageable for students with diverse learning needs. Although a number of factors, including density of information, text structure, and vocabulary, contribute to their difficulty, a large problem is the manner in which information is presented as lists of facts instead of strategies that promote general knowledge (Gehrke, Knapp, & Sirotnik, 1992, cited in Nolet & Tindal, 1994). History texts and instruction frequently are criticized as being a chronological sequence of events learned primarily by memorizing names, dates, and places (Brophy, 1990; Kinder & Bursuck, 1991). In general, history texts introduce far too much information and make far too few explicit connections (Carnine, Miller, Bean, & Zigmond, 1994). Beck, McKeown, and Gromoll (1989) found that textbook content did a poor job of helping students understand the underlying principles that account for historical events. Thus, the responsibility resides with the teacher or learner to make connections (a) between events, (b) between what is being learned to what has been learned previously, and (c) between what is being learned and what will be learned next.

An alternative presentation of history is a structure that emphasizes the relations and sameness between important events. For example, a big idea in history is a problem-solution-effect model that can provide a widely general strategy for understanding historical events and their interrelatedness (Carnine, Miller, et al., 1994). In this strategy, learners recognize a structure or sameness that underlies most historical problems. Specifically, "common problems in history can be attributed to (a) economic or (b) human rights issues" (Carnine, Miller, et al., 1994, p. 434).

Solutions to historical problems likewise can be classified into one of five types: moving, inventing, dominating, accommodating, or tolerating. Attempts to solve problems produce consequences or effects that frequently lead to other problems, reinforcing the relations between the parts. When instructional tools design information around such relational linkages, teachers' responsibilities can shift from designing to delivering information in ways that engage, involve, and motivate learners. Concomitantly, well-designed lessons that make content connections explicit further enhance the likelihood that students will relate historical events within the given period of time and also to more contemporary problems.

For example, U.S. history is filled with examples of individuals who, in the face of economic and human rights problems in their native countries, solved their problems by moving to a new country (Carnine, Miller, et al. 1994). The effect of moving eliminated the economic or human rights problems of some people. For others, moving resulted in new economic or human rights problems, which sometimes were more severe than the initial problem.

The colonists' flight from English rule is one example of a group of individuals who moved in an attempt to solve the problem of government control and the conflict between church and state. But the Tories' attempt to dominate through taxation created an even larger problem, escalating into a more severe form of domination: war. In relation to current events, parallel problems exist throughout the world, involving both economic (tariffs on imported automobiles) and human rights (e.g., Apartheid, Bosnia) issues. Through the problem-solution-effect model, these relations are made explicit, increasing the likelihood that students will retain the information.

Big ideas by themselves are important but insufficient and must be complemented with other effective design principles. For instance, in the problem-solution-effect model of history, conspicuous strategies are used to teach two general classes of problems (economic, human rights), five categories of solutions, (moving, inventing, dominating, accommodating, or tolerating) and three categories of effects (the problem ends, the problem continues, or a new problem is caused by the solution).

Scaffolding can be used to assist students in completing a problem-solution-effect outline. Teachers first might identify the problem, solution, and effect, gradually relinquishing the responsibility as students become proficient. This gradual transfer of responsibility to the learner is likely to increase (a) academic success, because students are given greater assistance early when they most need it, and (b) learning efficiency and depth, because students work systematically toward learning independence.

Strategic integration can be used to help students make the connections between past events, contemporary issues, and their own life experiences. For example, students might make the connection between historical and current immigration events in Florida and Haiti, and their own experiences with moving to a new place.

Mathematics

In mathematics, big ideas also can reduce the burden on students with diverse learning needs to memorize information. Many students learn to solve complex math problems by memorizing various formulas and applying the correct formula to a specific problem or task. Students with diverse learning needs will have difficulty adopting this strategy because, first, the sheer number of formulas may exceed their memory skills and, second, these students may lack conceptual understanding of how to determine which formula to apply.

Frequently, however, formulas can be reduced, changed, or grouped conceptually to aid organization and retrieval. Traditionally, seven different formulas using measures of length, width, height, diameter, and radius are applied to compute the volume of seven shapes (rectangle, wedge, triangular pyramid, cylinder, rectangular pyramid, cone, and sphere). These seven formulas can be reduced to one primary formula (base times height) with two slight variations based on the shape of the object (Carnine, Jones, & Dixon, 1994). Thus, rather than memorizing seven formulas and matching the correct one to a given shape to determine its volume, students need to learn one basic formula for volume and how to use variations of that formula to determine the volume of a given shape. In addition to simplifying the amount of information to memorize, students' conceptual understanding of volume will increase because, to calculate the volume of multiple shapes, students will have to understand why and how to apply variations on the base-times-height formula.

To be optimally effective, this big idea in mathematics has to be supported by additional instructional design principles. Determining volume using one formula instead of seven also depends on the strategic integration of specific math concepts. Students must understand the concept of geometric area to determine the base of shapes. After the concept of area is learned, the related concept of volume can be taught in the context of base (i.e., *area* of the base) times height (Carnine, Jones, et al., 1994). Using volume as the big idea, conspicuous strategies are aligned closely with scaffolding. The strategy for calculating volume is to determine the base times height of a shape (with two minor variations). Mediated scaffolding will ensure that students can perform simple aspects of this strategy in isolation (e.g., calculating the area of a base) before having them attempt complex problems (e.g., calculating the volume of a shape) or problems that require the analysis of information (e.g., story problems) to arrive at the answer.

Beginning Reading

Big Idea Phonological Awareness. In a review of reading research, the role and relation of phonological awareness to beginning reading acquisition garnered convincing and converging evidence (Smith, Simmons & Kameenui, 1995). Specifically, empirical evidence focused on the conclusion that beginning readers must be able to hear and manipulate sounds in words and understand the sound structure of language. Evidence derived from dozens of primary and secondary sources confirmed that children who are strong in phonological awareness usually learn to read more easily than children with delayed abilities (Juel, 1988; Smith et al., 1995; Stanovich, 1986; Torgesen, Wagner, & Rashotte, 1994).

Moreover, Smith et al. found converging evidence indicating that phonological awareness is (a) a complex process composed of many components; (b) a reliable predictor for later reading achievement; (c) causally related to reading development; and (d) developed successfully through instruction and practice. From this robust, foundational knowledge base, we ascertained that the ability to hear and manipulate sounds in language is a big idea and essential to early reading acquisition.

In beginning reading, big ideas are the unifying curriculum activities that enable learners to translate the alphabetic code into meaningful language. The research on phonological awareness provides compelling evidence that these skills are fundamental to beginning reading and deserve considerable attention in the early reading curriculum.

Big ideas represent perhaps the largest modification or shift in thinking for publishers, developers, and teachers. In a period when teachers are forced to make instructional choices, big ideas provide guidelines about essential components of beginning reading programs. Currently, we are analyzing kindergarten and first-grade basal reading programs to identify the quantity and quality of phonological awareness instruction with particular emphasis on big ideas, conspicuous strategies, and mediated scaffolding (Simmons et al., 1995). Preliminary findings indicate that the majority of basal programs incorporate the big idea of phonological awareness as a routine lesson component. Despite these activities, our review further suggests that design of instruction may not address the needs of students with diverse learning needs sufficiently.

Our analysis of basal reading programs indicated a tendency to identify a base activity, such as word-to-word matching or rhyming, and to use that activity across a series of lessons. In several basal reading programs the phonological awareness activity remained relatively constant and the letter-sound correspondence varied to correspond with the emphasis of the lesson. Though this consistency in curriculum design provides an anticipatory set for teachers and likely increases the predictability and usability of the materials, it likewise poses predictable limitations.

Reading research has documented that phonological awareness is a construct composed of multiple components (e.g., rhyming, blending, segmenting). These components relate differentially to reading acquisition; the processes of segmentation and blending correlate more strongly with reading acquisition than less complex processes such as sound isolation or rhyming (Yopp, 1988). The correlational nature of these data precludes definitive instructional decisions; nevertheless, a logical implication suggests that a curriculum provide beginning readers frequent opportunities to practice the phonological processes associated more highly with word reading.

Example. The example in Figure 13.1 is representative of the types of activities first-grade basal reading programs use to promote phonological awareness. According to the teacher's guide of a specific program, the objective of the activity is to develop phonemic awareness of /n/. The strategy requires learners to identify the sound of the letter at the beginning of *nest* and compare other words to determine whether the initial sound is a match with the initial sound of the target word. In essence, the task requires learners to make a word-to-word match based on the sameness of initial sounds. This example provides multiple pictures from which students discriminate those that begin the same as *nest* and those that do not. The task as presented in the teacher's guide is found in Figure 13.1.

Big Idea: Phonological Awareness

Existing Example: Lesson 4
Teach/Model
Inconspicuous Strategy: Word-to-Word Matching

Develop phonemic awareness of /n/.	Tell children they will be learning about the sound they hear at the beginning of *nest* and the letter that stands for that sound. Display the picture side of the picture cards for /n/ and assorted other picture cards. Identify the pictures with children. Have them sort the pictures by the names of pictures that begin the same as *nest* and those that do not. Have them say the names of the pictures that begin like *nest*.

Enhanced Example: Lesson 4
Teach/Model
Conspicuous Strategy: Word-to-Word Matching/Sound Isolation

Mediated Scaffolding	**Teacher**	**Model /n/ sound.** "Today you will be learning about the sound you hear at the beginning of *nest*. The beginning sound in nest is /n/." [Display picture cards that begin with /n/.] "Here are some pictures that begin with /n/. I'll name the picture and the beginning sound. Then you name the picture: net, /n/; nut, /n/; needle, /n/; newspaper, /n/."
	Student	**Listen to /n/ and say words that begin with /n/.**
	Teacher	**Assist student understanding of sound isolation.** "Here are other pictures that begin with /n/. I want you to name the picture and the beginning sound." [Display picture cards that begin with /n/.]
	Student	**Isolate beginning /n/ sound.**
	Teacher	**Assess student understanding of sound isolation.** "Here are some more pictures. Some begin with /n/, some begin with /h/, and some begin with /w/. When I show a picture, you name it and then say the beginning sound." [Display picture cards that begin with /n/, /h/, and /w/.]
	Student	**Isolate beginning /n/ sound and other sounds.**
	Teacher	**Assess student understanding of sound isolation.** "With these pictures, I want you to name each picture. Then put the pictures that begin with /n/ in one pile, those that begin with /h/ in a second pile, and those that begin with /w/ in a third pile." [Display picture cards that begin with /n/, /h/, and /w/.]
	Student	**Use beginning sounds to match and discriminate words.**

Figure 13.1 *Existing and Enhanced Examples*

The *existing* example requires students to sort through the instructional language to discern the objective of the task: to determine that /n/ is the target sound. Success of this task is predicated on learners' understanding the concept *beginning* and their ability to extract the desired objective from only one example of the target sound in a word. The complexity of the task is increased further by requiring students to discriminate words that begin the same as nest from those that do not before they have had sufficient practice with the target sound only.

This instruction may be sufficient for some learners in first grade; however, an increasing number of children require more than is specified currently in instructional manuals. The following recommendations may seem commonplace and straightforward; however, research indicates that these types of recommended modifications are not characteristic of basal reading programs.

We propose that the potential problems in the activity can be mediated by attending to the curriculum design principles of conspicuous strategies and mediated scaffolding. Conspicuous strategies in beginning reading are the steps that lead to effective and efficient word recognition. In phonological awareness, they are the steps a reader takes to recognize and figure out the sound structure of a word. Unfortunately, many learners do not intuit or figure out the processes of blending or segmenting sounds in words until much time has passed and many opportunities for learning have been exhausted. It is the process of making explicit the steps of manipulating the sounds in your head or figuring out a word that has to be conspicuous for students.

To rectify potential learning obstacles, we first recommend that the instructional strategy be more conspicuous. Through a sequence of teaching events and teacher actions, requirements of the task can be made more explicit. This is achieved by modeling the intended outcomes of the task as illustrated in the *enhanced* example in Figure 13.1. In this example, the teacher identifies the target sound and then names multiple pictures, all which begin with the target sound. Through explicit attention to the target sound and the use of multiple examples, students learn the commonalities in the target words and the task expectations.

In addition to conspicuous strategies, the enhanced example incorporates several forms of mediated scaffolding. First, teachers model the process of matching initial sounds of words. Next, initial learning is supported by focusing first on words with /n/. Before students are asked to discriminate pictures that begin with /n/ from those that do not, they practice identifying the initial sound in words that begin with /n/. Only after students have had multiple opportunities to hear the critical feature of words are discrimination words (e.g., *horse, window*) introduced.

An additional enhancement strategically structures the difficulty of the task by selecting words from which children discriminate. By limiting the discrimination tasks to words containing sounds that children know (e.g., *w* and *h*), have had sufficient practice with, and are not easily confused with the target sound n, learners are more likely to be successful.

Written Expression

Big Idea: Narrative Text Structure. In reading and writing, text structure represents an example of a big idea. The underlying text structure in narrative prose is story grammar. Story grammar refers to a set of rules and elements typically occurring in a story. Research provides evidence that instruction in story grammar enhances comprehension of stories for normally achieving and low-achieving students and for students with learning disabilities (Carnine & Kinder, 1985; Dimino, Gersten, Carnine, & Blake, 1990). Research also supports strategy instruction in story grammar to improve narrative composition skills for students with learning disabilities (Graham, & Harris, 1989). Building on the work of Dimino et al. (1990), Graves, Montague, and Wong (1990), and Nezworski, Stein, and Trabasso (1982), we developed an integrated strategy that relies on story grammar elements: setting, main character, additional characters, character development (including inferred descriptions), problem, attempts to solve, resolution (or failure to resolve), conclusion, and theme.

Strategic Integration: Reading and Writing. Reading and writing taught together seem to engage learners in a greater variety of reasoning operations than when taught separately. In a comprehensive examination of studies, including those with large and small sample sizes and varying subject ages, Tierney and Shanahan (1991) found consistent support for integrated instruction of reading and writing. Integrated reading and writing seemed to enhance thinking operations and learning of key concepts. In a 3-year study with 400 students in grades 9–11, Langer and Applebee (1986) concluded that essay writing following reading prompted students to focus more deeply on specific sections of text and prompted more written comments representing a greater variety of reasoning operations than note-taking or study guide questions. Reading followed by a writing exercise resulted in significantly more learning than did reading without some form of writing task (Langer & Applebee, 1986).

Besides enhancing thinking and comprehension, integrated reading and writing also may improve writing. Shanahan and Lomax (1986) found the influence of reading-to-write stronger than the influence of writing-to-read. Noyce and Christie (1985) concluded further that integrated instruction in reading and writing in complex syntactic structures produced greater gains in reading and writing than instruction in writing only. Likewise, Englert, Raphael, Anderson, Anthony, and Stevens (1991) found achievement gains by integrating the writing process and role of text structure knowledge in teaching writing strategies to students with and without learning disabilities.

Conspicuous Strategy: Writing Process. Several researchers (e.g., Graham and Harris, Seidenberg, Isaacson, and Englert) have addressed the effects of strategy instruction in writing. Research studies investigating writing strategy instruction for students with learning disabilities have examined the benefits of specific instructional components and have documented support for the teacher (a) explicitly introducing, explaining, and describing writing strategies, (b) modeling the strategy through think-alouds, (c) providing opportunities for students to interact and collaborate with the teacher and each other, (d) providing scaffolds and (e) training students in self-instructional strategies and self-monitoring. In particular, Englert et al. (1991) investigated teaching a writing process to students with and without learning disabilities using a writing strategy that consists of plan, organize, write, edit, and revise and known by the acronym POWER.

Mediated Scaffolding. Phases of individual scaffolding occurred in Englert's investigations of effective writing instruction. First, teachers introduced a writing strategy and think-sheets by modeling and thinking aloud. In the next phase, teachers and students jointly applied writing strategies. Finally, teachers provided guidance and opportunities for students to practice writing on topics of their own choice (Englert et al., 1991).

Another dimension of scaffolding is content presentation, the selection and sequence of content to enable students to learn and be successful. Dimino et al. (1990) scaffolded content by initially using shorter, less complex stories to teach easier, more obvious story grammar elements (character, problem, attempts, and resolution) before teaching more difficult story grammar elements (character clues based on inferences and theme). As students became more proficient at identifying story grammar elements, story length and complexity increased.

A third dimension of scaffolding, material prompts, provides external supports (procedural facilitation) for students (Scardamalia & Bereiter, 1986). In writing instruction, material prompts cue strategy use and help less experienced students emulate mature writers' performance (Scardamalia & Bereiter, 1986). Research studies have investigated a range of material prompts including think-sheets to activate planning, organizing, drafting, editing, and revising note sheets (Englert et al., 1991), for recording story grammar elements (Dimino et al., 1990), and story grammar cue cards, verbal reminders for character development, and metacognitive check-off procedures (Graves et al., 1990).

In task scaffolding, a fourth dimension of scaffolding, tasks gradually increase in difficulty. An example of scaffolded tasks is found in the work of Graham and Harris (1989). Students identified story grammar elements in stories, generated story grammar elements while looking at a picture, generated self-instruction statements to generate story parts, and practiced story writing strategies before composing stories independently. Another example of scaffolded tasks is providing students opportunities to write rough drafts and edit them, then write revised copies. This helps prevent students from feeling overwhelmed by attempting to write perfect papers. Students focus first on communicating ideas, then on mechanics.

Judicious Review. Reading and writing instruction requires an appropriate review schedule to reinforce and maintain knowledge and use of information. Based on review research, effective practice depends upon (a) time between repetitions, (b) frequency of repetitions, and (c) form of repetition (Dempster, 1991). Effective review also is cumulative, integrating skills and strategies and providing review opportunities over an extended time (Dixon, Carnine, & Kameenui, 1992). As skills and strategies for improving reading comprehension and writing are introduced, a firming cycle should be used. A firming cycle is the "repeated presentation of new and/or problematic tasks both throughout and at the end of a lesson to assure that students are firm on the information" (Kameenui & Simmons, 1990, p. 235).

The Effects of Educational Tools: Beyond the Instructional Veneer

In 1985, Gickling and Thompson coined the term *curriculum casualties* to refer to the interaction of curricula that move too fast in relation to learners' existing skills. They further noted that the cumulative effect of poorly designed curricula and instruction result is a failure cycle wherein learners become perpetually and increasingly discrepant from their peers. Dixon and Carnine (1993) reinforced curriculum effects proposing that "poorly designed instruction can have an effect on students that is less than poor learning: students can learn misconceptions that become stubborn impediments to all future remediation efforts" (p. 18).

A common tenet of instructional design is the power of the negative example (Engelmann & Carnine, 1982). Dixon and Carnine used the negative example skillfully to communicate what a curriculum would look like if it were designed intentionally to be difficult for students. (What would be the negative features of a curriculum for students with diverse learning needs?) Their analysis focused on mathematics; however, the principles generalize to other content areas. A curriculum designed intentionally to be difficult for students with diverse learning needs would:

- Teach very little thoroughly
- Avoid opportunities to work on the "hot spots" where many students predictably fail
- Avoid linking symbolic representations with concrete manipulation
- Encourage children to infer strategies
- Focus on rote acquisition
- Teach a topic or content and drop it, failing to give students the opportunity to apply content realistically.

Additional features we would add to Carnine and Dixon's list of "criteria for poorly designed curricula" are the following:

- Provide few explicit examples of how to perform a task
- Assume that learners have adequate background information and know when and how to use it
- Leave it entirely up to the learner to make the connections between information
- Allocate equal amounts of time to all instructional objectives
- Assume that instructional time is unlimited.

Currently, we have no easy or fully specified answers for how to optimize academic learning for the increasingly large number of children who fail to benefit adequately from current educational practices and tools. Instructional practices and educational curricula, however, currently are under scrutiny as states seek a cause and a solution to unprecedented rates of failure (Diegmueller, 1995). As proposed in this chapter and heralded historically by research on curriculum design, students who fail to respond to traditional instruction may require an intensity and an integrity of instruction different from past and present practices and educational tools. The diverse needs of children in today's schools are not likely to be resolved by adding instructional veneer to existing educational tools. Practitioners, administrators, educational researchers, publishers, developers, and personnel who prepare general and special educators alike must take seriously the role that educational tools play in learning and recognize the scientific body of knowledge available to guide curriculum design.

References

Armbruster, B., & Ostertag, J. (1993). Questions in elementary science and social studies textbooks. In B. K. Britton, A. Woodward, & M. Binkley (Eds.), *Learning from textbooks: Theory and practice* (pp. 69–94). Hillsdale, NJ: Erlbaum.

Baker, J., & Zigmond, N. (1990). Are regular education classes equipped to accommodate students with learning disabilities? *Exceptional Children, 56*, 515–526.

Bateman, B. (in press). *Legal research on what constitutes "specially designed instruction" and quality technology, media, and materials for students with disabilities.* (Tech. Rep.). Eugene: Oregon: University of Oregon, National Center to Improve the Tools of Educators.

Beck, I. L., McKeown, M. G., & Gromoll, E. W. (1989). Learning from social studies texts. *Cognition & Instruction, 12*, 118–132.

Brophy, J. (1990). Teaching social studies for understanding and higher-order applications. *Elementary School Journal, 90*, 353–417.

Carnine, D. (1993, December 8). Facts, not fads. *Education Week*, p. 40.

Carnine, D. (1994). Introduction to the mini-series: Educational tools for diverse learners. *School Psychology Review, 23*, 341–350.

Carnine, D., Jones, E. D., & Dixon, B. (1994). Mathematics: Educational tools for diverse learners. *School Psychology Review, 23*, 406–427.

Carnine D., & Kinder, D. (1985). Teaching low-performing students to apply generative and schema strategies to narrative and expository material. *Remedial & Special Education, 6*, 20–30.

Carnine, D., Miller, S., Bean, R., & Zigmond, N. (1994). Social studies: Educational tools for diverse learners. *School Psychology Review, 23*, 428–441

Carroll, J. B. (1963). A model of school learning. *Teachers College Record, 64*, 723–733.

Dempster, F. N. (1991, April). Synthesis of research on reviews and tests. *Educational Leadership, 48*, 71–76.

Diegmueller, K. (1995, June 14). California plotting new tack on language arts. *Education Week*, p. 1.

Dimino, J., Gersten, R., Carnine, D., & Blake, G. (1990). Story grammar: An approach for promoting at-risk secondary students' comprehension of literature. *Elementary School Journal, 91*, 19–32.

Dixon, B., & Carnine, D. (1993). The hazards of poorly designed instructional tools. *Learning Disabilities Forum, 18*(3), 18–22.

Dixon, R., Carnine, D. W., & Kameenui, E. J. (1992). *Curriculum guidelines for diverse learners.* Monograph for National Center to Improve the Tools of Educators. Eugene: University of Oregon.

Engelmann, S., & Carnine, D. W. (1982). *Theory of instruction: Principles and applications.* New York: Irvington.

Englert, C. S., Raphael, T. E., Anderson, L. M., Anthony, H. M., & Stevens, D. D. (1991). Making strategies and self-talk visible: Writing instruction in regular and special education classrooms. *American Educational Research Journal, 2,* 337–372.

Frymier, J., Barber, L., Carriedo, R., Denton, W., Gansneder, B., Johnson-Lewis, S., & Robertson, N. (1992). *Growing up is risky business and schools are not to blame.* Bloomington, IN: Phi Delta Kappa.

Fuchs, D., & Fuchs., L. (1994). Classwide curriculum-based measurement: Helping general educators meet the challenge of student diversity. *Exceptional Children, 60,* 518–537.

Gickling, E., & Thompson, V. (1985). A personal view of curriculum-based assessment. *Exceptional Children, 52,* 219–232.

Graham, S., & Harris, K. R. (1989). A components analysis of cognitive strategy instruction: Effects on learning disabled students' compositions and self-efficacy. *Journal of Educational Psychology, 81,* 356–361.

Graves, A., Montague, M., & Wong, Y. (1990). The effects of procedural facilitation on the story composition of learning disabled students. *Learning Disabilities Research, 5,* 88–93.

Hoffman, J. V., McCarthey, S., Abbot, C., Corman, L., Dressman, M., Elliott, B., Matherne, D., & Stahle, D. (1994). So what's new in the new basals? A focus on first grade. *Journal of Reading Behavior, 26,* 47–73.

International math and science study finds US covers more in less depth. (1994, June 24). *Education Week,* p. 10.

Juel, C. (1988). Learning to read and write: A longitudinal study of 54 children from first through fourth grades. *Journal of Educational Psychology, 80,* 437–447.

Kameenui, E. J. (1993). Diverse learners and the tyranny of time: Don't fix blame; fix the leaky roof. *Reading Teacher, 46,* 376–383.

Kameenui, E. J., Carnine, D. W., & Dixon R. C. (In press). Effective teaching strategies that accommodate diverse learners. In E. J. Kameenui (Ed.), *Effective teaching strategies that accommodate diverse learners.* Columbus, OH: Merrill.

Kameenui, E. J., & Simmons, D. C. (1990). *Designing instructional strategies: The prevention of academic learning problems.* Columbus, OH: Merrill.

Kauffman, J. M. (1994). Places of change: Special education's power and identity in an era of educational reform. *Journal of Learning Disabilities, 27,* 610–618.

Kinder, D., & Bursuck, W. (1991). The search for a unified social studies curriculum: Does history really repeat itself? *Journal of Learning Disabilities, 24,* 270–275.

Langer, J., & Applebee, A. (1986). Reading and writing instruction: Toward a theory of teaching and learning. In E. Rothkopf (Ed.), *Review of research in education* (Vol. 13) (pp. 171–194). Washington, DC: American Educational Research Association.

Longstreet, W. S., & Shane, H. G. (1993). *Curriculum for a new millennium.* Boston: Allyn & Bacon.

Mayer, R., Sims, V., & Tajika, H. (1995). A comparison of how textbooks teach mathematical problem solving in Japan and the United States. *American Educational Research Journal, 32,* 443–460.

McLeskey, J., & Pacchiano, D. (1994). Mainstreaming students with learning disabilities: Are we making progress? *Exceptional Children, 60,* 508–517.

Mosenthal, P. (1982). Designing training programs for learning disabled children: An ideological perspective. *Topics in Learning and Learning Disabilities, 2,* 97–107.

Nezworski, T., Stein, N. L., & Trabasso, T. (1982). Story structure versus content in children's recall. *Journal of Verbal Learning & Verbal Behavior, 21,* 196–206.

Nolet, V., & Tindal, G. (1994). Instruction and learning in middle school science classes: Implications for students with disabilities. *The Journal of Special Education, 28,* 166–187.

Noyce, R. M., & Christie, J. F. (1985). Effects of an integrated approach to grammar instruction on third graders' reading and writing. *Elementary School Journal, 84,* 63–69.

Porter, A. C. (1989, June-July). A curriculum out of balance: The case of elementary school mathematics. *Educational Researcher, 18*(5), 9–15.

Reading scores for high school seniors show drop. (1995, April). *Register Guard,* p. A7.

Scardamalia, M., & Bereiter, C. (1986). Research on written composition. In M. C. Wittrock (Ed.), *Handbook of research on education* (3d ed., pp. 778–803). New York: Macmillan.

Shanahan, T., & Lomax, R. G. (1986). An analysis and comparison of theoretical models of the reading-writing relationship. *Journal of Educational Psychology, 78*, 116–123.

Simmons, D. C., Gleason, M. M., Smith, S. B., Baker, S. K., Sprick, M., Thomas, C., Gunn, B., Chard, D., Plasencia-Peinado J., Peinado, R., & Kameenui, E. J. (1995, April). *Applications of phonological awareness research in basal reading programs: Evidence and implications for students with reading disabilities.* Paper presented at meeting of American Educational Research Association, San Francisco.

Simmons, D., Kameenui, E. J., Dickson, S., Chard, D., Gunn, B., & Baker, S. Integrating narrative reading and writing instruction for all learners. (1994). *Yearbook of the National Reading Council, 43*, 572–582.

Smith, P. L. & Ragan, T. L. (1993). *Instructional design.* New York: Merrill.

Smith, S. B., Simmons, D. C., & Kameenui, E. J. (1995). *Synthesis of research on phonological awareness: Principles and implications for reading acquisition* (Tech. Rep. No. 21). Eugene: University of Oregon, National Center to Improve the Tools of Educators.

Stanovich, K. E. (1986). Matthew effects in reading: Some consequences of individual differences in the acquisition of literacy. *Reading Research Quarterly, 21*, 360–406.

Tennyson, R., & Christensen, D. L. (1986, April). *Memory theory and design of intelligent learning systems.* Paper presented at meeting of American Educational Research Association, San Francisco.

Tierney, R. J., & Shanahan, T. (1991). Research on the reading-writing relationship: Interactions, transactions, and outcomes. In R. Barr, M. Kamil, P. B. Mosenthal, & P. D. Pearson (Eds.), *Handbook of reading research* (Vol. 2), (pp. 246–280). New York: Longman.

Torgesen, J., Wagner, R., & Rashotte, C. (1994). Longitudinal studies of phonological processing and reading. *Journal of Learning Disabilities, 27*, 276–286.

U. S. Department of Education (1994). *Sixteenth annual report to Congress on the implementation of the Individuals with Disabilities Education Act.* Washington, DC: Government Printing Office.

Worrall, R. S., & Carnine, D. (1994, March). *Lack of professional support undermines teachers and reform—A contrasting perspective from health and engineering.* Unpublished manuscript, National Center to Improve the Tools of Educators, College of Education, University of Oregon, Eugene.

Yopp, H. K. (1988). The validity and reliability of phonemic awareness tests. *Reading Research Quarterly, 23*, 159–177.

Zigmond, N., Jenkins, J., Fuchs, L. S., Deno, S., Fuchs, D., Baker, J. N., Jenkins, L., & Couthino, M. (1995, March). Special education in restructured schools: Findings from three multi-year studies. *Phi Delta Kappan, 76*(7), 531–540.

Part Three

Instructional Strategies for Students with Mild Disabilities

GLENN A. VERGASON, GEORGIA STATE UNIVERSITY
M. L. ANDEREGG, KENNESAW STATE COLLEGE (GEORGIA)

In educating students with mild disabilities, the three most important elements—management strategies, curriculum strategies, and instructional strategies—are contained in this book. The first two have been addressed already, leaving the ever critical elements of implementing instruction using the most effective instructional strategies available from current professional research.

Differences in instruction have been the heart of special education from its beginning. Only in fairly recent times have these differences been gathered into what has been termed strategies. Strategies are well thought-out sequences of presentation practices that enhance the student's learning, retention, and application of what has to be learned. The most systematic program, developed by Alley and Deshler (1979) has been well researched by Deshler (Deshler & Schumaker, 1986), his colleagues and students, and has been called learning strategies. Learning strategies, however, are not the only approaches presented here. We have gathered what we believe represents a strong continuum of effective approaches.

The editors of this book realize that specialized instruction (special education) can occur in a variety of settings, including the general education classroom. They also recognize that the debate of the geography of placement, whether parttime or fulltime, is not the determining factor. Instead, the authors of selections within this section and the editors who chose them believe that, without special education, some students are not likely to succeed. We further believe that, with the practices detailed in the readings that follow, effective instruction can occur in any environment with the right personnel and well developed programs. These latter two items can not be overemphasized.

The topics were carefully selected. The authors were invited to write chapters because of their relative areas of expertise. Some chapters address a specific category of disabilities rather than a more generic approach to students with mild disabilities. At the same time, the authors within this section encourage the reader to generalize across categories where characteristics are similar. Research has shown these strategies to be effective with students who have a variety of mild disabilities, including those with dual diagnoses.

The chapter by King-Sears (1997) discusses a program designed to provide instruction to students with mild disabilities in the general education setting. King-Sears presents 10 practices, well documented in the literature (Meyen, 1980; Vergason & Anderegg, 1991), that were chosen specifically to address problems common to special and general education. There is a general tendency for special education personnel to "spread themselves too thin," which means that students with mild disabilities may not always receive appropriate instruction.

The strategies discussed help teachers provide learning at the appropriate level by offering specific techniques to overcome learning difficulties. They afford a means of continuous monitoring of instruction and behavior and providing opportunities for greater instructional practice. These improvements are needed to enhance instruction in general education classes for those with disabilities as well as their peers without disabilities.

In their description of peer tutoring, Utley, Mortweet, and Greenwood (1997) go much further than King-Sears (1997) and Vergason and Anderegg (1991). Utley and colleagues specifically address the principles surrounding peer-mediated instruction (PMI), an alternative instruction in which peers are instructional agents or helpers in orchestrating student learning. This selection demonstrates how PMI can be used to provide incidental peer help, supervision, and support for direct instruction. The authors also discuss the research findings showing how PMI can increase academic instructional time on task for activities such as writing, reading, and mathematics. An indirect benefit of PMI arises from the social relationships that develop naturally from peer interaction focused on instruction. This form of socialization may be superior to the more contrived efforts to promote interaction that have characterized the inclusion movement.

Cole and McCleskey (1997) describe the operation of a successful inclusive high school program for students with mild disabilities. They first discuss the impediments and, then, how the program successfully provided instruction to students with disabilities in a general education setting. The case studies of how this worked for specific students and teachers offers encouragement to others engaged in similar endeavors. Teachers who are asking how inclusion can work at the secondary school level will find Cole and McCleskey's specific and detailed instructions highly beneficial.

Nolet and Tindal (1994), offer an inclusion model developed and used in Oregon and Maryland, which has succeeded in fostering collaboration between general and special education teachers. The program provides planned coordination that includes students who receive instruction for part of the day in a resource room.

The broadly accepted assumption is that special education and general education must collaborate and coordinate. The model presented by Nolet and Tindal has been tested and refined with the help of real-life, real-time teachers. It assumes that content is the area of expertise (the what of teaching) of the general education teachers, whereas instructional strategies (the how of teaching) are the purview of the special education teacher. The efficacy of using this curriculum-based collaboration (CBC) to accomplish effective instruction is documented. Both teachers, however, must know exactly what the other is attempting to teach. In addition, CBC employs a simple taxonomy that, if practiced, can assist both general education and special education teachers. This taxonomy is at the heart of effective instruction, learning, retention, and understanding for all students and is critical for those in special education.

Prater (1993) offers a set of procedures for designing instruction and teaching concepts to students with learning disabilities. Most teachers, even many basal textbook authors, can benefit from examining the practices outlined by Prater. She discusses how a teacher makes decisions about teaching concepts, their relative importance to all learning, and how to teach concepts on which so much of learning and understanding depends.

Among students with mild disabilities are those whose problems also relate to attention deficit disorder (ADD). ADD can compound their difficulty in learning and may result in an even greater academic deficiency than otherwise would be expected. Children with ADD learning characteristics present challenges that many teachers are ill equipped to handle. The chapter by Fiore, Becker, and Nero (1993) provides an intensive review of the literature indicating what works and what does not work when the ADD complication is present. The research reviewed is in the areas of behavioral therapies, cognitive therapy, and academic strategies for instruction with these students.

The chapter authored by Cook and Friend (1995) is designed to help teachers know which practices are effective in co-teaching. By co-teaching, they are referring to the practice of two or more professionals delivering instruction to a group of students in a single physical space. Their suggestions help teachers deal with the situation in which both teachers have a vested interest. The first step is to understand that one teacher is content-oriented and the other is focused on repairing learning when it is disrupted. Cook and Friend give examples for implementing instruction, including classroom organization and actual instructional delivery. These clearly center on the underlying structure of learning and teaching. The reader will recognize some of the themes reflected in the earlier chapter by Nolet and Tindal (1994).

The final selection, by Fisher, Schumaker, and Deshler (1995), examines validated inclusive practices, which have been sadly lacking in much of the literature on inclusive instruction. The authors recommend practices, based on research, that have been shown to be effective in practice. They give special attention to various forms of peer tutoring and cooperative learning approaches and emphasize specific instructional strategies that have worked well with students with learning problems. This selection provides teachers a sense of direction for what otherwise could be a difficult and frustrating situation.

Together, all of these chapters provide a spectrum of resources from which to draw. Those resources have a strongly documented efficacy and offer multiple alternatives for addressing the learning difficulties of students with mild disabilities within the general education classroom. The editors of this book and the authors of this section share a common belief in the value of these resources for teachers and students in general education and special education settings alike.

References

Alley, G. R., & Deshler, D. D. (1979). *Teaching the learning disabled adolescent: Strategies and methods*. Denver, CO: Love.

Cole, C. M., & McCleskey, J. (1997). Secondary inclusion programs for students with mild disabilities. *Focus on Exceptional Children, 29*(6), 1–15.

Cook, L., & Friend, M. (1995). Co-teaching: Guidelines for creating effective instruction practices. *Focus on Exceptional Children, 28*(3), 1–16.

Deshler, D. D., & Schumaker, J. B. (1986). Learning strategies: An instructional alternative for low achieving adolescents. *Exceptional Children, 52*, 583–589.

Fiore, T. A., Becker, E. A., & Nero, R. A. (1993). Educational interventions. *Exceptional Children, 60*, 163–173.

Fisher, J. B., Schumaker, J. B., & Deshler, D. D. (1995). Searching for validated inclusive practices: A review of the literature. *Focus on Exceptional Children, 38*, 1–20.

King-Sears, M. E. (1997). Best academic practices for inclusive classrooms. *Focus on Exceptional Children, 29*, 11–23.

Meyen, E. L. (1980). Quality instruction for students with disabilities. *Teaching Exceptional Children, 22*(2), 12–13.

Nolet, V., & Tindal, G. (1994). Curriculum-based collaboration. *Focus on Exceptional Children, 27*(3), 1–12.

Prater, M. A. (1993). Teaching concepts: Procedures for design and delivery of instruction. *Remedial and Special Education, 14*, 51–62.

Utley, C. A., Mortweet, S. L., & Greenwood, C. R. (1997). Peer-mediated instruction and interventions. *Focus on Exceptional Children, 29*(5), 1–23.

Vergason, G. A., & Anderegg, M. L. (1991). Beyond the regular education initiative and the resource room controversy. *Focus on Exceptional Children, 23*(7), 1–23.

14 Best Academic Practices for Inclusive Classrooms

MARGARET E. KING-SEARS

KING-SEARS THOROUGHLY EXPLORES programs that can enhance instruction of students with mild disabilities in general education settings. The chapter presents 10 practices, well documented in the literature, that can lead to the highest quality of instruction possible today. Teachers are encouraged to use this chapter as a template for program implementation.

Concerning the title of this chapter: What is meant by "best?" Best means the finest, the greatest, the highest. "Best" for whom? Effective inclusion is best for everyone, not just students with disabilities. "Academic" practices toward what type of goal? Is the academic goal for a given student in the cognitive, affective, or psychomotor domain of learning? For example, a student with a learning disability may be working on cognitive IEP goals that emphasize reading and writing skills. A student with emotional or behavioral disorders may have affective IEP goals that emphasize ways to deal effectively with frustration. If a student with severe cognitive disabilities has affective IEP goals related to communicating during social situations, is the communication considered a cognitive area, or even a psychomotor area, for that student? A student with a physical disability may have psychomotor IEP goals that relate to reaching, manipulating, and movement. For each of these students, academics can encompass any of the domains of learning. Academic practices, therefore, are not confined to traditional content achievement areas such as reading, mathematics, and science.

Conversely, are there best academic practices for exclusive, or segregated, settings? Baker (1994) contends that servicing students in separate environments came about through measurements that indicated a student was not successful in the mass educational system of the times, and not as a result of measures comparing students' success in noninclusive educational practices to inclusive ones. Similarly, Sobsey and Dreimanis (1993) note that a segregated service delivery model did not develop as a result of empirical research or evaluation.

More recently, court decisions have placed the burden of proof on school systems to provide data that describe students' performance in inclusive environments *with supplementary aids and services* prior to removing students from these environments to more segregated ones (Yell, 1995). Baker concludes that current evidence that does compare students' achievement in integrated to segregated environments does not support the use of noninclusive environments for the education of students with disabilities.

A mistaken impression of inclusion is that special education is not needed. The fallacy is that if more students with disabilities spend more time in general education classrooms, the numbers of students who need specialized services diminish such that the quantity of students for a special educator's caseload eliminates the need for as many special education teachers. On the contrary, the need for specialized services and special educators is not reduced when inclusion occurs. After reviewing empirical research about the effects of inclusion on students with and without disabilities, Sobsey and Dreimanis (1993) conclude:

> Research to date leaves little doubt that the vast majority of students with intellectual disabilities do better in integrated classrooms rather than special education programs. This finding should not be interpreted as implying that the total withdrawal of special supports and services would be in the best interests of students with intellectual disabilities. It is only the delivery of special education services in segregated settings that is called into question—not the need for individualized and intensive education. (p. 10)

"Inclusion" as a term means different things to different people. For purposes of this chapter, I use a definition from York, Doyle, and Kronberg (1992): Inclusion *is* students with disabilities (a) attending the same schools as siblings and neighbors, (b) being in general education classrooms with chronological age-appropriate classmates, (c) having individualized and relevant learning objectives, and (d) being provided with the necessary support. Inclusion is not students with disabilities who (a) must spend every minute of the school day in general education classes, (b) never receive small-group or individualized instruction, and (c) are in general education classes to learn the core curriculum only.

"Full inclusion" is not addressed in this chapter because of the misconceptions about what it is and if it even exists separate from inclusion. Despite considerable rhetoric about full inclusion in the literature, in my opinion it often is misrepresented. Brown et al. (1991) note that nowhere in the literature do they find any professional who is saying that all students with all disabilities should always receive all of their instruction in general education classrooms.

> Members of the 100% club argue that only by spending every minute of each school day in regular education classrooms can true, whole, full, meaningful, and pure integration/inclusion be realized....The 100% club may not have a member. The authors do not know anyone, nor could they find a printed reference, that argues that all the students of concern should spend 100% of their school time in regular education classrooms. (p. 40)

The best academic practices for inclusive classrooms are the methods that have the greatest desired impact in affective, psychomotor, and cognitive areas of academics for students with and without disabilities who are receiving most, if not all, of their differentiated, individualized, and appropriate learning, social, and instructional experiences together.

Placement and Quality Instruction

The focus for inclusion has to emphasize both where things are happening and what types of practices are being used. For example, Kluwin and Moores (1985) noted that secondary students with hearing impairments who were integrated into general math classes were achieving more than matched counterparts at segregated schools. Yet the factors impacting higher achievement levels (e.g., higher expectations, exposure to greater quantities of demanding material, availability of individual support, and teachers trained in mathematics), they contended, could have been used in the segregated placement as well.

In a second study on the mathematics achievement of students with hearing impairments who were taught in different placements, Kluwin and Moores (1989) again found that the quality of the instruction, not the placement, was the main predictor of students' achievement. Although they did find, not surprisingly, that student background factors were a primary determinant of achievement and that student achievement was considered when deciding whether or not to mainstream a youngster, the placement the youngster received in and of itself was not connected to achievement. Specific characteristics of quality placement included a supportive teacher, regular and extensive reviews of the material, direct instruction, a positive climate, and requirements that students work.

Similarly, Fewell and Oelwein (1990) found that the amount of time children with developmental disabilities spent in mainstreamed preschool settings was not a factor alone that could impact better developmental outcomes. They concluded that the curriculum used and the quality of instruction had powerful effects on the children's acquisition of skills.

Hunt, Farron-Davis, Beckstead, Curtis, and Goetz (1994) evaluated the effects of placement on students with severe disabilities in general education versus special education classes. In some areas these researchers found significant differences favoring the students who were included (e.g., taught in an academic context, student with others, and student actively engaged). Other areas may not have attained significant results, but more positive results accrued to the students in inclusion. Students who were included initiated more interactions with peers without disabilities, and peers without disabilities initiated more interactions with the students with disabilities. In other areas, the findings showed significant differences favoring students in the special classes (student working alone, taught basic skill/critical activities).

Although one may argue that placement is less important than the quality of instruction, that argument cannot be made without the stipulation that some opportunities for quality instruction for some students simply are not available in segregated programs. Furthermore, segregation can occur within school buildings. Students need not attend a separate school to feel isolated. A person also can be isolated within a group setting, such that physical presence in a group may not meaningfully include a student.

In short, the content and quality of an educational program are critical factors to consider when determining which service delivery option is appropriate for any given youngster with a disability. Not surprisingly, instructional variables also have consistently emerged for general education students as having the potential to influence their achievement positively (Wang, Haertel, & Walberg, 1993). Those researchers also found that instructional variables are correlated more powerfully with achievement than demographic, policy, and organizational variables. What may matter more than who the student is, or where he or she is from, or how the school system is organized, or what the educational policies are—is how good the instruction is for each student in the classroom.

Laying the Foundation for Inclusion

For inclusion to succeed, four foundational components are necessary upon which to "build" best practices. Foundational structures for inclusion are a shared vision, information about the change process, preparation, and ongoing support.

Shared Vision

Perhaps the most important start toward a shared vision that supports inclusion is that educators value and believe that students with and without disabilities should be together more in their learning and playing experiences at school. Misinformed preconceptions about inclusion and its effect on students can prohibit educators from envisioning an inclusive classroom with benefits for all students.

Research can provide information about students' progress in inclusive classrooms. For example, one concern about inclusion is the effect it will have on the academic achievement of students without disabilities. Parents, administrators, and general educators want to be satisfied that inclusion will not hold back other students. Several researchers have noted that academic achievement of typical students is not affected adversely under inclusion (e.g., Jenkins, Speltz, & Odom, 1985; Liddiard, 1991). Other researchers have found significant gains for students without disabilities when inclusion occurs (e.g., Bear & Procter, 1990).

Change Process

Planned educational changes typically have three stages—adoption or initiation, implementation, and incorporation—as a permanent feature of the system (Waugh & Punch, 1987). Some educators resist changing toward inclusion because they lack information. In those instances, information must be provided. Other educators may be unclear about how to use new methods; consequently, training is necessary. Other educators, especially people who are skilled in using their current methods of instruction, may be reluctant to take the risks necessary to become skilled with new methods. Educators also need to feel actively involved in their school's change toward inclusion, and they need to participate in decisions made about changes. If educators are not involved in the development and implementation efforts, changes toward inclusion are less likely to be sustained. Yell, Deno, and Marston (1992) reported that teachers and administrators alike acknowledged the difficulty of initiating change into the educational system as one of three major obstacles to implementing curriculum-based measurement. When new procedures are introduced, teachers will resist and become anxious. They need to know their principal's or system's commitment to the change and support for teachers while they are learning and refining the use of new methods. Furthermore, teachers' feelings of discomfort as they learn how to use instructional techniques new to them should be expected (Joyce & Weil, 1986), and corresponding support must be provided (Hord, Rutherford, Huling-Astin, & Hall, 1987).

Preparation and Ongoing Support

Preparation and ongoing support are intertwined; one should not occur without the other. Joyce and Weil (1986) note that high-quality training provides excellent results.

> Important new learning involves pain, and teachers are well able to withstand the discomfort. In many quarters teachers have been undersold as learners simply because inadequate training has been provided. (p. 469)

Staff development may be the most critical part of inclusive special education services, according to Roahrig (1993). He recommends that the amount of money needed for staff development for inclusion, especially at start-up, may be equal to that of one staff member, but that having the teachers determine how the staff development money is to be used, rather than hiring one person who would try to meet all staff's needs, may be more effective.

Similarly, Wolery, Werts, Caldwell, Snyder, and Lisowski (1995) report that special and general educators involved in inclusion consistently rated personal training and support as high-need areas for implementing successful inclusion. Educators consistently stated a discrepancy between resources they perceived they needed and those actually available to them. Educators who rated themselves as more successful with inclusion, however, had a lower discrepancy between needed and available resources. Furthermore, all staff training should not occur prior to teachers' trying out inclusion; some training and support should occur after teachers have had a chance to work in an inclusive situation and can target new areas of individualized training for themselves based on specific challenges.

Building the Structure for Inclusion

The structure for inclusion cannot weather the storm unless the foundation for inclusion has been firmly established. Changes toward inclusion are more likely to be sustained and institutionalized if the foundational components are sturdy. The 10 practices featured in Figure 14.1 and in the ensuing discussion should not be taken as stand-alone entities but should be used in combination. Using only one practice well is not sufficient for best practice.

The 10 practices described next should be individualized for specific school systems, schools, and students so the content of the practices and the process for implementing the practices are appropriate. Individualization of the content and process components, however, cannot adapt too many elements of the practices without compromising the desired results. Leaving out some elements of a practice (for example, leaving out the immediate corrective feedback in classwide peer tutoring, or collecting data for curriculum-based assessment but not using the data to make instructional decisions) could jeopardize the practice's effectiveness. These practices are applicable to all students, but what teachers have to understand is that systematic implementation of key elements of a method (e.g., in strategy instruction, one key element is that students attain mastery level at certain stages) for stu-

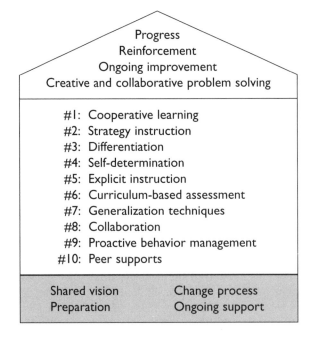

Figure 14.1 *Best Academic Practices for Inclusive Classrooms: Building and Supporting Heterogeneous Methods*

dents with disabilities who must have those elements may impact the method's effectiveness. Educators can—and should—personalize implementation but not delete critical elements that contribute directly to the power of the method.

Practice #1: Cooperative Learning

A variety of cooperative learning techniques have empirical support for students with and without disabilities, making these techniques a robust and powerful choice for educators to use in inclusive classrooms. Jenkins, Jewell, Leicester, O'Connor, Jenkins, and Troutner (1994) used Cooperative Integrated Reading and Composition (CIRC) with heterogeneous groups, along with cross-age and peer tutoring, phonics instruction for some learners, and in-class instructional support from specialists to investigate achievement in reading, spelling, and written expression for students with and without disabilities. Significant results were obtained for all groups of students on all academic measures.

The researchers note that, overall, the positive results indicate the power of cooperative learning techniques, but that some students still required direct intensive decoding instruction in addition to the cooperative learning techniques. An earlier study by these researchers (Jenkins, Jewell, Leicester, Jenkins, & Troutner, 1991) did not produce significant results, and they suggested that the results may have been a result of eliminating key elements of CIRC (e.g., family involvement and comprehension exercises).

Kamps, Leonard, Potucek, and Garrison-Harrell (1995) used CIRC in third- and fifth-grade classrooms that included typical students and students with disabilities (autism, learning disabilities, and behavioral disorders). When cooperative learning alone was used in the third-grade classroom, students equaled or increased their quiz scores. Then the students were taught a social skills strategy (Vernon, Schumaker, & Deshler, 1993) to promote cooperation and appropriate social interaction among the students. Students with and without disabilities increased their quiz scores even more when social skills instruction was combined with cooperative learning procedures. Individualizing reading levels was necessary for students with and without disabilities in the fifth-grade classroom; when all students were reading materials on their ability level, their performance improved.

Maheady, Sacca, and Harper (1988) used classwide peer tutoring (CWPT) in high school social studies classrooms where students with mild disabilities were included. Classwide peer tutoring is a procedure by which all students tutor each other in a reciprocal arrangement, with each student serving the role as tutor and tutee. CWPT has had good success for increasing students' active participation in learning, which has enhanced their achievement positively (Delquadri, Greenwood, Whorton, Carta, & Hall, 1986). Maheady and his colleagues found that CWPT virtually eliminated failing grades for all students, and that weekly test scores increased an average of 21 points.

Kamps, Barbetta, Leonard, and Delquadri (1994) investigated the use of CWPT in elementary classrooms that included full-time students with autism. Classwide peer tutoring was an effective technique for increasing students' reading fluency and comprehension. Concurrently, the researchers found that social interactions during unstructured situations increased between the students with autism and their typical peers.

O'Connor and Jenkins (1993) noted that large differences sometimes were present in the task involvement of special education students and the amount and kind of help students extend to each other in cooperative learning structures. They investigated how elementary students with mild disabilities fared when cooperative learning was used. Effective cooperative group learning occurred for the students with disabilities when (a) students received appropriate help from a group member, (b) students contributed to the group effort, and (c) students completed the assigned task. O'Connor and Jenkins found that only 40% of the students with disabilities participated successfully in cooperative learning. They attribute this to two special education practices: (a) one-to-one adult-student interactions occurred during times when groups were working together; and (b) shortened assignments for students with disabilities appeared inappropriate when this resulted in students who seemed to have permission to stop working before the group work was completed.

In addition to the expected teacher behaviors prior to cooperative group work of teaching students how to work cooperatively, the teacher behaviors during cooperative learning also could influence cooperation. Teachers who monitored by interfering actively with the group's processing seemed to negate the idea that peers were expected to help each other. Teachers who lowered standards unnecessarily for individual students with disabilities also inhibited those students' full group membership. O'Connor and Jenkins (1993) suggest that cooperative learning as an inclusion strategy may not be successful if traditional special education modifications (e.g., one-to-one assistance, shortened assignments) are used, and that the status of all group members' contributions can be heightened by the way in which teachers praise and provide feedback to students.

Practice #2: Strategy Instruction

Strategy instruction is described here as an alternative format for working with students with disabilities that minimizes a tutorial, watered-down instructional format and maximizes more strategy-based formats. In essence, a strategic format directs educators' effort away from helping a student keep up with the day-to-day demands of content learning and redirects it toward enabling the student to learn strategies by which to keep up with those demands himself or herself.

For example, students with learning disabilities who learned a test-taking strategy scored higher on tests across content areas, which minimized the need for an adult to tutor them for each test (Hughes & Schumaker, 1991). Park and Gaylord-Ross (1989) taught youngsters with mental retardation to use problem solving effectively to increase appropriate social interactions within their work settings. Schumaker and Deshler (1995) describe how the strategy instruction can enable students with disabilities to more independently think about, complete, and evaluate school tasks and assignments. Their research (see Deshler, Ellis, & Lenz, 1996, for a comprehensive description of strategy research and methods) emphasizes eight stages for teachers to use in teaching strategies to students:

1. Pretest and obtain students' commitment to learn a strategy.
2. Describe the strategy steps (typically a mnemonic is used to help students remember the strategy steps; pictures or icons can be used with younger students or students with more severe cognitive disabilities).
3. Model the strategy by talking aloud about thinking while performing the strategy.
4. Verbally practice the strategy steps until the student has memorized the steps.
5. Use controlled practice and feedback. Students perform the strategy on ability-level, or easier, content; feedback is structured explicitly to move from teacher feedback to students' self-evaluation.
6. Use advanced practice and feedback. Students' perform the strategy on advanced, or grade-level, content with feedback that promotes students' self-evaluation.
7. Posttest (same format as pretest; allows direct comparisons of student's performance before and after use of the strategy).
8. Generalize. Although this is a formal, last stage, a focus throughout strategy instruction has been on where, when, why, and how the student can use the strategy.

The stages of instruction require students to master information at key junctures: verbal practice, controlled practice, advanced practice, and posttest. Students' active involvement in learning is required throughout, with an emphasis on students' acquiring and using more proactive behaviors such as goal-setting and self-evaluation.

Strain, Kohler, Storey, and Danko (1994) describe instructional stages and mastery requirements for preschool children with autism who learned to self-monitor their social interactions in school and at home. The three stages of initial instruction were (a) demonstration and modeling, (b) practice with the adult and other children, with adult feedback, and (c) practice with other children. During the final stage, the children had to demonstrate mastery performance (e.g., exchange four skills within a 10-minute period) before they could move to the next phases of self-monitoring.

Irvine, Erickson, Singer, and Stahlberg (1992) taught high school students with moderate to severe mental retardation to use picture schedules to initiate tasks at school. Later the students used the same self-management system to initiate tasks at home. When the students were being trained to use the self-management system, mastery of 100% performance of the tasks without prompting was required. Although more time (all students mastered the required components after 5 consecutive days of practice) was necessary for the students to attain mastery, if the students could not perform the behaviors at a sufficient level during controlled situations, they could not be expected to perform the behaviors sufficiently in other situations.

Nelson, Smith, and Dodd (1992) found that the time duration of instructional sessions for students with learning disabilities who learned a summary skills strategy ranged from 43 minutes per session when initial instruction was occurring to 16 minutes per session for the final instructional session. A similar decrease in time was evident for the students when they used the strategy independently; independent reading sessions lasted 33 minutes initially and decreased to 16 minutes. The amount of time the students with disabilities need to achieve fluency and mastery of a strategy must be available, even if the rest of the class can acquire the elements of the strategy more quickly.

For teachers, the issue of competing demands is raised: If most of the class understands, what happens to the students who need more time to understand? What is the cost-benefit of proceeding with instruction when most of the students are ready to move on? What's the cost-benefit of proceeding with instruction when the few students who are not ready to move on also need to know the preceding information to move on and understand the new content? Mastering key pieces of information is necessary during instruction; students will not use the strategy independently if they do not achieve mastery (Scanlon, Deshler, & Schumaker, 1996).

A strategic approach to this dilemma is to minimize or eliminate special education instruction focusing solely on a tutorial approach that provides students with support to learn the day-to-day and week-to-week content (weren't most kids pulled for services like that?) and replaces that special education instruction with teaching robust strategic procedures in which the students learn how to make notecards (the FIRST Letter Mnemonic Strategy), how to understand more of what they read (the Paraphrasing Strategy), and how to decode multi-syllable words (the Word Identification Strategy). Whether the strategic instruction occurs in the general education classroom or in another setting should be less of an issue for inclusive classrooms than the issue of what students are learning how to do that they can use (a) independently, (b) in a variety of classes, and (c) to meet performance demands from a range of instructors.

The sessions for intensive and extensive strategic instruction may be a time when homogeneous groups of students who need to learn a strategy (the group may include students with disabilities, students who are at-risk for school failure, and so on) are formed to receive instruction that includes mastery and generalization of the instruction enabling them to more independently and correctly apply a set of rules, principles, or techniques across subjects, teachers, and materials. Although the concept of homogeneous groupings may seem to be in contrast to inclusive classrooms where heterogeneous groupings are emphasized, I contend they are not, *depending on what is taught*. If students are kept in heterogeneous groups all the time at the expense of a select subgroup of students learning strategies that will enable them to accomplish tasks across content areas more independently, that may be an inappropriate use of heterogeneous groups all the time.

Again, look at the cost-benefit for students. If they can spend one to two months of daily instruction learning a strategy they can use for the rest of the school year and the next school year and in out-of-school settings, too, what is the cost to them versus the benefit of the alternative of being tutored by someone who helps them pass each test and make the grade for each semester but doesn't teach them how to learn how to learn by themselves?

Stainback and Stainback (1990) emphasize the range of instructional possibilities available when teachers use differentiated techniques within heterogeneous groupings. They also acknowledge, however, that homogeneous groupings are appropriate at times.

> Heterogeneous grouping should occur whenever possible. However, some students may need to be homogeneously grouped occasionally for instruction within a class or across classes according to their interests, needs, and capabilities.... When such groupings occur, they should be based on the instructional needs of the students as they relate to the instructional focus of the class or grouping, rather than according to a categorical label such as retarded, normal, or gifted. Care also must be exercised to minimize such groupings to the greatest extent possible; but when they are used, they should be flexible, fluid, and short term to avoid the development of a tracking system and to allow students to move in, out, and across the groupings according to their needs and interest. (pp. 13, 14)

Practice #3: Differentiated Instruction

A fair amount of evidence suggests that even when students with mild disabilities (e.g., learning disabilities) are taught by general educators who are receptive to their presence and who promote their progress, the instruction is not differentiated systematically to meet their individual needs (see Schumm & Vaughn, 1995, for a research review). An issue becomes how much a general educator can differentiate his or her instruction. The factors underlying this issue include: (a) the quantity and quality of training experiences for that educator about student characteristics and effective practices for teaching a student with specific characteristics, (b) the extent to which an educator is willing to provide differentiated instruction, (c) the quantity and quality of support provided by a special educator who is knowledgeable about how to differentiate within general education curriculum and environments, and (d) how much educators know about how to effectively implement co-teaching, co-planning, and problem-solving activities.

Categories for Curriculum Differentiation

Switlick (1997) and Giangreco, Cloninger, and Iverson (1993) describe categories of curriculum differentiation for students with disabilities. Their categories are expanded in Table 14.1 to include curriculum differentiation for students who are high achievers or gifted. For some differentiation areas, the content and concepts are the same. According to Switlick:

1. An *accommodation* is a modification to the delivery of instruction or method of student performance that does not significantly change the content or conceptual difficulty of the curriculum. A student who is completing fewer math problem-solving activities than the other students may be receiving an accommodation.

2. An *adaptation* is a modification to the delivery of instruction or method of student performance that changes the content or conceptual difficulty of the curriculum. An example of an adaptation is to have the student attempt to

Table 14.1 *Differentiation of Curriculum for Students with Heterogeneous Learning Needs*

Curriculum			Content	Concept
		Enrichment	same	minor/major changes
Same		Standard	same	same
	Accommodation	Strategic	same	same
Multilevel	Adaptation		same	minor changes
		Parallel	same	major changes
Overlapping	Overlapping		different	different

identify the main characters and setting of a story while the other students focus also on the plot, subplots, problem, and resolution.

3. *Parallel instruction* is a modification of the delivery of instruction or method of student performance that does not change the content area but does significantly change the conceptual difficulty of the curriculum. An example of parallel instruction is to have most students work on solving fraction problems and a student with moderate disabilities work on counting from 1 to 10.

4. *Overlapping instruction* is a modification of the student performance expectations while all students take part in a shared activity or delivery of instruction that changes the content area and the conceptual difficulty of the curriculum. For example, in a cooperative group the students are tape-recording the rough draft of a play they are creating, and a student with physical and cognitive disabilities is using an adaptive switch to activate the recorder and working on following one-step directions and working on holding up his head for extended periods of time.

Table 14.2 provides explicit information about overlapping curriculum differentiation that can occur when a standard science curriculum (for typical students and students with mild disabilities) is used along with a functional life skills curriculum (for students with moderate to severe cognitive or developmental disabilities). All students are working together during science curriculum instruction, but the activities are differentiated for a student whose IEP goals stem from a functional life skills curriculum.

In the curriculum differentiation of Giangreco, Cloninger, and Iverson (1993):

1. The *same* curriculum is used with all students for whom no differentiation is needed.

■ **Table 14.2** *General Education Science and Functional Life Skills Curricula Overlapped*

Science—Solutions

General Education Science Curriculum	Life Skills Curriculum
1. Observe and describe the properties of substances.	1. Prepare tray. Measure dry materials by using a measuring cup and spoon. Mix materials into water and stir with spoon. Identify clear and cloudy.
2. Observe, identify, and classify a solution or a liquid.	2. Participate with peers. Get tray of materials. Practice turn-taking and communicating whether substance is cloudy or clear.
3. Observe, describe, and make inferences about the properties of liquids.	3. Fill bottles with warm water. Count aloud the number of drops to go into the water as another student uses the dropper. Clear materials from table.
4. Observe and describe the interaction of solids and liquids.	4. Participate with peers. Use stopwatch by pressing button to start and stop. Decide if tube is warm or cold.
5. Observe and describe the properties and interactions of substances.	5. Pass out trays. Have students stir the mixtures and communicate whether the crystals disappeared or stayed in the water. Stay within the group area.
6. Observe and describe the effects of temperatures on liquids.	6. Participate with peers. Stir substances into the water. Put materials away and clean area.

Source: From J. Hlass, J. Jorden, L. Lightner, & D. Nagle (1995). *Integration of life skills: General education curriculum and functional life skills curriculum* (p. 51). Unpublished manuscript, Johns Hopkins University, Rockville, MD. Used by permission.

2. In *multilevel* curriculum differentiation, all students work on the same content but some students may work on different levels of the content so the concepts may be different.
3. *Overlapping* curriculum is identical to Switlick's (1997) definition: Students are participating in the same activity, but a student may be working on different content and concepts altogether.

The version of curriculum differentiation shown in Table 14.1 expanded to include enrichment curriculum choices illustrates how teachers also differentiate for students who are high-achievers or are characterized as gifted. For general educators who already differentiate their instruction for students who are gifted, exposure to the three models in Table 14.1 provides more concrete information on differentiation that highlights what they are doing already for some groups of students, such as students who are gifted, and applies similar planning processes to include more groups of students (students at-risk, students with disabilities). Educators may find multiple intelligence theories and Dimensions of Learning frameworks to be useful guides in differentiating.

IEPs to Guide Differentiation

The content of IEPs, when they are developed by teams (including general educators, special educators, therapists, parents, and sometimes the student and the student's peers), can provide meaningful and valuable information. When IEP goals and objectives do provide qualitative and quantitative information, teachers can use them as a guide for determining appropriate modifications within general education classroom routines, activities, and instruction. Figure 14.2 provides an example of how modifications are linked to the IEP. Giangreco, Dennis, Edelman, and Cloninger (1994), however, found, in their analysis of IEP content, that for students who were deaf-blind and attended general education classes either full-time or part-time, goals and objectives frequently are (a) broad, inconsistent, and poorly connected to general education contexts (e.g., "improve communication skills"), (b) list content for staff (e.g., "reposition every hour") instead of content for the student, and (c) discipline-specific (e.g., "during therapy sessions..." or "improve occupational therapy skills") instead of team-specific. When IEP content does not provide sufficient information that can guide differentiation decisions, the education team should expand on its content so the accomplishment of IEP goals and objectives are connected more explicitly to classroom instruction and activities.

Higher-Order Thinking Skills

Carnine (1991) presents research on curricular interventions for teaching higher-order thinking to students with and without learning disabilities. Students with learning disabilities who were taught in middle or high school science, math, or health classes achieved high scores (in some studies the differences were statistically significant) on critical content related to higher-order thinking skills (e.g., reasoning, understanding concepts, problem solving). He makes an important distinction between curricular interventions and instructional approaches by describing curricular interventions as academic content that is analyzed and communicated via curricular materials to promote understanding, transfer, and retention among all students. Carnine contends that to accomplish higher order thinking skills (such as concepts, rules, strategies, algorithms), the underlying processes have to be taught, and that the primary underlying theory for each type of skill rests on the "sameness" features. He suggests that curricular content has to be organized around important samenesses as a means of teaching a larger variety of students with more heterogeneous learning patterns (such as students with mild disabilities and students at-risk for school failure).

Student: Jason, a student with significant fine-motor difficulties

IEP Goal: To grasp and release objects from assisted to unassisted using real-life situations

Activity: Jason is a 2nd grade student with multiple disabilities, including significant fine-motor difficulties. His IEP includes occupational therapy goals. The occupational therapist has suggested that Jason be given opportunities to practice his newly acquired skills in real-life situations. Jason's class eats lunch in the cafeteria and moves through the line to purchase items such as milk, juice, snacks, and a complete lunch. As the students are moving through the lunch line, Jason will:

(a) choose appropriate food items and place these items on his tray

(b) have a peer buddy place the items on the tray for him

Which modification would you use in this situation? _____

Answer: (a) Jason's IEP goal is to grasp and release objects. Moving through the cafeteria line and grasping and releasing food items provides a real-life opportunity to practice the skill. In this case, Jason should get the items for himself. Support may be provided by a peer who has been given direct instruction in how to assist without picking the items up for Jason.

Figure 14.2 *Linking Modifications to IEP Goals*

Source: From T. L. Bruff, J. C. Jacksits, L. A. Marchineck, & K. D. Sandleitner (1996). *Modifying instruction in diverse classrooms* (p. 43). Unpublished manuscript, Johns Hopkins University, Rockville, MD. Used by permission.

Multi-Age Groupings

Some schools are beginning to use multi-age groupings in which students from more than one grade receive differentiated instruction (Miller, 1995). Multi-age groupings can assist with some of the logistical components of differentiated instruction because more than one teacher is available, and when homogeneous groupings for direct instruction occur, the teachers can vary student groupings across grade levels. For example, in a first/second multi-age group, both teachers form reading groups according to skill level, and, when they combine the grades, they avoid duplicating skill groups across grades and within one classroom.

Flexible groupings that change as needed also characterize multi-age grades; they create an atmosphere in which all students are grouped differently and regrouped when their performance indicates the need to regroup. All students receive individualized instruction based on their performance levels, so no students are singled out for individualized instruction. Although student groupings are homogeneous for some content, large-group instruction and heterogeneous groupings—in which cooperative learning activities are used and differentiated learning objectives are targeted—are clearly evident.

Practice #4: Self-determination

Field and Hoffman (1994) propose a model for self-determination that includes five components for students:

1. Know yourself.
2. Value yourself.
3. Plan.
4. Act.
5. Learn.

Their definition of self-determination is the student's "ability to define and achieve goals based on a foundation of knowing and valuing oneself" (p. 164). Teaching students how to self-manage their behaviors can be used to promote self-determination. Self-management systems have enabled students with disabilities—across a wide range of ages, disability areas, severity levels, behaviors, and settings—to accomplish tasks and control behaviors more independently.

Moreover, when students with disabilities have been taught how to use self-management systems effectively, the onus for external behavior management systems shifts from needing an adult to manage and implement the external system to the student's being responsible for his or her own system of control. Effective inclusive classrooms do not just accommodate students with disabilities; methods that promote students' independence are evident. The range of possibilities for teaching students initial self-determination behaviors by using self-management systems is wide. Some examples follow.

- Middle school students with behavior problems substantially increased appropriate peer interactions and decreased inappropriate interactions after learning self-evaluation techniques (Falk, Dunlap, & Kern, 1996).
- Children with autism using self-management systems increased their appropriate play behaviors in unsupervised settings (Stahmer & Schreibman, 1992).
- An adolescent with learning disabilities and behavior disorders used self-monitoring to improve his on-task behaviors and academic skills across special and general education settings (Prater, Hogan, & Miller, 1992).
- Teenage students with autism were taught how to follow a schedule to make transitions in an after-school program; when students learned to make the transitions on their own, an adult no longer had to prompt them when it was time to move from one activity to another (Newman et al., 1995).

Van Reusen, Deshler, and Schumaker (1989) report that high school students with learning disabilities who were taught how to self-advocate during their individualized education program (IEP) conferences contributed important and relevant information to their educational plans. Furthermore, 86% of the goals on the IEPs for students who were taught how to participate effectively in their IEP conferences contained content they generated during the conference, in contrast to the IEPs for a control group of students, which contained only 13% content they identified.

Practice #5: Explicit Instruction

Gersten, Carnine, and Woodward (1987) describe direct instruction as having six critical features:

1. An explicit step-by-step model.
2. Development of mastery at each step.
3. Process corrections for student errors.
4. Gradual fading from teacher-directed activities to students' independence.
5. Use of adequate, systematic practice with a range of examples.
6. Cumulative review of newly learned concepts.

Direct instruction teaching procedures have enabled students with and without disabilities to learn content. More recently, however, educators have been exploring the use of constructivism, which is less structured and teacher-directed than direct instruction. Constructivist teaching and learning has been emphasized particularly in general education classrooms, leading to questions about how well that type of teaching results in efficient learning for students with, in particular, mild disabilities (Harris & Graham, 1996). Rosenshine and Stevens (1986) suggest that direct instruction procedures may be more effective when the content is more structured (e.g., vocabulary, grammar, factual information, general rules) than when content is less structured (e.g., appreciation, analysis of literature, problem solving in specific content areas, discussion of social issues).

What is emerging today regarding direct instruction versus constructivism is that students with disabilities (a) benefit most from direct instruction procedures, (b) can learn within a constructivist framework when teaching procedures are more explicit initially, and (c) should not be taught using an "either-or" perspective; both are needed to promote effective, efficient, and independent learning. Most students with disabilities will not thrive in a classroom setting that does not provide elements of explicit instruction that include demonstration, guided practice, independent practice, active learner involvement, and meaningful connections of content to real life.

Mercer, Jordan, and Miller (1996) describe effective math instruction for diverse learners that promotes students' active involvement in and self-regulation of learning. They note that a teacher's sole reliance on a traditional constructivist approach for math instruction (i.e., minimal teacher support, emphasis on discovery, eventual self-regulation) is not sufficient for learners who need more teacher support and explicit instruction. They note that a constructivistic classroom places many demands on learners—demands that many learners with learning disabilities, for example, have trouble meeting without explicit instruction from an expert—the teacher.

Their steps for explicit instruction are:

1. Introduce the lesson.
2. Describe and model the skill or strategy.
3. Use scaffolding to guide practice and interactions.
4. Conduct independent practice to mastery.
5. Provide feedback.
6. Teach for generalization and transfer.

Mercer et al. (1996) note that implicit instruction (e.g., when the teacher models the skills or strategy) also occurs throughout explicit instruction as a complement to the directed instruction. Discovery of rules and procedures is more directed and controlled so errors are not learned or practiced.

Practice #6: Curriculum-Based Assessment

Curriculum-based measurements (CBM—repeated measures on long-term goals) and curriculum-based assessment (CBA—repeated measures on long-term goals or short-term objectives) can indicate to teachers that their teaching methods are resulting in desirable achievement gains for individuals or groups of students (Marston, 1988). Teachers who collect data frequently (e.g., before, during, and after instruction) using direct observation techniques (e.g., the number of math problems the student can solve correctly, how well the student verbalizes the correct application of problem-solving methods) *and* use those data to make instructional decisions (is cooperative learning working? is more practice required?) have students who accomplish more and higher academic goals (Wesson, Skiba, Sevcik, King, & Deno, 1984).

Fuchs and Fuchs (1986) found an effect size of .70 on student achievement when teachers gathered and used systematically gathered formative evaluation measures. When teachers used data-evaluation rules (i.e., analyze student data at regular intervals and make instructional changes based on data) the effect size was higher than when teachers used judgment alone. When teachers graphed data, the visual stimulus of the graphed data resulted in higher effect sizes than when teachers simply recorded their data. Although the time needed for teachers to collect data and use it to make instructional decisions can be a barrier to using curriculum-based assessment, the benefits that promote student achievement *and* actively involve the students often can make it worth their while.

Gersten, Keating, and Irvin (1995) state that an assessment is not valid for informing instruction unless there is evidence that the assessment information is used by teachers as intended, and that it results in improved learning. One could extrapolate from their view, then, that teachers who use assessment only to give a grade or to fill in a score are not using valid assessments. Assessments must be used to improve learning for students, and they cannot be used to improve learning for students unless they also are used to guide teachers' decision-making *during* learning, not solely or primarily at the end of the unit of instruction.

Fuchs, Fuchs, Hamlett, Phillips, and Bentz (1994) investigated the use of curriculum-based measurement in general education classrooms where students with learning disabilities were included. They found that the students in classrooms where CBM that included specific instructional recommendations was used achieved greater gains. The CBM general educators used a computer program to facilitate implementation of CBM decision making and to involve the students in reading and interpreting their graphs and skills profiles. General educators in this study seemed to need specific recommendations, provided via the computer software program, to use the CBM student data for planning instruction.

Several researchers have looked at different assessment models, including curriculum-based assessment, as described above, and performance assessments based on the curriculum, and measured students' performance in heterogeneous settings. Dalton, Tivnan, Riley, Rawson, and Dias (1995) found that students with learning disabilities and students who were low-achieving and average-high achieving obtained significantly higher scores on a performance-based science assessment than when paper-and-pencil assessments were used. Those authors also note the value of diversifying assessment formats (for example, using multiple intelligence pathways) for all students so the assessment format does not prevent students from demonstrating their knowledge and application of skills and concepts learned.

When developing and using varied assessment formats, teachers must remain focused on what the learning goals are. Having demonstrated a procedure may tell you that a person can demonstrate the procedure but may not tell you why certain choices were made during the procedure and let you know that the student understands the underlying principles and concepts of that procedure—the learning goals.

Although facts tests and paper-and-pencil products receive criticism for not inducing higher-order thinking skills or being relevant/meaningful measures of content, teachers also must realize that the same criticisms can arise with performance-based or authentic assessments if they are not constructed carefully to measure critical thinking. For example, in one inclusive classroom of fourth graders (students with physical disabilities, cognitive disabilities, and typical students) who were learning geometry, the students were required to draw a picture of their bedrooms to illustrate the geometry patterns. Although the teacher may have considered this an authentic and performance-based assessment, some students could draw a picture of their bedroom but not identify the geometric patterns. Without also assessing the identity of the geometric patterns (which was the learning goal), the illustration itself does not demonstrate the intended learning outcome.

Another teacher who assigned projects based on multiple intelligence theory for the heterogeneous groups in her classroom (composed of typical students and students with serious emotional disturbance) realized midway through the unit that although students were enjoying the varied choices in projects and getting excited about making different projects, she had omitted the learning goals or standards that each project was supposed to accomplish. Some teachers have found grading rubrics useful to inform students at the beginning of instruction about standards that will be used in evaluating projects.

Tindal, Rebar, Nolet, and McCollum (1995) studied varied instructional outcomes for students with learning disabilities in content classes. They emphasize the impact of curriculum structure on assessment and instruction by noting that higher-order learning (which they claim can be measured in traditional and nontraditional formats) can be achieved for heterogeneous groups of students when a unit is reorganized to focus on concepts and principles. Students with and without learning disabilities whose teachers had reorganized their content and used content enhancements (e.g., graphic organizers) when delivering instruction scored comparably on assessment formats (that included selection and production responses), a range of knowledge forms (including facts, concepts, principles), and higher-order thinking skills (such as prediction, evaluation, and application). The relative standing of students with learning disabilities in some of the areas assessed (problem-solving essay) changed in that the students moved from well below the class average to very near it. The researchers further note that the ensuing instruction must be preceded by curricula shifting from a compilation of facts to be memorized to rearranged, reprioritized, and relevant concepts and principles.

When general educators use instructional methods with heterogeneous groups of learners, to look only at the group's average score is not sufficient. Disaggregated scores from heterogeneous groups can provide the teacher with more specific information about how each group, or representative students from each group, is performing. By looking at the performance of the varied groups within the classroom, the teacher can make more informed decisions about how well the instruction is working. In one method, called HALO (Deshler, 1992; King-Sears & Cummings, 1996), scores on assessments are separated for four groups of students within a classroom: *H*igh achievers or gifted students, *A*verage achievers or typical students, *L*ow achievers or students at-risk for school failure, and *O*ther students or students with disabilities. The progress for students' scores across HALO categories should indicate that all groups are progressing.

Practice #7: Generalization Techniques

Imperative in educators' knowledge of effective inclusive methods is educators' knowledge of where they are taking the whole class, as well as where they are taking each individual student, in any given curriculum. What students will be learning, why they are learning that information, and how that information applies in real-world living must be established at a macro level before selecting any method to use at a micro level.

Mundschenk and Sasso (1995) prepared typical peers to interact with students with autism during free-play sessions. As part of the training, the peers were involved in generating situations and social interaction behaviors instead of using situations and behaviors designed by the researchers. By using the peers' existing repertoire of behaviors and by eliciting their perspectives on situations, the researchers conjectured that more natural behaviors and opportunities for interacting with students with autism, rather than more artificial situations and behaviors, may have occurred in their study. During their baseline measures, Mundschenk and Sasso confirmed that peer interactions with the students with autism did not occur naturally; the peers needed training on how to interact. Consequently, the researchers were interested in how many typical peers had to be trained on interactions before generalization would occur. After analyzing data in which up to five peers were trained for interactions, the researchers concluded that only when three trained peers interacted within the free-play sessions did generalized initiations and responses from typical peers and the students with autism occur. Although they caution against assuming that three is a magic number, their results are instructive in that training all typical peers may not be necessary before interaction behaviors begin to have a ripple effect across a group of students.

Cole and Meyer (1991) studied students with severe disabilities in integrated and segregated environments. They found that the students in integrated environments scored significantly higher in four areas of social functioning. The integrated students initiated more contacts, obtained more cues, were more accepting of assistance, and indicated their preferences more than their counterparts in segregated environments. Furthermore, students in segregated environments tended to regress instead of making gains in several social functioning areas. The researchers conjectured that skills taught for community participation in segregated schools may not have offered the variety of natural opportunities available in integrated schools to allow those skills to generalize. In this situation, the placement *does* seem to matter as a pivotal part of the instruction; generalization environments must be readily available for generalization to occur.

Antia, Kreimeyer, and Eldredge (1993) studied the social interaction of young children with hearing impairments in integrated settings, and they compared two treatments conducted in small groups (four to six children). One group was taught a more structured social skills approach, and the other group was provided an integrated-activities intervention. Both groups were similar in increasing their interactions with peers of different hearing status, although more frequent interactions occurred for same-status peers than with different-status peers. Children in the integrated-activities approach, however, increased their interactions with each other significantly as a result of the intervention. The authors surmised that the integrated-activities approach was more amenable to generalization because the intervention occurred during typical play activities.

One also could surmise that the social skills approach was solely classroom-based without explicit instruction within the real environment. That is, the "controlled" environment of the classroom may have to be followed by the "advanced" or "real" environment of the playground as part of the social skills instruction. This situation could be akin to a traditional approach from special educators or related service personnel who note the discrepancy between what students with disabilities can do well within self-contained or controlled environments/materials/instructions, but the students' behaviors do not shift easily into the real environments. Teaching for generalization throughout instruction and as an explicit component of instruction continues to be necessary (Ellis, Lenz, & Sabornie, 1987; Haring & Liberty, 1990); if the generalization components are not evident then the chances for generalization are minimized greatly.

Not only do adults need to design and deliver generalization methods during instruction, but the students also need to be involved actively in the rationale for learning and using the specific content in other places, with other people, and during different circumstances. Connell, Carta, and Baer (1993) taught preschoolers with developmental delays how to self-assess and recruit teacher praise. When the children were taught how to both self-assess their behaviors and recruit reinforcement from adults, their active engagement during other classroom situations (outside the targeted situation) increased.

Students with disabilities who are taught how to use self-management procedures have used those systems more successfully to generalize their behaviors to other situations, settings, and people. Self-management (note that self-management also is used as a self-determination behavior) systems have enabled students with disabilities to (a) reduce disruptive classroom behaviors in special and general education classrooms (Rhode, Morgan, & Young, 1983), (b) interact appropriately in unsupervised settings (Pierce & Schreibman, 1994), and (c) increase appropriate social interactions in school and at home (Strain, Kohler, Storey, & Danko, 1994).

Practice #8: Collaboration

With a multitude of methods to choose from when implementing inclusion in general education settings (Bradley, King-Sears, & Switlick, 1997; Thousand & Villa, 1990; Udvari-Solner & Thousand, 1995), educators grapple with selecting effective and appropriate methods for individual students with disabilities, juggling the use of those methods in heterogeneous classrooms where other students may or may not benefit from the same methods, and monitoring students' progress to ensure that any method used is having the desired effects. The most effective inclusive methods are determined, implemented, and monitored by a team of people (including educators, parents, peers, other school personnel, and community agency personnel) who are collaborating. Warger and Pugach (1996) suggest that collaboration among educators toward inclusion starts with a careful and critical examination of the general education curriculum when including students with mild disabilities. The focus then moves from a more traditional emphasis on the student as the problem to a more progressive emphasis on the learning environment and how the demands of that environment affect all the students, not just a student with a learning problem.

Utley (1993) suggests a variety of ways by which to facilitate and measure teaming to promote inclusive services. Her endorsement of transdisciplinary teams, in which personnel provide direct and indirect services, is shared by many other professionals to accomplish inclusion (e.g., Downing & Bailey, 1990; Gallivan-Fenlon, 1994). Reed (1993) noted further that more comprehensive and coordinated recommendations can be done in less time when assessment teams use a transdisciplinary approach. A transdisciplinary approach to teaming is one in which each professional's unique skills, typically delivered to the student directly from that professional, are shared and transferred across people. Thus, the speech/language pathologist would be working within a transdisciplinary model to actively share information and skills with general educators, special educators, parents, and others; therapy is promoted throughout the youngster's day. In a transdisciplinary approach, a speech/language therapist would not cease providing direct services to the youngster, but the therapist would work more closely with other team members toward integrating the service across the day. A therapist also might deliver direct services within the context of the classroom environment instead of a more isolated therapy session. Co-teaching often is the form of delivery (Walther-Thomas, Bryant, & Land, 1996). Key components of a transdisciplinary approach are collaboration, cooperation, and coordination.

Effective inclusive classrooms feature collaboration not only among adults but also among students. Rainforth (1992) describes how general educators who had included students with severe disabilities in elementary classrooms learned more about disabilities both from adult teammates and from the typical students. One reason the students were able to inform the teachers was because this model for inclusion used an incremental approach beginning with kindergarten instead of the whole school. By the time the group of students reached first and second grades, their cohesiveness as a community of learners seemed well developed and their knowledge about how to include their peer with severe, profound, or multiple disabilities surpassed their teacher's knowledge. One teacher commented, "The kids are growing up learning sign language. The kids are growing up seeing things people used to call grotesque as commonplace" (p. 10).

Teachers involved in this program taught about disabilities in their classrooms both as a formal part of the curriculum and incidentally, as appropriate. Including the students with disabilities was not always easy and stress-free, but the teachers were not alone. Students also were active participants in collaborative problem-solving activities in which they partnered with adults to adapt activities. Several teachers found that involving the class in problem solving was more logical and natural because the students often saw the need for adaptations first, had a vested interest in solutions, and were influential in implementing solutions. Another teacher commented that students developed more creative, and sometimes easier, adaptations than the teachers did.

Effective inclusive classrooms are nurtured by collaboration both from students and from adults in the school. Many professionals, however, are realizing the magnitude of issues (e.g., violence, dysfunctional home life) that children today bring to the classroom that seem insurmountable even given the best and most school resources. While acknowledging the degree of success he and his colleagues attained using differentiated, cooperative methods in elementary classrooms, Jenkins et al. (1994) also despair that some of the students needed more intensive services than are available currently in public education. To better address the needs of some youth with (and without) disabilities, collaboration must extend beyond school personnel to include community agency personnel within a transdisciplinary model (Dikel, Bailey, & Sanders, 1994).

Practice #9: Proactive Behavior Management

Carpenter, Musy, and King-Sears (1997) synthesized research on effective behavior management methods and found that interventions occur at three levels within a school: schoolwide, classroom, and individual. Proactive behavior management interventions are those that most effectively prevent problems from occurring. These interventions are instructional in orientation, promote a positive learning climate, are made up of responsive and dynamic interventions, and benefit from teachers' experiencing collegial interactions. For example, features of an effective schoolwide discipline policy include (a) a proactive approach to managing behavior that is consistent across the school, (b) clear and consistent school rules, (c) frequent and positive communication with families, (d) collegial teams that support individual teachers and students, and (e) training and involvement that ensure a safe, secure school environment.

O'Neill, Williams, Sprague, Horner, and Albin (1993) found success in providing support for teachers working with students with severe problem behaviors (such as biting, kicking, hitting) by using a Teacher Support System. Case studies of seven students revealed that four of the students with moderate to severe mental retardation and/or autism were maintained in an inclusive placement after their teachers received assistance from members of the Teacher Support System. For the three students who were placed in more self-contained environments, the authors stated that staff turnover and inconsistent and ongoing program implementation were factors. The Teacher Support System's function was to provide technical assistance that went beyond consultation. Teachers needed initial training and assistance as they began to implement interventions, followed by ongoing support (including assistance in monitoring the effects of the interventions).

Flicek, Olsen, Chivers, and Kaufman (1996) report that students with emotional or behavioral disorders who were integrated into a combination fourth- and fifth-grade classroom increased their scores on a behavior checklist completed by their teachers such that by the end of the year in the Combined Classroom Model, their behaviors were within the average range. Furthermore, they (typical peers and peers with learning disabilities) maintained their academic standings and report card grades (decreases were not evident arising from their enrollment in this model). In addition, they achieved significant gains in mathematics applications. Techniques used in the Combined Classroom Model included (a) co-teaching, (b) weekly social skill lessons, and (c) behavior management level systems.

Practice #10: Peer Supports and Friendships

Staub, Schwartz, Gallucci, and Peck (1994) used observations, videotaped samples, and interviews to determine the effects of inclusion of four students with moderate and severe disabilities on four of their peers without disabilities. Two of the three classrooms the students were in used multi-age groupings and cooperative learning. In particular, friendships between the students with disabilities and their peers without disabilities were studied. What emerged were four descriptions of friendships, ranging from a helping relationship to more of a typical friendship. All of the friendships were developed outside of a tutorial or instructional context and were initiated by the students themselves, not by an adult.

The researchers noted that once the friendships were established, the students without disabilities began to take on more of a caretaker role in three of the four friendships. To place a subjective descriptor on this role for students without disabilities is difficult. In some instances the role of caretaker can be good, and in other instances the role of caretaker may inhibit the student with a disability from becoming more independent (Does a peer always prompt the student with a disability to complete classroom routines instead of the student completing those routines on his or her own when capable of doing so?).

Hunt, Alwell, Goetz, and Sailor (1990) found that high school students with severe disabilities who were taught to increase their conversation skills (both initiating and maintaining a conversation), with instruction occurring across a variety of school settings and with several general education students serving as communication partners, engaged in social interactions independently and decreased their inappropriate behaviors. The students with severe disabilities used communication books, photographs, and line drawings to assist them and their peers with dialogue.

Brady, Martin, Williams, and Burta (1991) investigated the influence of social play activities with nondisabled peers on the motor and social responses of students with severe, multiple disabilities. The peers were taught how to interact with the students during brief training sessions (15 minutes) across a week (total of 1 hour of initial training for the peers). The researchers concluded that the peers increased their social behavior toward the students. Also, targeted motor behaviors (e.g., reaching, holding head upright) increased for each of the students with severe, multiple disabilities. Interestingly, for the student whose motor behavior included reaching, the left arm was targeted because the student had preferred that arm over time as a result of limitations on his right side; however, during peer interactions the student's motor behavior increased with both arms. Several adults noted that this was the first time they had seen him reaching with his right arm and were surprised that he had that ability—one that seemed to "unlock" as a result of peer interactions.

Kamps, Leonard, Vernon, Dugan, and Delquadri (1992) found that first-grade students without disabilities and their peers with autism could be taught social skills effectively within small groups in which social skills were targeted for all students, not just the students with autism. The types of social skills that were instructed—participating in conversations, giving and receiving compliments, taking turns and sharing, helping others and asking for help, and including others in activities—were appropriate for all of the students. Furthermore, Kamps et al. determined that focusing instruction on fewer social skills with more practice activities was more efficient than teaching more skills without adequate practice. This concept of "less is more" seemed to benefit not only the students without disabilities but also the students with autism by providing more concrete demonstrations of appropriate behaviors.

Haring, Breen, Pitts-Conway, Lee, and Gaylord-Ross (1987) found that peer tutoring *or* a special friends program between typical high school students and students with autism, severe mental retardation, moderate mental retardation, and deaf/blindness was successful in increasing the social interactions between typical students and their peers with a variety of moderate to severe disabilities. A control group of typical peers who were not involved in either the peer tutoring or the special friends program experiences did not increase their social interactions. This research lends some credence to the argument that simply placing students in physical proximity may not alone induce interactions; that some type of training program has to occur; and that the type of training program (e.g., special friend, peer buddy) may not matter as much as that training does occur.

Ferguson et al. (1992) describe integration efforts in which physical proximity was a goal resulting in the creation of "bubble kids" or "velcro kids." They note that physical integration can be a "step on the way" to inclusion, and that true inclusion has the potential to flourish in the context of "reinvented" schools in which people develop "flexible, creative learning environments that include and are responsive to a full range of human diversity, including disability, race, culture, learning style, intelligence, personal preference, socioeconomic class, and family and community priorities" (p. 36).

Haring and Breen (1992) recruited junior high students to participate as part of a social network for two students with moderate and severe disabilities. The students with disabilities received the majority of their educational services in separate classrooms, but they were mainstreamed during lunch and transitions between classes. Teachers reported that during these unstructured parts of the day, the students had few appropriate interactions with their peers without disabilities. Typical peers were recruited to form a social network, taught how to interact (including the use of a self-evaluation scale), and assigned a specific time during the day to interact with the students with disabilities. Concurrently, one student with disabilities was taught to self-monitor his behaviors while interacting by pressing a wrist counter for each appropriate social response. By teaching the student with disabilities to self-monitor his interactions, the student himself became even more actively involved in the intervention versus being a passive recipient of an intervention.

Bimonthly network meetings were held for problem-solving and progress-reporting discussions. As a result of the social network, appropriate responding for one student with disabilities increased during the unstructured situations from 20% of the available opportunities (during baseline) to 38% (when students from the social network prompted and initiated interactions) to 81% (when the student used self-monitoring). Maintenance checks one and two months later indicated an ongoing high frequency of interactions. For the other student, appropriate responding skills increased to 78% (self-monitoring and maintenance phases were not implemented for this student).

Haring and Breen (1992) note that forming and supporting the social networks seems a more effective, efficient, and natural way for students with disabilities to learn how to participate in nonstructured contexts. Furthermore, direct adult support was not necessary to initiate and maintain these interactions. The intervention seemed to rely more on peer-controlled and peer-generated procedures (with the adult as the facilitator) than on adult-controlled procedures.

Peer supports and friendships may be more readily available when youngsters with disabilities participate in community activities, such as recreation programs.

Bernabe and Block (1994) found that modifying rules for a girls softball league to include a girl with moderate to severe disabilities did not affect her teammates' or other teams' performance. The girl's batting average, under the modified rule that she could use a batting tee, was not significantly different from the mean batting average for the rest of her team. The student also seemed to be well received by her teammates, which may not be surprising in this situation because she already was included in her neighborhood middle school. Her on-task behavior improved so that by the end of the season, she needed less frequent reminders to direct her attention to relevant aspects of the game.

Making Sure the Inclusive Structure Stands

Once teachers have received initial training in best practices for inclusion, one should not presume that those practices will be implemented correctly, systematically, and painlessly without additional support and technical assistance. Progress for students and adults should be evident, reinforcement for all should be available, ongoing improvement and refinement should be a goal, and creative, collaborative problem solving should continue. Waugh and Punch (1987) note that teachers want to know if their investment in new methods is likely to yield a greater return on factors such as student achievement and personal satisfaction. The progress of students—with and without disabilities—has to be evident. If teachers perceive that the personal cost of planning and implementing new methods is too great and results in little student progress, new methods may not be continued.

To feel comfortable all the way through change toward inclusion, even for people who want the change and are acting as the change agents, is not possible. Who has dieted and lost weight and enjoyed not eating their favorite foods? What makes the pain of dieting worth it? The benefit is derived when one looks better and feels healthier. What helps a person to stay on a diet despite the pain? Comments from others that reinforce dieting efforts and encourage one to "stick with it." What administrators and other change agents (the change agents for inclusion do not necessarily have to be the administrator; effective change efforts involve change agents from different levels and sources including teachers, other staff members, parents, and students) have to realize is that (a) change will not be easy and smooth, (b) support must be provided, and (c) support needs and methods will vary.

Scanlon, Deshler, and Schumaker (1996) note that secondary content teachers who learned and used strategic instruction designed to enhance learning for students with mild disabilities within heterogeneous settings were successful in using the methods but did not experience consistent significant academic gains for all students with disabilities. The teachers reported that, although they would have liked to have had more time to emphasize the strategic processes in their teaching and they realized how the instruction would benefit their students with and without disabilities, they perceived that they also faced competing demands for their time in class related to content coverage.

Gersten, Morvant, and Brengelman (1995) note that general educators are constantly balancing priorities. Increased success for students with disabilities is only one of many priorities competing for teachers' time. Similarly, Gelzheiser and Meyers (1996) found that general educators seem well aware of the benefits to individual students with disabilities when those students are included, but that more persuasive evidence for inclusion includes advantages for the teacher and the classroom as a whole. The cost of such instruction for some students has to be offset by the benefits for all students.

Greenwood et al. (1993) found that using a computer program designed to assist teachers as a "consultant" when they were implementing classwide peer tutoring programs was effective in prompting the teachers (a) when students were not being challenged enough or they were receiving material too difficult for their level, and (b) to examine varied reasons about why the method may not be being implemented correctly, such as too few sessions scheduled. The computer program was developed to help ensure fidelity of treatment, provide problem solving, and promote support. In a series of studies, Greenwood and his colleagues found that for teachers who still were working on getting the basic elements of ClassWide Peer Tutoring in place, the computer program typically responded with those elements and addressed differential group achievement. For teachers who had those basic elements in place, however, the computer program was able to focus on problems and concerns for individual students. What the computer program was able to do was to identify implementation problems and offer advice for addressing those problems.

Fuchs, Fuchs, and Hamlett (1994) also note how computer software can be used with curriculum-based measurement to enhance the effectiveness and efficiency with which teachers implement and use CBM. In particular, the use of technology was instrumental in complementing teachers' efforts to individualize instruction and make decisions on teaching based on students' data. When teachers are able to use such technology, the logistical barriers surrounding individualization can be minimized.

Gersten, Morvant, and Brengelman (1995) studied peer coaching as a way to bring research-based teaching practices into general education classrooms to improve the quality of reading instruction for students with learning disabilities. Over 3 years of working with general and special educators, they reached several conclusions that coincide with those of others who have studied the change process (Hall & Loucks, 1978; Joyce & Weil, 1986; Loucks-Horsley & Roody, 1990; Wisniewski & Alper, 1994):

1. Changed practices are implemented in an "up-and-down" pattern that reflect how hard it is to alter current practice and how tough it can be to integrate new patterns into a teacher's repertoire.

2. New practices, although they may seem uncomplicated for one professional, require extensive time to master. Joyce and Weil (1986) recommend 12 to 14 applications of a new practice to enable a person to feel more comfortable with that practice.

3. An implicit, yet unintended, message when teachers are told to use new practices is that they have been doing things "wrong" and they feel as if they are being evaluated, not assisted or coached, when they are trying something new. Ongoing refinement, continuous improvement, and risk taking have to be encouraged and supported.

4. Teachers report that what can offset the uncomfortable feelings of trying something new are the performance gains they see from their students as a result of the new practice.

5. Teachers have to be informed about the "why" of the new practice, not just the "what" and "how." The rationale is especially important for teachers to understand theory and research premises that support new practices.

What content should be taught in an educational program that effectively includes students with a range of disability labels and severity? What makes a quality program for those youngsters? And how can the appropriate content and quality instruction be delivered for them when different content and other types of quality instruction also have to be delivered to typical students in a general education setting? Educators who are creative and collaborative problem solvers are finding unique, practical, and effective ways to make inclusion work for them and their students (Thousand, Villa, & Nevin, 1994). Rarely can one person accomplish inclusion alone, and never can inclusion be successful using only one method. Just as a synergy occurs when people work together, so does a synergy occur when students with disabilities are exposed to a variety of effective practices.

The best academic practices for inclusion are instructional techniques that promote achievement, independence, and interdependence of individual students—with and without disabilities—within settings that include students who have a range of learning needs as a learning community. Heterogeneous groupings often are used, but not without individualization, differentiation, and heterogeneous techniques. The heterogeneously grouped settings should be (a) attained for the majority, if not all, of the school day, (b) individualized such that each student—with and without disabilities—achieves academically and socially, and (c) monitored so achievement gains are evident. Sometimes those practices may be delivered in small groups, frequently in large groups, and sometimes one-to-one instruction. What's most important for the students is the quality of instruction. What's most important about the instruction is that the content target meaningful and relevant learning. What's most important for teachers is the training and support that promote their comfort with effective inclusive practices. What's most important for the students is that they have multiple opportunities throughout their school careers to learn, work, and play with peers who are different from them, and that those differences are valued, accepted, and appreciated.

Consider this: How many practitioners, who today are responsible for developing, validating, and implementing inclusive practices, were schooled themselves in environments rich in such diversity? The prospect is exciting that tomorrow's practitioners—who may be receiving instruction right now in classrooms that promote acceptance and achievement by students with a wide range of learning needs—will be refining today's best practices in light of their own experiences. At no point can any of us rest on what we know now. Our challenge is to continually develop and refine techniques that work for each student within school classroom contexts and more accurately mirror the work and community contexts within which today's students will be living tomorrow.

References

Antia, S. D., Kreimeyer, K. H., & Eldredge, N. (1993). Promoting social interaction between young children with hearing impairments and their peers. *Exceptional Children, 60*, 262–275.

Baker, E. T. (1994). *Meta-analytic evidence for non-inclusive educational practices: Does educational research support current practice for special needs students?* Unpublished dissertation submitted to Temple University Graduate Board.

Bernabe, E. A., & Block, M. E. (1994). Modifying rules of a regular girls softball league to facilitate the inclusion of a child with severe disabilities. *Journal of the Association for Persons with Severe Handicaps, 19,* 24–31.

Bear, G. G., & Proctor, W. A. (1990). Impact of a full-time integrated program on the achievement of nonhandicapped and mildly handicapped children. *Exceptionality, 1,* 227–238.

Bradley, D. F., King-Sears, M. E., & Switlick, D. M. (1997). *Teaching students in inclusive settings: From theory to practice.* Needham Heights, MA: Allyn & Bacon.

Brady, M. P., Martin, S., Williams, R. E., & Burta, M. (1991). The effects of fifth graders' socially directed behavior on motor and social responses of children with severe multiple handicaps. *Research in Developmental Disabilities, 12,* 1–16.

Brown, L., Schwarz, P., Udvari-Solner, A., Kampschroer, E. F., Johnson, F., Jorgensen, J., & Gruenewald, L. (1991). How much time should students with severe intellectual disabilities spend in regular classrooms and elsewhere? *Journal of the Association for Persons with Severe Handicaps, 16,* 39–47.

Bruff, T. L., Jacksits, J. C., Marchineck, L. A., & Sandleitner, K. D. (1996). *Modifying instruction in diverse classrooms.* Unpublished manuscript at Johns Hopkins University, Rockville MD.

Carnine, D. (1991). Curricular interventions for teaching higher order thinking to all students: Introduction to the special series. *Journal of Learning Disabilities, 24,* 261–269.

Carpenter, S. L., Musy, T. L., & King-Sears, M. E. (1997). Behavior management methods. In D. F. Bradley, M. E. King-Sears, & D. M. Switlick, *Teaching students in inclusive settings: From theory to practice* (pp. 322–364). Needham Heights, MA: Allyn & Bacon.

Cole, D. A., & Meyer, L. H. (1991). Social integration and severe disabilities: A longitudinal analysis of child outcomes. *Journal of Special Education, 25,* 340–351.

Connell, M. C., Carta, J. J., & Baer, D. M. (1993). Programming generalization of in-class transition skills: Teaching preschoolers with developmental delays to self-assess and recruit contingent teacher praise. *Journal of Applied Behavior Analysis, 26,* 345–352.

Dalton, B., Tivnan, T., Riley, M. K., Rawson, P., & Dias, D. (1995) Revealing Competence: Fourth-grade students with and without learning disabilities show what they know on paper-and-pencil and hands-on performance assessments. *Learning Disabilities Research and Practice, 10,* 198–214.

Delquadri, J., Greenwood, C. R., Whorton, D., Carta, J. J., & Hall, R. V. (1986). Classwide peer tutoring. *Exceptional Children, 52,* 535–542.

Deshler, D. D. (1992). Lecture delivered to graduate students in an inclusion master's program at Johns Hopkins University, Rockville, MD.

Deshler, D. D., Ellis, E. S., & Lenz, B. K. (1996). *Teaching adolescents with learning disabilities: Strategies and methods* (2d ed.). Denver: Love Publishing.

Dikel, W., Bailey, J., & Sanders, D. (1994). Community mental health support services in a special education setting. *Behavioral Disorders, 20,* 69–75.

Downing, J., & Bailey, B. R. (1990). Sharing the responsibility: Using a transdisciplinary team approach to enhance the learning of students with severe disabilities. *Journal of Educational & Psychological Consultation, 1,* 259–278.

Ellis, E. S., Lenz, B. K., & Sabornie, E. J. (1987). Generalization and adaptation of learning strategies to natural environments: Part 2: Research into practice. *Remedial & Special Education, 8*(2), 6–23.

Falk, G. D., Dunlap, G., & Kern, L. (1996). An analysis of self-evaluation and videotape feedback for improving the peer interactions of students with externalizing and internalizing behavioral problems. *Behavioral Disorders, 21,* 261–276.

Ferguson, D. L., Willis, C., Boles, S., Jeanchild, L., Holliday, L., Meyer, G., Rivers, E., & Zitek, M. (1992). *Regular class participation system (RCPS): A final report.* (ERIC Document Reproduction Service No. ED 359 741)

Fewell, R. R., & Oelwein, P. L. (1990). The relationship between time in integrated environments and developmental gains in young children with special needs. *Topics in Early Childhood Special Education, 10,* 104–116.

Field, S., & Hoffman, A. (1994). Development of a model for self-determination. *Career Development of Exceptional Individuals, 17,* 159–169.

Flicek, M., Olsen, C., Chivers, R., & Kaufman, C. J. (1996). The combined classroom model for serving elementary students with and without behavioral disorders. Behavioral Disorders, 21, 241–248.

Fuchs, L. S., & Fuchs, D. (1986). Effects of systematic formative evaluation: A meta-analysis. *Exceptional Children, 53,* 199–208.

Fuchs, L. S., Fuchs, D., & Hamlett, C. L. (1994). Strengthening the connection between assessment and instructional planning with expert systems. *Exceptional Children, 61,* 138–146.

Fuchs, L. S., Fuchs, D., Hamlett, C. L., Phillips, N. B., & Bentz, J. (1994). Classwide curriculum-based measurement: Helping general educators meet the challenge of student diversity. *Exceptional Children, 60,* 518–537.

Gallivan-Fenlon, A. (1994). Integrated transdisciplinary teams. *Teaching Exceptional Children, 26*(3), 16–20.

Gelzheiser, L. M., & Meyers, J. (1996). Classroom teachers' views of pull-in programs. *Exceptionality, 6,* 81–98.

Gersten, R., Carnine, D., & Woodward, J. (1987). Direct instruction research: The third decade. *Remedial & Special Education, 8*(6), 48–56.

Gersten, R., Keating, T., & Irvin, L. K. (1995). The burden of proof: Validity as improvement of instructional practice. *Exceptional Children, 61,* 510–519.

Gersten, R., Morvant, M., & Brengelman, S. (1995). Close to the classroom is close to the bone: Coaching as a means to translate research into classroom practice. *Exceptional Children, 62,* 52–66.

Giangreco, M. R., Cloninger, C. J., & Iverson, V. S. (1993). *Choosing options and accommodations for children.* Baltimore: Paul H. Brookes.

Giangreco, M. F., Dennis, R. E., Edelman, S. W., & Cloninger, C. J. (1994). Dressing your IEPs for the general education climate. *Remedial & Special Education, 15,* 288–296.

Greenwood, C. R., Finney, R., Terry, B., Arreaga-Mayer, C., Carta, J. J., Delquadri, J., Walker, D., Innocenti, M., Lignugaris-Kraft, J., Harper, G. F., & Clifton, R. (1993). Monitoring, improving, and maintaining quality implementation of the classwide peer tutoring program using behavioral and computer technology. *Education & Treatment of Children, 16,* 19–47.

Hall, G. E., & Loucks, S. F. (1978). Teacher concerns as a basis for facilitating and personalizing staff development. *Teachers College Record, 80*(1), 36–53.

Haring, T. G., & Breen, C. G. (1992). A peer-mediated social network intervention to enhance the social integration of persons with moderate and severe disabilities. *Journal of Applied Behavior Analysis, 25,* 319–333.

Haring, T. G., Breen, C., Pitts-Conway, V., Lee, M., & Gaylord-Ross, R. (1987). Adolescent peer tutoring and special friend experiences. *Journal of the Association for Persons with Severe Handicaps, 12,* 280–286.

Haring, T. G., & Liberty, K. A. (1990). Matching strategies with performance in facilitating generalization. *Focus on Exceptional Children, 22*(8), 1–16.

Harris, K. R., & Graham, S. (1996). Constructivism and students with special needs: Issues in the class-room. *Learning Disabilities Research & Practice, 11,* 134–137.

Hlass, J., Jorden, J., Lightner, L., & Nagle, D. (1995). *Integration of life skills: General education curriculum and functional life skills curriculum.* Unpublished manuscript, Johns Hopkins University, Rockville, MD.

Hord, S. M., Rutherford, W. L., Huling-Austin, L., & Hall, G. E. (1987). *Taking charge of change.* Alexandria, VA: Association for Supervision & Curriculum Development.

Hughes, C., & Schumaker, J. B. (1991). Test-taking strategy instruction for adolescents with learning disabilities. *Exceptionality, 2,* 205–221.

Hunt, P., Alwell, M., Goetz, L., & Sailor, W. (1990). Generalized effects of conversation skill training. *Journal of the Association for Persons with Severe Handicaps, 15,* 250–260.

Hunt, P., Farron-Davis, F., Beckstead, S., Curtis, D., & Goetz, L. (1994). Evaluating the effects of placement of students with severe disabilities in general education versus special classes. *Journal of the Association for Persons with Severe Handicaps, 19,* 200–214.

Irvine, A. B., Erickson, A. M., Singer, G. H. S., & Stahlberg, D. (1992). A coordinated program to transfer self-management skills from school to home. *Education & Training in Mental Retardation, 27,* 241–254.

Jenkins, J. R., Jewell, M., Leicester, N., Jenkins, L. M., & Troutner, N. M. (1991). Development of a school building model for educating students with handicaps and at-risk students in general education classrooms. *Journal of Learning Disabilities, 24,* 311–320.

Jenkins, J. R., Jewell, M., Leicester, N., O'Connor, R. E., Jenkins, L. M., & Troutner, N. M. (1994). Accommodations for individual differences without classroom ability groups: An experiment in school restructuring. *Exceptional Children, 60,* 344–358.

Jenkins, J. R., Speltz, M. L., & Odom, S. L. (1985). Integrating normal and handicapped preschoolers: Effects on child development and social integration. *Exceptional Children, 52,* 7–17.

Joyce, B., & Weil, M. (1986). *How to learn a teaching repertoire. Models of teaching* (pp. 469–489). Boston: Allyn & Bacon.

Kamps, D. M., Barbetta, P. M., Leonard, B. R., & Delquadri, J. (1994). Classwide peer tutoring: An integration strategy to improve reading skills and promote peer interactions among students with autism and general education peers. *Journal of Applied Behavior Analysis, 27,* 49–61.

Kamps, D. M., Leonard, B., Potucek, J., & Garrison-Harrell, L. (1995). Cooperative learning groups in reading: An integration strategy for students with autism and general classroom peers. *Behavioral Disorders, 21,* 89–109.

Kamps, D. M., Leonard, B. R., Vernon, S., Dugan, E. P., & Delquadri, J. (1992). Teaching social skills to students with autism to increase peer interactions in an integrated first-grade classroom. *Journal of Applied Behavior Analysis, 25,* 281–288.

King-Sears, M. E., & Cummings, C. S. (1996). Inclusive practices of classroom teachers. *Remedial & Special Education, 17,* 217–225.

Kluwin, T. N., & Moores, D. F. (1985). The effects of integration on the mathematics achievement of hearing impaired adolescents. *Exceptional Children, 52,* 153–160.

Kluwin, T. N., & Moores, D. F. (1989). Mathematics achievement of hearing impaired adolescents in different placements. *Exceptional Children, 55,* 327–335.

Liddiard, H. J. (1991). *The academic achievement of second, third, and fourth grade regular education students involved in special education programs.* Unpublished thesis at Eastern Michigan University. (ERIC Document Reproduction Service No. ED 377 963)

Loucks-Horsley, S., & Roody, D. S. (1990). Using what is known about change to inform the regular education initiative. *Remedial & Special Education, 11*(3), 51–56.

Maheady, L., Sacca, M. K., & Harper, G. F. (1988). Classwide peer tutoring with mildly handicapped high school students. *Exceptional Children, 55,* 52–59.

Marston, D. (1988). The effectiveness of special education: A time series analysis of reading performance in regular and special education settings. *Journal of Special Education, 21*(4), 13–26.

Mercer, C. D., Jordan, L., & Miller, S. P. (1996). Constructivistic math instruction for diverse learners. *Learning Disabilities Research & Practice, 11,* 147–156.

Miller, W. (1995). Are multi-age grouping practices a missing link in the educational reform debate? *NASSP Bulletin, 79*(568), 27–32.

Mundschenk, N. A., & Sasso, G. M. (1995). Assessing sufficient social exemplars for students with autism. *Behavioral Disorders, 21,* 62–78.

Nelson, J. R., Smith, D. J., & Dodd, J. M. (1992). The effects of teaching a summary skills strategy to students identified as learning disabled on their comprehension of science text. *Education & Treatment of Children, 15,* 228–243.

Newman, B., Buffington, D. M., O'Grady, M. A., McDonald, M. E., Poulson, C. L., & Hemmes, N. S. (1995). Self-management of schedule following in three teenagers with autism. *Behavioral Disorders, 20,* 190–196.

O'Connor, R. E., & Jenkins, J. R. (1993). *Cooperative learning as an inclusion strategy: The experience of children with disabilities.* (ERIC Document Reproduction Services No. ED 360 778)

O'Neill, R., Williams, R., Sprague, J. R., Horner, R. H., & Albin, R. W. (1993). Providing support for teachers working with students with severe problem behaviors: A model for providing consulting support within school districts. *Education & Treatment of Children, 16*(1), 66–89.

Park, H., & Gaylord-Ross, R. (1989). A problem-solving approach to social skills training in employment settings with mentally retarded youth. *Journal of Applied Behavior Analysis, 22,* 373–380.

Pierce, K. L., & Schreibman, L. (1994). Teaching daily living skills to children with autism in unsupervised settings through pictorial self-management. *Journal of Applied Behavior Analysis, 27,* 471–481.

Prater, M. A., Hogan, S., & Miller, S. R. (1992). Using self-monitoring to improve on-task behavior and academic skills of an adolescent with mild handicaps across special and regular education settings. *Education & Treatment of Children, 15,* 43–55.

Rainforth, B. (1992). *The effects of full inclusion on regular education teachers.* (ERIC Document Reproduction Services No. ED 365 059)

Reed, M. L. (1993). The Revised Arena Format (RAF): Adaptations of transdisciplinary evaluation procedures for young preschool children. *Education & Treatment of Children, 16,* 198–205.

Rhode, G., Morgan, D. P., & Young, K. R. (1983). Generalization and maintenance of treatment gains of behaviorally handicapped students from resource rooms to regular classrooms using self-evaluation procedures. *Journal of Applied Behavior Analysis, 16,* 171–188.

Roahrig, P. L. (1993). *Special education inclusion: Fiscal analysis of Clark County schools inclusion site grant.* (ERIC Document Reproduction Services No. ED 373 528)

Rosenshine, B., & Stevens, R. (1986). Teaching functions. In M. C. Wittrock (Ed.), *Handbook of research on teaching* (pp. 376–391). New York: Macmillan.

Scanlon, D., Deshler, D. D., & Schumaker, J. B. (1996). Can a strategy be taught and learned in secondary inclusive classrooms? *Learning Disabilities Research & Practice, 11,* 41–57.

Schumaker, J. B., & Deshler, D. D. (1995). Secondary classes can be inclusive, too. *Educational Leadership, 52*(4), 50–51.

Schumm, J. S., & Vaughn, S. (1995). Getting ready for inclusion: Is the stage set? *Learning Disabilities Research & Practice, 10,* 169–179.

Sobsey, D., & Dreimanis, M. (1993). Integration outcomes: Theoretical models and empirical investigations. *Developmental Disabilities Bulletin, 21*(1), 1–14.

Stahmer, A. C., & Schreibman, L. (1992). Teaching children with autism appropriate play in unsupervised environments using a self-management treatment package. *Journal of Applied Behavior Analysis, 25,* 447–459.

Staub, D., Schwartz, I. S., Gallucci, C., & Peck, C. A. (1994). Four portraits of friendship at an inclusive school. *Journal of the Association for Persons with Severe Handicaps, 19,* 314–325.

Stainback, W., & Stainback, S. (Eds.). (1990). *Support networks for inclusive schooling.* Baltimore: Paul H. Brookes.

Strain, P. S., Kohler, F. W., Storey, K., & Danko, C. D. (1994). Teaching preschoolers with autism to self-monitor their social interactions: An analysis of results in home and school settings. *Journal of Emotional & Behavioral Disorders, 2,* 78–88.

Switlick, D. M. (1997). Curriculum modifications and adaptations. In D. F. Bradley, M. E. King-Sears,

& D. M. Switlick, *Teaching students in inclusive settings: From theory to practice* (pp. 225–251). Needham Heights, MA: Allyn & Bacon.

Tindal, G., Rebar, M., Nolet, V., & McCollum, S. (1995). Understanding instructional outcome options for students with special needs in content classes. *Learning Disabilities Research & Practice, 10,* 72–84.

Thousand, J. S., & Villa, R. A. (1990). Strategies for educating learners with severe disabilities within their local home schools and communities. *Focus on Exceptional Children, 23*(3), 1–24.

Thousand, J. S., Villa, R. A., & Nevin, A. (Eds.). (1994). *Creativity and collaborative learning: A practical guide to empowering students and teachers.* Baltimore: Paul H. Brookes.

Udvari-Solner, A., & Thousand, J. S. (1995). Promising practices that foster inclusive education. In R. A. Villa & J. S. Thousand (Eds.), *Creating an inclusive school* (pp. 87–109). Alexandria, VA: Association for Supervision & Curriculum Development.

Utley, B. L. (1993). Facilitating and measuring the team process within more inclusive educational settings. In L. Kupper (Ed.), *National symposium on effective communication for children and youth with severe disabilities* (pp. 55–77). (ERIC Document Reproduction Services No. ED 359 695)

Van Reusen, A. K., Deshler, D. D., & Schumaker, J. B. (1989). Effects of a student participation strategy in facilitating the involvement of adolescents with learning disabilities in the individualized educational program planning process. *Learning Disabilities: A Multidisciplinary Journal, 1*(2), 23–34.

Vernon, D. S., Schumaker, J. B., & Deshler, D. D. (1993). *The SCORE skills: Social skills for cooperative groups.* Lawrence, KS: Edge Enterprises.

Walther-Thomas, C., Bryant, M., & Land, S. (1996). Planning for effective co-teaching: The key to successful inclusion. *Remedial & Special Education, 17,* 255–265.

Wang, M. C., Haertel, G. D., & Walberg, H. J. (1993). Toward a knowledge base for school learning. *Review of Educational Research, 63,* 249–294.

Warger, C. D., & Pugach, M. C. (1996). Curriculum considerations in an inclusive environment. *Focus on Exceptional Children, 28*(8), 1–12.

Waugh, R. F., & Punch, K. F. (1987). Teacher receptivity to systemwide change in the implementation stage. *Review of Educational Research, 57,* 237–254.

Wesson, C., Skiba, R., Sevcik, B., King, R. P., & Deno, S. (1984). The effects of technically adequate instructional data on achievement. *Remedial & Special Education, 5*(5), 17–22.

Wisniewski, L., & Alper, S. (1994). Including students with severe disabilities in general education settings. *Remedial & Special Education, 15*(1), 4–13.

Wolery, M., Werts, M. G., Caldwell, N. K., Snyder, E. D., & Lisowski, L. (1995). Experienced teachers' perceptions of resources and supports for inclusion. *Education & Training in Mental Retardation & Developmental Disabilities, 30,* 15–26.

Yell, M. L. (1995). Least restrictive environment, inclusion, and students with disabilities: A legal analysis. *Journal of Special Education, 28,* 389–404.

Yell, M. L., Deno, S. L., & Marston, D. B. (1992). Barriers to implementing curriculum-based measurement. *Diagnostique, 18,* 99–112.

York, J., Doyle, M. B., & Kronberg, R. (1992). A curriculum development process for inclusive classrooms. *Focus on Exceptional Children 25*(4), 1–16.

15 Peer-Mediated Instruction and Interventions

CHERYL A. UTLEY, SUSAN L. MORTWEET, AND CHARLES R. GREENWOOD

THESE AUTHORS OFFER A PROGRAM for involving peers in the instruction of students with disabilities. The procedures they describe have been effective in getting students to spend more engaged time in instruction and to show academic benefits. The students not only monitor and assist but also may be trained to offer direct instruction to students with mild disabilities. These practices are recommended to all teachers who are instructing students with varying abilities and backgrounds.

Twenty years of research (1976–1996) investigating the inclusion of students with disabilities have consistently supported the finding that simply placing these students in general education classrooms without instructional supports for academic and social learning generally does not result in measurable academic and social benefits (Goodlad & Lovitt, 1993; Heller, Holtzman, & Messick, 1982; Stainback & Stainback, 1996; Ysseldyke, Algozzine, & Thurlow, 1992). For children with disabilities to be successful in inclusive settings, researchers have proposed that the development of academic skills and social competence, particularly with peers, become a major focus of school-based programs (Greenwood, Terry, Delquadri, Elliott, & Arreaga-Mayer, 1995). An inclusionary model of education must incorporate an analysis of effective teaching procedures and practices—what has to be done during instruction to produce optimal growth in students' learning. Classroom interventions must be available to teach appropriate academic and social behaviors and interactions among normally achieving students and students with disabilities.

In recent years the knowledge base and research studies supporting peer-mediated approaches to instruction have increased substantially. A rich knowledge base supports peer-mediated instruction and interventions (PMII) to facilitate learning in heterogeneous groups of students with varying abilities, interests, and backgrounds.

Numerous research studies have demonstrated that effective instructional process-es—engaged time, time management, success rate, academic learning time, moni-toring, structuring, and questioning—can be incorporated into PMII with important benefits (Greenwood, Carta, & Kamps, 1990). Further, the results of studies have consistently been positive and indicate peers can be trained, through specific PMII instructional procedures, to follow directions that lead to increased student outcomes.

Because PMII has major implications for the instruction of children with dis-abilities integrated in general education classrooms, we discuss PMII from two major perspectives:

1. We review the components of PMII that enlist sources of peer influence in support of instructional goals.[1] We define PMII as a viable instructional alter-native in which peers are used as instructional agents or helpers in orches-trating students' learning. Greenwood, Terry, Delquadri, Elliott, and Arreaga-Mayer (1995) stated that PMII is an increasingly sophisticated instructional technology consisting of "a set of practices and strategies that may be used to create the instructional processes known to be necessary to optimizing stu-dents' performance on standardized achievement tests" (p. 23). These strate-gies range from incidental peer help, supervision, and support for direct instruction in a subject matter (Greenwood, Carta, & Hall, 1988; Kalfus, 1984). In PMII, the teacher's role changes from delivering instruction to establishing monitoring and improving peer-teaching activities.
2. We describe instructional systems that incorporate PMII components with other elements of effective instruction and discuss recent findings support-ing their effectiveness.
3. We discuss implications for research and practice.

When studies have compared peer-mediated versus conventional teacher-medi-ated procedures (Greenwood, Delquadri, & Hall, 1989; Fantuzzo, Davis, & Ginsburg, 1995), results have demonstrated the relative effectiveness of PMII on instructional processes and student achievement. As illustrated in Table 15.1, PMII can offer a number of advantages, compared to conventional teacher-mediated instruction, in facilitating and creating processes known to result in academic out-comes. At the most basic level, the advantage of peer-mediated methods is the cre-ation of more favorable pupil-teacher ratios so the goals of individualization,

---

[1] Empirical studies in this review were located through many sources. A computer-assisted search of the ERIC and PSYCLIT databases was conducted for the years 1970–1995. Reference lists from articles also were examined for additional studies and relevant journals. Based on the importance of identifying effective peer-mediated instruction and interventions for students with disabilities, the following criteria for determining the inclusion or exclusion of empirical studies were estab-lished: participants between ages 5 and 19 years who were described as learning disabled (LD), educable mentally retarded (EMR), behaviorally disordered (BD), autistic, and severely disabled; data-based experimental or quasi-experimental evaluation of specific peer-mediated interventions; and quantitative measurement of academic (e.g., percent correct, accuracy, fluency) and social vari-ables (e.g., disruptiveness, social skill, social interaction, social acceptance).

■ **Table 15.1** *Active PMII Components*

Component	What They Do and How They Work
1. Peer modeling competent behavior	Exemplars and imitation of appropriate,
2. Peer initiation training	Opportunities to respond
3. Peer monitoring	Evaluation/feedback on responding
4. Peer networking	Peer support extended across time and settings
5. Peer tutoring	One-on-one instruction
6. Group-oriented contingencies	An individual's rewards are based in whole or in part on the successful performance of self and others

response supervision, error correction, and reinforcement are more likely to be achieved.

Compared to traditional forms of teacher-mediated instruction, research has confirmed that PMII increases time on academic tasks with behaviors such as writing spelling words, solving mathematical equations, oral reading, and task completion reliably produced by peer-tutoring programs. Another advantage is that PMII provides more opportunities to respond, in which students with and without disabilities can use teacher-student discussions, worksheets, workbooks or other written tasks, computer tasks, or structured projects, and peer interactions as contexts for using academic and social knowledge. In addition to increased opportunities to respond, PMII employs procedures that lead to (a) frequent error identification, (b) the practicing of correct responses, (c) immediate feedback and correction to increase rates of learning, and (d) help and encouragement from peers (Greenwood, Carta, Walker, Arreaga-Mayer, & Dinwiddie, Carta, & Kamps, 1990).

Other advantages of PMII include tapping the positive side of peer-group influence and providing powerful contexts for students to work together in cooperative and competitive learning situations to achieve common goals such as completing work tasks and earning points. Finally, when peer-mediated procedures are employed, students are able to motivate their peers to contribute their best performance to completing tasks and ensuring success (Greenwood, Terry, Delquadri, et al., 1995).

Components of PMII

Studies of peer influences and peer relations among children can be categorized as (a) naturalistic-observation studies, (b) manipulations of peer situations, the classroom context, and environment, and (c) peers as behavior-change agents (Field,

1984). In research conducted with young children with and without disabilities in general and special education classrooms, peer-related behaviors modeled by the typical students are accompanied by increases in the frequency of those behaviors by the students with disabilities. In studying various preschool classroom environments and the nature of peer and teacher interactions, researchers have found that (a) peer interactions are more frequent in classrooms featuring lower teacher-child ratios, (b) fewer teacher directives and free-play-oriented curricula contribute to more frequent peer interactions, and (c) less complex toys and equipment that are larger and less portable seem to facilitate peer interactions. Effective strategies that utilize peers as behavior-change agents are modeling or peer imitations, social reinforcement, and tutoring.

Researchers and practitioners have recognized the effectiveness of peer influences in improving classroom and academic performance. These influences, also referred to as components of PMII, consist of (a) peer modeling, (b) peer initiation training, (c) peer monitoring, (d) peer networking, (e) peer tutoring, and (f) group-oriented contingencies (see Table 15.2). These components are based on principles derived from applied behavior analysis (Greenwood & Hops, 1981), mastery learning (Keller, 1968), social learning theory (Bandura, 1968; Wagner, 1990), and process-products studies of effective instruction (Brophy, 1979). They are active ingredients of PMII and support specific teaching practices that create classroom processes that, in turn, lead to accelerated gains in students' performance on measures of achievement or social competence in general and special education classrooms. These components as shown by past research powerfully affect whether learning has or has not occurred.

Peer Modeling

Peer modeling encompasses a variety of instructional techniques that rely on the physical arrangement of an environment to include a child demonstrating appropriate behavior for a less skilled child to imitate (Strain, 1981). For example, in peer-proximity or peer-pairing interventions, a socially competent, untrained peer is paired with a child who is less competent to increase the opportunity for direct interaction (Odom & Strain, 1984). This approach has been investigated with withdrawn preschoolers (Furman, Rahe, & Hartup, 1979), students with autism (McHale, 1983), students with behavioral disorders (BD) (Mathur & Rutherford, 1991), and students with educable mental retardation (EMR) (Rucker & Vincenzo, 1970), with some success in increasing social interactions. Overall, however, improvements in the social behavior of the less competent child are not demonstrated, or the maintenance of positive results are not addressed or reported (Devoney, Guralnick, & Rubin, 1974; Guralnick, 1976; Odom & Strain, 1984; Rucker & Vincenzo, 1970; Strain & Odom, 1986).

Another peer modeling intervention is to have socially withdrawn or isolated children watch a film in which peer models demonstrate appropriate social behavior. Filmed interventions generally have been effective at increasing social interactions, particularly when an adult is commenting on the appropriate behavior being modeled

■ **Table 15.2** *Advantages and Disadvantages of Peer- and Teacher-Mediated Instructional Approaches*

Teacher Factor	Mediator	
	Teacher	**Peer**
Advantages		
Pupil/teacher ratio	High	Low
Engaged time	Variable	High
Opportunities to respond	Low	High
Opportunities for error correction	Low	High
Immediacy of error correction	Delayed	Immediate
Opportunities for help and correction	Few	Many
Opportunities for both competitive and cooperative learning experiences	Few	Many
Motivation	Teacher support	Peer plus teacher support
Disadvantages		
Peer training requirements	Few	Many
Quality control requirements	Few	Many
Content coverage	Good	Variable
Peer selection	Not required	Required
Curriculum adaptations	Few	Many
Costs	High	Low
Ethical concerns	Few	Increased

Source: "Teacher-Mediated Versus Peer-Mediated Instruction: A Review of Educational Advantages and Disadvantages," by C. R. Greenwood, J. J. Carta, & D. Kamps, In H. C. Foot, M. J. Morgan, & R. H. Shure (Eds.), *Children Helping Children* (pp. 177–205) (New York: John Wiley & Sons, Ltd., 1990).

in the film (O'Conner, 1972). Other researchers have added to the film a "coping" character who is talking about his or her own social situations as they are occurring. Results of these studies suggest that having a peer model narrate the various social scenarios in first-person is more effective at improving social behavior and increasing social interactions than having a third-person child narrate the film (Jakibchuck & Smeriglio, 1976). Filmed peer-modeling interventions may not be as useful for students with severe disabilities such as autism, who may not attend effectively to the salient social behavior the model in the film is trying to portray (Strain, 1981).

More recently and more typically, peer-modeling interventions are conducted "live" and are used in combination with other strategies (e.g., social skills training) (Elliott & Gresham, 1993; Hollin & Trower, 1988). For example, young children with mental retardation (MR) increased their appropriate social behavior after watching a typical peer modeling play behavior and being prompted and reinforced for imitating the behavior (Apolloni, Cooke, & Cooke, 1977). Positive results, including increased social skills and decreased inappropriate behavior, also have been reported for preschoolers with developmental delays who watched peer models demonstrate appropriate social behavior along with exposure to role-playing, direct instruction, and adult reinforcement (Matson, Fee, Coe, & Smith, 1991).

Peer modeling is an important component in many peer- mediated strategies, including peer-initiation training, peer tutoring, and cooperative learning, regardless of whether modeling is or is not reported as a specific strategy in the intervention. One premise of many peer-mediated interventions is that having a peer available to model appropriate behaviors to a less skilled child increases the likelihood of observational learning because of perceived similarity with the peer model (Kornhaber & Schroeder, 1975). Despite the potential effectiveness of peer modeling as a teaching strategy, simply placing students together without incorporating other intervention procedures most likely will not result in significant changes in the less skilled child's behavior (Guralnick, 1976; Odom & Strain, 1986; Vaughn & Lancelotta, 1990). This point is especially important to remember when considering the success of integrating a student with disabilities into a general education classroom, where instructional strategies for both academic and social behaviors are necessary to facilitate successful inclusion (Cullinan, Sabornie, & Crossland, 1992; Siperstein, 1992).

Peer Initiation Training

One of the most well researched and frequently used peer-mediated strategies to improve social behavior for children with disabilities is peer initiation training (Strain & Odom, 1986). Typically, peer initiation training requires a teacher to train peers how to evoke and maintain desired social and communicative behaviors from a target child (Antia, 1994; McEvoy, Odom, & McConnell, 1992; Odom & Strain, 1984). Some common behaviors that peers are taught to use to facilitate social behavior and interactions are (a) establishing eye contact, (b) suggesting play activities, (c) initiating conversation, (d) offering or asking for help, (e) describing ongoing social interactions, (f) expanding the content of the target student's speech, and (g) demonstrating affection (Goldstein & Wickstrom, 1986; Odom, Strain, Karger, & Smith, 1986; Storey, Smith, & Strain, 1993).

Peer initiation training has been used successfully to increase the appropriate social behavior and interactions of preschoolers who were withdrawn (Day, Powell, & Dy-Lin, 1982; Fantuzzo et al., 1988; Hecimovic, Fox, Shores, & Strain, 1985), preschoolers with autism (Odom, Hoyson, Jamieson, & Strain, 1985; Odom & Strain, 1986; Shafer, Egel, & Neef, 1984), and with school-aged children with autism (Brady et al., 1984; Handlan & Bloom, 1993; Strain, Kerr, & Ragland, 1979). For example, typical preschool peers were trained by teachers using role-play, prompting, and reinforcement to initiate social activities during freeplay with their peers who were withdrawn (Day et al., 1982). The results of these studies indicated an increase in typical peer social initiations and social interactions, including an increase in positive initiations by target students to trained typical peers (Strain, Shores, & Timm, 1977). Similar positive social outcomes have been reported for peer initiation training with students with autism (Strain et al., 1979).

Some evidence of generalization has been reported for social initiations by typical peers to nontarget children in the classroom and for social interactions in nontrained settings (Strain, Shores, & Timm, 1977). Peer initiation training with children who have more severe disabilities has been less successful in generalizing and maintaining social outcomes (Odom et al., 1985; Shafer et al., 1984). As with many social interventions, the generalization of social behaviors and interactions achieved with peer initiation training to other nontrained settings may not be obtained readily without additional programmed intervention (Mathur & Rutherford, 1991; McEvoy et al., 1992). In general, peer initiation training has been effective in facilitating social initiations and responses between children with disabilities and their typical peers, with less evidence reported for the maintenance and generalization of social outcomes.

Although peer initiation training is considered a peer-mediated instructional strategy, the level of teacher involvement can be intensive and necessary for success of the intervention (Antia, 1994; McEvoy et al., 1992). Peers may be trained in sessions separate from the planned curriculum (Day et al., 1982), teachers may be present during the initial social play situation to prompt and reinforce typical peers for displaying trained behaviors (Handlan & Bloom, 1993), or teachers may prompt and reinforce typical peers during the entire interaction (Goldstein & Ferrell, 1987). Shafer et al. (1984) reported a successful reduction in the level of teacher involvement needed to facilitate interactions between preschoolers with autism and their typical peers by including the students with autism in the training.

Despite some evidence that teacher involvement can be reduced, the level of teacher intervention necessary to ensure successful social outcomes still must be determined. In conclusion, although more research must be conducted to determine ways to increase maintenance and generalization of social outcomes and to decrease teacher involvement, peer initiation training may be considered a generally effective peer-mediated strategy for increasing the social behaviors and interactions of children with and without disabilities.

Peer Monitoring

One of the most important goals for special education and early childhood education is to teach children with and without disabilities how to cope with their environment, perform a wide variety of self-care tasks, and participate in social and preacademic activities (Sainato, 1990; Goetz, Ayala, Hatfield, Marshall, & Etzel, 1983). Completing these goals and tasks is problematic for children with disabilities. They may not have opportunities to practice (a) coping independently with the environment, (b) performing tasks without assistance from the teacher, and (c) performing activities without an enormous amount of teacher attention. In addition, individualized instruction may not allow children with disabilities to function independent of teacher monitoring and management.

One promising solution to teaching children with disabilities to function independently during the transition between classroom activities is peer-mediated intervention, the strategy by which children's behavior can be altered (Sainato, 1990). In an earlier study, Sainato, Strain, LeFebvre, & Rapp (1987) used a peer-monitoring system in which socially competent preschoolers acted as buddies for their peers who had autism. Preschoolers assisted their friends to make different transitions around the classroom. Prior to implementing the buddy system, the teacher modeled the desired behavior. Following the training session, the typical children were able to help their buddies make quicker transitions with less disruptive behavior across three different transition activities (circle to table, snack to bathroom, circle to language). Teachers considered the peer-monitoring strategy easy to implement because the buddy system promoted more social exchanges.

A series of earlier studies conducted by Carden-Smith and Fowler (1984) and Fowler (1986) showed that peer monitoring procedures (e.g., token systems) decreased disruptive behaviors during transition activities. Kindergarten children were assigned as team captains and distributed points for appropriate behavior to team members and to themselves on report cards depicting pictures of transition activities. Through role-playing activities, peers were trained to make point awards, prompt appropriate behavior, and provide corrective feedback based upon the children's behavior during transition time. Children were reinforced by participating in daily outdoor activities. Following the peer monitoring procedure, a self-monitoring procedure was implemented. Peer monitors were able to successfully initiate the token system without training by an adult to reduce disruptive behavior on the part of monitored peers. In addition, peers appointed as monitors continued that role throughout the day. Results also indicated that both the peer-monitored and the self-monitored interventions reduced inappropriate behaviors during transition time.

In one final study, Kohler, Schwartz, Cross, and Fowler (1989) implemented a peer-mediated strategy in a fifth-grade classroom during an independent work math period. Three students, identified as low-achieving, were selected as peer monitors for three students who engaged in high rates of off-task behavior such as looking around, and making paper airplanes during math class. The monitor training sessions consisted of rehearsing the roles of the monitor and point earner, and completing checklists that assessed on-task behavior, accuracy, neatness, and work completion. Peer monitors also were taught how to give verbal feedback to their partner about the quality of their work. The results indicated that (a) the peer-mediated intervention increased the appropriate study behaviors of the fifth-grade students during math class; and (b) the peer monitors and point earners produced comparable changes in their own appropriate behavior.

The major advantage of using peers as monitors was that the disciplinary and supervisory responsibilities of teachers were minimized. The benefits for children were twofold: (a) children who were peer monitors were placed in leadership roles; and (b) their participation in activities provided them opportunities to learn to make discriminations between appropriate and inappropriate behavior during transition times of the classroom.

Applicability to Students with Mild Disabilities

Researchers have demonstrated the efficacy of self-management and peer monitoring procedures with elementary-aged students with behavior problems (Nelson, Smith, & Colvin, 1995), students with mild disabilities (McCurdy & Shapiro, 1992; Rhode, Morgan, & Young, 1983), and junior high school aged students with mild disabilities (Smith, Young, West, Morgan, & Rhode, 1988). More recently, research has been conducted to determine the efficacy of self-management/self-monitoring procedures with high school-aged students with mild disabilities (Hogan & Prater, 1993; Smith, Nelson, Young, & West, 1992).

For example, a study conducted by Smith et al. (1992) compared teachers and peers as facilitators in the self-evaluation/management process and maintenance of behavioral gains in eight high school adolescents with learning disabilities (LD) during English classes. Eight typical peers enrolled in general education English classes served as peer facilitators. The criteria for selecting students with LD in general and special education classrooms included teacher reports of (a) off-task behaviors relative to peers during independent seatwork (e.g., failing to use academic materials appropriately, out of seat without permission, inattention to assigned tasks, talking to other students, swearing, and/or making inappropriate noises), and (b) inconsistent completion of assignments (e.g., independent seatwork, reading and answering chapter questions, dictionary work and grammar worksheets) relative to typical peers. A multiple baseline across experimental settings design was used to determine the effects of the self-management procedures on target behaviors and the generality of treatment effects across settings.

In summary, self-management procedures (self-recording, self-evaluation, self-reinforcement, self-instruction, and goal setting) with students with mild disabilities improved their academic and social behaviors in both general and special education classrooms. According to Nelson et al. (1995), researchers have incorporated several strategies to maximize the potential effectiveness of self-management procedures. Some of these are: (a) teaching students self-observation, self-recording, and self-evaluation procedures; (b) requiring students to make judgments about their behavior relative to an adult; (c) establishing contingencies for desirable behaviors; and (d) withdrawing procedures when students are controlling their own behavior reliably. In addition, peer-mediated self-management procedures are well suited for facilitating academic and behavior improvements across ages and disability groups and the generalization of these behaviors from special education to general education classrooms.

Peer Network Strategies

The literature is replete with interventions (e.g., peer-mediated) designed to increase the social competence and language development of students with autism. Inclusionary programs for students with autism have focused on interventions that increase their social-communicative behaviors and language development (Kamps, Barbetta, Leonard, Dugan, & Delquadri, 1992; McEvoy & Odom, 1987; Ostrosky

& Kaiser, 1995; Strain & Odom, 1986). In utilizing peer-mediated strategies, peers are instructional resources in which an adult trains a typical peer to interact effectively with students with autism. Following the training, student dyads are arranged for social activities and trained peers are instructed to prompt and encourage social responses from students with autism, as well as model and reinforce appropriate social behaviors (Farmer & Cairns, 1991; Goldstein, Kaczmarek, Pennington, & Shafer, 1992; Haring & Breen, 1992; Horner, Meyer, & Fredericks, 1987; Sasso, Garrison-Harrell, & Rogers, 1994). Procedural components include removing the adult from the intervention and using peers to engage in ongoing, age-appropriate interactions in natural social contexts.

Peer networks related to peer initiation interventions are defined as groups of individuals who demonstrate an interest in understanding the individual with disabilities and having an impact on that person's life (Chadsey-Rusch, 1986). The primary goal of peer network intervention is to promote a positive social environment for students with autism by creating a support system of friends and socially competent peers.

A limited number of studies have been published in support of peer networks. In studying the efficacy of peer networks with students with disabilities, Haring and Breen (1992) introduced a peer network within a peer clique during lunchtime activities. The criteria for selecting peers were that (a) both groups of students have classes together and know each other informally; and (b) that they share common interests, hobbies, and on-campus jobs. In the initial phase of the study, typical students were recruited to form four or five peer networks and discuss ways to include students with disabilities in the social activities within the school environment. Network peers outlined their schedules, chose specific times to interact socially with students with autism and other disabilities in school, and participated in out-of-school social events. Network peers were successfully taught strategies that mediate, reinforce, and maintain positive social interactions and responses. The frequency and quality of the social interactions were increased positively between the network peers and students with autism and disabilities.

More recently, Garrison-Harrell (1996) studied the social competence and social language of three elementary-aged children with autism. Appropriate social communication skills were taught via an augmentative communication system, and peer networks were formed during school-based activities that included language arts, reading, computer skills, lunch, and recess. Network peers were taught to interact socially during structured and unstructured activities and to use a variety of visual prompting systems (e.g., augmentative communication system, topic cards, and language strips) to increase the social-communicative behaviors of students with autism.

Peer network activities included training in the student's augmentative communication system and social interaction skills instruction (e.g., initiation of conversations, response to conversations, saying something nice, sharing, giving instructions, sharing ideas, and maintaining conversations). Positive findings were found suggesting that peer-mediated procedures and peer network strategies (a) facilitate communicative strategies and social and communication skills of students with autism, and (b) enhance and encourage friendships between students with autism and their typical peers.

Peer Tutoring Approaches

Peer tutoring, according to Foot, Shute, Morgan, and Barron (1990), represents an "unusual kind of social relationship in which children of relatively equal standing are given formal roles (by adults) in which their status is differentiated, possibly artificially or arbitrarily, for the purposes of promoting academic achievement and social competence" (p. 65). In the research-to-practice literature, peer tutoring represents a class of practices and strategies that employ peers as one-on-one teachers to provide individualized instruction, practice, repetition, and clarification of concepts (Greenwood et al., 1995; Jenkins & Jenkins, 1988; Topping, 1988; Wagner, 1990). Peer tutoring, as compared to conventional teacher-mediated instruction, increases (a) opportunities to respond, (b) academic engagement, and (c) relevant academic behaviors that are related to specific academic tasks (Greenwood & Delquadri, 1995; Greenwood, Dinwiddie, Terry, et al., 1984).

The benefits of students in the roles of tutor and tutee operate at the cognitive, affective, evaluative, and behavioral levels (Foot et al., 1990; Gartner, Kohler, & Reissman, 1971). At the cognitive level, tutors gain a deeper understanding of the material learned by having to teach it, and learning how to learn strategies may generalize to learning contexts other than the immediate learning task. At the affective level, tutoring may increase a sense of responsibility and concern for others. At an evaluative level, tutoring may enhance self-esteem and self-confidence. Last, at the behavioral level, tutoring may promote prosocial behaviors in students.

Peer Tutor Training Requirements

Peer tutoring strategies vary in the amount of training the interactors require. Peer tutoring strategies that require the tutor to employ a specific set of instructional behaviors have been reported to be more effective than those that only create pairs and then leave the tutoring procedures entirely to the tutor's discretion (Miller, Barbetta, & Heron, 1994; Niedermeyer, 1970). Using structured interactions between tutors and tutees increases training requirements.

In general and special education classrooms, tutors typically are trained in the instructional practices they are to provide. Deterline (1970) enumerated the following 10 goals for tutor training, which are prescriptive of the teaching strategies that children with and without disabilities are expected to learn: (a) putting the tutee at ease; (b) clarifying the prescribed task; (c) showing the tutee how to verify his or her answer; (d) directing the tutee to read each problem aloud; (e) having the tutee respond overtly before the tutor provides feedback; (f) having the tutee verify each response; (g) avoiding any form of punishment; (h) providing verbal praise when appropriate; (i) providing a tangible reward when appropriate; and (j) evaluating elements of mastery.

Training also may focus on materials to be used and what records of the tutee's performance are to be maintained. Tutor training for students without disabilities who participate as tutors for students with disabilities may include other kinds of information such as (a) an orientation describing cognitive, motivational, and behavioral characteristics of students with disabilities and how these characteristics may affect tutoring interactions, and (b) opportunities to observe students with disabilities before initiating a tutoring program observations (Whorton, Locke, Delquadri, & Hall, 1989).

Classroom Applications with Heterogeneous Student Populations

Numerous research studies and reviews pertaining to peer tutoring and students with disabilities (ADHD, EMR, LD, BD, moderate-severe disabilities, and autism) in general and special education classrooms may be found in the literature (Agran, Fodor-Davis, Moore, & Martella, 1992; Balenzano, Agte, McLaughlin, & Howard, 1993; Beirne-Smith, 1991; Bell, Young, Blair, & Nelson, 1990; Block, Oberweiser, & Bain, 1995; Byrd, 1990; Campbell, Brady, & Linehan, 1991; Cole, Vandercook, & Rynders, 1988; Cooke, Heron, Heward, & Test, 1982; Delquardri, Greenwood, Stretton, & Hall, 1983; DuPaul & Henningson, 1993; Fenrick & Petersen, 1984; Franca, Kerr, Reitz, & Lambert, 1990; Gable, Arllen, & Hendrickson, 1994; Goodman, 1990; Gordon, Vaughn, & Schumm, 1993; Greenwood, Delquadri, & Hall, 1984; Greenwood, Terry, Utley, Montagna, & Walker, 1993; Haper, Mallette, Maheady, Parkes, & Moore, 1993; Hogan & Prater, 1993, Kamps, Barbetta, Leonard, & Delquadri, 1994; Kamps, Locke, Delquadri, & Hall, 1989; Locke & Fuchs, 1995; Maheady, Harper, & Mallette, 1991; Maheady, Harper, & Sacca, 1988; Maheady, Sacca, & Harper, 1988; Mallette, Harper, Maheady, & Dempsy, 1991; Marston, Deno, Kim, Diment, & Rogers, 1995; Mathes & Fuchs, 1993, 1994; Mathes, Fuchs, Fuchs, & Henley, 1994; Odom & Strain, 1984; Osguthorpe, Eiserman, & Shisler, 1985; Osguthorpe & Scruggs, 1986; Romer, Busse, Fewell, & Vadasy, 1985; Santarsiero & Rotatori, 1994; Scruggs & Richter, 1988; Sideridis, 1995; Simmons, Fuchs, Fuchs, Hodge, & Mathes, 1994; Yasutake, Bryan, & Dohrn, 1996; Young, 1981).

This collective body of research supports the following conclusions: (a) peer tutoring is academically and socially beneficial for tutees and tutors alike; (b) benefits for tutors and tutees occur frequently and at consistently high rates; (c) students with disabilities can function effectively as tutors for other students; (d) the effects of peer tutoring interventions are aligned closely with the subject matter and reveal significant improvements in academic subjects; (e) social benefits are restricted to attitudes toward school, the academic content taught, and social interactions between tutors and tutees; and (f) the outcomes of peer tutoring strategies are related to the research design, experimental-control group comparisons, and pre-post treatment only group designs.

Peer tutoring strategies have been used effectively with students from ethnic, international, and multicultural/bilingual backgrounds (e.g., African-American and Hispanic-American groups) (Greenwood, Carta, Walker, Arreaga-Mayer, &

Dinwiddie, 1988; Greenwood, Delquadri, & Hall, 1989; Harper, Mallette, & Moore, 1991; King-Sears & Bradley, 1995; Maheady, Mallette, & Harper, 1991). Peer tutoring has occurred with multicultural/bilingual students of all languages, ages, achievement levels, socioeconomic levels, as well as diverse subject matter. Peer tutoring strategies with this population have been designed to meet a wide variety of purposes, including: (a) teaching basic skills in the primary and/or secondary languages, and (b) instructing students in foreign languages to allow for individualization, differential pacing through the curriculum, and to engage in supplementary drill and practice.

Because of the interactional context of tutoring, according to Greenwood et al., 1988, it is viewed as "particularly appropriate because second language acquisition naturally occurs in the context of talking to peers" (p. 6). The implementation of peer tutoring strategies results in many instructional and socioaffective benefits including the findings that (a) mastery learning in prespecified skill sequences is increased through practice and error correction opportunities; (b) communication skills are strengthened; (c) cross-cultural understanding occurs between tutors and tutees; and (d) positive relationships are established between second-language learners and fluent monolingual peers.

Cross-Age Tutoring

Cross-age tutoring is an innovative peer teaching program in which the tutors are students approximately two or more years older or younger than the students receiving the tutoring. The assumptions underlying this approach are that older students can benefit from tutoring experiences and they can effectively teach skills requiring individualized instruction (Gerber & Kauffman, 1981; Schrader & Valus, 1990; Topping, 1988). Research has demonstrated that older students with a range of disabilities have successfully tutored students with learning problems (Barbetta, Miller, Peters, Heron, & Cochran, 1991; Polirstok & Greer, 1986; Sindelar, 1982), students with LD (Kane & Alley, 1980; Lazerson, Foster, Brown, & Hummel, 1988), students with EMR (Csapo, 1976; Maher, 1984); students with severe disabilities (Vacc & Cannon, 1991), mainstreamed students with disabilities (Folio & Norman, 1981), and students with BD (Franca, 1983; Lane, Pollack, & Sher, 1972; Maher, 1982, 1984; Osguthorpe & Scruggs, 1986; Scruggs & Osguthorpe, 1986).

In cross-age tutoring situations, according to Foot, Shute, Morgan, and Barron (1990), social relationships differ qualitatively and quantitatively from same-age interactions in that cross-age interactions enhance and expand the social skills for each individual. For instance, caretaking roles are more observable in interactions with younger children, whereas dependency and modeling are more observable in interactions with older children. Further, in tutoring younger students, older students can make appropriate accommodations in how they use language to teach skills (e.g., using simpler words and shorter sentences) and put more effort into teaching group problem-solving tasks to compensate for differences between themselves and other children.

Cross-age tutors may be selected from older children within the same school (Miller, Barbetta, & Heron, 1994), nearby high schools (Barbetta et al., 1991), and universities and colleges (Miller, Miller, Armentrout, & Flannagan, 1995). Implementing cross-age tutoring programs requires careful scheduling between teachers and students involved in the program. Teachers must arrange and establish suitable tutoring schedules and routines. Older tutors may be scheduled to work with younger students when their class is doing individual work so older students are not affected adversely by lost instructional time.

The training of cross-age tutors may consist of tutors' learning sign language, problem-solving skills, behavior management techniques, classroom survival skills, and task analysis procedures in addition to specific tutoring procedures, error correction, and social and positive reinforcement. The amount of time required to train cross-age tutors may range from 45 minutes (Barbetta et al., 1991) to 5 hours (Folio & Norman, 1981) to 30 hours (Vacc & Cannon, 1991) to 6 weeks (Haisley, Tell, & Andrews, 1981).

The benefits of older students tutoring younger children are numerous. For counselors and teachers, cross-age tutoring provides opportunities to (a) reduce behavior problems, (b) allow individualized instruction, (c) help motivate students, (d) bridge the gap between teacher and student, and (e) build academic skills. Advantages for older students working with younger students with and without disabilities are that they can (a) give encouragement for establishing good work habits, (b) interpret to younger students the rewards they will have in learning to work, (c) help meet younger students' needs to be successful, important, appreciated, and growing in skills, and (d) help younger students to overcome their fears and gain self-confidence.

Reverse-Role Tutoring

Another innovative and promising peer-mediated approach is reverse-role tutoring, in which students with mild disabilities tutor younger students with and without disabilities. Because students with mild disabilities have proven to be effective tutors for younger students with disabilities, some researchers have hypothesized that they may be equally successful with younger students without disabilities (Maheady, Harper & Mallette, 1991). In a series of studies of reverse-role tutoring, Top and Osguthorpe (1987), Shisler, Osguthorpe, and Eiserman (1987), and Eiserman, Shisler, and Osguthorpe (1987) studied the academic skills and self-concepts of older students with mild disabilities (i.e., EMR, LD, and BD) who tutored younger peers without disabilities. In one study, Top and Osguthorpe (1987) used a nonequivalent control-group design and showed that students with mild disabilities designated as tutors and their tutees (i.e., typical peers) made significant gains in reading achievement and that students with mild disabilities improved significantly in their perceptions of their academic competence. The subjects' self-concepts, however, showed no significant improvements.

Eiserman et al. (1987) reported the findings of a comprehensive review of 13 studies of reverse-role tutoring as follows: (a) students with EMR spent significantly more time with their typical peers during freeplay, interacted more with general classroom peers, and increased their social interactions with typical peers; (b) students with LD showed significant gains in reading abilities, academic self-esteem, and attitudes about school and social acceptance; (c) students with BD were viewed more favorably by typical peers; and (d) students with LD and BD interacted more with their typical peers, made significant gains on criterion-referenced and standardized tests, improved their word attack skills, and increased their social acceptance among their typical peers.

Maheady, Mallette, & Harper, (1991) outlined several advantages to assigning students with mild disabilities as tutors. These authors pointed out that students with mild disabilities (a) can function effectively as tutors and make substantial academic gains themselves; (b) may become instructional assets and resources for general classroom teachers; and (c) may dispel negative stereotypes about disabilities that have persisted among general educators.

Group-Oriented Contingencies

In the natural classroom environment, peers are one of the most powerful sources of behavior change in academic and social settings (Gable & Arllen, & Hendrickson, 1994). They also are unique sources of information because they have opportunities to observe, interact, and informally assess aspects of an individual's behavior (e.g., peer relations, friends, and sportsmanship) during parts of the school day that are unavailable to teachers and parents (Rusch, Rose, & Greenwood, 1988). Further, the use of peers as behavior change agents may serve as a cue or as an aversive stimulus to: (a) facilitate academic accomplishments, (b) reduce instances of deviant and disruptive behavior, (c) increase work and study skills, (d) increase production and efficiency, and (e) teach social-interaction skills (Greenwood & Hops, 1981; Salend, Reeder, Katz, & Russell, 1992; Salend, Reid-Jantzen, & Giek, 1992).

Peer groups may consist of either typical/normally achieving students or students with disabilities in general and special education classrooms and may be categorized in the following ways: (a) peers are trained to be tutors or co-therapists in which they are taught to distribute points or reinforcers, record data, give instructions, and impose contingencies (Greenwood & Hops, 1981; Greenwood, Sloane, & Baskin, 1974), or (b) peers provide assistance through cooperative reinforcement contingencies in which they manipulate contingency arrangements so peers are given access to earned reinforcers and/or the reinforcement depends to some extent upon their behavior (Greenwood, Hops, Walker, et al., 1979).

Over the past 15 years, a behavioral technology—consisting of peer influence strategies and group-oriented contingencies—has emerged, with peers trained as social change agents in natural classroom settings. Peer influence strategies are those that take advantage of the natural social prompting and consequences that children in groups provide one another when working for a common goal or reward (Greenwood, Carta, & Hall, 1988). More specifically, peer influence includes social behaviors such as spontaneous prompts and encouragement (Alexander, Corbett, & Smigel, 1976), and assistance and spontaneous help to improve the performance of specific group members (Switzer, Deal, & Bailey, 1977). When tasks allow, students perform various task components at which they are most skilled, leading to group products or outcomes (e.g., tutoring) (Delquadri et al., 1983; Kohler & Greenwood, 1990; Greenwood, Dinwiddie, Bailey, et al., 1987; Polirstok & Greer, 1986).

As defined by Rusch et al. (1988, p. 255), group-oriented contingencies refer to "reinforcement programs in which earning the reinforcer is contingent upon the whole class or subgroups of the class." Examples of group-oriented procedures include the use of (a) uniform and groupwide behavior requirements (rules) for all students rather than individuals, (b) consolidated recording measures (e.g., a total score earned by the group) and standard contingencies to save teacher time and effort, (c) standard, naturally available consequences for groups rather than individually tailored reinforcers (Kohler & Greenwood, 1990), and (d) cooperative reward structures (Slavin, 1990). Utilizing group-oriented contingencies has several advantages over traditional methods of managing classroom behavior. Some of them are: (a) fostering group cohesiveness and cooperation among members, particularly culturally diverse students, (b) teaching responsibility to the group and enlisting support in solving classroom problems, (c) managing behavior efficiently and effectively, and (d) providing peers positive, practical, and appropriate methods for dealing with peer-related problems (Kohler, Strain, Hoyson, et al., 1995; Salend, 1994).

Early Childhood Research

One of the significant challenges facing early childhood education is the social integration of students with social and developmental delays. Research has addressed the social skills of young children with disabilities and consistently found that (a) these children are viewed by their typical peers to be less socially competent, (b) they experience more rejection on sociometric ratings than their typical peers, and (c) the sociometric rejections of these children often is represented in negative social interaction patterns during children's play activities. In preschool settings, a critical component of intervention programs for students with disabilities is social skills instruction involving the use of socially competent children to encourage or facilitate the social behavior of their classmates who exhibit delays (LeFebvre & Strain, 1989; Twardosz, Nordquist, Simon, & Botkin, 1983).

In reviewing the benefits of group-oriented contingencies, Kohler, Strain, Maretsky, and DeCesare (1990) and Kohler et al. (1995) noted that typical students and students with disabilities participating in these procedures exhibited corollary or untrained supportive behaviors. In the first Kohler et al. (1990) study, these authors examined the effects of individual and group-oriented reinforcement contingency procedures on the social and supportive interactions of two preschoolers with autism (ages 4 years old) and seven normally developing children (ages 3–4 years old) during dramatic play activities. Individual contingency procedures consisted of the teacher awarding Happy Faces to children who exchanged play organizers, shared, and offered assistance to other classmates. Group-oriented contingencies procedures consisted of the teacher pointing to a chart and showing a group of three elephants and stating, "Today is group day. To get a prize, every square on the Happy Face chart must be filled when the timer rings. That means that nobody gets a prize unless you earn all of your own Happy Faces and both of your friends earn all of the Happy Faces too." If one or more individuals did not meet this criterion, none of the children was permitted to select a reward. The results of this study showed that (a) individual and group-oriented contingencies both had equivalent effects on targeting children's social interaction with peers; (b) socially competent preschoolers exhibited few supportive prompts without direct training under group-oriented contingency conditions; and (c) socially competent children demonstrated high levels of supportive prompts after they had been taught to use these statements.

In the second study, Kohler et al. (1995) examined the effects of a modified peer-mediated strategy in which an entire class of preschoolers with disabilities and their typical peers received training for a wide range of diverse social skills and strategies. The participants were three preschoolers with autism (4 years old) and six of their typical classmates (3–5 years old) who were in engaged in manipulative play activities in groups of three (one target child and two socially competent peers). The peer-mediated intervention implemented was a programmed social skill training package developed by Odom, Kohler, and Strain (1987), in which all three target children and their peers learned the following skills: (a) play organizer suggestions, (b) share offers and requests, and (c) assistance, offers, and requests. Similar group reinforcement contingency procedures in the Kohler et al. (1990) study were implemented. In addition, classwide supportive skills were taught, whereby the target children and peers learned to remind one another to exchange, share, organize, and assist.

The results indicated that a comprehensive intervention package (a) increased the social interactions between the three students with autism and their typical peers, (b) socially competent preschoolers exchanged supportive prompts under group contingency conditions after they received training for these behaviors, and (c) supportive social interactions that contained supportive prompts were longer and more reciprocal in nature than those that did not.

Students with Mild Disabilities

Self-evaluation is one variation of group-oriented contingencies that decreases inappropriate behavior for students with BD (Rhodes, Morgan, & Young, 1983), for high school students (Smith, Young, West, Morgan, & Rhodes, 1988), for students with LD (McCurdy & Shapiro, 1992), for students with serious emotional disturbance (Clark & McKenzie, 1989), and for preschoolers with disabilities (Sainato, Strain, LeFebvre, & Rapp, 1990). According to Hughes, Ruhl, and Misra (1989) and Salend, Whittaker, and Reeder (1992), self-evaluation requires "a student to compare his or her behavior to a set criterion and make a judgment about the quality or acceptability of the behavior" (p. 203).

In group contingency management systems, a group of students or individual student behaviors to be changed are demonstrated by the teacher and modeled by peers. Students are aware of the target behaviors, are able to monitor their own performance, and are aware that other students in their group are observing their behavior. At the end of the class period, students are given time to reflect on their own performance and progress.

In one study, Salend et al. (1992) investigated a group evaluation system with two different groups of adolescent students with LD and ED in reading and English classes. The target behaviors to be modified through the program were the students' inappropriate verbalizations. The group-evaluation management system included the following procedures: (a) a review, explanation, and demonstration of the salient features of the target behavior; (b) an opportunity for students to identify and present examples and nonexamples of the target behavior; (c) an explanation, demonstration, and role play of the group-evaluation system; and (d) an assessment of the students' understanding of the target behavior and the intervention.

The results indicated that each group of students worked collaboratively to determine the class's behavior through a consensus method in which they discussed each member's perspective. Some of the group members used self-recording procedures to count the number of inappropriate verbalizations. In summary, the authors demonstrated that the group-evaluation system is an effective peer-mediated strategy that can be employed efficiently in the classroom.

Instructional Systems Built Around PMII Components

In the last five to 10 years, several instructional systems have emerged with compelling and supporting research to make classroom instruction more responsive to diverse learners. These include ClassWide Peer Tutoring (CWPT) and variations such as Peer-Assisted Learning Strategies (PALS), Classwide Student Tutoring Teams (CSTT), and Reciprocal Peer Tutoring (RPT). These systems have been used to improve the effectiveness of pull-out instructional programs for students at-risk in urban elementary schools (i.e., RPT) and to improve the effectiveness of general classroom instruction in which students with disabilities have been included (e.g., CWPT, PALS, and CSTT).

ClassWide Peer Tutoring (CWPT)

Developed in the 1980s, CWPT is an instructional design that originated in the general education classroom as a means of improving the spelling accuracy of students who were low-achieving and categorized as LD. Because the teacher did not want to teach students in different ability groups, she used CWPT as a way to include all students in classroom spelling instruction. As a result of its initial success, CWPT soon was expanded to other content-area subjects such as reading, mathematics, and vocabulary (Delquadri et al., 1983).

To include all students in instruction, the design of CWPT sought to take full advantage of PMII components, specifically including one-on-one peer tutoring and group contingencies of reinforcement (see Table 15.2). Other PMII components included in CWPT were (a) modeling of correct responses as an error-correction strategy and (b) peer initiations (task presentations and response opportunities presented by the tutor, peer monitoring of performance, and checking and recording of points earned by the tutor). Additional instructional components taken from research on effective instruction included (a) frequent opportunities to respond and practice, (b) reciprocal tutor-tutee roles, (c) immediate error correction, (d) frequent testing, (e) posting of performance, and (f) feedback on progress, mastery and content coverage (Greenwood, Terry, Delquadri, Elliott, & Arreaga-Mayer, 1995).

During CWPT sessions, all children are paired with a partner and each person is assigned to one of two competing teams. Tutor and tutee roles are reciprocal in that halfway through a session, tutors become tutees and vice-versa. The teacher's roles during these sessions are to supervise and monitor students' responding. Teachers are concerned with the quality of tutoring, and they award bonus points to tutors for using correct teaching behaviors. The teachers are concerned that the tutees are working quickly and that they are spelling words aloud as they write them.

Because of these components, CWPT is known be a system that engages the active academic responding of children focused on a specific subject matter lesson. Students commonly spend 60% to 80% of a session engaged in reading, writing, and talking about the subject matter. At the elementary school level, CWPT is designed to supplement traditional instruction and to replace seatwork, lecture, and oral reading group activities. At the secondary level, CWPT is focused on practice, skill building, and review of subject matter. Building and systems-level procedures also are available for supporting the implementation of CWPT programs schoolwide.

CWPT reorganizes individual class members into tutor-tutee pairs working together on two competing teams. Tutees earn points for their team by responding to the tasks their tutors present. Tutors earn points from the teacher according to their implementation of the tutoring role. The teacher's implementation is guided by a manual of procedures (Greenwood, Delquadri, & Carta, 1988; in press). The core procedures include:

- Review and introduction of new material to be learned
- Unit content materials to be tutored (e.g., reading passages, spelling word lists, or math fact lists)
- New partners each week
- Partner pairing strategies
- Reciprocal roles in each session
- Teams competing for the highest team point total
- Contingent individual tutee point earning
- Tutors providing immediate error correction
- Public posting of individual and team scores
- Social reward for the winning team

Added to these core procedures are subject matter specific procedures that accommodate peer teaching. For example, *when applied to passage reading*, tutees read brief passages from the curriculum to their tutor. The tutor provides points for correctly read sentences (2 points per sentence) and error correction (1 point per accurate correction). Teachers assess the fluency of the students' reading using oral reading rate measures.

When applied to reading comprehension, the tutee responds to who, what, when, where, and why questions provided by the tutor concerning the passage. The tutor corrects these responses, awards points, and gives feedback.

When applied to spelling, the tutee writes and spells words orally on a list. The tutor dictates the words to the tutee and corrects his or her performance. Similar variations are applied to *vocabulary, mathematics, and silent reading, as well as seatwork activities.*

CWPT lends itself to both teacher-prepared and standard commercial curriculum materials. CWPT enlists the rather extensive help and influence of the classroom peer group in the teaching process. Rewards of individual students in CWPT depend not just on their own performance but also on the collective performance of the individual's partner and team. Changing tutor-tutee pairs weekly and changing roles within daily sessions keep the children motivated. Each student also is provided with opportunities to learn teaching skills needed in the teacher's role.

At the end of the two tutoring sessions, students report their point totals to the teacher, who records them on their team chart. The totals are compared and both teams are applauded—the winning team for winning and the losing team for an excellent effort. Following this are transitional activities to the next lesson to be taught.

Research on CWPT has shown that students at-risk and with mild disabilities acquire literacy skills at a faster rate, retain more of what they learn, and make greater advances in social competence when using CWPT compared to conventional instructional methods. This research (Greenwood, Terry, Delquadri, et al., 1995) has addressed the issue of who benefits from CWPT (e.g., LD, low-achieving/non-LD), how it can be applied widely within local schools using an administrative/adoption model), and the role of technology (communication, training, and implementation quality information).

Perhaps the most dramatic findings have come from a 12-year experimental, longitudinal study (Greenwood & Delquadri, 1995). Results indicated that CWPT, compared to at-risk and a non-risk groups that did not receive CWPT (a) increased students' engagement during instruction, grades 1 to 3 (Greenwood, 1991a); (b) increased growth in student achievement at grades 2, 3, 4, and 6 (Greenwood, 1991b; Greenwood et al., 1989; Greenwood, Terry, et al., 1993); (c) reduced the number of CWPT students needing special education services by 7th grade (Greenwood, Terry, et al., 1993), and (d) reduced the number of CWPT students dropping out of school by 11th grade (Greenwood & Delquadri, 1995).

CWPT also has been used successfully as an integration strategy for a range of children with disabilities in addition to high-risk and students with LD. For example, Kamps et al. (1994) reported that CWPT improved the reading skills as well as peer interactions of students with autism and general education peers in an integrated setting. These students were a subgroup of high-functioning students with autism. They were children of normal intelligence but with serious deficits in social competence (e.g., rigid adherence to structure and schedules, a general disinterest in others, especially peers, and perseveration on objects or topics, or both).

DuPaul & Henningson (1993) and Fiore and Becker (1994) reported that CWPT was effective for students with ADHD in general education classrooms and it has been recommended as an effective strategy for this population of students. Harper et al. (1993) demonstrated improvements in spelling for students with mild disabilities including generalization of the words learned during CWPT spelling instruction to writing tasks in the absence of specific training. Sideridis (1995) reported improvements in students' weekly spelling accuracy, time engaged, and peer social interaction for students with MR when using CWPT. Arreaga-Mayer (personal communication) has completed work investigating the academic, language learning, and social benefits of CWPT adapted for students with limited English proficiency (LEP) and mild disabilities. In one study, she reported that English language use and practice were increased significantly when compared to traditional teacher-mediated instruction for LEP students with disabilities.

Consumers frequently have reported CWPT to be acceptable and useful.

> This model [CWPT] has impacted over 500 students and 65 teachers, both regular and special education throughout the district.... It has resulted in students making greater gains, both academically and socially, compared to traditional pull-out models. Quality implementation, finding the time to provide training, new methods of assessment, and evaluating student progress are pressing issues in our district addressed by CWPT. We must refine, not reinvent our current knowledge and practice. This project provides the technology and the resources needed to make it happen. *(comments of an inclusion coordinator)*

> We have used CWPT at every grade level with outstanding results. We have full inclusion of our special education population in regular education settings. . . . We continue to struggle with collaborative decision making, improvement in data management, and refinement of methods of assessment of student progress. Teachers use CWPT for reading and spelling in both literature and content settings. I have applauded [Juniper Gardens'] focus on academically engaged time and the pragmatic approaches suggested for increasing that. The results indicated that those strategies have merit. *(comments of an elementary school principal)*

Peer-Assisted Learning Strategies (PALS)

Developed in the early 1990s, PALS was an effort to provide general education teachers an effective, feasible, and acceptable intervention for the entire class in which students with LD were included. In a series of studies, Fuchs, Fuchs, and Bishop (1992a, 1992b), Fuchs, Fuchs, Hamlett, Phillips, & Bentz (1994), and Fuchs, Fuchs, Hamlett, Phillips, and Karns (1995) observed that general education teachers made fewer adaptations in their instruction to address the special needs of students with LD. This was the case even after teachers had been provided frequent information on the progress or lack of progress of individual students. To address the need for general educators to provide instruction across different types of learners, these authors recommended that general educators use curriculum-based measurement (CBM) within the context of classwide peer tutoring structures to differentiate instruction for students with LD.

PALS is built around CWPT, but it includes a number of different learning strategies and, in some cases, it is linked to computerized CBM (Fuchs, Fuchs, Phillips, & Karns, 1994). Thus, like CWPT, it joins PMII ingredients with the exception of peer networking to specific instructional tasks and strategies. PALS math, for example, provides teachers with group and individual reports on students' learning of specific math skills using classwide CBM. This enables teachers to gear instruction to the group as well as the needs of specific students. In the absence of CBM, teachers gear instruction to ability level groups of students and limited information is available for other students with diverse needs. PALS math instruction sessions last 40 minutes and may be implemented at least twice a week. The computer program identifies pairs of students (one who knows the skills and one who does not) to work together. This creates 13 to 15 unique pairings capable of working together all at the same time on individually tailored learning tasks instead of a single, whole-class, teacher-directed activity that may address the instructional needs of only a few students. PALS math tutoring is reciprocal, like CWPT, with each student in the role as a "player" and a "coach" during the session. The strongest student is identified as a coach first in the session, and the lower-performing student is identified as a player. Student pairings are changed every two weeks.

PALS math consists of skill coaching followed by practice. During coaching, the player solves a sheet of assigned problems. The coach guides the players responding by presenting a series of questions read from a prompt card. The questions break down the problem into its component parts (e.g., "Look at the sign, What kind of problem is it?"). The coach corrects responses and awards points much like CWPT. Midway through the sheet, they trade roles and continue. Practice follows after 15–20 minutes of coach. During practice, each student completes a problem sheet that contains easier problems combined with the problem type just coached. After 10–15 minutes, students exchange papers and correct the answers. The pair of students with the highest point total wins applause and the opportunity to collect the PALS folder, ending the session.

PALS reading is designed to be implemented three times per week during 35-minute sessions. Sessions are divided classwide activities that include: (a) partner reading, (b) paragraph shrinking, (c) prediction relays for 10 minutes each, and (d) a 2-minute story retelling after partner reading. The remaining few minutes are devoted to clean-up and transitional activities. Like PALS math, partners are formed to include high-performing and low-performing readers (heterogeneous pairs). From a ranking of students on reading ability, the strongest readers are assigned to tutor low-performing students.

Textbook materials are used during reading, and teachers may individualize reading materials for each pair, with a specific emphasis on the needs of the weaker reader. Like CWPT, both students read the assigned material. Both PALS and CWPT are designed to work with existing reading materials and approaches (e.g., phonics, whole language, or integrated reading methods).

During *Partner Reading/Story Retell*, the strongest student reads first (as a model) for 4 minutes; the lower-performing student reads the same material for 4 minutes; and then the lower-performing student sequences major events for 1–2 minutes. During *Paragraph Shrinking*, the higher-performing student resumes reading new text and stops after each paragraph to summarize the material for the next 4 minutes. The lower-performing student continues with new material and summarizes each paragraph. Prompt cards are used to direct readers to answer comprehension questions (e.g., who, what, where, when and why) in 10 or fewer words. During *Prediction Relay*, students continue reading new textbook material with the stronger student reading aloud for 5 minutes and stopping after each page to summarize information and make a prediction about what will happen next. The lower-performing student follows same procedure over next 5 minutes. Students earn points from the coaches for reading each sentence correctly, for summarizing what they read, for making reasonable predictions, and for working cooperatively with their partner.

As was the case for CWPT, research on the effectiveness of PALS provides convincing support for its superiority compared to conventional general education instruction in reading and math. Results indicated that all students with and without LD made measurably greater progress on test scores in the same amount of time. Teachers and students both reported high levels of satisfaction with PALS instruction (Mathes, Fuchs, Fuchs, Henley, & Sanders, 1994). In addition, these authors reported that students with LD were better liked, made friends, and were better known by peers during PALS instruction than in conventional teacher-led instruction. PALS reading and math also have won approval by the Program Effectiveness Panel, National Diffusion Network, and U.S. Department of Education.

Classwide Student Tutoring Teams (CSTT)

CSTT, a variation of CWPT, is designed for content-area classroom instruction at the secondary level (Maheady, Harper, Sacca, & Mallette, 1991). It has been used as a means of improving students' mastery of skills and concepts the teacher has previously introduced. The mastery of basic subject matter skills allows the teacher more time to focus on teaching higher-order skills. Developed during the late 1980s (Maheady, Sacca, & Harper, 1988), CSTT combined PMII ingredients (e.g., peer-teaching procedures of CWPT) with specific facets of the Teams-Games-Tournaments (TGT) program developed by Slavin and colleagues at John Hopkins University (DeVries & Slavin, 1978; Harper, Mallette, Maheady, & Brennan, 1993; Slavin, 1990).

As noted in the CSTT instructor's manual, a major antecedent requirement of CSTT is the development of study guides for the student teams (Maheady, Harper, & Mallette, 1991). This involves identifying important units of instruction that correspond to the subject matter to be taught during the week. Each study guide consists of questions that elicit student responses of practice, recall, and application and that reflect content instructional goals. Short exams then are developed and given as pre-post indicators of unit learning outcomes. It also is recommended that CSTT be used in the context of clear classroom behavior rules and that students be fully taught how to work and fulfill the roles of a CSTT team member. This peer-mediated intervention incorporates content-related discussions and review to support instruction in mathematics, social studies, science, and history.

The success of CSTT can be attributed to the use of study guides as a review strategy for subject matter introduced previously. The peer teachers in each team use study guides to focus student attention and eliminate the guesswork about what must be learned (Harper, Maheady, & Mallette, 1994). Thus, in contrast to CWPT and PALS, CSTT uses (a) three to five heterogeneous learning teams consisting of at least one high-, one average-, and one low-performing student to increase the probability and accuracy of peer teaching, help, and correction; and (b) teacher-developed study guides that identify the most important or relevant ideas, concepts, principles, or facts contained in each unit of instruction. The combination of these components seems to make CSTT effective, as well as interesting, to secondary-level teachers and older students.

In most academic environments, CSTT is relatively easy to implement. CSTT should be used after the instructional material has been presented and students have had the opportunity to discuss the content. CSTT may be incorporated into a teacher's instructional program twice a week with 30 minutes per session (Harper, Mallette, Maheady, & Brennan, 1993; Harper, Maheady, & Mallette, 1994; Maheady, Harper, Mallette, & Winstanley, 1991).

During a CSTT session, each team is given a folder containing a study guide for the week, paper and pencils, and a small deck of cards. The cards are numbered in correspondence to items in the study guide. Students rotate taking turns as the teacher. The teacher draws a card from the deck of cards and reads the corresponding item to the teams (e.g., "What does empiricism mean?"). Each student writes his or her answer. The peer teacher then checks each teammate's response against the answer guide, awarding 5 points if correct or supplying the correct answer if in error. A student may receive 2 points if he or she corrects the error and successfully writes the correct response three times. When all answers have been corrected, the study guide is passed to the next student to the left and the top card is selected, thereby designating the next study question for the group's tutor to read. The team continues working. If time remains after completing 30 items, they reshuffle the deck and continue the activity to earn additional points.

Like CWPT and PALS, the teacher's role in CSTT is one of (a) monitoring team teaching and (b) awarding bonus points for teaching steps, good manners, and constructive, supporting comments between and among team members. The teacher times the sessions, answers questions, collects team points, and posts winning point totals on the board. The noncompetitive reward system in CSTT ensures that (a) all teams that meet a minimum standard are recognized by the teacher, (b) the most improved team is recognized, and (c) the most outstanding team members are recognized.

In a series of research studies, Maheady, Sacca, and Harper (1988) demonstrated the effectiveness of CSTT compared to teacher-mediated procedures. In one study, these authors compared the effects of CSTT and teacher-led instruction on the math performance of six classes of low-achieving ninth- and tenth-grade pupils enrolled in a special district program for potential dropouts. These mainstreamed classrooms contained 28 students with mild disabilities and 63 typical peers.

During CSTT instruction, the students' weekly math quiz scores increased by approximately 20 per cent age points. The academic gains of the students with mild disabilities closely paralleled those of their typical peers. Students with and without disabilities were able to identify important content material and become better listeners. The students reported that they developed new friends and had more self-esteem.

Reciprocal Peer Tutoring (RPT)

Developed in the late 1980s, RPT has been used as a pull-out program for serving low-achieving, high-risk students in urban elementary schools. RPT has compiled an impressive record of measurably superior results in the math achievement of students who typically tested between the 20th and 50th percentiles. RTP also was designed to take advantage of PMII components including peer teaching and the interdependence of pairs of learners produced by group reward systems. In RTP, as in CWPT, PALS, and CSTT, students serve as both teachers and students during tutoring sessions, and they follow a structured format of interacting with each other. Like PALS math, in RPT an initial 20-minute session reciprocal coaching period is followed by a 7-minute worksheet-testing session. Peers select rewards and performance goals from a list prepared by the teacher. Peers monitor and evaluate their own performance (Fantuzzo, King, & Heller, 1992). Students are paired randomly in same-age dyads.

The students' responding in RPT is structured by four standard response opportunities for each problem (Try 1, Try 2, Help, and Try 3) (Fantuzzo, Davis, & Ginsburg, 1995). The peer teacher presents the student a problem to solve using a flashcard with the answer on the back. The student computes the problem in writing on a structured worksheet similar to that used in CWPT math/spelling. If the first try is correct, the teacher praises the student and presents the next problem. If incorrect, the peer teacher provides structured help (as described on the answer side of the flashcard) and coaching. The student then attempts the problem at Try 2. If still wrong, the teacher aide is called to coach the student in the correct-solution model, followed by a final effort by the student to solve it (i.e., Help). The student is provided an additional opportunity to solve the problem independently in Try 3. Following 10 minutes of RPT, the pair switches roles and continues for another 10 minutes. Last, as an assessment of learning, 20 minutes of RPT is followed by a 16-problem quiz covering the material taught. Following this session, the individual accomplishments of each student are combined and compared to the student's predetermined goal. If the student exceeds that goal, he or she scores a "win" for the day. After five "wins," the pair is permitted to obtain the previously selected reward.

Early controlled evaluations of RPT have demonstrated significant academic gains in achievement, better social interactions, and less disruptive behavior (Pigott,

Fantuzzo, & Clement, 1986). Subsequent replications and applications also indicated significantly improved math achievement with RPT students for low-income minority and non-minority groups in urban schools (Fantuzzo, Polite, & Grayson, 1990). In an investigation of the component procedures of RPT, Fantuzzo, King, & Heller (1992) reported that students did best when the RPT program combined structured peer tutoring with the group reward components. The structured peer tutoring component provided tutors training in the use of a script defining their instructional interactions with each other. The group reward component provided students rewards contingent on the combined average performance of each partner pair rather than their individual performance. Students significantly increased their academic gains compared to students in structure only, group reward only, and no structure and no reward comparison groups.

These findings confirmed the importance of using an explicit, well designed peer teaching procedure (script) and not relying on the tutor's own unique method of teaching (Fuchs, 1996; Fuchs, Fuchs, Bentz, Phillips, & Hamlett, 1994). And, by creating interdependence through the group reward system, it has been shown to make an important contribution to the overall effects of RPT in terms of increasing the concern, help, and support of the partner's progress during tutoring.

Recent studies have combined RPT at school with parent involvement at home. Heller and Fantuzzo (1993) and Fantuzzo, Davis, and Ginsburg (1995) reported that superior mathematics results on CBMs and standardized achievement tests were obtained by a group of African-American 4th- and 5th-grade students receiving both components compared to either one or a no-treatment control. Students receiving RPT rated themselves as more socially confident with peers than did students in the control group. Students and teachers in the RPT conditions rated their experiences highly.

Implications and Conclusions

PMII components, when applied to the design of general education instruction, provide a major assist in terms of better managing group and individual student teaching and learning. For example, high teacher-pupil ratio has remained a major roadblock to individualization of general education instruction and its effectiveness for students with diverse needs. Peer tutoring formats and peer initiation training offer efficient alternatives for providing one-on-one instruction/intervention for specific time periods or for individualization.

The workload involved in managing general education instruction also has been a problem, hindering its effectiveness. Peer monitoring provides an efficient and effective method of correcting and providing feedback to students and of managing the paperwork involved in general education instruction. The extra time and planning needed to devote to developing children's social skills traditionally has been a problem in making general education more effective. Peer modeling, peer tutoring, and group-oriented contingencies are powerful strategies for supporting social skills instruction that do not need extra time or work during regular instructional times, and that have academic as well as social benefits. The difficulty in individualizing and adapting instruction to all students' needs has been a barrier to instructing students with special needs in the general education classroom. PMII components provide support that enables individualization and adaption commensurate with the needs of many students at-risk and with specific disabilities.

PMII components, when added to intervention in the general education classrooms, are effective for students with special needs. Research evidence also suggests that, perhaps more than previously thought possible, students without disabilities also benefit academically and socially in ways unique to utilization of PMII in both general and special education classrooms. Thus, we believe PMII components have and will continue to have important implications for improving the responsiveness and effectiveness of general education for all students.

Systems of instruction and intervention demonstrate the successful use of PMII components. PMII components have been integrated with other educational technologies, such as classwide CBM and effective teaching strategies, to form instructional systems that teachers and students say they prefer over traditional, teacher-mediated instruction. CWPT, PALS, CSTT, and RPT are increasingly sophisticated instructional systems, based on multiple studies and evaluations of over a decade of work, designed to overcome barriers, individualize instruction, and improve academic and social outcomes of students with disabilities in general education classrooms.

References

Agran, M., Fodor-Davis, J., Moore, C., & Martella, R. C. (1992). Effects of peer-delivered self-instructional training on a lunch-making work task for students with severe disabilities. *Education & Training in Mental Retardation, 27*(3), pp. 230–240.

Alexander, R. N., Corbett, T. F., & Smigel, J. (1976). The effects of individual and group sequences on school attendance and curfew violations. *Journal of Applied Behavior Analysis, 9*, 221–226.

Antia, S. (1994). Strategies to develop peer interaction in young hearing-impaired children. *Volta Review, 96*, 277–290.

Apolloni, T., Cooke, S. A., & Cooke, T. P. (1977). Establishing a normal peer as a behavioral model for developmentally delayed children. *Perceptual & Motor Skills, 44*, 231–241.

Balenzano, S., Agte, L. J., McLaughlin, T. F., & Howard, V. F. (1993). Training tutoring skills with preschool children with disabilities in a classroom setting. *Child & Family Behavior Therapy, 15*(1), 1–36.

Bandura, A. (1968). Social-learning theory of identificatory processes. In D. A. Goslin (Ed.), *Handbook of socialization theory and research.* Chicago: Rand McNally.

Barbetta, P. M., Miller, A. D., Peters, M. T., Heron, T. E., & Cochran, L. L. (1991). Tugmate: A cross-age tutoring program to teach sight vocabulary. *Education & Treatment of Children, 14*, 19–37.

Beirne-Smith, M. (1991). Peer tutoring in arithmetic for children with learning disabilities. *Exceptional Children, 57*, pp. 330–337.

Bell, K., Young, K. R., Blair, M., & Nelson, R. (1990). Facilitating mainstreaming of students with behavioral disorders using classwide peer tutoring. *School Psychology Review, 19*, 564–573.

Brady, M. P., Shores, R. E., Gunter, P., McEvoy, M. A., Fox, J. J., & White, C. (1984). Generalization of an adolescent's social interaction behavior via multiple peers in a classroom. *Journal of the Association for Persons with Severe Handicaps, 9*, 278–286.

Block, M. E., Oberweiser, B., & Bain, M. (1995). Using classwide peer tutoring to facilitate inclusion of students with disabilities in regular physical education. *Physical Educator, 52*(1), 47–56.

Brophy, J. E. (1979). Teacher behavior and its effects. *Journal of Educational Psychology, 71*, 733–750.

Byrd, D. E. (1990). Peer tutoring with the learning disabled: A critical review. *Journal of Education Research, 82*(2), 115–118.

Campbell, B. J., Brady, M. P., & Linehan, S. (1991). Effects of peer-mediated instruction on the acquisition and generalization of written capitalization skills. *Journal of Learning Disabilities, 24*(1), 6–14.

Carden-Smith, L. K., & Fowler, S. A. (1984). Positive peer pressure: The effects of peer monitoring on children's disruptive behavior. *Journal of Applied Behavior Analysis, 17*, 213–227.

Chadsey-Rusch, J. (1986). Identifying and teaching valued social behaviors in competitive employment settings. In F. R. Rusch (Ed.), *Competitive employment issues and strategies* (pp. 273–287). Baltimore: Paul H. Brookes.

Clark, L. A., & McKenzie, H. S. (1989). Effects of self–evaluation training of seriously emotionally disturbed children on the generalization of their classroom rule following and work behaviors across settings and teachers. *Behavioral Disorders, 14*, 89–98.

Cole, D. A., Vandercook, T., & Rynders, J. (1988). Comparison of two peer interaction programs: Children with and without severe disabilities. *American Educational Research Journal, 25*, 415–439.

Cooke, N. L., Heron, T. E., Heward, W. L., & Test, D. W. (1982). Integrating a Down's syndrome child in a classwide peer tutoring system. A case report. *Mental Retardation, 20*(1), 22–25.

Csapo, M. (1976). If you don't know it, teach it! *Clearinghouse, 12*(49), 365–367.

Cullinan, D., Sabornie, E. J., & Crossland, C. L. (1992). Social mainstreaming of mildly handicapped students. *Elementary School Journal, 92*, 339–351.

Day, R., Powell, T., & Dy-Lin, T. (1982). An evaluation of the effects of a social interaction training package on mentally handicapped preschool children. *Education & Training of the Mentally Retarded, 17*, 125–130.

DeVries, D. L., & Slavin, R. E., (1978). Teams-games-tournaments (TGT): Review of ten classroom experiments. *Journal of Research & Development in Education, 12*, 28–38.

Delquadri, J., Greenwood, C. R., Stretton, K., & Hall, R. V. (1983). The peer tutoring game: A classroom procedure for increasing opportunity to respond and spelling performance. *Education and Treatment of Children, 6*, 225–239.

Deterline, W. C. (1970). *Training and management of students tutors*. (Final Report). Palo Alto, CA: General Programmed Teaching. (ERIC Doc. Rep. No. ED 048-133).

Devoney, C., Guralnick, M. J., & Rubin, M. (1974). Integrating handicapped and nonhandicapped preschool children: Effects on social play. *Childhood Education, 50*, 360–364.

DuPaul, G. J., & Henningson, P. N. (1993). Peer tutoring effects on the classroom performance of children with attention deficit hyperactivity disorder. *School psychology Review, 22*(1), 134–143.

Eiserman, W. D., Shisler, L., & Osguthorpe, R. T. (1987). Handicapped students as tutors: A description and integration of three years of research findings. B. C. *Journal of Special Education, 2*(3), 215–231.

Elliott, S. N., & Gresham, F. M. (1993). Social skills interventions for children. *Behavior Modification, 17*, 287–313.

Fantuzzo, J. W., Davis, G. Y., & Ginsburg, M. D. (1995). Effects of parent involvement in isolation or in combination with peer tutoring on student concept and mathematics achievement. *Journal of Educational Psychology, 87*, 272–281.

Fantuzzo, J. W., Jurecic, L., Stovall, A., Hightower, A. D., Goins, C., & Schachtel, D. (1988). Using multiple peer exemplars to develop generalized social responding of a autistic girl. In. R. B. Rutherford & C. M. Nelson (Eds.), *Monograph in severe behavior disorders of children and youth* (Vol. 7, pp. 17–26). Reston, VA: Council for Children with Behavioral Disorders.

Fantuzzo, J. W., King, J. A., & Heller, L. R. (1992). Effects of reciprocal peer tutoring on mathematics and school adjustment: A component analysis. *Journal of Educational Psychology, 84*, 331–339.

Fantuzzo, J. W., Polite, K., & Grayson, N. (1990). An evaluation of school-based reciprocal peer tutoring across elementary school settings. *Journal of School Psychology, 28*, 309–324.

Farmer, T. W., & Cairns, R. (1991). Social networks and social status in emotionally disturbed children. *Behavioral Disorders, 16,* 288–298.

Fenrick, N. J., & Petersen, T. K. (1984). Developing positive changes in attitudes towards moderately/severely handicapped students through a peer tutoring program. *Education & Training of the Mentally Retarded, 19*(2), 83–90.

Field, T. (1984). Early peer relations. In P. S. Strain (Ed.), *The utilization of classroom peers as behavior change agents* (pp. 1–30). New York: Plenum Press.

Fiore, T. A., & Becker, E. A. (1994). *Promising classroom interventions for students with attention deficit disorders*. Research Triangle Park, NC: Center for Research in Education, Research Triangle Institute.

Folio, M. R., & Norman, A. (1981). Toward more success in mainstreaming: A peer teacher approach to physical education. *Teaching Exceptional Children, 13*(3), 110–114.

Foot, H. C., Shute, R. H., Morgan M. J., & Barron, A. M. (1990). Theoretical issues in peer tutoring. In H. C. Morgan, M. J. Shute, & R. H. Shute (Eds.), *Children helping children.* (pp. 65–92). New York: John Wiley & Sons.

Fowler, S. A. (1986). Peer-monitoring and self-monitoring: Alternatives to traditional teacher management. *Exceptional Children, 52*, 573–583.

Franca, V. M. (1983). Peer tutoring among behaviorally disordered students: Academic and social benefits to tutor and tutee. *Dissertation Abstracts International, 44*, 459-A.

Franca, V. M., Kerr, M. M., Reitz, A. L., & Lambert, D. (1990). Peer tutoring among behaviorally disordered students: Academic and social benefits to tutor and tutee. *Education & Treatment of Children, 13*(2), 109–128.

Fuchs, L. S. (1996). Models of classroom instruction: Implications for children with learning disabilities. In D. L. Speece & B. K. Keogh (Eds.), *Research on classroom ecologies: Implications for inclusion of children with learning disabilities* (pp. 81–90). Mahwah, NJ: Lawrence Erlbaum.

Fuchs, L. S. Fuchs, D., Bentz, J., Phillips, N. B., & Hamlett, C. L. (1994). The nature of student interactions during peer tutoring with and without training and experience. *American Educational Research Journal, 31*, 75–103.

Fuchs, L. S., Fuchs, D., & Bishop, N. (1992a). Instructional adaptation for students at risk for academic failure. *Journal of Education Research, 86*, 70–84.

Fuchs, L. S., Fuchs, D., & Bishop, N. (1992b). Teacher planning for students with learning disabilities: Differences between general and special educators. *Learning Disabilities Research & Practice, 7*, 120–129.

Fuchs, L. S., Fuchs, D., Hamlett, C. L., Phillips, N., & Bentz, J. (1994). Classwide curriculum-based measurement: Helping general educators meet the challenge of student diversity. *Exceptional Children, 60*, 518–537.

Fuchs, L. S., Fuchs, D., Hamlett, C. L., Phillips, N., & Bentz, J. (1995). General educators' specialized adaptation for students with disabilities. *Exceptional Children, 61*, 440–459.

Fuchs, L. S., Fuchs, D., Phillips, N., & Karns, K. (1994). *Peer-mediated mathematics instruction: A manual*. Nashville, TN: Pea body College of Vanderbilt University.

Furman, W., Rahe, D., & Hartup, W. (1979). Rehabilitation of socially withdrawn preschool children through mixed-age and same-age socialization. *Child Development, 50*, 915–922.

Gable, R. A., Arllen, N. L., & Hendrickson, J. M. (1994). Use of students with emotional/behavioral disorders as behavior change agents. *Education & Treatment of Children, 17*(3), 267–276.

Garrison-Harrell, L. (1996). *Utilization of a peer network strategy to teach social-communicative skills to elementary-age students with autism in a public school setting*. Unpublished doctoral dissertation, University of Kansas, Lawrence.

Gartner, A., Kohler, M. C., & Reissman, F. (1971). *Children teach children: Learning by teaching*. New York: Harper & Row.

Gerber, M., & Kauffman, J. M. (1981). Peer tutoring in academic settings. In P. S. Strain (Ed.), *The utilization of classroom peers as behavior change agents* (pp. 155–188). New York: Plenum Press.

Goetz, E. M., Ayala, J. M., Hatfield, V. L., Marshall, A. M., & Etzel, B. C. (1983). Training independence in preschoolers with an auditory stimulus management technique. *Education & Treatment of Children, 6,* 251–261.

Goldstein, H., & Ferrell, D. (1987). Augmenting communicative interaction between handicapped and nonhandicapped preschool children. *Journal of Speech & Hearing Disorders, 52,* 200–211.

Goldstein, H., Kaczmarek, L., Pennington, R., & Shafer, K. (1992). Peer-mediated intervention: Attending to, commenting on, and acknowledging the behavior of preschoolers with autism. *Journal of Applied Behavior Analysis, 25,* 289–305.

Goldstein, H., & Wickstrom, S. (1986). Peer intervention effects of communicative interaction among handicapped and nonhandicapped preschoolers. *Journal of Applied Behavior Analysis, 199,* 209–214.

Goodlad, J. I., & Lovitt, T. C. (1993). *Integrating general and special education.* New York: Merrill.

Goodman, L. (1990). *Time and learning in the special education classroom.* Albany, NY: SUNY Press.

Gordon, J., Vaughn, S., & Schumm, J. S. (1993). Spelling interventions: A review of literature and implications for instruction for students with learning disabilities. *Learning Disabilities Research & Practice, 8*(3), 175–181.

Greenwood, C. R. (1991a). Classwide peer tutoring: Longitudinal effects on the reading, language, and mathematics achievement of at-risk students. *Journal of Reading, Writing, and Learning Disabilities International, 7*(2), 105–123.

Greenwood, C. R. (1991b). Longitudinal analysis of time, engagement, and achievement of at-risk versus non-risk students. *Exceptional Children, 57*(6), 521–532.

Greenwood, C. R. (1996). Research on the practices and behavior of effective teachers at the Juniper Gardens Children's Project: Implication for the education of diverse learners. In D. L. Speece & B. K. Keogh (Eds.), *Research on classroom ecologies: Implications for inclusion of children with learning disabilities* (pp. 39–67). Mahwah, NJ: Lawrence Erlbaum.

Greenwood, C. R., Carta, J. J., & Hall, R. V. (1988). The use of peer tutoring strategies in classroom management and educational instruction. *School Psychology Review, 17,* 258–275.

Greenwood, C. R. Carta, J. J., & Kamps, D. (1990). Teacher-mediated versus peer-mediated instruction: A review of educational advantages and disadvantages. In H. C. Foot, M. J. Morgan, & R. H. Shute (Eds.), *Children helping children.* New York: John Wiley & Sons.

Greenwood, C. R., Carta, J. J., Walker, D., Arreaga-Mayer, C., & Dinwiddie, G. (1988). Peer tutoring: Special education. In T. Husen & T. N. Postlethwaite (Eds.), *The international encyclopedia of education: Research and studies* (Supplementary Vol. 1) (pp. 1–9). New York: Pergamon Press.

Greenwood, C. R., & Delquadri, J. (1995). ClassWide peer tutoring and the prevention of school failure. *Preventing School Failure, 39*(4), 21–25.

Greenwood, C. R., & Delquadri, J. C., & Hall, R. V. (1984). Opportunity to respond and student academic performance. In W. L. Heward, T. E. Heron, J. Trap-Porter, & D. S. Hill (Eds.), *Focus on behavior analysis in education* (pp. 58–88). Columbus, OH: Charles Merrill.

Greenwood, C. R., & Delquadri, J. C., & Hall, R. V. (1989). Longitudinal effects of Classwide peer tutoring. *Journal of Educational Psychology, 81,* 371–383.

Greenwood, C. R., Delquadri, J., & Carta, J. J. (in press). *ClassWide Peer Tutoring (CWPT) for teachers.* Longmont, CO: Sopris West.

Greenwood, C. R., Dinwiddie, G., Bailey, V., Carta, J. J., Dorsey, D., Kohler, F. W., Nelson, C., Rotholtz, D., & Schulte, D. (1987). Field replication of Classwide peer tutoring. *Journal of Applied Behavior Analysis, 20,* 151–160.

Greenwood, C. R., Dinwiddie, G., Terry, B., Wade, L., Stanley, S., Thibadeau, S., & Delquadri, J. (1984). Teacher-versus peer-mediated instruction: An eco-behavioral analysis of achievement outcomes. *Journal of Applied Behavior Analysis, 17,* 521–538.

Greenwood, C. R., & Hops, H. (1981). Group-oriented contingencies and peer behavior change. In P. S. Strain, *The utilization of classroom peers as behavior change agents* (pp. 189–259). New York: Plenum Press.

Greenwood, C. R., Hops, H., Walker, H., Guild, J., Stokes, J., Young, K. R., Keleman, K., & Willardson, M. (1979). Standardized classroom management program: Social validation and replication studies in Utah and Oregon. *Journal of Applied Behavior Analysis, 12,* 235–253.

Greenwood, C. R., Sloane, H. N., & Baskin, A. (1974). Training elementary-aged peer behavior managers to control small group programmed mathematics. *Journal of Applied Behavior Analysis, 1,* 1–12.

Greenwood, C. R., Terry, B., Delquadri, J., Elliott, M., & Arreaga-Mayer, C. (1995). *ClassWide Peer Tutoring (CWPT): Effective teaching and research review.* Kansas City, KS: Juniper Gardens Children's Project.

Greenwood, C. R., Terry, B., Utley, C. A. Montagna, D., & Walker, D. (1993). Achievement, placement, and services: Middle school benefits of Classwide peer tutoring used at the elementary school. *School Psychology Review, 22*(3), 497–516.

Guralnick, M. J. (1976). The value of integrating handicapped and nonhandicapped preschool children. *American Journal of Orthopsychiatry, 42,* 236–245.

Haisley, F. B., Tell, C. A., & Andrews, J. (1981). Peers as tutors in the mainstream: Trained "teachers" of handicapped adolescents. *Journal of Learning Disabilities, 14,* 224–226.

Handlan, S., & Bloom, L. A. (1993). The effects of educational curricula and modeling/coaching on the interactions of kindergarten children with their peers with autism. *Focus on Autistic Behavior, 8,* 1–11.

Haring, T. G., & Breen, C. B. (1992). A peer-mediated social network intervention to enhance the social integration of persons with moderate and severe disabilities. *Journal of Applied Behavior Analysis, 25,* 319–333.

Harper, G. F., Maheady, L., & Mallette, B. (1994). The power of peer-mediated instruction: Why and how does it promote success for all students? In J. S. Thousand, R. A. Villa, & A. I. Nevin (Eds.), *Creativity and collaborative learning: A practical guide to empowering students* (pp. 229–241). Baltimore: Paul H. Brookes.

Harper, G. R., Mallette, B., & Maheady, L. (1995, November). *Peer-mediated instruction and multicultural child with mild disabilities.* Paper presented at annual meeting of Hawaii Federation Council for Exceptional Children, Honolulu.

Harper, G. F., Mallette, B., Maheady, L., & Brennan, G. (1993). Class wide student tutoring teams and direct instruction as a combined instructional program to teach generalizable strategies for mathematics word problems. *Education & Treatment of Children, 16,* 115–134.

Harper, G. F., Mallette, B., & Moore, J. (1991). Peer-mediated instruction: Teaching spelling to primary school children with mild disabilities. *Journal of Reading, Writing, & Learning Disabilities International, 7*(3), 137–151.

Harper, G. F., Mallette, B., Maheady, L., Bentley, A. E., & Moore, J. (1995). Retention and treatment failure in Classwide peer tutoring: Implications for further research. *Journal of Behavioral Education, 5*(4), 399–414.

Harper, G. F., Mallette, B., Maheady, L., Parkes, V., & Moore, J. (1993). Retention and generalization of spelling words acquired using a peer-mediated instructional procedure by children with mild handicapping conditions. *Journal of Behavioral Education, 3*(1), 25–38.

Hecimovic, A., Fox, J. J., Shores, R. E., & Strain, P. S. (1985). An analysis of developmentally integrated and segregated freeplay settings and the generalization of newly acquired social behaviors of socially withdrawn preschoolers. *Behavior Assessment, 7,* 367–388.

Heller, L. R., & Fantuzzo, J. W. (1993). Reciprocal peer tutoring and parent partnership: Does parent involvement make a difference? *School Psychology Review, 22,* 517–534.

Heller, K. A., Holtzman, W. H., & Messick, S. (1982). *Placing children in special education: A strategy for equity.* Washington, DC: National Academy Press.

Hogan, S., & Prater, M. A. (1993). The effects of peer tutoring and self-management training on on-task, academic, and disruptive behaviors. *Behavioral Disorders, 18*(2), 118–128.

Hollin, C. R., & Trower, P. (1988). Development and applications of social skills training: A review and critique. In M. Hersen, R. M. Eisler, & P. M. Miller (Eds.), *Progress in behavior modification* (Vol. 22, pp. 165–214). Newbury Park, CA: Sage.

Horner, R., Meyer, L. H., & Fredericks, H. D. (1987). *Education of learners with severe handicaps: Exemplary service strategies.* Baltimore: Paul H. Brookes.

Hughes, C. A., Ruhl, K. L. & Misra, A. (1989). Self-management with behaviorally disordered students in school settings: A promise unfulfilled? *Behavioral Disorders, 14,* 250, 262.

Jakibchuck, A., & Smeriglio, V. L. (1976). The influence of symbolic modeling on the social behavior of preschool children with low levels of social responsiveness. *Child Development, 47*, 838–841.

Jenkins, J. R., & Jenkins, L. M. (1988). Peer tutoring in elementary and secondary programs. *Focus on Exceptional Children, 17*, 10–12.

Kalfus, G. R. (1984). Peer mediated intervention: A critical review. *Child & Family Behavior Therapy, 6*, 17–43.

Kamps, D. M., Barbetta, P. M., Leonard, B. R., & Delquadri, J. (1994). Classwide peer tutoring: An integration strategy to improve and promote peer interactions among students with autism and general education peers. Special section: Behavior analysis in school psychology. *Journal of Applied Behavior Analysis, 27*(1), 49–61.

Kamps, D. M., Leonard, B. R., Vernon, S., Dugan, E. P., & Delquadri J. (1992). Teaching social skills to students with autism to increase peer interactions in an integrated first-grade classroom. *Journal of Applied Behavior Analysis, 25*, 281–288.

Kamps, D. M., Locke, P., Delquadri, J., & Hall, R. V. (1989). Increasing academic skills of student with autism using fifth grade peers as tutors. *Education & Treatment of Children, 12*(1), 38–51.

Kane, B. J., & Alley, G. R. (1980). A peer-tutored, instructional management program in computational mathematics for incarcerated, learning disabled juvenile delinquents. *Journal of Learning Disabilities, 13*, 148–151.

Keller, F. S. (1968). "Good-bye teacher..." *Journal of Applied Behavior Analysis, 1*, 79–89.

King-Sears, M. E., & Bradley, D. F. (1995). ClassWide peer tutoring: Heterogeneous instruction in general education classrooms. *Preventing School Failure, 40*(1), 29–35.

Kohler, F. W., & Greenwood, C. R. (1990). Effects of collateral peer supportive behaviors within the classwide peer tutoring program. *Journal of Applied Behavior Analysis, 23*(3), 307–322.

Kohler, F. W., Schwartz, I. S., Cross, J. A. & Fowler, S. A. (1989). The effects of two alternating peer invention roles on independent work skills. *Education & Treatment of Children, 12*(3), 205–218.

Kohler, F. W., Strain, P. S., Hoyson, M., Davis, L., Donina, W. M., & Rapp, N. (1995). Using a group-oriented contingency to increase social interactions between children with autism and their peers. *Behavior Modification, 19*(1), 10–32.

Kohler, F. W., Strain, P. S., Maretsky, S., & DeCesare, L. (1990). Promoting positive and supportive interactions between preschoolers: An analysis of group-oriented contingencies. *Journal of Early Intervention, 14*(4), 327–341.

Kornhaber, R. C., & Schroeder, H. E. (1975). Importance of model similarity on extinction of avoidance behavior in children. *Journal of Consulting & Clinical Psychology, 43*, 601–607.

Lane, P., Pollack, C., & Sher, N. (1972). Remotivation of disruptive adolescents. *Journal of Reading, 15*, 351–354.

Lazerson, D. B., Foster, H. L., Brown, S. I., & Hummel, J. W. (1988). The effectiveness of cross-age tutoring with truant, junior high students with learning disabilities. *Journal of Learning Disabilities, 21*, 253–255.

LeFebvre, D., & Strain, P. S. (1989). Effects of a group contingency on the frequency of social interactions among autistic and nonhandicapped preschool children: Making LRE efficacious. *Journal of Early Intervention, 13*, 329–341.

Locke, W. R., & Fuchs, L. S. (1995). Effects of peer-mediated reading instruction on the on-task behavior and social interaction of children with behavior disorders. *Journal of Emotional and Behavioral Disorders, 3*, 92–99.

Maheady, L., & Harper, G. (1987). A classwide peer tutoring program to improve the spelling test performance of low-income, third- and fourth-grade students. *Education and Treatment of Children, 10*, 120–133.

Maheady, L., Harper, G. F., & Mallette, B. (1991). Peer-mediated instruction: A review of potential applications for special education. *Reading, Writing, & Learning Disabilities, 7*, 75–103.

Maheady, L., Harper, G., Mallette, B., & Winstanley, N. (1991). Training and implementation requirements associated with the use of a classwide peer tutoring system. *Education & Treatment of Children, 14*, 177–189.

Maheady, L., Harper, G. F., & Sacca, M. K. (1988). Classwide peer tutoring programs in secondary self-contained programs for the mildly handicapped. *Journal of Research & Development in Education, 21*(3), 76–83.

Maheady, L., Harper, G. F., & Sacca, M. K. (1988). Peer-mediated instruction: A promising approach to meeting the diverse needs of LD adolescents. *Learning Disability Quarterly, 11*(2), 108–113.

Maheady, L., Harper, G. F., Sacca, M. K., & Mallette, B. (1991). *Classwide student tutoring teams (CSTT): Instructor's manual.* Fredonia, NY: State University of New York, College at Fredonia.

Maheady, L., Mallette, B., & Harper, G. F. (1991). Accommodating cultural, linguistic, and academic diversity: Some peer-mediated instructional options. *Preventing School Failure, 36*(1), 28–31.

Maheady, L., Sacca, M. K., & Harper, G. F. (1988). The effects of a classwide peer tutoring program on the academic performance of mildly handicapped students enrolled in 10th grade social studies classes. *Exceptional Children, 55,* 52–59

Maher, C. A. (1982). Behavioral effects of using conduct problem adolescents as cross-age tutors. *Psychology in the School, 19,* 360–364.

Maher, C. A. (1984). Handicapped adolescents as cross-age tutors: Program description and evaluation. *Exceptional Children, 51,* 51–63.

Mallette, B., Harper, G. F., Maheady, L., & Dempsy, M. (1991). Retention of spelling words acquired using a peer-mediated instructional strategy. *Education & Training in Mental Retardation,* 156–164.

Marston, D., Deno, S. L., Kim, D., Diment, K., & Rogers, D. (1995). Comparison of reading intervention approaches for students with mild disabilities. *Exceptional Children, 62*(1), 20–37.

Mathes, P. G., & Fuchs, L. S. (1993). Peer-mediated reading instruction in special education resource rooms. *Learning Disability Research & Practice, 8*(4), 233–243.

Mathes, P. G., & Fuchs, L. S. (1994). The efficacy of peer tutoring in reading for students with disabilities: A best-evidence synthesis. *School Psychology Review, 23*(1), 59–80.

Mathes, P. G., Fuchs, D., Fuchs, L. S., Henley, A. M., & Sanders, A. (1994). Increasing strategic reading practice with Peabody classwide peer tutoring. *Learning Disabilities Research & Practice, 9*(1), 44–48.

Mathur, S. R., & Rutherford, R. B. (1991). Peer-mediated interventions promoting social skills of children and youth with behavioral disorders. *Education & Treatment of Children, 14,* 227–242.

Matson, J. L., Fee, V. E., Coe, D. A., & Smith, D. (1991). A social skills program for developmentally delayed preschoolers. *Journal of Clinical Child Psychology, 20,* 428–433.

McCurdy, B. L., & Shapiro, E. S., (1992). A comparison of teacher-, peer, and self-monitoring with curriculum-based measurement in reading among students with learning disabilities. *Journal of Special Education, 26*(2), 162–180.

McEvoy, M. A., & Odom, S. L. (1987). Social interaction training for preschool children with behavioral disorders. *Behavioral Disorders, 12,* 242–251.

McEvoy, M. A., Odom, S. L., & McConnell, S. R. (1992). Peer social competence intervention for young children with disabilities. In S. L. Odom, S. R., McConnell, & M. A. McEvoy (Eds.) , *Social competence of young children with disabilities* (pp. 113–133). Baltimore: Paul H. Brookes.

McHale, S. (1983). Social intervention of autistic and nonhandicapped children during freeplay. *American Journal of Orthopsychiatry, 53,* 81–91.

Miller, A. D., Barbetta, P. M., & Heron, T. E. (1994). START tutoring: Designing, training, implementing, adapting, and evaluating tutoring programs for school and home settings. In W. L. Heward, T. E. Heron, D. S. Hill, & J. Trap-Porter (Eds.), *Focus on behavior analysis in education* (pp. 265–282). Englewood Cliffs, NJ: Merrill/Prentice Hall.

Miller, S. R., Miller, P. M., Armentrout, J. A., & Flannagan, J. W. (1995). Cross-age tutoring: A strategy for promoting self-determination in students with severe emotional disabilities/behavior disorders. *Preventing School Failure, 39*(4), 32–37.

Nelson, J. R., Smith, D. J., & Colvin, G. (1995). The effects of a peer-mediated self-evaluation procedure on the recess behavior of students with behavior problems. *Remedial & Special Education, 16*(2), 117–126.

Niedermeyer, F. C. (1970). Effects of training on the instructional behaviors of student tutors. *Journal of Educational Research, 64,* 119–123.

O'Conner, R. D. (1972). The relative efficacy of modeling, shaping, and the combined procedures for the modification of social withdrawal. *Journal of Abnormal Psychology, 79,* 327–334.

Odom, S., Kohler, F. W., & Strain, P. S. (1987). *Teaching strategies for promoting social interaction skills.* Unpublished manuscript, University of Pittsburgh, Early Childhood Research Institute.

Odom, S. L., & Strain, P. S. (1984). Peer-mediated approaches to promoting children's social interaction: A review. *American Journal of Orthopsychiatry, 54,* 544–557.

Odom, S. L., Hoyson, M., Jamieson, B., & Strain, P. S. (1985). Increasing handicapped preschoolers' peer social interactions: Cross setting and component analysis. *Journal of Applied Behavior Analysis, 18,* 3–16.

Odom, S. L., & Strain, P. S. (1984). Peer-mediated approaches to promoting children's social interaction: A review. *American Journal of Orthopsychiatry, 54,* 544–557.

Odom, S. L., & Strain, P. S. (1986). A comparison of peer initiation and teacher-antecedent interventions for promoting reciprocal social interaction of autistic preschoolers. *Journal of Applied Behavior Analysis, 19,* 59–72.

Odom, S. L., Strain, P. S., Karger, M. A., & Smith, J. D. (1986). Using single and multiple peers to promote social interaction of preschool children with handicaps. *Journal of the Division for Early Childhood, 10,* 53–64.

Osguthorpe, R. T., Eiserman, W. D., & Shisler, L. (1985). Increasing social acceptance: Mentally retarded students tutoring regular class peers. *Education & Training of the Mentally Retarded, 20*(4), 235–240.

Osguthorpe, R. T., & Scruggs, T. E. (1986). Special education students as tutors: A review and analysis. *Remedial & Special Education, 7*(4), 15–26.

Ostrosky, M. M., & Kaiser, A. P. (1995). The effects of a peer-mediated intervention on the social communicative interactions between children with and without special needs. *Journal of Behavioral Education, 5*(2), 151–171.

Piggott, H. E., Fantuzzo, J. W., & Clement, P. (1986). The effects of reciprocal peer tutoring and group contingencies on the academic performance of elementary school children. *Journal of Applied Behavior Analysis, 19,* 93–98.

Polirstok, S. R., & Greer, R. D. (1986). A replication of collateral effects and a component analysis of a successful tutoring package for inner-city adolescents. *Education & Treatment of Children, 9,* 101–121.

Rhode, G., Morgan, D. P., & Young, K. R. (1983). Generalization and maintenance of treatment gains of behaviorally handicapped students from resource rooms to regular classrooms using self-evaluation procedures. *Journal of Applied Behavior Analysis, 16,* 171–187.

Romer, L. T., Busse, D. G., Fewell, R., & Vadasy, P. F. (1985). The relative effectiveness of special education teachers and peer tutors. *Education of the Visually Handicapped, 17*(3), 99–115.

Rucker, C. N., & Vincenzo, F. M. (1970). Maintaining social acceptance gains made by mentally retarded children. *Exceptional Children, 36,* 679–680.

Rusch, F. R., Rose, T., & Greenwood, C. R. (1988). *Introduction to behavior analysis in special education.* Englewood Cliffs, NJ: Prentice Hall.

Sainato, D. M. (1990). Classroom transitions: Organizing environments to promote independent performance in preschool children with disabilities. *Education & Treatment of Children, 13*(4), 288–297.

Sainato, D. M., Strain, P. S., LeFebvre, D., & Rapp, N. (1987). Facilitating transition times with handicapped preschool children: A comparison between peer-mediated and antecedent prompt procedures. *Journal of Applied Behavior Analysis, 20,* 285–291.

Sainato, D. M., Strain, P. S., LeFebvre, D., & Rapp, N. (1990). Effects of self-evaluation on the independent work skills of preschool children. *Exceptional Children, 56,* 540–549.

Salend, S. J. (1994). Effective mainstreaming: Creating inclusive class rooms. New York: Macmillan.

Salend, S. J., Reeder, E., Katz, N., & Russell, T. (1992). The effects of a dependent group-evaluation system. *Education & Treatment of Children, 15*(1), 32–42.

Salend, S. J., Reid-Jantzen, N., & Giek, K. (1992). Using a peer confrontation system in a group setting. *Behavioral Disorders, 13*(3), 211–218.

Salend, S. J., Whittaker, C. R., & Reeder, E. (1992). Group evaluation: A collaborative, peer-mediated behavior management system. *Exceptional Children, 59*(3), 203–209.

Santarsiero, W. A., & Rotatori, A. F. (1994). Cooperative learning, peer tutoring, peer collaboration, and peer support in the REI. In A. F. Rotatori, J. O. Schwenn, & F. W. Litton (Eds.), *Advances in spe-*

cial education: Perspectives on the regular education initiative and transitional programs (Vol. 8, pp. 75–106). Greenwich, CT: JAI Press.

Sasso, G. M., Garrison-Harrell, L., & Rogers, L. (1994). The conceptualization of socialization and autism. In Scruggs, T. E. & Mastroperi, M. A. (Eds.), *Relevant research issues in developmental disabilities* (pp. 161–175). New York: Plenum Press.

Schrader, B., & Valus, V. (1990). Disabled learners as able teachers: A cross-age tutoring project. *Academic Therapy, 25*, 589–597.

Scruggs, T. E., & Osguthorpe, R. T. (1986). Tutoring interventions within special education settings: A comparison of cross-age and peer tutoring. *Psychology in the Schools, 23*, 187–193.

Scruggs, T. E., & Richter, L. (1988). Tutoring learning disabled students: A critical review. *Learning Disability Quarterly, 2,* 274–286.

Shafer, M. S., Engel, A. L., & Neef, N. A. (1984). Training mildly handicapped peers to facilitate changes in the social interaction skills of autistic children. *Journal of Applied Behavior Analysis, 17,* 461–476.

Shisler, L., Osguthorpe, R. T., & Eiserman, W. D. (1987). The effects of reverse-role tutoring on the social acceptance of students with behavioral disorders. *Behavioral Disorders*, 35–44.

Sideridis, G. D. (1995). *Classwide peer tutoring: Effects on the spell ing performance of social interactions of students with mild disabilities and their typical peers in an integrated instructional setting.* Unpublished doctoral dissertation, University of Kansas, Lawrence.

Simmons, D. C., Fuchs, D., Fuchs, L. S., Hodge, J. P., & Mathes, P. G. (1994). Importance of instructional complexity and role reciprocity to classwide peer tutoring. *Learning Disabilities Research & Practice, 9*(4), 203–212.

Sindelar, P. T. (1982). The effects of cross-aged tutoring on the comprehension skills of remedial reading students. *Journal of Special Education, 16*(2), 199–206.

Siperstein, G. N. (1992). Social competence: An important construct in mental retardation. *American Journal on Mental Retardation*, 966, iii–vi.

Slavin, R. E. (1990). *Cooperative learning: Theory, research, and practice.* Englewood Cliffs, NJ: Prentice Hall.

Smith, D. J., Nelson, J. R., Young, K. R., & West, R. P. (1992). The effect of a self-management procedure on the classroom and academic behavior of students with mild handicaps. *School Psychology Review, 21*(1), 59–72.

Smith, D. J., Young, K. R., West, R. P., Morgan, D. P., Rhodes, G. (1988). Reducing the disruptive behavior of junior high students: A classroom self-management procedure. *Behavior Disorders, 13*(4), 231–239.

Stainback, W., & Stainback, S. (1996). *Controversial issues confronting special education: Divergent perspectives.* Needham Heights, MA: Allyn & Bacon.

Storey, K., Smith, D. J., & Strain, P. S. (1993). Use of classroom assistants and peer-mediated interventions to increase integration in preschool settings. *Exceptionality, 4,* 1–16.

Strain, P. (1981). *The utilization of classroom peers as behavior change agents.* New York: Plenum Press.

Strain, P. S., Kerr, M. M., & Ragland, E. U. (1979). Effects of peer-mediated social initiations and prompting/reinforcement procedures on the social behavior of autistic children. *Journal of Autism & Developmental Disorders, 9*, 41–54.

Strain, P. S., & Odom, S. L. (1986). Effective intervention for social skills development of exceptional children. *Exceptional Children, 52*, 543–551.

Strain, P. S., Shores, R. E., & Timm, M. (1977). Effects of peer social initiations on the behavior of withdrawn preschool children. *Journal of Applied Behavior Analysis, 10*, 289–298.

Switzer, E. B., Deal, T. E., & Bailey, J. S. (1977). The reduction of stealing in second graders using a group contingency. *Journal of Applied Behavior Analysis, 10*, 267–272.

Top, B. L., & Osguthorpe, R. T. (1987). Reverse-role tutoring: The effects of handicapped students tutoring regular class students. *Elementary School Journal, 87*(4), 414–423.

Topping, K. (1988). *The peer tutoring handbook: Promoting cooperative learning.* London: Croom Helm.

Twardosz, S., Nordquist, V. M., Simon, R., & Botkin, D. (1983). The effect of group affection activities on the interaction of socially isolated children. *Analysis & Intervention in Developmental Disabilities, 3*, 311–338.

Vacc, N. N., & Cannon, S. J. (1991). Cross-age tutoring in mathematics: Sixth graders helping students who are moderately handicapped. *Education & Training of the Mentally Retarded, 26,* 89–97.

Vaughn, S., & Lancelotta, G. X. (1990). Teaching interpersonal social skills to poorly accepted students: Peer-pairing versus non-peer-pairing. *Journal of School Psychology, 28*, 181–188.

Wagner, L. (1990). Social and historical perspectives on peer teaching in education. In H. C. Foot, M. J. Morgan, & R. H. Shute (Eds.), *Children helping children* (pp. 21–42). New York: John Wiley & Sons.

Whorton, D., Locke, P., Delquadri, J., & Hall, R. V. (1989). Increasing academic skills of students with autism using fifth grade peers as tutors. *Education & Treatment of Children, 12*, 38–51.

Yasutake, D., Bryan, T., & Dohrn, E. (1996). The effects of combining peer tutoring and attribution training on students' perceived self-competence. *Remedial & Special Education, 17*(2), 83–91.

Young, C. C. (1981). Children as instructional agents for handicapped peers: A review and analysis. In P. S. Strain (Ed.), *The utilization of classroom peers as behavior change agents* (pp. 305–326) New York: Plenum Press.

Ysseldyke, J. E., Algozzine, B., & Thurlow, M. L. (1992). *Critical issues in special education.* Boston: Houghton Mifflin.

16

Secondary Inclusion Programs for Students with Mild Disabilities

CASSANDRA McCRORY COLE
AND JAMES McLESKEY

REALIZING THAT MOST of the practices and programs described in the literature have been directed at elementary inclusion, these authors decided to develop a program of inclusion for secondary-level students. Cole and McLeskey preface their discussion by addressing the difficulty of the task at the high school level. Then they describe how they overcame those obstacles. They also give numerous examples of how their program has worked in specific situations for students and teachers.

The movement toward more inclusive school programs has resulted in increasing numbers of students with mild disabilities (learning disabilities, mild mental retardation, and behavior disorders) who are educated in general education classroom settings (Espin & Foegen, 1996; Guterman, 1995; Scanlon, Deshler, & Schumaker, 1996; Smith, Polloway, Patton, & Dowdy, 1995). Although the effectiveness of inclusive school programs has remained controversial (Fuchs & Fuchs, 1994; McLeskey & Waldron, 1995; Zigmond et al., 1995), the movement toward these programs seems to be continuing unabated.

Until recently, much of the emphasis in the professional literature regarding inclusion focused on programs in elementary schools. Many of the efficacy studies that have been used to support inclusion have been conducted in elementary schools, and the model programs that have been described have primarily been elementary programs (Affleck, Madge, Adams, & Lowenbraun, 1988; Banerji & Dailey, 1995; Bear & Proctor, 1990; Zigmond, et al., 1995). Indeed, it seems likely that many more inclusion programs have been developed in elementary schools, and secondary schools have been much slower in moving toward developing and implementing these programs.

Barriers to Development of Secondary Inclusive School Programs

Many possible reasons exist as to why inclusive programs have developed more slowly at the secondary level when compared to elementary schools. These barriers to program development likely have contributed to the perceived resistance toward inclusive programs on the part of teachers and administrators in secondary schools. These barriers include the following:

1. At the secondary level, teachers emphasize complex curricular material; at the elementary level they teach basic academic and social skills.
2. There is a larger gap between the skill level of students and classroom demands at the secondary level. Students with disabilities at the secondary level lack the basic academic skills, as well as learning skills/strategies necessary for success (Rieth & Polsgrove, 1994; Schumaker & Deshler, 1988; Zigmond, 1990).
3. The secondary level has a much broader range of curricular content than the elementary level does. Not only are secondary schools responsible for curricular content such as mathematics across a range of skill levels, but they also must provide instruction related to careers/vocations, functional living skills, survival skills, transition from high school to a variety of settings, and so forth.
4. Secondary classrooms tend to be teacher-centered, in which instruction is most often didactic, directed to large groups, and infrequently differentiated for varying student needs. This results in teachers spending small amounts of time with large numbers of students each day, and limited contact with any single student (Schumaker & Deshler, 1988).
5. Teachers at the secondary level are trained as content specialists. Some cannot or are not inclined to make adaptations for students with disabilities who do not master the curricular content. In addition, teachers may be frustrated by the limited, slow progress that students with disabilities make in their classes (Smith, Polloway, Patton, & Dowdy, 1995).
6. Students are going through a complex, sometimes frustrating personal transition through adolescence, which affects their emotional, social, sexual, physical, and academic development (Mercer & Mercer, 1993). Even under the best of circumstances, academics tend not to be the primary interest of many of these students.
7. The pressure from outside agencies is greater in secondary schools. Accountability on the secondary school for providing students with certain skills and knowledge is demanded from businesses, state governments, colleges and universities, and the general public.
8. Secondary teachers tend to have significant autonomy as they develop their course offerings. This makes coordinating knowledge and skills across courses difficult (Schumaker & Deshler, 1988).

Given these barriers, it is not surprising that inclusive school programs have been slow to develop at the secondary level. This dearth of program alternatives has led to some controversy regarding just what inclusive programs at this level should entail. Most seem to agree that the programs should differ from elementary programs (Schumaker & Deshler, 1988) and that students should not necessarily spend 100% of the school day in general education classroom settings; some students, for example, should spend time in community or work settings or settings in which intensive support services may be provided (Kauffman, Lloyd, Baker, & Riedel, 1995; York & Reynolds, 1996).

In addition, considering the high rate at which students with disabilities are unsuccessful (or fail) in general education classrooms (Blackorby & Wagner, 1996; Rieth & Polsgrove, 1994; Schumaker & Deshler, 1988), it seems apparent that if students with mild disabilities are to be educated successfully in general education classrooms in secondary schools, these classrooms must be transformed so the organization, curriculum, and instruction provided is designed to meet the needs of a diverse group of students (Deshler & Schumaker, 1988). In spite of the general consensus regarding these issues, there is much less agreement regarding the emphasis that should be placed on various curricular content areas, the location in which this material should be presented, and who should present this information.

Secondary Curricular Content Needs for Students with Mild Disabilities

Decisions regarding which curricular content areas to emphasize are especially difficult because secondary teachers of students with disabilities have an acute shortage of time to address the many educational needs of secondary-level students (Deshler, Schumaker, Lenz, & Ellis, 1984). Curricular areas for which secondary-level teachers of students with disabilities may have partial or full responsibility include the following:

1. *Basic academic skills.* These skills involve instruction in basic skills such as reading, writing, and mathematics that are deficient for students with disabilities. Even among students with learning disabilities, basic reading, writing, and math skills are lacking when they enter adolescence (Espin & Foegen, 1996; Schumaker & Deshler, 1988; Zigmond, 1990). For example, Schumaker, Deshler, Alley, and Warner (1983) found that as these students enter the 10th grade, they tend to have basic skills that plateaued at the fourth or fifth grade level. Instruction in basic academic skills often is provided outside of the general education classroom, in a separate special education classroom by a teacher of students with disabilities (Zigmond, 1990).

2. *Tutorial programs* (Deshler, Schumaker, Lenz, & Ellis, 1984). This approach emphasizes tutorial support of students in general education content classes (e.g., English, mathematics, social studies, science). Tutorial

support typically is provided in separate resource classrooms by the teacher of students with disabilities.

3. *Compensatory programs and support in general education classes* (Deshler, Schumaker, Lenz, & Ellis, 1984). This approach is designed to facilitate the adaptation of general education classrooms so students with disabilities can succeed in these settings. Typically the general education and special education teachers work together to adapt classroom organization, curriculum, and instruction to meet the needs of all students in the setting. This approach may be used with content or vocational classes.

4. *Learning strategies programs* (Deshler, Schumaker, Lenz, & Ellis, 1984; Ellis, 1993). This approach is not designed to teach specific content but, rather, focuses on teaching students skills related to "how to learn." Much evidence indicates that students with disabilities lack these skills, which are critical for learning, solving problems, and completing tasks independently in general education classrooms. These skills may be taught in a separate setting by a teacher of students with disabilities or, as Ellis (1993) has proposed, as part of an Integrated Strategy Model that combines classroom content and general strategy instruction. In the latter model, the general and special education teachers teach these skills collaboratively.

5. *Instruction in survival skills* (Zigmond, 1990) and life skills (Polloway, Patton, Epstein, & Smith, 1993). Zigmond (1990) has proposed that secondary teachers of students with LD should teach these students skills they need to survive in school, including behavior control, teacher-pleasing behaviors, and study skills/test-taking strategies. Polloway et al. (1993) have proposed that students with disabilities at the secondary level would benefit from a life skills curriculum, which would teach them skills to support successful adjustment after they complete school. A teacher of students with disabilities teaches survival skills and life skills in a separate, special education classroom.

6. *Vocational training.* Vocational training is provided for students with disabilities as they prepare to make the transition from school to a work setting. This instruction frequently is provided by specialists in vocational education, assisted by teachers of students with disabilities in adapting for the needs of students with disabilities. Vocational instruction also is provided in work settings through work-study and supported employment programs.

7. *Transition planning.* Often included as part of vocational training, transition planning also may include a life skills curriculum, in which students are taught functional skills they need on the job and in other community settings (Polloway, Patton, Epstein, & Smith, 1993). The life skills curriculum is taught most often by a teacher of students with disabilities in a separate setting.

As the above list illustrates, secondary-level teachers of students with disabilities face a broad range of demands on their time to address these curricular areas. Clearly, priorities must be developed regarding which curricular areas should be emphasized, and teachers of students with disabilities must organize and use their time to maximize their efficiency and effectiveness. We readily admit that there are no easy answers regarding what inclusive school programs in secondary schools should entail, how they should be organized, what should be taught, where instruction should occur, and so forth. Indeed, from our perspective, each secondary program should be tailored to the specific needs of a given setting, thus precluding the possibility of a "one-size fits all" model program.

With these caveats in mind, the following section describes an inclusive school program currently in operation in a high school in a small midwestern city. This high school began developing an inclusive program eight years ago. The program subsequently achieved a high level of success and has been recognized as a model program for delivering inclusive school services (CEC, 1995).

Developing A Secondary-Level Inclusive School Program

Eleanor Roosevelt High School is located in a midwestern city with a population of approximately 50,000. A large state university is located nearby. A rich blend of small urban, suburban, and rural communities feeds into Roosevelt High School. The diversity of the community is illustrated by the fact that a major university is located in the same county that closed the last two-room school house in the state in 1965.

Eleanor Roosevelt High School has a student population of 1,350 students, 93% of whom are caucasian, 2% African-American, 4.5% Asian, and a small number of international students from more than 35 countries. Of the students at Roosevelt, 34% live in rural settings, 30% in suburban settings, and 36% in urban settings. Ten percent of the students at Roosevelt qualify for free or reduced lunches. Roosevelt employs approximately 80 full- and part-time professionals.

Implementation of the inclusive school program at Roosevelt High School began in the 1990–91 school year. Discussion regarding changes in the program, however, began two years prior to implementation, when members of the special education department began to assess and critically analyze special education services and student success. Roosevelt had a highly successful program for students with substantial needs; these students were being served in an age-appropriate building, attended general education classes with their peers, were provided vocational skills through a work study/supported employment program, and often left high school with paid employment.

Several faculty members in special education began to question the services provided for students with mild disabilities and believed this program was much less successful than the program for students with substantial needs. Even though students with mild disabilities most often left school with a diploma, they were not always able to secure paid employment and often had few skills that would enable them to become contributing members of the community. Overall, academic expectations for these students were extremely low. Based on these observations, several faculty members in special education thought they should begin to look at doing something different.

At about the same time, members of the special education department were becoming cognizant of the movement toward inclusion and the literature supporting the integration of students with disabilities into the general education classroom (Will, 1986). Discussions took place initially at staff meetings and in informal conversations. From these discussions, a team of teachers was convened to begin to plan seriously for teachers in general and special education to collaborate in teaching core content areas. This group drafted a written proposal and presented it to Roosevelt's Curriculum Council in October 1989. The rationale for changes that were proposed rested on five major points.

1. The English department was moving toward a more heterogeneous grouping of students. This provided an opportunity to include students with disabilities in these classes and to involve teachers of students with disabilities in the discussion, planning, and implementation of this new instructional arrangement.
2. Similar types of curricula were being used in the general math class and the special education math class. Both of these math classes were addressing basic arithmetic, and teachers from both courses believed the courses should be restructured totally to make them more applicable to the students' needs.
3. Both teachers of students with disabilities who would be involved initially in teaming with general educators had dual licensing in special education and the content area in which they would teach. This was important practically speaking because it satisfied the state's licensing requirements and eliminated the need for a waiver.
4. Collaborative efforts would result in growth experiences for students and teachers alike.
5. Teachers thought the wider diversity in student characteristics at Roosevelt would require all teachers to learn from each other and to share their expertise.

The initial proposal identified two sections designated for collaborative teaching: a ninth grade general math class and an 11th grade English class. The staff in special education was paired with general education faculty in each class section. All four individuals were voluntary participants. This core group then identified the following objectives for students:

1. To integrate students from general and special education.
2. To provide contact between same-age peers from general and special education.
3. To expose students to a greater variety of teaching strategies.
4. To develop in students appropriate skills in English and math.
5. To provide and share peer reinforcement.
6. To be exposed to a greater number of peer role models.

In addition, the following objectives were developed for faculty involved in the inclusive program:

1. To deliver services to a broader range of students.
2. To integrate faculty in general and special education.
3. To promote the use of effective educational practices for all students.
4. To introduce collaborative teaching techniques.
5. To give the teaching staff the opportunity to share expertise.
6. To encourage the use of a wide variety of teaching strategies.
7. To develop guidelines and directions for faculty members who may develop similar programs in the future.
8. To encourage teachers to view themselves as decision makers with respect to developing, presenting, and assessing collaborative teaching techniques.

The program at Roosevelt High School is beginning its seventh year of implementation. Self-contained special education classes have been reduced from 21 sections in the first year of the program to three at present. Collaborative teaching partnerships now extend to all core curricular areas, and teacher participation continues to be voluntary.

Decisions Regarding Curriculum

In developing an inclusive school program at Roosevelt High School, clear decisions were made regarding which areas of the curriculum would be emphasized and how teachers of students with disabilities would spend their time. These decisions were difficult, they involved compromise, and they are being adjusted continually to ensure a good fit with the student population. The following provides a brief description regarding these decisions and a rationale for making them.

The staff at Roosevelt High School decided not to offer separate-class special education programs in basic academic skill areas (reading and mathematics), for four basic reasons. *First,* teachers believed that students with mild disabilities had already had eight (or more) years of instruction in these basic skill areas, and this instruction most often had resulted in continuing poor performance in basic skills, as well as much frustration on the part of students when they addressed these topics in separate, special education classrooms. The staff also was aware that previous pullout, basic skills instruction at Roosevelt had not been effective. As Zigmond (1990) so aptly stated, students with learning disabilities tend to enter high school three to five years behind actual grade placement and "unfortunately...do not seem to recoup these basic skill deficiencies during their years of attending secondary school resource programs...and, in fact, the gap between achievement scores and grade expectancy level actually seems to widen as students with learning disabilities progress through high school" (p. 5).

Second, the faculty at Roosevelt realized that when students were in basic skills classes, they were missing important opportunities to be exposed to a rich curriculum, cooperative learning experiences, and classroom discussions that would provide beneficial learning experiences for them (see Oakes, 1985) for a discussion of curriculum inequality).

Third, the faculty made the decision to discontinue separate classes in basic skill instruction because they believed that the time of teachers of students with disabilities could be better spent in other activities (which will be described subsequently) that would provide more benefits for students with disabilities.

Fourth, evidence indicated that literacy skills learned in isolation (i.e., in separate reading classes) tended not to transfer to other academic or vocational content areas (Mikulecky, Albers, & Peers, 1994; Mikulecky & Lloyd, 1993). This finding, as well as experiences of the faculty at Roosevelt that supported this contention, led the faculty to decide that literacy and numeracy skills could be taught best within the context of content-area classes (i.e., English, science, vocational classes, and so forth) rather than teaching reading and mathematics as separate subject areas. Thus, the faculty did not "give up" on teaching literacy and numeracy skills to students with disabilities. For example, students would learn new vocabulary in an auto mechanics or a social studies class, read books in English classes, learn math skills in a practical mathematics class, and participate in a variety of other activities to increase their literacy and numeracy skills.

Faculty members who participated in general education partnerships realized the importance of tutorial services for students with disabilities. These services helped students organize their work, complete homework, study for tests, learn study skills related to content-area subjects, and so forth. The faculty also recognized that many students who were not labeled as having disabilities needed these services. To address the need for this type of support, a schoolwide program was developed to provide tutoring to all students who needed these services. The program involved administrators, teachers, paraprofessionals, peer tutors, and volunteers.

Teachers believed that learning strategies, survival skills, life skills, and transition planning were taught best within the context of ongoing classes that provided a natural setting for teaching and applying these skills. Indeed, some of the general education classes were transformed to offer some aspects of these curricular areas to a wide range of typical students as well as students with disabilities. Thus, separate special education classes addressing these topics were discontinued.

Vocational opportunities for students with mild disabilities continued to be offered through an area vocational school located on the campus of Roosevelt High School. The teachers of students with disabilities worked collaboratively with vocational staff and school counselors to develop programs to meet student needs. One major change in the vocational education program resulted from the success of the this program for students with substantial needs. These students were gaining important employment opportunities through a community-based supported employment/work study program. The faculty recognized that students with mild disabilities would benefit substantially from similar experiences. Thus, the community-based work study program was expanded to include students with mild disabilities, who were provided on-the-job training and community access skills during the school day.

Partnerships As the Foundation of Secondary Inclusive Programs

The foundation for the program in special education at Roosevelt High School was built on partnerships between general education teachers and teachers of students with disabilities, as they addressed the curricular area called "compensatory programs and support in general education classrooms." As the partnerships evolved, teachers changed their perspectives significantly regarding what this type of program should entail. Prior to development of the inclusive school program, "compensatory and support" programs were viewed primarily as support services provided by the teacher of students with disabilities to allow students with mild disabilities to succeed in the general education classroom. These programs did not question the curriculum, instruction, or classroom organization of the general education classroom. Thus, "the problem" was perceived to reside within the student, and the role of the teacher of students with disabilities was viewed as making sure the student could fit into the general education classroom.

As partnerships developed, teachers concluded quickly that this perspective had to change. They found that though students with mild disabilities indeed lacked some of the skills manifested by typical students, these deficits could be addressed best by changing the general education classroom and assisting students with disabilities within these settings to gain the skills necessary to succeed. Thus, as part of these partnerships, teachers worked to *transform* the general education classroom to better meet the needs of all students. The partnerships often resulted in significant changes in the curriculum of the general education classroom, methods of delivering instruction, and classroom organization. Classes also often became more student-centered and less teacher- or content-centered.

Through these partnerships, teachers work collaboratively to transform the general education classroom (organization, curriculum, and instruction) to better meet the needs of all students in the classroom, including students with disabilities. In the following section we describe how these partnerships develop, followed by an example.

Examining Current Practice

As collaborative partnerships begin to form in high schools, participants first must reflect on and understand the assumptions and specific training that teachers from special and general education bring to the classroom setting. In the initial stages of an inclusion program, as partnerships are beginning, teachers of students with disabilities typically enter into a minefield of uncertainties and begin to question the knowledge base and traditions that undergird their professional training. A critical examination and reappraisal of the practice of special education is important as it affords teachers an opportunity to address and challenge the basic assumptions and traditions in which their day-to-day decision making is grounded. It allows them to discuss options for students and teachers, which ultimately changes the way they view their profession.

To achieve this goal, special educators must ask themselves some difficult questions:

- What difference does it make for me and for my students if I enter into this partnership and no longer practice in a separate setting/system?
- What expertise do I have that is of value to the general education classroom?
- What about the current practice of special education is good and should be kept?
- What about the current practice of special education is not good and should be discarded?
- What role should I have in a general education classroom?

A critical examination and reappraisal of the practice of general educators entails asking questions similar to those above:

- What difference does it make for me and for my students if I enter into this partnership, and no longer practice in a separate setting/system?
- What expertise do I have that is of value to students with disabilities?
- What about my current instructional practices and curriculum is good and should be kept?
- What about my current instructional practices and curriculum is not good and should be discarded?
- What role should I have in a partnership with a teacher of students with disabilities?

By looking at their profession and practice in new and different ways, these teachers are able to consider their actions, intentions, and effects thoughtfully. They begin to plan for change based on what they know about themselves, their school, and their students.

Examining Contrasting Perspectives on Teaching and Learning

In addition to examining their own beliefs, teachers who are beginning partnerships must share this information and also examine how their beliefs and values differ from those of their partner. For example, in most instances the greatest difference between secondary-level general education teachers and teachers of students with disabilities relates to their perspectives on students and instruction.

As Cuban (1984) noted, general education teachers at the secondary level tend to be subject-focused and teacher-centered, whereas teachers of students with disabilities tend to be more student-centered. The experience and training of general education teachers has focused on ways to help students learn a specific subject: how to understand algebra, how to learn to write well, how to communicate, how to use a calculator. In contrast, the training of teachers of students with disabilities often centers on methods for ensuring student success by adapting instruction, altering curriculum, and so forth.

These different perspectives lead to differing practices in the classroom that must be addressed before a partnership can be successful. In a subject- or teacher-centered classroom, the teacher tends to talk more than students (much lecture is used to convey information efficiently), the classroom is organized to support lectures (with rows of desks facing the front of the room), and most instruction occurs with large groups. In contrast, in classes with student-centered instruction, students talk more and receive less lecture, the teacher uses more small-group and individual instruction, instructional materials and methods are more varied to address student needs, and the classroom is arranged to reflect these differences (to facilitate the use of cooperative groups).

Until teachers address and share these different perspectives on instruction and learning, developing successful partnerships is difficult, if not impossible. This process helps teachers to understand their partners' strengths, as well as their own strengths that they bring to the teaching partnership.

Determining Teacher Strengths

Teachers entering into a partnership must discuss their perception of their teaching strengths, as well as their shortcomings. This discussion will help the partners gain a new perspective on and respect for the strengths of their partner, as well as a better understanding of where their own strengths lie. When these discussions take place, the general education teacher's firm grasp of the course content and strong skills related to organizing this material and conveying it to large groups of students may become apparent. In contrast, teachers of students with disabilities often have less knowledge of the curriculum and more skills related to determining critical elements of the curriculum and adapting instruction to convey this information to small groups of students.

These complementary skills often form the foundation upon which partnerships are built, as both teachers feel good about the strengths they bring to the partnership and feel confident that their combined expertise will improve instruction for all students in the classroom. This is reflected in the following comment by a teacher of students with disabilities at Roosevelt.[1]

> You walk in and you see where a student is, emotionally, socially, academically, behaviorally. I mean, you start there. That's the only place I feel you can be effective. I think I take what the general education teacher sees in a general scope and make sure that it fits the individual students, tailoring the language, even the format of the worksheet, even the quantity of the work required. I will tailor or trim it down to the student who I just know is going to be mechanically slow on this. They can do it, but they are not going to do the quantity that somebody else will do.

---

[1]All quotes are taken from Cole (1995).

Risk Taking and Partnerships

In developing partnerships, the partners also have to clearly understand the risk involved for both participants. The partners often discover that the perception of the risk involved in moving into a collaborative teaching partnership varies greatly. Upon reflection, this difference is understandable.

Most frequently, general educators who become involved in a collaborative teaching effort do not believe they are taking a major risk. These teachers seem to understand that entering into a partnership might mean a change in how they normally would conduct one or two of their classes, but they do not feel at great risk personally or professionally. They still have a classroom, they still have the same number of (or a few additional) students they would have had if they had taught alone, and they feel confident about their expertise in the curricular area.

In contrast, teachers of students with disabilities entering into teaching partnerships often feel at great risk professionally and personally. These teachers often are required to change their entire professional identity as they enter into partnerships with general educators. Teachers of students with disabilities perceive that they must give up more than their partner does, including the loss of much of their identity as specialists, loss of their students and their classrooms, and loss of much of their autonomy as a teacher. In addition, these teachers often fear they lack the expertise to function effectively in a general education classroom, as they have little experience in this setting, are unfamiliar with the curriculum of the classroom, and are unaccustomed to teaching large groups of students.

Thus, as a partnership begins, a teacher of students with disabilities is attempting to define her role, learn the curricular content, and deal with 30 or more students in a classroom. In addition, these teachers may be in the process of developing partnerships with two, three, or more teachers. Under these circumstances, no wonder they often fear that entering into a teaching partnership will lower their professional status and that they may end up serving as a paraprofessional in the general education classroom.

Developing Trust and Respect

Trust and respect are necessary in co-teaching and collaboration. This takes several forms: trust and respect for teaching partners, for other colleagues involved in the program, and for administrators. Sharing responsibility and accountability takes time and depends in part on development of the partnership. Even though respect for a teaching partner may be present from the beginning, the trust of their partners as individuals takes some time.

Hartgraves (1993) proposes two dimensions to trust—predictability and common goals—and suggests that trust manifests itself as confidence instilled in persons or process. By responding to personal and professional concerns and by not bailing out at the first moment of stress, teachers begin to trust their partners. As this trust grows, the participants are better able to express their individual views, concerns, and ideas; they are able to be more vocal about the things that are important to them.

Trusting each other to make key decisions after years of being the sole decision maker in the classroom is a major change for teachers. As a math teacher at Roosevelt commented:

I think the other thing is the decision-making process. You are so used to doing it yourself that if you are going to get something done the way you want it done, you do it yourself. And even though you know the person you are with is very competent and can do it all, it is easier to do it yourself than to ask them to do it. Now I feel comfortable saying, "Hey, here is what I would like to do. What do you think?" and my partner will say "Okay, I'll make the test out and make sure we cover this," and there is no conversation about what should be on it, because I feel like the marriage has really settled in and we have become one.

Voluntary Participation

Along with trust and respect, involvement in co-teaching should be voluntary, not forced. Participants often liken it to a marriage; the interpersonal relationships necessary for co-teaching cannot be mandated. Giving educators this choice and allowing them to seek information and ask critical questions about the choice offers more ownership in the effort. Likewise, providing teachers with a choice gives them a sense that they have the support of their administration.

Administrative Support

Administrators play a major role in developing positive teaching partnerships. Teachers need to know that their administration will provide the necessary support. This may include having administrators cover teachers' classrooms so they can have time to meet to reflect on the program. It may mean that administrators facilitate staff development needs and ensure that schedules for students and staff are appropriate. Administrators need to provide the emotional support necessary when times got tough, and provide a "safety net" for teachers by communicating that they will not have the "limb chopped off" if they step out and try new and different things.

Communication

Communication is critical to the collaborative teaching effort. The necessary communication requires being able to speak as well as listen, sharing information and developing shared meaning, and being willing to provide and accept interpersonal feedback. Teachers have to "place the issues on the table," to talk about problems, both big and small. This communication has to be ongoing and may take place in a formal, structured fashion (as in a workshop or staff meeting) and in an informal way (in the hall, at lunch, in the parking lot, or at a social gathering.)

Communication might be both professional and personal in nature, addressing student and classroom needs as well as the personal needs of a teaching partner. Reflection and action must occur with respect to the students in the class as well as the relationship of the individual teachers as they work to form a teaching partnership. Rather than relying on standard responses to instructional problems, teachers should generate new thoughts and ideas to guide their actions in the classroom.

Problems are attendant to this type of interdependency. Working closely with another professional presents a new set of human relations issues. The conflicts that arise have to be dealt with both personally and professionally. Control issues, a lack of privacy, and sharing ownership of a class are concerns that have not been faced in a loosely coupled system wherein teachers have taught alone. Now they have to learn to communicate in new and different ways, to make time for each other, and to become more flexible. Talking about their practice in a critical, reflective way is something that teachers must learn over time.

Achieving Parity

Although some time is required for teachers in some partnerships to reach parity, there must be a clear notion that when presenting themselves to students, the teachers are co-teachers, not the special education teacher and the math teacher. As a math teacher said:

> We are co-teachers from the word go, from the ground up. He's not determining curriculum, I'm not determining curriculum. It's two heads are better than one. We tell students, "We are your teachers." We put the names up on the board, they stay up there all year long, and we go right into what the class is about and what they are going to experience this year, and we don't say another word about the roles we might play. We don't even explain it. I can't recall anybody asking, "Why are there two teachers in here?" They just kind of sit in here, and there are two teachers!

A teacher of students with disabilities further commented on this same partnership:

> From minute one we had to present ourselves as co-teachers. The minute the students get wind of "Oh, I see, you're just kind of a helper," as teachers we all know what is going to happen to your perception by those students. If you are seen as only helping certain students and not others, you'll be limited in your effect with all the students in that classroom. There are very concrete ways to present ourselves as co-teachers. It is always "we," "our policy, our restroom policy is, our feeling about textbooks is, today this is what we are going to do," as opposed to presenting only one teacher's viewpoint. We have found that has done wonders to start students right from the beginning as seeing us as co-teachers.

The classroom is a place to start sharing. The room that once belonged to one teacher now is home for two. Each teacher should have ownership of the room, whether it be sharing a desk or having two desks in the room. This not only makes a difference to the partner, but the students will benefit as well and not be confused with "who's the boss?" The students need to see the team in harmony to produce good results, and two teachers sharing a common goal of students' success is a good example for the student.

The parity issue must reach beyond sharing teaching responsibilities. Teachers, especially special education teachers, believe the little things are just as important to share. This includes physical space issues such as a desk, a chair, a place to put their things, and a file cabinet. Trivial as it may seem, issues such as this become important as the teams work toward being equal partners. As a teacher of students with disabilities stated:

> The fact that I have a desk is important. It is a table that I have in both of the classrooms that I go into, but that is my area, so I can say to a student who is supposed to turn in a book: "put your papers...your journals on my desk," and they know that. They see my partner and me as co-equals within that classroom. It becomes just one more tangible way of setting up the fact that we have equal responsibility and that kids can go to either one for help or answers to questions.

Developing trust, being committed to open communication, and clearly defining roles bring the individual teachers in each partnership to the co-equal relationship they often had envisioned from the beginning. Special educators may spend the beginning stages of a partnership defining their roles and establishing their contribution to co-teaching. Partnerships mature at different rates, but eventually each partnership should be able to develop a strong professional relationship, both within and outside of the classroom, and be able to share responsibility and accountability for all students in the classroom. The special educator cannot be viewed as a classroom assistant but must be seen as an equal partner.

Often in the beginning, individual teachers speak of "their" classroom or "their" lesson. Clearly, they have not yet merged as a teaching unit. Use of the word *I*, however, slowly becomes *we* as the partnerships grow and as parity is achieved. Parity is never completely resolved, though, as partnerships continue to grow and change over the years, and teacher roles, as well as related parity issues, must continue to be addressed.

Staff Development

Staff development is an important component in developing collaborative relationships. Formal training in conflict resolution and collaboration skills is helpful in the initial stages. What often proves to be most valuable for the participants as a whole, however, is the time afforded them to plan together and to reflect as a large group and as a partnership.

Classroom Make-Up

The classroom make-up in a high school program must be diverse and heterogeneous. Collaborative teaching programs are not intended to replicate the old special education classroom or track. Courses should not be overloaded with students who have disabilities. Generally, a classroom of 30 should have no more than 10 students with disabilities. In addition, the less "tracked" the course is, the better the class will be as a whole. While believing in the concept of heterogeneity in a classroom, teachers acknowledge the difficulties and challenges these classroom arrangements bring. As an English teacher stated:

The downside of it is that when you have that range, you obviously have some upper-end kids who really need to be challenged. You can't rely on them all the time to be the teacher. You have to allow them opportunities to expand their own knowledge and skills. And while they are achieving a lot in terms of self-esteem and true understanding of the concepts through teaching others—it is clarified for them and they are getting the benefits of that—the pace is one that is not really good for them. They can get bored with it, they feel like they are belaboring it when you do a review. So I think it is important to be able to provide opportunities for them to expand, to grow, and we work really hard at that.

Time

Time is a frequently mentioned concern of teachers. Time is important on two levels:

1. Time on a daily basis to talk and plan with the teaching partner;.
2. Time built into the school calendar to talk and make connections with others involved in this change initiative.

The time needed should not be added to the end of a busy day but, rather, built into the teachers' work day and year. Possibly, teachers value time more than any other factor because in the day-to-day life of teaching, teachers have little if any control over their time. Their days often are routine in terms of schedule, with little flexibility and limited power to change or adjust for extenuating circumstances. Teachers' time with students is improved as a result of their time with colleagues. Providing time for teachers to share must become a priority if ongoing reflection, renewal, and growth is to take place. Teachers consistently mention time as a key to the development of partnerships and professional growth.

Evolution of Teaching Partnerships

Participants in collaboration and co-teaching programs acknowledge that their involvement in the program makes them better teachers and better people. This does not happen immediately. Each teacher has to work out differences in teaching styles. Each teacher has to formulate ways to make public the ideas, concepts, and hunches that make up his or her teaching process, which are silent or unexamined when teaching alone. In addition, each special educator moves from a relatively secure environment (the resource classroom or a self-contained classroom) to an unknown environment. Defining new roles and dealing with interpersonal interests are two major issues that partnerships have to face.

Typically, teachers experience an evolutionary change over the course of the first year of a program. At first their concerns as participants are procedural or "how to" in nature: how to grade students, how to pace a lesson, how to deal with certain behaviors. It is as though the participants are seeking a recipe, something to grab onto to ensure that they are doing it right.

Once they acknowledge that there is not a recipe and that "doing it right" means different things for different partnerships, procedural concerns give way to reflections on teaching and learning. With time, the special education teachers define their roles further and begin to feel more confident as teachers. They begin to realize that they are having an impact on a larger number of students than they did in the past and that all students are accepting them as a teacher. This turns out to be a great ego builder. As a teacher of students with disabilities noted:

> It is wonderful to walk down the hall and be able to say "hi" to that number of kids and know you have had an impact on them. As a special ed person, I never had that before. There was my own little separate group, and that was it. That for me makes it really great.

Benefits of Partnerships

Teachers who have been involved in partnerships at Roosevelt High School agree that many benefits accrue from these programs. These benefits can be summarized as follows:

1. Administrative duties (e.g., attendance taking, grading, copy machine duties, parent phone calls) are shared.
2. Having two teachers in the classroom allows them to give more attention to problem behaviors and crisis situations without disrupting the entire class.
3. More time is available to give students individual attention and get to know them better.
4. Evaluation and feedback from a colleague allows teachers to fine-tune lessons on a daily basis.
5. Daily contact with a colleague provides opportunities for problem solving, bouncing ideas off one another, risk taking, and being creative regarding challenging student behaviors.
6. Renewal and reinforcement come from watching good teaching and working together.
7. Teachers model collaboration and cooperation for students.
8. Each teacher is able to use his or her strengths to address student needs. For example, if one teacher has difficulty addressing a challenging student behavior, the other teacher can step in and provide support.

General education teachers, too, frequently comment on how the skills they gain while teaching with a partner generalize to other classes. One teacher addressed the changes made in a class where he works with a partner by stating:

> Now that Gary and I have worked together for two years, I find myself thinking about [these changes] an awful lot in every class, not just in the general math class [where the partnership occurred]. I don't know that I can prove it, but my guess is that calculus instruction is better, in a measurable way, than in the past as a result of the partnership.

An Example of a Partnership at Work

The greatest benefits from partnerships relate to the transformations in general education classrooms. The following example illustrates the outcome of a partnership between a high school math instructor (also head of the mathematics department) and a teacher of students with disabilities. These teachers developed a partnership to teach a general math class. As with all partnerships at Roosevelt High School, students with disabilities in this class formerly had been taught in a separate, special education classroom. In large part, this example is described in the words of the two teachers who formed the partnership. The quotes are taken from interviews by the first author of this chapter, conducted as part of her dissertation research (Cole, 1995).

Background—General Math

As the partnership began, both teachers had strong reservations regarding the extent to which the general math class was meeting the needs of typical students, or the extent to which the class would meet the needs of newly enrolled students with disabilities. The math teacher put this well in stating:

> To give you a little background about the general math course we teach, general math has been around since the rocks cooled off, and I don't think that ever during that time it has been completely satisfactory for the vast majority of kids in the class. I felt free to experiment with general math because it has been so unsuccessful for decades, not just at this school, but everywhere.

This teacher went on to describe the basic content of the course, as it had been taught for many years.

> The prevailing idea of general math was, "Let's make one more effort at teaching arithmetic." The skills that were being practiced were nothing new. It is built around two components: There were these problems where you get fifty whole-number division problems...and verbal problems. It had grown up historically around a lot of drill work.

An experience common to both teachers early in the first year of their partnership served to solidify their perspectives on the types of changes that had to occur in the general math class.

> (We) had an experience that also contributed to the mix. The local Chamber of Commerce had started what it called a Partners in Education Program. This was a collaborative effort on the part of educators and business leaders. As a part of that program, the teachers involved spent a week in local industries. I spent a week at Westinghouse, and Gary at RCA. In that shared experience, he and I brought together some notes about what we had seen at those factories, and it was plain as day to us that the kinds of situations our kids are going to be leaving high school and entering are nothing like the general math class was preparing them for.

This realization led Gary and Adam to begin examining the curriculum of the general math class, as well as what students were learning from that curriculum:

> I've got kids who knew that September was whole-number division month, and it was going to be followed by whole-numbers tracking week, and they were going to be followed by whole-number multiplication month, and so forth. It dawned on me that they are not solving problems. You give them a verbal problem and they weren't

very successful at story problems. Why? Because they see a problem, they pick out the numbers, they know it is whole-number addition week, so they add the whole numbers together, and zip, they go right on. When we presented situations where they had to determine whether those numbers should be added or subtracted, it was a whole new ballgame. I was real impatient to do something about general math in a major way.

Altering Curriculum and Instruction

Gary and Adam then began exploring alternatives for the general math curriculum. They questioned initially whether they could build the curriculum around a textbook. The following comments illustrate the evolution of their thinking on this matter.

> The textbooks are written well, more or less. There is a great variety in those, but there aren't very many that can really help a kid learn.
>
> Textbooks need to cut out the superfluous language and put the info into a clear and concise language that students can use.
>
> We made a decision to take the textbook and throw it away.
>
> We both thought the textbook was too unwieldy for not just the students with special needs but also for the math student period. So our goal was to basically rewrite the textbook in a language that would be concrete, understandable, readable, clear, and still be workable to use the math in their world. We didn't want it to be so simplistic that it was unusable in the real world.

The alternative that Gary and Adam decided upon for the general math class was to "run the entire class on the basis of the *Math Manual*." The format and content for the *Math Manual* was designed by the teachers, modeled after some of their experiences in observing workplaces.

> What we decided was to build the course around the concept of an operator's manual—a manual of procedures for the job, the tasks the job is composed of. The Math Manual ends up looking like a folder. Because what we saw in those workplaces was a collection of people whose jobs are so complex that they can't keep it all in their heads at once—the way we ask kids to memorize multiplication tables, know the area of triangles, and so forth. In fact, what we have provided our students is a set of reference materials.

Thus, these teachers moved from having students memorize facts (such as multiplication tables) to helping students solve problems and understand the process used to solve problems. The *Math Manual* was developed by students.

> Students have compiled this folder through several means. They have taken notes off the board, and we have taught note taking by doing that. We have done some pages and handed them out and used them in class. And we have a hybrid of the two—some pages that we hand out and go through them in class and they fill in blanks. There is a table of contents at the beginning that they have kept up-to-date. We check this periodically for a grade.

As Gary and Adam described the purpose of the *Math Manual*, this manual clearly reflects a significant change in teaching philosophy for both teachers.

This is a big change for most teachers. A major part of the course is devoted to using the manual. The only way to pass tests is to have that manual available, because some of the questions say, "Do not answer the question; just tell us what page you would look at to help you answer the question." That is a reference skill.

They elaborate regarding how the *Math Manual* is used in their class.

That manual—and this is the key—is used all the time—for tests, quizzes, projects, homework, and so forth. That manual is an integral part of what they do.... A major portion of the course is devoted to using the manual. Change we did—and essentially we have written our own curriculum.

This change in curricular focus also emphasized lessening student dependence on teachers and helping them discover that they could solve problems independently.

I have held their hands for too long. I've tried to get away from that and point out that it is okay to get stuck. The important thing is to know what you do when you get stuck. How do you behave at that point? Do you throw up your hands in disgust? Or do you go back to the point where you understood things last and go over that territory again, or maybe with someone else?

What we have found was students coming to us with this attitude: "I don't know how to do this, and I'm not going to do it. I don't know how to reduce a fraction, so I'm not going to reduce a fraction. I'll go on to the next question." That is in direct conflict to what we saw in the workplace. That attitude is incompatible with success in the workplace. You don't say, "I don't know how to make the Big Mac; therefore I'm not going to make a Big Mac for this customer." Yet, we found our students internalizing that kind of learning philosophy, so what we have done is add a qualifier to the statement, "I don't know how to do this, so I'm going to go find a place where I can find out how to do this." That seems to parallel the workplace, in an assembly line, a retail place, a restaurant, or just about anything you do outside of school.

One of the teachers synopsized this perspective when he stated:

They don't remember how to add fractions, and frankly I don't care. That's something they could find out if they had to. They know it is written down someplace, and if they need that kind of information, they can do it.

In some ways, the general math class borrowed from perspectives of many general educators, as instruction took on a more "constructivist" or process learning model of instruction (Heshusius, 1995). The teachers also adopted methods used widely in special education. The criterion they used for selecting instructional approaches was, "Does it work with our students?" For example, with some of the course content, they emphasized breaking down tasks into incremental steps for instruction:

The incrementals, the tiny step-by-step is the sort of thing we all probably should be doing. Textbooks, standard published materials, probably don't do it. They make huge assumptions about how far a kid can go within the space on one problem. Try someday to sit down and figure out how you know how to read a ruler. I haven't found a textbook yet that describes that.

We've spent a lot of time thinking over the tiny little details that someone needs to go though to learn how to do something that most of us take for granted. Drawing a line with a ruler—we took two days just talking about the technique, how to hold it, how to use it. Then we did some exercises that resulted in some really nice designs.

There was also much more emphasis on hands-on activities in this class rather than lecturing, drill, and practice.

We have gone to a lot of hands-on types of activities. One of the things that bothered me as a parent, for my own kids, was that they could read about measurement, but they never actually did any measuring. In our class, kids measure tire pressure, they measure lumber, and we find out that those things are valuable. We have concentrated on a lot of hands-on things.

Changes in Expectations and Student Evaluation

Both teachers recognized that in the past they had expected far too little of their students.

We are both pleasantly surprised at the capability of these students. When we raised our expectations of them, we found that we can go higher, faster; we can go into things that we never even ventured into last year. It's like the more we try, the more we find these students are capable of doing.

At least part of this success is attributed to the emphasis on modeling the classroom after the workplace.

There are a number of things we want students to do, and we're asking them to do a better job of what they're doing and holding them to a higher standard by maintaining this workplace analogy as much as we can.

Today kids are making drawings with a ruler. They are actually doing what would pass for mechanical drawing, from a thumbnail sketch of a house. They are measuring; they are looking; they are trying to figure stuff out. We gave them a sloppy sketch of a house with dimensions all over it and they had to come up with a nice drawing that was accurate. And that's an important skill for kids to have when they leave this school, to have at least encountered. And it was not part of the general math curriculum. It's not in a textbook anywhere.

Evaluating Student Progress

These altered expectations, as well as changes in curriculum and instruction, were reflected in altered methods of evaluating student progress. Putting together the *Math Manual* constitutes a major part of each student's grade. Further, tests often focus on use of the *Math Manual* to solve problems or to find information that will aid the student in solving problems. These changes were a new experience for most, if not all, of the students, and it took some time for the students to adjust.

Initially students balked. [One of the first tests] just threw them for a loop. They thought we were kidding. [They said], "What do you mean we don't answer these?"

> This was an entire math test, and it took about 50 minutes of simply going through
> their *Math Manual* and finding the page number where they would get the answers
> to those questions. That was really foreign to those students because they come in
> with a mentality of, "Look, all we have to do is get this done." Now they are so used
> to this that it is real comfortable for them to do these kinds of process exercises. We
> have some students [looking through] each page. You will see others getting the gist
> of what the question is and going to the table of contents.

To reflect further the emphasis on the workplace, the teachers also included
group activities on some tests.

> On some tests a component of the test was group work. The test that you would see
> isn't a test in the traditional sense. We begin by emphasizing the resources they have
> available: They have their group that they can call on; they have notes they've made
> on the geometry unit; they have a textbook they can use as a resource rather than the
> central focus of the class. They have their calculators that we not only hand to them
> but teach them how to use. [Calculators] become an object of instruction as well.

> The test consisted of several tasks they were to perform together as group—sup-
> porting one another, and we go around supporting the group interaction. We are
> kind of coaching them: Can you learn from one another? Here's someone who
> knows what's happening. Help that person explain to other members in the group.

Conclusion

The experience of Roosevelt High School is one example of how inclusion can work
effectively. The indispensable aspect of this program is the collaborative partnerships used to transform classrooms into settings in which the needs of a broad range
of students can be met. These partnerships require significantly different roles for
teachers of students with disabilities, as well as for content-area teachers. They also
require that teachers become equal partners in the education of all students.
Periodically integrating teachers of students with disabilities into the general education classroom on an "as needed" basis was not possible or sufficient to achieve
these goals.

At Roosevelt, only through the teamwork of the teaching partnerships were
classes transformed. Indeed, the curriculum and instruction were "reinvented" to
better meet the needs of all students. Through these transformations classes became
more learner-centered rather than remaining traditional, content-centered classes,
teachers shared their expertise and learned to adapt instruction to the needs of a
broad range of students, and assessment and evaluation were altered to better reflect
student needs.

Considering the complexity of secondary schools and classrooms, we must recognize that effective inclusive programs cannot be developed short of collaborative
partnerships of teachers who bring a range of expertise to these endeavors. There is
no "one-size-fits-all" approach for secondary level inclusive programs. Only
through sharing the best ideas available in a given secondary setting can effective
programs, tailored to the individual needs of a given school, be developed.

References

Affleck, J. Q., Madge, S., Adams, A., & Lowenbraun, S. (1988). Integrated classroom versus resource model: Academic viability and effectiveness. *Exceptional Children, 54*, 339–348.

Banerji, M. & Dailey, R. (1995). A study of the effects of an inclusion model on students with specific learning disabilities. *Journal of Learning Disabilities, 28*(8), 511–522.

Bear, G. G., & Proctor, W. A. (1990). Impact of a full-time integrated program on the achievement of nonhandicapped and mildly handicapped children. *Journal of Exceptionality. 1*, 227–238.

Blackorby, J. & Wagner, M. (1996). Longitudinal postschool outcomes of youth with disabilities: Findings from the National Longitudinal Transition Study. *Exceptional Children, 62*(5), 399–413.

Council for Exceptional Children (CEC) (1995). *Creating schools for all our students: What 12 schools have to say*. Reston, VA: Author.

Cole, C. (1995). *A contextualized understanding of teachers' practice, their collaborative relationships, and the inclusion of students with disabilities*. Unpublished doctoral dissertation (AAC9601781), Indiana University, Bloomington.

Cuban, L. (1984). *How teachers taught: Constancy and change in American classrooms 1890–1980*. New York: Longman.

Deshler, D., Schumaker, J., Lenz, K., & Ellis, E. (1984). Academic and cognitive interventions for LD adolescents: Part II. *Journal of Learning Disabilities, 17*(3), 170–179.

Ellis, E. (1993). Integrative strategy instruction: A potential model for teaching content area subjects to adolescents with learning disabilities. *Journal of Learning Disabilities, 26*, 358–383.

Espin, C., & Foegen, A. (1996). Validity of general outcome measures for predicting secondary students' performance on content-area tasks. *Exceptional Children, 62*(6), 497–514.

Fuchs, D., & Fuchs, L. (1994) Inclusive schools movement and the radicalization of special education reform. *Exceptional Children, 60*, 294–309.

Guterman, B. (1995). The validity of categorical learning disabilities services: The consumers' view. *Exceptional Children, 62*(2), 111–124.

Hartgraves, A. (1993). Individualism and individuality: Reinterpreting the teacher culture. In J. Little & M. McLaughlin (Eds.), *Teachers' work*. New York: Teachers College Press.

Heshusius, L. (1995). Holism and special education: There is no substitute for real life purposes and processes. In T. Skrtic (Ed.), *Disability and democracy: Reconstructing (special) education for postmodernity* (pp. 166–189). New York: Teachers College Press.

Kauffman, J., Lloyd, J., Baker, J., & Riedel, T. (1995). Inclusion of all students with emotional and behavioral disorders? Let's think again. *Phi Delta Kappan, 76*(7), 542–546.

McLeskey, J., & Waldron, N. (1995). Inclusive elementary programs: Must they cure students with learning disabilities to be effective? *Phi Delta Kappan, 77*(5), 300–303.

Mercer, C., & Mercer, A. (1993). *Teaching students with learning problems* (4th ed.). New York: Macmillan.

Mikulecky, L., Albers, P., & Peers, M. (1994). *Literacy transfer: A review of the literature* (Technical report TR 94-05). Philadelphia: University of Pennsylvania, National Center on Adult Literacy.

Mikulecky, L., & Lloyd, P. (1993). *The impact of workplace literacy programs: A new model for evaluating the impact of workplace literacy programs* (Technical report TR 93-2). Philadelphia: University of Pennsylvania, National Center on Adult Literacy.

Oakes, J. (1985). *Keeping track: How students structure inequality*. New Haven, CT: Yale University Press.

Polloway, E., Patton, J., Epstein, M., & Smith, T. (1993). Comprehensive curriculum for students with mild disabilities. In E. Meyen, G. Vergason, & R. Whelan (Eds.), *Educating students with mild disabilities* (pp. 255–272). Denver: Love Publishing.

Rieth, H., & Polsgrove, L. (1994). Curriculum and instructional issues in teaching secondary students with learning disabilities. *Learning Disabilities Research & Practice, 9*(2), 118–126.

Scanlon, D., Deshler, D., & Schumaker, J. (1996). Can a strategy be taught and learned in secondary inclusive classrooms? *Learning Disabilities Research and Practice, 11*(1), 41–57.

Schumaker, J., & Deshler, D. (1988). Implementing the regular education initiative in secondary schools: A different ballgame. *Journal of Learning Disabilities, 21*(1), 36–42.

Schumaker, J., Deshler, D., Alley, G., & Warner, M. (1983). Toward the development of an intervention model for learning disabled adolescents. *Exceptional Education Quarterly, 4*(3), 295–304.

Smith, T., Polloway, E., Patton, J., & Dowdy, C. (1995). *Teaching children with special needs in inclusive settings.* Boston: Allyn & Bacon.

Will, M. (1986). Educating children with learning problems: A shared responsibility. *Exceptional Children, 52,* 411–415.

York, J., & Reynolds, M. (1996). Special education and inclusion. In J. Sikula (Ed.), *Handbook on research on teacher education* (2d ed.) (pp. 820–836). New York: Macmillan.

Zigmond, N. (1990). Rethinking secondary school programs for students with learning disabilities. *Focus on Exceptional Children, 23*(1), 1–22.

Zigmond, N, Jenkins, J., Fuchs, L., Deno, S., Fuchs, D., Baker, J., Jenkins, L, & Couthino, M. (1995). Special education in restructured schools: Findings from three multi-year studies. *Phi Delta Kappan, 76*(7), 531–540.

17 Curriculum-Based Collaboration

VICTOR NOLET AND GERALD TINDAL

WITHIN INCLUSIVE SETTINGS, special education teachers and general education teachers have been forced to work more closely together. This selection presents a model that has been implemented successfully in several states. It provides the necessary ingredients for effective instruction of all students, and especially those with disabilities.

Collaboration occurs when two or more individuals work together to complete a project, create a product, or solve a problem. When people collaborate, they enter into a purposeful, goal-directed relationship with equitable contributions from all participants. In schools, collaboration could involve teachers working together to plan lessons, develop curricula, team teach, engage in peer coaching, or adapt instruction for a particular student.

When collaborative relationships develop among teachers, benefits accrue for them and for their students. Teachers gain increased opportunities to learn content, improve practice, and receive feedback. They develop a greater sense of collegiality and community, and they experience less professional isolation (Firestone & Pennel, 1993). At the same time, peer collaboration among teachers has been identified as an effective strategy for accommodating students who have special needs in general education classrooms (Johnson & Pugach, 1991; Phillips & McCullough, 1990). For all of these reasons, enthusiasm continues to grow for the creation of collaborative relationships among general education and special education teachers with the goal that students who have special needs can effectively be included in general education classrooms. Given the apparent benefits of collaboration among teachers, it is surprising that it doesn't occur more regularly in schools, but, unfortunately, ongoing collaboration among teachers is still the exception rather than the norm.

Organizational as well as cultural forces work to limit both opportunities and motivation for collaboration among teachers. The physical organization of schools tends not to facilitate collaboration. Each teacher works in a separate classroom and rarely has opportunities to interact substantially with peers. Scheduling and staffing patterns in many schools also prevent development of collaborative relationships. Virtually every minute of many teachers' workdays is consumed with directly supervising or teaching students. Furthermore, to maintain adequate "coverage" of classes, teachers' planning periods often are scheduled when the individuals with whom teachers could most profitably collaborate are engaged in teaching. It is not uncommon for teachers at all grade levels to report that they go through entire school days in which they have few if any conversations with other adults.

Even when schools are organized to facilitate collaboration, cultural and attitudinal factors may limit the extent to which it can occur. Many teachers lack both specific skills associated with collaboration as well as a general sense of the purpose and benefits of collaboration. Strong norms of privacy permit social interactions, but they limit discussions about teaching practice (Little, 1990). General education classroom teachers and "specialized" support personnel, such as special education teachers or school psychologists, may have different levels of training and knowledge, so that potential collaborators may not view themselves as equals.

One of the biggest barriers to effective collaboration in middle and high schools may be that the actual practice of special education differs dramatically from the practice of general education, and often there is a lack of a mutual understanding of the different roles and responsibilities different teachers fill. Indeed, special education and general education teachers working at the middle and high school levels may actually adhere to fundamentally different belief systems about the goals of education.

General education content teachers often enter the profession because they wish to share a commitment to and appreciation for their particular domain. For them, fidelity to their content implies that it is not enough that their students learn "anything at all" but that they learn some very specific things about a domain such as history, biology, earth science, or geography. Many content area teachers consider the learning of science, history, or math vital to an adequate quality of life for all students, and their goal in working with a special education or remedial teacher is to find ways to help students develop a deeper appreciation or understanding in a particular content area. However, because general education is oriented toward groups of students, content teachers tend to be rewarded for allocating time and expertise to ensure that the greatest number of students in their classes learn content information.

Contrast this orientation with that of many special education teachers who view requirements that students take certain content classes or pass minimal competency tests as irrelevant distractions from the goal of teaching their students to read or write more effectively or to find and keep a job. Special education teachers view success in relative terms with respect to individual students. A special educator may be less concerned that a particular student masters a particular domain such as history or biology than that the student demonstrates improved use of basic literacy or vocational functioning skills. For these teachers, the goal of working with content teachers is to find the straightest path to helping their students "get past" required classes.

To be effective, collaboration models aimed at supporting students who have special needs must bridge organizational and attitudinal roadblocks such as these so that special education and general education teachers can communicate effectively about content and pedagogy. Both the general educator's and the special educator's perspectives are needed. It is in the best interest of many students who have special needs to learn to use key information in the content domains. At the same time, literacy and career development must continue to be a priority for many students whose options after high school will be severely limited by diminished proficiency in basic skills in reading, written expression, and math.

Curriculum-Based Collaboration

Curriculum-based collaboration (CBC) is based on the notion that the expertise, perspectives, and attitudes that general education and special education teachers bring to the classroom are distinct and complementary. The model incorporates the combined expertise of special education and general education teachers in an ongoing process that focuses on specific information presented in mainstream content classes such as social studies or general science. Curriculum-based collaboration was developed by the authors in an ongoing program of research at the University of Oregon and the University of Maryland. The model has been implemented in suburban and urban middle school classrooms in the Pacific Northwest and in two large East Coast cities. Throughout the development process, general education and special education teachers have been integrally involved in formulating and field testing each component of the model.

The goal of curriculum-based collaboration is for students who have special needs to receive most of their content-area instruction from content-area classroom teachers whose background and experiences are based in a content domain such as one of the sciences or social studies. These students could include those served in special education resource room programs or other students who may be at risk of school failure, for example, those who speak English as a second language. However, CBC is not necessarily intended as a mechanism to facilitate full-time inclusion of all students in general education classes. Some students who have special needs may occasionally be best served in settings other than the general education classroom. Also, for some students to benefit fully from instruction in general education, special education, remedial, or other classes, support teachers may need to provide supplemental instruction in basic skills or in social skills or strategies.

With CBC, we view the primary goal of instruction in middle and high school content classes as teaching students to think and communicate in real-world contexts (Cole, 1990; Nickerson, 1989). Achievement is defined not as acquisition of a specific body of content knowledge but as development of expertise in using that information in complex intellectual operations. For students to learn to think like historians, geographers, or biologists, they need to serve cognitive apprenticeships (Brown, Collins, & Duguid, 1989) with content-area teachers who can model the kind of thinking used by real-world practitioners in a domain.

In curriculum-based collaboration, the content-area teacher is viewed as an expert in the domain in which instruction occurs. We realize that not all teachers, particularly in middle schools, have educational degrees in the subject matter they teach, and the actual expertise teachers bring to the classroom may vary greatly. However, when compared with a special education teacher, a general education content teacher who teaches a particular content area on a daily or weekly basis probably has a richer sense of the important information students would be expected to learn as well as anticipated performance outcomes. Therefore, we use the perceptions of the general education content teacher regarding which information is most important for students to learn as the basis for instructional planning.

Generally, curriculum-based collaboration occurs between two teachers, one of whom is a general education classroom teacher and one of whom is a special education or other support or remedial teacher. The general education and special education teachers each have specific knowledge and skills they contribute to the relationship, but they function as equal partners. The content-area teacher brings to this relationship expertise in a particular domain that permits the teacher to identify key knowledge forms (facts, concepts, principles, and procedures) around which content instruction can be organized. The special education teacher, in turn, brings pedagogical expertise related to methods for designing instruction, managing the classroom, and motivating at-risk learners. Information transfer is two-way in that both teachers are expected to gain new skills and knowledge as a result of the relationship. Interactions focus on the knowledge contained in content-area curricula, content-area pedagogy, as well as specific methods or strategies that are effective with students who have special needs.

Curriculum-based collaboration involves a combination of direct and indirect service delivery from both the general education and special education teacher, with teaching and planning responsibilities shared or divided by agreement. Content instruction occurs in the general education classroom, but supplemental pull-out or pull-in services may be provided in either the general education classroom or in special education settings. Often teachers engaged in curriculum-based collaboration use team or cooperative teaching, with both teachers working in one classroom; however, at times, services may be delivered in the context of a traditional resource room or remedial program. Curriculum-based collaboration is particularly well suited for use in classrooms that employ peer tutoring or cooperative learning because a wide range of activities and assessment formats typically are developed. Planning and communication meetings take place outside of instructional times, but because interactions are frequent and structured around content knowledge forms, meetings tend to be short, often lasting less than 15 minutes.

Curriculum-based collaboration consists of the six components shown in Figure 17.1. First the key information associated with a particular unit of instruction is

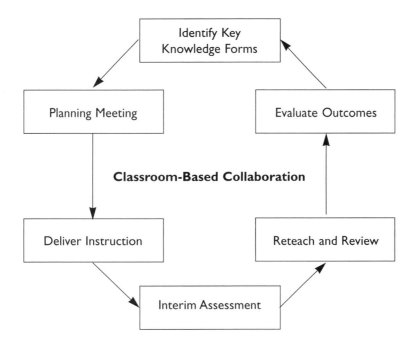

Figure 17.1 *Steps in Curriculum-Based Collaboration*

identified by the general education teacher. Next, the collaborating teachers meet to clarify activities and responsibilities. After the information to be taught has been specified and activities planned, both teachers deliver initial instruction. Next, interim data are collected to assess the effectiveness of planning and instruction. Based on these data, the teachers decide whether some information needs to be retaught or reviewed during the final phase of instruction. Finally, various forms of assessment strategies are used to evaluate the overall outcomes of instruction, and this evaluation then triggers the next cycle of collaboration. Each of these components is described in detail here.

Identify Key Content

One of the problems general education and special education teachers face when they attempt to collaborate to teach content information is that they don't share a vocabulary for communicating about the content of instruction. Consider this situation:

When a special education teacher with whom we worked asked a sixth-grade general science teacher what she was planning to teach during a two-week period, the reply was "I'm going to cover Chapter 13. I'll teach fossil fuels." The special education teacher then proceeded to teach three special needs students placed in that science teacher's classroom to decode and tell the meaning of five examples of fossil fuels listed at the end of Chapter 13. However, when the authors observed in the science teacher's classroom, we found that most of the instruction centered on renewable alternatives to fossil fuels rather than examples of fossil fuels. Indeed, only one of the examples listed in the textbook was ever discussed in class. Furthermore, students spent very little time interacting with the textbook, so their ability to read and understand the vocabulary terms, although important in the larger context of literacy, was not central in developing the understanding of fossil fuels valued by the classroom teacher.

Clearly, these two teachers had very different ideas about what it meant to "teach fossil fuels" or "cover Chapter 13." The general education teacher based her instruction on her understanding of the implications of the characteristics of fossil fuels (i.e., they're nonrenewable), whereas the special education teacher based her instruction on prior knowledge of the students' skills (i.e., their reading ability was insufficient to comprehend the textbook). Neither of these approaches to "covering Chapter 13" was wrong, they were just unsynchronized. The result was that the three students with special needs were no better prepared to learn and use the information valued by their science teacher as a result of the instruction they received in special education. At the same time, they had few opportunities to practice the study skills and comprehension strategies they had been taught in the resource room.

Knowledge Forms and Intellectual Operations

To facilitate clear communication between collaborating teachers, curriculum-based collaboration employs an analysis of the conceptual knowledge contained in each unit of instruction presented in content classes. We use a taxonomy of knowledge adapted from one first presented by Roid and Haladyna (1982) that includes four forms of knowledge and five intellectual operations, or formats for using information. The four types of knowledge forms are facts, concepts, principles ("if-then" relationships), and procedures, which generally are formatted as a chain of principles. Information can be used in one of five intellectual operations: summarization, illustration, prediction, evaluation, and explanation.

The first step in curriculum-based collaboration is for the general education content teacher to identify the specific facts, concepts, and principles deemed critical for understanding the content of a particular unit of instruction. These key knowledge forms are then shared with the special education teacher, and together they plan activities that incorporate the intellectual operations in a range of instructional and assessment formats. By using operationalized definitions of the knowledge forms and intellectual operations, it is possible for teachers to succinctly and effectively communicate with one another about the exact information to be presented in a unit of instruction, thus preventing the kind of misunderstanding illustrated earlier.

Facts are defined as simple associations between names, objects, events, and places that use singular exemplars. For example, the statement "Columbus is the capital of Ohio" is a fact because there is only one example of the capital of Ohio.

Because facts describe only one relationship, they may be grouped together in descriptions of unique events, objects, or places. In a chapter in a world geography textbook, a section describing the Indian subcontinent might include specific facts about climate and topography grouped together under the subtitle "Four Greats of India" (great rivers, great winds, great mountains, and great plateau). However, each individual fact (for example, the name of each of the rivers or the location of the great plateau) would need to be taught and remembered as a specific name or place. In this respect, facts may not be difficult to teach or test but they are especially difficult to learn because they must be memorized and have little explanatory power beyond the specific relationship they describe.

Concepts are clusters of events, names, dates, objects, and places that share a common set of defining attributes or characteristics. A concept may be thought of as a category having a rule that defines its relevant characteristics, a name, and a set of instances or exemplars that share the key attributes. In this definition, rules provide the basis for organizing the attributes of the concept; these attributes, in turn, provide the criteria for distinguishing examples of the concept from nonexamples. This is a classical view of concepts that does not cover every contingency encountered in content classes, but it does provide a framework within which teachers can share information about what should be taught and how to teach it. Indeed, many concepts encountered in content classes are quite complex, with conditional or nested attributes or membership in multiple categories. When such concepts are targeted, collaborating teachers must clarify attributes and examples through discussion during the planning meeting.

Principles indicate causal or covariant relationships among different facts or concepts, more often the latter. A principle usually represents an if-then or cause-effect relationship, although this relationship may not be stated explicitly. A principle generally involves multiple applications in which the fundamental relationship among the relevant concepts is constant across virtually all examples of the concepts. For example, the law of supply and demand may be taught as the principle "when supply goes up, demand goes down," with comparable applications found in the contexts of medieval European city-states, a child's lemonade stand, and the 1929 stock market crash.

Procedures involve the steps or phases required to complete a process. For example, the topic "Scientific Method" may be taught in seventh-grade science class as a series of steps proceeding from formation of a hypothesis, construction of an experiment, collection of data, and evaluation of results. However, procedural knowledge involves more than simply "knowing what" the steps are, but focuses on "knowing how" to execute those steps in an actual experiment (Anderson, 1983). Often procedures can be formatted as a set of principles that comprise a decision chain of the form "If A occurs, then I do B. If C occurs, then I do D." Execution then follows a series of decisions based on results obtained at each preceding step. For example, writing a research paper might involve a series of decisions about where to obtain information, which information to include, and the order in which information should be presented.

Concepts and principles form the bedrock of curriculum-based collaboration. Concepts have greater explanatory power than facts in that they can be broad enough to be applicable across multiple contexts within a domain but often are specific to a particular body of content. Similarly, while there may only be one or two key principles associated with a body of content or domain, they may link together as many as eight or ten key concepts in a few overarching relationships. Knowing the attributes and examples of the key concepts then sets the occasion for understanding the principles.

Concepts and principles can be used in a wide range of intellectual operations. These operations are arranged in increasing complexity, where summarization represents a less complex operation and prediction, evaluation, and explanation represent higher levels of complexity. Summarization is either a near-verbatim reproduction or a paraphrase (rewording or condensation of specific content previously presented in instruction). *Illustration* is generation or identification of an example of a concept or principle that was not presented previously during instruction. Because the student must attend to the key attributes or relationships of the concept or principle rather than simply recall an example presented during instruction, illustration involves the manipulation of information rather than simple recall. *Prediction* is description of a likely outcome, given a set of antecedent circumstances or conditions. *Evaluation* is analysis of a problem that requires a judgment to make a decision. Evaluation is a two-step process in which the student first makes a decision and then supports it with a rationale or an argument. *Explanation* is description of the antecedent circumstances or conditions that would be necessary to bring about a given outcome. Explanation is the reverse of prediction. The student must use information about a concept or principle to work backwards from the circumstances presented and tell what happened to create it.

Content Planning Worksheet

Using the framework just described, the general education teacher identifies the most important concepts and principles associated with a unit of instruction that is expected to last two to three weeks. This information is then summarized on a content planning worksheet that is shared with the special education teacher with whom she or he is collaborating. An example of a content planning worksheet for a unit on Europe in the Middle Ages is shown in Figure 17.2.

This form has three components that specify (a) the proposed schedule for instruction, (b) key knowledge forms that the teacher considers minimally essential for understanding the unit of instruction, and (c) activities and specific tasks that represent the outcomes expected to result from instruction. The general education content teacher completes the top two sections of the form, and the collaborating teachers work together to specify activities and tasks during the content planning meeting.

The schedule identifies the specific topic or unit that will be taught during a two- to three-week period, and the specific topic or activities that will be taught each day. In middle schools, this amount of time usually corresponds to one or two chap-

CONTENT PLANNING WORKSHEET

Teachers *Smithers/Newhall*   Class *World History*   Begin Date *November 14*

Schedule

Topic	Monday	Tuesday	Wednesday	Thursday	Friday
Middle Ages		When were the Middle Ages?	Life on the manor	Serfs, vassals, lords, knights	Quiz
City-States	City-states	Travel between city-states	The economy	Quiz	Coat of arms
	Make a shield	The plague	Castles	Review	Test

Knowledge Forms

	Attributes/If	Examples/Then
Trade	An exchange of goods/buying and selling	Imports/exports
Castle	A fortified group of buildings held by a vassal or a ruler in feudal societies	Windsor Castle Examples on page 85
Knight	A trained, armored horseman who fought wars in the early Middle Ages	Soldier or armored horseman
Plague	A widespread sickness	Bubonic plague in Europe in the 1340s AIDS

Activities and Tasks

Instructional Activity	Planning Tasks	Due Date
Reading Chapter 12, section 1 Chapter 12, section 2	Study guide for Chapter 12: Key concepts (S) Model illustration and evaluation of concepts (N)	November 17 November 22
Projects Make a shield with coat of arms	Study strategies for researching coat of arms (S)	November 20
Assignments Questions on page 97 Report: What did knights do?	Review key attributes of city-state and knights (S) Short evaluation essay on knight vs. lord(N)	November 16 November 20
Worksheets How were castles constructed?	Review attributes of castle (S)	November 21
Assessments Evaluation essay: Middle Ages vs. now, tell why. Test	Make up three practice essays for review (S) Review attributes of key concepts (S) .Make up test items (S & N)	November 22

Figure 17.2 *Content Planning Worksheet*

ters in a typical content-area textbook. At the high school level, it might correspond to a unit consisting of two to four chapters. The goal is to make the schedule realistic in terms of comprehensiveness but not so full of information that planning becomes impossible. At the same time, schedules that focus on too little content or too short a period of time are unnecessarily labor-intensive when additional planning worksheets must be completed or planning meetings held.

Typically, content teachers identify eight to ten key concepts and one or two principles in middle school classes and slightly more in high school classes. Many of the content-area teachers with whom we have worked have had difficulty in deciding what are the most important concepts or principles in a unit and subsequently in specifying the attributes of those knowledge forms. Their tendency often has been to include too much factual information (for example, names, dates, etc.) or to identify broader themes that have indefinite attributes or examples rather than specific concepts or principles. However, as teachers have become more comfortable with the framework of knowledge forms and intellectual operations presented here and as they engage in more conversations with other content teachers and special education teachers, they have tended to identify more focused lists of concepts and principles.

Outcomes are framed in the form of intellectual operations. For example, a teacher may wish to have students generate examples of (i.e., illustrate) key concepts or make predictions using key principles. On the content planning worksheet, outcomes are listed as activities and tasks. Instructional activities are the specific instructional and assessment events that take place during the two- to three-week period during which the unit is taught. Generally, activities are associated with specific materials such as the textbook or worksheets. Planning tasks refer to the things each teacher will do to help students accomplish the activities. On the planning worksheet shown in Figure 17.2, the initial of the teacher responsible for each task is included in parentheses after each task statement, as determined during the planning meeting.

In a sense, the content planning worksheet represents an agreement that is negotiated between the collaborating teachers. The knowledge forms and expected outcomes listed on the content planning worksheet represent the minimal requirements of performance for mastery of the topic covered in the two- to three-week unit. If a student is able to use the concepts or principles listed in the intellectual operations specified in the activities and tasks, then both teachers will agree that the student has mastered the topic. A more formal variation on this theme was described by Tindal and Germann (1991), *where mainstream consultation agreements* were used to specify the grade a student could earn and the responsibilities of the general and special education teachers and the student for ensuring that the student demonstrates sufficient mastery of secondary content material.

The content planning worksheet should function as a thumbnail sketch rather than a detailed blueprint of instruction in a content classroom. The general topic and overall content should remain stable, but the day-to-day activities can vary according to the needs of the teachers and students. As the collaboration process becomes more comfortable for the collaborators, the content planning worksheet actually functions more as a proposal, with specific details to be worked out during a face-to-face planning meeting. This is particularly true with respect to the outcomes and activities listed on the lower part of the form. The content teacher suggests expected outcomes, but the specific instructional activities and planning tasks get worked out during a planning meeting.

Planning Meeting

After the general education content teacher has identified the key knowledge forms and desired outcomes for the unit of instruction, the form is shared with the special education or remedial teacher collaborator and a meeting is scheduled. The purpose of the meeting is to finalize the schedule of instruction, clarify the attributes and examples associated with the knowledge forms, and plan the activities and tasks that will be implemented.

Depending on the nature of the relationship that has developed between the collaborating teachers, the planning meeting may be quite informal or fairly structured. When two teachers have been working together for some time, are in agreement about the nature of the knowledge forms to be targeted, and have established norms and responsibilities for designing and implementing instruction, planning meetings can be as brief as 10 minutes and take place "on the fly" after or before school or over lunch in the teachers' lounge. When two teachers are just beginning to collaborate, they may need to invest more time during planning meetings developing consensus about the nature of facts, concepts, and principles, and clarifying attributes and examples. Some teachers find it useful to hold planning meetings in installments, where the first session focuses on the key knowledge forms and subsequent meetings focus on planning activities and assessment tasks that use complex intellectual operations. This arrangement keeps the amount of time devoted to any one meeting to a minimum. In the early stages of development of a collaborative relationship among two teachers, it is useful to use a checklist such as the one illustrated in Figure 17.3 to structure the meeting. Such a form helps to keep the meeting focused on the key information that must be shared and ensures that the critical instructional activities, assessment formats, and planning tasks are discussed.

The key tasks to be accomplished during the planning meeting are shown on the checklist. These focus on completion of the content planning worksheet, but also include explicit reference to the areas that must be agreed upon during the collaboration process. Specifically, the teachers must decide what intellectual operations will be modeled or prompted in the various activities and tasks. For example, in a unit on plate tectonics, collaborating teachers might decide whether students would be required to simply recognize examples of different types of faults or evaluate the potential damage various faults could cause in a specific scenario.

Development of a timeline for completion of assignments and tasks is the final task to be accomplished during the planning meeting. This step ensures that the teachers' instruction stays coordinated throughout the unit and is especially important if instruction is delivered in separate settings. On the content planning worksheet, the column labeled "Due Date" specifies the schedule of events.

Planning Meeting Checklist			
Date of Meeting _____			
Teachers _____			
Task	Yes/No		Comment
Topic Identified	yes	no	
Schedule Outlined	yes	no	
Knowledge Forms Identified	yes	no	
Attributes/Examples Identified	yes	no	
Reading Tasks	yes	no	
Problem-Solving Tasks	yes	no	
Assignments Specified	yes	no	
Final Test Discussed	yes	no	
Grading Negotiated	yes	no	
Pull-Away Schedule Discussed	yes	no	
Student Reminders	yes	no	
Notes:			

Figure 17.3 *Planning Meeting Checklist*

Deliver Instruction

To the maximum extent possible, students who have special needs are expected to participate in the general education classes, with supportive services scheduled at another time during the day. Therefore, much of the instruction delivered in curriculum-based collaboration takes place in the general education classroom, with special education and general education teachers working cooperatively to plan and provide instruction for all students in the class. They may co-teach, with each collaborator taking responsibility for some aspect of instruction, or they may run separate groups in the same classroom.

However, CBC does not necessarily imply that *all* lessons are delivered with both teachers working in the general education classroom. Scheduling constraints or the preferences of the collaborating teachers may result in support services being delivered in settings outside the content classroom. For example, in many middle and high schools, during any one class period, students scheduled into a resource room may represent different grade levels and take a variety of content classes. It would be impossible for the special education teacher to co-teach in a content class during this period.

When students do receive assistance in another setting during the class period, the collaborating teachers plan activities and tasks to ensure that students don't miss new information presented in the general education classroom. For example, the class may be scheduled to work individually on reports or projects or pursue an enrichment activity not directly related to the key knowledge forms. Supportive instruction provided by a special education or remedial teacher focuses primarily on the key knowledge forms and intellectual operations targeted on the content planning worksheet. At the same time, while instruction in the general education classroom may involve additional information or activities, the key knowledge forms represent the basis for all other instruction. Naturally, the exact methods of instruction, specific activities, curriculum materials, and so on vary from teacher to teacher; however, supportive services provided by a special education or remedial teacher tend to be effective when they are aimed at (a) previewing, (b) modeling, (c) providing practice in using key knowledge forms, and (d) reviewing the key knowledge forms.

Previewing involves teaching students who have special needs the attributes and examples of key concepts and principles before they are presented to the rest of the class. Previewing provides students with two advantages. First, students have the maximum amount of time possible to learn and practice using the concepts and principles associated with a unit, particularly, complex or abstract information that might be difficult to master. Second, when a particular concept is then presented in the general education classroom, the student already is familiar with it and can participate more fully in class discussions or benefit from demonstrations or explanations presented by the general education teacher. Previewing can be particularly effective when the general education teacher subsequently models the key knowledge forms during instruction and provides students with opportunities to practice using them in complex intellectual operations (Nolet & Tindal, 1994).

Modeling occurs when teachers model the use of key concepts in complex intellectual operations. Their students tend to use those concepts more frequently in authentic problem-solving tasks and they tend to answer correctly test items that pertain to those concepts (Nolet & Tindal, 1993). Teachers can model the use of key knowledge forms in each of the intellectual operations by posing questions or scenarios and then engaging in a think-aloud process to make the thinking process visible for students. Here is an example of an instructional dialogue that models the intellectual operation evaluation with the concepts of fossil fuels, acid precipitation, and nonrenewable energy:

Teacher: Newtopia is a planet in a galaxy not far from here. The people who live there have just discovered fossil fuels. Should they develop them or not?

Student: Well...Yeah, I guess so....

Teacher: Fossil fuels are formed over millions of years when trees and animals decay and are placed under tons of pressure. Fossil fuels are nonrenewable. When they are used up, there are no more. If the people develop the fossil fuels, they will run the risk of creating air pollution and acid precipitation. Also, they could run out of fossil fuels. No one on Newtopia knows how much fossil fuel they have. On the other hand, they could develop the fossil fuels and have a much higher quality of life. They could have all the modern conveniences we have. This would give them more time to create music and art and go to school. We would have to decide which is better: to have a clean planet like the people of Newtopia have now or to have a higher quality of life like we have now.

Development and administration of *frequent practice activities* are critical tasks for the teacher providing supplemental support. Practice activities could be in the form of short problem-solving tasks requiring a written or oral response, questions that prompt intellectual operations, or other activities such as worksheets or cooperative learning activities. Often, when one of the collaborating teachers develops practice activities, they are implemented in the general education classroom, and they provide a powerful interface between the general and special education programs.

Reviewing occurs when a teacher reteaches the key concepts or principles after they have been presented in the general education content class. Reviewing can occur any time in the unit after a knowledge form has been taught in the general education class and involves explicit reteaching of the key information. For example, if a general education science teacher taught the attributes of a fossil fuel during class on Monday, the special education teacher might ask students to give an example and attributes of fossil fuels on Wednesday. Ideally, the collaborating teachers time the presentation of new material in the general education classroom with supportive previewing, modeling, and reviewing so students, in effect, receive massed practice in using key knowledge forms.

Interim Assessment

To support ongoing communication and instructional planning, teachers using curriculum-based collaboration collect information about student learning on an ongoing basis throughout the two- to three-week period a unit is taught. Measures can include short problem-solving tasks that require students to use key knowledge forms in complex intellectual operations or perception probes in which students list the terms they think are most important for understanding the topic being taught (Tindal & Nolet, in press). Other interim measures that can contribute to instructional decision-making include informal observations and traditional criterion-referenced quizzes that require students to summarize or illustrate key knowledge forms. Interim assessments can be administered to the entire class or to a subgroup of students and usually are administered after about one third to one half of the information that is to be taught in the unit has been presented. They usually focus on the knowledge forms and intellectual operations the collaborating teachers view as most important in the instruction that has been delivered to that point. Responsibility for developing, administering, and scoring the interim assessments is finalized in the initial planning meeting.

Problem-Solving Tasks

Problem-solving tasks require students to apply the targeted facts, concepts, principles, and procedures in one of the intellectual operations described earlier by making predictions or decisions or developing explanations. Students might be asked to respond in writing with a brief essay or orally in a short interview. Generally, interim problem-solving tasks take no more than 10 minutes to administer. Scoring is conducted using holistic sorting or analytic rating scales focusing on the accuracy and effectiveness of students' use of the key knowledge forms. The intent of interim problem-solving tasks is to inform instruction by revealing student misconceptions or factual errors, and they are not used to grade student performance or generalized learning.

Perception Probes

Perception probes focus on students' opinions of which information they view as most important for understanding the content of instruction, regardless of their actual comprehension of content. Perception probes are administered one or two times during a unit and take approximately 10 minutes. Students are simply asked to list the most important words and ideas in the unit. Scoring involves tallying the most frequently occurring words and the targeted knowledge forms on the perception probes completed by the class. Perception probes permit the collaborating teachers to check the alignment of student perceptions with their own goals for instruction. If it turns out that very few students list as important the terms the collaborating teachers want them to understand, instruction needs to focus student attention on those terms specifically. On the other hand, if student perceptions about which information is most important match the teachers', the instructors can present additional knowledge forms or use information in more complex intellectual operations.

Reteach and Review

Based on the information collected during interim assessments, the collaborating teachers hold at least one interim planning meeting in which they finalize plans for instruction for the remainder of the unit. This meeting is analogous to the high altitude camp climbers establish before their final assault on the summit of a very high mountain. The collaborating teachers review the content planning worksheet to adjust the schedule and to jettison or reprioritize the knowledge forms and activities and tasks they expect to accomplish. During the remainder of the time the unit will be taught (that is, the final assault on the summit), instruction will focus on the most important knowledge forms and on that information about which students seem to have the weakest understanding.

As with the initial planning meeting, some of the teachers with whom we have worked have used a fairly formal meeting process, employing a meeting checklist similar to that shown in Figure 17.3, while others have developed informal methods for sharing information. Interim planning meetings generally are held after about two-thirds of the content has been presented.

During the final phase of instruction, when information is reviewed and retaught, collaborating teachers often arrange to co-teach some of the lessons. This allows both teachers to obtain "on-line" information about student learning and to deliver instruction in small groups of various configurations based on students' needs and understandings. It is particularly useful during this final phase of instruction for the teachers to model use of information in complex intellectual operations and for students to have adequate practice, with feedback, in using key information and intellectual operations. Therefore, the teachers may arrange more hands-on problem-solving tasks, peer tutoring, or cooperative learning activities during this time.

Evaluate Outcomes

The final phase in curriculum-based collaboration is to collect student performance data to evaluate the effectiveness of instruction. Measures can include more elaborate versions of the problem-solving tasks used in interim assessments and criterion-referenced tests that focus on the key knowledge forms used in various intellectual operations (Roid & Haladyna, 1982). Generally, development of outcome measures is a collaborative process, with both collaborating teachers contributing tasks or test items and assisting with scoring. Outcome data can be evaluated using a norm-referenced perspective in which the overall performance of the class is summarized or an individual-referenced perspective in which the performance of specific students is compared over time.

In a norm-referenced perspective student performance can be summarized by knowledge form. In our work we have used the average item easiness (i.e., percentage of students who passed each item) for all items pertaining to specific concepts. For example, suppose an assessment task administered to a class of 20 students contains three items that pertain to the concept "dual economy." The items are passed by 18, 15, and 20 students, respectively. The first item has an easiness of .90, the second an easiness of .75, and the third an easiness of 1.0. Thus the easiness rating for the concept "dual economy" is .88. This easiness rating can be compared with that for other concepts tested, and the teachers can develop a profile of the extent to which each concept was mastered by the class.

We also have used short essays and brief interview tasks in norm-referenced perspective. Students are presented with a task employing one of the intellectual operations that involves manipulation of information, such as evaluation or explanation. These tasks are then scored using an analytic scoring system that rates students' effectiveness in making a decision and supporting it with content information (Nolet & Tindal, in press). Normative data can involve these qualitative ratings as well as the frequency with which students use targeted concepts in essays or oral responses. If the class masters a sufficient number of key knowledge forms in a desired range of intellectual operations, instruction can move on to the next unit. If performance does not meet teacher expectations, the collaborating teachers can decide whether to modify instruction or reteach certain information.

In an individual-referenced perspective, the performance of a particular student is compared with her or his previous performance on similar tasks. Growth over time is evaluated, using a time-series approach to data analysis. We have used two measures of student learning in individual-referenced evaluations. One is performance on targeted concepts on criterion-referenced tests. For example, if a student answers correctly two out of the three items pertaining to "dual economy" on the test in the previous example, her score for that concept would be 67%. If the test samples four other concepts, for which she receives scores of 100%, 90%, 50%, and 75%, her combined concept score is 76% for that unit. Concept scores can be plotted for each unit to observe whether she is maintaining an adequate level of performance. Because the content changes with each unit, decision rules may be tied to maintenance of a particular level of performance (for example, at least 75%) rather than to a rate of growth as might be the case with curriculum-based measures (Fuchs & Deno, 1991).

The second individual-referenced measure we have used is student ratings on use of intellectual operations on problem-solving tasks such as interviews or essays. This rating is then plotted and compared with ratings on previous tasks that required the same intellectual operation. For example, a student's performance in using social studies content to make a decision and support it with a cogent rationale can be evaluated by comparing tasks that require the intellectual operation of evaluation. Again, because the scale contains only five anchors, and because the content of units is constantly changing, we are more interested in observing whether students "hold their own" and show growth over longer periods of time than on short-term growth. However, it is possible to make valid decisions about the success of a student in a content class by systematically evaluating their growth in complex thinking within the context of specific content material.

Making Collaboration Work

For curriculum-based collaboration to be successful, it must be implemented in an environment in which there exists a collaborative ethic. According to Phillips and McCullough (1990), in an organization where this ethic exists, all professionals share joint responsibility for problems as well as joint accountability and recognition for problem solution. A collaborative ethic involves a belief that pooling talents and resources is advantageous and that the outcomes of collaboration are desirable (Phillips & McCullough, 1990).

Clearly, the kind of collaborative relationships we have described here do not develop overnight, and in schools where collaboration is not currently occurring, considerable time and energy will need to be expended to gain peer and administrative support for such efforts. We offer the following suggestions for those interested in initiating curriculum-based collaboration:

1. *Gain administrative support.* In schools where a collaborative ethic doesn't yet exist, organizational barriers may prevent individual teachers from going beyond small-scale collaboration efforts. However, when building and district administrators understand and support the goals of collaborative service delivery, organizational barriers can be addressed at the system level. Keep administrators informed of the goals of collaboration and share data that demonstrate success.
2. *Begin small.* Work with one teacher on one unit and with a few students. As relationships develop, more elaborate interventions can be tried.
3. *Collect data regularly that can support valid inferences about student performance in content classes.* Perception probes or short problem-solving tasks can be administered to individual students or classes, even when collaboration isn't ongoing. These data can serve as the basis for beginning a conversation with potential collaborators.

References

Anderson, J. R. (1983). *The architecture of cognition.* Cambridge, MA: Harvard University Press.

Brown, J. S., Collins, A., & Duguid, P. (1989). Situated cognition and the culture of learning. *Educational Researcher, 18*(1), 32–42.

Cole, N. S. (1990). Conceptions of educational achievement. *Educational Researcher, 19*(3), 2–7.

Firestone, W. A., & Pennel, J. R. (1993). Teacher commitment, working conditions, and differential incentive policies. *Review of Educational Research, 63*, 489–525.

Fuchs, L. S., & Deno, S. L. (1991). Paradigmatic distinctions between instructionally relevant measurement models. *Exceptional Children, 57*, 489–500.

Johnson, L. J., & Pugach, M. C. (1991). Peer collaboration: Accommodating students with mild learning and behavior problems. *Exceptional Children, 57*, 454–455.

Little, J. W. (1990). The persistence of privacy: Autonomy and initiative in teachers' professional relations. *Teacher College Record, 91*(4), 509 534.

Nickerson, R. S. (1989). New directions in educational assessment. *Educational Researcher, 18*(9), 3–7.

Nolet, V. W., & Tindal, G. (1993). Special education in content classes: Development of a model and practical procedures. *Remedial and Special Education, 14*(1), 36–48.

Nolet, V. W., & Tindal, G. (1994). Instruction and learning in middle school science classes: Implications for students with learning disabilities. *Journal of Special Education, 28*, 166–187.

Nolet, V. W., & Tindal, G. R. (in press). Essays as valid measures of learning in middle school science classes. *Learning Disabilities Quarterly.*

Phillips, V., & McCullough, L. (1990). Consultation-based programming: Instituting the collaborative ethic in schools. *Exceptional Children, 56*, 291–304.

Roid, G. H., & Haladyna, T. M. (1982). *A technology for test item writing.* New York: Academic Press.

Tindal, G., & Nolet, V. W. (in press). Serving students with learning disabilities in middle school content classes: A descriptive study of critical variables linking instruction and assessment. *Journal of Special Education.*

Tindal, G. R., & Germann, G. (1991). Mainstream consultation agreements in secondary schools. In G. Stoner, M. Shinn, & H. Walker (Eds.), *Interventions for Achievement and Behavior Problems.* Washington, DC: National Association of School Psychologists.

18 Teaching Concepts: Procedures for the Design and Delivery of Instruction

MARY ANNE PRATER

SO MUCH OF WHAT STUDENTS LEARN depends on their development of concepts. Students with mild disabilities have difficulty with concepts, especially if they do not have a concrete basis. This selection affords the type of understanding that general education and special education teachers alike must have to design and deliver effectively the concepts on which most of learning is dependent.

Concepts are the fundamental structure for thought throughout a human being's lifetime. As Ausubel (1968) stated,

> anyone who pauses long enough to give the problem some serious thought cannot escape the conclusion that man lives in a world of concepts rather than a world of objects, events, and situations.... Reality, figuratively speaking, is experienced through a conceptual or categorical filter. (p. 505)

Although most students learn many concepts through observation and experience, learning concepts consumes an integral part of any school curriculum (Markle, 1975). In fact, all of the content of school learning may be reduced to skill learning, problem solving, or concept learning (Shumway, White, Wilson, & Brombacher, 1983).

Normal development of concept knowledge "depends upon the abilities to abstract, generalize, and categorize and to establish relationships between symbols and referents" (Lovitt, 1989, p. 152). Students with disabilities often do not demonstrate this normal development of concept formation (Lerner, 1988; Wiig & Semel, 1984); for example, they often demonstrate limited knowledge of concepts (Kirk &

Chalfant, 1984; Lerner, 1988; Myers & Hammill, 1990). Social and/or perceptual difficulties may inhibit their ability to accurately learn concepts through their personal experiences or observation of the world around them (Kirk & Chalfant, 1984). Students with mental retardation also demonstrate this difficulty. Individuals with retardation, often described as less efficient in formal learning situations, "are especially deficient in acquiring information and skills in informal or naturally occurring situations" (Kramer, Piersel, & Glover, 1988, p. 43).

Language plays an important role in concept development (Lerner, 1988). Students with mild disabilities often demonstrate limited language skills. This is true of students with learning disabilities (Dudley-Marling, 1985; Dudley-Marling & Searle, 1988; Feagens & Appelbaum, 1986; Vellutino, 1977; Wiig, 1984) and students with mild mental retardation (Abbeduto, Furman, & Davies, 1989; Abbeduto & Nuccio, 1991). Elementary-aged students with mild mental retardation, for example, have been shown to have significant deficits in understanding and using basic concepts, such as directional (e.g., left, right) and positional (e.g., on, under, between) (Nelson & Cummings, 1981, 1984). Some students with learning disabilities have demonstrated restricted or only literal understanding of word meanings (Candler & Hildreth, 1990; Lerner, 1988; Lovitt, 1989; Wiig & Semel, 1984).

Students with mild disabilities reportedly have particular difficulty grasping abstract concepts (Hardman, Drew, Egan, & Wolf, 1990; Myers & Hammill, 1990). Authors describing instructional procedures for these students generally advocate the use of concrete demonstrations and examples and suggest that teachers move gradually from the concrete to the semiconcrete to the abstract (e.g., Mercer & Mercer, 1989; Nelson, Cummings, & Boltman, 1991; Polloway, Patton, Payne, & Payne, 1989).

Effective concept instruction remains important for all students. However, inasmuch as students with disabilities (a) often fail to learn concepts accurately through observation and experience, (b) often demonstrate language difficulties, and (c) have particular difficulty with abstract concepts, concept instruction for this population is particularly vital. Special and remedial educators must be appropriately prepared to design and deliver instruction so that they do not teach or promote misconceptions (Prater, 1987b).

What follows are suggested procedures from a "classical" or traditional point of view for the design and implementation of concept instruction. Researchers have suggested that concepts that meet the classical or traditional framework are primarily, but not exclusively, science and mathematics concepts (Fleming, 1987). Many other concepts cannot be characterized in the classical framework as presented in this chapter. Consequently, the procedures outlined here must be viewed as inherently limited in scope.

In addition to the outlined procedures, a brief discussion of the role of technology in concept instruction follows. Prior to the suggested procedures, concept learning, as well as characteristics of and relationships between concepts from the classical point of view, is described.

Concept Learning

A concept, when considered as a mental construct, consists of "a person's organized information about an item or a class of items that enables the person to discriminate the item or the class of items from her items and also to relate it to other items and classes of items" (Klausmeier, 1990, p. 94).

Concepts have *defining attributes*, or attributes that differentiate the example of a concept from examples of other concepts. Attributes that do not differentiate the example of a concept from examples of other concepts are called *variable attributes*. The defining attribute of the concept *round* is the shape we define as round. Variable attributes would include such things as the size or color of the shape, and whether it is an object, a picture of an object, or a line drawing.

Concepts with two or more defining attributes require rules for joining them together. These rules can be divided into at least three types: conjunctive (*and*), disjunctive (*and/or*), and relational (Bruner, Goodnow, & Austin, 1956; Martorella, 1972; Merrill & Tennyson, 1977; Stanley, 1984). Conjunctive concepts have two or more essential or defining attributes, all of which must be present for an example to be a member of the concept set. For example, a *chord* is defined as three or more musical tones sounded simultaneously. To be an example of a chord, there must be three or more musical tones *and* they must sound simultaneously. Three tones sounded, but not simultaneously, or only one or two musical tones that are sounded simultaneously, are not examples of the concept *chord*.

Disjunctive concepts are unlike conjunctive concepts in that they have alternative sets of defining attributes, each of which might define the concept. A commonly used example of a disjunctive concept is a *strike* in baseball (e.g., Bruner et al., 1956; Martorella, 1972; Merrill & Tennyson, 1977). A strike is a pitched ball that is in the strike zone and missed *or* a pitched ball that is swung at but not hit fair.

A relational concept is one in which one defining attribute is the spatial or temporal relationship between two or more attributes. A *trochaic meter*, an example of a relational concept, is a line of verse or prose in which each poetic foot consists of a stressed syllable *followed by* an unstressed syllable (Merrill & Tennyson, 1977).

The most common type of concepts and, generally speaking, the easiest to learn are conjunctive (Bourne & O'Banion, 1971). To design appropriate instruction, one must have a clear understanding of the type of rule used to connect the attributes so that a concept may be taught appropriately.

Words used as concept labels provide a means of communication in any language. In fact, most of the words used in any given language refer to concepts (Merrill & Tennyson, 1977). It must be remembered, however, that words are not concepts per se, but rather symbols that name concepts (Klausmeier, 1990). Most, but not all, concept labels are words. For example, mathematical signs, such as =, –, and +, also represent concepts (Novak, 1990).

Concepts may differ in many ways. One way they differ is across a continuum of concreteness to abstractness. Concepts with attributes that are readily observable are more concrete, and, conversely, those with unobservable or less observable attributes fall on the abstract end of the continuum (Klausmeier, 1990; Tennyson & Cocchiarella, 1986). The concepts *apple* and *tomato* are usually considered concrete, and the concepts *liberal* and *conservative* are considered abstract.

Concepts may also be categorized across a continuum of complexity. Concepts with dimensions that remain constant are less complex and generally not affected by context, whereas concepts with variable dimensions are affected by context and may be classified as more complex (Tennyson & Cocchiarella, 1986). "The concept *poem* has constant dimensions (because it is a piece of poetry), whereas the concept *poetry* has variable dimensions (because it may convey a variety of meanings beyond that of a verse)" (Tennyson & Cocchiarella, 1986, p. 55). The concept *poem* would be classified as less complex than the concept *poetry.*

The number of attributes of a given concept can also add to its complexity. As the number of possible attributes increases, so does the complexity of the concept (Tennyson & Cocchiarella, 1986). In addition, not only do complex concepts have "fuzzy borders," but also the examples that are used have a gradient of representativeness (Fleming, 1987).

Basic concepts are usually difficult to describe verbally. Good examples of basic concepts are colors. The characteristics of the concepts *red, blue,* and *yellow* are very difficult to describe in words; examples must be used to teach the color concepts. One must teach the color red by presenting objects and pictures that are red and comparing those with objects and pictures that are not red.

Relationships Between Concepts

The concepts of a subject field can be organized into taxonomies, whole-part relationships (e.g., chair, legs, seat), dependency relationships (e.g., observing is a prerequisite of predicting), or other schematic arrangements (Klausmeier, 1990). *Superordinate, subordinate,* and *coordinate* concepts are ways of describing the relationships among concepts that can be organized into taxonomies. If one superordinate concept can be divided into several subordinate concepts, then the subordinate concepts are usually coordinate concepts. For example, a partial taxonomy for the concept *parts of speech* appears in Figure 18.1. The superordinate concept is *parts of speech. Noun, verb, adjective,* and *adverb* are all subordinate to *parts of speech* and are coordinate concepts. In the above example, *noun* is a concept subordinate to *parts of speech,* coordinate to *verb,* and superordinate to *common noun* and *proper noun.*

To teach the relationships among concepts, the teacher can present the hierarchy of concepts to the learner (Driscoll & Tessmer, 1985; Kember, 1991; Markle, 1977). Providing graphic organizers to students, or teaching students with disabilities to create graphic organizers, has been demonstrated to be an effective tool in teaching relationships among concepts (Darch & Carnine, 1986; Foster-Havercamp, 1988; Horton, Lovitt, & Bergerud, 1990; Weisberg & Balajthy, 1987). The use of conceptual relationship hierarchies, however, does not imply that students must

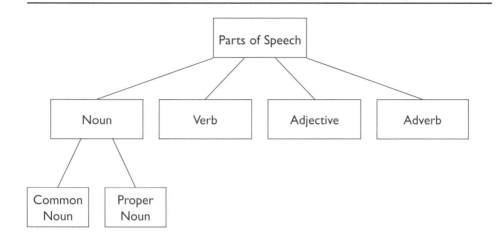

Figure 18.1 *An Example of a Partial Concept Taxonomy*

learn concepts in a certain order. Concepts are not learned in the same hierarchical, sequential fashion as tasks often are. "A valid hierarchy of...skills immediately locks an instructional designer into a sequential approach to teaching. Skills at lower levels must be taught first. No such locked-in sequencing is dictated by a knowledge structure" (Markle, 1977, p. 15). For example, young children understand the concept *dog* before acquiring the superordinate concept *animal,* or the subordinate concept *breed of dog*.

Procedure for Designing Instruction

A step-by-step process of designing instruction to teach concepts follows. Although written from the perspective of designing and delivering concept instruction, the procedures outlined may also be used to evaluate published materials designed to teach concepts. A listing of the steps appears in Table 18.1. Each step is elaborated on according to research and/or theory regarding effective concept instructional design. Whenever possible, research studies that have demonstrated effectiveness of a design component will be discussed. Well-grounded theories that have not as yet been demonstrated empirically are also included.

Analyze the Concepts to Be Taught

Analysis of the concepts being taught involves three stages: (a) examining the content structure, (b) formulating a definition, and (c) generating examples and nonexamples.

■■■■ **Table 18.1** *Steps for Instructional Design of Concept Instruction*

A. Analyze the concept to be taught.
   1. Examine the content structure of the concept.
   2. Identify the attributes of each concept.
   3. Determine whether context is important to defining the concept.
B. Formulate a definition of the concept.
C. Generate a list of examples and nonexamples.
   1. List examples and nonexamples that are matched on the variable attributes and differ on the defining attributes.
   2. Vary the variable attributes between matched pairs of examples/nonexamples.
   3. Arrange examples/nonexamples across a continuum from easy to difficult.
D. Design the teaching sequence.
   1. Define the instructional objectives.
   2. Analyze the task that will be used to demonstrate knowledge of the concept.
   3. Provide the definition and label.
   4. Select the appropriate number and sequence of examples/nonexamples.
   5. Elaborate the defining attributes.
   6. Incorporate immediate feedback.
E. Construct a diagnostic classification test.
   1. Use novel examples and nonexamples that are representative of the concept.
   2. Examine the task used to demonstrate knowledge on the test.
   3. Randomly order the test items.
   4. Provide means for analyzing and correcting student errors.

1. *Examining the content structure of the concepts.* If the concepts being taught fit into a taxonomy, one must determine the relationships among the concepts to be taught, and their relationships to additional concepts (i.e., Are they coordinate, subordinate, or superordinate to one another?). Outlining the relationship among the concepts into a taxonomy or hierarchy may prove helpful in determining this structure.

One should examine the structure in which a concept is placed and use this information to assist in selecting effective teaching strategies. Although some models of concept instruction indicate that concepts should be taught one at a time (Kameenui & Simmons, 1990), other instructional designers indicate that coordinate concepts can be taught simultaneously, because an example of one concept is a nonexample of another concept (Markle, 1977). There is some documentation that simultaneous presentation of coordinate concepts can be more effective than successive or collective presentations (Tennyson, Tennyson, & Rothen, 1980). So, when teaching the coordinate concepts *nouns* and *verbs,* nouns could act as nonexamples of verbs and vice versa. It has also been demonstrated that separating concepts that are easily confused can enhance understanding of the concepts being taught

(Carnine, 1980a). This separation should be provided over time (Carnine, 1989b). Whether concepts should be taught one at a time or simultaneously may depend on factors such as learner's sophistication and prior knowledge and the complexity and similarities of the concepts being taught.

2. *Identifying the attributes of each concept.* To teach a desired concept, the teacher must make certain that the attributes that are defining and those that are variable are well defined. A clear list of the defining and variable attributes will facilitate (a) generating of examples and nonexamples, (b) selection of the appropriate number of examples and nonexamples, and (c) sequencing of the examples and nonexamples throughout instruction. Defining attributes are the attributes that differentiate the example of a concept from examples of other concepts; attributes that do not differentiate the example of a concept from examples of other concepts are called *variable attributes.* The defining attributes of chord, for example, include *three or more musical tones and sounded simultaneously.* Variable attributes may include the type of musical tone, quality of the musical tone, musical pitch, and volume, and number and type of sources from which the tones came (e.g., one piano, string quartet, music box, trio of singers).

3. *Determining whether context is important to defining the concept.* The role that context plays, if any, in defining the concept needs to be determined. As stated earlier, concepts with dimensions that remain constant are generally not affected by context, whereas concepts with variable dimensions are affected by context. The definition of *freedom fighter* changes across context, from a national liberator to someone considered a terrorist, depending on the context in which it is used (Tennyson & Cocchiarella, 1986). Special education classification categories, such as mental retardation, learning disabilities, and behavior disorders, change within context (Ferrara, Prater, & Baer, 1987). The definitions of these categories have changed over time and vary across states and school districts at any given time (Prater & Ferrara, 1990). Context must be considered when developing a definition of the concept.

Formulate a Definition of the Concepts

As stated earlier, basic concepts are difficult to describe verbally. Although it is possible to write definitions of basic concepts, the complexity of the definition would not assist most learners.

> [We] could define the color *red* by noting that it is a primary color or a spread of colors at the lower end of the visible spectrum, varying in hue from bloodred to pale rose or pink. However, it's unlikely that a naive learner who doesn't know the color *red* will understand this definition. (Kameenui & Simmons, 1990, p. 150)

Complex or defined concepts can be taught most efficiently through presentation of definitions along with examples and nonexamples. The verbal definition of the concept must communicate to the learner all of the defining attributes and the relationships among those attributes (Carroll, 1964). If possible, the definition should also include the name of the concept superordinate to the target concept or a more inclusive concept name (Klausmeier, 1976). For example, if teaching the concept name *equilateral triangle,* the teacher could include either *isosceles triangle* or polygon could be included in the definition, because they are superordinate to the target concept. For most students, however, the term *triangle* better conveys the general concept being taught (Klausmeier, 1976).

Teachers need to ensure that the definition is written in vocabulary appropriate to the target population (Feldman & Klausmeier, 1974). A vocabulary list including the concept name, defining attribute names, and other key words may be used when initiating instruction, to ensure that students understand necessary prerequisite vocabulary (Klausmeier, 1990). Using appropriate vocabulary and ensuring that the students understand the meaning of the words used are particularly important considerations for special learners.

Generate a List of Examples and Nonexamples

Instruction often includes only examples (Fleming, 1987), but both examples and nonexamples are necessary for teaching what is distinctive about the concept. Providing both examples and nonexamples is vital regardless of the types of concepts being taught (Richey, 1986). The examples and nonexamples to be used in instruction should be matched on the variable attributes, but should differ on the defining attributes. In addition, they should vary between matched pairs on the variable attributes, and the pairs should represent a continuum from easy to difficult items. Both examples and nonexamples are called *instances* (Merrill & Tennyson, 1977). Further elaboration follows.

1. *List examples and nonexamples that are matched on the variable attributes and differ on the defining attributes.* By matching instances (examples and nonexamples) on variable attributes, one is demonstrating that the variable attributes are not important in distinguishing examples from nonexamples. The nonexamples should differ only subtly from their matched examples (Engelmann & Carnine, 1982; Kameenui & Simmons, 1990). Generally speaking, learners who practice comparing instances that are very similar generalize their understanding of the concept better than those who compare instances that are very different (Hamilton, 1986). By matching on variable attributes, one is teaching the students to use the defining attributes in distinguishing between examples and nonexamples. When students can distinguish previously encountered nonexamples that share some characteristics with previous examples is being different from the examples, they have learned to discriminate (Gagné, Briggs, & Wager, 1988; Markle & Tiemann, 1970). It may be advantageous to select nonexamples that the student already knows (Kameenui & Simmons, 1990). For example, if a student already knows the concept *blue,* blue objects and pictures can be matched with red ones, particularly when initially introducing the concept *red.*

If the concept being taught is *round,* the students could be presented with two figures that are both red, but one that is round and the other square. The variable attribute would be the color of the object, and the defining attribute would be the round shape. If teaching the concept *noun,* matched examples and nonexamples that share variable attributes (in parentheses) might include *Paula/Pretty* (capital letter); *kitchen/kill* (lowercase letters); Mount Rushmore/most rundown (both have two words); Please turn out the *light*/The bag was very *light* (same word, same placement in the sentence); I lost my *watch*/Please *watch* my purse (same word, different placement in the sentence). In each of these examples the instances are matched as closely as possible on the variable attributes. These variable attributes were selected because they represent typical errors students make. For example, *proper nouns*, a subcategory of the concept *noun,* are always capitalized. Students need to learn, however, that capitalization is not a defining attribute of all nouns (e.g., *Pretty* as a nonexample). In the last two sets of instances, the same words (*light* and *watch*) are used but have different functions in their sentences. The context in which these two words are used determines whether they represent an example of a noun or adjective (*light*) or a noun or verb (*watch*).

2. *Vary the variable attributes between matched pairs of examples/nonexamples.* Presentation of the instances is most effective when the matched pairs vary widely on variable attributes (Tennyson, Woolley, & Merrill, 1972). This provides a wide range of both examples and nonexamples. Divergence with respect to both variable attributes and contexts is necessary (Merrill, Reigeluth, & Faust, 1979). When teaching the concept *two*, for example, teachers should present students with "objects as vastly different in other characteristics as two dots on a page, two persons, two buildings, or two baseballs" (Gagné et al., 1988, p. 60). Nonexamples would be the same objects but in different numbers. When teaching fraction concepts, teachers should use fractions with various numerators and denominators, as well as pie charts or other visual representations, and these should represent values less than, greater than, *and* equal to 1 (Engelmann, Carnine, & Steely, 1991).

3. *Arrange examples/nonexamples across a continuum from easy to difficult.* To adequately teach concepts, one must be concerned not only with teaching discrimination between examples and nonexamples, but also with generalization beyond the instances used in instruction (Gropper, 1983). Generalization has occurred when the student can perform the behavior under conditions different from those under which it was acquired (Alberto & Troutman, 1986), including across cues, materials, formats, trainers, and settings. One way in which generalization of concept acquisition can be demonstrated is through accurate classification of an example that is novel or differs in some way from previously encountered examples (Markle & Tiemann, 1970). Using instances that range from easy to difficult and providing instances that differ greatly from one another helps facilitate generalization and helps avoid developing misconceptions (Carnine, 1980b; Kelly, Gersten, & Carnine, 1990; Ranzijn, 1991).

Merrill and Tennyson (1977) outlined one method for estimating difficulty level of instances. They suggested presenting the definition and the instances to a group of students similar to those who will be taught and asking them to classify the instances based on the definition only. The percentage of students who correctly identify the instance provides the estimated difficulty level. The suggested cutoffs are 0% to 30%, difficult; 30% to 70%, medium; and 70% to 100%, easy. Appropriate proportions of each difficulty level of instances (approximately equal numbers of difficult, medium, and easy instances) are used during instruction.

Design the Teaching Sequence

To create a teaching sequence, six steps are outlined: (a) defining the instructional objectives, (b) analyzing the task used to demonstrate knowledge, (c) providing the definition and label, (d) selecting the appropriate number of examples and nonexamples, (e) elaborating the defining attributes, and (f) incorporating immediate feedback.

1. *Defining the instructional objectives.* Instructional objectives define the purpose of the lesson. Effective teachers create clear and appropriate instructional objectives and present these objectives to their students (Rosenshine & Stevens, 1986). This is also the case with concept learning (Archer, 1962).

Knowledge of a concept can be divined in various ways. First, students could be given the concept label and asked to identify or produce the definition. Although labeling, recognizing, or recalling a definition may be, under some circumstances, desirable instructional objectives, these should not be confused with understanding a concept or demonstrating classification behavior (Gagné et al., 1988; Markle, 1977). Second, students could be given the concept label and asked to create examples of that concept. Additional explanation by the student as to why these instances are or are not examples would provide further information about his or her real understanding (Gropper, 1983). Third, students could be asked to produce the concept structure describing the relationships among superordinate, subordinate, and coordinate concepts to demonstrate understanding (Driscoll & Tessmer, 1985; Markle, 1977). The fourth and most common method of assessing concept knowledge is to provide instances that the student identifies as either examples or nonexamples of a given concept and/or classifies them into groups (Gagné et al., 1988). The remaining procedural steps were designed for using the last method, providing students instances to be classified or identified as examples or nonexamples.

Both generalization and discrimination should be included in the instructional objectives (Harris, 1973). That is, learners should be expected to recognize new examples (generalization) as well as new nonexamples (discrimination) of the concept (Gagné et al., 1988). This is of particular concern to the special educator, in that students with disabilities have well-documented difficulty with generalizing new information (Taylor, 1988).

2. *Analyzing the task that will be used to demonstrate knowledge of the concepts.* This step ties very closely with the previous step, defining the instructional objectives. A task "consists of some sort of directions to the learner and some requirement for the learner to respond" (Engelmann & Carnine, 1982, p. 135). The required task should be carefully examined to ensure that students are capable of completing it.

Although understanding concepts may be considered a cognitive process, demonstration of knowledge needs to be overt. Therefore, the task must not interfere with students' abilities to demonstrate their knowledge. A critical question to ask is, Can one be certain that the failure to accurately respond is due to lack of knowledge, or are the demonstration tasks interfering? If it is possible that there is task interference, then both the concepts and the tasks need to be taught or the tasks changed. This is particularly important for students with disabilities.

Tasks used to demonstrate knowledge of concepts can vary widely. For example, if one were teaching a student the concept *truck,* the child would touch pictures of trucks, draw a circle around pictures of trucks, point to toy or real trucks, or draw a truck. If these are the tasks used, the child needs to know how to touch or how to draw a circle around or how to point to or how to draw in order to demonstrate knowledge of *trucks.*

3. *Providing the definition and label.* Presenting the student with a meaningful concept label along with the concept examples facilitates his or her concept learning (Fredrick & Klausmeier, 1968). Unless teaching basic concepts that are difficult to describe verbally, the teacher can use concept definitions to recall for the student component elements of a framework of the concept (Tennyson & Boutwell, 1974). Presenting and even displaying the definition in terms of an organized list of defining attributes may improve the student's learning of concepts (Markle, 1975).

Although it has been argued that presentation of a few simple and clear examples prior to presentation of the definition may be an effective introductory procedure (Fleming, 1987), usually the definition should be presented to the learner before the examples and nonexamples (Tennyson & Park, 1980). Examples presented before the definition may not be necessary if it is anticipated that students will clearly understand the verbal definition (Fleming, 1987).

Definitions, rather than additional demonstrations of examples and nonexamples, can economize the teaching sequence, especially with more sophisticated learners (Anderson & Kulhavy, 1972; Merrill & Tennyson, 1971). In addition, it has been demonstrated that with some populations, presenting the concept definition reduces the number of examples they need to learn the concept (Tennyson & Park, 1980).

4. *Selecting the appropriate number and sequence of examples/nonexamples.* Including the appropriate number of examples and nonexamples is often considered a matter of judgment, with the rule being as follows: Include enough examples to adequately represent the concept and enough nonexamples to clearly differentiate the concept from other, similar concepts (Eggen, Kauchak, & Harder, 1979). Although some researchers have discovered that students who are taught via best examples, defined as clear cases of the concept, score higher than students given the defining attributes of the concept (Park, 1984; Tennyson, Youngers, & Suebsonthi, 1983), other researchers report to the contrary (McKinney, Gilmore, Peddicord, & McCallum, 1987). Rather than just best examples, a sufficient range should be provided (Kameenui & Simmons, 1990). The examples and nonexamples should adequately represent the class of possible instances that the student will likely encounter in the real world (Merrill et al., 1979).

A rational set of concepts consists of as many nonexamples as there are defining attributes of the concept and as many examples as there are variable attributes

(Markle & Tiemann, 1970). Each nonexample should have one or more of the defining attributes and may have only one fewer defining attribute than its matched example. Additionally, each example should have variable attributes that are also present in its matched nonexample. With this approach, the appropriate number of examples and nonexamples to be presented is directly related to the number of defining and variable attributes of the concept being taught. Other characteristics of the concept, such as the level of abstraction, should also be considered (Tennyson & Park, 1980).

Learner characteristics should also be considered. Studies indicate that learner characteristics, such as age, prior knowledge, aptitude, on-task performance, and cognitive style, may all contribute to the number of examples needed for mastery of a given concept (Pazzani, 1991; Tennyson & Park, 1980; Tennyson & Rothen, 1977). Prior knowledge, cognitive style, and on-task performance, among other learner characteristics, often differentiate students with disabilities from their peers. Consequently, additional attention may need to be provided to special and remedial education students to ensure that they receive an adequate number of examples and nonexamples for learning a concept. This should be considered in the design and delivery of instruction for special populations.

Once the instances have been listed, they should be ordered for presentation to the learner. It has been suggested that the sequence of matched examples and nonexamples should be presented to the student from the most simple to the most complex (Fleming, 1987). It does appear most important to present the easiest examples first, but not to group all the difficult instances at the end of instruction. The difficult instances should be distributed throughout the sequence (Carnine, 1989a).

5. *Elaborating the defining attributes.* The optimum conditions allowing students to learn concepts occur when "the obviousness of the relevant information is maximized and the obviousness of irrelevant information is minimized" (Archer, 1962, p. 619). Directing student attention to the attributes and/or concept rules is more effective than allowing students to discover them unaided (Clark, 1971). Inasmuch as students with disabilities often demonstrate difficulty with identifying and/or attending to relevant attributes (Kirk & Chalfant, 1984), making the attributes explicit is important for this population regardless of the complexity of the concepts being taught. "If attention-focusing help is not provided, the student may miss important attributes...[and guess] whether or not a given attribute is important" (Merrill et al., 1979, p. 190). One should use some kind of attention-focusing device to direct student attention to (a) the defining attributes present in a specific example and (b) the absence of the defining attributes in a specific nonexample (Merrill & Tennyson, 1977).

Defining attributes within the definition, the examples, and the nonexamples can be made obvious in several ways. If the material is printed, these attributes can, for example, be highlighted, colored, underlined, or printed in bold. Additional attention-focusing devices include drawings, special symbols, notes, and simplified illustrations. When presenting information orally, the instructor can change oral intonation or stress to emphasize the defining attributes.

6. *Incorporating immediate feedback.* Feedback is important for practice items. Feedback may be confirming or corrective: Confirming feedback should be provided in situations where the student cannot obtain feedback independently (Klausmeier, 1990); corrective feedback may be provided through emphasizing the defining attributes (Merrill & Tennyson, 1977). If the attributes are emphasized, students will be more likely to see *why* the instance is an example. Otherwise, if only correctness is given, students may fail to understand why. With instances used for practice, feedback should follow each student response. This differs from test feedback, whereby the feedback is withheld until the student has responded to the whole set of instances.

Construct a Diagnostic Classification Test

In creating an opportunity for students to demonstrate their ability to discriminate between examples and nonexamples and to generalize to new instances, four steps should be followed: (a) developing a new set of examples and nonexamples for students to classify, (b) evaluating the task used to demonstrate knowledge, (c) sequencing the test items in a random order, and (d) analyzing and correcting errors.

Although the term *test* is used throughout this section, it is not used in a traditional sense. Tests given in typical school situations usually consist of written responses. There are situations, however, when the tests require verbal or overt demonstrations. For example, if one were teaching the concepts *over* and *under*, students' verbal (or signed) responses to the placement of a cup under or over the table would be more appropriate than a written test. Consequently, here the term *test* is used to refer to any task, whether written, verbal, or an overt demonstration, that is required of the students for demonstrating their knowledge of a given concept.

1. *Using novel examples and nonexamples that are representative of the concept.* To assess discrimination and generalization, tests must contain novel examples and nonexamples (Harris, 1973). That is, the items on a test should not be the same as the instances used in instruction (Engelmann & Carnine, 1982; Merrill & Tennyson, 1977).

Additionally, the items on the test should represent a valid and divergent sample of examples of the concept. The examples should have variable attributes that are as different from one another as possible, and the examples and nonexamples should have variable attributes as similar to one another as possible (Merrill & Tennyson, 1977).

2. *Examining the task used to demonstrate knowledge on the test.* As mentioned under "creating the teaching sequence," the tasks need to be examined to ensure that the students are capable of demonstrating knowledge of the concept. This applies to both the instructional setting and the testing situation.

3. *Randomly ordering the test items.* Unlike the matched examples and nonexamples presented in order of increasing difficulty during instruction, the test items should be sequenced randomly throughout the test or arranged so that the order does not provide any prompts for accurate responding (Merrill & Tennyson, 1977).

4. *Providing means for analyzing and correcting student errors.* Error correction follows analysis of test performance. Merrill and Tennyson (1977) suggested that students who incorrectly classify one third or more of the items have not mastered the concept. Major classification errors have been described as overgeneralization, undergeneralization, and misconception. Overgeneralization errors occur when the student identifies nonexamples that share some variable attributes with examples, as examples. When making undergeneralization errors, the student does not recognize all examples as examples of the concept; and misconceptual errors occur when the student identifies a variable attribute as a defining attribute of the concept (Merrill & Tennyson, 1977). Misconception errors are the most difficult to correct. Regardless of the type of error, the definition and defining attributes of the concept should be retaught (Park, 1981).

Technology

Instructional procedures for the design and implementation of concept instruction have been described. This set of procedures was presented from the framework of the teacher designing, delivering, and/or evaluating the instruction. Technological tools have recently been applied to the development and delivery of concept instruction. These tools are receiving increasing attention and warrant a brief discussion. In particular, intelligent computer-assisted instruction, expert systems, and videodisc technology have been demonstrated to be effective and efficient modes of concept instruction. Each is briefly described below.

Intelligent computer-assisted instruction (ICAI) differs from conventional computer-assisted instruction in that ICAI allows students to interact with the computerized tutor, which is in some ways similar to a human tutor, rather than just responding to the tutor's directives (Tennyson & Park, 1987; Thorkildsen, Lubke, Myette, & Parry, 1985). One advantage of ICAI as a tool for teaching concepts may be the potential of learner control in determining the pace, sequence, and content of the instruction. Research indicates that although ICAI student control does not necessarily improve instruction, it is motivational for the learner (Murphy & Davidson, 1991). Students with disabilities are often described as being unmotivated, passive, self-doubting, and dependent on others (Gresham, 1988; Polloway et al., 1989). Providing them some control may enhance their motivation, provide success, and assist with teaching them independence and active participation.

Expert systems are computer programs designed to replicate the best experts' logic and decision-making processes. An expert system may be viewed in the same manner as a consultant, who, based on information given, provides advice about a decision or outcome (Hofmeister & Ferrara, 1986). Expert systems are usually created through interviews with experts. The creation of expert systems and the development of effective concept instruction procedures are similar processes. For example, the defining attributes of a concept are joined together through rules in a concept definition. Identifying defining and variable attributes and formulating the concept definition in terms of rules is similar to the interview process of identifying defining and variable attributes of the experts' decisions and creating programmable rules to represent the experts' decisions (Prater, 1987a). Defining attributes of the experts' decisions includes those factors or variables that make a difference in the outcome of the decision; variable attributes are those factors that do not make a difference in the outcome.

The similarities between concept analysis and creating expert systems have allowed expert systems not originally designed as training tools to be successfully modified and used for training. For example, an expert system originally designed to provide a second opinion regarding the appropriateness of a learning disabilities classification was restructured and combined with the strategies of effective concept instruction to create an instructional package used to train school personnel to more accurately identify students qualifying for special education as having learning disabilities (Prater & Ferrara, 1990). Although this area needs further investigation, expert systems appear particularly appropriate for teaching complex concepts.

Videodisc programs have been tested with students with disabilities and found to be extremely effective in teaching concepts (Carnine, 1989b). For example, a videodisc program entitled Mastering Fractions has been demonstrated to be effective in teaching fraction concepts (e.g., least common denominators, fraction equivalence) to general education students and to students with mild disabilities in mainstream settings (Miller & Cooke, 1989). This technology may be advantageous compared to teacher presentations in that principles from the effective teaching literature and procedures for conceptual instruction can be combined to provide efficient and effective instruction that, once captured, remains consistent and available for future presentation (Hofmeister, 1989). The capability of using graphics and simulations to demonstrate concepts that are difficult to visualize is another advantage.

Both computer programs and videodiscs hold promise for the advancement of concept instruction. The value of these tools in enhancing instruction for students with disabilities has just begun to be explored.

Conclusions

Students with mild disabilities, particularly those with learning disabilities and mild mental retardation, often have difficulty learning concepts accurately through experience or observation. Special and remedial educators need to integrate the systematic instruction of concepts into their curriculum. To assist them in doing so, an overview of some key instructional design strategies for concept instruction from the classical or traditional framework has been presented. Both research findings and instructional design theory have been applied in formulating this set of procedures. These guidelines were designed to assist teachers in designing and implementing instructional procedures for teaching concepts. A brief description of current technological advances, including intelligent computer-assisted instruction, expert systems, and videodiscs, and their role in the current and future delivery of concept instruction, was also presented.

References

Abbeduto, L., Furman, L., & Davies, B. (1989). Relation between the receptive language and mental age of persons with mental retardation. *American Journal on Mental Retardation, 93,* 535–543.

Abbeduto, L., & Nuccio, J. B. (1991). Relation between receptive language and cognitive maturity in persons with mental retardation. *American Journal on Mental Retardation, 96,* 143–149.

Alberto, P. A., & Troutman, A. C. (1986). Applied behavior analysis for teachers. Columbus, OH: Merrill.

Anderson, R. C., & Kulhavy, R. W. (1972). Learning concepts from definitions. *American Educational Research Journal, 9,* 385–391.

Archer, E. J. (1962). Concept identification as a function of obviousness of relevant and irrelevant information. *Journal of Experimental Psychology, 63,* 616–620.

Ausubel, D. P. (1968). *Education psychology: A cognitive view.* New York: Holt, Rinehart & Winston.

Bourne, L. E., Jr., & O'Banion, K. (1971). Conceptual rule learning and chronological age. *Developmental Psychology, 5,* 525–534.

Bruner, J. S., Goodnow, J. J., & Austin, G. (1956). *A study of thinking.* New York: Wiley.

Candler, A. C., & Hildreth, B. L. (1990). Characteristics of language disorders in learning disabled students. *Academic Therapy, 25,* 333–343.

Carnine, D. (1980a). Two letter discrimination sequences: High-confusion alternatives first versus low-confusion alternatives first. *Journal of Reading Behavior, 12*(1), 41–47.

Carnine, D. (1980b). Relationships between stimulus variation and the formation of misconceptions. *Journal of Educational Psychology, 72,* 452–456.

Carnine, D. (1989a). Designing practice activities. *Journal of Learning Disabilities, 22,* 603–607.

Carnine, D. (1989b). Teaching complete content to learning disabled students: The role of technology. *Exceptional Children, 55,* 524–533.

Carroll, J. B. (1964). Words, meanings, and concepts. *Harvard Educational Review, 34,* 178–202.

Clark, D. C. (1971). Teaching concepts in the classroom: A set of prescriptions derived from experimental research. *Journal of Educational Psychology Monograph, 62,* 253–278.

Darch, C., & Carnine, D. (1986). Teaching content area material to learning disabled students. *Exceptional Children, 53,* 240–246.

Driscoll, M. P., & Tessmer, M. (1985). *Applications of the concept tree and rational set generator for coordinate concept learning.* Tallahassee: Florida State University. (ERIC Document Reproduction Service No. ED 257 875)

Dudley-Marling, C. (1985). The pragmatic skills of learning disabled children: A review. *Journal of Learning Disabilities, 18,* 193–199.

Dudley-Marling, C., & Searle, D. (1988). Enriching language learning environments for students with learning disabilities. *Journal of Learning disabilities, 21,* 140–143.

Eggen, P. D., Kauchak, D. P., & Harder, R. J. (1979). *Strategies for teachers: Information processing models in the classrooms.* Englewood Cliffs, NJ: Prentice Hall.

Engelmann, S., & Carnine, D. (1982). *Theory of instruction: Principles and applications.* New York: Irvington.

Engelmann, S., Carnine, D., & Steely, D. G. (1991). Making connections in mathematics. *Journal of Learning Disabilities, 24,* 292–303.

Feagens, L., & Appelbaum, M. I. (1986). Validation of language subtypes in learning disabled children. *Journal of Educational Psychology, 78,* 358–364.

Feldman, K. V., & Klausmeier, H. J. (1974). Effects of two kinds of definition on the concept attainment of fourth and eighth graders. *Journal of Educational Research, 67,* 219–223.

Ferrara, J. M., Prater, M. A., & Baer, R. (1987). LD Trainer: Modification of an expert system for complex conceptual training. *Educational Technology, 27*(5), 43–46.

Fleming, M. L. (1987). Displays and communication. In R. M. Gagné (Ed.), *Instructional technology: Foundations* (pp. 233–260). Hillsdale, NJ: Erlbaum.

Foster-Havercamp, M. (1988). Twin strategies for reading improvement. Vocational Education Journal, 63, 36-37.

Fredrick, W. C., & Klausmeier, H. J. (1968). Instructions and labels in a concept-attainment task. *Psychological Reports, 23*, 1339–1342.

Gagné, R. M., Briggs, L. J., & Wager, W. W. (1988). *Principles of instructional design* (3rd ed.). New York: Holt, Rinehart & Winston.

Gresham, F. M., (1988). Social competence and motivational characteristics of learning disabled students. In M. C. Wang, M. C. Reynolds, & H. J. Walberg (Eds.), *Handbook of special education: Research and practice* (Vol. 2, pp. 283–302). Oxford, England: Pergamon Press.

Gropper, G. L. (1983). A behavioral approach to instructional prescription. In C. M. Reigeluth (Eds.), *Instructional-design theories and models: An overview of their current status* (pp. 101–161). Hillsdale, NJ: Erlbaum.

Hamilton, R. (1986). Role of adjunct questions and subject ability levels on the learning of concepts from prose. *American Educational Research Journal, 23*, 1–12.

Hardman, M. L., Drew, C. J., Egan, M. W., & Wolf, B. (1990). *Human exceptionality* (3rd ed.). Boston: Allyn & Bacon.

Harris, R. C. (1973). Concept learning as a function of type, identifiability, and variety of instructional instances. *The Journal of Education Research, 67*, 182–189.

Hofmeister, A. M. (1989). Teaching with videodiscs. *Teaching Exceptional Children, 21*, 52–56.

Hofmeister, A. M., & Ferrara, J. M. (1986). Expert systems and special education. *Exceptional Children, 53*, 235–239.

Horton, S. V., Lovitt, T. C., & Bergerud, D. (1990). The effectiveness of graphic organizers for three classifications of secondary students in content area classes. *Journal of Learning Disabilities, 23*, 12–22.

Kameenui, E. J., & Simmons, D. C. (1990). *Designing instructional strategies: The prevention of academic learning problems*. Columbus, OH: Merrill.

Kelly, B., Gersten, R., & Carnine, D. (1990). Student error patterns as a function of curriculum design: Teaching fractions to remedial high school students and high school students with learning disabilities. *Journal of Learning Disabilities, 23*, 23–29.

Kember, D. (1991). Instructional design for meaningful learning. *Instructional Science, 20*, 289–310.

Kirk, S. A., & Chalfant, J. C. (1984). Academic and developmental learning disabilities. Denver: Love.

Klausmeier, H. J. (1976). Instructional design and the teaching of concepts. In J. R. Levin & V. L. Allen (Eds.), *Cognitive learning in children: Theories and strategies* (pp. 191–217). New York: Academic Press.

Klausmeier, H. J. (1990). Conceptualizing. In B. F. Jones & L. Idol (Eds.), *Dimensions of thinking and cognitive instruction* (pp. 93–138). Hillsdale, NJ: Erlbaum.

Kramer, J. J., Piersel, W. C., & Glover, J. A. (1988). Cognitive and social development of mildly retarded children. In M. C. Wang, M. C. Reynolds, & H. J. Walberg (Eds.), *Handbook of special education: Research and practice* (Vol. 2, pp. 43–53). Oxford, England: Pergamon Press.

Lerner, J. (1988). *Learning disabilities: Theories, diagnosis, and teaching strategies* (5th ed.). Dallas: Houghton Mifflin.

Lovitt, T. C. (1989). *Introduction to learning disabilities*. Boston: Allyn & Bacon.

Markle, S. M. (1975). They teach concepts don't they? *Educational Researcher, 4*(6), 3–9.

Markle, S. M. (1977). Teaching conceptual networks. *Journal of Instructional Development, 1*, 13–17.

Markle, S. M., & Tiemann, P. W. (1970). *Really understanding concepts: Or in frumious pursuit of the jabberwock*. Champaign, IL: Stipes.

Martorella, P. H. (1972). *Concept learning: Designs for instruction*. Scraton, OH: Intext Educational Publishers.

McKinney, C. W., Gilmore, A. C., Peddicord, H. Q., & McCallum, R. S. (1987). Effects of a best example and critical attributes on prototype formation in the acquisition of a concept. *Theory and Research in Social Education, 15*, 189–201.

Mercer, C. D., & Mercer, A. R. (1989). *Teaching students with learning problems* (4th ed.). Columbus, OH: Merrill.

Merrill, M. D., Reigeluth, C. M., & Faust, G. W. (1979). The instructional quality profile: A curriculum evaluation and design tool. In H. F. O'Neill, Jr. (Ed.), *Procedures for instructional systems development* (pp. 165–204). New York: Academic Press.

Merrill, M. D., & Tennyson, R. D. (1971). *The effect of types of positive and negative examples on learning concepts in the classroom* (Final Report USOE No. 0-H-014). Provo, UT: Brigham Young University.

Merrill, M. D., & Tennyson, R. D. (1977). *Teaching concepts: An instruction design guide.* Englewood Cliffs, NJ: Educational Technology Publications.

Miller, S. C., & Cooke, N. L. (1989). Mainstreaming students with learning disabilities for videodisc math instruction. *Teaching Exceptional Children, 21*(3), 57–60.

Murphy, M. A., & Davidson, G. V. (1991). Computer-based adaptive instruction: Effects of learner control on concept learning. *Journal of Computer-Based Instruction, 18*, 51–56.

Myers, P. I., & Hammill, D. D. (1990). *Learning disabilities: Basic concepts, assessment, practices, and instructional strategies* (4th ed.). Austin, TX: PRO-ED.

Nelson, R. B., & Cummings, J. A. (1981). Basic concept attainment of educable mentally handicapped children: Implications for teaching concepts. *Education and Training of the Mentally Retarded, 16*, 303–306.

Nelson, R. B., & Cummings, J. A. (1984). Educable mentally retarded children's understanding of Boehm Basic Concepts. *Psychological Reports, 154*, 81–82.

Nelson, R. B., Cummings, J. A., & Boltman, H. (1991). Teaching basic concepts to students who are educably mentally handicapped. *Teaching Exceptional Children, 23*(2), 12–15.

Novak, J. D. (1990). Concept maps and Vee diagrams: Two metacognitive tools to facilitate meaningful learning. *Instructional Science, 19,* 29–52.

Park, O. (1981). A response-sensitive strategy in computer-based instruction: A strategy for concept teaching. *Journal of Educational Technology Systems, 10*, 187–197.

Park, O. (1984). Example comparison strategy versus attribute identification strategy in concept learning. *American Educational Research Journal, 21*, 145–162.

Pazzani, J. M. (1991). Influences of prior knowledge on concept acquisition: Experimental and computational results. *Journal of Experimental Psychology: Learning, Memory, and Cognition, 17*, 416–431.

Polloway, E. A., Patton, J. R., Payne, J. S., & Payne, R. A. (1989). *Strategies for teaching learners with special needs* (4th ed.). Columbus, OH: Merrill.

Prater, M. A. (1987a). *Expert system technology and concept instruction: Training educators to accurately classify learning disabled students.* Unpublished doctoral dissertation, Utah State University, Logan.

Prater, M. A. (1987b). Is a tomato a fruit? Using examples to teach concepts. *Academic Therapy, 23*(1), 37–43.

Prater, M. A., & Ferrara, J. M. (1990). Training educators to accurately classify learning disabled students using concept instruction and expert system technology. *Journal of Special Education Technology, 10*, 147–156.

Ranzijn, F. J. A. (1991). The number of video examples and the dispersion of examples as instructional design variables in teaching concepts. *Journal of Experimental Education, 59,* 320–330.

Richey, R. (1986). The theoretical and conceptual bases of instruction design. New York: Nichols.

Rosenshine, R., & Stevens, R. (1986). Teaching functions. In M. C. Wittrock (Ed.), *Handbook of research on teaching* (pp. 376–391). New York: Macmillan.

Shumway, R. J., White, A. L., Wilson, R., & Brombacher, B. (1983). Feature frequency and negative instances in concept learning. *American Educational Research Journal, 20*, 451–459.

Stanley, W. B. (1984). Approaches to teaching concepts and conceptualizing: An analysis of social studies methods textbooks. *Theory and Research in Social Education, 11*, 1–14.

Taylor, R. L. (1988). Psychological intervention with mildly retarded children: Prevention and remediation of cognitive deficits. In M. C. Wang, M. C. Reynolds, & H. J. Walberg (Eds.), *Handbook of special education: Research and practice* (Vol. 2, pp. 59–75). Oxford, England: Pergamon Press.

Tennyson, C. L., Tennyson, R. D., & Rothen, W. (1980). Content structure and instructional control strategies as design variable in concept acquisition. *Journal of Educational Psychology, 72,* 499–505.

Tennyson, R. D., & Boutwell, R. C. (1974). Methodology for the sequencing of instances in classroom concept teaching. *Education Technology, 14*(9), 45–59.

Tennyson, R. D., & Cocchiarella, M. J. (1986). An empirically based instructional design theory for teaching concepts. *Review of Educational Research, 56,* 40–71.

Tennyson, R. D., & Park, O. (1980). The teaching of concepts: A review of instructional design research literature. *Review of Educational Research, 50,* 55–70.

Tennyson, R. D., & Park, O. (1987). Artificial intelligence and computer-based learning. In R. M. Gagné (Ed.), *Instructional technology: Foundations* (pp. 319–342). Hillsdale, NJ: Erlbaum.

Tennyson, R. D., & Rothen, W. (1977). Pretask and on-task adaptive design strategies for selecting number of instances in concept acquisition. *Journal of Educational Psychology, 69,* 586–592.

Tennyson, R. D., Woolley, F. R., & Merrill, M. D. (1972). Exemplar and nonexemplar variables which produce correct concept classification behavior and specified classification errors. *Journal of Education Psychology, 63,* 144–152.

Tennyson, R. D., Youngers, J., & Suebsonthi, P. (1983). Concept learning by children using instructional presentation forms for prototype formation and classification-skill development. *Journal of Educational Psychology, 75,* 280–291.

Thorkildsen, R. J., Lubke, M. M., Myette, B. M., & Parry, J. D. (1985). Artificial intelligence: Applications in education. *Educational Research Quarterly, 10,* 2–9.

Vellutino, F. R. (1977). Alternative conceptualizations of dyslexia: Evidence in support of a verbal deficit hypothesis. *Harvard Educational Review, 47,* 334–354.

Weisberg, R., & Balajthy, E. (1987, December). *Effects of training in constructing graphic organizers on disabled readers' summarization and recognition of expository text structures.* Paper presented at the annual meeting of the National Reading Conference, Clearwater, FL.

Wiig, E. H. (1984). Language disabilities in adolescents: A question of cognitive strategies. *Topics in Language Disorders, 4,* 41–58.

Wiig, E. H., & Semel, E. (1984). *Language assessment and intervention for the learning disabled* (2nd ed.). Columbus, OH: Merrill.

19 Educational Interventions for Students with Attention Deficit Disorder

THOMAS A. FIORE, ELIZABETH A. BECKER, AND REBECCA C. NERO

THIS DISCUSSION of the effectiveness of various approaches with students with attention deficit disorder (ADD) is based on a careful examination of the literature. The authors show how the behavioral approaches, the cognitive approach, and careful organization of academic instruction can benefit students with ADD as well as their teachers.

In this chapter, we review and organize the current research-based knowledge on nonpharmacological interventions relevant to educating students with attention deficit disorder (ADD).

We conducted a search of the literature through an iterative process designed to identify work of historical significance, as well as ongoing projects. Our search methods included (a) computer searches of databases in education, psychology, and medicine; (b) requests to ADD organizations for intervention materials and reference lists; (c) letters to leading researchers who have published work related to educational interventions; and (d) pursuit of reference trails from research articles, review articles, and book chapters. Because the criteria for defining and identifying attention deficits have changed over time, we included studies with subjects whom researchers identified as having characteristics or behaviors associated with ADD, whether or not formally diagnosed. Though our focus was on nonpharmacological interventions, we included studies that compared drug therapy with other interventions.

After screening for subject characteristics, applicability in education settings, recency (or historical importance), and methodological soundness, we identified

137 empirically based articles for inclusion in an electronic database. The articles we cite here are either representative of that body of work, particularly noteworthy for their clarity on various topics, or unique in their findings. In the following sections, we review the empirical evidence according to four topic areas of interest to educators: behavior management, academic instruction, home-school collaboration, and comprehensive programming.

Before describing the empirical evidence related to each of these topics, we must note two important limitations that affect the validity of the work we describe. First, investigators have collected relatively few data on interventions in public school classrooms. Clinical psychologists, neuropsychologists, and physicians conducted most of the reported research in laboratory or clinic settings (including clinic-based classrooms); only 21 of the 137 studies reported on interventions in actual classroom settings. If we had limited our review to those studies set in actual schools, we would have had little to report.

Second, the subjects for the studies we reviewed are far from a homogeneous group. A great range of characteristics guided the investigators as they identified the children with attention deficits who served as subjects, partly because the definition of ADD has changed over time. In addition, for many studies, the investigators determined that subjects had attention deficits based on screening instruments rather than through formal diagnostic protocols. For other studies, the investigators were interested in a single ADD characteristic (such as hyperactivity) and thus chose subjects on measures of that characteristic alone. These subject-selection issues raise concerns about the generalization of the findings to other children or youth with ADD and signal a need for caution in making comparisons across studies.

Behavior Management

Research in behavior management with children with ADD has focused on increasing on-task behavior, task completion, compliance, impulse control, and social skills while reducing hyperactivity, off-task behavior, disruptive behavior, and aggression. The following overview examines studies that employed behavioral or cognitive-behavioral strategies—the two nonpharmacological treatments for managing children with ADD that have been most extensively investigated.

Behavior Therapy

Behavior therapy, behavior modification, and contingency management all refer to strategies that use reinforcement and punishment to establish or reduce target behaviors. Behavior therapy techniques have the advantages of being cost effective, relatively easy and quick to implement, and adaptable to multiple settings. To special educators familiar with contingency management, the research on children and youth with ADD offers few surprises. The ADD literature does suggest, however, a special emphasis on three common behavioral interventions: positive reinforcement, punishment, and response cost.

Positive Reinforcement

Research provides evidence that positive reinforcement procedures (most often using secondary reinforcers) can be effective in reducing activity level, increasing time on task, and improving academic performance of students with ADD. O'Leary and her colleagues reported on a series of studies (Friedling & O'Leary, 1979; O'Leary, Pelham, Rosenbaum, & Price, 1976; Rosenbaum, O'Leary, & Jacob, 1975) indicating the effectiveness of carefully implemented token economies. Their work provides examples of successful behavioral treatments that included group reward contingencies and parent rewards for progress toward goals set in a clinic school. Using social praise as a reward, Douglas and Parry (1983) found that reward improved reaction time for subjects with hyperactivity but only continuous reward reduced response variability. They concluded that children with hyperactivity are unusually sensitive to rewards and that partial rewards are less effective than continuous rewards. When Pelham, Milich, and Walker (1986) examined different schedules of reinforcement using a token economy, however, they found no difference on spelling tasks between continuous and partial reinforcement conditions.

Ayllon, Layman, and Kandel (1975) studied three children with learning disabilities and hyperactivity using a token reinforcement condition focused on reading and mathematics performance. Under the reinforcement condition, the students' hyperactivity was reduced to levels comparable to the levels achieved with methylphenidate; and, in contrast to the students' performance while taking methylphenidate, the establishment of the token economy led to dramatic improvements in academic performance. Other investigators have questioned the relative effectiveness of behavior therapy compared to stimulant medication. For example, Gittelman-Klein et al. (1976) found methylphenidate to be more effective in improving conduct, attention, hyperactivity, and disruptive behavior than a positive reinforcement program that included home and school use of token reinforcers; and combining the behavior therapy with methylphenidate did not produce results beyond those obtained with methylphenidate alone.

Punishment

A number of behavior therapy studies have examined the effects of negative feedback or reprimands, which are specific forms of punishment, on the performance of students with ADD. (We use the term "punishment" in the behaviorist sense—a contingency that reduces the frequency of a behavior. Research on subjects with ADD has employed only mildly aversive contingencies.) Specifically, these mild corrections have proven effective in decreasing off-task behavior and, to some extent, in increasing academic productivity. Worland (1976) compared positive feedback, negative feedback, and no feedback and found that hyperactive children were on task significantly more under negative feedback than the other two conditions; but negative feedback significantly increased their errors on a spelling correction task. In a pair of similar experiments, Abramowitz, O'Leary, and Rosén (1987) compared the effects of teacher encouragement, teacher reprimands, and no feedback on off-task behavior. They found significantly lower off-task rates with reprimands.

Abramowitz's work on reprimands (or redirection) is noteworthy because it demonstrates how empirical evidence can contribute to the refinement of a simple and common classroom technique. Abramowitz, O'Leary, and Futtersak (1988) demonstrated that short reprimands resulted in significantly lower rates of off-task behavior, compared with long reprimands; and they found a similar, though non-significant, trend in improvement of academic performance. The authors conjectured that long reprimands, because they involve more adult attention, may serve as positive reinforcers. Abramowitz and O'Leary (1990) found that immediate reprimands yielded much lower rates of interactive (involving another student) off-task behavior than did delayed reprimands; regardless of timing, however, reprimands did not affect noninteractive off-task rates. Futtersak (1988) compared the effectiveness of consistently strong verbal reprimands to reprimands that gradually increased in strength. He found that the sudden introduction and maintenance of strong reprimands resulted in more overall suppression of unwanted behavior and reduced the overall level of negative consequences needed in the classroom, while exposure to a gradually strengthening series of reprimands led to increased persistence of unwanted behavior that continued even after the reprimands became strong.

Response Cost

Research also indicates that response cost programs—a combination of positive reinforcement and punishment—can be effective in improving attention, on-task behavior, and completion of academic tasks. Sullivan and O'Leary (1990) compared reward-only and response cost and found that both programs were effective in producing immediate gains in students' on-task behavior; after the programs were faded out, however, students who were more hyperactive and aggressive maintained on-task behavior better under the response cost condition. In two single-subject design experiments, Rapport, Murphy, and Bailey (1980) also found that response cost was more effective than positive reinforcement in improving on-task behavior and completion of academic assignments.

Pelham et al. (1986) investigated the interaction effects between psychostimulant medication and a response cost program and reported that the combination of methylphenidate and response cost yielded significant improvements over a no-reinforcement/placebo condition. Rapport et al. (1980) found that methylphenidate combined with response cost slightly increased on-task behavior but did not increase assignment completion. Rapport, Murphy, and Bailey (1982) compared the effectiveness of differing dosages of methylphenidate versus a response cost system. Analyses of on-task behavior and phonics and math performance indicated that methylphenidate and response cost were effective, but the greatest improvement occurred during response cost.

Researchers have also obtained promising results with commercially available electronic devices, placed on children's desks, that automatically credit children with points and allow teachers using remote control devices to deduct points. Using such a device, DuPaul, Guevremont, and Barkley (1992) investigated the effects of a response cost program on two boys with ADD enrolled in a self-contained public school classroom for children with behavior disorders. The response cost program resulted in improvements for both boys in on-task behavior, attention, product completion, and overall level of ADD behavior (such as fidgeting and vocalizing). In a clinical setting, Gordon, Thomason, Cooper, and Ivers (1991) obtained similar results with an electronic device. Five out of six children improved in attention to academic tasks during attention training. The training effect dissipated quickly, however, once they discontinued use of the device. Though commercially available electronic apparatuses make implementation of a response cost program practical in a general classroom setting, acceptance by target students and classmates has not been adequately examined.

Cognitive-Behavioral Therapy

Although behavior therapy offers a limited but time-tested and practical course for educators, cognitive-behavioral therapy is the most intuitively appealing intervention because it combines behavioral techniques with cognitive strategies designed to directly address core problems of impulse control, higher order problem solving, and self-regulation. Some evidence, though virtually none without contradiction, suggests that cognitive-behavioral therapy may produce positive changes in sustained attention, impulse control, hyperactivity, and self-concept.

In a series of studies, Brown and his colleagues (Brown, Borden, Wynne, Schleser, & Clingerman, 1986; Brown, Wynne, & Medenis, 1985; Brown, Wynne et al., 1986) examined the effectiveness of cognitive therapies in combination with or in contrast to drug therapy. Comparing the effects of methylphenidate therapy, cognitive training, and a combination of the two, they found that only the medication conditions (with medication continuing through posttesting) produced significant improvements in sustained attention, cognitive impulsivity, academic achievement, and teacher and parent behavioral ratings. When they discontinued medication before posttesting, the medication effects dissipated rapidly; and posttest measures showed no significant main treatment effects or interactions. In none of the studies did the combination of medication and cognitive therapy produce results beyond medication alone.

Inconsistent findings on cognitive-behavioral interventions persist throughout the research literature. When Hall and Kataria (1992) investigated the relative effectiveness of behavior modification and cognitive training implemented with and without medication, none of the treatments significantly improved sustained attention; the combination of cognitive training and medication was the only intervention that significantly improved subjects' abilities to delay impulsive responding. Douglas, Parry, Marton, and Garson (1976) trained boys with hyperactivity to use self-verbalizations and self-reinforcement during cognitive tasks, academic problems, and social situations. The trained group showed significantly greater improvement on several posttest and follow-up measures, but not on a teacher rating scale. Hinshaw and Melnick (1992) reported improved behavior for two cases in which they used cognitive-behavioral interventions, in combination with behavior strategies and methylphenidate, to enhance self-monitoring and self-evaluation skills and to train anger management.

Kendall and Braswell (1982) compared the effects of cognitive-behavioral treatment and behavioral interventions for elementary school students with ADD. The cognitive-behavioral group improved significantly on teacher ratings of self-control and hyperactivity, child self-concept reports, academic performance measures, and on-task behaviors; but parent ratings indicated no significant improvements in self-control or in hyperactivity. After 1 year, no significant differences could be found across treatment conditions. In an elementary school-based study, Bloomquist, August, and Ostrander (1991) compared the short-term efficacy of multicomponent cognitive-behavioral therapy, teacher-only cognitive-behavioral therapy, and no treatment. The multicomponent cognitive-behavioral therapy included child training, teacher training and consultation, and parent training. On classroom observations, teacher ratings, and student self-reports, the researchers found posttreatment benefits to the multicomponent group only in reduction of off-task/disruptive behavior.

Citing research that shows the importance of considering the match between children's cognitive capacities and the requirements of training tasks, Borden, Brown, Wynne, and Schleser (1987) examined the influence of cognitive development level (derived from basic Piagetian conservation tasks) on the ability of children to benefit from cognitive therapy. Contrary to the hypothesis, measures of sustained attention, distractibility, academic achievement, academic aptitude, and behavioral ratings of teachers and parents produced no statistically significant differences across developmental groups. Only on cognitive impulsivity did the researchers find significant group differences, but these favored the nonconserving group.

In preliminary investigations, Paniagua (1992) and Paniagua, Morrison, and Black (1990) demonstrated the potential of a strategy with features similar to cognitive-behavioral therapy. They tested the effectiveness of correspondence training, which trains a relationship between verbal and nonverbal behavior. In the two studies, the researchers used training activities designed to decrease inappropriate behaviors of hospitalized children with ADD by evoking promises to inhibit problem behaviors. They rewarded the children for making promises, fulfilling them, and accurately reporting what they had done. On measures that included observations of inattention, overactivity, and conduct problems, correspondence training resulted in the consistent reduction of inappropriate behaviors. Less elaborate in implementation than traditional cognitive-behavioral therapy, correspondence training may prove to offer educators a practical school-based technique.

As reviewers (most notably Abikoff 1987, 1991) have demonstrated, the weight of the empirical evidence is against the efficacy of cognitive-behavioral therapy. As implemented and tested to date, cognitive-behavioral therapy has not consistently demonstrated positive effects on a magnitude that would recommend its widespread use, especially considering the relatively high staff investment required for implementation. Nevertheless, experienced clinicians (e.g., Barkley, 1990;

Goldstein & Goldstein, 1990; Hinshaw & Erhardt, 1991) advocate additional study of cognitive-behavioral therapies, especially as components of comprehensive intervention programs.

Academic Instruction

Though researchers have focused a relatively large amount of effort on testing strategies to increase behaviors, such as sustained attention, that may indirectly increase academic productivity of students with ADD, much less work has directly addressed instruction and learning. A limited, but promising, body of work focuses on characteristics of academic instruction or materials for students with ADD. Zentall's exploration of optimal stimulation theory is particularly intriguing and offers promise for finding an academic treatment (based on optimally stimulating instruction and instructional materials) that may be uniquely effective with students with ADD.

Conte, Kinsbourne, Swanson, Zirk, and Samuels (1987) studied varying presentation rates with children with ADD with and without hyperactivity by presenting paired-associate learning tasks at slow, fast, and mixed rates. Results indicated that children with ADD failed to benefit from consistently slow presentation compared with fast presentation, but did benefit from slow-rate items within a mixed-rate task. The authors concluded that the children with ADD were affected by the slow rate over an extended time period and suggested that, because average event rate rather than individual item duration was the relevant variable, situational context plays an important role in regulating the behavior of children with ADD.

On communication tasks, Zentall and Gohs (1984) found that subjects with hyperactivity took significantly longer to complete tasks when initial information was detailed rather than global; and subjects with hyperactivity requested significantly more cues when their initial cues were detailed, suggesting that the difficulties children with hyperactivity experience as receivers of verbally communicated information occur in response to detailed rather than global information. Shroyer and Zentall (1986) varied rate of auditory presentation and level of content stimulation of stories to examine the effects of those variables on listening comprehension, activity level, and off-task behavior and found that the subjects with hyperactivity were least active and most on task when the story was read fast without added non-relevant detail. But the subjects performed best on comprehension when the story was read slowly without added detail, suggesting that high activity level and poor performance are independent problems for children with hyperactivity.

In a series of studies, Zentall and her colleagues explored the effects of color added to instructional materials. Comparing children's performances on colored and noncolored versions of a search task, Zentall (1985) found that color added to search-attentional tasks improves the performance of children with hyperactivity; but after children have adapted to task and color novelty, performance gains diminish more rapidly for children with hyperactivity than for those without. On repetitive-copying tasks with adolescent boys, Zentall, Falkenberg, and Smith (1985) compared copying performances across multiple conditions of stimulation and information and found that, on most of the copying tasks, the boys with attention problems performed significantly better with high than with low stimulation; but the information-added conditions had no effect. On spelling-recognition tasks (Zentall, 1989), subjects with hyperactivity outperformed those without hyperactivity when black-letter trials preceded color-letter trials.

In an attempt to channel excessive activity into constructive active responses, Zentall and Meyer (1987) investigated whether motor responses added to rote tasks would reduce sensation-seeking activity and impulsive errors of children with hyperactivity. They tested children on two experimental tasks requiring sustained auditory attention and simple word recognition. Under the active-response condition, children had opportunities for simple motor responses. On a variety of behavior and performance variables, the children with hyperactivity performed significantly better under the active-response condition.

Home-School Collaboration

The issue of collaboration between home and school to improve outcomes for children with ADD has not been studied directly. The literature contains no empirical studies of strategies or programs designed specifically to implement or promote home-school collaboration. From the literature, however, we can identify strategies in two areas, tested with children with ADD in clinical settings. These strategies have implications for ways educators and parents can work together. Both approaches involve parents in enhancing or extending professional treatment.

The first of these two areas is quite limited. Some behavior therapy studies have included a component of parent collaboration, usually with parents providing rewards for positive behavior at school or in a treatment program. For example, O'Leary et al. (1976) evaluated the effectiveness of a combined home-school behavioral treatment for elementary school children and found that the behavioral treatment program, which included parent reward of the child for progress toward daily goals, led to significant improvements in hyperactive behaviors. Hoza, Pelham, Sams, and Carlson (1992) reported similar success with an intervention program that included parent reward for positive school behaviors.

The second area of strategies with implications for home-school collaboration involves parent training and the direct use of parents to provide treatment. The literature contains many examples of parent-training programs (typically instructing parents in behavioral strategies) that have demonstrated some effectiveness in reducing activity level, conflict, and anger intensity and in increasing on-task behavior and compliance. Significantly, none of the studies we identified involved school personnel. Instead, these studies reported on the efforts of clinic-based psychologists and physicians, and thus tested a component of clinic-home collaboration. Nevertheless, these studies are suggestive of the potential of similar home-school collaborations, and we describe some of this work in the following paragraphs.

Many studies have compared the effects of parent training (in behavioral strategies) and medication on child outcomes. Thurston (1979) found that both methylphenidate and parent training resulted in significant reductions in activity levels, while parent ratings of overall improvement showed parent training to be superior to both drug therapy and no treatment. Firestone, Kelly, Goodman, and Davey (1981) found that subjects receiving each treatment alone, or the two treatments in combination, made academic, behavioral, and emotional adjustment gains; but parent training with methylphenidate did not produce benefits over methylphenidate alone. Pelham, Schnedler, Bologna, and Contreras (1980) reported that parent and teacher behavioral training improved on-task behavior, but the training was not maximally effective until combined with methylphenidate. Interestingly, the investigators also reported a drug-therapy-by-parent-training interaction whereby children required smaller doses of medication following parent training. Pollard, Ward, and Barkley (1983) found that both methylphenidate and parent training decreased the number of parental commands and improved parents' ratings of deviant child behavior in the home, whereas only parent training increased parents' use of praise and attention following child compliance; the combination of treatments did not prove more effective than either treatment alone.

Other studies have compared parent training with child cognitive-behavioral therapy. With children of elementary school age, Horn, Ialongo, Popovich, and Peradotto (1987) reported that behavioral parent training, child self-control instruction, or a combination of the two treatments all significantly improved behaviors in the home at posttest and follow-up; but differential improvements across treatments occurred in only 1 of 32 possible comparisons. Using a single-subject design, Guevremont, Tishelman, and Hull (1985) examined a child self-instructional training program that used the subjects' mothers as adjunct therapists and reported improvements in classroom work completed, self-control, and hyperactivity. Barkley, Guevremont, Anastopoulos, and Fletcher (1992) found that three different family treatment approaches with adolescents all produced improvements in communication, conflicts, anger intensity, and school adjustment, according to mother and child reports; but clinical measures of the same variables showed only slight improvements with no significant differences among the treatment groups. Horn, Ialongo, Greenberg, Packard, and Smith-Winberry (1990) reported that a combined program of behavioral parent training and child self-control instruction did not produce effects that endured longer or generalized better than either treatment alone, though, as reported by parents, the combined treatment did produce a significantly greater proportion of improvements in some behavior; none of the groups made significant gains on measures of academic achievement or cognitive style.

Studies of parent training with preschoolers with ADD have also produced mixed results. Erhardt and Baker (1990) described two case studies of family-based behavioral interventions with preschool boys and reported modest gains attributable to parent training. Pisterman et al. (1989) evaluated the effectiveness of a parent information and training program to improve compliance of preschoolers. On every measure of compliance, the experimental group showed significant improvements that were maintained at a 3-month follow-up; but the researchers found no generalization across settings. As a follow-up to this and another study with similar positive results, Pisterman et al. (1992) found that parents who participated in training groups reported significantly decreased parenting stress and an increased sense of competence following treatment and at follow-up. In a study of low-income parents of preschoolers with behavior problems (over half of whom had attention deficits), Strayhorn and Weidman (1989) used research assistants, with cultural roots in the communities, to train parents to have fun with and to instruct their children. The experimental intervention exceeded the control treatment on 7 out of 15 outcome measures, but failed to show a significant effect on the children's classroom behavior at initial follow-up. Teacher ratings at a 1-year follow-up (Strayhorn & Weidman, 1991), however, indicated that the behavior of children in the experimental group evidenced much greater improvement than that of children in the control group.

Comprehensive Programming

Comprehensive programming encompasses efforts to develop effective general and special education programs that will ensure appropriate educational opportunities for students with ADD. As with home-school collaboration, researchers have not directly addressed the development of comprehensive educational programs for these students. Findings in two areas, however, have implications for program development. First, some studies have demonstrated the potential benefits of multimodal interventions (e.g., Barkley et al., 1992; Hall & Kataria, 1992; Hinshaw, Henker, & Whalen, 1984; Hinshaw & Melnick, 1992; Pelham et al., 1980). Though not without contradiction (e.g., Bloomquist et al., 1991; Firestone et al., 1981; Horn et al., 1987, 1990), the findings from these multimodal studies suggest that treatments may have additive or interactive effects. Effective comprehensive programming for students who are difficult to serve may well require the exploration of multiple interventions, using resources within and outside the school community.

The second area of findings with implications for educational programs is the between-subject variation that many investigators have reported. This variation suggests that results based on groups or averages may not be as relevant as individual case findings. For example, in investigating the effects of low, moderate, and placebo methylphenidate doses in combination with two intensities of teacher reprimands, Abramowitz, Eckstrand, O'Leary, and Dulcan (1992) found that optimal intervention combinations varied across subjects, suggesting that a simple behavioral intervention can be as effective as medication for some, but not all, children with ADD. When Hoza et al. (1992) administered varied doses of methylphenidate and different potencies of behavior therapy to two boys, both responded well to behavior therapy. For one boy, however, the behavior therapy combined with a low dose of methylphenidate proved to be the most effective intervention, whereas the other boy responded most favorably to a high dose of methylphenidate combined with the most potent behavioral contingency.

Conclusion

Intervention research on children with attention deficits has moved well beyond the concept, associated with the era of "minimal brain dysfunction," of serving students with attention deficits in barren cubicles (e.g., Cruickshank, Bentzen, Ratzeburg, & Tannhauser, 1961). Instead, researchers have focused on training or shaping specific desirable target behaviors, reducing the frequency of undesirable behaviors, creating optimally stimulating learning tasks, and refining multimodal intervention programs. Overall, however, the empirical evidence in favor of nonpharmacological interventions to promote the education of students with ADD is weak. Although some evidence supports behavior therapy, cognitive-behavioral therapy, parent training, and task stimulation, the findings are invariably inconsistent.

The teacher or school administrator seeking guidance from the literature must also keep in mind other significant limitations of the research. First, generalization is problematic because the samples for the reported studies are far from homogeneous and represent children with a great diversity of behavior or learning difficulties. Second, researchers drew subjects almost exclusively from elementary school-age children, making application of findings to older students questionable. Third, we have grouped treatments in categories, the actual interventions within these categories varied considerably across studies. Fourth, the dependent measures also varied greatly and were often too broad to capture subtle distinctions between treatments. Fifth, and perhaps most important, because the research comes almost exclusively from the fields of medicine and clinical psychology, researchers tested few interventions in school settings, and even fewer in regular classrooms.

From an educational perspective, researchers have devoted too much effort to peripheral questions. Perhaps because the population is inadequately defined, investigators have often labored to identify performance differences between children with attention deficits and those without, rather than comparing treatments with randomly assigned groups of children with ADD. Similarly, investigators have frequently compared nonpharmacological interventions to drug therapy. Although this provides one valid standard against which treatments can be measured, the merit of an intervention relative to medication is a moot point for educators who must use nonpharmacological interventions to improve the performance of students who may or may not be on medication.

Most important, many key questions have not been addressed:

- What specific curricula or instructional materials do students with ADD need?
- What role can computers and other technologies play in the education of students with attention deficits?
- What interventions can be applied by teachers in general education classrooms?
- What implications for interventions does the presence of multiple disorders have?

- Do interventions that are effective with students with learning disabilities or emotional and behavioral disorders, such as time-out, need to be modified to be effective with students with ADD?
- What strategies are most effective in teaching social skills to students with ADD?
- At school, what related services do students with ADD need?
- How should responsibility be shared among schools, social agencies, and medical professionals?

In describing the current state of practice, Hinshaw and Erhardt (1991) effectively summed up the challenge educators face:

> It is stressed that no intervention strategies to date, whether employed singly or in combination, have proved clinically sufficient and durable for the troubling and troublesome problems of these youngsters, thus necessitating the continuing search for integrated components—cognitive, behavioral, and pharmacologic—that will constitute an adequate treatment package. (p. 99)

Overall, the literature on educationally relevant interventions for children and youth with ADD is exploratory, not prescriptive. Though the problem of attention deficits is pervasive, investigators have tested relatively few interventions that speak to the day-to-day issues teachers face or to the larger issues related to developing comprehensive programs for these students. From the research, we have some sense of what might work in the classroom—redirection, response cost, correspondence training, color added to repetitive tasks—but not enough information to make definitive, categorical decisions about educational programming for students with ADD.

References

Abikoff, H. (1987). An evaluation of cognitive behavior therapy for hyperactive children. In B. Lahey & A. Kazdin (Eds.), *Advances in clinical child psychology* (Vol. 10, pp. 171–216). New York: Plenum.

Abikoff, H. (1991). Cognitive training in ADHD children: Less to it than meets the eye. *Journal of Learning Disabilities, 24,* 205–209.

Abramowitz, A. J., Eckstrand, D., O'Leary, S. G., & Dulcan, M. K. (1992). ADHD children's responses to stimulant medication and two intensities of a behavioral intervention. *Behavior Modification, 16,* 193–203.

Abramowitz, A. J., & O'Leary, S. G. (1990). Effectiveness of delayed punishment in an applied setting. *Behavior Therapy, 21,* 231–239.

Abramowitz, A. J., O'Leary, S. G., & Futtersak, M. W. (1988). The relative impact of long and short reprimands on children's off-task behavior in the classroom. *Behavior Therapy, 19,* 243–247.

Abramowitz, A. J., O'Leary, S. G., & Rosén, L. A. (1987). Reducing off-task behavior in the classroom: A comparison of encouragement and reprimands. *Journal of Abnormal Child Psychology, 15,* 155–163.

Ayllon, T., Layman, D., & Kandel, H. J. (1975). A behavioral-educational alternative to drug control of hyperactive children. *Journal of Applied Behavior Analysis, 8,* 137–146.

Barkley, R. A. (1990). *Attention-deficit hyperactivity disorder: A handbook for diagnosis and treatment.* New York: Guilford Press.

Barkley, R. A., Guevremont, D. C., Anastopoulos, A. D., & Fletcher, K. E. (1992). A comparison of three family therapy programs for treating family conflicts in adolescents with attention-deficit hyperactivity disorder. *Journal of Consulting and Clinical Psychology, 60,* 450–462.

Bloomquist, M. L., August, G. J., & Ostrander, R. (1991). Effects of a school-based cognitive-behavior intervention for ADHD children. *Journal of Abnormal Child Psychology, 19,* 591–605.

Borden, K. A., Brown, R. T., Wynne, M. E., & Schleser, R. (1987). Piagetian conservation and response to cognitive therapy in attention deficit disordered children. *Journal of Child Psychology and Psychiatry, 28,* 755–764.

Brown, R. T., Borden, K. A., Wynne, M. E., Schleser, R., & Clingerman, S. R. (1986). Methylphenidate and cognitive therapy with ADD children: A methodological reconsideration. *Journal of Abnormal Child Psychology, 14,* 481–497.

Brown, R. T., Wynne, M. E., Borden, K. A., Clingerman, S. R., Geniesse, R., & Spunt, A. L. (1986). Methylphenidate and cognitive therapy in children with attention deficit disorder: A double-blind trial. *Developmental and Behavioral Pediatrics, 7,* 163–170.

Brown, R. T., Wynne, M. E., & Medenis, R. (1985). Methylphenidate and cognitive therapy: A comparison of treatment approaches with hyperactive boys. *Journal of Abnormal Child Psychology, 13,* 69–87.

Conte, R., Kinsbourne, M., Swanson, J., Zirk, H., & Samuels, M. (1987). Presentation rate effects on paired associate learning by attention deficit disordered children. *Child Development, 57,* 681–687.

Cruickshank, W. M., Bentzen, F. A., Ratzeburg, F. H., & Tannhauser, M. T. (1961). *A teaching method for brain-injured and hyperactive children.* Syracuse, NY: Syracuse University Press.

Douglas, V. I., & Parry, P. A. (1983). Effects of reward on delayed reaction time task performance of hyperactive children. *Journal of Abnormal Child Psychology, 11,* 313–326.

Douglas, V. I., Parry, P., Marton, P., & Garson, C. (1976). Assessment of a cognitive training program for hyperactive children. *Journal of Abnormal Child Psychology, 4,* 389–410.

DuPaul, G. J., Guevremont, D. C., & Barkley, R. A. (1992). Behavioral treatment of attention-deficit hyperactivity disorder in the classroom: The use of the Attention Training System. *Behavior Modification, 16,* 204–225.

Erhardt, D., & Baker, B. L. (1990). The effects of behavioral parent training of families with young hyperactive children. *Journal of Behavior Therapy & Experimental Psychiatry, 21,* 121–132.

Firestone, P., Kelly, M. J., Goodman, J. T., & Davey, J. (1981). Differential effects of parent training and stimulant medication with hyperactives. *Journal of the American Academy of Child Psychiatry, 20,* 135–142.

Friedling, C., & O'Leary, S. G. (1979). Effects of self-instructional training on second- and third-grade hyperactive children: A failure to replicate. *Journal of Applied Behavior Analysis, 12,* 211–219.

Futtersak, M. W. (1988). *The effects of consistently strong and increasingly strong reprimands in the classroom.* Unpublished doctoral dissertation, State University of New York at Stony Brook.

Gittelman-Klein, R., Klein, D. F., Abikoff, H., Katz, S., Gloisten, A. C., & Kates, W. (1976). Relative efficacy of methylphenidate and behavior modification in hyperkinetic children: An interim report. *Journal of Abnormal Child Psychology, 4,* 361–379.

Goldstein, S., & Goldstein, M. (1990). *Managing attention disorders in children.* New York: Wiley.

Gordon, M., Thomason, D., Cooper, S., & Ivers, C. L. (1991). Nonmedical treatment of ADHD/hyperactivity: The Attention Training System. *Journal of School Psychology, 29,* 151–159.

Guevremont, D. C., Tishelman, A. C., & Hull, D. B. (1985). Teaching generalized self-control to attention-deficient boys with mothers as adjunct therapists. *Child and Family Behavior Therapy, 7,* 23–37.

Hall, C. W., & Kataria, S. (1992). Effects of two treatment techniques on delay and vigilance tasks with attention deficit hyperactive disorder (ADHD) children. *The Journal of Psychology, 126,* 17–25.

Hinshaw, S. P., & Erhardt, D. (1991). Attention-deficit hyperactivity disorder. In P. C. Kendall (Ed.), *Child and adolescent therapy: Cognitive-behavioral procedures* (pp. 98–128). New York: Guilford Press.

Hinshaw, S. P., Henker, B., & Whalen, C. (1984). Cognitive-behavioral and pharmacologic interventions for hyperactive boys: Comparative and combined effects. *Journal of Consulting and Clinical Psychology, 52,* 739–740.

Hinshaw, S. P., & Melnick, S. (1992). Self-management therapies and attention-deficit hyperactivity disorder: Reinforced self-evaluation and anger control interventions. *Behavior Modification, 16,* 253–273.

Horn, W. F., Ialongo, N., Greenberg, G., Packard, T., & Smith-Winberry, C. (1990). Additive effects of behavioral parent training and self-control therapy with attention deficit hyperactivity disordered children. *Journal of Clinical Child Psychology, 19,* 57–68.

Horn, W. F., Ialongo, N., Popovich, S., & Peradotto, D. (1987). Behavioral parent training and cognitive-behavioral self-control therapy with ADD-H children: Comparative and combined effects. *Journal of Clinical Child Psychology, 16,* 57–68.

Hoza, B., Pelham, W. E., Sams, S. E., & Carlson, C. (1992). An examination of the "dosage" effects of both behavior therapy and methylphenidate on the classroom performance of two ADHD children. *Behavior Modification, 16,* 164–192.

Kendall, P. C., & Braswell, L. (1982). Cognitive-behavioral self-control therapy for children: A components analysis. *Journal of Consulting and Clinical Psychology, 50,* 672–689.

O'Leary, K. D., Pelham, W. E., Rosenbaum, A., & Price, G. H. (1976). Behavioral treatment of hyperkinetic children: An experimental evaluation of its usefulness. *Clinical Pediatrics, 15,* 510–515.

Paniagua, F. A. (1992). Verbal-nonverbal correspondence training with ADHD children. *Behavior Modification, 16,* 226–252.

Paniagua, F. A., Morrison, P. B., & Black, S. A. (1990). Management of a hyperactive-conduct disordered child through correspondence training: A preliminary study. *Journal of Behavior Therapy and Experimental Psychiatry, 21,* 63–68.

Pelham, W. E., Milich, R., & Walker, J. L. (1986). Effects of continuous and partial reinforcement and methylphenidate on learning in children with attention deficit disorder. *Journal of Abnormal Psychology, 95,* 319–325.

Pelham, W. E., Schnedler, R. W., Bologna, N. C., & Contreras, J. A. (1980). Behavioral and stimulant treatment of hyperactive children: A therapy study with methylphenidate probes in a within-subject design. *Journal of Applied Behavior Analysis, 13,* 221–236.

Pisterman, S., Firestone, P., McGrath, P., Goodman, J. T., Webster, I., Mallory, R., & Goffin, B. (1992). The effects of parent training on parenting stress and sense of competence. *Canadian Journal of Behavioral Science, 24,* 41–58.

Pisterman, S., McGrath, P., Firestone, P., Goodman, J. T., Webster, I., & Mallory, R. (1989). Outcome of parent-mediated treatment of preschoolers with attention deficit disorder with hyperactivity. *Journal of Consulting and Clinical Psychology, 57,* 628–635.

Pollard, S., Ward, E. M., & Barkley, R. A. (1983). The effects of parent training and Ritalin on the parent-child interactions of hyperactive boys. *Child and Family Behavior Therapy, 5,* 51–69.

Rapport, M. D., Murphy, A., & Bailey, J. S. (1980). The effects of a response-cost treatment tactic on hyperactive children. *Journal of School Psychology, 18,* 98–111.

Rapport, M. D., Murphy, H. A., & Bailey, J. S. (1982). Ritalin vs. response-cost in the control of hyperactive children: A within-subject comparison. *Journal of Applied Behavior Analysis, 15,* 205–216.

Rosenbaum, A., O'Leary, K. D., & Jacob, R. G. (1975). Behavioral intervention with hyperactive children: Group consequences as a supplement to individual contingencies. *Behavior Therapy, 6,* 315–323.

Shroyer, C., & Zentall, S. S. (1986). Effects of rate, nonrelevant information, and repetition on the listening comprehension of hyperactive children. *The Journal of Special Education, 20,* 231–239.

Strayhorn, J. M., & Weidman, C. S. (1989). Reduction of attention deficit and internalizing symptoms in preschoolers through parent-child interaction training. *Journal of the American Academy of Child and Adolescent Psychiatry, 28,* 888–896.

Strayhorn, J. M., & Weidman, C. S. (1991). Follow-up one year after parent-child interaction training: Effects on behavior of preschool children. *Journal of the American Academy of Child and Adolescent Psychiatry, 30,* 138–143.

Sullivan, M. A., & O'Leary, S. G. (1990). Maintenance following reward and cost token programs. *Behavior Therapy, 21,* 139–149.

Thurston, L. P. (1979). Comparison of the effects of parent training and of Ritalin in treating hyperactive children. *International Journal of Mental Health, 8*, 121–128.

Worland, J. (1976). Effects of positive and negative feedback on behavior control in hyperactive and normal boys. *Journal of Abnormal Child Psychology, 4*, 315–326.

Zentall, S. S. (1985). Stimulus-control factors in search performance in hyperactive children. *Journal of Learning Disabilities, 18*, 480–485.

Zentall, S. S. (1989). Attentional cueing in spelling tasks for hyperactive and comparison regular classroom children. *The Journal of Special Education, 23*, 83–93.

Zentall, S. S., Falkenberg, S. D., & Smith, L. B. (1985). Effects of color stimulation and information on the copying performance of attention-problem adolescents. *Journal of Abnormal Child Psychology, 13*, 501–511.

Zentall, S. S., & Gohs, D. E. (1984). Hyperactive and comparison children's response to detailed vs. global cues in communication tasks. *Learning Disability Quarterly, 7*, 77–87.

Zentall, S. S., & Meyer, M. J. (1987). Self-regulation of stimulation for ADD-H children during reading and vigilance task performance. *Journal of Abnormal Child Psychology, 15*, 519–536.

20 Co-Teaching: Guidelines for Creating Effective Practices

LYNNE COOK AND MARILYN FRIEND

IN INCLUSIVE PROGRAMS, teachers in general education and special education increasingly have to learn how to work with each other and determine whose authority lies where. Cook and Friend examine the issue of co-teaching—how teachers work as a team in planning and organizing the classroom. They offer many specific suggestions that can help teachers work together more effectively.

Although the isolation of the teaching profession long has been recognized and has often been commented upon (Barth, 1990; Lortie, 1975), for the past three decades educators also have been intrigued with the possibilities created by two teachers' sharing one classroom. As early as the 1960s (e.g., Trump, 1966), co-teaching was recommended as a strategy for reorganizing secondary schools in the United States as well as in England (Warwick, 1971). A variation of co-teaching—team teaching, in which teachers share planning responsibilities for instruction while they continue to teach separately—was adopted in many open-concept schools during the 1970s (Easterby-Smith & Olive, 1984). More recently, renewed interest in co-teaching has emerged as part of the middle school movement and other school reform efforts (MacIver, 1990).

As a service delivery option in special education, pairs of special educators used co-teaching to share their responsibilities for students in self-contained class-rooms (Garvar & Papania, 1982). Further, co-teaching grew rapidly in response to factors recognized during the early days of mainstreaming, including the need for special education teachers and general education teachers to work in constructive and coordinated ways (Bauer, 1975; Walker, 1974) and increasing expectations that students with disabilities be educated in classrooms with their nondisabled peers. By the late 1980s, co-teaching was discussed most often as a means for special education teachers to meet students' needs in general education settings.

Much of the current literature on co-teaching as it relates to special education consists of educators' detailed anecdotal accounts of successful co-teaching programs and experiences (e.g., Adams & Cessna, 1991; Howell, 1991; White & White, 1992). Others have raised questions or dedicated entire articles or chapters to discussions of the limitations of and problems with co-teaching and its collaborative elements (e.g., Fuchs & Fuchs, 1992; Pugach & Johnson, 1995; Reeve & Hallahan, 1994). In the meantime, schools planning to include co-teaching as part of their inclusive practices are asking how to go about setting up co-teaching programs that are responsive to the needs of students as well as feasible in the eyes of teachers.

The purpose of this chapter is to raise and discuss many of the issues and concerns that can guide the thinking and practice of professionals as they strive to design and implement responsible co-teaching programs. Our intent is not so much to provide a single set of "right" answers as to try to ensure that the questions have been asked so that professionals planning to co-teach can make deliberate and reflective choices concerning this service delivery option.

Ten Questions to Guide Co-Teaching Program Development

What Do We Mean by Co-Teaching?

When teachers discuss co-teaching, a similar understanding of the co-teaching concept is important. Our definition is as follows:

> two or more professionals delivering substantive instruction to a diverse, or blended, group of students in a single physical space.

This definition includes four key components which are elaborated here. *First,* co-teaching involves *two educators**, and occasionally, more. For purposes of the discussion here, one of the professionals is a general education teacher and the other is a special educator—either a special education teacher or a specialist in one of the related services such as a speech/language therapist. Another configuration of teachers falling under the rubric of co-teaching may be two middle school teachers teaching English and social studies in an integrated block. The intent here, however, is to focus on the somewhat unique possibilities that occur from the different but complementary perspectives of the professionals involved: *General educators,* who specialize in understanding, structuring, and pacing curriculum for groups of students are, paired with *special educators,* who specialize in identifying unique learning needs of individual students and enhancing curriculum and instruction to match these needs. Related services professionals also may be involved. This is elaborated

---

* We use the terms *educator, teacher,* and *professional* throughout this chapter to designate professionally prepared and licensed teachers and related services providers.

further in the section, "Who Should Be Involved in Co-Teaching?" This linking of educational perspectives becomes a strategy for creating classroom communities in inclusive schools (Friend, Reising, & Cook, 1993).

More than two educators can be present in the classroom. Moreover, in some co-taught classes, paraprofessionals, parent volunteers, or older student volunteers also have roles in assisting the teachers. But these arrangements do not meet the definition of co-teaching as we have articulated it.

The second part of our co-teaching definition specifies that the educators *deliver substantive instruction*. They do not supervise a study hall, support a single student, monitor students who are listening to a guest speaker, or assist in delivering instructional add-ons that are related only marginally to the curriculum of the general education classroom. This definitional component emphasizes that both professionals are involved actively in the *instruction* of students.

Third, the educators teach a *diverse group of students*, including students with disabilities. Co-teaching involving special educators or related services specialists is undertaken because students with individualized educational programs (IEPs) have educational needs that can be met by moving their supports to the general education classroom through this instructional arrangement.

Finally, in co-teaching the instruction is delivered primarily in a *single classroom or physical space*. This does not preclude the possibility of occasionally separating groups of students for instruction that involves considerable activity with possible high levels of noise and distraction, but it does eliminate from consideration situations in which teachers coordinate instruction (for example, plan an integrated unit together) but deliver it to separate groups of students in separate locations. The latter is sometimes a recommended instructional practice and well may be an excellent example of collaborative planning, sometimes referred to as co-planning, but it does not involve the considerably more complex set of issues that arise when two teachers share instruction in one classroom.

Variations in Practice

Co-teaching is just one of several structures or arrangements used by professionals who collaborate in providing special education and related services to special needs students in general education classrooms. Ideally, co-teaching includes collaboration in all facets of the educational process. It encompasses collaboratively assessing student strengths and weaknesses, determining appropriate educational goals and outcome indicators, designing intervention strategies and planning for their implementation, evaluating student progress toward the established goals, and evaluating the effectiveness of the co-teaching process.

What is ideal and what is pragmatic, however, are often different. Variations in student needs, caseloads and class size, competing professional responsibilities, and scheduling are among the reasons that collaboration in the full range of activities that support co-teaching is not always possible. Although we encourage professionals to collaborate as fully as possible throughout their teaching and service delivery, we will limit our discussion of co-teaching here to the collaborative *delivery of instruction*.

Further Sorting Vocabulary

A deeper understanding of the meaning of co-teaching can be derived by distinguishing it from other activities on behalf of students as we have done above. For example, we agree with others who clarify that co-assessment (Choate, 1993), problem solving and intervention planning teams (Graden, 1989; Phillips & McCullough, 1990; Pugach & Johnson, 1989), consultation (Heron & Harris, 1993), and individualized educational planning teams (Friend & Cook, 1996) are distinct activities in which educators might participate collaboratively to enhance education and services. Co-teaching will benefit from educators' collaborative efforts in all of these and similar activities. Co-teaching, however, is uniquely different from these activities in that it is an approach for special educators and related services professionals to provide *direct* service to students with special needs during instruction within the general education classroom.

Collaborative problem-solving approaches and joint planning efforts, in contrast, are generally *indirect* services, as the special educators interact directly with the teachers, who then interact directly with the students. The special educator or related services provider serves the student indirectly in this fashion.

Finally, though co-teaching—as well as the other activities mentioned—contributes to inclusive practices, it is not synonymous with inclusion. Inclusion can be accomplished in many ways depending on the students' needs just as co-teaching may be done to accomplish many goals other than inclusion. Yet co-teaching is clearly just one approach that is valuable for facilitating the inclusion of some students.

What is the Rationale for Co-Teaching?

Before deciding to begin a co-teaching program, professionals should have opportunities to clarify what they hope to accomplish by using this approach to meet student needs, particularly since it places new demands on the adults involved and requires them to reconsider their professional roles. The following are among the most salient elements of a rationale for co-teaching:

1. Increase instructional options for all students.
2. Improve program intensity and continuity.
3. Reduce stigma for students with special needs.
4. Increase support for teachers and related service specialists.

Increasing Instructional Options

Any discussion of reasons for co-teaching should begin with an understanding of the potential benefits to students. For example, co-teaching can be characterized as a means of bringing the strengths of two teachers with different expertise together in a manner that allows them to better meet student needs (Bauwens, Hourcade, & Friend, 1989; Walsh, 1992). From this perspective, a primary rationale for co-teaching is that it increases opportunities for student success through expanding instructional approaches. Although research supporting the value of co-teaching is limited, some is beginning to emerge demonstrating greater academic gains for students when their teachers receive consultation and participate in co-teaching (Schulte, Osborne, & McKinney, 1990).

One way of understanding this part of a co-teaching rationale is to think of co-teaching as an opportunity to increase the instructional options for *all* students. For example, although co-teaching occurs because students with disabilities need support services in a general education classroom, gifted and talented students may also benefit because more options can be created for individualizing their learning. Likewise, students who struggle to learn but who are not eligible for special education or other support services gain the benefit of a reduced student-teacher ratio and the instructional variety that co-teaching brings.

Improving Program Intensity and Continuity

A second reason for co-teaching concerns the intensity and integrity of students' educational programs. First, in co-taught classes, students can receive more instruction and are involved more systematically in their learning than would be possible in a classroom with only one teacher. Moreover, the combination of two teachers reduces the student-teacher ratio and provides opportunities for greater student participation and engaged time. Also, co-teaching enables students who otherwise might leave the classroom for their special education or related services to spend more time in one instructional environment (the general education classroom), thereby reducing wasteful interruptions to student programs.

As you think about this point, consider any "pullout" situations. Quite conservatively, the process of stopping an instructional activity in the general education classroom, "packing up" to go to a special service, walking to that location, re-orienting to the instruction offered there, and then reversing all those steps upon returning to the general education classroom takes 15 minutes. Using this conservative estimate, students who leave the classroom one time each day for a special service are losing 75 instructional minutes each week just to get to their services.

In addition, the curriculum for a student in a pullout program often is fragmented. When general education and special services are separate, either a separate curriculum or lack of congruence in the curriculum and services is the common result. Even if general and special educators work collaboratively outside of class to plan an integrated curriculum, no matter how skilled the special educator, students often have difficulty generalizing what they have learned in a separate setting to activities in the general education setting. Thus, two types of program fragmentation may be reduced through co-teaching: (a) temporal continuity of the student's learning opportunities; and (b) curricular continuity of the instruction and instructional process.

Reducing the Stigma for Students

A third part of a student-centered rationale for co-teaching concerns the stigma often associated with leaving the general education classroom to receive special education or related services (Redditt, 1991). The stigma derives from uninformed attitudes of students and teachers regarding special needs students' requirements for special education, related services, or remedial education. Although general education teachers and students may have little knowledge about what specific supplementary services entail, they associate negative attributes to them—and they often, however subtly, convey those perceptions to the special needs students. Some evidence suggests that students prefer to receive supports in classrooms with their peers rather than leave the classroom for special services (Walsh, 1992).

Although providing required supports for students in the general education classroom may be preferable to pulling them out for any number of reasons, a note of caution is warranted. The co-teaching framework to which we subscribe emphasizes that students with disabilities are taught the general education curriculum with needed modifications and support. They are included in instruction of the general education curriculum. We have seen many classrooms in which efforts to provide in-class services resulted in students with disabilities simply being pulled to the side to receive their instruction. In essence, these classrooms constitute a pullout model within the general education classroom and sometimes are referred to as "pull in" or "pull aside" approaches. The stigmatizing of students using this approach can be as great if not greater than in traditional special education pullout services, and few of the other benefits of co-teaching accrue to the student.

Increasing Professional Support

Another part of the rationale for co-teaching relates to the professionals and the extent to which they feel supported. For example, many co-teachers in elementary schools joke that the greatest benefit of co-teaching to them is that someone in the classroom gets their jokes! More seriously, co-teachers talk about the notions that they can relieve each other during instruction or help to clarify their partners' presentation, that they share the understanding that can come only from having been there for the best and worst moments of instruction, and that they can work together to more sensitively gauge student needs at any particular moment of instruction.

When is Co-Teaching the Appropriate Instructional Option?

Clearly, students' needs and skills and their match with the general education curriculum are the primary considerations when deciding if co-teaching is appropriate for a specific situation. The instructional strengths and needs of special needs students and typical students alike should be examined and deemed to be compatible and manageable by two teachers within a single classroom. In assessing the extent to which students will benefit from co-teaching, a number of factors arise that will assist in determining the appropriateness of co-teaching. Several key questions are

- Is the content of the general education curriculum appropriate for the student?

- How much and what type of modifications and other support will the student require to benefit from the general education curriculum?
- Does the student require direct intervention or instruction that is entirely different from instruction other students receive?
- Is the ecology of the classroom appropriate for diverse learners?
- Do other students in this classroom need modified curriculum or instruction?

These same questions provide a framework for making decisions about instructional design and modification. These topics are not discussed here but require serious consideration.

First, questions have to be asked about appropriateness of the general education curriculum for the student with a disability and the nature and intensity of support the student will need to benefit from participating in the general education instruction. Is the match between content and learning demands of the general education curriculum and the skills and learning needs of the student close enough to justify co-teaching? Although minor or major modifications in the level and amount of content, as well as modifications in the methods of instruction, probably will be required, the basic content of the general education curriculum should be determined to be appropriate for the student.

When a student requires direct intervention or instruction that is entirely different from what other students receive in the general education classroom, in-class delivery of the intervention most likely will not meet the definition of co-teaching. The individualized decision-making process used to design the student's IEP should be followed to determine if these specialized services would be delivered most appropriately in the general education classroom or elsewhere (MacDonald & York, 1991).

The next area of student needs to consider when deciding if co-teaching is a viable option focuses on the ecology of the specific class in which the student will participate and its appropriateness for the student. White and White (1992) have noted the importance of getting the right mix of students in one class. In doing so, we have to examine the learning needs of the students without disabilities and the composition of the group assigned to the potentially co-taught classroom. Is the ecology of the classroom likely to be conducive to co-teaching, to the inclusion of special needs students, and to the presence of a second teacher on a scheduled basis? For instance, is this class characterized by a wide range of diversity in teaching and learning styles? If the class already has several nondisabled students who might be at risk or who may have special learning needs, the addition of a limited number of students with disabilities probably will not alter the instructional demands of the overall classroom group significantly. At the same time, the accompanying addition of another teacher most likely will improve the quality of instruction, increase the intensity of instruction, and expand the instructional options for students.

Even though students might benefit from inclusion in general education classes and might be excellent candidates for co-teaching situations, a handful of classrooms and teachers will not be able to provide appropriate experiences for them. If a general education teacher is rigid or inflexible regarding student needs and classroom expectations or if the teacher treats students with little respect when they struggle to learn, *many* students assigned to that classroom likely will receive a poor education. This is a supervisory issue concerning professional performance and is a matter for administrative action. Attempting to use co-teaching as a remedy or substitute for a poor teacher would be a serious misuse of the approach.

What Does Co-Teaching Look Like?

One of the benefits of co-teaching is that the unique perspectives and strengths of general educators and special educators or other specialists are brought together to create teaching approaches and instructional strategies that could not occur if just one teacher were present (Friend, Reising, & Cook, 1993). To accomplish this, co-teachers develop an array of classroom arrangements for their shared instruction. The following common co-teaching approaches, as outlined by Cook and Friend (1993), can serve as a starting point for considering how co-teaching might look in a classroom. They also are depicted schematically in Figure 20.1.

All the approaches have variations depending on the subject matter being taught, age and maturity of the students, and creativity of the teachers. No one approach is best or worst; each has a place in a co-taught class. In fact, each of the approaches—or some variation—is likely to be used alone or with another in any session of a co-taught class. They are presented here in what often proves to be a developmental order in terms of the amount of planning, trust, and comfort with one another that each requires of the teachers. Finally, all the approaches are presented as they would be used with instructional groups characterized by diverse student needs and including students with disabilities. Students with disabilities are dispersed among the instructional groups.

One Teaching, One Assisting

In this type of co-teaching, both educators are present, but one takes a clear lead in the classroom while the other observes students or drifts around the room, assisting them as needed. This approach is simple, limited teacher planning is required, and it provides the basic support to students that can make a class with diverse learning needs successful. It also has serious liabilities, though. When one teacher only observes or assists, especially if this role is assigned to the special educator, he or she may feel like a glorified teaching assistant. Students might question that teacher's authority in the classroom, too. These problems might be surmounted if the teachers alternate the lead and supportive roles.

As an example, consider the U.S. history class taught by Mr. Miles and the special education teacher Ms. Anderson. Although Mr. Miles takes the lead in much of the instruction because he has the content expertise in history, Ms. Anderson has a key role in the classroom. On Tuesdays she leads a current events activity while Mr. Miles assists in the classroom. On Thursdays, during the last part of the class, Ms. Anderson leads students through a review of material covered and shows students how history affects contemporary society. The teachers planned these opportunities

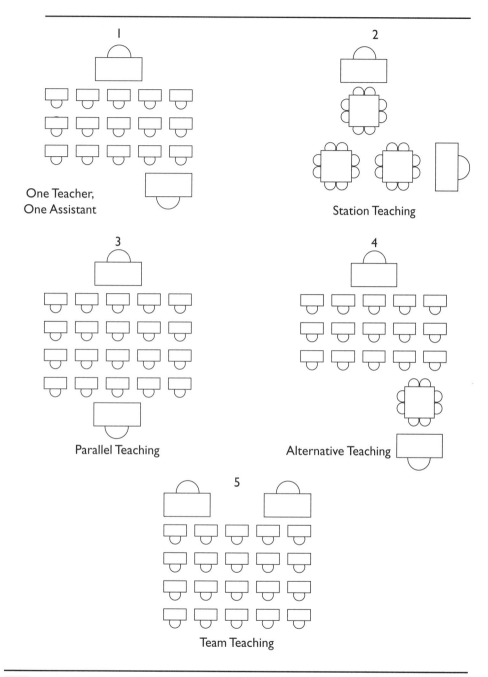

■ **Figure 20.1** *Approaches to Co-Teaching*

Source: Adapted from *Including Students with Special Needs: A Practical Guide for Classroom Teachers* (p. 87), by M. Friend and W. Bursuck, 1996, Boston: Allyn & Bacon.

to add variety to the instruction for students and to make clear to students that Ms. Anderson is a "real" teacher.

Station Teaching

In station teaching, teachers divide instructional content into two, three, or more segments and present the content at separate locations within the classroom. With two teachers and two stations the teachers teach their half of the material and then trade student groups and repeat the same instruction. If students are able to work independently, a third station sometimes is created in which students work alone or with a partner on a related project or assignment. Although this approach requires that the teachers share responsibilities for planning sufficiently to divide the instructional content, each has separate responsibilities for delivering instruction.

This separating of instruction can increase the comfort level of inexperienced co-teachers. Students benefit from the lower teacher-pupil ratio, and students with disabilities can be integrated into all the groups instead of being singled out. Furthermore, equal teacher status in the classroom is not a serious concern because both teachers have active teaching roles. Potential drawbacks to station teaching include noise and a high activity level. Another challenge is that the teachers have to be able to pace their lessons well so the students are able to transition from one station to another at scheduled times. If one teacher extends the station time consistently while the second stays on schedule, conflict might arise.

Stations can be used at any grade level. In a first-grade classroom, students might spend 20 minutes at each of two math stations, one for introducing a new concept and one for practicing the concept taught last week. In an eighth-grade science class, students at one station complete an experiment while the other half of the class reviews for an upcoming test. In a high-school English class, students might go to a single station for an entire class period, rotating to new stations on subsequent days. One day students look at social and political influences on society during a particular era. On another day, they read two examples of short stories from that era. On yet another day, they work with a learning partner to complete a short biographical sketch of a famous person from that time period. Station teaching has to be arranged so the order of material presented does not matter, but in many lessons this is not a serious issue.

Parallel Teaching

Parallel teaching also lowers the student-teacher ratio, so it often is used when students need opportunities to respond aloud, to engage in hands-on activities, or to interact with one another. In parallel teaching the teachers plan the instruction jointly, but each delivers it to a heterogeneous group consisting of half the class. For this approach to be successful, teachers have to coordinate their efforts so the students receive essentially the same instruction in approximately the same amount of time. This type of co-teaching lends itself to drill-and-practice activities, projects requiring close teacher supervision, and discussion of activities. As with station teaching approaches, noise and activity levels sometimes are problematic.

Teachers create a number of adaptations for this co-teaching approach. One of particular interest is using parallel teaching to teach students different perspectives on a topic, then having them share with one another. For example, in a unit on the environment, both groups receive instruction about endangered species, but one group is given the perspective of those who want to protect wildlife and the other learns about the economic problems that occur when wildlife protection leads to the loss of jobs. The students later discuss this issue together and use a problem-solving approach to address their differing points of view.

Alternative Teaching

Sometimes students with disabilities or other exceptional learning needs benefit from instruction in a smaller group than is customary in station or parallel teaching arrangements. In alternative teaching one teacher works with the small group (e.g., 3–8 students) while the other instructs the large group. For example, in a *pre-teaching group* students learn the vocabulary that will be introduced with tomorrow's lesson or pre-read the next short story or chapter. In *re-teaching*, already taught information is reviewed or taught using additional techniques or materials. Students who elect to have extra review or make up material missed during absences often ask to participate in re-teaching groups. This approach also can be used to ensure that all students receive opportunities to interact with a teacher in a small group. Other uses of alternative teaching include providing an *enrichment group*, allowing an *interest group* to pursue a specific interest, and creating opportunities for an *assessment group* in order to check the development of student skills.

The greatest risk in this approach is stigmatizing students with disabilities by grouping them for re-teaching repeatedly, with or without other students included as group members. This risk can be avoided by varying groupings and ensuring that all students are periodically included in a group.

One interesting variation on this co-teaching approach is to use it for addressing a student's social skills. A student with need is targeted, and a small group of positive peer models is selected to join that student. The lesson taught is essentially the same as the one the large group is receiving, but an emphasis is placed on turn-taking, talking appropriately with others, or any other needed skill.

Team Teaching

In team teaching, both teachers share the instruction of students. The teachers might take turns leading a discussion, or one may speak while the other demonstrates a concept, or one might speak while the other models note taking on a projection system. The teachers who are teaming also role play and model appropriate ways to ask questions. This approach requires a high level of mutual trust and commitment. It is an approach with which some co-teachers might never be comfortable. On the other hand, many veteran co-teachers report that they find this type of co-teaching rewarding. They note that it gives them a renewed energy in their teaching and prompts them to try new ideas for reaching their students.

Two teachers team taught an introductory lesson on debate using this approach. One of the teachers began the class and worked into the conversation her opinion that Tonya Harding's much publicized fall from favor was an example of media shaping public opinion in the absence of any concrete information. The other teacher jumped into the conversation by declaring that Nancy Kerrigan's career was nearly ended because of Harding's actions and that the press had nothing to do with the facts. Not surprisingly, within in a matter of minutes the teachers had the undivided attention of their class as the students anticipated how the teachers would solve their disagreement. After a short period of debate, the teachers transitioned into their lesson, using their own impromptu debate for examples to illustrate concepts.

Clearly, approaches to co-teaching should be selected on the basis of student characteristics and needs, teacher preferences, curricular demands, and pragmatics such as the amount of teaching space available. Most experienced co-teachers use many approaches, sometimes two or three even within a single lesson. They often also comment that one or two of the approaches just do not seem to fit their instructional setting. What is most crucial is to experiment with approaches, adapting them to fit specific situations to produce variety and appropriate use of teacher skills in the delivery of instruction.

Who Should Be Involved in Co-Teaching?

The personal characteristics and the professional roles of the prospective co-teachers will influence the success of the co-teaching relationship and service. Consideration of these factors should precede decisions to co-teach.

Co-teacher Characteristics

Co-teaching is not a comfortable arrangement for all professionals. The issues of sharing responsibility, modifying teaching styles and preferences, and working closely with another adult represent serious challenges for some educators. Yet for others these same issues are a source of excitement that can lead to renewed enthusiasm about teaching. Thus, a first step for most co-teachers is to examine carefully their own readiness for the professional and personal demands of co-teaching, particularly the demands related to working closely with another professional. For example, co-teachers might use the following questions to reflect on their co-teaching readiness and to structure discussion among teaching partners. The discussion will help to initiate important communication between and among co-teachers.

1. To what extent am I willing to let someone else carry out teaching tasks at which I am particularly skilled?
2. How willing am I to allow a colleague to see aspects of my teaching in which I am not particularly skilled?
3. To what degree do I believe that there is more than one right way to carry out almost any teaching/learning task?
4. How willing am I to tell a colleague when I disagree about an issue or have a concern?

In addition to a general readiness to co-teach, several specific characteristics are associated consistently with successful co-teachers. Flexibility and commitment to the concept of co-teaching are considered essential (Armbruster & Howe, 1985; Gelzheiser & Meyers, 1990; Redditt, 1991). Strong interpersonal and communication skills, including collaborative problem-solving and decision-making skills, also are essential (Bauwens & Hourcade, 1995; Pugach & Johnson, 1995). Based on our work with co-teaching teams, we add strong clinical judgment as another essential characteristic for co-teachers. Co-teachers must have well developed judgment so they can evaluate the information they gain from colleagues and use it in their teaching and decision making.

Many writers, as well as the many teachers with whom we have worked, tell us that voluntariness on the part of the teachers is critical (Armbruster & Howe, 1985; Dettmer, Dyck, & Thurston, 1996) just as it is in all other forms of collaboration (Friend & Cook, 1996). As in any close relationship, having skills and attitudes that foster collaboration and trust also is necessary. As many co-teachers report, "Co-teaching is like a marriage." We agree. It is a form of professional marriage.

Professional Roles

Although most new co-teaching programs emphasize general education and special education teachers sharing a classroom and some of our discussion here implies such arrangements, many different specialists can be involved in co-teaching. Indeed, the program planning and clinical literature includes numerous examples of successful co-teaching among vocational and special educators (Mori, 1979; Phelps & Lutz, 1977), general educators and speech-language clinicians (Brush, 1987; Goodin & Mehollin, 1990), and general educators and occupational therapists (Embers & Robles, 1994). A key factor in determining if co-teaching is appropriate for related services professionals is the degree to which the students' related services needs can be met through modification of the general education curriculum. As examples, an occupational therapist might co-teach art, handwriting, or a hands-on vocational class, or a physical therapist might be present to co-teach an exercise or a game, while modifying as needed. As we noted earlier, decisions about these variations of co-teaching are to be made by an IEP team.

How Much Co-Teaching Should Take Place?

If you are considering co-teaching for the first time or thinking about improving your current co-teaching activities, you probably are entertaining the same questions that many professionals ask:

1. How can I physically co-teach in that many classrooms every day?
2. What happens to the students on my caseload who require special curriculum and instruction apart from the general education classroom?
3. When and how am I going to have time to plan with my co-teachers?
4. How can I manage to co-teach and still keep up with the other responsibilities of my position?

Perhaps you will be encouraged to know that these questions, or some variation of them, are among those asked most frequently by school professionals as they embark upon co-teaching. Our unqualified and definitive response to these questions is, "It depends!" Readers who are challenged positively by this response and its elaboration are likely to be the kinds of professionals who will consider and weigh the factors upon which co-teaching depends and use their ingenuity to develop the type of co-teaching program that will meet the needs of their students and the ecology of their schools.

Before considering the factors upon which co-teaching designs are built, readers should reflect on some of the notions presented in the previous section, namely, (a) not everyone is able to co-teach, and (b) successful co-teachers are flexible and use good clinical judgment. These two characteristics are important for a number of reasons, not the least of which is the responsibility that co-teachers have for problem solving and decision making as they collaboratively design programs and services to meet the individual needs of groups of students.

A large number of factors individually and collectively influence the amount of co-teaching that any one professional may do, just as they influence the number of students and classrooms that will be involved in the co-teaching program in a specific school. Several of the most salient factors are

- Size and grade levels of the schools
- Number of students with IEPs and their class/age distribution
- Number and disciplines of the specialists available to co-teach
- Level of administrative support
- Role responsibilities of potential co-teachers
- Stability of school enrollment and caseload composition
- Relevance of IEP to general education curriculum.

Clearly, the differences between large and small schools; among elementary, middle, and high schools; and among rural, suburban, and urban schools will influence the amount of co-teaching that can be offered. Related to these concerns is the number of specialists and whether they are available full time or part time as well as the range of available options for placing and scheduling students. Although these appear to be straightforward, they all interact to add complexity to the unique situations that typify individual schools.

Moreover, in most schools these factors are dynamic rather than stable. As one factor changes, it influences the others. For example, consider a school in an agricultural area where enrollments and, hence, caseloads fluctuate with seasons of the year because of the influx and outflow of migrant workers and their families. A program designed to meet student needs and school ecology during a season of low enrollment may be unable to expand to meet the needs of a large migrant population. If factors are considered in advance, they may be avoidable.

Ultimately the decision regarding the amount of co-teaching that is possible and desirable must be made at the local district and school levels. Strategies that veteran co-teachers have used successfully to increase their co-teaching opportunities include these:

1. Schools that have more than one special educator or related service provider assign special educators to serve students with IEPs who may not be on their caseloads.
2. The amount of specialized direct service the students require is reevaluated and the service is reduced when appropriate modifications can be made in the general education classroom.
3. Some students with IEPs are clustered in specific classes (or teams in secondary or year-round schools) without being seriously overrepresented in any class or program.
4. When writing the IEP, the general education context is examined and students' goals and objectives are written to be as compatible as possible with the core curriculum.
5. The schedules of students with disabilities are prepared before those of other students. This may require hand-scheduling in secondary schools, and it may create more structured schedules in elementary schools, but this option increases opportunities for serving students appropriately.

Potential co-teachers often fear that the first of these strategies will increase caseloads. This is not the intent. Rather, it is an approach to meeting identified student needs in general education classrooms without having a traffic jam with many different specialists darting in and out of the classrooms. For example, a speech-language specialist co-teaching with a sixth-grade teacher may provide instruction in organizing thoughts and ideas for written reports. If that also is an identified need for the two students with learning disabilities who are not on her caseload but are in that class, she may include them along with several unidentified students who need this instruction. The arrangement in this example ensures that the students with learning disabilities receive appropriate services from a qualified professional. It also frees some of the direct service time for the special education teacher who has these students on his caseload to co-teach in another classroom.

Each of these strategies could be discussed in depth. Our point is simply to raise a range of possibilities for consideration. Many co-teachers with whom we have worked have benefited from using the list as a stimulus for brainstorming alternative strategies that will be effective in their schools.

How Can Co-Teachers Maintain a Collaborative Working Relationship?

Successful co-teaching is more than planning lessons in which both educators are integral. It also relies on effective and ongoing communication. It is surprising how simple matters, if clarified, are easily resolved, but if not clarified sometimes lead to misunderstandings that interfere with co-teaching success (Redditt, 1991). For example, two teachers in an elementary classroom share the responsibility for leading the lesson. One, however, prefers that students who have to sharpen their pencils do it at any time, including during large-group lessons, while the other wants students to remain in their seats and listen during large-group instruction. The first teacher's rationale is to take away from some students the game of asking to sharpen pencils. To the second, pencil-sharpening is distracting and interferes with the instruction of all students. Neither is right or wrong, but they do need to discuss this matter before it becomes more than a source of annoyance for one or the other.

Major Topics for Discussion

The following are some of the topics that we discuss regularly with co-teachers to help them build and maintain positive working relationships. Questions that might be raised related to each are included in Table 20.1. Most co-teaching teams find that they have to add a few other topics to their discussion list and make a commitment to address them while they are still small matters rather than wait until they become major issues. We have found that using the topics as a discussion guide to be reviewed before beginning to co-teach and then periodically throughout the relationship helps to facilitate the open communication that is so essential to success in co-teaching.

Instructional Beliefs

Teachers' shared beliefs about teaching and learning are fundamental to successful co-teaching (Adams & Cessna, 1991). If partners for co-teaching do not agree on their beliefs about the ability of all children to learn, the rights of children to experience success in their classroom, regardless their ability level, and their own role in student learning, they are likely to encounter difficulties when they share a classroom. Further, because teachers' instructional beliefs guide their practice, they also could find they do not agree on the general atmosphere that makes teaching and learning successful or the amount of activity and responsibility that students and teachers have during instruction.

Planning

A frequent concern of co-teachers is finding opportunities to plan. Even if time is limited, both teachers have to sense the direction the class is headed and how they play a role in it. Administrators need to recognize the importance of shared planning time and provide it for co-teachers (Cook & Friend, 1993). Teachers committed to co-teaching often find unusual ways to create planning time. Some choose to meet before or after school, or to stay late one afternoon every other week. One clever teaching pair realized that they both liked to walk for exercise, so they brought walking shoes to school so they could exercise and plan at the same time.

A second part of planning concerns assigning responsibility for lesson planning tasks. Who will duplicate materials? Who will grade homework? There is no single, appropriate way to assign these types of responsibilities, and care must be taken not to overwhelm a special educator who might be co-teaching in four or five different classrooms. Yet, if planning is not shared, the general education teacher often feels

Table 20.1 *Questions for Creating a Collaborative Working Relationship in Co-Teaching*

Topic	Questions
Instructional beliefs	• What are our overriding philosophies about the roles of teachers and teaching, and students and learning? • How do our instructional beliefs affect our instructional practice?
Planning	• When do we have at least 30 minutes of shared planning time? • How do we divide our responsibilities for planning and teaching? • How much joint planning time do we need? • What records can we keep to facilitate our planning?
Parity signals	• How will we convey to students and others (for example, teachers, parents) that we are equals in the classroom? • How can we ensure a sense of parity during instruction?
Confidentiality	• What information about our teaching do we want to share with others? • Which information should not be shared? • Which information about students can be shared with others? • What information should not be shared?
Noise	• What noise level are we comfortable with in the classroom?
Classroom routines	• What re the instructional routines for the classroom? • What are the organizational routines for the classroom?
Discipline	• What is acceptable and unacceptable student behavior? • Who is to intervene at what point in students' behavior? • What are the rewards and consequences used in the classroom?
Feedback	• What is the best way to give each other feedback? • How will you ensure that both positive and negative issues are raised?
Pet peeves	• What aspects of teaching and classroom life do each of us feel strongly about? • How can we identify our pet peeves so as to avoid them?

overburdened and the special educator feels as though he or she is not an integral part of the instruction.

Parity Signals

Earlier we mentioned that a goal in co-teaching is to have students respond to the teachers as classroom equals. To achieve and maintain this parity, teachers can arrange visual, verbal, and instructional signals that convey their equality. For example, teachers who co-teach daily can put both teachers' names on the board and on correspondence that goes to parents. They can arrange for two teachers' desks, or share a large work table instead of having one teacher camping at a student desk. They can be sure that both take the lead on delivering instruction, and they both can grade papers to make clear to students that both contribute to grades or other student evaluation. In new co-teaching programs in particular, listing all the ways that parity can be signaled sometimes is helpful.

Confidentiality

Co-teachers have to agree on which of their activities are to be public and which are to be confidential classroom matters. Even well intentioned co-teachers can inadvertently miscommunicate on this matter. For example, a special educator so enjoyed a teaching technique a general education teacher used that she shared it with several other teachers in the building, crediting the general education teacher from whom she had learned it. The teacher, however, took issue with the special educator's actions: She felt as though a teaching idea that was uniquely hers had been "stolen." Also, she thought the other teacher's actions put her in the awkward position of being singled out as an extraordinary teacher, something that violated the culture of the school. With a brief conversation, this and other issues about confidentiality could have been resolved.

Noise

Teachers have different levels of tolerance for the noise level of a classroom. Part of their working relationship requires taking into account the other person's preferences and reaching agreement on what is an acceptable noise level. Noise includes teacher as well as student voices, instructional activities (e.g., an experiment with humming equipment), and environmental sounds. The discussion also should include the signals that are used to quiet a class that is beyond acceptable noise limits.

Classroom Routines

As a matter of practicality, all classrooms, whether special education or general education, have routines. One type of routine is organizational. Organizational routines include the systematized ways in which the classroom is operated. Examples of organizational routines include how students prepare to leave a classroom, what they are to do when they enter class at the beginning of the day or class period, whether permission is given during instruction for students to leave the class, and so on.

The second type of routine is instructional. Instructional routines include the ways in which students are to organize their written assignments, including paper headings, lab and other report formats, and other conventions (for example, is work done in pencil or ink?). They also include ways students are to seek assistance, whether from another student or from the teacher, how they are to turn in assignments, and whether they are to keep assignment notebooks.

Sometimes teachers are surprised to learn how many routines operate in their classrooms. Both teachers, however, must know the routines, even if they tend to be those the general education teacher follows. At the very least, this shared knowledge prevents students from playing the teachers off against one another by seeing who will give them an answer they prefer.

Discipline

Many teachers have strong beliefs about acceptable classroom behavior. These beliefs are tied to the instructional beliefs mentioned already and can vary significantly among co-teachers. Co-teachers generally discuss what they expect of students in terms of behaviors, and the system of rewards and consequences used in the classroom. If some students in a co-taught class have behavior disorders, co-teachers typically discuss what the alternative expectations will be for those students so their message for them, as well as for other students, is clear.

Feedback

Co-teaching, especially when it is highly collaborative, includes providing feedback to one another on all aspects of the teaching and learning in the classroom. Co-teachers, however, might know and be able to tell their teaching partners the way they prefer to receive feedback. Some teachers want to know right away how their co-teacher viewed the lesson; others would prefer to gain the perspective of waiting a day. Some teachers prefer to discuss a positive lesson before discussing any problems that occurred; others prefer the reverse order. When we ask teachers with whom we work how to best give them feedback, a surprising number of them immediately say something like, "Bring chocolate!" Their irreverent comments might contain a grain of truth, especially if the feedback includes raising a concern or an issue.

Pet Peeves

Nearly every teacher has pet peeves about some aspect of teaching or the classroom environment that could interfere with a positive working relationship if it is not brought to the other teacher's attention. For example, some teachers are adamant that no one should open their desk drawers. Imagine their reaction if an unsuspecting teacher partner needs a pencil and heads for the desk. Other teachers are particular about how they want grades recorded or papers graded. Still others want teachers' manuals kept in a certain location or condition.

Other pet peeves relate to students. Students who rock on their chairs might be a pet peeve, or students who call their teachers "Teacher" instead of by name, or students who whine when they need to ask for help. The point is this: Part of co-teaching is respecting the other person's quirks as a teacher. Knowing your partner's pet peeves—as long as the list is relatively short—is one way to accomplish this.

What Do Co-Teachers Need to Be Successful?

A number of studies and reports identify what teachers and schools need to be successful whether they are offering traditional or more innovative services (e.g., Berman & McLaughlin, 1978; Council for Exceptional Children, 1994). The two most critical needs that have not been addressed directly elsewhere in this chapter are professional preparation and administrative support.

Professional Preparation

School professionals have been formally prepared and socialized to operate in isolation (Barth, 1990; Friend & Cook, 1996). To be successful in collaborative activities such as co-teaching, these professionals require opportunities for additional skill development in communication skills, instructional strategies, and collaborative planning. They will also need to acquire new knowledge and skills in program planning. Initial preparation should address the mutual needs of all involved. The preparation or training activities should focus on developing communication and collaboration skills, assessing one's readiness for collaboration and co-teaching, and designing the parameters of the co-teaching relationships. Instructional strategies and methods for joint delivery of instruction make up the instructional methods to be studied and developed. The special educators may need additional knowledge regarding specific curriculum areas. And the general educators may need to learn more about students with disabilities (Friend & Cook, 1990). These specialized needs may be met through subsequent co-teaching experience.

The approach to professional preparation is particularly important. Ideally, readiness for co-teaching and other collaborative approaches will be promoted in preservice programs, which also should provide some initial experiences with collaborative planning and instruction. The most intensive professional development for co-teaching will occur when teachers and other specialists are in service and have opportunities to implement what they learn. Our experiences in providing both preservice and in-service education and our technical assistance experiences in co-teaching have demonstrated the necessity for preparation at both levels.

Administrative Support

Nearly every study of teacher performance and satisfaction finds that administrative support is essential to teachers' success (Berman & McLaughlin, 1975). The research is less clear on the nature of the support teachers seek and the specific actions administrators can take to provide that support. Anecdotal and focus-group information suggests what administrative actions are needed to support co-teaching (Cook & Friend, 1993).

Administrators can support professional partners who co-teach by modeling desirable traits that promote collaboration and by fostering those traits in others. Among the strategies that administrators have used successfully to support co-teaching are (a) to help the co-teachers to plan and schedule their programs, (b) to provide incentives and resources that allow co-teachers to design and reflect about desirable changes in the way they provide services, and (c) to assist teachers in setting priorities that will protect their limited time. Committing resources to enhancing the preparation of co-teaching partners, participating with them in training activities, and scheduling additional planning time for co-teachers also are valued signs of administrative support.

How Do We Plan for a Co-Teaching Program?

Regardless of the extent of the co-teaching effort, some basic planning should precede implementation of a new program or service. Although successful co-teaching programs or other innovations can begin casually without systematic planning, these are rare. Planning not only is useful in preparing for implementation, but also is important in clarifying, for all involved, the specific expectations and changes that the program entails. This is discussed further in the later section on communicating with others. Planning allows everyone to start "on the same page" and identifies potential misunderstandings or problems in advance. Through these efforts, many future roadblocks can be avoided and facilitating conditions can be put into place.

Program planning and initiation are complex tasks that often are shortchanged because of time restrictions and other demands faced by the professionals involved. Planning of this sort is rather straightforward—perhaps so much so that it can be naively overlooked or considered unnecessary. Through our experiences with co-teaching, we have come to highly respect appropriate advance planning, particularly as it helps to reduce the frustration and stress resulting from badly planned change. Other sources that provide more detailed discussions of program planning include Adams and Cessna (1991), Friend and Cook (1990), and Reisberg and Wolf (1986). Here we provide an overview of the most basic steps in program planning.

Establish a Planning Structure

Whether it is for a large-scale, school-wide effort or just two professionals interested in providing more in-class services, the way in which planning will proceed will have to be decided jointly. Some schools establish a committee or task force of people who will be most involved. Other task forces have broader representation by including nonparticipating professionals, parents, and community members. In some cases the planning group may be small initially with co-teaching teams meeting together to design their own programs. We caution, however, that small planning teams may have logistical appeal but have less impact than larger groups that involve more stakeholders. If program expansion is planned, the participation of a larger group will become advisable.

Describe the Program

Co-teachers should agree on the general description of their co-teaching efforts. Mutually deciding what the program will be called (e.g., co-teaching, team teaching, teaching partners) often is helpful, along with a two- or three-sentence written description of the program. The description may be disseminated to others, but its greatest value probably derives from the sheer act of preparing it. When two or more individuals come together to *commit to paper* a description of what it is they are attempting to do, they discover points of confusion and ambiguity in their individual and mutual expectations. Identifying and resolving these points will be extremely beneficial in helping to ensure that their continued planning and their communication with others will be as clear and rational as possible.

Specify Goals and Objectives

Program goals and objectives will indicate the expected outcomes of the effort and provide a basis for subsequent evaluation. As with any changes designed and implemented in schools, new co-teaching programs often begin with general goals and objectives, which become defined more fully as the effort progresses. Goals and objectives are most realistic when they are developed with attention to factors including student needs, staff receptivity, and availability of time for general education teachers and special educators alike to interact and engage in joint planning. These and other factors will influence attainment of the desired outcomes.

Determine Who is Eligible

Once the desired program outcomes are specified, the next step is to decide who should receive services in a co-taught classroom. The issues raised earlier on deciding if co-teaching is an appropriate instructional option may assist in developing specific statements about eligibility. Asking the questions suggested in Table 20.1 relative to a specific population of students may help to clarify, in concrete ways, criteria for selecting students to participate. These criteria should be written and discussed thoroughly so eligibility for the program is clear.

Specify Responsibilities

Another planning task that is significant to participants as well as to interested others, is the specification of role responsibilities. Listing distinct responsibilities for all individuals affected by the co-teaching program will help everyone involved to understand the nature of the program and its potential impact for them. Obviously the co-teachers and any participating paraprofessionals will experience role changes, and their responsibilities will change. The responsibilities of others, such as administrators, other teachers or specialists, and multidisciplinary team members may change also. Resistance that may arise might reflect concerns about changing responsibilities. Providing adequate information can alleviate this resistance as well as provide a framework for continued planning.

Outline the Types of Service

Clarifying the nature of the services to be offered in a co-teaching program is the final step. The earlier discussions about appropriateness of co-teaching and eligibility for service will assist in decisions regarding instructional services, but what of offering related services in a co-teaching format? The same considerations are likely to be useful here as well. The central consideration should be: Can the student receive appropriate related services while participating in the general education curriculum? For example, a student may be able to receive needed language development instruction by the speech therapist while participating in the general education social studies class.

Design Evaluation Strategies/Measures

Evaluation is a vital component of any innovation in school-based services. Co-teaching is no exception. Both formative and summative evaluation are needed to develop and implement an effective co-teaching program adequately. Formative evaluation is needed to gather information that will signal the need to make modifications to goals, objectives, and strategies during initial implementation. This is the information that guides refinement and clarification of objectives and implementation strategies. Summative evaluation, conducted annually or more often, provides information that may lead to rethinking and revising the overall design of the co-teaching program. The summative evaluation is best conducted after the program has had an opportunity to have results. The evaluation should be designed to assess progress toward the desired outcomes specified in the program objectives.

Meaningful evaluation data have numerous sources. Quantitative measures of students' academic and social outcomes are extremely important to many stakeholders in evaluating co-teaching. Formal and informal measures of achievement, social relationships, and student behaviors also are useful. In some instances portfolio assessment is the most illuminating. Other extant data, such as attendance records, academic products, and discipline records, provide meaningful information regarding the program's effect on students. More qualitative sources also should be explored, as these often provide rich information that elaborates or clarifies the objective measures. Anecdotal information should be collected throughout the program, and various approaches for assessing perceptions of the students, parents, and professionals should be considered.

How Do We Introduce Co-Teaching and Communicate with Others About It?

Some schools invest considerable time in planning and preparing for co-teaching as a school-wide program. In other schools teachers enter into co-teaching in a much less systematic way. They see it as a good idea, agree on some initial principles, and "just do it." Regardless of the magnitude of the co-teaching effort and the amount of planning, the professionals involved are advised to communicate with others about their intent to offer services through co-teaching approaches. What information is shared and how it is communicated influence significantly how others view, and subsequently respond, to the co-teaching effort.

Information to be Shared

Stakeholders are bound to have questions and information needs that indicate specific levels of concern (Loucks-Horsley & Hergert, 1985), and they need answers to these questions before they will be ready to accept a program change. Their questions reveal real concerns about the students' welfare and sometimes reflect a more generalized sense of resistance. We have been more successful in assuming that all questions stem from concern about student success rather than general resistance to change.

The stated concerns of the parents, administrators, students, teachers, and other adults will provide the framework for the information to be shared. The 10 planning questions presented in this chapter represent some of those asked most frequently as programs are introduced. Moreover, the planning steps described above (program description, goals and objectives, eligibility, responsibilities, types of services, and evaluation) yield the types of information that others will want to know about the program. If information from these two sources does not satisfy the stakeholder questions, it often is helpful to become an avid listener and promote discussion with the hope of identifying and alleviating unspoken concerns.

At least three areas of concern commonly arise and require consideration in advance.

1. *The impact co-teaching may have on the nondisabled students.* Will the nature of instruction and the standards for performance of all students be lowered to accommodate learners with special needs? Will nondisabled students receive less attention? At first blush lower standards and less instructional attention may seem to be consequences of co-teaching. Addressing these concerns is imperative.

2. *The extent and purpose of co-teaching.* Teachers, parents, paraprofessionals, related services professionals, and administrators all may fear that co-teaching will become the preferred approach to delivering services to students with special needs. Their concerns actually may reflect their fear of full inclusion, loss of services, loss or change in employment, significant role changes, and the like.

3. *The need to schedule time for co-teaching and joint planning to prepare for co-teaching.* This concern usually is restricted to the professionals in the schools because parents generally are unaware of the individual schedules of teachers and other school professionals. Scheduling services and planning time will be an important issue during program development and implementation.

The information presented previously should clarify what we intend co-teaching to mean and how we believe it should be used. These same questions and concerns will have to be addressed at local district and school levels. Experiences of implementers should be shared with interested parties to demonstrate solutions to the ever present challenges and to provide opportunities for others to help develop solutions.

Approaches to Communication

Various mechanisms are used for communication with individuals in varying roles in the educational community. Individuals who will be affected most by the program will have the greatest and most immediate need for information. The teachers and parents of the students in the co-taught classes, as well as the students themselves, may have the greatest interest in knowing about the program. Administrators also are on the front line in terms of information needs. The group with the next most pressing information needs will be individuals who may be affected by the program at a later date—teachers, specialists, parents, and students who are not participating currently but who may be expected to become involved sometime.

Schools have used several strategies to communicate about the development of new programs. When first planning a program, inviting key stakeholders to participate in the planning process is often helpful. Before implementing any changes, the parents of affected students should be informed through individual conferences, group meetings, or a letter sent to their homes. At the same time teachers and other specialists should be made aware of the change in service through an announcement at faculty or department meetings or through the established channels of communication at the school (e.g., faculty bulletins, electronic or other bulletin boards).

As the co-teaching effort matures, has evaluation or other data to support its expansion, and involves more professionals and students, more formalized mechanisms are appropriate. At this stage, letters or newsletters describing the project and any potential changes might be sent to all parents and other members of the school community. Depending upon the credibility of the data that support the project, schools also may choose to communicate with the broader community through news releases to a newspaper and to local organizations.

Regardless of which strategies seem to be most efficient, maintaining a balance of communication strategies is important. Too much reliance on one-way communication (e.g., from the school to the parents via written material) becomes ineffective because those who are informed do not have opportunities to question or clarify the information they receive. Equally troublesome, school professionals miss out on learning how parents respond to the information. People are more likely to accept and decide to participate in a new program or approach when they have been involved in its development at some level. Receiving and responding to information about the program being developed is one low-intensity activity that allows others to be involved in program development.

Summary

Co-teaching is defined as two or more professionals delivering substantive instruction to a group of students with diverse learning needs. This approach increases instructional options, improves educational programs, reduces stigmatization for students, and provides support to the professionals involved. Co-teaching is an appropriate service delivery approach for students with disabilities who can benefit from general education curriculum if given appropriate supports. Teachers and related service professionals who are flexible and have good clinical judgment are likely to be successful in this role.

Various approaches to co-teaching include instructional support as well as station, parallel, alternative, and team teaching. The optimum amount of co-teaching in a school depends on a number of factors and must be determined by professionals at the site. Co-teachers need preparation, administrative support, and opportunities to nurture their collaborative relationships. Co-teaching programs should be planned and implemented systematically. Deliberate and ongoing communication among everyone involved is essential.

References

Adams, L., & Cessna, K. (1991). Designing systems to facilitate collaboration: Collective wisdom from Colorado. *Preventing School Failure, 35*(4), 37–42.

Armbruster, B., & Howe, C. E. (1985). Educators team up to help students learn. *NASSP Bulletin, 69*(479), 82–86.

Barth, R. S. (1990). *Improving schools from within.* San Francisco: Jossey-Bass.

Bauer, H. (1975). The resource teacher-A teacher consultant. *Academic Therapy, 10,* 299–304.

Bauwens, J., & Hourcade, J. J. (1995). *Cooperative teaching: Rebuilding the school house for all students.* Austin: Pro-Ed.

Bauwens, J., Hourcade, J. J., & Friend, M. (1989). Cooperative teaching: A model for general and special education integration. *Remedial & Special Education, 10*(2), 17–22.

Berman, P., & McLaughlin, M. L. (1978). The analysis of verbal interactions occurring during consultation. *Journal of School Psychology, 13,* 209–226.

Brush, E. (1987). *Public school language, speech and hearing services in the 1990s.* Paper presented at annual convention of American Speech-Language-Hearing Association, New Orleans, November 1987. (ERIC Document Reproduction Service No. ED 295 383)

Choate, J. S. (1993). Co-assessment of special learners: A call for special and general education to unite. *Preventing School Failure, 37,* 11–15.

Cook, L., & Friend, M. (1993). *Co-Teach! Strategies for creating teaching teams.* (In preparation).

Cook, L., & Friend, M. (1993). Educational leadership for teacher collaboration. In B. Billingsley (Ed.), *Program leadership for serving students with disabilities.* Richmond, VA: State.

Dettmer, P. A., Dyck, N. T., & Thurston, L. P. (1996). *Consultation, collaboration, and teamwork for students with special needs* (2d Ed.). Boston: Allyn & Bacon.

Easterby-Smith, M., & Olive, N. G. (1984). Team teaching: Making management education more student-centered? *Management Education & Development, 15,* 221–236.

Embers, P., & Robles, M. H. (1994). Occupational therapists in the classroom. *Co-Teaching Network News, 2*(3), 2.

Friend, M., & Cook, L. (1990). Pragmatic issues in the development of special education consultation programs. *Preventing School Failure, 35*(1), 43–46.

Friend, M., Reising, M., & Cook, L. (1993). Co-teaching: An overview of the past, a glimpse at the present, and considerations for the future. *Preventing School Failure, 37*(3), 6–10.

Friend, M., & Cook, L. (1996). *Interactions: Collaboration skills for school professionals* (2d Ed.). White Plains, NY: Longman.

Fuchs, D., & Fuchs, L. S. (1992). Limitations of a feel-good approach to consultation. *Journal of Educational and Psychological Consultation, 3,* 93–98.

Garvar, A. G., & Papania, A. (1982). Team teaching: It works for the student. *Academic Therapy, 18*(2), 191–196.

Gelzheiser, L. M., & Meyers, J. (1990). Special and remedial education in the classroom: Theme and variations. *Journal of Reading, Writing, and Learning Disabilities, 6,* 419–436.

Goodin, G., & Mehollin, K. (1990). Developing a collaborative speech-language intervention program in the schools. In W. A. Secord & E. H. Wiig (Eds.), *Best practices in school speech-language pathology.* San Antonio, TX: Psychological Corp.

Graden, J. (1989). Redefining "prereferral" intervention as intervention assistance: Collaboration between general and special education. *Exceptional Children, 56,* 227–231.

Heron, T. E., & Harris, K. C. (1993). *The educational consultant: Helping professionals, parents, and mainstreamed students* (3d ed.). Austin, TX: Pro-Ed.

Howell, P. (1991). Taking AIM to assist middle school students with special needs. *Preventing School Failure, 35*(4), 43–47.

Lortie, D. (1975). *Schoolteacher: A sociological study*. Chicago: University of Chicago Press.

Loucks-Horsley, S., & Hergert, L. F. (1985). *An action guide to school improvement.* Andover, MA: ASCD The NETWORK.

MacDonald, C., & York, J. (1991). *Including students with disabilities in general education classes. What's working?* Minneapolis: Minnesota Inclusive Education Technical Assistance Program.

MacIver, D. J. (1990). Meeting the needs of young adolescents: Advisory groups, interdisciplinary teacher teams, and school transition programs. *Phi Delta Kappan, 71*, 458–464.

Mori, A. A. (1979). Vocational education and special education: A new partnership in career education. *Journal of Career Education, 6*(1), 55–69.

Phelps, L. A., & Lutz, R. J. (1977). *Career exploration and preparation for the special needs learner.* Boston: Allyn & Bacon.

Phillips, V., & McCullough, L. (1990). Consultation-based programming: Instituting the collaborative ethic in schools. *Exceptional Children, 56*, 291–304.

Pugach, M. C., & Johnson, L. J. (1989). Prereferral interventions: Progress, problems, and challenges. *Exceptional Children, 56*, 217–226.

Pugach, M. C., & Johnson, L. J. (1995). *Collaborative practitioners, collaborative schools*. Denver: Love Publishing.

Redditt, S. (1991). Two teachers working as one. *Equity & Choice, 8*(1), 49–56.

Reeve, P. T., & Hallahan, D. P. (1994). Practical questions about collaboration between general and special educators. *Focus on Exceptional Children, 26*(7), 1–11.

Reisberg, L., & Wolf, R. (1986). Developing a consulting program in special education: Implementation and interventions. *Focus on Exceptional Children, 19*(3), 1–14.

Schulte, A. C., Osborne, S. S., & McKinney, J. D. (1990). Academic outcomes for students with learning disabilities in consultation and resource programs. *Exceptional Children, 57*, 162–176.

Trump, J. L. (1966). Secondary education tomorrow: Four imperatives for improvement. *NASSP Bulletin, 50*(309), 87–95.

Walker, V. (1974). The efficacy of the resource room for educating retarded children. *Exceptional Children, 40*, 288–289.

Walsh, J. M. (1992). Student, teacher, and parent preference for less restrictive special education models—Cooperative teaching. *Case In Point, 6*(2), 1–12.

Warwick, D. (1971). *Team teaching*. London: University of London.

White, A. E., & White, L. L. (1992). A collaborative model for students with mild disabilities in middle schools. *Focus on Exceptional Children, 24*(9), 1–10.

Author Index

A

Abbeduto, L., 418
Abbott, M. S., 82
Abikoff, H., 442
Abramowitz, A. J., 440, 446
Achenbach, T. M., 74, 75
Adams, A., 375
Adams, L., 454, 468, 473
Addams, J., 62
Affleck, J. Q., 375
Agran, M., 350
Agte, L. J., 350
Aichorn, A., 58
Albers, P., 382
Alberto, P. A., 119, 149, 425
Albin, R. W., 328
Aldinger, L. E., 241
Alexander, R. N., 353
Algozzine, B., 208, 339
Algozzine, R. F., 230
Allen, M. G., 214, 232
Allen, T., 94
Alley, G., 177, 301, 351, 377
Alper, S., 332
Altman, K., 81
Alwell, M., 329
American Psychiatric Association, 71
Anderegg, M. L., 302
Anderson, J. R., 405
Anderson, K., 80
Anderson, L. M., 268, 294
Anderson, L. W., 180
Anderson, R. C., 427

Anderson, T. H., 164
Andrews, J., 352
Anastopoulos, A. D., 445
Anthony, H. M., 294
Antia, S., 325, 344
Apolloni, T., 344
Appelbaum, M. I., 418
Applebee, A., 294
Apter, S. J., 83
Archer, E. J., 426, 428
Arllen, N. L., 350, 353
Armbruster, B., 164, 279, 465
Armentrout, J. A., 352
Armstrong, S., 178
Arreaga-Mayer, C., 339, 340, 341, 350, 357
Asher, S. R., 137
Atkinson, B., 168
August, G. J., 442
Austin, G., 419
Ausubel, D. P., 417
Axelrod, S., 83
Ayala, J. M., 345
Ayllon, T., 439

B

Bacon, S. B., 63
Baddeley, A. D., 96
Baer, D. M., 79, 82, 184, 326
Baer, R., 423
Bahr, C., 263, 269
Bailey, B. R., 326
Bailey, D. B., 147, 158
Bailey, J., 327, 353, 440
Bailey, V., 354
Bain, A., 137
Bain, M., 350

Baker, B. L., 445
Baker, E. T., 305
Baker, J., 209, 277, 279, 377
Balajthy, E., 420
Balenzano, S., 350
Bambara, L. M., 119
Bandura, A., 73, 79, 342
Banerji, M., 375
Barbetta, P. M., 311, 347, 349, 350, 351, 252
Barclay, W., 28
Barkley, R. A., 440, 442, 445, 446
Barr, R., 266, 268
Barrish, H. H., 19
Bartel, N. R., 177, 186
Barth, R. S., 453, 472
Barton, E. J., 152
Barritt, L., 29
Barron, A. M., 349, 351
Baskin, A., 353
Bateman, B., 278
Bauer, H., 453
Bauwens, J., 456, 465
Bean, R., 288
Bear, G. G., 308, 375
Beattie, J., 212, 230
Beck, I. L., 288
Becker, E. A., 303, 359
Becker, L. D., 178, 183, 186
Beckstead, S., 307
Beekman, T., 29
Beirne-Smith, M., 350
Bell, K., 350
Bender, W. N., 210
Bentz, J., 322, 359, 364
Benz, M. R., 256

Benedetti, L., 164, 169
Bentzen, F. A., 447
Bereiter, C., 295
Bergerud, D., 163, 164, 167, 169, 420
Berler, E. S., 157
Berliner, D. C., 179
Berman, P., 472
Bernabe, E. A., 331
Bijou, S. W., 82
Biklin, S. K., 29
Binkoff, J. A., 77
Birch, J., 257
Bishop, N., 359
Black, H., 3
Black, S. A., 442
Blackorby, J., 377
Blackwell, S. L., 96
Blair, M., 350
Blake, G., 294
Blankenship, C., 180, 181
Blanton, L. P., 115
Blanton, W. E., 115
Bleeker, H., 29
Block, J., 33
Block, M. E., 331, 350
Bloom, L. A., 344, 345
Bloomquist, M. L., 442, 446
Blum, G., 85
Bogden, R. C., 29
Bologna, N. C., 445
Boltman, H., 418
Borden, K. A., 441, 442
Bos, C. S., 184
Botkin, D., 354
Bourne, R. E., Jr., 419
Boutwell, R. C., 427
Bracey, G. W., 212

481

Subject Index